AMERICAN LAW YEARBOOK 2001

ISSN 1521-0901

AMERICAN LAW YEARBOOK 2001

AN ANNUAL SOURCE PUBLISHED
BY THE GALE GROUP AS A
SUPPLEMENT TO
WEST'S ENCYCLOPEDIA OF
AMERICAN LAW

GALE GROUP

★

TM

THOMSON LEARNING

Detroit • New York • San Diego • San Francisco
Boston • New Haven, Conn. • Waterville, Maine
London • Munich

Jeffrey Lehman, *Editor*
Brian J. Koski, *Associate Editor*
Laura L. Brandau, Rebecca Parks, Jeffrey Wilson, *Contributing Editors*
Shelly Dickey, *Managing Editor*

Maria Franklin, *Permissions Manager*
Margaret Chamberlain, *Permissions Specialist*
Julie Juengling, Ryan Thomason, *Permissions Assistants*

Mary Beth Trimper, *Composition and Electronic Prepress Manager*
Evi Seoud, *Assistant Composition and Electronic Prepress Manager*

Kenn Zorn, *Product Design Manager*
Barbara J. Yarrow, *Imaging/Multimedia Content Manager*
Randy Bassett, *Image Database Supervisor*
Pamela A. Reed, *Imaging Coordinator*
Robyn Young, *Imaging Project Manager*
Luke A. Rademacher, *Imaging Specialist*

CONTENTS

The need for a layperson's comprehensive, understandable guide to terms, concepts, and historical developments in U.S. law has been well met by *West's Encyclopedia of American Law* (*WEAL*). Published at the end of 1997 by West Group, the foremost legal professional publisher, *WEAL* has proved itself a valuable successor to West's 1983 publication, *The Guide to American Law: Everyone's Legal Encyclopedia*.

Since 1998, the Gale Group, a premier reference publisher, has extended the value of *WEAL* with the publication of *American Law Yearbook* (*ALY*). This supplement adds entries on emerging topics not covered in the main set. It also updates cases, statutes, and issues in *WEAL* through July 2001. A legal reference must be current to be authoritative, so *ALY* is a vital companion to a key reference source. Uniform organization by *WEAL* term and cross-referencing make it easy to use the titles together, while inclusion of key definitions and summaries of earlier rulings in supplement entries— whether new or continuations—make it unnecessary to refer to the main set constantly.

**Understanding the American
Legal System**

The legal system of the United States is admired around the world for the freedoms it allows the individual and the fairness with which it attempts to treat all persons. On the surface, it may seem simple, yet those who have delved into it know that this system of federal and state constitutions, statutes, regulations, and common law decisions is elaborate and complex. It derives from the English common law, but includes principles older than England, along with some principles from other lands. The U.S. legal system, like many others, has a language all its own, but too often it is an unfamiliar language: many concepts are still phrased in Latin. *WEAL* explains legal terms and concepts in everyday language, however. It covers a wide variety of persons, entities, and events that have shaped the U.S. legal system and influenced public perceptions of it.

FEATURES OF THIS SUPPLEMENT

Entries

This supplement contains 176 entries covering individuals, cases, laws, and concepts. Entries are arranged alphabetically and, for continuation entries, use the same entry title as in *WEAL*. There may be several cases discussed under a given topic. Entry headings refer to court decisions by case name; others are identified by their subject matter.

Profiles of individuals cover interesting and influential people from the world of law, government, and public life, both historic and contemporary. All have contributed to U.S. law as a whole. Each short biography includes a timeline highlighting important moments in the subject's life. Persons whose lives were detailed in *WEAL*, but who have died since publication of that work, receive short obituary entries in *ALY*.

Definitions

Each entry on a legal term is preceded by a definition, which is easily distinguished by its sans serif typeface.

Cross References

To facilitate research, two types of cross-references are provided within and following entries. Within the entries, terms are set in small capital letters (e.g. DISCLAIMER) to indicate that they have their own entry in *WEAL* or in *ALY*. Cross references at the end of an entry refer readers to additional relevant topics in *WEAL*.

In Focus Pieces

In Focus pieces present complex and controversial issues from different perspectives. These pieces, which are set apart from the main entries with boxed edges and their own logo, examine some of the difficult legal and social questions that confront attorneys, judges, juries, and legislatures. The trend of increasing punishment for DWI offenses and the apparent politicization of the U.S. judiciary are among the high-interest topics in this yearbook.

Appendix

For the first time, *ALY* includes a glossary of difficult or uncommon legal words and phrases found within its pages. The appendix also features the text of documents complementary to the main entries, such as the law making English Utah's official language and Louisiana's covenant marriage statute.

Index of WEAL's Appendix and Milestones in the Law

This section indexes a number of primary documents included in the main set. Primary documents included in *ALY* are included in the Index by Name and Subject.

Table of Cases Cited and Index by Name and Subject

These features make it quick and easy for users to locate references to cases, people, statutes, events, and other subjects. The Table of Cases Cited traces the influences of legal precedents by identifying mentions of cases throughout the text. In a departure from *WEAL*, references to individuals have been folded into the general index to simplify searches. Litigants, justices, historical and contemporary figures, as well as topical references are included in the Index by Name and Subject.

Citations

Wherever possible, *American Law Yearbook* includes citations to cases and statutes for readers wishing to do further research. The citation refers to one or more of the series called "reporters" that publish court opinions and related information. Each citation includes a volume number, an abbreviation for the reporter, and the starting page reference. Underscores in a citation indicate that a court opinion has not been officially reported as of *ALY*'s publication. Two sample citations, with explanations, are presented below.

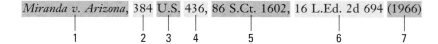

1. *Case title.* The title of the case is set in italics and indicates the names of the parties. The suit in this sample citation was between Ernesto A. Miranda and the state of Arizona.

2. *Reporter volume number.* The number preceding the reporter abbreviation indicates the reporter volume containing the case. The volume number appears on the spine of the reporter, along with the reporter abbreviation.

3. *Reporter abbreviation.* The suit in the sample citation is from the reporter, or series of books, called *U.S. Reports,* which contains cases from the U.S. Supreme Court. Numerous reporters publish cases from the federal and state courts; consult the abbreviations list at the back of this volume for full titles.

4. *Reporter page.* The number following the reporter abbreviation indicates the reporter page on which the case begins.

5. *Additional reporter citation.* Many cases may be found in more than one reporter. The suit in the sample citation also appears in volume 86 of the *Supreme Court Reporter,* beginning on page 1602.

6. *Additional reporter citation.* The suit in the sample citation is also reported in volume 16 of the *Lawyer's Edition,* second series, beginning on page 694.

7. *Year of decision.* The year the court issued its decision in the case appears in parentheses at the end of the cite.

Brady Handgun Violence Prevention Act, Pub. L. No. 103-159, 107 Stat. 1536 (18 U.S.C.A. § § 921-925A)

1   2   3   4   5   6   7   8

1. *Statute title.*

2. *Public law number.* In the sample citation, the number 103 indicates this law was passed by the 103d Congress, and the number 159 indicates it was the 159th law passed by that Congress.

3. *Reporter volume number.* The number preceding the reporter abbreviation indicates the reporter volume containing the statute.

4. *Reporter abbreviation.* The name of the reporter is abbreviated. The statute in the sample citation is from *Statutes at Large.*

5. *Reporter page.* The number following the reporter abbreviation indicates the reporter page on which the statute begins.

6. *Title number.* Federal laws are divided into major sections with specific titles. The number preceding a reference to the U.S. Code stands for the section called Crimes and Criminal Procedure.

7. *Additional reporter.* The statute in the sample citation may also be found in the *U.S. Code Annotated.*

8. *Section numbers.* The section numbers following a reference to the *U.S. Code Annotated* indicate where the statute appears in that reporter.

COMMENTS WELCOME

Considerable efforts were expended at the time of publication to ensure the accuracy of the information presented in *American Law Yearbook 2001.* The editors welcome your comments and suggestions for enhancing and improving future editions of this supplement to *West's Encyclope-* *dia of American Law.* Send comments and suggestions to:

American Law Yearbook
Gale Group
27500 Drake Rd.
Farmington Hills, MI 48331-3535

ACKNOWLEDGMENTS

SPECIAL THANKS

The editor wishes to acknowledge the contributions of the writers who aided in the compilation of *American Law Yearbook*. The editor gratefully thanks Rose Blue, Daniel E. Brannen, Jr., Halle I. Butler, Richard Cretan, Frederick K. Grittner, Lauri R. Harding, Corinne J. Naden, April Scheiner, Scott D. Slick, Kelly B. Willis, and Richard R. Willis. Valuable content review of entries came from: Frederick K. Grittner, Lauri R. Harding, Scott D. Slick, Kelly B. Willis, and Richard R. Willis.

PHOTOGRAPHIC CREDITS

The editor wishes to thank the permission managers of the companies that assisted in securing reprint rights. The following list—in order of appearance—acknowledges the copyright holders who have granted us permission to reprint material in this edition of *American Law Yearbook*:

Abraham, Spencer, Republican Senator of Auburn Hills, MI, photograph by Lennox McLendon. AP/Wide World Photos. **Brooks, Diana,** photograph. AP/Wide World Photos. **Bannigan, Eugene** (far left) with legal team, (l-r) John Gordan, Michele Connaugton and Steve Zelinger, all representing Visa International, photograph. AP/Wide World Photos. **Montgomery, Betty, Ohio Attorney General,** with Mike Allen (l), Hamilton County Prosecutor, and Michael G. Spahr, photograph by Terry Gilliam. AP/Wide World Photos. **Ashcroft, John,** photograph by Arnold Sachs.

Archives Photos. **Boies, David,** photograph by Bui Khue. AP/Wide World Photos. **New Hampshire state map.** The Gale Group. **Bauer, Dean,** leaving Dirken Federal Courthouse, photograph by Stephen J. Carrera. AP/Wide World Photos. **La Mont, Alfredo** (center), and his attorney Lee Foreman (left) leaving federal court, photograph by Douglas C. Pizac. AP/Wide World Photos. **Penry, Johnny Paul,** convicted murderer, looking out from visiting area cell, photograph by David Phillip. AP/Wide World Photos. **Carnahan, Mel,** speaking to reporters, photograph by Kelley McCall. AP/Wide World Photos. **Harris, Kevin,** in courthouse, photograph by Jeff T. Green. AP/Wide World Photos. **Edwards, Edwin Washington, Jr.,** speaking to his staff and members of the media, photograph by Bill Haber. AP/Wide World Photos. **Artist's rendition of Ali Mohamed** (second from left), standing with attorneys before U.S. District Judge Leonard B. Sand in Manhattan Federal Court, photograph by Andrea Shepard. AP/Wide World Photos. **Isikoff, Mike,** standing inside NBC studios, photograph by Leslie E. Kosoff. AP/Wide World Photos. **Bolton, Michael,** holding his 1990 Grammy Award, photograph by Doug Pizac. AP/Wide World Photos. **Cranston, Alan MacGregor, speaking** at a news conference in Los Angeles, photograph by Kevok Djansezian.

AP/Wide World Photos. **Casey, Martin,** in Austin, Texas, 1998, photograph by LM Otero. AP/Wide World Photos. **Ash, Milton,** answers reporter's question, as Patricia Garrett watches, photograph by Stephen J. Boitano. AP/Wide World Photos. **Dixon, Julian C.,** photograph. AP/Wide World Photos. **Metro-Dade police officer** displaying Marijuana leaf. AP/Wide World Photos. **Breathalyzer test administered** by Santa Monica police officer, © Shelley Gazin/Corbis. **LePore, Theresa,** Palm Beach County (Fla.) Supervisor of Elections (l), Judge Charles Burton, Palm Beach County Voting Canvassing Board Chairman (c), unidentified Republican observer (r). © AFP/Corbis. **Aerial view of Microsoft** Corporate headquarters, photograph. © Microsoft Corporation. **Nehring, Ronald,** presiding over lawsuit to throw out Utah's official English law, photograph by Ryan Galbraith. AP/Wide World Photos. **Wen Ho Lee, leaving** courthouse, with his attorneys Mark Holscher, to his right, and John Kline, Lee's daughter, Alberta Lee, in back, photograph by L.M. Otero. AP/Wide World Photos. **Pope, Edmond,** sitting in Moscow City Court, photograph by Alexander Zemlianichenkko. AP/Wide World Photos. **Palazzolo, Anthony,** standing on undeveloped land, beside Winnapaug Pond, in Westerly, Rhode Island, photograph by Stew Milne. AP/Wide World Photos. **Reilly, Thomas F.,** sitting in front of bank of microphones, photograph by William Plowman. AP/Wide World Photos. **Love, John,** standing outside Charles McArthur's trailer, in Nichols Trailer Court, photograph by Randy Squires. AP/Wide World Photos. **Kyllo, Danny Lee,** standing outside house, photograph by Don Ryan. AP/Wide World Photos. **Gamblers playing video poker games,** Riverfront Station, St. Charles, Missouri, 1996, photograph. AP/Wide World Photos, Inc. **Dees, Morris,** 1996, photograph by Laurence Agron. Archive Photos, Inc. **Grand Central Station** with cars driving past and people walking outside lower level, photograph. Archive Photos. **Brock, David,** looking around courtroom, photograph by Jim Cole. AP/Wide World

Photos. **Atwater, Gail,** sitting with her children, Anya (c), and Mac, at home, after Atwater was jailed for family not wearing seat belts, photograph by Pat Sullivan. AP/Wide World Photos. **Barry, Hank,** (l), standing with (l-r) Andreas Schmidt, Thomas Middelhoff, and Shawn Fanning, displaying t-shirts bearing Napster logo, photograph by Louis Lanzano. AP/Wide World Photos. **America Online Headquarters,** photograph by Willia, Philpott. AP/Wide World Photos. **Clean up after Exxon** *Valdez* oil spill, photograph by Merjenburgh. Greenpeace. **Levi, Edward H(irsch),** briefing reporters at the White House, photograph. AP/Wide World Photos. **Lindsay, John V.,** photograph. The Library of Congress. **Carlisle, Troy,** age 28, at Rankin County Courthouse, Mississippi, photograph by Rogelio Solis. AP/Wide World Photos. **Ronghi, Frank,** photograph. AP/Wide World Photos. **Swango, Michael,** is escorted by a U.S. Marshal out of federal court in Uniondale, New York, photograph by Ed Betz. AP/Wide World Photos. **Stayner, Cary,** being escorted into a Mariposa County courtroom, photograph by Paul Sakuma. AP/Wide World Photos. **Carruth, Rae,** listening as witnesses testify during his murder trial, photograph by Jeff Siner. AP/Wide World Photos. **Lewis, Ray Anthony,** testifying in Fulton Superior Court, photograph by Kimberly Smith. AP/Wide World Photos. **Skakel, Michael,** (center) leaving with his attorney after a court hearing, photograph by Douglas Healey. AP/Wide World Photos. **Mascot Eddie Eagle, and Wayne LaPierre,** executive vice-president of the National Rifle Association, during a news conference in Washington, photograph by Dennis Cook. AP/Wide World Photos. **Olson, Ted, with George W. Bush,** photograph by Kenneth Lambert. AP/Wide World Photos. **Transplant waiting list,** showing the eight most common organs requested for transplant. Coloradohealthnet. **Artist's impression of conjoined twins** identified only as Mary (l) and Jodie (r), photograph by Priscilla Coleman. AP/Wide World Photos. **DNA being examined,** photograph by Sinclair

Stammers. Photo Researchers, Inc. **Deutschendorf, Emma,** mother of the late singer John Denver, and her son Ron arrive for public memorial service honoring Denver at the Faith Presbyterian Church in Aurora, Colorado, photograph by Fred Prouser. Reuters/Fred Prouser/Hulton. **King, Don,** gives the "V" for victory sign, photograph by Adam Nadel. AP/Wide World Photos. **U.S. Navy crewmen** aboard U.S.S. *Blue Ridge* carry two Vietnamese refugee children brought in by a Vietnamese Air Force helicopter, photograph. National Archives and Records Administration. **Rogers, William Pierce,** in a news conference in Washington, D.C., photograph. AP/Wide World Photos. **Ruff, Charles F.C.,** David Kendall, Gregory Craig (sitting behind name plate), Washington, D.C., 1998, photograph by Joe Marquette. AP/Wide World Photos. **Collection of London newspapers** with headlines reporting the NATO bombing of Serbia, photograph by Martin Cleaver. AP/Wide World Photos. **Pollard, Sharon B.,** at her home near Memphis, Tennessee, photograph by John L. Focht. AP/Wide World Photos. **McSorley, Marty, and Tie Domi** fight, California, 1997, photograph by Paul Sakuma. Associated Features, Inc. **U.S. Supreme Court,** ground level view across a paved distance, people gathered outside, photograph by Michael BeBari, Jr. AP/Wide World Photos. **Workers maintaining a cellular telephone tower** in Clackamas, Oregon, photograph. John Gress/Getty Images. **Mementos on fence** outside Murrah Federal Building, photograph by J. Pat Carter. AP/Wide World Photos. **Ahmed, Nasser,** photograph. AP/Wide World Photos. **Aerial view of the nose section of Pan Am Flight 103** lying in a field outside the village of Lockerbie, Scotland, after the plane was downed by a terrorist bomb, photograph by Martin Cleaver. AP/Wide World Photos. **Jury members in Florida class-action lawsuit against tobacco industry** learn about second phase of trial from judge at Miami Dade County Courthouse, photograph by Tony Gutierrez. AP/Wide World Photos. **Kellogg's Tony the Tiger** at press conference, photograph by Richard Drew. AP/Wide World Photos. **A bar scene from the television sitcom, *Cheers*** with (l-r) Coach behind the bar, George Wendt as Norm, John Ratzenberger as Cliff, Ted Danson as Sam, and Shelley Long as Diane, photograph. Archive Photos, Inc. **Abraham, Lynne, holding up a photograph of a Benetton ad,** photograph by Louise Sabina Pierce. AP/Wide World Photos. **Vento, Bruce Frank,** laughing with reporters, photograph by Jim Mone. AP/Wide World Photos. **Blaskic, Tihomir,** sitting at a desk in the Croatian Army's chief inspector's office, photograph by Jovo Pavkovic. AP/Wide World Photos. **Combs, Sean "Puffy,"** 1998, photograph. AP/Wide World Photos. **Bakaly, Charles,** Washington, D.C., 1998, photograph. AP/Wide World Photos. **Whitman, Christie,** photograph. AP/Wide World Photos. **Smith, Anna Nicole,** crying as she testifies against E. Pierce Marshall, in probate court, photograph by Carlos Antonio. AP/Wide World Photos. **Garcia, Jose Guillermo,** photograph by Kathy Willens. AP/Wide World Photos. **Miller, David,** embracing his daughter, as they enter a news conference, photograph by Damian Dovarganes. AP/Wide World Photos. **Branch Davidian compound** in flames, 1995, Waco, Texas, photograph. AP/Wide World Photos.

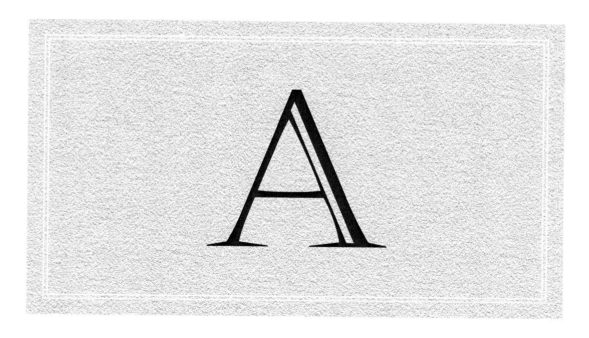

ABORTION

The spontaneous or artificially induced expulsion of an embryo or fetus. As used in legal context, usually refers to induced abortion.

Okpalobi v. Foster

Though the Supreme Court has upheld the right of a woman to obtain an abortion, many state legislatures that are opposed to abortion have sought to make it harder to exercise this right. The state of Louisiana may have sought to discourage providers of abortion services from continuing these services by enacting a law that made providers liable in TORT to any woman who suffers any injury caused by the abortion. A three-judge panel of the Court of Appeals for the Fifth Circuit, in *Okpalobi v. Foster*, 190 F.3d 337 (5th Cir.1999), ruled the law unconstitutional because it placed an undue burden on a woman's right to seek an abortion. The panel also found the statute unconstitutionally VAGUE. However, the entire court, sitting *en banc*, reversed this decision. Because Louisiana's governor and attorney general were named as defendants in the case, they ruled that these officials could not enforce the law, nor did they cause any of the alleged injuries. The court dismissed the case for lack of jurisdiction.

Dr. Ifeanyi Charles Anthony Okpalobi, two fellow physicians, and five health care clinics challenged the Louisiana law and asked the federal district court to stop it from becoming effective in August 1997. They contended that they would cease to provide abortion services because the act left the clinics and physicians open to significant liability. The court granted a temporary RESTRAINING ORDER and in January

1998 ruled on the MERITS of the case. It concluded that the law "had the purpose and effect of infringing" on a woman's right to an abortion and permanently ENJOINED the enforcement of the law. The state then appealed to the Fifth Circuit.

The appeals court panel, on a 2–1 vote, upheld the lower court decision. Judges Jacques L. Wiener and Robert M. Parker, in a joint opinion, devoted a significant part of their decision to jurisdictional issues. They concluded that the plaintiffs had the right to name the governor in the lawsuit, as officials are normally named personally in federal civil rights lawsuits. In addition, the plaintiffs had STANDING to bring the lawsuit, as they demonstrated they would be affected by the law.

Addressing the merits of the case, the judges pointed out that they were governed by U.S. Supreme Court decisions, which stated that where an undue burden exists for a woman to obtain an abortion, the law is invalid. The law must be held invalid if its purpose or effect places a substantial obstacle in the path of a woman seeking an abortion. They also acknowledged, however, that the Supreme Court had provided little instruction on how a lower court should determine whether a law has the "purpose" of imposing an undue burden on a woman's right to seek an abortion. Therefore, Wiener and Parker looked to other fields of CONSTITUTIONAL LAW for direction.

Louisiana asserted that the plaintiffs could not successfully challenge an abortion statute's purpose unless the state admitted an improper motive. The judges disagreed, holding that leg-

Edward Spencer
Abraham

islative history along with the social and historical context of the legislation can demonstrate an improper purpose. In this case the state argued that the purpose of the law was to encourage a physician to inform a woman of the risks associated with having an abortion. The judges rejected this argument, stating that the law's "plain language refutes such a contention." The act ignored INFORMED CONSENT because it expressly stated that the signing of a consent form by the mother before the abortion did not foreclose a CAUSE OF ACTION. A valid consent form only reduced the amount of DAMAGES she could recover. Viewed this way, the court found the purported legislative purpose unpersuasive. The majority ruled that the true purpose was "to ensure that a physician cannot insulate himself from liability by advising a woman of the risks, physical or mental, associated with abortion."

The majority then looked to the effect of the statute if it was implemented. They held that the law "undoubtedly would drive Louisiana's qualified and responsible abortion providers out of business," thereby imposing an undue burden on a woman's right to seek an abortion. The court pointed out that the plaintiffs currently provided 80 percent of all abortions in the state.

On rehearing, the appeals court ignored the substantive issues and concentrated on the jurisdictional ones. Judge E. Grady Jolly, writing for the majority, held that Louisiana was immune from suit under the ELEVENTH AMENDMENT, since no enforcement connection existed between the statute and Louisiana's governor and attorney general, who had been named personally in the suit. Judge Jolly also found that the plaintiff providers lacked standing to sue because the governor and attorney general did not cause any injury to them. Moreover, the defendant public officials could not redress the alleged actual or threatened injury. Finally, the court ruled that state officials must have a causal connection to a plaintiff's injury and powers to redress the injury in order for the plaintiff to have standing to sue the officials. Therefore, the court dismissed the action for lack of standing. Considering the always controversial nature of abortion-related issues, such elements may have influenced the court to focus on the jurisdictional issues of the case instead.

CROSS REFERENCES

Appendix: Louisiana's Abortion Malpractice Statute; Injunction

ABRAHAM, EDWARD SPENCER

On January 20, 2001, Edward Spencer Abraham, better known as Spence, was sworn in as the tenth Secretary of the U.S. Department of ENERGY after his appointment by President GEORGE W. BUSH and a confirmation by the U.S. Senate. Abraham is an experienced politician and has been a powerful member of the Republican Party for decades.

Born on June 12, 1952, in Lansing, Michigan, Abraham began his career in politics at the young age of 18 when he orchestrated Nelson Rockefeller's presidential campaign for the state of Michigan. He graduated with honors from Michigan State University in 1974 with a B.A. in political science. That same year, and again in 1976, he managed the congressional campaign for Michigan politician, Cliff Taylor. Abraham went on to Harvard Law School, where he co-founded the Harvard Journal of Law and Public Policy. He graduated in 1979 *cum laude* and returned to Michigan to teach law at Thomas Cooley School of Law and practice with the Danfield, Timmer and Taylor law firm in Lansing.

In 1983 Abraham was elected to serve as the chairman of the Michigan Republican Party. At 30 years of age, he was the youngest in the nation to serve in such a role. At the time he took over, the state party was deeply in debt and did not hold many state government positions. Within two years, however, Abraham paid off the $450,000 debt and led the Republicans in the 1984 elections, where they won eleven of thirteen state seats, all eight state board of education seats, and a state supreme court judgeship. Under his leadership, the Michigan Republican Party became one of the strongest state parties in the country and served as a model for others. Abraham's success did not go unnoticed by the Republican National Committee, which elected him to serve as chairman of the Republican Party Rules Committee.

In January 1990 Abraham was selected to serve as deputy chief of staff for Vice President Dan Quayle, in which role he assumed the management of the vice president's office, including budget and staff, for two years. He also served as liaison between the vice president and Republican leaders, a role that increased his visibility and political influence on a national basis. Throughout his tenure as deputy chief of staff, Abraham remained the Michigan Republican Party chairman and assisted in the campaign of his good friend, John Engler, who was elected governor of Michigan in 1990. In 1991, after

EDWARD SPENCER ABRAHAM

1952	Born in Lansing, Michigan
1979	Graduated from Harvard Law School
1983–1991	Served as Michigan Republican Party Chairman
1990–1991	Served as Deputy Chief of Staff for Vice President Dan Quayle
1991–1993	Served as National Republican Congressional Committee co-chairman
1995–2001	Represented the state of Michigan in the U.S. Senate
2001	Appointed Secretary of the U.S. Department of Energy

completing his third term as state party chairman and finishing his duties as deputy chief of staff, Abraham took on the co-chairman position for the National Republican Congressional Committee. Until 1993 he helped to manage the transition in the U.S. House of Representatives from a Democratic to a Republican majority.

Abraham was elected to represent the state of Michigan in the U.S. Senate in 1994, making him the first Michigan Republican Senator in twenty-two years. While in Congress, he served on several committees: Budget; Commerce, Science and Transportation; Judiciary; and Small Business. He chaired the Manufacturing and Competitiveness subcommittee as well as the Immigration subcommittee. As a senator, he supported free trade, legal and regulatory reform, and tax reform. He authored twenty-two bills that were signed into law, including the Electronic Signature in Global and National Commerce Act, which established federal guidelines for on-line contracts and signatures.

The grandson of Lebanese immigrants, Senator Abraham also supported an increase in legal immigration and sponsored a bill to increase visas for foreign technical workers. Abraham earned a reputation in the Senate as a hard worker, and during his six years in the Senate he never missed a roll call. Perhaps because he

spent so much of his time and energy in Washington instead of politicking in Michigan, he lost his Senate seat to the charismatic Democrat Debbie Stabenow in November 2000.

In January 2001, however, incoming President GEORGE W. BUSH rewarded him for his hard work and loyalty by appointing him to be the Secretary of the Department of Energy (DOE). Many were surprised by this appointment. After all, in 1996 and 1999, Abraham co-sponsored legislation that proposed to close the DOE and transfer its functions to other departments or to the private sector. During his confirmation hearings, Abraham explained that during those times the energy markets were stable, and, further, he had concerns about the department's operation. He assured the Senate, however, that since the Nuclear Security Administration Act of 2000 restructured and improved the agency's management, he no longer supported the dissolution of the DOE.

Environmental groups have expressed their concerns about Abraham's Senate record and views. As a senator, he, together with more than thirty other senators, opposed higher fuel efficiency standards for automobiles and trucks. Of course, he was a representative of Michigan, which is home to the U.S. automobile industry, so perhaps such opposition was to be expected. Many are also concerned about his support of increased oil drillings in the United States, including the Arctic National Wildlife Refuge in Alaska.

Abraham has set goals for the DOE, the first being to increase domestic production of energy, which he promised to do in an environmentally responsible manner, thereby decreasing reliance on imported oil. He also pledged to increase the use of renewable energy and to develop new technologies that would conserve fossil fuels and reduce energy-related pollution. The need for such energy solutions took on an urgency in 2001 when California experienced an energy crisis that included such emergency measures as rolling blackouts. Abraham's negotiation of that difficult situation will likely determine the success of his tenure in that office.

AFFIRMATIVE ACTION

Employment programs required by federal statutes and regulations designed to remedy discriminatory practices in hiring minority group members; i.e. positive steps designed to eliminate existing and continuing discrimination, to remedy lingering cost effects of past discrimination, and to create systems and procedures to prevent future discrimination; commonly based on population percentages of minority groups in a particular area. Factors considered are race, color, sex, creed, and age.

University of Michigan Admissions Policies Challenged

On December 13, 2000, U.S. District Judge Patrick J. Duggan upheld the University of Michigan's undergraduate admissions policy as a constitutional way to achieve diversity among races in *Gratz v. Bollinger*, 122 F.Supp.2d 811 (E.D.Mich. Dec 13, 2000). He wrote, "A racially and ethnically diverse student body produces significant educational benefits such that diversity, in the context of higher education, constitutes a compelling government interest." On March 27, 2001, in *Grutter v. Bollinger*, 137 F.Supp.2d 821 (E.D.Mich. Mar 27, 2001), U.S. District Judge Bernard A. Friedman struck down the admissions policy of Michigan's law school, saying "All racial distinction is inherently suspect and pre-emptorily invalid." The dean of the law school, Jeffrey S. Lehman, said the two opinions are "completely irreconcilable." Both decisions will be appealed and seem headed for the U.S. Supreme Court.

The undergraduate system upheld by Duggan uses race to a far greater degree in admitting students than does the law school's policy. Freshmen applying to the University of Michigan (UM) are judged on a 150-point scale; 80 points are given for a perfect grade point average (GPA) of 4.0, and 12 points are awarded for high scores on standardized tests. A student must have 100 or more points to be admitted. If the student has a 3.0 GPA, for example, he or she gets 60 points on the GPA scale. MINORITIES—including blacks, Hispanics, and Native American—with the same GPA are automatically given another 20 points, thereby boosting their scores to 80. That puts the minority student on the same level as white students or "unfavored minority" students—such as Asians—with a perfect GPA. Other, non-racial advantages are also allowed, such as 4 points to children of UM alumni and 10 points to residents of Michigan. About 13 percent of the university's 38,000 member student body, both undergraduate and graduate, are minorities: nearly 8 percent black, about 4 percent Hispanic, and six-tenths of a percent Native American. Michigan has spent more than $4 million pursuing its policy of affir-

mative action, and since 1987 minority enrollment has doubled.

The suit against the undergraduate admissions system, which has been in use since 1999, was filed by two white students denied admission, which they claimed was in favor of less qualified minority applicants. They were represented by the Center for Individual Rights, a conservative group that won its affirmative action case against the University of Texas law school in 1996. In upholding the system, Duggan issued judgments without holding a trial.

The admissions policy that governs the University of Michigan law school shows that white students have a slightly higher chance of entry. For example, in 2000, the student body was 38 percent white and 35 percent black. However, as Friedman wrote, "The evidence indisputably demonstrates that the law school places a very heavy emphasis on race in deciding whether to accept or reject." In 1995, for example, of five African Americans with GPA scores of 3.25–3.49 and law school admissions test scores of 154 or 155, four were admitted. Of 51 white students within that same range, only one was admitted.

Reactions to both rulings were mixed on campus. University president Lee Bollinger felt that Duggan's decision was a victory for UM, but "more important it is a victory for higher education and society." But a lawyer for the Center for Individual Rights disagreed with the idea that a public university has the right to engineer a certain racial mix of students. After the Friedman ruling, a lawyer on the plaintiff side said that the decision "moves us beyond the point where race matters." Some students on campus called Friedman a "relic from the era of Jim Crow."

The rulings from these judges, both appointed by President RONALD REAGAN, seem headed for the higher courts. They both stem from interpretations of the 1978 Supreme Court decision in REGENTS OF UNIVERSITY OF CALIFORNIA V. BAKKE 438 U.S. 265, 98 S. Ct. 2733, 57 L. Ed. 2d 750. A white student, Bakke, applied for admission to the UC-Davis medical school. Rejected twice, he filed a lawsuit against the university, claiming that 16 of the openings were filled through a special program catering to minorities. In a 5–4 decision, the Court ruled that race may be "part" of the admissions process as long as "fixed quotas" are not used. LEWIS FRANKLIN POWELL, however, was the only justice to declare that for an institution of higher education, "diversity" is constitutional as a goal. Although universities have followed that idea ever since, Friedman declared that diversity was not a standard to be articulated in the *Bakke* decision. These and other differences in interpretation of previous rulings make fairly certain that these decisions will find their way to the higher courts.

CROSS REFERENCES
Education Law

ALIENS

Foreign-born persons who have not been naturalized to become U.S. citizens under federal law and the Constitution.

Zadvydas v. Davis

The federal government is authorized to regulate immigration. Over the years, Congress has imposed various schemes to prevent or discourage illegal immigration. The public is most acquainted with the patrolling of the U.S.-Mexico border, yet the Immigration and Naturalization Service (INS) also deals with aliens who have legally been admitted to the United States but who have committed FELONY-level crimes in the United States. Apart from serving time in a U.S. prison, aliens are subject to DEPORTATION to their country of origin. This solution becomes problematic, however, when the alien's home country refuses to accept his or her return or when the country does not have a repatriation treaty with the United States. This difficulty has led to the indefinite detention of aliens with criminal records in federal immigration facilities. Critics have charged that this confinement violates the FIFTH AMENDMENT's DUE PROCESS Clause and entitles aliens to seek release through the use of the writ of HABEAS CORPUS.

The Supreme Court, in *Zadvydas v. Davis*, ___U.S.___, 121 S.Ct. 2491, ___L.Ed.2d___ (2001), agreed with these critics, ruling that aliens should not be held indefinitely. Moreover, the Court established as a maximum a six-month detention period. At that point, the alien may provide information as to why removal to the country of origin is not likely in the foreseeable future. If the government cannot rebut this information, the alien must be released from confinement. Finally, the Court declared that the FEDERAL COURTS are the proper place to review these issues, rejecting the government's claim that immigration is strictly the province of the executive branch.

The case involved the deportation of two resident aliens, Kestutitis Zadvydas and Kim Ho Ma. Zadvydas was born to Lithuanian parents in a displaced persons camp in Germany in 1948 and came to the United States in 1956. He became involved in crime and compiled a long list of convictions, including drug crimes and attempted ROBBERY and BURGLARY. Zadvydas was paroled and taken into INS custody and was ordered deported to Germany in 1994. Germany refused to accept him, however, as did Lithuania. Two years later the Dominican Republic refused to accept Zadvydas, whose wife is from that country. By 1998, four years after being held in detention, Zadvydas failed to obtain Lithuanian citizenship. Zadvydas began his legal fight in 1995 to escape detention by filing for a writ of habeas corpus. Though a federal DISTRICT COURT ordered him out of custody and into supervised release, the Court of Appeals for the Fifth Circuit reversed this ruling. It permitted Zadvydas to remain under supervised release, however, until the case was resolved.

Kim Ho Ma was born in Cambodia in 1977. He came to the United States in 1984 with his family. In 1996 he was convicted of MANSLAUGHTER in a gang-related shooting. After serving two years in prison, Ma was turned over to the INS. The INS determined that he should remain in custody because of his criminal record and his participation in a prison hunger strike. In 1999 Ma filed a writ of habeas corpus, arguing that because Cambodia did not have a repatriation treaty with the United States, it was virtually impossible for Ma to be deported. The district court agreed and ordered Ma released. The Court of Appeals for the Ninth Circuit upheld this decision, setting the stage for the Supreme Court to hear the cases and resolve issues among the circuit courts of appeal.

The Court, in a 5–4 decision, concluded that the federal courts had a role to play in resolving these types of deportation actions. Justice STEPHEN G. BREYER, writing for the majority, noted that the main federal habeas corpus law conferred jurisdiction on the federal courts to hear immigration appeals of this type. Though Congress had amended the immigration laws to restrict judicial review in certain kinds of cases, this type of case was not one of them. Therefore, the threshold issue of federal court jurisdiction came down on the side of aliens challenging their detention.

Justice Breyer remarked that a law "permitting indefinite detention of an alien would raise a serious constitutional problem." The denial of a person's liberty invokes the protection of the Fifth Amendment's Due

Process Clause. In these cases the civil detention of aliens could not be justified in light of the law's stated purposes: the need to prevent the flight of the alien and protect the community. It was unlikely a person in Zadvydas's or Ma's position had anywhere to flee. As to community protection, Justice Breyer agreed that this was a valid purpose but pointed out that the pair's civil confinement "is not limited, but potentially permanent." Moreover, the majority affirmed the distinction between an alien who has entered the country legally and an alien who has entered illegally. The former is afforded constitutional protections not given to the latter.

These constitutional concerns were compounded by the fact that Congress had not specifically given the attorney general, who oversees the INS, the power to confine indefinitely an alien who has been ordered removed. Breyer admitted that if such an intent had been expressed in statute, the Court would have allowed such a practice.

Finally, Justice Breyer addressed the practicalities of federal courts addressing similar cases. The Court declared that it was unlikely that Congress contemplated all removals could be accomplished in ninety days but "there is reason to believe that it doubted the constitutionality of more than six months' detention." Therefore, for "the sake of uniform administration in the federal courts," the INS can hold an alien ordered for removal for six months. After this period, the alien can file a petition for habeas corpus and seek to show there is "no significant likelihood of removal in the reasonable foreseeable future." If the government fails to rebut this showing, the alien must be released from confinement.

CROSS REFERENCES
Habeas Corpus; Jurisdiction

ANTITRUST LAW

Legislation enacted by the federal and various state governments to regulate trade and commerce by preventing unlawful restraints, price-fixing, and monopolies, to promote competition, and to encourage the production of quality goods and services at the lowest prices, with the primary goal of safeguarding public welfare by ensuring that consumer demands will be met by the manufacture and sale of goods at reasonable prices.

Sotheby's and Christie's Agree to Settlement

On February 22, 2001, in the U.S. District Court for Southern New York, Judge Lewis A. Kaplan gave final approval to a $537 million settlement reached between lawyers representing 130,000 plaintiff buyers/sellers and the defendant auction houses, New York-based Sotheby's Holdings Inc. and London-based Christie's International over alleged price-fixing charges pending against them. The civil lawsuit settlement was premised upon a four-year JUSTICE DEPARTMENT criminal investigation focusing on documents showing "years of secret meetings by top officers" of the auction houses, aimed at collusive PRICE-FIXING and other illegal business practices.

Under the initial settlement proposed in September 2000, each auction house was to pay $256 million of a $512 million proposal—an equivalent approximating three or four years' annual pre-tax profits for each of the corporate defendants, which jointly control approximately "95 percent of the $4 billion worldwide auction market." The final settlement, however, required that each auction house pay $206 million in cash and another $62.5 million in discount coupons applicable to future auction purchases. In March 2001 the judge briefly threatened to RESCIND the settlement approval, unless and until the defendant auction houses notified customers in foreign AUCTIONS of their right to sue in the United States—a provision not part of the original settlement agreement. This action followed the filing of objections, including those articulated by a client, the J. Paul Getty Trust, regarding the settlement's ostensible inapplicability to foreign auctions, and a general dislike for settlement proceeds in the form of "certificate" coupon vouchers for future auctions.

Concurrent with the civil settlement, Judge Kaplan accepted a criminal plea deal of $45 million in fines against Sotheby's. The amount of the fine was well below federal sentencing guidelines, but Sotheby's was only CULPABLE for half of the wrongdoing, thus justifying the reduced fine. The criminal plea bargain followed earlier admissions by former Sotheby's president and CEO, Diana D. Brooks, who pleaded guilty to fixing commission prices and fees in COLLUSION with Christie's top officials. As of Spring 2001, Brooks was awaiting sentencing, which was expected to be delayed until sentencing of two others indicted in the matter: A. Alfred Taubman, billionaire former chairman of

Diana Brooks, CEO of Sotheby's, takes a bid during the sale of items from Jacqueline Kennedy Onassis's estate in New York City, 1996.

Sotheby's, and Anthony J. Tennant, former head of Christie's. Both Taubman and Brooks had resigned from Sotheby's following the charges. As part of her previous plea, Brooks had implicated Taubman, stating that he had ordered the secret meetings. In May 2001, a federal GRAND JURY indicted Taubman and Tennant on the antitrust charges. In conjunction with cooperation from Brooks and Christie's, federal prosecutors agreed not to prosecute other former or current employees of the auction houses. Following indictment, Tennant published a statement to the press in which he indicated that he was "not subject to jurisdiction by the U.S. courts and accordingly will not be taking part in any of the pending proceedings." Notwithstanding, both men face up to three years in prison and $350,000 in penalty fines if convicted. To settle ongoing civil problems with the courts, Taubman had agreed to pay $156 million of Sotheby's share of the civil settlement, but this concession did not affect continued federal investigation and prosecution.

Moreover, Sotheby's agreed to settle a *third* related matter: a shareholders' lawsuit for $70 million, stemming from the same antitrust charges and alleging breach of FIDUCIARY duties and deceit. The essence of all the alleged wrongdoing focused on claims that since 1993, Sotheby's and Christie's had secretly colluded and agreed to charge buyers the same rates for services. Furthermore, they claimed, since 1995 the companies had done the same with sellers.

The suits also alleged that the auction houses ceased their previous practices of negotiating the amounts of sellers' commissions with some of their more affluent clients. Top officials allegedly participated in secret meetings to discuss commission rates, even agreeing to which one would first publish new non-negotiable fee schedules. They were also charged with collusion to fix prices and stifle competition from other auction houses.

U.S. Department of Justice v. Visa and MasterCard

The two-year-old anti-trust battle between the U.S. Department of JUSTICE (DOJ) and the Visa and MasterCard credit card companies heated up during the summer of 2000 when the parties faced off during a ten-week trial in FEDERAL COURT. Both sides claimed victory, but a final decision has yet to be rendered by the presiding judge.

The lawsuit began on October 7, 1998, when the DOJ brought a complaint against Visa U.S.A., Inc., Visa International Corp., and MasterCard International Inc. Filed in the U.S. District Court for the Southern District of New York, the complaint alleged that the two credit card giants have been engaging in monopolistic practices in violation of the SHERMAN ANTITRUST ACT. 15 U.S.C.A. § 1. Specifically, the defendants were charged with conspiring to restrain trade by restricting banks that are authorized to issue Visa cards, MasterCards, or both,

Lawyers for Visa International during the U.S. Justice Department's antitrust suit return to courthouse. (*left-right*): Eugene Bannigan, John Gordan, Michele Connaugton, and Steve Zelinger.

from also offering competitors' credit cards, such as American Express cards and Discover cards. The complaint stated that the defendants' monopolistic practices suppressed competition, deprived consumers of full choice, increased credit card interest rates, and impeded development of new credit card products. The complaint also alleged that the defendants' two networks are unlawfully controlled by a small number of banks sitting simultaneously as board members on both credit card companies. Judge Barbara S. Jones was assigned to preside over the case without a jury.

The trial was originally scheduled to begin on October 29, 1999, but the defendants objected to this date as overly ambitious. The court then rescheduled the trial to begin on February 8, 2000. Miscellaneous disputes between the parties delayed the proceedings and pushed the date back further, this time to June 12, 2000. One pre-trial dispute centered on who would pay for a DISCOVERY request made by the plaintiff, which had asked Visa to retrieve and recreate E-mail from a system that had been replaced. Visa estimated the cost of complying with the request at $130,000. The court ordered Visa to front the costs of producing the E-mail initially but reserved judgment as to who would be held ultimately responsible for the expenses. In another dispute Discover credit card filed a motion to intervene in the lawsuit on the side of the government. Discover, a unit of the New York securities firm Morgan Stanley Dean Witter & Co., argued that the government's proposal to permit Visa and MasterCard banks to issue cards for American Express and Discover would actually hurt Discover because, as the smallest of the

four networks of credit card banks, it could have a hard time attracting partner banks. The court denied Discover's motion because it said that the Justice Department's role was to represent the public interest in competition, not just the private interests of Discover.

When the trial finally began, the government presented its opening statements first. Melvin A. Schwarz, the Justice Department's special counsel for civil enforcement, told Judge Jones that the government's case had two prongs. He called the first one the "duality" prong. He argued that although Visa and MasterCard appear to be comprised of two separate networks of member banks that are authorized to issue one particular brand of credit card, in reality the two companies behave as one huge monolith. Visa and MasterCard, Schwarz said, are jointly run by a small group of banks who sit on the board of directors at both companies and control many of the important committees at both companies. Schwarz maintained that the line separating the two companies is further blurred by the fact that most member banks in both networks are authorized to issue either credit card to consumers, and neither company targets the other in advertising campaigns.

Schwarz called the second prong of the government's case the "exclusionary-rules" prong. The DOJ's attorney argued that the operating rules for both companies prohibit member banks from issuing credit cards for rival brands. Schwarz said that those same rules allow Visa and MasterCard to remove banks from their networks when they conduct business with rival credit card companies. Even when the defendants did not directly invoke these operating rules to remove member banks from their networks, Schwarz contended, Visa and MasterCard made their message clear by pressuring member banks against dealing with competitors. Since Visa and MasterCard issue 75 percent of the nearly 500 million credit cards in circulation in the United States, Schwarz reasoned that this pressure was substantial.

Schwarz stated that the result of this allegedly monopolistic behavior was decreased competition between Visa and MasterCard, as the interlocking board members realized that the two companies would only hurt themselves if they took aggressive action against each other in the marketplace. The DOJ's attorney also stated that the defendant's behavior had decreased competition with smaller credit card companies who found it difficult to expand their clientele with businesses already in the exclusive Visa and

MasterCard networks. Finally, Schwarz maintained that the defendants' stranglehold on the market had stifled technological development. He cited as an example the slow development of so-called "smart" cards that enable secure purchases over the Internet via an electronic transaction identity system.

The defendants' opening statements were much shorter. Ken Gallo was MasterCard's lead attorney, while Laurence Popofsky spoke on behalf of Visa. Both attorneys argued that competition between Visa and MasterCard and other credit card companies had been vigorous. They told the court that their witnesses would testify about thousands of credit card products that are currently on the market. They said that defense witnesses also would show how competitors take business away from Visa and MasterCard through lower interest rates and cash rebates. Finally, they argued that Visa and MasterCard have been conducting business the same way for twenty years, and the government tacitly consented to their business practices by waiting so long to object.

Harvey Golub, chairman and chief executive officer for American Express Co., testified on behalf of the plaintiff. He compared Visa and MasterCard to Coca-Cola and Pepsi-Cola in the soft-drink industry. The defendants' behavior in this case, Golub testified, was tantamount to Coke and Pepsi entering an agreement that required U.S. supermarkets to carry both Coke and Pepsi if they wanted to sell either brand but prohibited the supermarkets from carrying any rival brand. Coke and Pepsi are so strong that the supermarkets would have to capitulate, Golub suggested, just like the member banks have capitulated to the defendants' exclusive-dealing arrangements in the credit card industry.

Visa and MasterCard countered Golub's testimony with a series of witnesses who tried to blame American Express for its inability to compete with the defendants. Executives from both companies testified that American Express had lobbied the government to pursue this case for several years. They testified that American Express lost customers by maintaining high annual fees, uncompetitive interest rates, and exclusive-dealing agreements of their own with corporate credit card customers. In effect, the witnesses suggested, American Express was trying to win in the courtroom a battle it lost in the marketplace due to its own poor business decisions.

The last witness testified on August 22, 2000. Closing arguments were scheduled for October 16, but Judge Jones canceled them at the last second, prompting speculation that a final ruling was imminent. She had yet to issue a ruling as of July 2001.

APPEAL

Timely resort by an unsuccessful party in a lawsuit or administrative proceeding to an appropriate superior court empowered to review a FINAL DECISION on the ground that it was based upon an erroneous application of law.

Becker v. Montgomery

U.S. law contains both substantive and procedural components. Though substantive law receives the most public attention, many cases are lost because of procedural defects or irregularities. Federal and state court systems maintain rules of procedure to insure uniformity, fairness, and administrative efficiency. Though courts routinely dismiss cases for failure to comply with procedural requirements, the modern trend has been to allow litigants an opportunity to correct the mistake before such a dismissal. In some cases, however, the defect is characterized as jurisdictional. This term means that the mistake is fatal to the case, and the court cannot allow for a subsequent correction.

In a rare occurrence, the Supreme Court of the United States confronted such a procedural issue in *Becker v. Montgomery*, ___U.S.___, 121 S.Ct. 1801, 149 L.Ed.2d 983 (2001). The Court, in a unanimous ruling, held that a prisoner's failure to sign his name on his notice of appeal to a federal circuit COURT OF APPEALS did not justify dismissal of his appeal. The Court made clear that in such cases the APPELLANT must be given the opportunity to provide a signature.

Dale G. Becker, an inmate in an Ohio state prison, filed a federal CIVIL RIGHTS lawsuit without an attorney, challenging his confinement because he was exposed to second-hand cigarette smoke. The federal DISTRICT COURT dismissed his lawsuit because he had failed to "exhaust prison administrative remedies" and because he had not stated a claim upon which relief could be granted. Becker then filed an appeal with the U.S. Court of Appeals for the Sixth Circuit. He used a notice of appeal form, which lists the title of the case, the parties, and the judgment from which he was appealing. Above the space listed as "Counsel for Appellant" Becker typed his name. He also typed his address and the date of the notice in the appropriate places. Though Becker should have

Betty Montgomery, Ohio Attorney General (*center*), makes an announcement to the press in Columbus, Ohio, 2000.

Capital Justice Initiative:
Post-Conviction DNA Protocol

signed his name instead of typing it, there were no instructions on the form telling him to do so.

The district court accepted and docketed Becker's notice and sent a copy to the AP-PELLATE COURT. Becker received a letter from the Clerk's Office for the Sixth Circuit, notifying him that costs would be waived because he was indigent and that he needed to submit his brief by a certain date. Becker filed his brief two weeks before the deadline and signed the brief as required by appellate rules. However, six months later he received an order from the court dismissing his appeal because he had failed to sign the notice of appeal. The court informed Becker that it had no jurisdiction to consider his appeal because of this defect. Becker filed a motion for reconsideration of this order and attached a new notice of appeal that he had signed. The appeals court denied this motion. Becker petitioned the Supreme Court, and, in an unusual move, the Attorney General of Ohio filed a response that agreed with Becker's position. Faced with no party to defend the court's order, the Supreme Court granted the petition and named two attorneys as FRIENDS OF THE COURT to represent the appellate court's interests.

In a unanimous ruling, the Court overruled the Sixth Circuit. Justice RUTH BADER GINSBURG, writing for the Court, stated that the Sixth Circuit case on which it based its decision was faulty precedent. That decision com-

bined two rules, one from the Federal Rules of Appellate Procedure and one from the Federal Rules of Civil Procedure (which generally govern trial matters.) The appellate rule requires that a notice of appeal must be filed with the district court within 30 days after the judgment or order is entered. The civil rule requires that every paper filed in district court must be signed. The Court agreed that the "governing Federal Rules call for a signature on notices of appeal." However, the Court rejected the Sixth Circuit's "ruling that the signature requirement cannot be met after the appeal period expires."

The Court also rejected Becker's claim that a typed signature satisfies the signature requirement. Though technology has begun to provide for electronic and digital signatures, the Court concluded that only a rules change could allow more leeway in the interpretation of the signature requirement. Instead, the Court focused on the civil signature rule, pointing out that the rule allows the "omission of a signature . . . [to] be corrected promptly after being called to the attention of the attorney or party." The Court held that this rule should be read as a whole. In its view, Becker had followed the spirit of the rule by proffering a duplicate of the notice of appeal with his signature once the defect had been brought to his attention. Therefore, Becker "should not have suffered dismissal of his appeal for nonobservance of that rule."

ARBITRATION

The submission of a dispute to an unbiased third person designated by the parties to the controversy, who agree in advance to comply with the AWARD—a decision to be issued after a hearing at which both parties have an opportunity to be heard.

Eastern Associated Coal Corp. v. Mine Workers

Employers and labor unions have historically had a difficult time in resolving personnel disputes. Many COLLECTIVE BARGAINING AGREEMENTS, however, now contain arbitration provisions, which authorize the appointment of a neutral party to determine whether the employer has JUST CAUSE to discharge an employee. Employers sometimes disagree with an arbitrator's decision and ask a court to issue an order that refuses to enforce the arbitration. The U.S. Supreme Court, in *Eastern Associated Coal Corporation v. United Mine Workers of America, District 17*, 531 U.S. 57, 121 S.Ct. 462, ___ L.Ed.2d. ___ (2000), examined the enforceability of an arbitration award when the employee in question had twice tested positive for marijuana. The Court upheld the arbitrator's decision, ordering the employer to reinstate the employee.

Eastern Associated Coal Corporation and the United Mine Workers (UMW) entered into a collective bargaining agreement with arbitration provisions. The agreement specified that, in arbitration, in order to discharge an employee, Eastern must prove it has just cause. Otherwise the arbitrator will order the employee reinstated. The arbitrator's decision is final.

James Smith worked for Eastern as a member of a road crew, a job that required him to drive heavy vehicles on public highways. As a truck driver, Smith was subject to Department of TRANSPORTATION (DOT) regulations requiring random drug testing of workers engaged in "safety-sensitive" tasks. In March 1996 Smith tested positive for marijuana. Eastern sought to discharge him. The union went to arbitration, and the arbitrator concluded that Smith's positive drug test did not amount to just cause for discharge. Instead the arbitrator ordered Smith's reinstatement, provided that Smith accept a suspension of 30 days without pay, participate in a substance-abuse program, and undergo drug tests at the discretion of Eastern or an approved substance-abuse professional for the next five years. However, in July 1997 Smith again tested positive for marijuana. Eastern again sought to discharge him, and the union went to arbitration. The arbitrator again concluded that Smith's use of marijuana did not amount to just cause for discharge, in light of two mitigating circumstances: Smith had been a good employee for 17 years, and he had testified about a family problem that caused a one-time lapse in drug usage.

The arbitrator once more ordered Smith's reinstatement with provisions. Smith had to accept a new suspension without pay, this time for slightly more than three months. He had to reimburse Eastern and the union for the costs of both arbitration proceedings. Smith also had to continue to participate in a substance abuse program and undergo random drug testing. Finally, he was to provide Eastern with a signed, undated letter of resignation, to take effect if Smith again tested positive within the next five years.

Eastern filed a lawsuit in federal court seeking to have the arbitrator's award vacated, arguing that the award contravened a public policy against the operation of dangerous machinery by workers who test positive for drugs. The district court, in *Eastern Associated Coal Co. v. United Mine Workers of America*, 66 F.Supp.2d 796 (S.D.W.Va. Sep 30, 1998), rejected this argument and ordered Smith reinstated. The Court of Appeals for the Fourth Circuit upheld this decision in *Eastern Associated Coal Co. v. United Mine Workers of America, Dist. 17*, 188 F.3d 501, (4th Cir.(W.Va.) Aug 20, 1999). The Supreme Court agreed to hear Eastern's appeal because there was a conflict in the circuit courts over whether a court had to order reinstatement of an employee who had used illegal drugs.

The Court unanimously agreed that Smith should be reinstated, with Justice STEPHEN G. BREYER writing for seven of the justices. Breyer noted that the key question was whether the contractual reinstatement should be unenforceable because it is contrary to public policy. Breyer made clear that the question was not whether Smith's drug use itself violated public policy but whether the agreement to reinstate him did so. He also pointed out that the public policy exception is a narrow one.

The company argued that the DOT rules against truck drivers using illegal drugs were based on the important policy of public safety. Justice Breyer agreed that this was an important public policy but also found that enforcing arbitration awards was an equally compelling public policy. Moreover, Breyer determined that the DOT's rules went beyond public policies against drug use. The rules also included a policy that favored rehabilitation of employees who use drugs. Finally, Breyer concluded, "the relevant statutory and regulatory provisions must be read in light of a background labor law policy that favors determination of disciplinary questions through arbitration when chosen as a result of labor-management negotiation."

Based on these principles, Breyer ruled that the reinstatement did not violate public policy, as the award did not condone the employee's drug use or its impact on public safety. In addition, the arbitrator punished Smith by placing conditions on his reinstatement. Justice Breyer also concluded that just because Smith was a RECIDIVIST did not tip the balance in favor of discharge. Therefore, Smith should be reinstated.

Green Tree Financial Corp. v. Randolph

The use of arbitration is designed to avoid costly litigation in the court system, yet the courts are often called upon to determine the legality of arbitration provisions and whether they should be enforced. In certain sectors of U.S. business, the sellers of products routinely require the buyer to sign a contract that requires the buyer to submit to arbitration if a dispute arises. This procedure is used in the manufactured home industry, where purchasers of mobile homes must agree to arbitration when obtaining financing on their homes. Because of the disparity in bargaining power between the purchaser and the finance company, courts look closely at the terms of arbitration agreements to see if they should be enforced. The provisions of the Federal Arbitration Act shape their analysis. The U.S. Supreme Court, in *Green Tree Financial Corp. v. Randolph*, 531 U.S. 79, 121 S.Ct. 513, 148 L.Ed.2d 373, (U.S.Ala. Dec 11, 2000) (NO. 99–1235), addressed these questions, ruling that a purchaser could appeal a final court decision on whether to arbitrate. However, the Court also ruled that the failure of an arbitration agreement to mention arbitration costs and fees is not automatically unenforceable on the theory that it fails to protect a party from potentially steep arbitration costs.

Larketta Randolph purchased a mobile home from a company in Opelika, Alabama. She financed her purchase through Green Tree Financial Corporation, a national company that specializes in the financing of mobile homes. Green Tree required Randolph to purchase insurance that protected Green Tree against the costs of repossession in the event Randolph defaulted on the loan. "The agreement also provided that all disputes relating to the con-

tract. . .would be resolved by binding arbitration."

Randolph later sued Green Tree, contending that "they violated the TRUTH IN LENDING ACT by failing to disclose as a finance charge" the repossession insurance requirement. She also claimed that Green Tree violated the Equal Credit Opportunity Act by requiring her to arbitrate her statutory causes of action. The federal district court dismissed Randolph's case and ordered her to arbitrate her claims. She then appealed. The Court of Appeals for the Eleventh Circuit first held that it had jurisdiction to review the district court's order because that order was a final decision. The court of appeals looked to the Federal Arbitration Act (FAA), 9 U.S.C. § 16, which governs appeal from a district court's arbitration order, and specifically § 16(a)(3), which "allows appeal from a final decision with respect to an arbitration that is subject to this title." The court concluded that a final, appealable order within the meaning of the FAA is one that disposes of all the issues framed by the litigation, leaving nothing to be done but execute the order. The Court of Appeals found the District Court's order within that definition. The court also ruled that the arbitration agreement failed to provide the minimum guarantees that Randolph could vindicate her statutory rights under the Truth-in-Lending Act. It observed that the arbitration agreement was silent with respect to payment of filing fees, arbitrators' costs, and other arbitration expenses. On that basis, the court held that the agreement to arbitrate posed a risk that the respondent's ability to vindicate her statutory rights would be undone by "steep" arbitration costs, and therefore was unenforceable.

The Supreme Court agreed unanimously with the Court of Appeals on the jurisdictional issue but split 5–4 in reversing the unenforceability ruling. Chief Justice WILLIAM H. REHNQUIST, writing for the Court on the jurisdictional issue, agreed that the district court's decision was "final" and thus appealable. He reasoned that the term "final decision" had "a well-developed and longstanding meaning. It is a decision that 'ends the litigation on the merits and leaves nothing more for the court to do but execute the judgment.'"

Rehnquist, writing for the majority, overturned the second part of the Eleventh Circuit's decision. The fact that Randolph's agreement did not specify arbitration costs did not render it unenforceable. The purpose of the FAA was to reverse "longstanding judicial hostility to arbitration agreements . . . and to place [them] upon the same footing as other contracts." Randolph had agreed to arbitrate all claims when she signed the agreement. Though Rehnquist acknowledged that large arbitration costs might deter Randolph from pursuing her claims, he concluded that she had failed to put into the record that she would bear such costs. To make the arbitration agreement unenforceable because of its silence on costs "would 'undermine the liberal federal policy favoring arbitration agreements.'"

Justice RUTH BADER GINSBURG, in a dissenting opinion joined by Justices JOHN PAUL STEVENS, DAVID H. SOUTER, and STEPHEN G. BREYER, argued that the Court should have sent the case back to the district court to develop more facts about potential arbitration costs. If they were deemed prohibitive, the minority believed the arbitration agreement should be rendered unenforceable.

CROSS REFERENCES
Contracts; Drugs and Narcotics; Labor Law

ASHCROFT, JOHN DAVID

In twenty-five years, John Ashcroft has gone from Assistant State Attorney General for the state of Missouri to U.S. Attorney General. The political road to the JUSTICE DEPARTMENT has been paved by this conservative right-wing Republican with his hard work and strong ethics.

John David Ashcroft was born on May 9, 1942, in Chicago, Illinois. His family moved to rural Springfield, Missouri, when he was just a young boy. Springfield is the home of the Pentecostal Assembly of God church, and since Ashcroft's father and grandfather were Pentecostal ministers, it seemed only natural that the family would make Springfield their home. While the church forbids smoking, drinking, and dancing, it does promote gospel singing. Ashcroft took up playing the guitar and singing gospel when he was young, and it has been a passion of his ever since.

After high school, Ashcroft headed east to Yale where he received a degree in history in 1964. Ashcroft then returned to the Midwest and studied at the University of Chicago Law School. There he met his wife, Janet. They both graduated from the University of Chicago in 1967 and went on to teach business law at Southwest Missouri State University.

JOHN DAVID ASHCROFT

1942	Born in Chicago, Illinois
1967	Graduated from University of Chicago Law School
1976	Elected Attorney General for the state of Missouri
1984	Elected Governor of Missouri
1994	Elected to the U.S. Senate
2001	Appointed U.S. Attorney General by President George W. Bush

In 1972 Ashcroft decided to run for a spot in the U.S. House of Representatives. While he lost the race, he still found his way into politics when he was named assistant ATTORNEY GENERAL for the state of Missouri in 1975 under then-attorney general, John Danforth. While working there, Ashcroft found himself working side by side with future U.S. Supreme Court Justice CLARENCE THOMAS.

In 1976 Danforth decided to run for the U.S. Senate, leaving Ashcroft the opportunity to campaign for this soon to be vacated State Attorney General position. Ashcroft won the election and, in this new role, established his conservative reputation when he vehemently opposed court-ordered SCHOOL DESEGREGATION in St. Louis and Kansas City. While he could not please everybody, he managed to please many as he was re-elected to another term, before then becoming the fiftieth governor of Missouri.

John David Ashcroft

Ashcroft accomplished a great deal for the state of Missouri. He balanced budgets without increasing taxes. He also focused on WELFARE reform and education by imposing tougher testing requirements for student advancement. As a validation of these efforts, Ashcroft was re-elected to a second term as governor with an impressive 65 percent of the vote. State law did not allow him to run for a third term.

In 1994 Ashcroft again followed the footsteps of John Danforth, who was retiring from the Senate. Ashcroft was elected to the U.S. Senate and sworn in at the beginning of 1995. While in Congress, Ashcroft proposed and supported very conservative legislation, most of which did not become law. He was pro-life, against GUN CONTROL, and against AFFIRMATIVE ACTION. He sponsored the Human Life Amendment, which defined life to begin at conception and banned all abortions, including those involving incest or rape, except when needed to save the life of the mother. The legislation did not become law. He was also unsuccessful in his support for term limits for congressmen and prayer in schools. Ashcroft was, however, successful with his Charitable Choice provision, which made it into the welfare reform legislation in 1996. The provision granted funding to religious organizations in order to provide social welfare programs.

In 1998 Ashcroft published a book, *Lessons from a Father to his Son*, about his father's preachings, his Christian faith, and how it influenced his life. Also in 1998 the Ronnie White confirmation hearings branded him by some as a racist. White was the first African-American Missouri Supreme Court Justice. Then-President BILL CLINTON appointed him for the federal bench. During White's confirmation hearings, Ashcroft focused on a dissent that White made in a CAPITAL PUNISHMENT case and argued that White was soft on crime. Yet, White had actually voted to uphold the death penalty in 41 of the 59 cases that he heard on the bench, and some argued that Ashcroft attacked White because of his race. Ultimately, the Senate voted down White, making him the first federal judicial nominee to be defeated since ROBERT BORK. Meanwhile that same year, Ashcroft seriously considered running for the Republican Party nomination for U.S. president. After a short-lived campaign, however, he withdrew his name and supported GEORGE W. BUSH.

In 2000 Aschroft ran once again for his Senate position, this time against Missouri Governor MEL CARNAHAN. Carnahan had died in a plane crash with his son three weeks *before* the election but still won the vote by a slim margin. Ashcroft was a gracious loser, and Carnahan's widow was appointed to replace her deceased husband in the Senate.

In 2001 Ashcroft was appointed by President George W. Bush and confirmed by Congress for the position of U.S. attorney general, one of the most powerful positions in the country. As attorney general, Ashcroft is head of the Justice Department and oversees many powerful segments of the federal government, including the Drug Enforcement Administration, the Immigration and Naturalization Service, the Federal Bureau of Investigation, and the U.S. Marshals. He is the country's chief prosecuting attorney who will, among other things, decide how to proceed with the Microsoft antitrust case after their inevitable appeal. He also will have input on the president's appointments for the federal bench, including the U.S. Supreme Court.

CROSS REFERENCES
Attorney General; Justice Department

BOIES, DAVID

Some call David Boies the greatest trial lawyer alive or "the Michael Jordan of the courtroom." He has successfully handled cases for IBM, CBS, Texaco, Westinghouse and, perhaps most notably, the U.S. government in its victory over Microsoft.

Boies was born on March 11, 1941, in the small town of Marengo, Illinois. The son of two high school teachers and the eldest of five children, he developed a hard work ethic and down-to-earth Midwestern charm. Boies exhibits this non-pretentious character in his courtroom attire, which usually consists of black tennis shoes, simple suits, knit ties, and a $35 watch that he wears on his sleeve so he can always be aware of the time. While today he is known for his keen memory, Boies could not read until the third grade due to a mild form of dyslexia. He believes it may have been the challenges he faced with his dyslexia that enabled him to develop the ability to remember key facts, legal citations, and contradictory testimony in the middle of trial without a single note in front of him.

For his college level work, Boies managed to complete three years of studies in just two at the University of Redland. He then entered Northwestern University School of Law but transferred to Yale to study in a two-year program in law and economics. He graduated second in his class and went on to work with the well established law firm, Cravath, Swaine and Moore, in New York City.

Boies worked diligently for Cravath, typically billing seventy hours per week while still teaching a course at the New York University

Law School. In 1969 he successfully defended IBM in a major ANTITRUST action. This accomplishment helped him earn partnership at Cravath at the young age of 31. In 1977 Boies took a sabbatical from the firm to work as chief counsel for the Senate Antitrust committee. After returning to Cravath, Boies was retained in 1982 to defend the television network, CBS, in a LI-BEL suit brought against them by VIETNAM WAR General William Westmoreland. This case was Boies's first libel suit, yet spectators in the courtroom nicknamed him "Jaws" for his bloody, yet successful, cross examinations of the plaintiff's witnesses. Before the trial came to a close, General Westmoreland dropped the lawsuit. In November 1986 Texaco recruited Boies to represent them in an appeal to overturn the $10.6 billion jury verdict in favor of Penzoil in a case involving Penzoil's purchase of Getty Oil. He won the appeal and saved Texaco from financial ruin.

Boies continued to make headlines during the 1990s. In 1992 he worked with the FEDERAL DEPOSIT INSURANCE CORPORATION (FDIC) in recovering a $1.1 billion settlement from Michael Milken and his firm, Drexel Burnham Lambert. And in 1993, he successfully defended Westinghouse against accusations by the Philippine government that the company bribed former President Marcos for a power plant contract.

In 1995 Boies was retained by George Steinbrenner to represent the New York Yankees. In 1997 the Yankees brought an antitrust suit against Major League Baseball. One of the defendants, the Atlanta Braves baseball team, had recently been purchased by Time Warner, a

David Boies

15

DAVID BOIES

1941	Born in Marengo, Illinois
1966	Earned Yale Law School degree
1969	Successfully defended IBM in antitrust case
1984	Successfully defended CBS in libel suit
1992	Recovered $1.1 billion for FDIC from Michael Milken and Drexel Burnham Lambert
1999–2000	Aided Justice Department in Microsoft antitrust lawsuit
2000	Represented Al Gore in election recount battle

prominent client of his law firm, Cravath, Swaine, and Moore. Boies had to choose between the Yankees and the law firm, which he had worked with for nearly thirty years. As Boies had, over the years, grown distant from Cravath, he decided the time had come for him to leave, so he chose the Yankees. His departure from Cravath, Swaine, and Moore made the front page of the *New York Times*.

Free of the constraints of a large, institutional law firm, Boies and Washington lawyer, Jonathon Schiller, formed their own firm. This new freedom allowed Boies to accept an invitation to join the JUSTICE DEPARTMENT's litigation team in the antitrust case against Microsoft, the world's largest computer software company. Boies's performance was cited as brilliant, especially during the twenty-hour deposition of Microsoft chairman, Bill Gates, where many believe he reduced the genius billionaire into an argumentative, belligerent, non-credible witness. Not surprisingly, Gates did not testify at trial. Judge Thomas Penfield Jackson found that Microsoft violated the federal antitrust laws by exploiting its powers to destroy its competitors. And in spite of his notoriety and expertise, Boies only charged the government $40 per hour for his services.

Known for his ability to handle many matters at one time, Boies continued to represent many clients during the Microsoft trial, including his CLASS ACTION lawsuit against the vitamin

CARTEL for PRICE-FIXING. The case resulted in a settlement of $1.17 billion—of which Boies's firm collected $40 million—the largest award ever to be given in an antitrust case. Later, Boies was appointed to handle a class-action suit against two leading art AUCTION companies, Christie's and Sotheby's, which resulted in a $537 million settlement (*see* Antitrust Law: Sotheby's and Christie's Agree to Settlement).

More recently, Boies has taken on the big record companies, representing Napster, the website where over a half billion songs are downloaded free of charge. Most of these songs are copyrighted, leading to the fundamental issue in the case: the definition of COPYRIGHT on the Internet. Boies has also taken on the Health Maintenance Organizations (HMOs), accusing them of nondisclosure to patients when it comes to financial impacts on medical care decisions.

Perhaps the greatest and most monumental challenge for Boies in the new millennium was his representation of presidential hopeful AL GORE in his post-election fight for a recount. While Boies celebrated early victories in the ordeal, in the end the Supreme Court of the United States rejected his arguments, resulting in a small margin of victory for now President GEORGE W. BUSH. Boies continues to be in high demand. He represents large conglomerates such as AOL-Time Warner, as well as celebrity clients including fashion designer Calvin Klein, radio personality Don Imus, and actor Gary Shandling.

BOUNDARIES

Natural or artificial separations or divisions between adjoining properties to show their limits.

New Hampshire v. Maine

It is not uncommon for individual owners of real property to dispute the boundaries of their property. Trial courts routinely hear cases where boundary lines are at the heart of the dispute. More unusual are boundary disputes between states, as these boundaries may date back to the eighteenth century. The Supreme Court of the United States was called upon to resolve just such a dispute between New Hampshire and Maine. In *New Hampshire v. Maine* ___U.S.___, 121 S.Ct. 1808, 149 L.Ed.2d 968 (2001), the Court concluded that the state of Maine's boundaries include the Portsmouth Harbor and the Portsmouth Naval Shipyard. In its ruling, the Court employed the doctrine of judicial ESTOPPEL, a theory that is rarely used but which seeks to guard "the integrity of the judicial process."

The territory in dispute involves the Piscataqua River, which lies at the southeastern end of New Hampshire's boundary with Maine. The river runs seaward into the harbor. New Hampshire filed a lawsuit with the Supreme Court in March 2000 under the Court's ORIGINAL JURISDICTION over such disputes between states. New Hampshire claimed that the Piscataqua River boundary entended to Maine's shore and thus all of the Piscataqua River and all of Portsmouth Harbor belonged to New Hampshire. Maine responded by asking the Court to dismiss the complaint. It asserted two GROUNDS in support of its motion. First, it contended that King George II of England had settled the current boundaries in 1740. Second, it asserted that a 1977 consent judgment between the states had set the boundary between the states at the middle of the Piscataqua River's main navigation channel. Therefore, New Hampshire was bound by this interpretation. Justice DAVID H. SOUTER recused himself from the case because he had served as New Hampshire ATTORNEY GENERAL.

The Supreme Court, in a unanimous decision, sided with Maine and dismissed the complaint. Justice RUTH BADER GINSBURG, writing for the Court, noted that King George's 1740 DECREE located the river boundary at the "Middle of the River." More telling, however, was New Hampshire's ASSENT to this interpretation in the 1977 boundary proceeding. The 1977 dispute involved lobster fishing rights between the two states. Though the Supreme Court did not issue a ruling, the parties entered into a consent agreement that stated that the "Middle of the River" referred to the middle of the Piscataqua's main navigation channel. A special master appointed by the Supreme Court contended, however, that the geographic middle of the river and not its main navigation channel was the correct interpretation of the 1740 decree. Nevertheless, the Court deferred to the states and entered the consent judgment based on the middle of the navigation channel.

In its 2000 complaint, New Hampshire asserted sovereignty over the entire river. Maine countered that the 1977 consent judgment legally prohibited—or, estopped—New Hampshire from arguing for a new boundary definition. Justice Ginsburg concluded that judicial estoppel was the appropriate doctrine to apply to the dispute. Noting that the doctrine has rarely been discussed or applied, Ginsburg

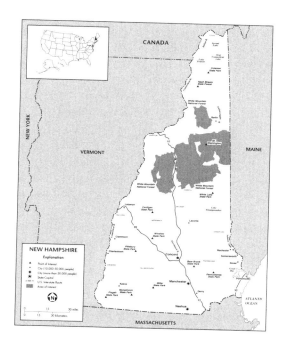

Map of New Hampshire showing the state's boundaries as of 2001.

stated that where a party assumes a certain legal position and succeeds in maintaining that position, the party may not assume a contrary position at a later time merely because the party's interests have changed. Ginsburg, citing *Scarano v. Central R. Co.*, explained that the doctrine "prevents parties from playing 'fast and loose with courts'," and it maintains the integrity of the judicial process. Although the application of judicial estoppel must be applied on a case-by-case basis, Ginsburg identified several factors that will determine whether estoppel is warranted. First, "a party's later position must be clearly inconsistent with its earlier position." Second, "the party has succeeded in persuading a court to accept its earlier position." A third factor is whether the party "would derive an unfair advantage or impose an unfair detriment on the opposing party if not estopped."

In applying these three factors, Ginsburg concluded that New Hampshire's boundary claim was "clearly inconsistent" with its 1977 interpretation of the "Middle of the River." This interpretation located the middle of the river "somewhere other than the Maine shore of the Piscataqua River." Second, the Supreme Court in 1977 accepted the agreement that contained New Hampshire's definition of the middle of the river. Ginsburg noted that New Hampshire had endorsed the consent agreement as being in the "best interest of each State." Ginsburg rejected New Hampshire's claim that the 1997 consent decree was entered with a thorough search of the historical record and that it would not have entered into the agreement if it had known what it later came to find were the true historical facts. In analyzing the "new" historical evidence, Ginsburg found that none of it supported New Hampshire's position. Moreover, the evidence had been available in 1977, and New Hampshire had the opportunity to consult it then. Nothing had changed in 25 years to alter this fact. Finally, it would be unfair to Maine to accept the new boundary, as the state had relied upon the 1977 definition. Therefore, the Court dismissed the complaint.

BRIBERY

The offering, giving, receiving, or soliciting of something of value for the purpose of influencing the action of an official in the discharge of his or her public or legal duties.

Illinois's Governor Tainted by Driver's License Scandal

A two-year investigation into a bribery scandal involving the sale of drivers' licenses threatened to ensnare Illinois Governor George Ryan in July 2000. An indictment charged that Dean Bauer, inspector general during Ryan's terms as Illinois SECRETARY OF STATE (1991–1998), ignored charges of corruption even though a whistleblower reported the scandal. Ryan himself had telephoned the whistleblower to meet with Bauer, according to federal prosecutors, who cited the meeting as an attempt to cover up the bribery scheme. Investigators also indicated that the licensing scam enriched

Dean Bauer, former inspector general, leaving Dirken Federal Courthouse, after being charged with covering up evidence of corruption to protect Governor George Ryan.

Ryan's campaign-for-governor fund by some $170,000. Bauer had already been scheduled for trial on charges of covering up the scandal to save the new governor's reputation. However, the second indictment tended to link Ryan directly with the bribery operation.

Ryan's authority as secretary of state included the Illinois driver's license program. Investigators charge that, beginning about 1996, hundreds of people paid bribes to pass road tests and written exams in order to obtain truckers' and other commercial licenses. Many of them could not speak English and gave false addresses. The practice was uncovered when an employee in an Illinois driver's license office noticed that many truck drivers with Florida licenses were exchanging them for licenses from Illinois. Most of the drivers were able to obtain Illinois licenses without additional testing.

Federal investigators were notified, and in the spring of 1998, the U.S. attorney in Chicago, Scott Lassar, along with the FEDERAL BUREAU OF INVESTIGATION (FBI) and other government agencies, began an inquiry, called Operation Safe Road. The early probes involved mainly license examiners and driving instructors, who were accused of accepting money without administering the tests. Drivers who bought the fraudulent licenses testified that they slipped money to the employees by various methods and that much of the money was funneled into Ryan's campaign for governor. They also testified that sometimes Illinois driving schools participated in a plan that had the license buyers purchase tickets to fund-raising events for Ryan.

Although Ryan himself has not been accused, the investigation moved closer to the governor when Bauer was charged with the cover-up. For the first time, Ryan himself was acknowledged as being personally involved by allegedly calling a meeting between the whistleblower and Bauer. The unidentified worker from the DeKalb drivers' licensing center gave a television interview, with her identity hidden, in which she spoke of corruption in the secretary of state's office. Investigators charge that instead of looking into the accusation, Bauer, who is now retired, tried to block all avenues of inquiry. He is also charged with failing to look into a 1994 accident that killed six children in Wisconsin. The truck driver who caused the accident, Ricardo Guzman, testified that he did not have his truck inspected, although he was warned that something was wrong with the tail light assembly, because he was afraid his Illinois license would be found invalid. The assembly broke off on a highway and hit a minivan, which exploded and killed six children of one family. The man to whom Guzman paid a bribe was sentenced to 18 months in prison. He testified that he passed along most of the money obtained in such a manner to Ryan's political fund raisers. Investigators say that other drivers obtaining licenses by bribes have been involved in fatal accidents as well.

When Jesse White became Illinois secretary of state in 1998, he ordered the retesting of all drivers who obtained licenses under questionable conditions. That may mean the retesting of about 10,000 people. In November 2000, his office reported that of 295 drivers who were retested, 218 failed and another 175 did not show up when ordered to report for retesting. Their licenses were revoked.

Governor Ryan denies all connections with the bribery scheme and says that he supports Operation Safe Road. A popular Republican, Ryan was born in Kankakee, south of Chicago, in 1934. He served in the army in Korea and graduated from Ferris State College in Big Rapids, Michigan, with a degree in pharmacy. Charismatic and outgoing, he first entered politics in 1972 when he won election to the Illinois House of Representatives where he served five terms. He was speaker of the house from 1981 until 1983 and then served two terms as lieutenant governor in the administration of James R. "Big Jim" Thompson. After eight years as secretary of state, Ryan ran for governor in 1998 in a campaign marred by charges of illegally obtained campaign funds. Ryan himself was not implicated, however, and he was elected with 51 percent of the vote.

Known as a "doer" and popular with both Democrats and Republicans, Ryan still has the backing of his colleagues during this scandal. His popularity with the voters has slipped, however: a poll by the *Chicago Tribune* in 2000 reported that 38 percent of the people held an unfavorable opinion since the bribery investigation, and 78 percent believed that if the governor did not know about the driver's license scheme, he should have. Said Ryan in his State of the State address in 2000, "I am not going to let anything get in the way of me being the best governor I can be for the people of this great state."

According to a March 2001 *Washington Post* article, more disclosures about campaign fund irregularities came February 13, when Anthony De Santis, a suburban businessman, was subpoenaed to testify before a federal grand jury about occasions in 1997 and 1998 when he gave $2,500 in personal checks to Ryan and his wife while Ryan was secretary of state. De Santis claimed the checks were political contributions, but Ryans deposited the money into a personal account. Assistants to Ryan then claimed the checks were gifts, which were technically not illegal under Illinois law at the time they were given. Further, a Ryan spokesman claimed that the gifts were not included on Ryan's state ethics disclosure report due to an "inadvertent oversight" and that the governor instructed staff to correct the disclosure reports to include the De Santis checks. No allegation of Ryan's financial misconduct has resonated with the public as much as comment by Willis, the father of the six dead children, at a news conference. An emotional Willis called on Ryan to step down due to his ongoing troubles. "I do believe that there is enough evidence to show that the governor had knowledge of this and that he hid that knowledge," Willis said. "And it would be refreshing to see somebody come up and say, 'Yes,' and admit to it and to step down."

Olympic Officials Indicted in Salt Lake City Bid Scandal

Two former officials on the Olympic bid committee to bring the 2002 Winter Olympic Games to Salt Lake City, Utah, were indicted in July 2000 on charges of wire and MAIL FRAUD, CONSPIRACY, and interstate travel in aid of RACKETEERING. Tom Welch, president of the bid committee in 1997, and David Johnson, vice

Former U.S. Olympic official, Alfredo La Mont (*right*) and attorney Lee Foreman leave federal court after La Mont agreed to plead guilty to charges.

president of the committee in 1999, were charged with paying an official of the U.S. Olympic Committee (USOC) to give the selection edge to Utah's capital. In addition, Alfredo La Mont of Colorado Springs, Colorado, former international relations director of the USOC, pleaded guilty to accepting bribes, filing false tax returns, and conspiring with bid officials to designate Salt Lake City as the site of the 2002 Games.

The INDICTMENT states that Welch and Johnson secretly paid La Mont for help in choosing the city, paid $1 million to influence votes of several International Olympic Committee (IOC) members, and diverted some $130,000 of the bid committee's income. It was further charged that false contracts and altered books helped to conceal these activities. The charges each carry a maximum sentence of five years, a $250,000 fine, or both. The investigation was carried out by agents of the FEDERAL BUREAU OF INVESTIGATION (FBI), INTERNAL REVENUE SERVICE (IRS), and the U.S. Customs Service, as well as prosecutors from the U.S. JUSTICE DEPARTMENT's Fraud and Public Integrity Sections of the Criminal Division. In March 2001, federal prosecutors reported that they would use tax returns of the bid committee to prove that an attempt was made to hide the bribes extended to IOC members. Welch and Johnson insisted, however, that the unlisted payments on the bid committee's tax returns were intended as grants for poor athletes or as scholarships, not bribes.

The IOC, a nonprofit, international organization based in Lausanne, Switzerland, was formed in 1894 to promote and manage the modern Olympic Games. It is headed by a president who is elected for an eight-year term that is renewable in four-year terms, and an executive board comprised of four vice presidents and six other members, each elected for four-year terms. IOC members are elected by the organization. Each member must be a citizen of a country in which there is a National Olympic Committee (NOC), and each country is limited to one IOC member. A second member is allowed for countries that have been the hosts for Olympic Games.

When news of the Salt Lake City scandal broke, ten members resigned or were expelled from the IOC. In addition, the charges started a flurry of reorganization activity within the group in an effort to restore its tarnished image. In March 2000, at its 110th session in Lausanne, the IOC enacted some 50 reforms. The proposals include the following: providing that the president will serve one eight-year term with only one possible renewal of four years; providing that member travel will be more tightly regulated and expenses paid only by the IOC; and causing new members, who must retire by age 70, to be more carefully evaluated before admission. Without reforms, the U.S. Congress had threatened to remove the tax-exempt status from the IOC.

The United States Olympic Committee was also deeply tarnished by the scandal. An independent ethics panel, led by former Maine Senator George Mitchell, criticized the organization for not doing more to prevent abuses such as those at Salt Lake City. The panel called for a complete overhaul of USOC practices. It especially called for stricter control of the bidding procedures in U.S. cities to host future games.

In the aftermath, work proceeded cautiously on construction for the 2002 Games, and officials promised that Salt Lake City would be ready. Although many residents were dismayed at the charges of bribery and other allegations, the majority now support the Games and the efforts of the USOC to reform their practices. Mitt Romney, chief executive of the Salt Lake Organizing Committee (SLOC), promised to get the job done on time and within budget so that the city itself does not incur indebtedness as a result of the Games. Some city officials, however, admit to worrying that the scandal may repel sponsors, a vitally important factor in making the Olympic Games a financial success for any city. Romney says his goal is to sign one or two sponsors a month until the games open. Although enthusiasm is growing in the state capital, some cynicism prevails.

Tom Welch and Dave Johnson were to be on trial beginning July 30, 2001, when jury selection would begin.

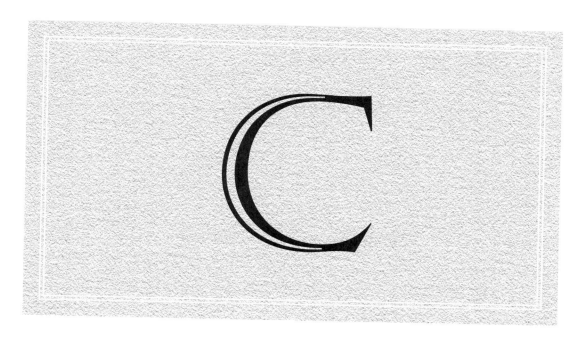

CAMERAS IN COURT

Proposal to Televise Supreme Court Sessions

In September 2000 a BILL to require television coverage of U.S. Supreme Court sessions was introduced in the Senate by Senators Arlen Specter and Joseph Biden. The proposed coverage did not include in-chambers discussion or debate but only the oral arguments before the Court on the 70 to 80 cases it hears each year. There was no Supreme Court response to the bill, and it ended in oblivion with the 2000 elections. On November 27, 2000, however, the Court, through Chief Justice WILLIAM H. REHNQUIST, delivered a letter to cable-news station C-Span chairman-CEO Brian Lamb, declining electronic coverage on the historic December 2000 arguments concerning Florida's vote-counting controversy and related legal battles in the 2000 presidential elections. In the statement, Rehnquist said, "Today the Court took up the question of televising these proceedings and a majority of the Court remains of the view that we should adhere to our present practice of allowing public attendance and print media coverage of argument sessions, but not to allow camera or audio coverage." Though it does not allow live sound broadcasts of oral arguments, the Court does audiotape its arguments and makes the tapes available to the public after each term. In this case, Rehnquist offered to make a transcript of the hearing available on an expedited basis, which in fact was read by nearly every news agency in America minutes after it was made available.

The ban on cameras in all federal courts dates back to 1937. There was a partial interruption for several years by a now-ended experiment permitting individual FEDERAL COURTS the discretion to allow electronic coverage of courtroom proceedings. Also pending before the Senate in 2000 was a companion bill that would again let presiding federal judges decide whether to allow electronic media coverage on a case-by-case basis. Congress has the authority to legislate Supreme Court-operations that do not interfere with the independent JUDICIARY or challenge the Supreme Court's dispositive interpretations of the U.S. Constitution.

Specter worked on the bill for several years and had solicited feedback from the Supreme Court. In 1996 Rehnquist wrote to Specter that the justices "periodically consider the question of allowing live television and radio coverage . . . and a majority are of the view that it would be unwise to depart from our current practice." Rehnquist himself has conducted a tour of the courtroom for a TV-coverage advocate, even going so far as to indicate where he would want cameras to be placed. He made it clear, however, that he would never allow camera coverage if even one of the justices disapproved. A number of the justices strongly disapprove, including Justice DAVID H. SOUTER who has twice appeared before a congressional subcommittee on the issue. He remarked that "cameras will come in only over [his] dead body." Souter told the subcommittee that TV would bring "entertainment values" to the serious business of the Court. Another concern voiced by Souter was the importance of not letting the judicial

IS DEATH BY ELECTROCUTION CRUEL AND UNUSUAL UNDER EVOLVING STANDARDS?

The Georgia Supreme Court, in a March 2001 ruling, indefinitely delayed the execution of convicted killer Kenneth Spivey, declaring that it wanted to review the matter further. Spivey's attorneys had argued that his impending death in the electric chair constituted "cruel and unusual punishment" under the EIGHTH AMENDMENT and the FOURTEENTH AMENDMENT to the Constitution of the United States. In the 4–3 majority opinion, Justice Leah J. Sears wrote, "Electrocution offends the evolving standards of decency that characterize a mature, civilized society." *Spivey v. State of Georgia*, No. S01A0837 (6 March 2001). Georgia's ATTORNEY GENERAL and a county prosecutor asked the court for reconsideration.

In early May 2001, several radio stations, including WYNC in New York, aired audiotapes of electrocutions in Georgia's prisons spanning a period from 1983 to 1998. The recordings were made by state officials to protect themselves from litigation over the manner in which they followed policies to ensure smooth executions. The tapes were void of emotion and merely recorded the voices of the executing officials during the process. There were no shouts or cries of pain, but several tapes contained the final words of the inmates. The tapes might support the argument that electrocution, when properly conducted, is as humane as other alternatives.

Dr. Chris Sparry, Chief Medical Examiner for the State of Georgia, who has testified on the matter, stated:

The best evidence that exists to indicate that people who are judicially executed never feel any conscious pain or suffering rests in the tens of thousands of people who have sustained accident electrocutions and have survived. None of those people can eve[r] remember the event if the current goes through their head[s] . . . consciousness is obliterated instantly when the current is passed through the body because the amount of the current is so very, very great.

Georgia is one of four states still employing the use of electric chairs for execution of condemned criminals, although both Georgia and Florida changed their *primary* means of execution to lethal injection for the newly-convicted starting in 2000. Nebraska and Alabama continue to use their electric chairs as the sole means of execution, however, both states are considering legislation to change their modes to lethal injection as well.

It must first be said that a two-thirds majority of Americans in the latest April 2001 Gallup poll said they favored the death penalty. Despite some of the media's characterization of declining support, the percentage has remained consistently above 60 percent for at least the preceding five years. The all-time

branch be subject to the same publicity as the political branches of government.

There is nothing in the Constitution that prohibits such electronic capturing or monitoring of Court sessions. At least forty state courts have allowed cameras inside their walls for civil cases, and almost as many have allowed them in criminal matters. In *Estes v. Texas*, 381 U.S. 582, 85 S.Ct. 1628, 14 L.Ed.2d 543 (1965), the U.S. Supreme Court reversed a criminal conviction, finding that the televising and broadcasting of the trial, in which there was widespread public interest, had violated the defendant's fundamental right to a fair trial guaranteed by the DUE PROCESS Clause of the FOURTEENTH AMENDMENT. In a later decision involving a Florida criminal trial, *Chandler v. Florida*, 449 U.S. 560, 101 S.Ct. 802, 66 L.Ed.2d 740 (1981), the Supreme Court clarified that not all televised trials violate constitutional rights and outlined several considerations to be used in assessing whether such broadcasting would have an adverse effect on the judicial process, including jury deliberation and ADJUDICATION.

At the level of the U.S. Supreme Court, however, the televising of oral arguments carries other considerations, as exemplified by Justice Souter's statements. In general, Rehnquist and other justices have argued that television cameras in the courtroom would lead to distraction and disruption and perhaps degrade the proceedings. After announcement of the Court's decision, CNN and the Radio-Television News Director Association submitted papers asking the Court to reconsider its decision, but there were no changes.

CAPITAL PUNISHMENT

The lawful infliction of death as a punishment; the death penalty.

Penry v. Johnson

Though the Supreme Court of the United States has upheld the constitutionality of the

high for supporting capital punishment was in 1994 at 80 percent; the low of 42 percent was in 1966. The manner by which execution is accomplished is a different matter toward which there is growing sensitivity.

In many states, condemned persons are given the opportunity to elect the method by which they will die. Some Americans bristle at the thought that "humane consideration" should be given to those who have wreaked heinous inhumanity upon others. There remains a palpable undercurrent of opinion/attitude that execution should hurt, not only because it may serve to deter future wrongdoers but also because of the belief that death is intended as a punishment, not an escape.

Still, as of Spring 2001, thirty-six of the thirty-eight states with death penalty laws employed lethal injection as the preferred method. Lethal injection involves a painless process where a person is first put to sleep with sodium pentothal, after which other drugs are administered to paralyze the body and stop the heart. The person never regains consciousness.

The Supreme Court of the United

States, over the decades, has provided guidance as to what should constitute "cruel and unusual" punishment under the Eighth Amendment. It is clear from the sum total of its opinions that the standard is evolving and dynamic. "Difficulty would attend the effort to define with exactness the extent of the constitutional provision which provides that cruel and unusual punishments shall not be inflicted; but it is safe to affirm that punishments of torture [such as drawing and quartering, emboweling alive, beheading, public dissecting, and burning alive], and all others in the same line of unnecessary cruelty, are forbidden by that amendment to the Constitution," the Court said, more than 100 years ago, in *Wilkerson v. Utah*, 99 U.S. 130 (1878), which upheld an execution by firing squad. Twelve years later, in *In re Kemmler*, 136 U.S. 436 (1890), the Court, under the Fourteenth Amendment's DUE PROCESS clause, found electrocution to be a permissible method of execution. Moreover, in assuming the applicability of the Eighth Amendment to the States, the Court, many years later, held that a second electrocution, resulting from the

failure of the first one, did not violate the proscription. "The cruelty against which the Constitution protects a convicted man is cruelty inherent in the method of punishment, not the necessary suffering involved in any method employed to extinguish life humanely," the majority opinion stated. *Louisiana ex rel. Francis v. Resweber*, 329 U.S. 459 (1947).

In *Trop v. Dulles* 356 U.S. 86 (1958), the Supreme Court, in referring to the United States as "an enlightened democracy," held that "The [Eighth] Amendment must draw its meaning from the evolving standards of decency that mark the progress of a maturing society." That language was repeated again in *Gregg v. Georgia* 428 U.S. 153 (1978), wherein the Court noted that the Eighth Amendment was to be interpreted "in a flexible and dynamic manner to accord with evolving standards of decency." Most likely, this is the language from which Georgia's Chief Justice Sears formed her comment in the March 2001 *Spivey* ruling. The ultimate question for Georgia then may be whether electrocution offends an "evolving standard of decency."

death penalty, this has not foreclosed appeals based on procedural and substantive grounds. One substantive issue involves the constitutionality of imposing capital punishment on a defendant who is mentally retarded. Those who argue for the unconstitutionality of this practice took heart when the Supreme Court agreed to hear the HABEAS CORPUS appeal of John P. Penry, a Texas inmate guilty of capital murder. Penry's attorneys argued that he is mentally retarded. However, the Court avoided the substantive issue in *Penry v. Johnson*, ___U.S.___, 121 S.Ct. 1910, ___ L.Ed.2d ___ (2001) and instead overturned his death sentence on narrow procedural grounds. Nevertheless, this decision demonstrated the importance the Court places on procedural fairness in death penalty cases.

Penry's litigation over his death sentence has spanned three decades. In 1980 he was convicted of capital murder and sentenced to death. During his trial Penry's attorney offered evidence of Penry's mental retardation and the severe abuse he suffered as a child. However, the

court never instructed the jury that it could consider this evidence in deciding whether to sentence him to death. Penry's appeal reached the Supreme Court in 1989. In this first decision the Court overturned the conviction because of this failure to clearly instruct the jury that it could use this mitigating evidence. Texas retried Penry in 1990, and he was found guilty of capital murder for a second time. During the penalty phase of the trial, Penry's attorney presented even more detailed evidence from expert witnesses on Penry's mental retardation and childhood abuse. On cross-examination by the prosecutor, one expert noted that he had reviewed a prior psychiatric examination from a 1977 rape prosecution. He told the jury that this evaluation indicated that if Penry were released from custody he would be dangerous to other persons. Following testimony and closing arguments, the judge gave the jury the same three written questions that were asked in Penry's first trial: Had Penry acted deliberately when he murdered the victim? Was there a probability he would be

Johnny Paul Penry, condemned murderer, looking out from visiting area cell.

dangerous in the future? Did Penry act unreasonably in response to provocation? If the jury answered all three questions affirmatively, Penry would be sentenced to death. If the jury answered no to any of the three questions, he would be sentenced to life imprisonment. In addition, the judge orally instructed the jury that if it found any mitigating circumstances (mental retardation, child abuse), it could take these into account when answering the three questions. However, the instruction was very long and convoluted. Most important, it was not included on the verdict form, though it was attached to the form. The jury answered all three questions affirmatively, and Penry was sentenced to death.

Penry exhausted his direct appeals and postconviction remedies in the Texas state courts and then filed a habeas corpus petition in FEDERAL COURT. The lower federal courts upheld the sentence, rejecting both of Penry's claims. He contended that his expert's disclosure of the 1977 evaluation as to "his future dangerousness violated his Fifth Amendment" right to confront witnesses. It was unfair to allow this testimony, which had nothing to do with the murder case, into evidence without giving him a chance to cross-examine that medical witness from 1977. Second, he argued that the jury instructions had been constitutionally inadequate.

The Supreme Court, in a 6–3 decision, overturned the lower courts and threw out Penry's death sentence. Justice SANDRA DAY O'CONNOR, writing for the majority, rejected

Penry's FIFTH AMENDMENT claim. She noted that prior court rulings that seemed to support Penry were inapplicable because of factual differences. Moreover, O'Connor explained, even if the precedents applied, Penry could not show that this error had a "'substantial and injurious effect or influence in determining the jury's verdict'." Texas had presented a number of witnesses who had stated that Penry would commit violent criminal acts if released from prison. In light of this evidence, the isolated statement from 1977 could not have played a substantial role in the jury's decision.

Justice O'Connor was more troubled by the judge's instructions to the jury. She concluded that the Texas court had "misapprehended" the Supreme Court's prior decision involving Penry. That decision "did not hold that the mere mention of 'mitigating circumstances' to a capital sentencing jury satisfies the Eighth Amendment." Nor did the decision mean that a jury could "consider" mitigating circumstances. O'Connor declared that the first decision meant that the jury must be able to "consider and *give effect to*" the defendant's mitigating evidence in imposing a sentence. After analyzing the jury instruction on mitigating circumstances, O'Connor found it to be ambiguous and confusing. In addition, the instructions on the three questions conflicted with the mitigation instruction. O'Connor stated that "it would have been both logically and ethically impossible for a juror to follow both sets of instructions." The jurors had to ignore either the verdict form or the supplemental instruction in coming to its verdict. Thus, the supplemental instruction "provided an inadequate vehicle for the jury to make a reasoned moral response to Penry's mitigating evidence." O'Connor sternly noted that the Court's first decision "provided guidance as to how the trial court might have drafted the jury charge." The first jury instruction could have defined the word "deliberately" in a way that would have brought in Penry's mitigating evidence as it bore on personal culpability. Alternatively, a written "catchall instruction on mitigating evidence also might have complied" with the Court's prior decision. In light of these procedural problems, the Court concluded that the jury's determination was "objectively unreasonable" and vacated Penry's death sentence.

Justice CLARENCE THOMAS, in a dissenting opinion joined by Chief Justice WILLIAM H. REHNQUIST and Justice ANTONIN SCALIA, complained that the majority had gone too far in its analysis of the case and had sought to propose "the ideal instruction on how a jury should take into account evidence" regarding Penry's mental retardation and childhood abuse. Thomas concluded that the jury instruction on mitigating evidence was not objectively unreasonable.

Shafer v. South Carolina

The U.S. Supreme Court has upheld the constitutionality of capital punishment, but it has also required that states revise their trial procedures to ensure that the defendant's rights are fully protected. For example, the Court has ruled that when the only sentencing alternative to death is life imprisonment without the possibility of parole, the jury must be told of the defendant's parole ineligibility. This issue came back to the Court in *Shafer v. South Carolina*, ___ U.S. ___, 121 S.Ct. 1263, 149 L.Ed.2d 178 (2001), when the South Carolina legislature changed its sentencing practices in cases potentially involving the imposition of the death penalty. The Court reaffirmed its prior holding, mandating that jurors be informed that life without parole is an option in lieu of the death penalty.

Aaron Shafer, Jr., was charged with the 1997 murder of a Union County, South Carolina, convenience store cashier that occurred during an armed robbery. Under South Carolina law, juries in capital cases consider guilt and sentencing proceedings. This bifurcated trial resulted in a jury finding Shafer guilty of the murder. During the sentencing phase, the jury had determine beyond a reasonable doubt whether there were any statutory aggravating circumstances (such as kidnapping or rape), and if not, it could not seek the death penalty. The judge would then sentence the defendant to either life imprisonment without parole or a mandatory minimum 30-year prison term. During the sentencing phase, Shafer's attorney sought to inform the jurors of these terms. The judge refused, and when the jury later asked the judge if Shafer might have a chance of parole if sentenced to life, the judge told the jury that the parole issue was "not for your consideration." The jury then resumed deliberations and found that Shafer had committed the murder during a ROBBERY, which was an aggravating factor. The jury recommended the death penalty, which the judge imposed.

To appeal the sentence, Shafer took his case to the South Carolina Supreme Court. The court upheld the sentence and rejected Shafer's contention that the U.S. Supreme Court required that jurors be informed if life imprison-

ment carried with it no chance of parole. The South Carolina Supreme Court concluded that the precedent did not apply because the new South Carolina sentencing scheme did not limit the sentencing choices to death or life imprisonment. The mandatory 30-year sentence meant that at the time the jury started deliberating, there were three alternative sentences available. Therefore, the South Carolina Supreme Court concluded that the U.S. Supreme Court precedent was inapplicable.

The U.S. Supreme Court, in a 7–2 decision, rejected this interpretation. Justice RUTH BADER GINSBURG, writing for the majority, noted that "South Carolina has consistently refused to inform the jury of a capital defendant's parole eligibility status." She noted that the precedent rejected by the South Carolina Supreme Court had been announced to prevent jurors from being misled that if they sentenced a person to life imprisonment the defendant might later be paroled. Faced with that prospect, jurors might be very reluctant not to impose the death penalty. Due process required that the impossibility of parole should not be concealed from the sentencing jury.

Justice Ginsburg was not persuaded that South Carolina's new sentencing scheme, with three sentencing alternatives, changed anything. She stated, "This reasoning might be persuasive if the jury's sentencing discretion encompassed the three choices the South Carolina court identified." However, the new scheme did not work this way. The jury does not make the sentencing decision until it finds an aggravating circumstance. When the jury makes that decision, as in this case, it has only two sentences available, death or life imprisonment without parole. At that stage of the sentencing process, the South Carolina law does not give the jury the option of sentencing the defendant to a mandatory minimum 30-year term. When, as here, the future dangerousness of the defendant is at issue, the jury must be informed that a life sentence carries no possibility of parole. Therefore, the Court vacated the death sentence and remanded the case for a new hearing on Shafer's future dangerousness.

Justices ANTONIN SCALIA and CLARENCE THOMAS wrote dissenting opinions. Justice Thomas argued that the court's instructions were sufficient to inform the jury in Shafer's case what the term "life imprisonment" meant. In addition, Justice Thomas questioned the propriety of the Court in getting involved in such an issue. He stated, "It is not this Court's role to micromanage state sentencing proceedings or to develop model jury instructions." In his opinion, such matters were best left to the states.

CROSS REFERENCES
Appeal; Due Process; Fifth Amendment; Sentencing

CARNAHAN, MELVIN EUGENE

Melvin Eugene
Carnahan

On October 16, 2000, a twin-engine Cessna 335, carrying Missouri Governor Mel Carnahan and two others, plunged 3,200 feet from the sky and crashed to the earth about 25 miles south of St. Louis. Killed instantly were the 66-year-old Carnahan, his 44-year-old son Roger, and the governor's chief aide, Chris Sifford, 37. Son Roger, an amateur pilot with 1,600 flying hours to his credit, was attempting to pilot the plane through a fog and rain storm, but reported operational trouble to air traffic controllers just minutes before the plane disappeared from radar.

At the time of the tragedy, Carnahan was on the way to a Democratic Party campaign rally in New Madrid, Missouri, to raise money for his 2000 bid for the U.S. Senate. A two-term popular governor, Carnahan and his opponent, Republican incumbent Senator John Ashcroft, were engaged in one of the nation's closest Senate races. Following the crash, Carnahan's name remained on the state's ballot because the deadline for changes had already passed. As it turned out, Carnahan posthumously defeated Ashcroft in a race so tight that results remained controversial until the following morning. Carnahan's victory marked the first time in U.S. history that a deceased candidate had ever won election to the U.S. Senate, although a few House members had been elected posthumously.

Melvin Eugene Carnahan was born into politics. The son of a seven-term congressman, he was a native of Birch Tree, Missouri, where he was born on February 11, 1934. His parents, A.S.J. and Mary Catherine (Schupp) Carnahan, were rural schoolteachers in the nearby Ozark Mountains. A.S.J. Carnahan also served 14 years in the U.S. House of Representatives and was appointed the first ambassador to Sierra Leone by President JOHN F. KENNEDY.

Carnahan earned a Bachelor of Arts degree from George Washington University in 1954. He then served for two years with the U.S. Air Force, aspiring to become a pilot but failing to pass the requisite physical exam. He returned to his hometown after leaving the military, and, in 1959, earned a law degree from the University of Missouri in Columbia. Within two years,

MELVIN EUGENE CARNAHAN

1934	Born in Birch Tree, Missouri
1963	Elected to Missouri House of Representatives
1976–1980	Practiced law
1992	Elected governor of Missouri
1996	Re-elected governor of Missouri
2000	Died in plane crash

Carnahan's first election win was as a municipal judge in Rolla, Missouri. In 1963 he was elected to the Missouri House of Representatives, where he stayed for two terms. Becoming majority floor leader during his tenure there, Carnahan was named Outstanding Democrat of the Missouri House of Representatives in 1965 by the *St. Louis Globe.*

Carnahan married Jean Carpenter in 1954, with whom he had four children. A fervent Baptist, he became a deacon for his church and also served as president of the local Rolla School board, as well as president of the Rolla Chapter of Kiwanis and member of the Masons and Shriners. In his personal time, Carnahan eventually earned his private pilot's license and often flew with his son for recreational escape from a busy life.

In 1966, he sought the Democratic nomination for the Missouri Senate but lost. Afterward, he practiced law while also serving as president of the Rolla School Board from 1976 to 1980. Earning a political reputation as a straight-arrow with high ethical standards, Carnahan returned to public life in 1980 when he was elected state treasurer, a post he held until 1984. By 1989, he had become Lieutenant Governor of Missouri. In 1992, he won the governorship by a landslide and was soundly reelected to a second term in 1996. By state law, he could not run for a third term and decided to seek the Senate seat for the 2000 election.

Carnahan's tenure as governor marked a prosperous era for Missouri, which enjoyed record economic gains in the 1990s. During his first term, plagued by the devastating floods of the

Missouri and Mississippi Rivers in 1993, Carnahan nonetheless enacted a $315 million tax increase to benefit public education after a state judge had thrown out the state's education funding system. It remained his proudest achievement, notwithstanding other impressive measures, including the development of Missouri's first strategic economic plan. Carnahan also signed a number of crime-fighting laws into existence and allocated several million dollars for new prisons. Additionally, 300,000 new jobs were created during his first term. More recently, Carnahan had made headlines during Pope John Paul II's visit to St. Louis in 1999. A staunch supporter of the death penalty, Carnahan honored a personal request from the pope to spare the death penalty for a convicted murderer.

Dubbed Missouri's "education governor," the laid-back Carnahan enjoyed a popular rapport with young and old alike. He and his wife opened up the governor's mansion every year to welcome Halloween trick-or-treaters, greeting them in full and elaborate costume. He also was known to have "pardoned" a boy who had told a fib and was grounded by his parents.

Following Carnahan's untimely death, Lt. Governor Roger Wilson was sworn in to complete the term. After the Missouri Board of State Canvassers certified Carnahan's posthumous victory for the Senate seat, Wilson announced that he would appoint Carnahan's widow, Jean, to occupy that seat until a senator is selected in the November 2002 election. Jean accepted, and was sworn into office on January 3, 2001.

CHILD SUPPORT

A payment that a non-custodial parent makes as a contribution to the costs of raising his or her child.

L.W.K. v. E.R.C.

State and federal laws mandate that a man who divorces his spouse must contribute child support to help pay for the expenses attributed to raising the couple's children. In addition, a person who through a PATERNITY action has been adjudged the father of a child also must contribute child support. Collection efforts began to intensify in the late 1980s as government social service agencies sought to make "deadbeat" parents honor their child support obligations. These obligations may even continue after a parent dies. In *L.W.K. & another v. E.R.C., executrix & others*, 432 Mass. 438, 735 N.E.2d 359 (2000), the Supreme Judicial Court

of Massachusetts ruled that although a father could disinherit a child born out of wedlock, the court-ordered child support must be paid from the deceased father's ESTATE.

The father in this case died in November 1994 at the age of fifty-five. Divorced at the time of his death, he was survived by two children, an adult daughter from his only marriage, and a minor child born in 1990, to the mother, L.W.K., to whom he was not married. The mother, who was forty-two years old at the time of the child's birth, brought a paternity action to establish him as her child's father. In 1992, after a hearing, a judge determined paternity and ordered the father to pay child support of $100 a week to the mother. The order was to remain in effect "until further order of the Court." The father paid the required child support until his death. Five months before his death the father executed a will that disinherited his minor child, leaving to her the amount of one dollar. The will provided that his estate be given to a TRUST he had set up in 1977 and that all proceeds be given to his sister and his adult daughter. After the father's death, the sister was appointed executrix of his estate. She filed a federal estate tax return that listed the father's total gross estate at over $800,000.

On the death of the father, the mother filed a claim for Social Security benefits on her child's behalf based on the father's participation in the Social Security system. The child was awarded a monthly benefit of $849, a benefit she would receive until she turned eighteen. This was the child's only source of income apart from her mother's income. Though the mother eventually agreed to settle all claims against the estate for $10,000, the GUARDIAN AD LITEM—a court-appointed attorney to represent the best interests of the child—objected, insisting that the child support payments continue until the child reached eighteen. The probate court certified the questions surrounding the case to Massachusetts's highest court.

In a 4–2 decision, the court ruled that the death of the father did not end his child support obligation. Writing for the majority, Chief Justice Margaret H. Marshall noted, "Testamentary freedom is not absolute, and certain preexisting obligations have priority over all testamentary dispositions." In the court's view, "a legally enforceable obligation to pay child support [took] precedence over other testamentary dispositions and must be satisfied." Chief Justice Marshall declared that a parent with a child support obligation could not nullify that obligation by disinheriting the child. However, once that obligation was satisfied, a parent was free to disinherit the child from all other parts of his or her estate.

The court based its decision on statutory interpretation (MA ST 191 § 20 and MA ST 119A § 1). Marshall stated that the court was not legislating new policy but was "applying unequivocal policy mandates of the Legislature to the specific facts of this case." One underlying legislative policy was the obligation of parents to support their minor children, a policy the legislature directed the courts to liberally construe to achieve its purposes. Second, Marshall noted the "recent and profound" changes in state and federal laws that have increased the obligation of parents to support their children. Moreover, it made no difference if the child support order came out of a divorce proceeding or a paternity action.

The court noted laws (e.g., MA ST 209C § 1) that unambiguously directed parents to support their children until they turned eighteen. The underlying court order in this case carried out this mandate and remained in effect until the child reached majority or the court issued a new order. Neither of these contingencies had occurred. Therefore, the father remained responsible for paying child support. In addition, there was nothing in the statutes that prohibited the court's construction.

The court found that the support obligation could be paid out of the trust assets that were part of his estate. The court also ruled, however, that the trial court could not issue a new order directing that a college fund be established for the child. Marshall looked to the statute again, finding that a child had to reach eighteen before requesting educational support. The child also had to be residing with a parent and be financially dependent. Because the child was ten, she could not meet these contingencies. Therefore, the court ruled that the court had no statutory authority to establish an educational trust fund.

CROSS REFERENCES
Parent and Child; Paternity

CIVIL RIGHTS

Personal liberties that belong to an individual owing to his or her status as a citizen or resident of a particular country.

Buckhannon Board and Care Home, Inc. v. West Virginia Department of Health and Human Resources

Congress enacted the Civil Rights Attorney's Fee Awards Act to encourage attorneys to take civil rights cases that might be viewed as unprofitable. The act permits the federal district court to award reasonable attorney's fees to a "prevailing party." For a litigant to be considered a prevailing party, the plaintiff must either secure a final judgment in a court action or vindicate rights through a consent order approved by the court. In addition, for many years the circuit COURTS OF APPEAL had endorsed the use of a "catalyst theory" to award such fees. Under this theory, if the plaintiff's federal lawsuit led the defendant to change its course of disputed conduct, then the plaintiff's attorney was entitled to receive attorney's fees from the defendant. In a major reversal of judicial thinking, the Supreme Court of the United States rejected the catalyst theory in *Buckhannon Board and Care Home, Inc. v. West Virginia Department of Health and Human Resources* , ___U.S.___, 121 S.Ct. 1835, 149 L.Ed.2d 855 (2001). The Court ruled that attorney's fees may only be awarded upon the entry of a court judgment, whether following a trial or through a settlement entered as a consent decree. The decision was attacked by the four dissenting justices as a means of undermining civil rights enforcement.

The case grew out of a nursing home safety enforcement action by the West Virginia state fire marshal. The marshal concluded that some of the residents of the Buckhannon Board and Care Home could not adequately take care of themselves as required by state laws. For failing this self-preservation element of the law, the state department of health and human resources subsequently ordered the Buckhannon closed. In October 1997, prior to closing, Buckhannon filed a class action lawsuit against the state of West Virginia, arguing "that the 'self-preservation' requirement violated the federal Fair Housing Amendments Act of 1998 (FHAA) and the Americans with Disabilities Act of 1990." The state agreed to allow the home to remain open during the litigation. However, in 1998 the West Virginia legislature enacted two laws that removed the self-preservation provision. The state then successfully petitioned the DISTRICT COURT to dismiss the lawsuit, as the requirement was no longer in effect.

Buckhannon then asked for attorney's fees as the prevailing party, claiming that under the catalyst theory it had obtained the desired end due to its lawsuit. Because the U.S. Court of Appeals for the Fourth Circuit (which had appellate jurisdiction over the case) was the only appeals court that did not recognize the catalyst theory, the district court denied the request. The Fourth Circuit affirmed this order and the Supreme Court agreed to hear the case to resolve the disagreement among the appellate circuit courts.

The Supreme Court, in a 5–4 decision, sided with the Fourth Circuit in rejecting the catalyst theory. Chief Justice WILLIAM H. REHNQUIST, writing for the majority, noted that in most cases the "American Rule" prevails. Under this rule, a court does not award a prevailing party attorney's fees unless there is explicit statutory authority. Congress made an exception for civil rights cases when it passed the Civil Rights Attorney's Fees Awards Act of 1976. However, in employing "prevailing party," Congress used a "legal term of art" that is commonly defined as a party "in whose favor a judgment is rendered." This definition along with prior Court decisions led Rehnquist to conclude that a prevailing party "is one who has been awarded some relief by the court." Thus, when the court enters a judgment after a hearing on the issue in question, the court may award attorney's fees. In addition, Chief Justice Rehnquist found "that settlement agreements that are enforced through a consent decree" entered by a court also may trigger an award of fees.

In contrast, the catalyst theory did not employ a court-ordered judgment. Rehnquist stated that the theory "allows an award where there is no judicially sanctioned change in the legal relationship of the parties." Just because a defendant makes a voluntary change in conduct that the plaintiff sought to change through the lawsuit, this result "lacks the necessary judicial imprimatur on the change." Though Rehnquist acknowledged that most of the circuit courts had endorsed the catalyst theory, he concluded that the Supreme Court had never fully considered the issue. He characterized the circuit courts' reliance on Court dicta (statements in an opinion not directly germane to the issues at hand) as misplaced. The Court had never awarded attorney's fees for a "nonjudicial" change in circumstances.

The majority rejected a reading of the legislative history of the Civil Rights Attorney's Fees Award Act that supported the catalyst theory. Chief Justice Rehnquist concluded that this reading of history is "at best ambiguous" and

cannot support the theory. In addition, he rejected the claim that abandonment of the catalyst theory would allow defendants to change their behavior to avoid paying attorney's fees and would discourage attorneys from taking civil rights cases out of fear that they will not be paid. Rehnquist reexamined these issues and found that the catalyst actually could serve as a disincentive for the defendant to "voluntarily change its conduct, conduct that may not be illegal." Finally, Rehnquist sought to prevent a second round of litigation on attorney's fees. The catalyst theory seemed prone to such contests because a court has to establish a factual record to determine if the claim for fees is justified.

Justice RUTH BADER GINSBURG, in a dissenting opinion joined by Justices JOHN PAUL STEVENS, DAVID H. SOUTER, and STEPHEN G. BREYER, argued that the majority's decision "upsets long-prevailing Circuit precedent applicable to scores of federal fee-shifting statutes." In her view, "the 'catalyst rule' . . . is a key component of the fee-shifting statutes Congress adopted to advance enforcement of civil rights." She contended that nothing in "history, precedent, or plain English" warranted a restricted reading of the term "prevailing party."

Justice Department Settles Civil Lawsuit Over Ruby Ridge

In September 2000 the U.S. JUSTICE DEPARTMENT settled the final civil lawsuit resulting from the shootout eight years earlier between U.S. marshals and white separatists at Ruby Ridge, Idaho. Kevin Harris, wounded by a FEDERAL BUREAU OF INVESTIGATION (FBI) sniper during the standoff, had sued the government for violating his civil rights. He received $380,000. In 1995 Randall Weaver, whose wife and son were killed at Ruby Ridge, was paid $3.1 million. A deputy marshal also died in the exchange of gunfire.

A white separatist who espoused anti-Semitic and racist ideologies, Weaver had moved to northwestern Idaho with his wife and four children in the early 1980s. Their cabin, which lacked electricity or a telephone, was located in a remote wooded area on Ruby Ridge, overlooking the Kootenai Valley. Although the Weavers tended to distance themselves from neighbors at first, they gradually embraced some of the beliefs of the Identity Christians and Aryan Nations groups in the area. Weaver became well known locally for his white supremacist and separatist beliefs and preachings.

Kevin Harris is seen here in an Idaho courthouse after murder and assault charges against him were dismissed in 1997.

In the summer of 1992, U.S. marshals began surveillance of the Weaver cabin, seeking Randy Weaver's arrest on a 1991 weapons charge. Weaver had failed to appear in a Boise court to answer charges for possession of a sawed-off shotgun and had told the press in an interview that he would not be taken alive if federal agents came for him. The officers believed that Weaver, his wife, Vicki, and their four children were in the cabin, as well as Harris, a young man who had lived with them on and off since 1984. Harris's stepfather, Brian Pierce, later described Harris as a "big, lovable boy" who was brainwashed by Weaver's teachings. Pierce said that the family had tried many times unsuccessfully to induce Harris to leave the Weaver cabin.

Although the marshals knew that Weaver and his family often practiced target shooting on their land, they did not know how much ammunition was stored in the fortress-like cabin. They did not regard their mission as a "routine arrest." And despite their numbers, they were hesitant about launching a full-scale assault, fearing that the Weaver children might be hurt in any exchange of gunfire. During the August 21 arrest attempt, the marshals' fears were realized when a shoot-out between the Weavers and federal agents occurred, resulting in the deaths of Weaver's 14-year-old son, Sam, and Deputy U.S. Marshal William Degan of Massachusetts. One of the service's most decorated members, Degan had flown in from Boston a week earlier

for the mission. His body was returned to Massachusetts for burial.

On August 22, the second day of the standoff, the marshals were joined by members of the FBI hostage rescue team. They had a murder warrant for 24 year-old Harris, whom they believed to have shot Degan. They also brought with them a telephone, which they managed to deliver to the cabin door. It is not known whether Weaver communicated with the agents via the telephone. By this time, hundreds of law enforcement officers on foot, in helicopters, and in armored cars had surrounded the cabin on remote Ruby Ridge. Neighbors in the area, who had been evacuated for safety, accused authorities of violating Weaver's civil rights. Red Cross workers joined the siege to bring food to the law officers, which tended to infuriate Weaver's neighbors further.

During the second day, Harris, Randy Weaver, and daughter Sara Weaver ventured outside the cabin in an attempt to get to the shed where Sam's body lay. The FBI fired on them, forcing a retreat back to the house. At that point FBI sniper Lon Horiuchi fired through the cabin door, wounding Harris and killing Vicki Weaver. She had been standing behind the door holding one of her children. With every adult in the cabin now dead or severely wounded, the Ruby Ridge stand-off came to an end. A long investigation into what went wrong was just beginning though.

Both Weaver and Harris were acquitted of murder and CONSPIRACY charges. No charges were filed against Weaver for gun violations, although that had been the initial cause of the siege. Harris testified during a Senate hearing in September 1995 that the gunfire killing Weaver's son and Marshal Degan occurred while he and the boy "were just walking along the trail, making a perfect target of ourselves." One of Weaver's friends who witnessed the standoff testified that the U.S. marshals were the first to fire on August 21 and that they were slow in identifying themselves as law officers. Also at the hearing, the Senate committee criticized FBI agent Thomas Miller for saying that the shooting of Vicki Weaver was justified.

Both Weaver and Harris filed civil rights suits against the U.S. government. Weaver, who moved to Iowa after the incident, was paid $3.1 million in return for dropping his initial $10 million lawsuit. However, the government did not admit any LIABILITY while making the payment. Harris charged that U.S. marshals and FBI agents had violated his constitutional rights in the shooting on Ruby Ridge. He received $380,000. As with Weaver, the U.S. government did not admit liability. Harris later moved to the state of Washington.

Criminal charges against agent Horiuchi, whose shot killed Vicki Weaver and wounded Harris, were dropped. Horiuchi said that Harris was armed when he fired and he believed the young man was a threat to the other agents. Harris, who admitted he probably shot agent Degan, claimed that he had fired his gun only after being fired on.

A few FBI agents were investigated for trying to cover up their role in the Ruby Ridge standoff. Only one supervisor, E. Michael Kahoe, was charged with OBSTRUCTION OF JUSTICE. One deputy director, Larry Potts, was demoted but left the service before the discipline was enacted.

Of the incident and aftermath, Assistant Attorney General David Ogden said the settlement "resolves this long-pending case in a way that is fair to the United States and all involved." And although the U.S. government did not admit liability in the charges, the siege at Ruby Ridge did lead to new rules that govern how and when FBI agents can fire their guns.

CONSPIRACY

An AGREEMENT between two or more persons to engage jointly in an unlawful or criminal act, or an act that is innocent in itself but becomes unlawful when done by the combination of its actors.

Louisiana Governor Guilty of Racketeering and Extortion

Former Louisiana Governor Edwin Edwards, or "Fast Eddie" as he was often called, served four terms as governor of Louisiana, during which time he evaded two charges of corruption. On November 6, 1998, at the age of 72, however, he was indicted on 34 counts of conspiracy and racketeering for extorting payoffs from businessmen who were applying for riverboat casino licenses. This criminal enterprise was said to have occurred during Edwards's final term in office and during the past year since then. He was charged with being in direct violation of the RACKETEER INFLUENCED AND CORRUPT ORGANIZATIONS ACT (RICO), a crime punishable by up to twenty years in jail and a fine of up to $250,000. With many witnesses and exhibits, the prosecutor was able to prove that Edwards; his son, Steven Edwards; his office

Edwin Edwards speaks to his staff and members of the media during the last press conference of his governorship in December 1995.

aide, Andrew Martin; cattleman, Cecil Brown; and businessman, Bobby Johnson were guilty of being part of this criminal enterprise.

Prosecutors generated much of the evidence against Edwards from his wire-tapped home telephone and a microphone that had been hidden in his law office for three years. Edwards contends that this WIRETAPPING was illegal. Judge Frank Poloza rejected the argument that the wiretapping constituted illegally obtained evidence. Another large part of the prosecution's case depended on the testimony of other suspects. They plea-bargained for release in exchange for their testimony at trial, testifying that they all had paid millions of dollars in EXTORTION to Edwards in an attempt to obtain riverboat casino licenses. Edwards responded by contending that the jury should have been made aware of the witnesses' criminal status as participants in the crimes for which he stood trial as a legitimate reason to doubt the testimony against him. He also called the allegations against him a personal vendetta by the JUSTICE DEPARTMENT, which had been trying to catch him in a criminal enterprise for years.

The charges that Edwards faced at trial included extortion, MAIL FRAUD, wire fraud, MONEY LAUNDERING, interstate travel for the purpose of racketeering, direct violations of the RICO Act, and false statements. On May 9, 2000, a jury of seven, with the approval of Judge Poloza, convicted the former governor of seventeen charges of extortion and racketeering, in addition to a number of lesser charges. The other four defendants in this case were also found guilty of lesser charges. It had been argued that they were convicted for little more than "guilt by association" with the former governor, but testimony and records showed enough evidence for conviction according to Judge Poloza. He applied the sentencing guidelines that required both a prison term and fees paid by each convicted defendant. Edwin Edwards was sentenced to ten years in a federal prison in Texas and fined $250,000.

Edwards's attorney immediately filed for an appeal with the hope that those convicted would be allowed to remain free prior to the appellate hearing, which would take longer than a year. During this time all parties involved in the case were issued a GAG ORDER. Two issues were involved when deciding whether the convicts could remain free pending appeal. First, they had to indicate that there was sufficient evidence that could alter their conviction. This standard was met, although not without significant controversy. Second, they had to show that they were of no danger to the community and that would not seek to flee justice. The defendants were allowed to remain free since the bail hearing board decided that this standard also had been met, again with a great deal of controversy. U.S. Attorney Rosenberg said that freedom during appeal is a mistake due to past actions committed by Edwards during his prior cases in which he evaded conviction. This point suggested that the defendants may indeed be a danger to the community. Furthermore, the enormous amount of money and resources that the defendants had accumulated made it difficult for the prosecution to believe that they were not likely to try to avoid further prosecution.

A number of arguments were raised upon appeal before an independent panel. The defendants argued that presiding judge Poloza should have removed himself from this case due to BIAS. This claim stemmed from the fact that he allowed the admissions from wiretapping and particular witnesses to be entered as evidence in the trial. Furthermore, defense attorneys again contended that the wiretapping, which provided the core of the prosecution's case, was illegally obtained when the government misled two judges into allowing this electronic surveillance. Excusing Juror 68 from the trial due to his misbehavior, which included carrying books into deliberations, was another argument on appeal. Edwards's attorney claimed that this would not have occurred if the juror had not been on the side of acquittal of the defendants. Yet there was evidence that Juror 68 was also being badgered by the other jurors due to his stance for acquittal, which *would* allow for his dismissal if extreme.

Possibly the most controversial argument was that the jury should not have been anonymous. Prosecutors claimed that anonymity was necessary due to jury tampering during Edwards's previous two hearings. Some legal experts claimed that using an anonymous jury ought to be a judgment of last resort. The defense argued that using an anonymous jury denied Edwards a fair trial because it made the jurors believe that they had something to fear from him and the other defendants. Furthermore, the defendants' attorneys were denied the advantage of being able to evaluate juror biases due to their anonymity. Until all of these arguments could be addressed by the appellate board, the defendants remained free.

If he loses on appeal, Edwards would serve his prison sentence in a secured medical facility due to his advanced age. His attorney contended that the ten-year sentence amounted to life imprisonment. The others received lighter sentences and fines but also would serve prison time if Edwards's appeal is rejected.

United States v. Mohamed

On October 20, 2000, 48-year-old Ali A. Mohamed pleaded guilty to five counts of conspiracy, including conspiring to kill U.S. nationals; conspiring to murder, kidnap, and maim outside the United States; conspiring to murder in general; and conspiring to destroy U.S. buildings and property. The charges stemmed from the August 7, 1998, terrorism at U.S. embassies in Nairobi, Kenya, and in Dar es Salaam, Tanzania. Two hundred and twenty-four people were killed in the attacks, and more than 5,000 were injured. Twelve of those killed were American citizens.

The human tragedy wrought by the bombings was enough in itself to focus attention on the U.S. government's case against Mohamed, but the case also generated national interest in part because of Mohamed's status as a former U.S. Army officer. The case attracted international attention because Mohamed implicated Osama bin Laden in the bombings. Bin Laden, a reputed terrorist, is wanted by law enforcement officials in several countries and tops the FEDERAL BUREAU OF INVESTIGATION (FBI) Most Wanted List. In addition to Mohamed, U.S. authorities captured four men suspected of par-

An artist's rendition of Ali Mohamed (*second from left*) as he stands with attorneys before U.S. District Judge Leonard B. Sand in a Manhattan Federal Court.

ticipating in the embassy-bombing conspiracy, while authorities in London are holding three other suspects. Fourteen more suspects remain at large, including bin Laden.

Mohamed was born in Egypt in 1951. After graduating from high school at the age of 20, he enlisted in the Cairo military academy where he quickly became an officer. His duties included recruiting intelligence officers for Egypt's army. Ten years later he visited the United States for the first time, when he received training in intelligence operations from American soldiers at Fort Bragg, North Carolina. During this training he told friends that the Egyptian army was hostile to devout Muslims like himself, and that he was philosophically aligned more with Islamic radicals who carried out the assassination of Egyptian Prime Minister Anwar Sadat in 1981. In 1984 Mohamed worked briefly for the CENTRAL INTELLIGENCE AGENCY (CIA). The CIA soon discovered, however, that he had revealed his alignment with Middle-East terrorists, and his services were immediately terminated.

On September 6, 1985, Mohamed formally took up residence in California for the purpose of becoming a naturalized U.S. citizen. The next year he enlisted in the U.S. Army and was assigned to the Special Operations Command at Fort Bragg, where the Army trains its Special Forces. Fort Bragg is also home to the elite anti-terrorist commando unit known as the Delta Force. (Foreign-born persons are permitted to join the American military if they have attained permanent resident status.) Mohamed was trained as a paratrooper and achieved the rank of sergeant before being honorably discharged in 1989.

Upon his discharge Mohamed renewed his contacts with the Egyptian "Islamic Jihad," a radical group he had secretly associated with since the early 1980s. In 1991 he was recruited by the terrorist network known as al Qaeda, a group headed by bin Laden. One of Mohamed's first assignments was to help smuggle bin Laden from Pakistan to Sudan, where the two later established a headquarters in Khartoum. At his plea hearing Mohamed testified that he was responsible for training bin Laden's bodyguards. He also said that he had arranged for a meeting between bin Laden and a leader of Hezbollah, a militant Islamic organization suspected of orchestrating the 1983 car bombings that killed 241 Marines at a U.S. barracks in Beirut, Lebanon.

Mohamed testified that bin Laden's goal was to use the Beirut bombing as a model to drive the United States and its allies from the Middle East. In 1993 bin Laden asked Mohamed to scout possible sites in Kenya to target for similar terrorist attacks. At the time, Mohamed was a naturalized U.S. citizen, and as such he traveled to Nairobi, where he took photographs of the U.S. embassy, drew diagrams, wrote a report, and then personally delivered his findings to bin Laden in Sudan. Mohamed testified that when bin Laden saw the photographs, he pointed to a spot near the Nairobi embassy where a truck full of explosives could be parked. Mohamed testified that bin Laden's plans came to fruition five years later with the simultaneous attacks against the two U.S. embassies in Africa.

Already under investigation by a New York GRAND JURY for lying to the FBI about his contacts with terrorist organizations in the Middle East, Mohamed emerged as a suspect in the embassy bombings when an alias he commonly used turned up on correspondence found near the rubble in Nairobi. Confronted about his role in the bombings, Mohamed told investigators that he knew who carried out the attacks but would not identify the attackers unless he was first given a deal by prosecutors. The FBI arrested Mohamed on September 10, 1998.

Escorted into the Manhattan federal district courtroom wearing leg irons, Mohamed took the witness stand before Judge Leonard B. Sand. Mohamed spoke in a calm voice while detailing the last 20 years of his life. Never expressing remorse, Mohamed precisely described his relationship with bin Laden, whom he said had masterminded and bankrolled the embassy attacks. Prosecutors said it was the first time a close associate of bin Laden had implicated the reputed terrorist in open court. Mohamed also implicated Wadih El-Hage in the attacks. A naturalized U.S. citizen born in Lebanon, the 40-year-old El-Hage is accused of aiding the broader conspiracy as bin Laden's top aid.

On February 5, 2001, El-Hage went on trial with co-defendants Mohamed Rashed Daoud al-'Owhali, Mohamed Sadeek Odeh, and Khalfan Khamis Mohamed in a Manhattan federal DISTRICT COURT. The proceedings were expected to last at least six months, but on March 29, 2001, all four defendants were found guilty of all 302 counts. To the surprise of some, Ali Mohamed was not a key witness at that trial. Mohamed did not disclose at his hearing whether his guilty plea was entered in exchange for a deal to turn STATE'S EVIDENCE. During the hearing Judge Sand initially said that Mohamed would receive no less than 25 years in prison, but after a conference with attorneys for both sides, Sand retracted his statement and said that sentencing would be for an unspecified number of years. He then ordered the plea agreement sealed, leading some to conjecture about Mohamed's role in the upcoming trial.

CROSS REFERENCES
Terrorism

CONTRACTS

AGREEMENTS between two or more persons that create an obligation to do, or refrain from doing, a particular thing.

Julie Hiatt Steele v. Michael Isikoff

Julie Hiatt Steele sued *Newsweek* journalist Michael Isikoff in U.S. District Court for the D.C. District over a 1997 article, claiming he broke his promise not to use her name. The article, which concerned allegations about one of President BILL CLINTON's sex scandals, ultimately led to Steele's becoming a target of prosecution by Independent Counsel KENNETH STARR. She subsequently sued Isikoff, *Newsweek*, and the magazine's owner, the Washington Post Company, alleging fraud and breach of contract. On September 6, 2000, a federal judge dismissed both claims.

The case began with investigative reporting, sexual scandal, and lying. In March 1997 Isikoff's research into allegations about the president's sexual impropriety led him to Kathleen Willey. Privately, the former White House volunteer and employee made a lurid accusation: she claimed that President Clinton had groped her sexually four years earlier. Willey told Isikoff to interview her friend, Steele, for corroboration. At the time a 51-year old divorcee living in Richmond, Virginia, Steele met with the reporter and confirmed the groping allegation. Later, she changed her mind, called Isikoff, and said the story was untrue. She claimed that Willey had asked her to lie.

Five months later, Isikoff published his article. Naming Steele as a key source, he recounted both versions of her story, the initial account and her later recantation in which she claimed to be lying at Willey's behest. Though the article contained neither the first nor the last allegation of sexual impropriety to be leveled against Clinton, it nevertheless ignited a new White House scandal.

Steele soon felt its impact, too. In January 1998 she agreed to provide Clinton's legal team with an AFFIDAVIT stating that Willey asked her to lie. In March, INDEPENDENT COUNSEL Starr sent the FEDERAL BUREAU OF INVESTIGATION (FBI) to interview her. Swiftly, Steele was enmeshed in Starr's wide-ranging investigation. Twice he subpoenaed her, and then her brother and daughter, for GRAND JURY testimony. Ultimately indicted on three counts of OBSTRUCTION OF JUSTICE and one of making false statements, she was prosecuted in 1999, with the case ending in a MISTRIAL. Willey, who testified against Steele, never faced prosecution because Starr granted her immunity in exchange for testimony.

In 1998 Steele filed suit. Rather than alleging the more common claims of LIBEL and DEFAMATION, the lawsuit's central claim was based on the law of contracts. It contended that her interview statements were made only after Isikoff agreed that they would be considered off the record—traditionally, an agreement between reporters and sources that the sources' names will not be disclosed. Steele's suit asserted that Isikoff's promises on two occasions constituted separate contracts, both of which the reporter had breached. In this connection, the lawsuit invoked a legal doctrine recognized by some states called PROMISSORY ESTOPPEL. Essentially concerning gratuitous promises made by one party to another party, the doctrine permits injured parties to sue by showing that reliance upon the promise harmed them. Separately, the lawsuit accused the defendants of fraud.

The defendants denied both claims. *Newsweek* stood by Isikoff, who maintained that the Steele interview was never considered off the record. In a public comment upon the lawsuit, the magazine's Washington bureau chief, Ann McDaniel, called the plaintiff's claim "pure fantasy."

Initially, the defendants filed a motion to dismiss the suit, but this action proved unsuccessful. U.S. District Court Judge Colleen Kollar-Kotelly rejected the motion in light of the Supreme Court of the United States's decision in *Cohen v. Cowles Media Co.*, 501 U.S. 663, 111 S. Ct. 2513, 115 L. Ed. 2d 586 (1991), which permits certain suits by sources against journalists for enforcement of promises. Notably, *Cohen* holds that the FIRST AMENDMENT does not forbid promissory estoppel actions against journalists because the doctrine is a general one available in private civil actions that does not specifically target the press.

The DISTRICT COURT ultimately dismissed the lawsuit anyway. The promissory estoppel claim failed because Judge Kollar-Kotelly determined that the case was governed by Virginia law, which does not recognize the doctrine. Even if state law recognized the claim, the judge held that Steele would have been prevented from using it due to her failure to tell Isikoff the

Mike Isikoff stands inside NBC studios after appearing on *Meet the Press* in 1998.

truth. Moreover, the judge ruled that any agreement Isikoff might have made to keep Steele's comments off the record was not legally a contract; as such, no breach of contract had occurred. In rejecting the fraud claim, the judge had sharp words for the plaintiff. "Painful as the glaring spotlight may be," she wrote, "Steele's harm is rooted in her own lie, a deception by which she alone tied herself to a sordid news story that dominated all types of media." Steele reportedly was weighing whether to appeal.

COPYRIGHT

An intangible right granted by statute to the author or originator of certain literary or artistic productions, whereby, for a limited period, the exclusive privilege is given to the person to make copies of the same for publication or sale.

New York Times v. Tasini

The history of publishing has pitted the writer against the publisher when compensation is the issue. Apart from celebrities and best-selling authors, few writers can expect to earn a sizable amount of money. Those who stand lowest on the ladder are freelance authors, those whom publishers designate as INDEPENDENT CONTRACTORS and who are paid for their writing based on a page length or word count. Until the mid-1970s, the U.S. copyright law gave freelancers who wrote for newspapers, magazines, or books such as encyclopedias, little opportunity to share in the revenues when a publisher resold or repackaged their articles. With the 1976 revision of the copyright law, however, the law recognized both a copyright in the publisher's collective work and a separate copyright for each author's contribution to the work. This change gave authors the ability in theory, if not in practice, to negotiate compensation for the right of publishers to reuse their works at a later time.

Though the law seemed clear at the time, the revision occurred just before the computer revolution of the 1980s and the rapid expansion of electronic databases and the development of CD-ROM disks that contain thousands of pages of text. By the early 1990s, some freelancers began to object to the sale of their articles to companies that produced these databases and disks, arguing that they were not being paid as they were entitled to under the 1976 Copyright Act. This dispute ultimately led Jonathan Tasini and five other freelance writers to sue the publishers of the *New York Times*, *Newsday*, and *Time* for copyright violations, arguing that they should be paid for their copyrighted work that had been published in electronic media.

The Supreme Court, in *New York Times v. Tasini*, ___U.S.___, 121 S.Ct. 2381, ___ L.Ed.2d ___ (2001), ruled in favor of the writers. The Court ruled that the publishers had failed to show that they came within a PRIVILEGE granted them in the Copyright Act that allowed them to distribute additional or revised versions of the collective works without obtaining permission of the freelance writers. The Court made clear that electronic databases are not "revisions" of past collective works.

The federal DISTRICT COURT dismissed the case but the Court of Appeals for the Second Circuit reversed this ruling. The appeals court rejected the lower court's conclusion that an electronic database containing the works in question was a revision that invoked the publisher's privilege of reproduction. Moreover, the court rule that databases in general were not collective works as defined by the copyright law. Though the databases might serve as ever-changing "anthologies," they were not revisions "of particular editions of periodicals in the Databases."

The Supreme Court, in a 7–2 decision, upheld the Second Circuit ruling. Justice RUTH BADER GINSBURG, in her majority opinion, revisited the legislative history behind the 1976 Copyright Law revision and examined the form and function of electronic databases and CD-

ROMs. Her reading of the legislative history led her to conclude that Congress had sought to protect the copyright of freelance writers: "If there is demand for a freelance article standing alone or in a new collection, the Copyright Act allows the freelancer to benefit from that demand; after authorizing initial publication, the freelancer may also sell the article to others."

In the present case there was no dispute that Tasini and the other writers held copyrights for the articles. The only issue was whether the electronic databases and CD-ROMs qualified under the law as revisions of the original collective work. Justice Ginsburg focused her analysis through the eyes of database users and considered whether they would perceive these as revisions of the collective work. She noted that databases shear the context away from each article. Moreover, a constantly growing information database was not by itself a revision: "The massive whole of the Database is not recognizable as a new version of its every small part."

The publishers had argued that databases and CD-ROMs were analogous to microfilm and microfiche, in which articles are archived in a different medium for research. These types of media were accepted by the law as reproductions of the original collective works that did not require authorial permission. Justice Ginsburg rejected this argument, noting that the pages of newspapers and magazines were photographed on microfilm. Thus, the collective work would retain its original context. In contrast, in a database "the articles appear disconnected from their original context." Though publishers warned of "dire consequences" if freelancers were allowed to make claims on articles in databases, Ginsburg refused to base the decision on a forecast. Moreover, she pointed out that the decision would give publishers and writers the opportunity to negotiate agreements for the electronic use of the authors' works. Commentators had observed that since the filing of the lawsuit publishers had routinely inserted a clause in their standard contracts giving them the right to use the works in electronic form.

Justice JOHN PAUL STEVENS, in a dissenting opinion, argued that the electronic versions of the collective works in question were "revisions" under the Copyright Act and that the "aggregation" of these revisions fell within the publisher's right to reproduce without author's permission.

Three Boys Music Corporation v. Bolton

Popular songs generate millions of dollars in ROYALTIES to their composers. Every year individuals file lawsuits alleging that composers have taken their songs and claimed them as their own. U.S. copyright laws give the holders of copyrighted songs the right to sue for DAMAGES and profits when they believe their material has been misappropriated. Many of these lawsuits are frivolous and are quickly dismissed. In a small number of cases, however, the plaintiff does prove that the songwriter did borrow from copyrighted material. This was the case in *Three Boys Music Corporation v. Bolton*, 212 F.3d 477 (9th Cir.2000), where the Isley Brothers, a famous rhythm and blues group, won a copyright INFRINGEMENT action against singer-songwriter Michael Bolton, his co-writer Andrew Goldmark, and Bolton's record company, Sony Music. The court of appeals affirmed the jury verdict, which awarded the Isley Brothers $5.4 million. The court concluded that the jury had reasonable grounds to believe Bolton and Goldmark had used significant parts of the 1966 Isley Brothers song "Love is a Wonderful Thing," when they released a song with the same title in 1991.

The facts of the case illustrate the ways in which copyright infringement may be proved. The Isley Brothers wrote and recorded "Love is a Wonderful Thing" in 1964, but the record company did not release it until 1966. The song was not released on a long-play album but on a 45-record as a single. Though industry insiders thought it would be a big hit, it never cracked the Top 100 charts. The song received strong airplay in New York and Connecticut, however. At the time of the song's release, Bolton and Goldmark were Connecticut teenagers. Moreover, Bolton was an avid collector of rhythm and blues music and he had access to his older brother's extensive record collection. In 1991 Bolton released the album "Time, Love and Tenderness," which contained his song entitled "Love is a Wonderful Thing." It became the first single release to promote the album, which finished 49th on Billboard's year-end pop chart. That same year the Isley Brothers' "Love is a Wonderful Thing" was issued on compact disc.

In early 1992, the Isley Brothers, through their Three Boys Music Corporation, filed a copyright infringement action against Bolton, Goldmark, and Sony Music. The trial on these charges began in 1994. The plaintiffs had to prove either that Bolton and Goldmark had access to the Isley Brothers song at the time they

Michael Bolton holds his 1990 Grammy Award for Best Male Pop Vocalist, honoring the song "How Am I Supposed to Live Without You."

wrote *their* song or that the two songs were substantially similar. As to the access issue, the Isley Brothers established through the testimony of disk jockeys that they had played the Isley Brothers song in 1966 and that Bolton could have heard it. Second, Ronald Isley testified that Bolton had approached him at a concert in 1988 and said he had everything the group had recorded and that he knew "everything" Roland Isley had done. A third piece of evidence was the songwriting session for "Love is a Wonderful Thing" that Bolton and Goldmark had recorded on tape. Bolton is heard on the tape asking if they were copying a Marvin Gaye song called "Some Kind of Wonderful." Though Bolton introduced the tape to show he and Goldmark had independently composed the song, the tape communicated the idea that Bolton was not sure if what they were doing was rewriting an old soul song.

As to the substantial similarity claim, the Isley Brothers produced an expert witness on music who analyzed both songs and made comparisons as to various elements. He concluded that the two songs shared a combination of five elements: the title hook phrase, the shifted cadence, the instrumental figures, the verse/chorus relationship, and the fade ending. Bolton and Goldmark sought to prove that their arranger contributed two of these elements. The court observed that the arranger's contributions to Bolton and Goldmark's song were described by the appellants' own expert as "very common." The court also said, "Although the appellants presented testimony from their own expert musicologist, Anthony Ricigliano, he conceded that there were similarities between the two songs and that he had not found the combination of unprotectible elements in the Isley Brothers' song 'anywhere in the prior art'."

The Court of Appeals for the Ninth Circuit upheld the jury's verdict that there had been infringement. Judge D.W. Nelson concluded that the jury had reasonable GROUNDS to conclude the defendants had access to the song, despite the fact that the song was 25-years old and fairly obscure. Though he acknowledged the case of access was weak and that the case of substantial similarity was based on circumstantial evidence, Nelson noted that it is not the role of the APPELLATE COURT to retry the case and second-guess the jury.

The defendants also challenged the $5.4 million award, which was based on apportioning the profits from Bolton's album based on the song and then attributing a portion of the song's profits based on the infringing elements. The jury found that 28 percent of the album's profits derived from the song and that 66 percent of the song's profits resulted from infringing elements. Judge Nelson upheld these findings, ruling that Sony Music had the burden of proving lower percentages of profits and that the jury chose not to believe Sony's experts. On January 22, 2001, the Supreme Court of the United States denied CERTIORARI to Bolton's appeal of the circuit court's ruling.

CROSS REFERENCES
Music Publishing; Publishing Law

CRANSTON, ALAN MACGREGOR

Alan MacGregor Cranston

Former U.S. Senator Alan Cranston, retired four-term liberal Democrat from California, died of natural causes at his Los Altos home on December 31, 2000. A fierce proponent of nuclear arms control and world peace, the high-profile activist had served a total of 24 years in the Senate before resigning under a cloud of controversy in 1993, which largely overshadowed his previous accomplishments. He was 86 at the time of his death.

Alan MacGregor Cranston was born to William MacGregor and Carol Dixon Cranston in Palo Alto, California, on June 19, 1914. He studied at Pomona College and the University of Mexico before graduating from Stanford University, where he earned his bachelor's degree in 1936. Upon graduation, Cranston be-

ALAN MACGREGOR CRANSTON

1914	Born in Palo Alto, California
1945	Published *The Killing of the Peace*
1953–1958	President of the California Democratic Council
1969	Elected to the U.S. Senate
1993	Resigned Senate seat following reprimand for involvement in Keating scandal
2000	Died in Los Altos, California

came a foreign correspondent for the International News Service, traveling throughout England, Italy, Germany, and Ethiopia for two years. By 1942, he had become chief of the foreign language division for the U.S. Office of War Information in Washington, D.C.

At the height of World War II in 1944, Cranston entered the U.S. Army but was released one year later when the war ended. That same year, in 1945, Cranston published his first book, *The Killing of the Peace*, about the Senate struggle over the LEAGUE OF NATIONS. Also during 1945, Cranston served as executive secretary of the Council for American-Italian Affairs, Inc., in Washington.

After the war, Cranston became seriously involved in politics. Joining the United World Federalists, he served as its national president from 1949 to 1952. He was an active member of the California Democratic Council, rising to the presidency from 1953 to 1958, and also served as a member of the executive committee of the California Democratic Central Commission. From 1959 to 1967, Cranston was CONTROLLER for the State of California and also ran unsuccessfully for a Senate seat.

Coinciding with his political ambitions—as well as his journalistic and writing endeavors—was Cranston's interest in the real estate and construction industry. This lead to a partnership in the Ames-Cranston Company in 1947, an entrepreneurial building and real estate firm that kept him busy for the next several years.

After leaving the position of state controller in 1967, Cranston served as president of Homes for a Better America, Inc., and as vice president of Carlsberg Financial Corporation. He was a columnist for the *Los Angeles Times* and several other newspapers and decided to bid for a seat in the Senate again. This time he was elected as U.S. Senator from California in 1969. Thus began a 24-year congressional career that ended anti-climactically in 1993.

Cranston's years in the Senate were marked by serious controversy as well as noteworthy success in moving difficult legislation through Congress. From the onset, he was heavily involved in international affairs, drawing on his experiences as a foreign correspondent and his tenure with the Office of War Information. In his very first year, Cranston became chairman of the Senate Veterans Affairs Committee, the Housing & Urban Affairs Subcommittee and the East Asian & Pacific Affairs Subcommittee. He was an outspoken advocate for nuclear arms control, which became central to his platform for decades to come. In later years, he served as a member of the Banking, Housing & Urban Affairs Committee and the Foreign Relations Committee & Select Committee on Intelligence, which he also chaired. Cranston later became Senate majority whip. In 1984 he made an unsuccessful run to win the Democratic presidential nomination.

Cranston's political reputation was later marred by his association with Lincoln Savings & Loan president Charles Keating, who had been indicted on securities fraud charges. Cranston and four other U.S senators—known as "the Keating five"—were the subjects of a Senate Ethics Committee investigation for their intervention with federal regulators on Keating's behalf. At the time, Cranston had received $1.2 million from Keating in campaign funds. Ultimately in 1991, Cranston was formally reprimanded for engaging "in an impermissible pattern of conduct in which fund raising and official activities were substantially linked in connection with Mr. Keating and Lincoln." The other senators received lesser sanctions. Cranston resigned from his four-term Senate seat, announcing that he would not seek a fifth term. Although his public approval rating was at a record low at the time, he cited only his diagnosis of prostate cancer as a reason for not running.

After leaving the Senate in 1993, Cranston receded into the background of public life but remained involved in many international organizations. Until 2000 he chaired the Gorbachev Foundation USA, a thinktank founded by former Soviet President Mikhail Gorbachev to work for world peace and nuclear disarmament. He also served as chairman of the U.S.-Kyrgiz Business Council from 1993 to 1996, and as its honorary chairman from 1997 to 2000. Concurrently, he remained active in the State of the World Forum from 1995 to 1999, and lent his expertise to Boston's Schooner Capital Corporation as its senior international adviser. In 1999 Cranston became president of Global Security Institute, a position he held until his death.

Cranston died peacefully at his home in Los Altos, California on the eve of the millennium. He was survived by one son, Kim. Another son was killed in 1980 following an automobile accident.

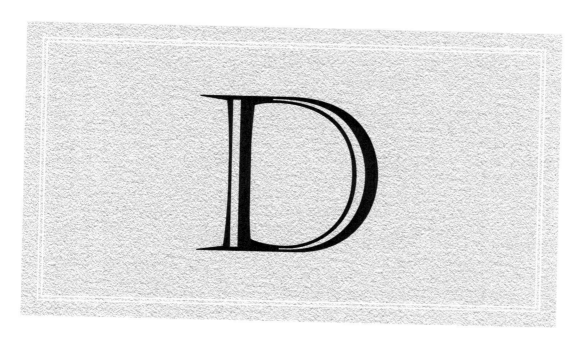

DAMAGES

Monetary compensation that is awarded by a court in a CIVIL ACTION to an individual who has been injured through the wrongful conduct of another party.

Cooper Industries, Inc. v. Leatherman Tool Group, Inc.

In a civil lawsuit the plaintiff typically seeks an AWARD of money damages from the defendant. The damages are based on the actual injuries suffered by the plaintiff and must be grounded in the evidence presented at trial. In some cases, however, the court will also permit the jury to award PUNITIVE DAMAGES. Punitive damages are similar to a criminal fine in that such an award is meant to deter the defendant from committing similar injuries. Moreover, the amount of a punitive damage award is not tied to the plaintiff's actual injuries, which often results in a large punitive damage amount. The awarding of excessive punitive damages, though, has led many state legislatures to limit them. In addition, the U.S. Supreme Court has set out rules on how courts must assess the reasonableness of any punitive damage award.

The Court was required to resolve an ongoing conflict in the federal CIRCUIT COURTS of appeal over what standard of review must be applied to punitive damages at the appellate court level. In *Cooper Industries, Inc. v. Leatherman Tool Group, Inc.,* ___U.S.___, 121 S.Ct. 1678, 149 L.Ed.2d 674 (2001), the Court ruled that APPELLATE COURTS must conduct DE NOVO review rather than apply an ABUSE OF DISCRETION standard. This ruling means that fed-eral appellate courts have great freedom to review and reduce punitive damages based on previous Supreme Court standards. The decision is one more example of the Court expressing its desire to control excessive punitive damage awards.

The case involved the competition between two companies for a share of the pocket tool business. Leatherman Tool Group developed in the 1980s what it called the "Pocket Survival Tool" (PST). The PST was an elaboration of the popular Swiss Army Knife, which contains a number of handy tools within a compact handle. Leatherman's innovations included pliers that could be folded and unfolded in an instant. In 1995 Cooper Industries entered the PST market with the hope of capturing about five per cent of the business. It planned to copy Leatherman's tool and add some additional features. The new tool, dubbed "ToolZall", was introduced at a national trade show in 1996. Cooper had not yet manufactured the ToolZall and needed to display it to interested customers. Therefore, it made a mock-up by using a Leatherman PST. It deleted Leatherman's TRADEMARK and retouched photographs to remove distinctive features of the PST. This photograph was used at the trade show and later on promotional materials distributed around the United States.

Leatherman sued Cooper under the LANHAM ACT, the federal trademark law, for infringing on its PST design and for using the PST in its promotional material. A jury awarded Leatherman $50,000 in general damages and $4.5 million in punitive damages. Cooper asked the judge to reduce the punitive damage award, as the trial judge can use REMITTITUR to alter the verdict. Under remittitur the judge directs the plaintiff either to accept a lower award or face a new trial. In this case the judge concluded that the punitive damages award was reasonable and therefore upheld the verdict. On appeal, the Ninth Circuit Court of Appeals upheld the trial court. The court based its analysis on the abuse of discretion standard. This standard is very deferential to the trial court's actions, allowing the appeals court to overturn a decision only if the trial judge clearly abused his or her authority. Cooper had argued that the appeals court must conduct a de novo review. This type of review empowers the appeals court to review all the evidence on punitive damages without regard to the trial court's decision. This fresh review gives the court enormous latitude in judging the issue.

The Supreme Court agreed to hear Cooper's appeal because the federal circuits were divided over the appropriate standard of review for punitive damages. The Court, in an 8–1 decision, ruled that federal appeals courts must apply a de novo review. Justice JOHN PAUL STEVENS, writing for the majority, concluded that the nature of punitive damages demanded that appeals courts conduct a fresh inquiry. He noted the similarities of punitive damages to criminal fines and cited various criminal cases dealing with the proportionality of sentences that relied on de novo review. Moreover, Stevens rejected the idea that when a jury awarded punitive damages, it was making a finding of fact that could not be disturbed by an appeals court unless it was clearly erroneous.

Justice Stevens justified a fresh review in part because of the "[d]ifferences in the institutional competence of trial judges and appellate judges." Under the Court's previous rulings, a court that evaluates a punitive damages award must assess "(1) the degree or reprehensibility of the defendant's misconduct, (2) the disparity between the harm . . . suffered by the plaintiff and the punitive damages award, and (3) the difference between the punitive damages . . . and the civil penalties authorized or imposed in comparable cases." Stevens acknowledged that a trial judge would "have a somewhat superior vantage over courts of appeal" in assessing the defendant's misconduct. As to the second factor, Stevens concluded that either a trial or appellate court was capable of analyzing the disparity between harm and damages. An appeals court was most capable of reviewing the third factor, however, "which calls for a broad legal comparison."

Stevens then applied the de novo standard to assess the strength of the punitive damages award. He concluded that Cooper's conduct was relatively innocuous and that the size of the award appeared disproportionate based on the use of the doctored photograph. Finally, he noted that the state's unlawful trade practices act mandated a $25,000 fine for a violation similar to Cooper's. A de novo review would appear to justify a punitive damages award of that amount rather than $4.5 million. Though the Court did not rule on the punitive damages award directly, it sent a strong signal to the Ninth Circuit that it should drastically reduce the amount on REMAND.

Tri County Industries, Inc. v. District of Columbia

In civil lawsuits tried before a jury, the jurors are charged with determining the facts of the case, which includes whether the plaintiff is entitled to money damages and in what amount. Though in theory the jury is the ultimate factfinder, in practice, trial judges have the authority to set aside verdicts they deem excessive or unsupported by the evidence. A common practice in such a situation is for the judge to give the plaintiff two options. The plaintiff either agrees to accept a smaller damages award, which is called REMITTITUR, or the judge throws out the verdict and orders a second trial. In most cases a plaintiff accepts the reduced award to avoid the uncertainty of a new trial. A plaintiff is free to appeal such a decision, however. Such was the case in *Tri County Industries, Inc. v. District of Columbia*, 200 F.3d 836 (D.C.Cir. 2000), where the federal district court judge had thrown out a $5 million dollar verdict after the plaintiff refused to accept $1 million in remittitur. The second trial resulted in the plaintiff receiving "nominal damages of one hundred dollars." The appeals court held that the trial judge had abused his discretion in throwing out the original damages award verdict. The U.S. Supreme Court initially agreed to hear the defendant's appeal, but later dismissed the WRIT of CERTIORARI, thereby failing to resolve authoritatively how much discretion a federal district court judge has to review damage awards made by juries.

Tri County Industries obtained permission from the District of Columbia to convert an abandoned warehouse into an installation that would decontaminate polluted soil. Tri County acquired building and air quality permits and were allowed to bypass the required environmental impact statement requisite under the law. For several months after obtaining the needed permits, Tri County could not proceed with operations because of equipment delays. Nevertheless, it began storing soil on the site. The District issued a citation for this storage because Tri County needed to obtain a certificate of occupancy first. Tri County did not respond to the citation, which led the District to suspend the building permit. At the same time community leaders became aware of the proposed use for the site and started to mount a campaign to prevent Tri County from operating there. After a few more months the District rescinded the other permits and the environmental impact statement waiver. Tri County's attorney told the company that because of political maneuvering and community opposition there was no way to know how long the appeal might take. Faced with high rental costs for the building and the need to purchase expensive equipment, Tri County abandoned the project and filed a CIVIL RIGHTS lawsuit in federal district court alleging that the District of Columbia had violated its DUE PROCESS rights.

At the trial Tri County brought forth witnesses to support its damages claims. Tri County asked for damages to cover the amount of money it had invested in the project and for damages to compensate it for future lost profits. The District did not put on any expert witnesses and was not allowed by the judge to introduce evidence about "health and safety concerns." The judge ruled that because the District had granted all the necessary permits, all health and safety issues had been resolved as a matter of law in Tri County's favor. The jury ultimately found for Tri County and awarded it $5 million. The District asked the judge to grant it a new trial. After Tri County refused the judge's remittitur offer of $1 million, the judge threw out the jury award as being grossly excessive and ordered a new trial.

At the second trial, the judge allowed the District to present health and safety evidence. Furthermore, the District summoned experts to contest the fact that Tri County would have been allowed to operate at the site. This time the jury agreed with the District and "awarded nominal damages of one hundred dollars." Not surprisingly, Tri County appealed.

The Court of Appeals for the District of Columbia Circuit reversed the trial judge's original determination that the $5 million verdict was grossly excessive. Judge Karen LeCraft Henderson, writing for the court, stated that the appeals court could reverse the trial judge if the judge had abused his discretion. Turning to the trial judge's reasons for granting a new trial,

Henderson rejected all three of his justifications. First, he had concluded that Tri County's failure to try to seek reinstatement of the building permit was "unreasonable" as a matter of law in light of its claims of lost profits. Judge Henderson rejected this conclusion, finding that whether or not Tri County was reasonable under the circumstances was a jury question. She noted that Tri County had offered the jury an explanation for why it had not appealed the permit rescission, citing the political influences surrounding the process.

Judge Henderson also rejected the judge's finding that, "Tri County's evidence of lost profits was too speculative and remote and that the award of less than half of the amount Tri County estimated was 'grossly excessive'." Henderson pointed out that Tri County had produced evidence by economists and other experts of lost profits in excess of $11 million. Case law clearly stated that proof of the amount of damages could be based on a reasonable estimate. The estimates provided by these experts were "largely unchallenged" by the District. The appeals court also noted that the jury had awarded less than half of the total amount claimed and that "the award was within the reasonable range within which the jury may properly operate." Given these circumstances, the appeals court ruled that the trial judge had abused his discretion. Therefore, the appeals court dismissed the second trial verdict and reinstated the original $5 million verdict.

CROSS REFERENCES
Civil Procedure; Due Process; Trademarks

DISABLED PERSONS

Persons who have a physical or mental impairment that substantially limits one or more major life activities. Some laws also include in their definition of disabled persons those people who have a record of or are regarded as having such an impairment.

Casey Martin Sues PGA

The Americans with Disabilities Act of 1990 (ADA) has provided disabled persons with legal rights that have changed employment laws and removed architectural barriers in public accommodations. In addition, the ADA has focused on many societal practices and forced departures from tradition. Such was the case in *PGA Tour, Inc. v. Martin*, ___U.S.___, 121 S.Ct. 1879, 149 L.Ed.2d 904 (2001), where profes-

Casey Martin plays golf in Austin, Texas, 1998.

sional golfer Casey Martin requested permission to use a golf cart instead of walking the golf course during tournaments. Martin, who has a serious circulation disorder, sought a "reasonable accommodation" under the ADA. However, the Professional Golfers Association (PGA) tour denied his request. The Supreme Court of the United States ruled that the PGA must allow Martin to use a golf cart, as the golf tour was a public accommodation under the ADA and the use of the cart would not fundamentally change the nature of the golf competitions.

Martin was a golf prodigy, who won 17 golf events in Oregon before he was 15. He went on to play golf at Stanford University. He joined the Nike Tour (now called the Buy.com Tour) in 1998, which is one level below the PGA Tour. After two successful years on the tour, Martin qualified for the PGA Tour in 2000. However, Martin has been afflicted from birth "with Klippel-Trenaunay-Weber Syndrome, a degenerative circulatory disorder that obstructs the flow of blood from his right leg back to his heart." The disease is progressive and Martin's right leg has atrophied. Before leaving Stanford, Martin could no longer walk an 18-hole golf course. The Pacific 10 Conference and the NCAA allowed Martin to use a golf cart because of his medical condition, in part because if Martin walked he would be prone to developing blood clots and fracturing his leg.

Martin gained access to the Nike Tour by entering a three-stage qualifying tournament known as the "Q-School." Anyone can enter the Q-School by paying a $3000 entry fee and submitting two letters of recommendation from

PGA or Nike Tour members. The third step is to participate in a series of tournaments. The finalists qualify either for the PGA or Nike Tours. Though Martin was allowed to use a cart during the first two rounds of competition, he was denied the use of a cart for the final stage. He then sued in federal court, alleging that the PGA Tour had violated his rights under the ADA. The district court granted Martin a preliminary injunction to compete using the golf cart.

The PGA sought to dismiss the complaint, arguing that it was a private club or alternatively not a public accommodation and thus was exempt from Title III of the ADA. The judge rejected these arguments. At trial the PGA did not contest that Martin had a disability covered by the ADA or that this disability prevented him from walking the entire course during a round of golf. Instead, the PGA argued that the waiver of the rule would "fundamentally alter the nature of" the competition. The judge agreed that physical fatigue played a part in this rule and could affect the shot-making skills of the golfer. However, walking the course for non-disabled golfers was less taxing than the fatigue Martin suffered in walking over a mile even when he used a golf cart. The court ultimately sided with Martin, and the PGA appealed to the U.S. Circuit Court of Appeals for the Ninth Circuit. The appeals court upheld the ruling and found that the PGA tournaments were public accommodations for ADA purposes.

The Supreme Court, in a 7–2 decision, upheld the Ninth Circuit ruling. Justice JOHN PAUL STEVENS wrote the majority opinion. Stevens noted that the threshold issue was whether Title III of the ADA, which deals with public accommodations, applies to a golf tournament. Reviewing the categories of public accommodations, Stevens concluded that the PGA "golf tour and their qualifying rounds fit comfortably within the coverage of Title III, and Martin within its protection." Golf courses are specifically mentioned as a place of public accommodation, and the PGA operates these golf courses during tournaments. The PGA contended that competing golfers are not members of the class protected by Title III, as they are independent contractors who perform entertainment for the public. As such, they are not the "clients or customers" of the golf course as defined by Title III, and they are not employees protected by Title I. Justice Stevens rejected this argument, finding that Title III's general rule against discrimination does not contain an express clients or customers limitation. Moreover, the Q-School from which Martin progressed was open to all members of the public who could meet the entrance requirements. Thus, Martin had been a client or customer at that stage of competition.

Turning to the PGA's argument that Martin's use of the cart would fundamentally alter competition, Stevens concluded that the waiver would not change an essential aspect of the game nor give Martin an unfair advantage over others. Stevens pointed out that golf carts are used in the qualifying rounds of PGA tournaments and are permitted on the Senior PGA Tour. In addition, it was impossible to guarantee every competitor the same conditions during a round of golf. The weather may change, and the golf course may become harder or softer because of rain, sun, and wind. In Stevens's view, "pure chance may have a greater impact on the outcome of elite golf tournaments than the fatigue resulting from the enforcement of the walking rule." In the end, shot making rather than walking was the essence of golf. Therefore, Martin was entitled under the ADA to use a golf cart during PGA tournaments.

University of Alabama v. Garrett

The Americans with Disabilities Act (ADA) places state governments under its provisions regarding the right of employees to sue for money DAMAGES when they allege discrimination based on a disability. At the time that Congress enacted the ADA this provision appeared unremarkable, as Congress has subjected state governments to many civil rights laws. By the mid-1990s, however, the states had found an ally in the Supreme Court of the United States, which began to limit federal authority over the states. The Court relied primarily on the ELEVENTH AMENDMENT, which prohibits a citizen of one state suing the government of another state. Prior Supreme Court rulings dating back to 1890 had extended this prohibition to lawsuits filed by citizens against their own states. In *Board of Trustees of University of Alabama v. Garrett*, 531 U.S. 356, 121 S.Ct. 955, 148 L.Ed.2d 866, the Court employed the Eleventh Amendment to strike down the ADA's applicability to damage lawsuits involving alleged disability employment discrimination by state governments.

Patricia Garrett was the director of nursing for a major department at the University of Alabama's Birmingham hospital. In 1994 she was diagnosed with breast cancer and had to spend more than a year away from work undergoing treatment. When she returned in mid-1995, her supervisor told Garrett "that she would have to give up her director position." Garrett then took another, lower paying position as a nurse manager. She then sued the University of Alabama for monetary damages under the ADA. The university asked the federal DISTRICT COURT to dismiss the action because it alleged that Congress had exceeded its authority to ABROGATE the state's Eleventh Amendment immunity. The

Milton Ash answers reporters' questions as Patricia Garrett watches during a news conference.

court granted the motion to dismiss (*Garrett v. Board of Trustees of University of Alabama at Birmingham*, 989 F.Supp. 1409, [N.D.Ala. Jan 13, 1998]), but the Court of Appeals for the Eleventh Circuit reversed this decision (*Garrett v. University of Alabama at Birmingham Bd. of Trustees*, 193 F.3d 1214 [11th Cir.(Ala.) Oct 26, 1999]), ruling that Congress had acted within its authority. Because the circuit courts of appeals had split on this issue, the Supreme Court agreed to hear the university's appeal.

The Court, in a 5–4 ruling, reversed the Eleventh Circuit and found that Congress had failed to demonstrate that it had enough justification to remove state immunity granted by the Eleventh Amendment. Therefore, the ADA's provisions applying to employment discrimination could not be applied to the states. Chief Justice WILLIAM H. REHNQUIST, writing for the majority, noted that the Court had permitted Congress to abrogate state immunity when Congress unequivocally expresses the intention to do so and when it acts pursuant to a "valid grant of constitutional authority." In the present case the Court found that only the second issue was in question.

Chief Justice Rehnquist based his analysis on a line of cases and reasoning that center on the FOURTEENTH AMENDMENT. This amendment, which was enacted after the CIVIL WAR, prohibits the states from denying any citizen DUE PROCESS OF LAW, EQUAL PROTECTION of the law, or PRIVILEGES AND IMMUNITIES accorded by law. Its passage signaled a major shift of power from the states to the federal government. Congress is authorized under Section 5 of the amendment to enact legislation to enforce the substantive guarantees found in its first section. Case law required Section 5 legislation that reaches beyond the scope of the amendment's actual guarantees must exhibit "congruence and proportionality between the injury to be prevented or remedied and the means adopted to that end."

The key to the case was the Fourteenth Amendment's protection of disabled persons. Rehnquist cited an earlier case (*Cleburne v. Cleburne Living Center, Inc.*, 473 U.S. 432 [1985]) that involved a group home for mentally retarded persons to support the proposition that disabled persons are not given increased constitutional protection. Instead, the state can merely provide a RATIONAL BASIS to justify legislation or action. For the Court's majority, this meant that the states are not required "to make special accommodations for the disabled so long as their actions towards such individuals are rational." Rehnquist admitted that the states could "quite hard headedly—and perhaps hardheartedly—hold to job-qualification requirements which do not make allowance for the disabled."

Congress could only be authorized to include the states within the ADA's reach if it identified "a history and pattern of unconstitutional employment discrimination" against disabled persons. Rehnquist concluded, however, that the legislative record "simply fails to show that Congress did in fact identify a pattern of irrational state discrimination in employment against the disabled." Rehnquist asserted that Congress published only a handful of incidents to support this conclusion. Absent a compelling historical pattern of discrimination, such as the racial discrimination against African Americans that justified the VOTING RIGHTS ACT OF 1965, Chief Justice Rehnquist saw no merit in stripping states of their immunity from citizen lawsuits for money.

Justice STEPHEN G. BREYER, in a dissenting opinion, argued that the majority had ignored hundreds of incidents in the legislative record that involved state agencies. Based on these examples, Breyer believed, "Congress expressly found substantial unjustified discrimination against persons with disabilities."

CROSS REFERENCES
Eleventh Amendment; Fourteenth Amendment

DISBAR

To revoke an attorney's license to practice law.

Arkansas Moves to Disbar Former President Clinton

On June 30, 2000, the Arkansas Supreme Court's Committee on Professional Conduct, which governs the licensing and disciplining of attorneys within the state, filed suit to disbar then-president BILL CLINTON from the practice of law. The suit followed an earlier recommendation made by a court advisory panel, which charged that Clinton's dishonesty about his relationship with White House intern Monica Lewinsky damaged the legal profession and demonstrated his "overall unfitness" to practice law. The lawsuit marked an unprecedented action against a sitting president. Clinton had thirty days to respond to the five-page complaint filed in Pulaski County Circuit Court.

The complaint was premised upon a 1999 decision by U.S. District Court Judge Susan Webber Wright, who found Clinton in CON-

TEMPT of court and fined him $90,000 for OB-STRUCTION OF JUSTICE. Wright ruled that Clinton had knowingly tendered "misleading statements" during a January 1998 deposition in which he, as a defendant in a lawsuit brought by Paula Corbin Jones, testified under oath that he did not remember ever being alone with Lewinsky and that he did not have, or engage in, sexual relations with her.

Another complaint had been filed by the Atlanta-based Southeastern Legal Foundation, which also petitioned for disbarment. Clinton previously had been impeached by the U.S. House of Representatives, which charged that his denials in the same matter had amounted to PERJURY. He was later acquitted by the Senate in February 1999. KENNETH STARR's successor as INDEPENDENT COUNSEL, Robert W. Ray, investigated into this and other issues, however, including the WHITEWATER real estate and Arkansas land deals scandal, the White House's improper gathering of FEDERAL BUREAU OF INVESTIGATION (FBI) files involving the Clintons, and the firing of White House travel employees. All investigations remained open and active at the time of the suit to disbar Clinton.

Clinton stated that the Arkansas committee was acting too harshly and that his attorneys would fight it. Four Pulaski Circuit Court judges RECUSED themselves from the case, citing conflicts of interest with the former Arkansas governor. A fifth, Judge Leon Johnson, accepted the case for his docket.

Attorneys for Clinton defended that the events alleged in the complaint did not arise out of Clinton's practice of law; that the Paula Jones case was ultimately dismissed, albeit with an $800,000 settlement from Clinton to Jones; and that disbarment was too harsh a discipline against a lawyer not in active practice who had not pleaded guilty or been convicted of a crime. Conversely, the committee's attorneys requested formal admission or denial from Clinton that he intentionally mislead lawyers in the Paula Jones case. They also requested the court to compel from Clinton either an admission or a denial of the body of evidence previously used against him by Judge Wright in finding Clinton in contempt. In this non-political forum, Clinton's denial would be responded to with a plethora of incriminating evidence: his admission would constitute a violation of the professional code for attorneys and, thus, would be GROUNDS for disbarment. Such an admission could also, in turn, be used in any pending criminal proceeding.

As Clinton's tenure in the Oval Office neared its end, his attorneys fought to work out a deal that would spare him a criminal INDICTMENT. Concurrent negotiations continued with the Arkansas Supreme Court disbarment committee as well as independent counsel Ray. No resolution appeared viable.

On January 19, 2001, Clinton's very last day in office, he acknowledged for the first time that he had made false statements under oath. The formal admission presented to the court was combined with Clinton's surrender of his law license as part of an arrangement with independent counsel Ray and federal prosecutors. In return, they agreed to drop the $55 million six-year investigation and no longer pursue a GRAND JURY indictment. An order of discipline, signed by Clinton, was entered with the court, which stated that "Clinton admits . . . that he knowingly gave evasive and misleading answers 'prejudicial to the administration of justice'." Both Democrats and Republicans expressed relief that the matter could finally be put to rest and that the nation was spared the possibility of seeing a former chief executive face criminal charges. Independent counsel Ray stated, "The nation's interests have been served. This matter is now concluded."

Prior to his career in politics, Clinton had practiced law only briefly and sporadically. He was serving as a law professor at the University of Arkansas when he won an election for state ATTORNEY GENERAL. From there, he sprang to the governorship and then the presidency. Clinton said in his January 19th statement, "I tried to walk a line between acting lawfully and testifying falsely, but I now recognize that I did not fully accomplish this goal. . . ."

CROSS REFERENCES
Whitewater

DISCRIMINATION

In CONSTITUTIONAL LAW, the GRANT by STATUTE of particular privileges to a class arbitrarily designated from a sizable number of persons, where no reasonable distinction exists between the favored and disfavored classes. Federal laws, supplemented by court decisions, prohibit discrimination in such areas as employment, housing, voting rights, education, and access to public facilities. They also proscribe discrimination on the basis of race, age, sex, nationality, disability, or religion. In addition, state and local laws can prohibit discrimination in these areas and in others not covered by federal laws.

Boy Scouts Win Suit but Lose Funds

In January 2000 the Supreme Court of the United States ruled in *Boy Scouts of America v. Dale* that the Boy Scouts of America (BSA), as a private organization, had a FIRST AMENDMENT constitutional right of FREEDOM OF ASSOCIATION and expression. Accordingly, the group may exclude avowed homosexuals from organizational positions of leadership or policy-making. The case centered on assistant scoutmaster James Dale, who was denied a leadership position with the Scouts after he publicly declared himself to be homosexual. After the court's decision, the Scouts reaffirmed the right "to ask all of our members to do their best to live the Scout Oath and Law." Such oath includes pledges to revere God and be "morally straight," which the leaders interpret as excluding unrepentant homosexuals.

Prior to the decision, several *state* high courts had issued opposite opinions regarding the inclusion or exclusion of the Boy Scouts under their respective state CIVIL RIGHTS laws. The California Supreme Court ruled in favor of the Scouts while New Jersey's Supreme Court found that the Scouts had violated its anti-discrimination laws. The Connecticut Human Rights Commission ruled that the Scout's anti-homosexual policy violated the state's GAY AND LESBIAN RIGHTS law, and as such, state employees can no longer deduct charitable contributions for the Boy Scouts from the state's payroll deduction plan.

The seeming victory with the Supreme Court was short-lived when, within days, several private and public entities began withdrawing fund commitments to the Scouts or otherwise displaying their dissatisfaction with the court's decision. Many companies who previously sponsored or donated funds to the Scouts suddenly found themselves in the position of having corporate employment policies that contradicted the policy enunciated in the high court's decision. Among the first to revoke contributions were Levi Strauss, Wells Fargo, Textron, Chase Manhattan Corporation, and Merrill Lynch & Company.

Nationwide, nearly one million Boy Scouts in 19,000 troops meet in public schools or community centers, often without being charged. Soon the trend of fund revocation reached local governments, churches, and schools. Some of these entities expressed concern that, if they had local policies, ordinances, or laws prohibiting discrimination based on sexual preference, they could no longer contribute funds or confer special benefits to the Boy Scouts. New York City's school chancellor prohibited the Scouts from bidding on any contracts with the school system. The Los Angeles City Council severed ties with the Scouts and blocked troops from using city property *gratis*, as it had before. In Seattle, a coalition called Safe Schools requested that the school district curb the troops' access to students and the use of public buildings. The Fort Lauderdale City Commission refused a $10,000 grant of public money to the Boy Scouts, and Florida's largest school district, the Miami-Dade Public Schools, indefinitely postponed the Scouts' annual recruitment drive until it could be determined whether it violated school board policy against discrimination. About 12 of 1,400 local United Way chapters in various cities issued public statements that they would no longer fund the Boy Scouts. Even famed movie director Steven Spielberg announced that he would leave his post on the advisory board of the Boy Scouts in protest of the organization's anti-gay policies.

Despite what appeared to be widespread protestation, youth enrollment in the Boy Scouts actually grew by 4.2 percent in 2000. Boy Scout spokesman Gregg Shields has stated publicly that it is still too early to predict the effect of corporate withdrawals but that funding has remained stable. In 1999 the organization received approximately $11 million in charitable contributions. The Boy Scouts of America boasts a membership of six million.

A particularly meaningful show of support came from the U.S. House of Representatives in September 2000, when the House voted 362–12 to reject a proposal by Representative Lynn Woolsey (D-CA) to revoke the Boy Scouts' federal CHARTER because of its policy of excluding homosexuals. While it confers no special benefit, a federal charter is a mark of prestige and an honorary title granted to only 90 entities for their patriotic, charitable, or educational contributions. Other grantees include the American Legion, the National Ski Patrol, and Future Farmers of America. Representative Cass Ballenger (R-NC) stated that half the members of the House were former scouts and would defend an organization "as American as apple pie and baseball."

More support was on the way. As of March 2001 state legislatures in Arizona, Connecticut, and Florida began discussing bills to prevent local governments from withholding funds for the Boy Scouts. In early May, the Illinois Appellate Court lifted a seven-year injunction that blocked the Chicago Area Council of the Boy Scouts of America from considering sexual orientation when screening applicants for staff positions. The APPELLATE COURT cited the Supreme Court decision in its opinion, which also made clear that the Scouts could not automatically reject all homosexual applicants for clerical or low-profile positions. The court further ordered a review of the underlying facts in the discrimination case, *Richardson v. Chicago Area Council of Boy Scouts of America*, that led to the 1992 injunction. Plaintiff G. Keith Richardson, a former Eagle Scout, had told the Chicago Area Council that he is gay "and very interested in any job opening with the [council]." After investigation, the court determined that Richardson's claim to be interested was false and vacated the DAMAGES award but upheld its injunction upon further review.

Similarly, the BSA came under attack from the AMERICAN CIVIL LIBERTIES UNION (ACLU) when it filed a religious discrimination lawsuit against Portland, Oregon, schools and the state Department of Education in April 2001 on behalf of an atheist mother whose son did not meet the Scout requirement of belief in God. An earlier suit filed by the ACLU had alleged that city and state educators had violated the separation of church and state by allowing the Scouts to recruit at public schools. The case was dismissed by a state judge but was being appealed to the Oregon Court of Appeals.

CROSS REFERENCES
First Amendment; Freedom of Association; Gay and Lesbian Rights

DISTRICT OF COLUMBIA

Adams v. Clinton

For years many residents of the District of Columbia have complained about their second-class citizenship. Residents are not permitted to elect voting members to the House of Representatives and the Senate. Political efforts to change the status quo have failed. In 1998 this issue led to the filing of lawsuits alleging that excluding residents from electing voting representatives to Congress violated the Constitution. However, a three-judge panel in *Adams v. Clinton*, 90 F.Supp.2d 35 (D.C. 2000), ruled against these claims.

Lois Adams and 75 other D.C. residents filed the lawsuit, arguing that it was unjust that they pay taxes and defend the country in times war yet cannot send elected representatives to vote on taxes and war. They argued that this situation violated their "rights to equal protection of the laws and to a republican form of government." They also alleged these deprivations violate "their right to due process and [abridge] their privileges and immunities as citizens of the United States." A three-judge panel was appointed to hear the case.

The panel, in a *per curiam* (unsigned) opinion, rejected these constitutional arguments. The panel devoted a substantial part of its opinion to reviewing the jurisdictional issues surrounding the case. The legislative and executive branches, which were the defendants, argued that the courts had no jurisdiction even to consider the merits of the claims. They argued that the central issue was a "political question" that should only be considered by Congress via the political process. Despite this and other jurisdictional objections, the judicial panel agreed that it could examine the issues presented by the plaintiffs.

The plaintiffs argued that Article I of the Constitution guarantees district residents the right to vote in congressional elections. The panel noted, however, that Article I makes repeated references to "each state," thereby making clear that the term did not refer generally to all the people of the United States but to citizens of individual states. Therefore, the panel concluded that Article I's language demonstrated "how deeply Congressional representation is tied to the structure of statehood." Based on this reading, residents of U.S. territories are not entitled to vote in federal elections, even though they are U.S. citizens. Based on history and judicial precedent, the court also rejected the plaintiffs' claim that district residents can be characterized as citizens of a state as the term was intended under Article I.

The panel also rejected an alternative argument, relying on a theory of "residual citizenship," that district residents be permitted to vote in congressional elections through Maryland. This theory depends on the fact that residents of the land ceded by Maryland to form the district continued to vote in Maryland elections between 1790 and 1801, when Congress assumed jurisdiction and provided for the district's government. The panel noted that this theory had been rejected in a 1964 court case. In that case the court concluded that former residents of Maryland lost their state citizenship when the District of Columbia separated from Maryland. The Supreme Court affirmed this decision, thereby requiring the judicial panel to accept this as binding precedent.

The panel also stated that if there had been no precedent, the residual citizenship theory would fail "because the Maryland citizenship of the District's inhabitants was extinguished upon the completion of the transfer of the seat of the national government to the territory of the District." Once Congress accepted the cession of land and passed the 1801 law providing for the government in the District of Columbia, the jurisdiction of the governments of Virginia and Maryland over the persons in this territory ceased. Even if district residents voted in Maryland elections during this early period, the states ceased treating district citizens "as state citizens eligible to vote in their elections" by 1801. Since then district residents have been unable to vote in either Maryland or Virginia.

The panel also analyzed the plaintiffs' DUE PROCESS OF LAW, EQUAL PROTECTION, and PRIVILEGES AND IMMUNITIES claims. The panel agreed "defendants have failed to offer a compelling justification for denying District residents the right to vote in Congress." Nevertheless, constitutional provisions cannot be challenged for illegal classifications, as can legislative and executive actions: "[T]he classification complained of here is not the product of presidential, congressional, or state action. Instead, as we have just concluded, the voting qualification of which plaintiffs complain is one drawn by the Constitution itself." Therefore, the panel could not employ the Equal Protection Clause to strike down a classification in another part of the Constitution.

Similar issues undercut the due process and privileges and immunities arguments as well. Therefore, the panel concluded it lacked authority to grant plaintiffs the relief they sought, remarking, "If they are to obtain it, they must plead their cause in other venues." As to the claim that residents were denied a REPUBLICAN form of government, the court rejected the argument that the District of Columbia Financial Responsibility and Management Assistance Authority was illegitimate. The Constitution clearly gives Congress the power of "exclusive legislation" over the District of Columbia. Thus, it has the power to set up a form of government to manage the District. Plaintiffs were not denied a republican form of government because they lacked representation on the Authority board.

CROSS REFERENCES
Equal Protection; Separation of Powers; Voting

DIXON, JULIAN C.

Julian C. Dixon

Representative Julian Dixon, who served the West Los Angeles District for twenty-two years in Congress, died on December 8, 2000, at the age of 66 in Inglewood, California. Dixon left a legacy as a supporting legislator on CIVIL RIGHTS and national security matters. He also will be remembered for the differences he made in California and in the District of Columbia in his various roles serving in the U.S. House of Representatives.

Julian C. Dixon was born in Washington, D.C., in 1934. He moved to Los Angeles, California, with his family at the age of ten. He grew up and attended public school in Los Angeles. In 1957 he left to serve his country in the Army but returned in 1960 to receive his degree from California State University in 1962. Dixon then went on to earn his law degree from Southwestern State University in Los Angeles in 1967.

Dixon spent only a few years in the private practice of law before entering a life devoted to politics and public service. In 1972 he was elected to the California State Assembly, where he served for six years. In 1978 he was elected to serve in the U.S. House of Representatives. He served his constituents in the 32nd District of California for twenty-two more years in the House.

Throughout his career, Julian Dixon was a strong advocate for civil rights causes. During the 1980s he was chairman of the Congressional Black Caucus. He also created a Martin Luther King, Jr., Memorial in Washington, D.C. The Human Rights Campaign, this nation's largest lesbian and gay political organization, views Dixon as an advocate for their cause, citing his introduction of the $8.6 billion relief bill after the 1994 earthquake in Los Angeles. The bill, for the first time ever in a federal law, specifically outlawed discrimination of disaster victims on the grounds of sexual orientation. Dixon was also co-sponsor of the Employment Non-Discrimination Act and Hate Crimes Prevention Act, both of which seek to reduce discrimination against minority groups.

From the beginning of his career on Capitol Hill, Dixon earned the respect of his peers and

JULIAN C. DIXON

1934	Born in Washington, D.C.
1967	Graduated from law school at Southwestern State University in Los Angeles
1972–1978	Member of the California State Assembly
1978	First of 11 elections to U.S. House of Representatives
1989	House Ethics Committee Chairman
2000	Died in Inglewood, California

served as chairman of several committees. In 1984 he was Rules Committee chairman of the Democratic Convention. He also served as chairman of the Committee on Standards of Official Conduct, better known as the Ethics Committee. This position proved to be Dixon's most challenging position, particularly in 1989 when then-House Speaker, Jim Wright, a Democrat from Texas, was being investigated for ethics violations. Georgia Republican NEWT GINGRICH backed the Republicans in their attacks against the speaker, which predictably sparked a defensive tone from Democrats. As chairman of the Ethics Committee, Dixon emerged as a bi-partisan leader who focused on the facts and the true issues presented. In June 1989, Wright resigned. As a result of his leadership in this episode, Dixon was commended by members of both sides of the House for his fairness and judgment.

More recently, Dixon was ranking Democrat on the House Permanent Select Committee on Intelligence. Additionally, he served on a panel to determine defense spending. Here, he fought on behalf of his constituents for the appropriation of funds to aid Southern California communities hurt by base closings and defense budget cuts.

Dixon was also a senior member of the Appropriations Committee and, during the mid-1990s, chaired the Washington, D.C., subcommittee where he was able to make a difference in the city of his birth by focusing on public safety and education. During his leadership of the subcommittee, Congress began a crackdown on the scandal-ridden administration of Mayor Marion Barry, leading the way for a federal takeover of the finances for Washington, D.C. Because of his efforts in Washington, Dixon is still heralded by the leadership of Capitol Hill and the citizens of the city.

Dixon is, of course, highly regarded and remembered by his own constituents in western Los Angeles. He always came through with aid in times of emergency. In 1992 the streets of Los Angeles were rocked as buildings were broken into, looted, and burned after a verdict of "not guilty" was issued in the trial of two white police officers who beat motorist RODNEY KING in a highly-broadcast, videotaped incident. Dixon acquired emergency funds for the businesses of Los Angeles that suffered in the riots. He also came to the aid of his city after the 1994 Northridge earthquake.

Perhaps his most lasting contribution to the Los Angeles community, however, was the effort he put into establishing the MTA, the commuter rail system in Los Angeles. Dixon was well aware that the city needed a solution to its major traffic problems, and high-speed public transportation seemed to be a good answer. The city and MTA recognized his efforts; they renamed one of the busiest rail stations the "Julian Dixon Metro Rail Station." Dixon was so highly revered by his constituents that he won re-election the month before he died with 84 percent of the vote.

DRUGS AND NARCOTICS

Drugs are articles intended for use in the diagnosis, cure, mitigation, treatment, or prevention of disease in humans or animals, and any articles other than food intended to affect the mental or body function of humans or animals. *Narcotics* are any drugs that dull the senses and commonly become addictive after prolonged use.

United States v. Oakland Cannabis Buyers' Cooperative

For many decades the federal government has classified marijuana as a controlled substance that cannot be used legally except for scientific research projects. Though state governments continue to make the possession, distribution, and use of marijuana a crime, nine states have legalized the use of the drug for medical use. Voters through the use of ballot initiatives approved these so-called "medical marijuana" laws in eight of these states, including California.

A Metro-Dade police officer displays a marijuana leaf confiscated after raiding a hydroponics lab.

Advocates contend that persons afflicted with serious illnesses such as AIDS, cancer, and multiple sclerosis are helped by smoking marijuana. The federal government contested the legality of these laws, believing that federal drug laws prevented the states from making exceptions. The federal government's efforts to end the distribution of medical marijuana in California led to a Supreme Court of the United States decision. In *United States v. Oakland Cannabis Buyers' Cooperative*, ___U.S.___, 121 S.Ct. 1711, 149 L.Ed.2d 722 (2001), the Court agreed with the federal government, concluding that the federal Controlled Substances Act did not recognize the use of marijuana for medical purposes.

The case grew out of a 1996 vote by California citizens that enacted an initiative called the Compassionate Use Act of 1996. The law sought to provide seriously ill persons with legal clearance to purchase marijuana for medicinal use. It permitted patients and their primary caregivers to possess or cultivate marijuana for medical purposes if approved by a physician. Following the law's enactment, numerous organizations started "medical cannabis dispensaries" to distribute marijuana to eligible patients. The Oakland Cannabis Buyers' Cooperative was one of these organizations. The nonprofit cooperative employed a doctor and registered nurses to screen prospective members through a personal interview and a review of the treating physician's written statement. If the person met the requirements, the cooperative issued the person an identification card that entitled the person to purchase marijuana from the organization.

The federal government sued the cooperative in 1998 and asked the federal district court to issue an injunction banning the cooperative from distributing and manufacturing marijuana. The court agreed that the cooperative had violated the federal controlled substance law and issued the injunction. On appeal to the Ninth Circuit Court of Appeals, the court reversed the lower court decision. The court ruled that a "medical necessity exemption" existed and that the district court could apply its equitable discretion and permit such an exemption to be asserted by the cooperative. The government then appealed to the Supreme Court.

The Court, in an 8–0 decision, reversed the appeals court. (Justice STEPHEN G. BREYER recused himself from the case because his brother, federal district judge Charles Breyer, issued the original ruling granting the government's injunction.) Justice CLARENCE THOMAS, writing for the Court, looked to the provisions of the Controlled Substances Act to determine whether the courts could make medical necessity a defense. Thomas noted that marijuana is classified as a "schedule I" substance. Schedule I drugs are the most tightly regulated and restricted substances, as they have "no currently accepted medical use," they have a "lack of accepted safety for use . . . under medical supervision" and they have "a high potential for abuse." The only express exception to the unlawfulness of possession, manufacture or distribution is for government-approved research projects. Taking these provisions into account, Justice Thomas concluded that there was clearly no statutory exemption.

The cooperative had argued that the law was subject to implied exceptions, including medical necessity. Though Thomas admitted that the common law had recognized the NECESSITY defense for hundreds of years, he also pointed out that defense is inapplicable "when the legislature has made a determination of values." Congress, in passing the Controlled Substances Act, had declared that marijuana had no medical benefits by placing it within schedule I. He also rejected the cooperative's assertion that the statute's restrictions only applied to drugs placed into schedule I by the attorney general. Because Congress had placed marijuana into schedule I, the cooperative claimed medical necessity was a legitimate defense. Justice Thomas found this reasoning illogical and found that Congress had not created "two tiers of schedule I narcotics."

The cooperative also contended that marijuana was medically necessary even though the law classified it as having "no currently accepted medical use." Though marijuana may not have reached the level of "general acceptance as a medical treatment," it still had benefits to particular types of patients. Justice Thomas refused to accept this line of reasoning because the statutory language was clear. Without a statutory exception, medical marijuana was not legal. The Court would not ignore the "legislative determination manifest" in the Controlled Substances Act.

Finally, Justice Thomas ruled that the federal courts could not use their equitable powers to make such an exception. A court sitting in equity could not ignore Congressional pronouncements as to what is prohibited activity. It could only exercise discretion in choosing the means of enforcing the statute.

CROSS REFERENCES
Necessity

DUE PROCESS OF LAW

A fundamental constitutional guarantee that all legal proceedings will be fair and that one will be given notice of the proceedings and an opportunity to be heard before government acts to take away one's life, liberty, or property. Also, a constitutional guarantee that a law shall not be unreasonable, arbitrary, or capricious.

Lujan v. G&G Firesprinklers, Inc.

The Due Process Clause of the FOURTEENTH AMENDMENT prohibits state governments from depriving an individual of liberty or property without due process of law. The concept of due process is a fundamental part of American law, as it seeks to prevent government abuse and insure that procedural rules are followed in every case. Though defendants frequently use due process arguments in criminal cases, due process issues sometimes arise in civil cases. Such was the case in *Lujan v. G&G Firesprinklers, Inc.*, ___U.S. ___, 121 S.Ct. 1446, ___L.Ed.2d.___ (2001), in which the Supreme Court of the United States considered whether a state government must hold a hearing before withholding money and imposing penalties on a building subcontractor. The Court ultimately concluded that the state's summary actions did not violate the due process clause because the subcontractor was free to sue the state for breach of contract in state court.

The State of California's Labor Code requires contractors and subcontractors on state-funded projects to pay the prevailing wage in the construction industry. The use of the prevailing wage encourages the hiring of union workers, as a contractor has no financial incentive to hire non-union workers because they will be paid the same. To enforce this requirement, the code authorizes the state government to withhold the payments due a contractor on a public works project if a subcontractor fails to pay the prevailing wage. The code also permits the contractor to withhold that sum from the subcontractor. Finally, the LABOR LAW permits the contractor or the contractor's assignee to sue the state for an alleged breach of contract to recover the payments and the penalties withheld by the state.

In 1995 the California Division of Labor Standards Enforcement concluded that G&G Sprinklers had failed to pay the prevailing wage to its workers who installed fire sprinklers in state buildings. Therefore, it invoked the Labor Code provisions and withheld more than $135,000 from the general contractor's payment. In turn, the contractor withheld that amount from its subcontractor, G&G. The subcontractor then filed a federal CIVIL RIGHTS lawsuit in FEDERAL COURT alleging that the state had deprived it of property without due process of law as guaranteed by the Fourteenth Amendment. The company contended that it should have been given notice before the payment was withheld and the opportunity to present its side of the case in a hearing. The federal DISTRICT COURT agreed and entered judgment for G&G. The Ninth Circuit Court of Appeals upheld this ruling in *G&G Fire Sprinklers, Inc. v. Bradshaw*, 156 F.3d 893, 898 (CA9 1998). The APPELLATE COURT first had to deal with the issue of whether the withholding of the payment by the general contractor was a state action, for the Due Process Clause only applies to state and local government. The panel ruled that the general contractor had been directed to withhold the money by the state and had no discretion to refuse this demand. Therefore, the state was the controlling authority, and the general contractor acted under COLOR OF LAW. Turning to the substantive issue, the appeals court found that G&G had a property interest. This interest required the state to conduct a hearing before it withheld the payment.

The U.S. Supreme Court, in a unanimous ruling, overturned the Ninth Circuit decision. Chief Justice WILLIAM H. REHNQUIST, writing for the Court, assumed for the sake of argument

SHOULD PUNISHMENT BE STRICTER FOR REPEAT DWI OFFENDERS?

By 2001 nearly 16,000 lives were lost each year in alcohol-related automobile accidents. Even though drunk driving had declined 41 percent from 1982, not much progress had been made in getting repeat offenders off the road. Eight out of ten drunk driving fatalities are caused by repeat offenders.

Horror stories of justice gone wrong made headlines in many cities and states. In Wisconsin, a convicted drunken driver, awaiting trial on a previous drunken driving charge, slammed his vehicle into a car carrying four high school students coming home from their prom. All were killed. In Florida, a man with fourteen previous driving while under the influence (DWI) convictions received a one-year jail sentence, to the shock of the community. Existing Florida law required at least two DWI convictions in the seven years prior to the present charge in order to be charged with a FELONY. The man had only one prior conviction in the preceding seven years, however, so the maximum charge available to prosecutors was a

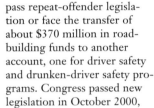

IN FOCUS

MISDEMEANOR, which carries a one year maximum sentence. Incidents like these have ignited several moves toward tougher legislation and enforcement efforts on the part of federal, state, and local governments.

In 1998 federal transportation legislation gave states until October 2001 to pass repeat-offender legislation or face the transfer of about $370 million in road-building funds to another account, one for driver safety and drunken-driver safety programs. Congress passed new legislation in October 2000, defining "legally drunk" as the term for anyone with a blood alcohol level (BAC) of .08 percent. Most states use a .10 percent standard. The new federal law also required states with .10 percent standards to adopt the stricter federal standard within the following seven years or forfeit federal highway funds. This newer legislation was not directed toward repeat offenders, unlike the 1998 bill.

Notwithstanding these legislative efforts, the NATIONAL TRANSPORTA-

TION SAFETY BOARD (NTSB) released a report in late 2000, indicating that it would not be able to meet its goal of reducing alcohol-related fatal crashes to 11,000 or fewer annually by 2005, unless a more comprehensive national program, with stricter penalties for what it termed "hardcore drinkers," was put into place. The National Highway Traffic Safety Administration concluded that repeat offenders account for less than 1 percent of drivers on the road on a typical weekend night, but they account for 40 percent of alcohol-related fatalities.

Barbara Harsha, executive director of the National Association of Governors' Highway Safety Representatives (NAGHSR), stated that the NAGHSR was not going to push states to do anything more than what they were already being made to do under the 1998 and 2000 federal laws. By 2000, forty-five states had enacted or introduced new legislation that met the more strict federal requirements for sentencing repeat offenders, including a one-year suspension of driving privileges, the installation of ignition interlocks on the driver's vehicle or impoundment of the vehicle,

that the withholding of the payment took place "under color of state law" and that G&G had a property interest in the claim on its contract. Therefore, the only issue was whether the withholding of payment without a prior hearing violated due process. The Court concluded that such a hearing was not a constitutional prerequisite.

Chief Justice Rehnquist found that the Ninth Circuit had misapplied previous Court rulings dealing with due process. The forfeiture of a person's house or the suspension of an occupational license required a hearing before such actions could be taken because the person "exercised ownership dominion over real or personal property" or a "gainful occupation." Such was not the case with G&G's claim. It had only been deprived of a payment it claimed it deserved under the terms of its contract. This interest, while substantial, was merely a claim.

Therefore, G&G's interests could be "fully protected by an ordinary breach-of-contract suit." In the Court's view, the opportunity under the statute to sue for breach of contract guaranteed G&G its day in court. This was sufficient due process under the Fourteenth Amendment. Although the Court acknowledged that it might take several years for G&G to recover its payments, this delay was not unusual or unwarranted. Chief Justice Rehnquist noted, "Lawsuits are not known for expeditiously resolving claims." Therefore, however long it took, due process would be served.

DWI

An abbreviation for *driving while intoxicated,* which is an offense committed by an individual who operates a motor vehicle while under the influence of ALCOHOL or DRUGS AND NARCOTICS.

and an automatic assessment for alcohol abuse syndrome. The NTSB had recommended these sanctions, along with a provision wherein states would eliminate "community service" as an alternative to incarceration. The Board argued that diversion programs, because they keep prosecutions off offenders' records, actually contribute to RECIDIVISM. It also recommended a "zero tolerance" policy for repeat offenders, although implementation of such a policy would admittedly be difficult.

Publicly-elected judges and prosecutors had also come under increasing fire for what was perceived as sentencing leniency in repeat-offense cases. Many states were not waiting for federal deadlines and were taking the initiative, albeit, through political platforms, to change laws by mandating minimum punishments. On September 6, 2000, the national group Mothers Against Drunk Driving (MADD) observed its twentieth anniversary at a rally outside the U.S. capitol, where 600 surviving victims and activists urged Congress to continue its efforts in reducing vehicular accidents caused by drunken drivers. MADD also supported the lower BAC reading of .08 percent.

Private industry, including Anheuser-Busch—the world's largest beer brewer

and one of the largest theme-park operators in the United States—joined in the campaign. For example, in June 2001, Anheuser-Busch encouraged its Illinois beer distributors to write letters and make phone calls to Illinois's Governor George Ryan. They urged him to sign two bills, House Bills 2265 and 2266, addressed at keeping repeat-offenders off the roads by giving judges more latitude in sentencing alternatives. The bills would allow judges to impose increasingly stiffer fines and mandatory jail time, order the installation of alcohol ignition interlock devices on vehicles, and impose other punishments proven effective in repeat-offense drunken driving cases.

In Waco, Texas, Lynnwood Anthony Vrba had amassed eight DWI convictions, including two felonies, in addition to a murder conviction. He was sentenced in early 2000 to sixty years in prison for his ninth conviction. Obviously able to avoid serious punishment the previous eight times, Vrba this time swerved in front of a Texas Alcoholic Beverage Commission agent. Since Vrba had two previous felony convictions, he was classified as a habitual criminal and, thus, was subject to more stringent sentencing.

In March 2001 a California APPELLATE COURT overturned the twelve-year

prison sentence of drunken driver Johnny Castro, stating that his eight previous DWI convictions made him eligible for life imprisonment. His prior convictions were not discovered until after the jury had rendered a verdict, however. Prosecutors tried to amend their complaint to apply a 1997 California law punishing drunk drivers who kill someone with at least fifteen-years in prison and at most life. The district trial judge ruled that the amendment would violate the defendant's DUE PROCESS rights, but the appellate court disagreed. And in May 2001 a South Carolina court sentenced a 24-year-old Clemson University student to fifteen years in prison after his drunken driving caused the death of another driver.

Another trend in state law in recent years has been to prosecute drunken drivers who cause fatalities in vehicular accidents for felony murder. Although the laws may be used to prosecute first-time offenders as well, repeat-offenders are disproportionately caught in the sieve because of their disproportionately high involvement in alcohol-related traffic fatalities. In states where felony murder is a capital offense, the prospect of facing the death penalty because of a drunk-driving fatality may be a sobering thought to prevent such accidents.

Congress Imposes National DWI Standard

Since the 1980s states have imposed tougher laws on persons who are convicted of driving while intoxicated (DWI) offenses. They have imposed longer prison sentences, and many have turned DWI into a FELONY-level crime for repeat offenders. However, the more controversial issue in this national debate has been the effort to reduce the blood alcohol concentration (BAC) needed to charge a person with DWI from .10 to .08 percent. Proponents have argued that such a reduction is the most effective way to prevent drunken driving deaths. Opponents contend that the .08 is too low and will ensnare drivers who are not truly impaired. Though many states have adopted the .08 standard, proponents sought a national solution. After experiencing defeat in 1998, the proponents won an enormous victory in October 2000 when Congress enacted, and then-President BILL CLINTON signed, the transportation appropriation

bill. Included in the act was a provision that requires states to enact a .08 BAC as the legal limit or lose part of their federal highway funding. This enactment has led state legislatures to begin considering amending their DWI laws.

Evidence suggests a strong correlation between a BAC greater than .05 percent and risk of serious injury or death while operating a motor vehicle. After a person's BAC reaches .08 percent or more, the probability of a crash climbs rapidly. The National Highway Traffic Safety Administration (NHTSA) estimates that in 1998, "alcohol was involved in 39 percent of all fatal crashes (almost 16,000 fatalities) and 7 percent of all crashes." NHTSA also predicted that three out of ten Americans will be involved in an alcohol-related crash sometime during their lives.

These kinds of statistics helped convince eighteen states and the District of Columbia to

A Santa Monica police officer uses a breathalyzer to test the blood-alcohol level of the individual shown.

1998, but it failed to pass the House of Representatives. As a compromise, Congress provided $500 million of incentive grants over six years to states that have enacted and are enforcing a .08 BAC law. Proponents of the lower BAC renewed their efforts in the next Congress.

Proponents of the national standard introduced evidence about the effects of alcohol on an individual. According to the NHTSA, a 170-pound man can consume approximately four drinks "in an hour on an empty stomach" before reaching a .08 BAC. A 137-pound woman could consume "three drinks in an hour on an empty stomach" before reaching .08. Research studies also have shown that the risk of a fatal crash at .08 is at least 11 times greater than that of a sober driver. In addition, the risk rises sharply to at least 29 times that of a sober driver at .10 BAC, the limit in 32 states as of 2001. Proponents also pointed to statistics that suggested that 500 highway deaths could be prevented annually if every state adopted the .08 limit.

change the BAC threshold to .08 before the 2000 congressional act. These states are Alabama, California, Florida, Hawaii, Illinois, Indiana, Kansas, Kentucky, Maine, New Hampshire, New Mexico, North Carolina, Oregon, Texas, Utah, Vermont, Virginia, and Washington. The remaining 32 states still define intoxicated driving as .10 BAC. Though organizations such as Mothers Against Drunk Driving (MADD) lobbied these states, they met strong opposition from the alcohol and hospitality industries. Rather than fight 32 battles, .08 BAC proponents concentrated their efforts on the passage of a uniform federal standard. Such an approach worked in 1984 when Congress established a national uniform drinking age of 21, thus eliminating serious problems between states with different minimum drinking age laws.

The Clinton administration supported the national approach but met congressional resistance. The Senate passed the .08 BAC law in

Congress agreed to adopt the .08 limit but only after adjusting the timing and severity of penalties for states that refuse to lower their legal limits. Under the law, states have until October 1, 2003, to pass a .08 BAC law that would meet the provisions of the existing federal incentive grant program. If states do not meet this deadline they will lose two percent of their federal highway construction funds. States that do not pass a .08 law by October 1, 2004, will lose four percent of their construction funds, and the penalty increases to six percent in 2005 and eight percent in 2006. If states lose funding in 2003, they have four years to pass the .08 BAC. If they do so, the money withheld will be returned to the states.

CROSS REFERENCES
Transporation Department

ELECTION CAMPAIGN FINANCING

Federal Elections Commission v. Colorado Republican Federal Campaign Committee

The continuing debate over campaign finance reform has largely taken place in the political arena. The FEDERAL COURTS, however, have been called upon to review federal campaign finance reform laws to determine the constitutionality of certain provisions. The Federal Election Campaign Act of 1971, which was amended in 1974 in the wake of the WATERGATE scandal, places limits on the amounts that individuals and political parties may contribute to candidates for federal office. Though the Supreme Court struck down some provisions as unconstitutional, others have remained in effect for thirty years. Under the 1974 amendments, the FEDERAL ELECTIONS COMMISSION (FEC) was established to enforce these contribution and campaign expenditure limits.

In 1996 the Supreme Court struck down spending limits that the federal law imposed on political parties that were deemed independent expenditures—in other words, spending that was not coordinated with a candidate's congressional election campaign. This decision, which involved the Colorado Republican Party's efforts to support a Republican senate candidate, also returned to the lower courts a separate question for further consideration: Did the federal provision that limited expenditures by political parties for spending done in coordination with a candidate's campaign violate the FIRST AMENDMENT?

On REMAND, the Colorado Republican Party argued that any restriction on its ability to support a candidate financially violated its freedom of expression. The FEC argued that allowing unlimited expenditures by a political party would subvert the goals of the law and give parties an advantage over individuals and political action committees (PACs). Moreover, having no restrictions on party spending would encourage political corruption. The federal DISTRICT COURT sided with the party. The Court of Appeals for the Tenth Circuit affirmed this ruling, setting the stage for a full review by the Supreme Court.

The Court, in *Federal Elections Commission v. Colorado Republican Federal Campaign Committee*, __U.S.__, 121 S.Ct. 2351, __ L.Ed.2d __ (2001), reversed the Tenth Circuit in a 5–4 decision. Justice DAVID H. SOUTER, writing for the majority, reemphasized the distinction between campaign contributions and campaign expenditures. Because restrictions on expenditures "generally curb more expressive and associational activity than limits on contribution do," the Court more closely scrutinized such restrictions. In addition, expenditures have been viewed as less susceptible to political corruption. Despite the Court's general intolerance toward independent expenditure limits, Justice Souter noted that the legal landscape changed when "the independence of the political spending cannot be taken for granted." Once a party coordinated its expenditures with a candidate, these "expenditures" looked the same as "contributions" under the law. Hence the need to resolve the coordinated expenditures issue.

The Colorado Republican Party argued that its free speech rights were restricted when it was prevented from supporting a candidate.

Financial support of a candidate is an essential function of a political party. The FEC countered that Congress equated coordinated expenditures and contributions because it was the only way to prevent parties and candidates from circumventing contribution limits placed on individuals and corporations. Allowing coordinated expenditures would encourage those persons who wanted to influence a candidate to contribute to the party after they had reached the individual contribution limit.

Though Justice Souter acknowledged that both positions were "plausible at first blush," in the end the FEC's claims made more sense. Souter endorsed the FEC's "characterization of party coordinated spending as the functional equivalent of contributions." He brushed aside the party's claim that coordinated spending was essential, pointing out that such a practice had not occurred for thirty years and that the party had not suffered.

Souter focused his analysis on how the "power of money actually works in the political structure." It was naïve to believe political parties merely worked to elect particular candidates. PACs and individuals with special interests contributed to the parties in hopes of advancing their interests. Viewed this way, parties were "instruments" for some contributors who sought the candidate's support on their narrow interest.

Based on these perceptions, Justice Souter concluded that it would be unfair to allow parties to contribute as much as they want to a candidate when individuals are limited to $2,000. Moreover, Souter continued, "The same donor may give as much as another $20,000 each year to a national party committee supporting the candidate." If the law were overturned, political candidates would likely pursue these larger amounts and ignore individual donors. This behavior would enhance the threat of political corruption, which the law seeks to prevent. Therefore, political parties are restricted in how much they can contribute directly to a political candidate. Justice CLARENCE THOMAS, in the dissent, summed up their opposition to the majority thus: "Because this provision sweeps too broadly, interferes with the party-candidate relationship, and has not been proved necessary to combat corruption."

CROSS REFERENCES
Elections

ELECTIONS

The process of voting to decide a public question or to select one person from a designated group to perform certain obligations in a government, corporation, or society.

Chicago Board of Election Commissioners v. Voteauction.com

Overshadowed by the flood of state and federal lawsuits engulfing the disputed returns in the state of Florida during the 2000 presidential election, another series of lawsuits focused attention on the integrity of the voting process in the United States. A website known as Voteauction.com was offering to collect absentee ballots from across the country for the purpose of selling them over the Internet to the highest bidder. An Illinois court was the first to order the website to cease business, but courts in other states soon issued similar orders when the website reappeared under a different name. Eventually, the website's Internet Service Provider (ISP) closed Voteauction.com shortly before the election. On election day the website's owner held a press conference at which he announced that Voteauction.com had been created as a publicity stunt to raise consciousness about the corrupting influencing of money in American politics.

The controversy began when James Baumgartner first launched the Voteauction.com website on a server in Wisconsin during August 2000. Baumgartner, a native of Overland Park, Kansas, told reporters that he created the site in conjunction with the master's thesis he was writing as a graduate student at Rensselaer Polytechnic Institute in Troy, New York. Despite his ostensible academic interest, Baumgartner said he was also interested in influencing the way presidents are elected in the United States.

Under the current political system, Baumgartner said, corporations give soft money to presidential candidates, who, after they get elected, reward their biggest donators by making decisions that profit them. Baumgartner's goal was to eliminate the middle-man by giving voters the opportunity to profit directly from their vote rather than having it bought and sold by people whom they never meet. The website's tag line was *Bringing Capitalism and Democracy Closer Together*.

At first observers were not sure what to make of the new website. On the one hand, buying and selling votes is prohibited by every state in the country, regardless of whether the candidate is running for president of the United States or a local school board. It is also prohibited by federal law. 42 U.S.C.A. § 1973i. Deborah Phillips, president of the Virginia-based Voting Integrity Project, criticized the site for sullying American politics and urged Congress to investigate. On the other hand, political satire and parody are protected by the FIRST AMENDMENT to the U.S. Constitution. Peter Eisner, managing director at the Center for Public Integrity, said he supported the site as political satire because he felt that society needed to be made more aware that "soft money is undermining democracy."

Legal authorities were less equivocal in their approach. A few weeks after the website was launched, Baumgartner was flooded with inquiries from state and federal law enforcement agencies. The volume of correspondence, phone messages, and electronic mail (E-mail) made it difficult for him to maintain the website. As a result, in late August he sold the site to Hans Bernhard of Vienna, Austria. The purchase price was one euro, an amount worth less than one American dollar at the time. Bernhard is also the owner of Ubermorgen.com, a website known for its shock-drama marketing concepts and consulting. Sometimes called a "guerrilla marketer," Bernhard has been responsible for launching several successful Internet campaigns aimed at galvanizing public opinion about various issues involving law and technology.

Following the sale, Baumgartner hinted that the site was in fact intended to raise consciousness through satire. "Our candidates are for sale, and by selling themselves they are treating the election as a commodity," Baumgartner said. "By treating elections as commodities the next step is to treat votes like commodities." He said, "at no time was it my intent to have people buy and sell votes."

Hans Bernhard took a different tack after he bought the website. The new owner told CNN that Voteauction.com was a "serious business in which we can make money." Bernard said the website was offering to collect absentee ballots from voters, verify them, and then sell them at an auction to the highest bidder who could decide how to cast them. Approximately 21,000 voters in fifteen states had already shown an interest in selling their votes, Bernhard stated, more than 1,000 from Illinois alone. He also indicated that bidders were actively pursuing these votes, though he refused to disclose their names. Bernhard said that bidders were offering

$19.61 on average for California votes, while votes in Illinois and Wisconsin were bringing a lower price.

On October 16, 2000, the Chicago Board of Election Commissioners (CBOEC) responded to the new owner's intensified rhetoric by filing a lawsuit. Two days later Cook County Circuit Court Judge Michael J. Murphy ordered Bernhard to temporarily shut down the website until the lawsuit was resolved. By October 20 Bernhard had complied with the judge's order, but three days later Bernhard moved the website from a server in Wisconsin to a server in Austria. He also registered the site under a slightly different name—he added a hyphen between "vote" and "auction". The additional hyphen did not fool anyone.

Five states were taking legal action against Bernhard: Illinois, Massachusetts, Michigan, Missouri, and Wisconsin. California, Delaware, and New York were contemplating lawsuits. By the first week in November a Missouri judge had ordered the website to disclose that buying and selling votes is illegal under state law. Massachusetts and Wisconsin state courts issued similar orders. CBOEC went back to court asking Judge Murphy to find Bernhard in CONTEMPT for violating the October 16th order. However, the need for further legal action was eliminated when the website's Austrian ISP voluntarily stopped Vote-auction.com. On November 7, 2000, the day of the election, Bernhard held a press conference at which he said the website had served the purpose of raising awareness about how money can corrupt politics. He concluded his remarks by saying:

> It will be obvious, even to the legal folk, that there are people out there buying and selling votes, but that it is not us. We just gave you the showcase. The real dealers do their businesses quite openly in Washington. Vive la difference!

Cook v. Gralike

In the 1980s and early 1990s a national movement arose that sought to limit the number of terms an individual could serve in Congress. Popular dissatisfaction with career politicians led states to pass laws or constitutional amendments that aimed to prevent individuals from serving more than a set number of terms in office. However, in 1995 the U.S. Supreme Court dealt the term limit movement a severe blow when it ruled unconstitutional an Arkansas measure that prohibited "congressional candi-

THE ELECTORAL COLLEGE

The 2000 presidential election, wrongly or rightfully, inspired calls to reform or eliminate the nation's electoral college. Among the earliest to announce such requests were JESSE JACKSON; Senator Arlen Specter, the first to introduce a CONSTITUTIONAL AMENDMENT; newly-elected Senator and former First Lady HILLARY RODHAM CLINTON, who stated that she would sponsor legislation "to do away with [it]"; the presidential nominee from the Socialist Party USA; and the AMERICAN CIVIL LIBERTIES UNION. In the months following the election many states reconsidered their methods for appointing ELECTORS and also looked at instituting changes directed toward more control over electors' votes. The electoral college system was adopted by the Constitutional Convention of 1787, however, and is not likely to be "done away with."

The actual term "electoral college" appears nowhere in the Constitution of the United States. Article II, Section I of the Constitution states that the president and vice-president be elected as fol-

lows: "Each State shall appoint, in such Manner as the Legislature thereof may direct, a Number of Electors, equal to the whole Number of Senators and Representatives to which the State may be entitled in the Congress." Article II also prohibits a Senator or Representative or "Person holding an Office of Trust or Profit under the United States" from being appointed as an elector.

IN FOCUS

It was the original design and intention of the 1787 Convention's delegates to create a system that would include a voice from the general populace, but as ALEXANDER HAMILTON wrote, "It was equally desirable that the immediate election [of a president] should be made by men most capable." Thus, the advantage of the devised electoral college was that "a small number of persons, selected by their fellow citizens from the general mass, will be most likely to possess the information and discernment requisite to so complicated an investigation." The number of electors allocated by the 1787 Convention represented a compromise between large and small states. The

large states wanted presidential voting electors to be premised upon population such as the House of Representatives was, while the smaller states wanted each state to have the same number of votes, such as in the Senate. The difference was split, with each state being given a number of electors equal to its combined total of House and Senate seats in Congress.

In 2000 there were 538 electors: one for each of the 435 members of the House of Representatives and 100 Senators, and three for the District of Columbia. The decennial census is used to reapportion the allocation of electors among states, as it is used to apportion House seats. At one time, the actual electors were chosen almost exclusively by state legislatures. But because there is no Constitutional provision mandating elector loyalty—that is, requiring that an elector vote for a certain candidate—most electors are now chosen by the political parties. According to the U.S. Office of the FEDERAL REGISTER, for the 2000 election, 27 states had laws in effect that bound their electors to vote for the same candidate as the majority of the general populace in that

dates from appearing on the general election ballot if they had already served two Senate terms or three House terms." Term limit proponents then succeeded in having a number of states pass laws that placed labels beside the names of candidates who had failed to support national term limit legislation or take a pledge to do so if elected. Though lower courts threw out most of these laws, the Supreme Court, in *Cook v. Gralike*, ___ U.S. ___, 121 S.Ct. 1029, 149 L.Ed.2d 44 (U.S. Feb 28, 2001), settled any doubts when it ruled that a Missouri constitutional AMENDMENT violated the U.S. Constitution's Elections Clause.

The case arose when Don Gralike decided to run for the U.S. House of Representatives from Missouri's Third District. He filed a lawsuit in federal court alleging that the Missouri term limit labeling amendment violated several provisions of the U.S. Constitution. The amendment "instructed" Missouri Congress

members to pass a federal term limits constitutional amendment. The words "DISREGARDED VOTERS' INSTRUCTION ON TERM LIMITS" would be placed on ballots next to the names of candidates "who failed to take certain legislative acts in support of the federal amendment." The amendment further provided that the phrase "DECLINED TO PLEDGE TO SUPPORT TERM LIMITS" be printed alongside the names of non-incumbents who were unwilling to promise to work toward term limits.

The federal district court agreed with Gralike that the amendment violated the U.S. Constitution and struck down the amendment. The Circuit Court of Appeals for the Eighth Circuit affirmed this ruling, and the Supreme Court agreed to hear the case to settle the law on this issue. The Court unanimously voted to affirm the lower courts, though four separate opinions were written to explain what the jus-

elector's state, while 24 states did not. Of all the areas of proposed reform, this is one that has been visited by many states.

For purposes of general summation, on Election Day (November 7, 2000), citizens went to the polls and voted for a presidential/vice-presidential ticket. Within each state, the presidential candidate who won the most popular votes then received all the electoral votes from that state, referred to as the "winner-takes-all" feature. Only two states, Maine and Nebraska, allocated their electoral votes proportionally according to the popular vote. The "winner-takes-all" feature is the second most frequently visited area of the electoral college system identified for possible reform. The Constitution clearly permits states to choose their electors by whatever system they wish, but many believe the system would be improved by following Maine's or Nebraska's split system.

On the first Monday after the second Wednesday in December (December 18, 2000), the electors met in their respective states and went through the formality of casting their votes for the candidates from the party that elected them. Each state then reported its totals to Congress, utilizing "Certificates of Ascertainment," which list names of the electors appointed and the number of votes received by each, and "Certificates of Votes," which list all persons voted for as president and the number of electors voting for each person and which also separately list all persons voted for as vice president and the number of electors voting for each person. The Congress met in joint session at 1:00 P.M. on January 6, 2001, to conduct the official tally of electoral votes. If, perchance, no candidate for president had a majority, the House of Representatives would choose a president from among the top three receiving the most electoral votes, using a procedure calling for one vote per state, regardless of state size or congressional seats.

The battle over the 2000 presidential election focused on Florida's twenty-five electoral votes. Florida is a "winner-takes-all" state. (A month after the election, *USA Today* analyzed and reconstructed the 2000 vote *proportionally*, as used by Maine and Nebraska. It found that Bush would still have received 271 electoral votes to Gore's 267.) Many believe that, for example, the risks of 25 electoral votes hinging on the popular vote of a single county (as in Florida) could be more fairly and judiciously eliminated with proportional representation of electors. The argument can be made that, in a "winner-takes-all" system, re-calculation of votes in *any* county in *any* state could potentially alter an entire election.

The framers of the Constitution emphatically intended to create a constitutional republic, with power allocated by representation, not by direct popular vote. However, nothing precludes states from endorsing a system that allocates electoral votes by proportionality according to the states' popular vote. Since the 2000 election, California, Indiana, and Texas have introduced bills to change to proportional voting. More states are expected to consider this and other options, and reform at the state level appears more viable than a Constitutional amendment.

No electoral reform has made it through Congress since 1804, when adoption of the 12th Amendment required electors to specify separate candidates for president and vice-president. The 2000 election was not the first controversy and is not expected to be the last, but most agree that it would be better to reform the electoral system than to eliminate it.

tices felt was unconstitutional about the amendment. Justice JOHN PAUL STEVENS, writing for five of the justices, rejected Missouri's contention that the term limit label amendment could be upheld based on the TENTH AMENDMENT and on the Constitution's Election Clause. Stevens found the Tenth Amendment argument dubious. The Tenth Amendment states, "The powers not delegated to the United States by the Constitution, nor prohibited by it to the States, are reserved to the States respectively, or to the people." Missouri claimed that its term limits amendment was an exercise of the "right of the people to instruct" their representatives and that this was a reserved power under the Tenth Amendment.

Justice Stevens noted that the state failed to overcome three hurdles to validly exercise such a reserved power. First, the historical basis on which Missouri relied for the proposition that the states have such a reserved power were distinguishable. Second, Stevens found contrary historical evidence. Third, and most importantly, the process used to distribute the instructions—ballots for congressional elections—was unsatisfactory unless it was a permissible exercise of the state's power to regulate the manner of holding elections for senators and representatives. Justice Stevens concluded that such means were not permissible.

Stevens then turned to Missouri's claim that the amendment was constitutional because the U.S. Constitution's Election Clause permits the states to regulate the manner in which elections are held. Therefore, the labeling requirement merely provided information to the voters about congressional candidates. Stevens rejected this argument, noting that the states may regulate procedural elements of federal elections and work to prevent voter fraud and corrupt practices. In this case, however, Missouri imposed a requirement that was "plainly designed to favor candidates who are willing to support the particular form of a term limits amendment set forth in its text and to disfavor those who either oppose term limits entirely or would prefer a different proposal." Such a label, which the Court acknowledged was a "Scarlet Letter," conveyed "substantial political risk" for the candidate who refuses to agree to the amendment's point of view. The amendment violated the Elections Clause because it attempted to "dictate electoral outcomes."

Chief Justice WILLIAM H. REHNQUIST, in a separate opinion joined by Justice SANDRA DAY O'CONNOR, argued that the amendment was unconstitutional because it infringed on the FIRST AMENDMENT rights of political candidates. They reasoned that the "Scarlet Letter" wording was to be imposed by the same state that granted the candidate's right to be on the ballot in the first place. Justice ANTHONY M. KENNEDY believed that, per the Elections Clause, the state "simply lacks the power to impose any conditions on the election of Senators and Representatives, save neutral provisions as to the time, place, and manner of elections." Justice CLARENCE THOMAS disagreed with Kennedy's assessment of the Elections Clause. Thomas restated the crux of his dissenting opinion from another case on state-created term limits, *U.S. Term Limits, Inc. v. Thornton*, 514 U.S. 779 (1995), yet had to vote with the majority because both parties in the case at hand stipulated to the validity of an interpretation of the Elections Clause equivalent to Kennedy's.

Election 2000

The presidential election of 2000 was unlike any in history. For thirty-five days after election night, nobody knew who had become the 43rd U.S. president. The outcome awaited recounts in Florida, where a few hundred votes out of nearly six million cast separated Democratic candidate AL GORE and Republican candidate GEORGE W. BUSH. As recounts began by machine and by hand, uncertainty turned to accusation. Both parties traded charges of inaccurate counting, voter disenfranchisement, undue political influence, and outright efforts to steal the election. Vice President Gore contested the results as debate raged over which government body had the authority to end the standoff. By the time it was over, multiple lawsuits had streaked through Florida's court system to the Supreme Court of the United States, which intervened for a second and final time on December 12. One day later, Bush was president-elect.

Even before election night, the race was distinct from previous campaigns. Besides Gore and Bush, two major independent candidates put forward their names: longtime liberal activist RALPH NADER ran as the Green Party candidate, and conservative commentator PATRICK J. BUCHANAN ran on the Reform Party ticket. The entry of these dark-horse candidates, who were sharply critical of the mainstream candidates, led to unique pre-election maneuvers. Worried that either man might tip the results, mainstream party activists canvassed strongly to shore up voter unity, and some Democrats sympathetic to Nader suggested vote-trading arrangements with his supporters in order to prevent a Bush victory.

The pre-election jockeying for support was only a foretaste of the chaos to come on election night. So close was voting that by mid-evening it became clear that the next president would be whoever won Florida's critical twenty-five electoral votes. This crucial result proved elusive as television networks first reported Gore to be the victor in Florida and then, around 1:30 A.M., gave the victory to Bush. Gore called his opponent to concede, but minutes later, stunningly telephoned again to retract his concession after learning he was guaranteed a recount under Florida law. By 3:40 A.M., the TV networks reported the race was too close to call.

Over the next several days as the election continued to hang in the balance, the realization mounted that something had gone wrong, but what, exactly, was a matter of debate. Both parties sent elder statesmen to Florida as spokesmen: former secretaries of state Warren Christopher and James Baker for the Democrats and Republicans, respectively. The Democrats maintained that Florida was awash in irregularities: ballots were missing, machines had failed to count valid ballots, African American voters had been improperly delayed or turned away from the polls, elderly voters had been confused by a bizarre ballot design, and the state had erroneously identified some citizens as felons who were thus ineligible to vote. The fact that Bush's brother, Jeb Bush, was governor of Florida was frequently cited, although the governor quickly RECUSED himself from any involvement in the recount.

Republicans saw things differently. Secretary Baker declared the Bush camp was unaware of any irregularities in Florida. Elsewhere, however, the GOP decried devious machinations: in Milwaukee, Wisconsin, for instance, Democratic Party campaigners had been caught dis-

Supervisor of Elections Theresa LePore (*left*), Voting Canvassing Board Chairman Judge Charles Burton (*center*), and a Republican observer inspect a questionable ballot in Palm Beach.

tributing cigarettes to homeless voters. Republicans accused Democrats of making excuses, for instance, in complaints about the so-called butterfly ballot used in Palm Beach. This type of ballot drew fire for its design in which Democratic candidates' names were listed second, but only by punching what appeared to be the third hole could a voter select them. Republicans drily pointed out that a Democrat had designed it.

Upon completion of a machine recount on November 11 giving Bush a 288-vote lead, Republicans called upon Democrats to concede. Instead, Gore pushed for hand recounts and the post-election battle moved into litigation. As both sides went to court, three major issues emerged: 1) the legality of hand recounts; 2) the authority of Florida's SECRETARY OF STATE to set the date and terms for certifying the final vote; and 3) the legality of certain overseas ballots.

Sharply divisive, the debate over hand recounts struck to the core of the dispute: what was the fairest way to count the votes? Democrats maintained that aging, inaccurate machines had failed to tally paper ballots in which holes had not been punched out completely. They argued that such ballots revealed a voter's intent and that only a hand recount could properly interpret this indented, dimpled, or dangling "chad." Republicans mocked the very idea, maintaining that hand recounts polluted the count with subjectivity. Democrats responded that several states provided for such, including Bush's home state of Texas.

Republicans sued to stop hand recounts but initially lost. The federal courts did not see a constitutional issue. On November 16, the Florida Supreme Court approved hand recounts by grounding its decision in the state constitution's right to vote and citing an Illinois Supreme

Court decision. As hand recounts proceeded in the Democratic strongholds of Palm Beach, Broward, and Miami Dade counties, both parties stationed observers. High drama followed in Miami-Dade on November 22, where dozens of GOP protesters angrily chanted until officials decided to stop recounting. Democrats accused the protesters of intimidating election officials, although officials denied the charge.

The second major controversy arose over the authority of Florida Secretary of State Katherine Harris. As an active campaigner for Bush, Harris came under scathing attack for the appearance of bias when she tried to swiftly certify the election. Refusing to give Democrats more time to complete a hand recount, Harris said she lacked such discretion under law. Democrats claimed she was only trying to sew up the election for Bush. Her subsequent refusal to include hand recounts brought more accusations. On November 26, after Harris certified the election results giving Bush a 537-vote victory, Gore officially contested the election. "This is America," he said in a televised speech. "When votes are cast, we count them."

In response to a Gore lawsuit, the Florida Supreme Court on November 21 extended the seven-day STATUTORY deadline for certification and ordered Harris to include hand recounts in the final tally (*Palm Beach Canvassing Bd. v. Harris*, ___ So. 2d ___ [2000]). Republicans responded furiously, with Baker accusing the justices of "changing the rules in the middle of the game" and "rewriting" Florida election laws. Dramatically, he asked the Florida legislature to effectively overturn the court's decision. Leaving nothing to chance, the Republican-controlled legislature proceeded to hold a special session on December 8 to appoint the state's electors—this in preparation for the possibility that the U.S. Congress might ultimately have to choose the president.

The third major issue concerned absentee ballots. With the election hanging in the balance, both sides hungrily eyed the overseas ballots cast by U.S. military members and citizens living abroad. On December 6, Democrats sued to have 25,000 ballots thrown out in Seminole and Martin counties, alleging that Republican election officials filled in data on ballots in order to prevent their being rejected. Republicans bitterly accused Democrats of trying to disenfranchise soldiers, who traditionally had supported their party. The Democrats lost two lawsuits in CIRCUIT COURT on December 8.

The endgame was played out in the U.S. Supreme Court. On December 4, granting a request by Bush, the nation's highest court set aside the Florida Supreme Court's extension of the certification deadline in *Bush v. Palm Beach County Canvassing Bd.*, 531 U.S. 70 (2000) [Bush I]. The unsigned—and therefore presumably unanimous—PER CURIAM opinion ordered the Florida high court to clarify its decision. Before responding to this order, the Florida justices did something different: in a 4–3 ruling on December 8, they ordered manual recounts of some 40,000 ballots to resume immediately, *Gore v. Harris*, ___ So. 2d, ___ (2000). That decision seemed to revive Gore's chances, but the U.S. Supreme Court granted an emergency request by Bush to intervene. On December 9, it halted the recount; on December 11, it heard oral arguments; and on December 12, in a stunning historic decision, the Court reversed the Florida Supreme Court's decision.

The decision in *Bush v. Gore*, 531 U.S. 98, 121 S.Ct. 525, 148 L.Ed.2d 388 (2000), effectively ended the election. The Court issued six opinions: an unsigned majority per curiam opinion supported by five justices; a concurrence by Chief Justice WILLIAM H. REHNQUIST and Justices ANTONIN SCALIA and CLARENCE THOMAS; and four dissenting opinions. Seven justices found constitutional problems with the Florida Supreme Court's order, but only five of these formed the majority that reversed the state court. That majority held that varying recount standards from county to county violated the FOURTEENTH AMENDMENT's guarantees of EQUAL PROTECTION and DUE PROCESS. They also observed that any recount was too late because December 12—the deadline established by federal law for resolving federal election controversies—had passed. Two justices, DAVID H. SOUTER and STEPHEN G. BREYER, disagreed with the majority's remedy; they preferred to order Florida to set acceptable standards and then resume recounting. In the most vehement dissent of all, JOHN PAUL STEVENS declared that the true loser in the election was "the nation's confidence in the judge as an impartial guardian of the rule of law."

Announcing respectful disagreement with the decision, Gore promptly conceded. On December 13, president-elect Bush declared that "our nation must rise above a house divided." Divided it was, between critics of the Supreme Court decision questioning Bush's election legitimacy and supporters of the president declaring these critics sore losers. In critical respects, the election controversy continued. The U.S. Civil Rights Commission pursued an ongoing investigation into claims of voter disenfranchisement. Legislators began examining voting machine reform options. And the counting continued in Florida, too, albeit unofficially, as several newspapers undertook a manual recount of their own. The majority of these independent vote-counters determined that Bush would have won the election even if the hand recount had been allowed to continue. In addition, Florida passed a new election reform law that officially ended the use of the controversial butterfly ballots.

CROSS REFERENCES
Appendix: Missouri's Term Limits Amendment; Voting

EMPLOYMENT LAW

The body of law that governs the employer-employee relationship, including individual employment contracts, the application of TORT and contract doctrines, and a large group of statutory regulation on issues such as the right to organize and negotiate COLLECTIVE BARGAINING AGREEMENTS, protection from discrimination, wages and hours, and health and safety.

Microsoft Settles with Temporary Workers

After being enmeshed in protracted litigation for eight years, the much-watched employment CLASS ACTION case of *Vizcaino v. Microsoft*, 97 F.3d 1187 (9th Circuit 1996) finally settled out of court on December 12, 2000. Microsoft, the world's largest computer software company, agreed to pay $97 million to several thousand long-term current and former "temporary" employees who were denied certain employee benefits because of their temporary status. As the Supreme Court of the United States twice refused to review the matter on Microsoft's appeal from the U.S. Circuit Court of Appeals for the Ninth Circuit, corporate counsel around the country were advising their clients to heed the Ninth Circuit's opinion following the settlement announcement.

The case's central question was the legal distinction between temporary and permanent employment with Microsoft, and the consequence of such distinction upon entitlement to company employment benefits. At issue were certain employment practices of the software giant which resulted in employees being classified as "temporary" for as long as fourteen years.

At any given time prior to 1990, Microsoft employed at least a few thousand "temporary workers," referred to by the company as either "INDEPENDENT CONTRACTORS" or "freelancers." Importantly, there was no ambiguity or equivocal understanding on the part of the workers as to their temporary employment status: upon hire, they were informed of their ineligibility for benefits and were made to sign "Microsoft Corporation Independent Contractor Copyright Assignment and Non-Disclosure Agreement(s)." No plaintiff in the subsequent action alleged that Microsoft ever promised benefits. The temporary workers also signed documents acknowledging their understanding and agreement to pay their own federal and state taxes, withholding, social security, insurance, etc. Microsoft gave these temporary employees separate E-mail addresses, differently colored badges, had them attend separate orientation meetings, and did not invite them to official company functions. Microsoft additionally required that these workers submit invoices for work performed, and it paid them through the accounts receivable rather than payroll department. They also were not paid overtime wages.

Notwithstanding this different corporate treatment, in 1989 and 1990 the INTERNAL REVENUE SERVICE (IRS) examined Microsoft's employment records for tax compliance and concluded that, for tax purposes, Microsoft's freelancers were to be considered "employees." The IRS came to this conclusion by applying COMMON LAW principles defining the employer-employee relationship. As a result, it required Microsoft to begin paying withholding taxes and the employer's portion of the Federal Insurance Contribution Act (FICA) tax for their "temporary" workers.

Thereafter, Microsoft issued retroactive W-2 forms to the freelancers, allowing them to recover Microsoft's share of FICA taxes which they had been required to pay and also agreed to pay them "retroactively for any overtime they may have worked." The company then began to convert all temporary freelancers or independent contractors to either permanent employment or to employment with an independent temporary employment agency. The agency would provide payroll services, withhold taxes, and pay FICA—in other words, the employment agency would be their employer. The day-to-day work of the temporary staff remained

WHAT DOES OSHA REQUIRE FOR WORK-AT-HOME EMPLOYEES?

The OCCUPATIONAL SAFETY AND HEALTH ACT OF 1970 is the source of authority for the Occupational Safety and Health Administration (OSHA). The Act creates the agency and vests in it the authority to establish and enforce occupational safety and health standards. The Act itself contains no standards but does contain minimum procedural requirements for creating standards, comparable to the public-participation process employed by other federal agencies in their lawmaking responsibilities. Those procedures include "notice-and-comment rulemaking" which ostensibly ensures that all interested parties—including, employers, employees, unions, and safety and health professionals—have an opportunity to review proposed rules, regulations, and standards, and provide feedback for the agency's consideration and response.

After OSHA publishes the final form of a rule or standard, it avails itself to the public for advice and counsel on COMPLIANCE issues. When questions regarding AMBIGUITIES or contradictions are posed to the agency, it mostly relies on what are referred to as "letters of interpretation" (LIs), authored and issued by its representatives—commonly referred to as "opinion letters" or "advisory letters." While these letters are not official regulations, FEDERAL COURTS give them great evidentiary weight in

legal disputes, and, following a 1991 U.S. Supreme Court decision, give them presumptive authority if there is a question about correct interpretation of an OSHA standard or STATUTE, provided that the interpretation is "reasonable." Under the auspices of the Department of LABOR (DOL), OSHA also conducts scheduled inspections of employment worksites and has the authority to issue CITATIONS and fines for violations of OSHA safety and health standards.

The stage having thus been set, there occurred in 2000 one of the most disruptive, controversial, and usurping series of events within the agency in all its thirty-year history. It all started over a November 15, 1999, opinion letter to Texas-based Credit Services Company (CSC), which asked for guidance regarding a handful of sales employees who would be performing some of their job duties from computers and telephones in their homes and the company's responsibilities under OSHA's standards.

The responsive opinion letter (LI), signed by none other than Richard Fairfax, OSHA's Director of Compliance Programs in Washington, stated, in part: "All employers, including those that have entered into 'work-at-home' agreements with employees, are responsible for complying with the OSH Act and with safety and health standards." The

LI also held employers accountable for "reasonably foreseeable hazards created by their at-home employment" and went on to state that "reasonable diligence may necessitate an on-site examination of the working environment by the employer." Finally, the LI noted that employers would have to take steps to "reduce or eliminate any work-related safety or health problems they become aware of through on-site visits or other means." As usual, the LI was posted on OSHA's official website as a guideline.

Apparently, the letter went unnoticed until January 4, 2000, when it was published by various news reporting entities and made national headlines. The ramifications of the LI's contents were astounding. Some 20 million estimated Americans work for their employers from their homes. Employers, employees, politicians, human resource managers, and safety and health professionals became entangled in a mass of confusion over a seeming requirement they knew nothing about until January 4. The news had particular relevance in light of the newer ergonomic standards that had recently been published by OSHA, although Congress removed them in the Spring of 2001 with new legislation.

In less than 24 hours, Alexis Herman, Secretary of the U.S. Department of Labor, issued a formal statement by press release, alluding to the November LI "to one employer [providing] guid-

unaltered, however, as did any other terms and conditions of employment.

After learning of the IRS rulings, a few "temporary" workers approached Microsoft to seek certain previously denied employee benefits, specifically, enrollment in Microsoft's Savings Plus Plan (SPP) and its Employee Stock Purchase Plan (ESPP). After Microsoft rejected their claims, they sought review with the Microsoft plan administrator. Following panel review, the workers were formally found ineligible for the stated benefits for two reasons: first, they

"had contractually waived any rights" to benefits upon acceptance of employment as temporary staff, and second, they were not "regular, full time employees in approved headcount positions."

Because of the administrator's ruling, eight workers filed federal suit in the U.S. District Court for the Western District of Washington in 1992. Plaintiff Donna Vizcaino had been discharged after refusing to convert to a "temporary agency employee," but most other plaintiffs had converted. Jurisdiction was based

ance to him on his employees working at home." Herman continued, "While this employer has received the guidance he needs, the letter has caused widespread confusion and unintended consequences for others. Therefore OSHA is withdrawing the letter today." Herman went on to say that there would be a national dialogue "to determine what the rules and policies should be for America's workers."

Herman's official statement may have rescinded the November 15 *cause celebre*, but it did little to quell the controversy. By noting that the original employer had received the guidance he needed, Herman seemed to imply that the LI was content-valid but applicable only to certain employers. Why would there be a national dialogue after the fact? Why had employers not been apprised of this? What happened to the "notice-and-comment rulemaking" which, to some, constituted a condition precedent to final lawmaking?

Later in January 2000, Congressional subcommittees began investigating OSHA's policies for rulemaking and record-keeping. Testifying before a House of Representatives subcommittee, which requested that the Department of Labor clarify *its* position on the issue, Charles Jeffries, assistant secretary for the Labor Department's OSHA, stated, "I regret the confusion caused by the letter of November 15. Let me state that we have not inspected home offices; and we have no intention of inspecting home offices. The letter suggested OSHA policy where no such policy exists, and I regret the unintended consequences it caused."

Things got worse. Congressmen then confronted the DOL with copies of internal E-mail messages that DOL officials sent to employees on the day before Herman rescinded the LI. In one E-mail addressed "for internal circulation only," Fairfax wrote, "The issues raised are political and not safety and health related . . . no one has found fault with our letter." Another e-mail read, "For your information, the letter accurately articulates the position of the Department and the Agency; however, for now, don't engage in the discussion." When asked by subcommittee members to defend those statements, Fairfax replied that they were intended as internal "morale-boosters" only.

Needless to say, Congress requested an internal AUDIT by the Office of the Inspector General, which ultimately found, among other things, that OSHA staff published the November 15 letter without proper consideration of its policy and without inspection by senior officials. Prior to the publication of its results, OSHA formally published Directive No. CPL-2–0.125, "Home-Based Worksites," on February 25, 2000. The stated purpose in the directive was to provide guidance to OSHA's compliance personnel "about inspection policies and procedures concerning worksites in an employee's home." Section 9, "Policy for Home Offices," expressly stated, "OSHA will not conduct inspections of employees' home offices. OSHA will not hold employers liable for employees' home offices, and does not expect employers to inspect the home offices of their employees. If OSHA receives a complaint about a

home office, the complainant will be advised of OSHA's policy." The directive went on to explain that OSHA would conduct inspections of "other" home-based worksites, such as home manufacturing operations, only when OSHA received a complaint or referral that indicated a violation of a safety or health standard that threatened physical harm or where an imminent danger existed, including reports of a work-related fatality. Importantly, the directive stated, "Employers are responsible in home worksites for hazards caused by materials, equipment, or work processes which the employer provides or requires to be used in an employee's home." On the same day, OSHA's Office of Public Affairs released a plain-language version of the directive to the press. OSHA later testified to another House subcommittee that it had learned from its mistakes and had instituted internal procedures to ensure that senior officials were apprised of outgoing opinion letters.

In April 2001 President GEORGE W. BUSH's administration announced plans to call for an amendment to the Occupational Safety and Health Act to preclude home office inspections where employees primarily work on the telephone, computer, and/or with other electronic devices. As part of the administration's larger "New Freedom Initiative," the move was intended to help disabled workers buy computers and other equipment needed to work at home, without OSHA intervention, in return for tax incentives to encourage employers to provide such equipment.

upon a federal claim under the Employee Retirement Income Security Act (ERISA) that the plaintiffs were entitled to savings benefits under the SPP. A second claim alleged that, under Washington state law, plaintiffs were entitled to the stock option benefits under Microsoft's ESPP. Both claims were premised upon plaintiffs' assertion that they were common law employees of Microsoft, incorporating the reasoning of the IRS.

The DISTRICT COURT first certified the plaintiffs and others similarly situated as repre-

sentatives of a class of "common-law employees," ultimately affecting some 8,000 to 12,000 workers. It then granted SUMMARY JUDGMENT against the plaintiffs on all counts, thereby dismissing the case *in toto*. Plaintiffs appealed to the Ninth Circuit *Vizcaino v. Microsoft*, 97 F.3d 1187 (1996). The matter was again heard EN BANC in 1997, resulting in agreement with the panel decision in the first appeal.

The court of appeals concluded that plaintiffs were, indeed, common law employees who were improperly excluded from participation in

The corporate headquarters of the Microsoft Corporation is located in Redmond, Washington.

the subject benefit plans. Regardless of any label or designation of employment status conferred by a company, common law principles look to the essential work relationship between worker and company. The critical legal test is and has been the amount of control the company exercises over the worker's or contractor's work product or performance. The more control, the more indicative of "employee" status. In this case, Microsoft's temporary workers often worked on the same teams as regular employees, performing identical functions, working the same core hours, and reporting to the same supervisors. Moreover, some of the workers had been temporarily employed by Microsoft for as long as fourteen years.

The Microsoft ruling is significant in that it places higher priority on the common law definition of the employer-employee relationship than on any agreement between worker and company. Even where employers are careful to define temporary employees as nonpermanent, casual, or seasonal, managers' actions may affect employee classification. Providing temporary workers with company tools, office space, or training may be further indications that the workers are essentially employees and not temporary independent contractors.

In addition to the PECUNIARY portion of the settlement, Microsoft made several changes to its staffing and worker classification practices. It now limits temporary employment to twelve months and requires a 100-day break between assignments. It also has become more selective in the use of temporary employment agencies, utilizing those which offer better benefit packages to their workers.

CROSS REFERENCES
Appendix: OSHA Letter on Work-at-Home Employees; Independent Contractor

ENGLISH-ONLY LAWS

Laws that seek to establish English as the official language of the United States.

Alexander v. Sandoval

The CIVIL RIGHTS ACT of 1964 contains a number of sections, called titles, that deal with distinct areas of discrimination. Proscribed discrimination is generally one of two types: direct, intentional discrimination against a person or persons within a protected class; or discrimination that occurs as a result of a practice, policy, law, etc. which may be neutral on its face, but has an adverse or discriminating effect on a protected class of persons as a whole. This is referred to as "disparate impact" discrimination.

Title VI of the Act, which deals with recipients of federal funds and other federal assistance, prohibits recipients from discriminating on the basis of race, color, or national origin. An amendment to the 1964 act, Title IX, is almost identical to Title VI but extends the prohibition to gender as well. The Supreme Court of the United States has interpreted § 601 of Title VI to allow private citizens to sue institutions receiving federal aid for intentional discrimination. Under § 602 of Title VI, agencies of the federal government are authorized to promulgate regulations that proscribe discriminatory practices for aid recipients. For over 20 years the lower FEDERAL COURTS also allowed private Title VI lawsuits based on disparate-impact discrimination.

In *Alexander v. Sandoval*, ___U.S.___, 121 S.Ct. 1511, 149 L.Ed.2d 517 (2001), the Supreme Court held that private individuals cannot file lawsuits for disparate impact against those who violate Title VI discrimination regulations. In so ruling, the Court emphasized that Congress had not explicitly granted individuals this private right of action and that the courts have no business creating such rights.

The case arose after the Alabama Department of Safety moved to an English-only policy in 1991. Because the voters of Alabama had amended the state constitution in 1990 to make "English the official language of the state of Alabama," the department stopped administering the driver's license test in 13 non-English languages. Martha Sandoval, a Mexican immigrant living in Mobile, Alabama, sued the department in federal court, alleging that the department's policy violated Title VI. Sandoval noted that the department received federal grants and funds, thus making it subject to federal regulations. One such regulation forbade recipients from using methods that had the effect of subjecting individuals to discrimination based on race, color, or national origin. Sandoval did not seek money damages but rather the end of the English-only policy. Armed with these federal laws and regulations, Sandoval persuaded both the DISTRICT COURT and the Eleventh Circuit Court of Appeals that she was correct in her interpretation of the discriminatory effect of the Alabama policy, which allegedly had a disparate impact on non–English speaking persons. The Eleventh Circuit ordered reinstatement of the multi–language driver's tests in Alabama.

However, the Supreme Court disagreed. In a 5–4 decision the Court rejected the idea that Title VI contained a private right of action that allowed Sandoval to make her case. The Court, in reaching this result, never examined the English-only policy. Instead, it devoted its decision to the collateral issue of whether private citizens had a right to file such suits. The result surprised many commentators because no federal circuit COURT OF APPEALS had ever disputed the private right of action under Title VI, whether for intentional discrimination or disparate impact.

Justice ANTONIN SCALIA, in his majority opinion, stated that Title VI law was clear in three areas. First, private citizens could sue to enforce Title VI's § 601 for intentional discrimination. Second, only intentional discrimination was prohibited by § 601. Third, for purposes of the argument, federal "regulations promulgated under § 602 may validly proscribe activities that have a disparate impact on racial groups, even though such activities are permissible under § 601."

Beyond these three aspects, Justice Scalia found little that helped Sandoval's private right of action. Much of the case law that Sandoval believed supported her action was inapplicable in Scalia's view because these cases were based on intentional discrimination. Moreover, an examination of Title VI demonstrated that a private right of action based on disparate impact cannot come from § 601, which governs intentional discrimination. Scalia concluded that such a right of action can only be based, if at all, on § 602, which authorizes federal agencies to promulgate regulations. In the majority's view there was no evidence that Congress intended to con-

vey a private right of action in this section. Justice Scalia noted that without clear congressional INTENT on this issue, "a cause of action does not exist and courts may not create one." After a review of § 602, Scalia found no such intent. The section only gives the federal government the power to enforce regulations by terminating funding to the offending program or by using any other appropriate means authorized by law. The precise procedural process given in the regulations for terminating funding demonstrated that Congress never intended that a private citizen be allowed to intrude on this regulatory scheme. Scalia also rejected the idea that Congress had ratified the private right of action in later amendments to Title VI.

Justice JOHN PAUL STEVENS, in a dissenting opinion joined by Justices DAVID H. SOUTER, RUTH BADER GINSBURG, and STEPHEN G. BREYER, accused the majority of misreading the Court's prior cases on Title VI. In addition, Stevens argued that Congress had clearly wanted to permit such private lawsuits.

Utah's Voter-approved English-only Law Upheld by State Court

In the general elections of November 2000, Utah's voters approved "Initiative A" by a 2–1 margin. Initiative A is a new law acknowledging English as the official language of the state. The law's language had been carefully drafted to avoid some of the legal challenges that proved fatal to a similar initiative in Arizona. Utah's measure contained exceptions for law enforcement of public safety needs, judicial proceedings, and tourism promotion, including the 2002 Olympics to be held in Utah. The measure does not prohibit public officials from speaking with constituents in other languages but does require that official meetings be conducted in English. The state of Utah has a culturally and ethnically diverse population, with an estimated 120 different languages spoken by its citizens.

The new law was immediately challenged by the AMERICAN CIVIL LIBERTIES UNION (ACLU), Salt Lake City's mayor, and the Utah Hispanic Chamber of Commerce. State DISTRICT COURT judge Ronald Nehring accordingly blocked the law's enforcement in early December, citing FIRST AMENDMENT concerns raised by the challenges. Nehring issued a TEMPORARY RESTRAINING ORDER and scheduled a full hearing for December 14, 2000.

Following the December hearing, Judge Nehring, representing Utah's Third Judicial District Court, affirmed the constitutionality of

Ronald Nehring presides over the lawsuit to throw out Utah's English-only law.

Initiative A in a ruling issued on March 5, 2001, that effectively dismissed the ACLU's and others' challenge. Mauro E. Mujica, the chairman and chief executive officer of "U.S. ENGLISH"—the nation's first and largest citizen action group for preserving the English language as a unifying element—commented on the decision to the press: "As the voters clearly understood, the key to unity and understanding among the state's increasingly diverse population is communication through a common language." Mujica himself is an immigrant from Chile whose first language is Spanish. U.S. ENGLISH was founded in 1983 by the late Senator S.I. Hayakawa of California and has a nationwide membership of approximately 1.4 million.

Notwithstanding the court's finding that the STATUTE was constitutional, the ACLU again tried to block the court's decision. The organization filed another injunctive motion for STAY of the decision. On the other side, U.S. ENGLISH, "Utahns for Official English," and Utah's ATTORNEY GENERAL all filed formal objections to the ACLU's motion. On May 9, 2001, Utah's Third District Court denied the ACLU's motion. Although the ACLU was planning to appeal the decision, a recent opinion of the Supreme Court of the United States in a related matter was expected to influence the appeal.

In the case of *Alexander v. Sandoval*, ___U.S.___, 121 S.Ct. 1511, 149 L.Ed.2d 517 (2001), Alabama's Department of Public Safety stopped issuing drivers' tests in other languages when the state adopted an English-only law in 1990. Plaintiff Martha Sandoval, a house cleaner in Mobile, was not fluent in English. Sandoval

sued the agency with the help of the Southern Poverty Law Center, claiming that since it received federal funds, it was subject to Title VI of the CIVIL RIGHTS ACT of 1964, which bars discrimination based on race or national origin. The Circuit Court of Appeals for the Eleventh Circuit upheld the decision in 2000, ruling that the English-only policy violated federal law because it had a "disparate impact" on non-English-speaking individuals. The appeals court ordered reinstatement of the multi-language driver's tests in Alabama. However, the U.S. Supreme Court reversed the appellate and district courts on the collateral issue of legal STANDING to sue, ruling that an individual has no private right of action to enforce disparate impact regulations promulgated under Title VI.

An estimated 26 other states have made English the official language, however, in some states the initiative has been largely symbolic. For example, Florida passed its English-only law in 1988 but rarely restricts state documents and services to English. Its drivers' tests can be taken in Spanish or Creole in some areas. Approximately 38 states offer written drivers' tests in other languages. In California, the test is given in 30 languages.

Meanwhile, by the year 2000, immigration into the United States was at its highest level in history: more than 1.1 million annually. The U.S. Commission on Immigration Reform had proposed to cut back on legal immigration and wholly eliminate illegal immigration, but Congress was slow to respond with legislation. The healthy economy was driven partially by businesses' continued need for both skilled and unskilled workers. Still, 2000 Gallup polls, as well as public votes on initiatives such as Utah's English-only law and California's Proposition 187, reflect an increasing wariness toward new arrivals into immigrant-heavy states such as in the Sunbelt and a general frustration in having to accommodate multiple language and cultural barriers in order to communicate effectively. Following the Supreme Court's decision in *Sandoval*, challenges to English-only laws may need to show direct, intentional discrimination and not merely disparate impact in order to have legal standing.

CROSS REFERENCES
Appendix: Utah's "Initiative A"; Civil Rights; Discrimination

ENVIRONMENTAL LAW

An amalgam of state and federal STATUTES, regulations, and COMMON LAW principles covering air pollution, water pollution, hazardous waste, the wilderness, and endangered wildlife.

Solid Waste Agency of Northern Cook County v. U.S. Army Corps of Engineers

Congressional power to regulate the environment derives from Article I of the federal Constitution (USCA CONST Art. I § 8, cl. 3), which gives Congress the authority to regulate commerce among the several states, also known as interstate commerce. If, for example, a river has an effect on interstate commerce, the Commerce Clause will come into play, and Congress will have the authority to regulate actions that take place or affect the river. On the other hand, an isolated stream or pond that has no discernible connection to interstate commerce is usually not subject to federal regulation. In this case the *state* has authority to regulate the use of the stream or pond.

When Congress enacted the Clean Water Act (CWA; 33 USCA 1251 et seq.), it gave the U.S. Army Corps of Engineers the authority to regulate "the discharge of dredged or fill material into 'navigable waters.'" Since the 1970s, the Corps has given an increasingly broad reading to the term "navigable waters," including waters that provide habitat to migratory birds, whether or not they are navigable. The Supreme Court of the United States, in *Solid Waste Agency of Northern Cook County v. U.S. Army Corps of Engineers*, 531 U.S. 159, 121 S.Ct. 675, 148 L.Ed.2d 576 (2001), rejected this broad interpretation, ruling that the Corps had gone beyond its STATUTORY authority in extending its regulatory control to waters that are not navigable. The Court held that states had jurisdiction to regulate ponds and other small bodies of water that have no connection to interstate commerce.

The Solid Waste Agency of Northern Cook County is a consortium of Chicago cities and villages that joined forces to locate and develop a disposal site for nonhazardous solid waste. In the early 1990s, the agency located a 533-acre parcel of land that had been a sand and gravel pit-mining operation until 1960. Since that time the land had returned to nature and had become the home for more than 121 bird species, which took advantage of the land's permanent and seasonal ponds of water. These ponds varied in size from one-tenth of an acre to several acres and ranged in depth from several inches to several

feet. The agency applied for a landfill permit from the Corps of Engineers, but the permit was denied based on the Corps's so-called Migratory Bird Rule. Under this rule, the Corps asserted it had jurisdiction to regulate intrastate waters that were used as habitat by birds protected by migratory bird treaties, birds that crossed state lines, and birds that were endangered species. Therefore, the Corps believed it had the authority to deny the agency the use of these wetlands for the landfill.

The agency filed a lawsuit in federal court challenging both the Corps of Engineer's jurisdiction over the sight and the merits of its permit denial. The court ruled in favor of the Corps (191 F.3d 845, [7th Cir.(Ill.) Oct 07, 1999]), and the Court of Appeals for the Seventh Circuit (998 F.Supp. 946 [N.D.Ill. Mar 25, 1998]) affirmed this decision. The APPELLATE COURT found that destruction of the bird habitat would have an aggregate effect on interstate commerce because millions of Americans cross state lines to hunt and observe birds, in the process spending over a billion dollars a year on these activities.

The U.S. Supreme Court, on a 5–4 vote, reversed the Seventh Circuit decision. Chief Justice WILLIAM H. REHNQUIST, writing for the majority, noted that though Congress passed the Clean Water Act to preserve and protect the nation's waters, it recognized that the states have primary responsibility in this area. Moreover, the act authorized the Corps of Engineers to regulate navigable waters, which the statute defined as "the waters of the United States, including the territorial seas." Rehnquist acknowledged that the Court had previously reviewed the meaning of the term "navigable waters." In a prior ruling the Court had allowed the Corps to regulate wetlands that were not navigable but were immediately adjacent to navigable waters. However, in this case the wetlands were neither navigable nor adjacent to any navigable bodies of water.

Chief Justice Rehnquist concluded that the 1972 CWA would not allow an extension of federal jurisdiction to wetlands not adjacent to open water. The Corps argued that it had expanded its definition of navigable waters in 1975 to include "isolated wetlands and lakes" and that Congress had not tried to change this interpretation when it amended the CWA in 1997. Rehnquist rejected this argument, noting that "congressional acquiescence to administrative interpretations" must be analyzed with "extreme care." There are many reasons why a bill can be proposed and rejected, making it difficult to determine whether Congress truly intended to affirm a regulation by inaction. The Court concluded that the Corps had failed to make the necessary showing that the failure of a 1977 bill demonstrated congressional acquiescence to the Corps's regulation or the 1986 Migratory Bird Rule.

The majority found that the CWA did not give clear guidance to the Corps to make this expansive interpretation. Chief Justice Rehnquist stated that when "an administrative interpretation of a statute invokes the outer limits of Congress's power, we expect a clear indication that Congress intended that result." He justified this position as a way "not to needlessly reach constitutional issues." Moreover, the Court wished to tread carefully when the Corps's interpretation "alters the federal-state framework by permitting federal encroachment upon a traditional state power." Therefore the Court struck down the Corps's definition and the Migratory Bird Rule. Regulation of the gravel pit wetland properly belonged to the State of Illinois.

Justice JOHN PAUL STEVENS, in a dissenting opinion, argued that the CWA was a milestone piece of legislation that "endorsed fundamental changes in both the purpose and the scope of federal regulation of the Nation's waters." The dissenters believed the Corps's regulations served the broad purposes of the act.

Whitman v. American Trucking Associations, Inc.

Federal agencies are responsible for implementing laws passed by Congress. Agencies administer these laws, which are often general mandates, through regulations. The regulatory process can be highly controversial, and critics often charge that an agency has exceeded its STATUTORY authority or has used improper standards in setting its rules. Such was the case when the federal ENVIRONMENTAL PROTECTION AGENCY (EPA) issued final rules on air quality standards pursuant to the Clean Air Act (CAA; 42 USCA § 7401 et seq.). Manufacturers and other businesses waged a legal battle that ultimately was rejected by the Supreme Court of the United States in *Whitman v. American Trucking Associations, Inc.*, 531 U.S. 457, 121 S.Ct. 903, 149 L.Ed.2d (U.S.Dist.Col. Feb 27, 2001). The Court, in a landmark ruling, held that the EPA could set air pollution standards without balancing the public health benefits against compliance costs.

The Clean Air Act requires the EPA to promulgate national air quality standards for each type of air pollutant. In 1997 the EPA revised its standards on ozone and particulate matter, which triggered lawsuits by a number of private business associations and several states. The District of Columbia Circuit Court of Appeals ruled in *American Trucking Associations, Inc. v. U.S. E.P.A.*, 175 F.3d 1027 (5/14/99) that the EPA's interpretation of the STATUTE, which delegated power to the EPA to set standards to protect public health, delegated legislative power to the EPA "in contravention of the Constitution." The APPELLATE COURT also endorsed the rule that the EPA did not have to consider implementation costs in setting national air quality standards. Finally, the court held that the EPA's ozone regulations concerning areas that had exceeded maximum allowable levels was unlawful because it ignored specific congressional language.

The Supreme Court unanimously ruled that the EPA had the authority to set ozone and soot standards and that it did not have to consider implementation costs in devising its standards. However, the Court agreed with the appeals court that the ozone regulations in "nonattainment areas" were unlawful. Justice ANTONIN SCALIA, writing for the Court, stated that the CAA did not permit the EPA to consider costs in setting air quality standards. He noted that other parts of the CAA expressly granted the EPA the authority to consider implementation costs. Therefore, the consideration of costs could not be inferred from ambiguous provisions of the act. In addition, the air quality standards provision of the act was the "engine" that drove nearly all of that section of the CAA. It made no sense, Scalia wrote, to conclude that Congress would alter a regulatory scheme's "fundamental details . . . in vague terms or ancillary provisions." Finally, Justice Scalia pointed out that the cost factor urged by the businesses was "*both* so indirectly related to public health *and* so full of potential for canceling the conclusions drawn from direct health effects that" Congress would have had to expressly mention it if it wanted that factor to be considered.

Justice Scalia rejected the appeals court ruling that Congress had improperly delegated legislative authority to the EPA. Congress had directed the EPA to set air quality standards that allowed an adequate margin of safety to protect public health. The appeals court had found that this section did not "provide an intelligible principle to guide the EPA's exercise of authority in setting" national air quality standards. Justice Scalia agreed that "an agency could not cure an unconstitutional standardless delegation of power by declining to exercise some of that power," however, in this case, the delegation was constitutional. The CAA language was similar to that found in drug and occupational safety statutes that the Court had upheld as appropriate limits on agency discretion. Justice Scalia also concluded that Congress had provided sufficient guidance to the EPA on setting air standards. The Court had never demanded, as the court of appeals had, that statutes provide a "determinate criterion" for saying how much of the regulated harm is too much. Therefore, the EPA had the authority to set national air quality standards.

Justice Scalia also examined whether the EPA had properly exercised its authority to implement the revised air quality standards for ozone for areas that exceeded maximum levels. The EPA had interpreted the CAA so as to use one part of the act to guide its implementation. The appeals court had overturned this interpretation, finding that other sections of the act must be read together to control the implementation of revised ozone standards. Scalia rejected the EPA's contention that the policy had not been finalized and thus was not ripe for JUDICIAL REVIEW. Turning to the MERITS of the issue, Scalia affirmed the appeals court and found that the EPA's interpretation of the statute was unreasonable. Therefore, the EPA had to revise this regulation to make it lawful.

Though the Court voted 9–0 in this case, only parts I and IV of Justice Scalia's opinion were unanimous. Furthermore, Justices STEPHEN G. BREYER, JOHN PAUL STEVENS, and CLARENCE THOMAS filed concurring opinions detailing where and how their decisions to vote differed from Justice Scalia's.

CROSS REFERENCES
Administrative Law and Procedure; Commerce Clause; Endangered Species

ESPIONAGE

The act of securing information of a military or political nature that a competing nation holds secret. It can involve the analysis of diplomatic reports, publications, statistics, and broadcasts, as well as spying, a clandestine activity carried out by an individual or individuals working under a secret

identity for the benefit of a nation's information gathering techniques. In the United States, the organization that heads most activities dedicated to espionage is the CENTRAL INTELLIGENCE AGENCY.

Chinese Scientist Accused of Leaking Nuclear Secrets

In December 1999, 60 year-old Wen Ho Lee was arrested and charged with mishandling classified nuclear secrets at Los Alamos National Laboratory. The charge followed months of controversial investigations by the FEDERAL BUREAU OF INVESTIGATION (FBI) and the JUSTICE DEPARTMENT into what some government officials believed was a spy operation supported by China. Considered a security risk, Lee was placed, by the government, in guarded solitary confinement for nine months in a Santa Fe, New Mexico, county jail cell with no opportunity to raise the $1 million bail. Lee was held on 59 counts of illegally copying design secrets as well as destroying seven tapes, to which his plea was not guilty. The government then offered Lee a plea bargain in which the other charges would be dropped if he pleaded guilty to one count of downloading classified data to a non-secure computer. Lee finally agreed to plead guilty to this minor felony charge. As part of the plea bargain, Lee was also required to provide detailed information as to what happened to the tapes.

The Justice Department soon came under fire for its treatment of Lee. U.S. District Judge James A. Parker, the presiding federal judge in New Mexico who had been assigned the case, questioned why the government had chosen not

Wen Ho Lee exits the courthouse with his attorneys Mark Holscher (*right*) and John Kline (*left*), and his daughter Alberta Lee (*back*).

to pursue a voluntary polygraph test or allow Lee to make statements about why he had downloaded such sensitive material onto an unsecured computer and destroyed certain tapes. Even President BILL CLINTON, who had appointed JANET RENO to the attorney general position, disagreed with her about Lee being denied bail for so long. Both President Clinton and Judge Parker agreed that if these things were provided, the previous nine months would have been much less taxing for Lee.

Judge Parker went further. He stated that the treatment of Lee was an embarrassment to the whole nation. Parker's statement was partly based on the fact that key witnesses for the prosecution later admitted that they had provided misleading and even false information during their testimonies at Lee's bail hearing in December 1999. Judge Parker went out of his way to apologize to Lee and bitterly condemned the Clinton administration's tactics in this case. He sentenced Lee to the time he had already served since his arrest, and the 58 other charges were dropped.

Attorney General Janet Reno claimed that representatives of the Justice Department made the best decision they could based upon the evidence and the law. Reno flatly denied Parker's allegations. She disagreed with Parker's apology to Lee, stating that Lee had been held because he had refused to cooperate with investigators. Reno said that Lee would not answer questions regarding why he had downloaded the classified files and would not give a detailed explanation of what had happened to the tapes that contained the files. Had he cooperated, there would have been no reason to hold him in custody.

FBI Director Louis Freeh also countered Judge Parker's accusations. Freeh stated that the plea bargain with Lee was in the best interests of the country because the deal protected the nation's secrets, which would have come out in court if the case went to trial. The plea bargain also would allow the FBI to determine what had happened to the files that Lee had downloaded and removed from Los Alamos. Freeh was quick to point out that, contrary to Parker's statement, the government did have a case against Lee. The FBI had evidence, according to Freeh, that Lee had tried to remove any traces that he had taken the files and that, after he became aware of the investigation, Lee had attempted to delete files that he had manipulated and access the Los Alamos system after his clearance had been revoked.

Russia Convicts then Frees American Businessman Accused of Spying

On December 7, 2000, Edmond Pope became the first American to be convicted of spying in Russia since 1960, when U-2 pilot Francis Gary Powers was shot down, convicted, and then exchanged for a convicted Soviet spy. Russian Judge Nina S. Barkova's verdict gave Pope the maximum prison sentence of 20 years for trying to buy classified information about Russia's Shkval, or Squall, the fastest torpedo in the world. One week later, Russian President Vladimir V. Putin pardoned Pope for humanitarian reasons and to foster good relations with the United States. Pope, who at 54-years old has a rare form of bone cancer, maintained his innocence throughout the ordeal, saying he was buying unclassified information that Russia had been selling to foreign governments for five years.

The case grew out of the murky intersection between business and espionage that developed in 1991 with the collapse of the Soviet Union. Russian scientists, factories, and laboratories looking for work began meeting with international business people who sought to buy Russian technology for commerce and industry. At the same time, governments worldwide sought opportunities to acquire Russian technology for military applications.

In the early 1990s, Edmond Pope was a Navy captain who worked in the U.S. Office of Naval Research as an intelligence advisor and director of security. Upon retiring from the Navy in 1994, he moved to State College, Pennsylvania, to work at the Advanced Research Laboratory (ARL) of Pennsylvania State University, which has close ties with the Office of Naval Research. Three years later, Pope left Penn State to be a freelance technology consultant through his own companies, CERF Technologies International and TechSource Marine Industries. Pope's goal was to acquire little-known foreign technologies that might have commercial value in the United States.

Business was slow at first, so Pope developed sideline businesses, such as importing Russian malachite wall art, lacquered boxes, and nesting dolls, or "matryoshka," to market with Penn State's insignia. Eventually Pope landed a couple contracts to develop technology concerning the Squall, a 27-foot torpedo that spews air bubbles from its nose to surround itself with a friction-reducing sheath, allowing it to travel as fast as 300 miles per hour. U.S. torpedoes do not yet have such technology or capability. In 1999

Pope signed a contract with Region, a torpedo plant in Russia, and with Russian Technologies, a Russian government export agency, to commercialize various technologies used in the Squall. He also had a contract with the Office of Naval Research to study ways to apply the Squall's propulsion system to the commercial ferry industry. Meanwhile, ARL had a contract with the Navy to research the guidance and control of undersea vehicles, including torpedoes.

In March 2000, Pope went to Russia with ARL scientist Daniel Kiely to buy information about the Squall's propulsion system from Anatoly Babkin, a professor at Bauman State Technical University in Moscow. On April 3, 2000, as he met with Babkin in a hotel room to pay $30,000 for the information, Pope was shocked when armed agents from Russia's Federal Security Service ("FSB") barged into the room and arrested Pope, Kiely, and Babkin. Russia eventually released Kiely and Babkin after forcing them to sign confessions in Russian stating that they had trafficked in state secrets. Kiely did not understand Russian, and Babkin publicly retracted his confession, saying it was coerced. Babkin even produced tape recordings of FSB agents threatening to send him to Siberian prison camps unless he stuck to his confession. Pope, however, was destined to stand trial for espionage.

In the months leading up to Pope's trial, his wife, Cheryl Pope, lobbied hard for his release. During four prison visits, Cheryl saw her husband lose 25 pounds and two teeth, probably from malnutrition. Pope's appearance made Cheryl fear that her husband's bone cancer, which had been in remission, had returned. Cheryl Pope and Republican Senator John E. Peterson urged Russia to release Pope so he could return home for proper medical attention. Even after a call from then-President BILL CLINTON, Russia refused to release Pope, saying that numerous medical examinations by its own doctors revealed that Pope's cancer was still in remission.

Pope's trial began on October 18, 2000. It was a secret affair, closed to the public, which prevented Americans from even knowing the specific charges against Pope. According to reports, the Squall's designer, Genrikh V. Uvarov, testified that Babkin offered Pope too much information about the Squall's secret metal fuel system, which could be used to propel rockets in oxygenless environments such as outer space. Russia used the confessions signed by Kiely and

Edmond Pope sits in the Moscow City Court's defendant's cage during his trial on espionage charges.

Babkin as well as Pope's membership in the Navy Federal Credit Union and the American Legion to implicate Pope in espionage.

Pope's lawyer, Pavel Astakhov, said his client had no idea that he was buying secret information. In fact, Pope's contract with Babkin made it clear that Babkin was not to deliver any classified information. Attorney Astakhov further argued that Pope's contract with Region and Russian Technologies led Pope to believe that Squall's technology was unclassified. Arsenty Myandin, a Russian scientist, testified that he had spoken publicly and openly about the Squall for 15 years. Astakhov argued that Russia had freely described the Squall-E—one version of the torpedo—in textbooks and other open reference sources. Astakhov also explained that Russia had marketed the Squall to foreign governments at public arms shows during the 1990s and had even sold 40 units to China.

At the trial's conclusion, Judge Barkova delivered a guilty verdict and a 20-year sentence as Pope stood in a steel cage holding his wife's hands through the bars. Astakhov questioned how the judge could prepare a 20-page opinion in just two and a half hours after closing arguments, leading to speculation that the result was preordained. Three days later, President Putin said he would accept the advice of his pardon commission to release Pope. Members of the commission said "that 'spy mania' had gone too far with the case." Chairman Anatoly I. Pristavkin said, "[W]e are a magnanimous people, although legends circulate in the world about our cruelty." Commission member Marietta O. Chudalova added, "The investigative organs in our country still bear the marks of the Soviet system, more so than in society in general."

Pope returned to freedom on December 14, 2000. Although he remained fairly silent after his release to save his story for a book deal and for testimony before a U.S. Congressional investigative committee, Pope said he believes there is a small power group in Moscow that wants to go back to the old ways of the Soviet Union. Pope also thinks that this same group orchestrated his conviction from the beginning. Meanwhile, speculation arose that Pope's arrest and prosecution was Russia's way of retaliating for Canada's failed efforts to buy the Squall from a Russian defense plant that has authorization to promote the torpedo but not to sell it.

Back in the United States in time for the winter holidays, Pope traveled first to his boyhood hometown of Grants Pass, Oregon, to visit his mother and father, the latter of whom was dying of bone cancer. Pope then returned with his wife to their home in State College, where he saw his two sons for the first time since leaving for Russia in March 2000. Pope, who acknowledged that his bone cancer remained in remission during his imprisonment, considered a lawsuit against the Russian government. Pope also spent time reestablishing relationships with his family, changed his Pennsylvania automobile license plate to read "NO SPY," and wrote a book, *Torpedoed*, which was due to be released by New York publisher Little, Brown in November 2001.

CROSS REFERENCES
Federal Bureau of Investigation; Justice Department

EX POST FACTO LAWS

[*Latin, "After-the-fact" laws*] Laws that provide for the infliction of punishment upon a person for some prior act that, at the time it was committed, was not illegal.

Rogers v. Tennessee

The Ex Post Facto Clause of the U.S. Constitution prohibits the Congress from passing laws that would criminalize an act previously committed or add more punishment to a crime previously committed. All state constitutions have adopted a similar provision. The clause, which is rarely litigated, resurfaced as an issue in

the Supreme Court of the United States case of *Rogers v. Tennessee*, ____U.S.____, 121 S.Ct. 1693, 149 L.Ed.2d 697 (2001). The Court examined the relation of the clause to the FOURTEENTH AMENDMENT's Due Process Clause and to common law rules. It ruled that the clause did not apply to a state supreme court decision that abolished a common law rule dating back to Medieval England. The "year and a day rule," which prohibited a defendant from being convicted of murder if the victim of the assault died more than 366 days after the act, has been repealed or abolished as an historical anachronism that makes no sense in the modern age.

Wilbert K. Rogers stabbed James Bowdery with a butcher knife on May 6, 1994. One wound struck Bowdery's heart, which led to cardiac arrest and severe damage to his brain and kidneys. Bowdery remained in a coma for 15 months and died on August 7, 1995 from a kidney infection. The medical examiner certified that the knife wound caused the death. Rogers was charged and convicted of second-degree murder in Tennessee state court and sentenced to 33 years in prison. On appeal, Rogers asserted that the year and a day rule barred his conviction for homicide, even though the rule was not contained in the Tennessee criminal code. Instead, Rogers contended that Tennessee common law, which is judge-made law based on individuals cases, still recognized the rule. In addition, he argued that if the courts did not apply the rule, such action "constituted an *ex post facto violation*." The Tennessee court of appeals rejected these arguments, as did the state's supreme court. The state supreme court, though it acknowledged it had recognized the year and a day rule in a 1907 decision, pointed out that most states had "legislatively or judicially" abolished it. Finding that the Tennessee legislature had not expressly abolished it in a 1989 criminal law reform act, the supreme court took the occasion to terminate the rule. As to the ex post facto argument, the court found it inapplicable, as the state and federal constitutional provisions only referred to legislative, not judicial, actions.

The U.S. Supreme Court, in a 5–4 decision, upheld the Tennessee courts. Justice SANDRA DAY O'CONNOR, writing for the majority, ruled that the courts had not violated the Fourteenth Amendment's Due Process Clause by abolishing the rule. Rogers had sought to use the "incorporation doctrine" to include the specific prohibitions of the Ex Post Facto Clause within the Fourteenth Amendment. This doctrine has been used by the Supreme Court to incorporate most provisions of the Bill of Rights into the Fourteenth Amendment, thereby making them applicable to the states. Justice O'Connor held that while certain "core due process concepts" do apply to the application of ex post facto issues, this did not mean that the clause extended to "the context of common law judging." In limiting the reading of a prior ruling, Justice O'Connor found that the appropriate concepts of due process to apply in such cases as Rogers's were notice, foreseeability, and the right to fair warning.

Justice O'Connor's refusal to extend the Ex Post Facto Clause to judicial decisions was based on a concern for the judicial system as a whole. Apart from the fact that its text indicated that only legislative acts were applicable, the Court noted that Rogers's interpretation "would be incompatible with the resolution of uncertainty that marks any evolving legal system" and "would unduly impair the incremental and reasoned development of precedent that is the foundation of the common law system."

The majority concluded that the abolition of the year and a day rule did not violate due process because its abolition was not unexpected and indefensible. Modern medicine had changed the underlying rationale for the rule, which presumed that a person could not survive more than a year from a violent assault. Moreover, the abolition of the rule by legislatures and courts had made its demise in Tennessee not unexpected. Finally, the Court found that the rule had never served as a ground of decision in any murder prosecution in Tennessee history. Taking these factors together, Justice O'Connor concluded that the abolition of the rule in Rogers's case was not unfair or arbitrary.

Justice ANTONIN SCALIA, in a dissenting opinion joined by Justices JOHN PAUL STEVENS, CLARENCE THOMAS, and STEPHEN G. BREYER, argued that Rogers had been convicted "for a murder that was not murder (but only manslaughter) when the offense was committed." Scalia contended that judges, who are unelected, should not be given the power to retroactively make an action a crime when that power is not given to elected legislatures. In his view, "the law . . . was altered after the fact."

CROSS REFERENCES
Due Process of Law; Fourteenth Amendment

FIFTH AMENDMENT

Nguyen v. Immigration and Naturalization Service

Gender discrimination is commonly thought to apply only to women, yet there are areas in the law where discrimination against men has been common. Most of these types of gender discrimination focus on family law. For most of the twentieth century it was presumed that a mother should have custody of her child. The justification for this presumption was based on the biological ties between mother and child and the cultural belief that females are more nurturing than males. Though many of these distinctions have been abandoned through litigation, lawmaking and or cultural changes, there remain isolated examples. Such was the case in *Nguyen v. Immigration and Naturalization Service,* ___U.S.___, 121 S.Ct. 2053, ___ L.Ed.2d ___ (2001). In this case a provision of the immigration and naturalization laws makes it more difficult for a citizen father of a child born out of wedlock to an alien mother to establish citizenship for his son or daughter. In contrast, a child born out of wedlock to a citizen mother and an alien father acquires U.S. citizenship at birth. The Supreme Court of the United States upheld the constitutionality of these requirements, ruling that the differing requirements did not violate EQUAL PROTECTION as mandated by the Fifth Amendment.

The events that led to the case were a product of U.S. involvement in Vietnam. Tuan Ahn Nguyen was born in Saigon, Vietnam in 1969 to Joseph Boulais, a U.S. citizen, and a Vietnamese mother. The couple did not marry. Nguyen came to the United States in 1975, when he was almost six years of age. Boulais raised his son in Texas. Though Nguyen was a lawful permanent resident, Boulais took no steps to obtain citizenship for his son. In 1992 Nguyen was convicted in Texas of two counts of sexual assault on a child and sentenced to eight years in prison. In 1995 the IMMIGRATION AND NATURALIZATION SERVICE (INS) started deportation proceedings against Nguyen, as federal law mandated such action when an alien has been convicted to crimes of moral turpitude. The Board of Immigration Appeals and the Court of Appeals for the Fifth Circuit upheld Nguyen's deportation, despite the fact that Boulais obtained a Texas state court order of paternity based on a DNA test. Nguyen and Boulais in their joint appeals argued that the immigration law governing the granting of citizenship to children born out of wedlock violated equal protection because a father has to do more to establish citizenship for his child with an alien parent than a mother. The Supreme Court agreed to hear their appeal because the courts of appeal were divided over whether these differing requirements constituted illegal gender discrimination.

The Court, in a 5–4 decision, upheld the law's constitutionality. Justice ANTHONY M. KENNEDY, writing for the majority, noted that the law required a father with U.S. citizenship could establish the citizenship of a child born of an alien mother if he concluded the process before the child turned 18. The father could establish citizenship by either (1) marrying the mother; (2) acknowledging paternity in writing under oath; or (3) having a court establish paternity through a court proceeding. In Nguyen's case, Boulais had not taken these steps before his son turned 18. His son was now over 30. In contrast, if Nguyen had been born of a U.S. mother and a Vietnamese father, the law provides that he would "have acquired at birth the nationality status of his mother." The question before the Court was whether these differing requirements for establishing citizenship constituted illegal gender-based classifications.

Justice Kennedy employed the "heightened scrutiny" test that is required when examining the constitutionality of gender-based classifications. Under this test the government must show that the classifications serve "important governmental objectives and that the discriminatory means employed" are "substantially related to the achievement of those objectives." Therefore, Justice Kennedy reviewed the law's provisions to determine what government objectives underlay the law and whether these objectives had been met.

Kennedy found that one important interest was "assuring that a biological parent-child relationship exists." The mother's relationship seemed apparent, as the relation is "verifiable from the birth itself." Moreover, the mother's status is usually documented in a birth certificate or hospital records. Such was not the case for fathers. Kennedy pointed out that fathers do not have to be present at birth, and even if they are present their presence does not prove paternity. Therefore, the three options for a father to establish paternity under the federal law were "designed to ensure an acceptable documentation of paternity." Justice Kennedy rejected the claim that a DNA test establishing paternity was sufficient to meet the legal standard. There was no constitutional requirement that Congress require or permit a DNA test.

Justice Kennedy also found that the law furthered the government's interest in insuring that the "child and citizen parent have some demonstrated opportunity or potential to develop" a relationship that consists of "real, everyday ties." In the majority's view this opportunity for a citizen mother and child "inheres in the very event of birth." However, the same opportunity does not result for the unwed father "as a matter of biological inevitability." A father may not know of the pregnancy, and the mother may not be sure of the father's identity. With U.S. male military personnel posted all over the world and fathering out of wedlock children, this concern appeared acute to Justice Kennedy.

Justice Kennedy concluded that these government objectives were legitimate and that the statute furthered them. Moreover, the three options that Boulais could have chosen were not onerous and could have been satisfied on the day of Nguyen's birth or up until he turned 18. The statute did not constitute gender discrimination, as the "difference between men and women in relation to the birth process is a real one." Congress was entitled to address the "problem at hand in a manner specific to each gender."

Justice SANDRA DAY O'CONNOR, in a long and impassioned dissenting opinion that was joined by Justices DAVID H. SOUTER, RUTH BADER GINSBURG, and STEPHEN G. BREYER, argued that the majority had completely misapplied the heightened scrutiny test and had ignored court precedents on gender discrimination.

Palazzolo v. Rhode Island

The Fifth Amendment's Eminent Domain Clause—also called the Takings Clause—bars the government from taking private property for public purposes without paying the owner just compensation. Since the late 1890s, this clause has applied to state and local governments through the FOURTEENTH AMENDMENT'S DUE PROCESS Clause. Though state court systems regularly hear lawsuits from property owners who believe they were not paid enough when the government exercised its power of EMINENT DOMAIN, a more recent type of lawsuit deals with a different type of taking. This theory asserts that government regulations, especially environmental rules, prevent the economic development of the property. Owners have successfully recovered compensation for this type of taking, asserting either a total deprivation of the use of the property or some reduction in its economic value.

The Supreme Court has reviewed several cases that have dealt with this "reverse" taking theory and has upheld the viability of this cause of action. Certain issues have remained unanswered, however, especially those concerning the knowledge of the property owner about restrictions on development at the time of purchase. The Court tried to resolve this and another procedural issue in *Palazzolo v. Rhode Island*, ___U.S.___, 121 S.Ct. 2448, ___ L.Ed.2d ___ (2001). The Court declared that property owners may file lawsuits without filing additional permit applications. Most importantly, the Court overturned a ruling that barred property owners from filing suit if they took possession of the property after the environmental regulations had been enacted.

Anthony Palazzolo stands on his undeveloped land, beside Winnapaug Pond in Westerly, Rhode Island.

The genesis of the dispute reaches back to 1959, when Anthony Palazzolo and several business associates formed a corporation to purchase three parcels of undeveloped land along the beach front of Westerly, Rhode Island. The land is salt marsh, which is subject to tidal flooding. Soon after the purchase Palazzolo bought out his associates and took total control of the corporation. He first submitted a plan to subdivide the land into 74 lots; this required dredging to fill up the land so as to prevent the flooding. This application was denied, as were two later ones in 1963 and 1966. The last application reduced the amount of fill that would be brought to the site and proposed a beach club. Environmental concerns led the Rhode Island Department of Natural Resources to deny approval. Palazzolo tried again in the early 1980s, but the regulatory framework had grown more complex. The state legislature had established the Rhode Island Coastal Resources Management Council to administer an environmental resources program. Also in the late 1970s, Palazzolo's corporate CHARTER was revoked for failure to pay taxes. This action made Palazzolo personally the owner of the land.

The council denied Palazzolo's 1983 application to fill the entire marsh area, as it conflicted with the management plan. He returned in 1985 with a proposal to construct a beach club, which would have entailed filling eleven acres with gravel. The council turned down this plan as well, ruling that under its management plan the proposal lacked a public purpose. Palazzolo then filed suit in state court, alleging a Fifth Amendment taking without just compensation. Ultimately, the Rhode Island Supreme Court ruled against Palazzolo. The court concluded that his case must be dismissed because it was not ripe for legal action and that even if he could sue, the fact that he took the property in 1978 as a private owner barred such a suit. The court reasoned that the 1978 law creating the council and setting up a plan had put him on notice that development was unlikely. Finally, it found that he could develop a portion of the land away from the beach for a home estimated at $200,000. Therefore, he had not lost all economic value in the property.

The U.S. Supreme Court overturned the state court on the first two issues but agreed that Palazzolo had not suffered a total loss in value. The Court, in a 5–4 decision, sought to clarify when a property owner may file a reverse takings case and what, if any, notice, may foreclose a recovery. Justice ANTHONY M. KENNEDY, writing for the majority, first examined the RIPENESS issue. Under the Constitution, there must be a case or CONTROVERSY for a court to hear. The Supreme Court has developed doctrines that eliminate disputes because of the failure to meet this standard. Ripeness simply means that a real controversy is presented. In this case's context, the state court had found that Palazzolo could have filed additional applications with the council that might have been accepted. Justice

Kennedy concluded that this was wrong. The council had made a final decision on the beach club proposal, and its denial was enough to trigger a lawsuit. Kennedy explored several other ripeness arguments, but in each case he found that Palazzolo had been correct in bringing the lawsuit.

Kennedy was more troubled by the state supreme court's conclusion that a property owner could not sue for compensation if he or she took the property with notice of the environmental regulations. In certain circumstances, property owners may assert that government regulations are "so unreasonable or onerous as to compel compensation." It made no sense to allow a state to avoid suit simply because of a transfer of legal title to the property. Kennedy explained: "A state would be allowed, in effect, to put an expiration date on the Takings Clause. This ought not to be the rule. Future generations, too, have a right to challenge unreasonable limitations on the use and value of land."

Though Kennedy sided with Palazzolo's right to assert his rights in court, he agreed with the state court that his ability to build and sell a home worth $200,000 negated his claim of total economic loss. The Court remanded the case to the state court to apply a balancing test to see what, if any, amount of loss Palazzolo was entitled to be compensated for because of the regulatory scheme.

CROSS REFERENCES
Appendix: Nationality Statute on Children Born out of Wedlock; Discrimination; Eminent Domain; Equal Protection; Immigration and Naturalization Service

FIRST AMENDMENT

American Target Advertising, Inc. v. Giani
Though the First Amendment protects FREEDOM OF SPEECH, government can regulate commercial activities that involve the expression of ideas. However, the government must demonstrate that its regulations are content-neutral and are narrowly tailored to protect an important government interest. Controversies over laws that regulate commercial speech often find their way to the courts, where judges must determine whether the regulation violates the First Amendment. In *American Target Advertising, Inc. v. Giani*, 199 F.3d 1241 (10th Cir. 2000), a professional fundraising company that provided direct mail services to various nonprofit organizations challenged a Utah statute that set requirements for charitable solicitations. The law required fundraising services organizations to register with the state, pay a registration fee, and post a $25,000 bond. The Court of Appeals for the Tenth Circuit upheld most provisions of the act as constitutional but threw out two provisions.

American Target, a Virginia corporation, challenged the Utah Charitable Solicitation Act (U.C.A. 1953 § 13–22–1 et seq). American Target provided services to Judicial Watch, a nonprofit organization headquartered in Washington, D.C. Under its contract with Judicial Watch, American target managed a national, direct-mail fundraising campaign. Because the Utah law classified American Target as "a professional fundraising consultant," it was required to file for a permit to conduct business in the state. To obtain the permit, the business had to complete a registration form, pay a $250 annual fee, and "post a bond or letter of credit in the amount of $25,000." American Target refused to comply with the law and, therefore, could not help Judicial Watch solicit funds in Utah. It filed a lawsuit in federal district court alleging that the act violated the First Amendment. The district court upheld the statute's constitutionality, and American Target appealed.

The Tenth Circuit three-judge panel upheld most of the statute and ruled that two provisions violated the First Amendment. It severed these two provisions and allowed the rest of the law to remain in effect. Judge Deanell Reece Tacha, writing for the court, reviewed the legal setting for charitable solicitations. Judge Tacha cited U.S. Supreme Court precedent that charitable solicitations are protected speech for First Amendment purposes. Therefore, the court was required to examine the Utah law to determine whether the law was content neutral. She concluded that the law was not designed to "suppress the expression of unpopular views but rather to control the 'secondary' effects of speech." Secondary effects include undesirable effects unrelated to content or to the communicative impact of *speech.*

Judge Tacha found that the Utah law targeted "the secondary effects of professional solicitation," which included "increased fraud and misrepresentation." She viewed the law as a means of "oversight of mailers' backgrounds and methods." Because the statute was content neutral, the state of Utah had to prove that the act "served a substantial government interest," and it was "narrowly drawn to serve that interest without unnecessarily interfering with First Amendment freedoms." Therefore, the appeals court analyzed each provision of the act according to this test. As to the registration and disclosure requirement, Judge Tacha found the law on solid constitutional footing. The Supreme Court had ruled that registration and disclosure provisions do not implicate the First Amendment. This requirement served the interest of combating fraud, and it did not interfere with American Target's protected speech.

The appeals court also upheld the $250 annual registration fee. Judge Tacha concluded that the fee was not excessive and was needed to defray the costs of administering the law. The court had trouble, however, with the $25,000 bond requirement. American Target had testified that it could not afford to post the bond; therefore, it could not conduct business in Utah. It argued that this restrained its free speech. Judge Tacha agreed, pointing out that the purpose of the bonding requirement was different from the rest of the statute. The bond provided a victim relief fund for those injured by companies violating the act. If the state vigorously enforced the other provisions, it would "diminish the likely need for a victim compensation fund." Because the bond requirement would discourage companies from applying for the permit, the provision violated the First Amendment. Nevertheless, Judge Tacha ruled that this provision could be severed from the act and the rest of the act could remain in effect.

The court also struck down a provision that gave the director of the consumer protection division the authority to request "any additional information the division may require." It found this provision acted as a PRIOR RESTRAINT on speech because it gave the director "unbridled discretion" to "demand any piece of information from an applicant and lawfully deny a permit if the applicant refuses such request." The court severed this provision from the act but upheld the overall registration scheme. Judge Tacha concluded that the act served a legitimate governmental interest and the remaining provisions were narrowly drawn to protect the speech of fundraising organizations. The Tenth Circuit Court's rulings were contested to the U.S. Supreme Court where CERTIORARI was denied in *Giani v. American Target Advertising, Inc.*, 121 S.Ct. 34, 148 L.Ed.2d 14 (U.S. Oct 02, 2000).

Bartnicki v. Vopper

With the dramatic growth in use of cellular telephones, the airwaves are now filled with conversations that can be intercepted and overheard by anyone. Though federal and state laws prohibit the interception and disclosure of elec-

tronic communications, the courts have been called upon to determine whether the use of such communications by the news media is barred. The Supreme Court of the United States addressed this issue in *Bartnicki v. Vopper*, ___U.S.___, 121 S.Ct. 1753, 149 L.Ed.2d 787 (2001), ruling that the First Amendment rights establishing FREEDOM OF THE PRESS take precedence over the PRIVACY rights of those who use cellular phones.

The facts of the case demonstrate how a supposed private conversation dealing with sensitive issues can be transformed into a public statement. In 1993, Anthony Kane, the teachers' union president in Wyoming, Pennsylvania, spoke to Gloria Bartnicki, the union's negotiator in a protracted contract dispute. Bartnicki used a cell phone during the conversation. During this conversation, Kane expressed his frustration over the school board's pay raise proposal and suggested that "we're gonna have to go to their . . . homes . . . To blow off their front porches." Someone intercepted and recorded this conversation and dropped a tape in the mailbox of the leader of a group opposed to the teachers' union wage demands. He in turn gave a copy to a local radio station, where Frederick Vopper, an on-air personality, played the tape many times over the air. The local newspaper and another radio station also published the contents of the recording.

Bartnicki and Kane were outraged over the disclosure and filed suit in federal DISTRICT COURT against Vopper for DAMAGES. The plaintiffs based their civil action on federal and state laws that make it illegal to record and disclose telephone conversations. After the district court refused to dismiss the case, Vopper appealed to the Third Circuit Court of Appeals (200 F.3d. 109), arguing that he had not intercepted the call or illegally obtained the tape. He claimed that the federal WIRETAPPING laws violated his First Amendment right as a member of the news media to disclose such information. At this point the federal government intervened to argue for the constitutionality of the wiretapping laws. The circuit court concluded that the laws were illegal because they deterred more speech than necessary to protect individual privacy rights.

The Supreme Court, in a 6–3 decision, affirmed the circuit court. Justice JOHN PAUL STEVENS, writing for the majority, noted that the federal wiretapping law, which was part of the Omnibus Crime Control and Safe Streets Act of 1968, sought "to protect effectively the privacy of wire and oral communications." The act, which provides criminal penalties for violations, has been amended several times to incorporate new technologies, including wireless communications. It prohibits both the intentional interception and intentional disclosure of such communications. A person could be found liable if he or she has "reason to know" the communications were illegally intercepted.

Because the appeal came so early in the litigation, Justice Stevens assumed for the purposes of argument that the interception of the conversation was intentional and that Vopper had reason to know that the interception was illegal. Based on these assumptions Vopper clearly violated the law. The larger issue, however, was whether the law violated Vopper's First Amendment rights. Stevens acknowledged that Vopper had no role in the illegal interception and that he obtained the tape recordings lawfully. Most importantly, Stevens concluded that the information contained in the recordings was "a matter of public concern." The statements would have been newsworthy if they had been made in public or if they had been "inadvertently overhead" in a public place.

With these legal and factual assumptions in place, Stevens examined the First Amendment argument. He pointed out that the Court, in the 1971 Pentagon Papers case (NEW YORK TIMES v. UNITED STATES), upheld the right of the press to publish important information of concern to the public, even though Daniel Ellsberg had stolen it. In the present case the narrow question was whether, under similar facts, the government could punish the publication because the information was obtained in violation of the wiretapping laws.

For the government to prevail, it had to convince the Court that there were sufficient reasons to justify the restriction on free speech. Justice Stevens rejected the government's assertion that the wiretapping laws removed an incentive for people to intercept private communications. It was inapplicable in this case because Vopper had not intercepted the call and, therefore, had no incentive or disincentive to violate the law. Stevens noted that in most wiretapping violations the identity of the person intercepting and disclosing the conversation had been known. Moreover, he found no evidence that Congress believed the act would deter or reduce the number of illegal interceptions.

The government also argued that the laws sought to protect the privacy of, and minimize the harm to, persons whose conversations had been illegally intercepted. Though Stevens found this argument much stronger than the first, he ultimately concluded that these privacy interests were outweighed by "the interest in publishing matters of public importance." Because Bartnicki and Kane were public figures, engaged in public matters, they had surrendered some of their privacy rights.

Chief Justice WILLIAM H. REHNQUIST, in a dissenting opinion joined by Justices ANTONIN SCALIA and CLARENCE THOMAS, contended that the need to protect privacy was sufficient to uphold the constitutionality of the wiretapping laws. He argued that "'the interest in individual privacy' at its narrowest must embrace the right to be free from surreptitious eavesdropping on, and involuntary broadcast of, our cellular telephone conversations."

City News and Novelty, Inc. v. City of Waukesha

The U.S. Supreme Court continues to review the rights of municipalities to ban or curtail adult-oriented establishments that traffic in explicit sexual materials or activities. In a series of closely-watched cases, the Court has sought to balance the rights of communities to protect their citizens from these types of establishments against the rights guaranteed to all persons under the First Amendment. In *City News and Novelty, Inc. v. City of Waukesha*, ___ U.S. ___, 121 S.Ct. 743, 148 L.Ed.2d 757, (U.S.Wis. Jan 17, 2001), the Court avoided these issues, however, dismissing a First Amendment case because it found that the business that had filed the complaint was no longer in operation.

The City of Waukesha, Wisconsin, required sellers of sexually explicit materials to obtain and annually renew adult business licenses. City News and Novelty obtained such a license in 1989, operating an adult-oriented shop in downtown Waukesha. In November 1995, City News applied for a renewal of its license, which was due to expire in January 1996. In December the Waukesha Common Council denied the application, finding that City News had violated the city's ordinance by permitting minors to loiter on the premises, failing to maintain an unobstructed view of booths in the store, and allowing patrons to engage in sexual activity inside the booths. Waukesha's refusal to renew City News's license was upheld in administrative proceedings and on JUDICIAL REVIEW in the state courts. City News then appealed to the U.S. Supreme Court.

The Supreme Court, in a unanimous opinion, dismissed City News's appeal. Justice RUTH BADER GINSBURG, writing for the Court, noted that it had accepted the appeal to resolve a conflict in the lower courts over the interpretation of a 1990 case, *FW/PBS, Inc. v. Dallas*, 493 U.S. 215, 110 S.Ct. 596, 107 L.Ed.2d 603. In *FW/PBS* the Court examined a municipal ordinance conditioning the operation of sexually oriented businesses on receipt of a license. Unsuccessful applicants for an adult-business license, according to the opinion in *FW/PBS*, must be accorded "an avenue for prompt judicial review." In *City News and Novelty v. Waukesha*, however, Justice Ginsburg pointed out that courts had divided over the meaning of the "prompt judicial review requirement." Some courts held that the unsuccessful applicant for an adult business license must be assured a prompt judicial determination on the merits of the permit denial. Other courts, like the state of Wisconsin in this case, have held that prompt access to court review suffices.

The legal situation for City News changed two months after it petitioned the Supreme Court. It notified the city that it was withdrawing its renewal application and would close its business if the city council granted a license to a potential competitor with which City News felt it could not effectively compete. After the city granted the license to this new corporation in June 2000, City News ceased to operate as an adult business and no longer sought the license renewal.

Justice Ginsburg concluded that the case was now MOOT because City News no longer sought the license and had no "legally cognizable interest in the outcome." City News wanted to keep the case alive, though, and proposed two arguments. First, it had "never promised not to apply for a license in the future." It pointed to *Erie v. Pap's A.M.*, 529 U.S. 277, 120 S.Ct. 1382, 146 L.Ed.2d 265 (2000), which involved the licensing of a nude dancing club. While on appeal to the Supreme Court, Pap's attempted to have the appeal dismissed because it had sold the club to a new owner who had closed the business. Such a dismissal would have preserved the Pennsylvania Supreme Court's ruling in Pap's favor. In City News's case, Justice Ginsburg ruled that there were critical differences in the two cases. The most important was that the nude dancing business had prevailed in the lower courts. If the Court had dismissed the case, the municipality would have been "saddled" with the ongoing injury of having the law struck down. In the case of City News, how-

ever, it was the loser, not the winner, in the earlier legal proceedings. Therefore, a dismissal would not "keep Waukesha under the weight of an adverse judgment, or deprive Waukesha of its victory in state court."

City News's second argument was that it "experienced an ongoing injury because it was barred from reopening as an adult business until 2005." It noted that the city ordinance banned licensing for five years after a violation. Though the five-year ban expired in 2000, City News had continued to operate without a license into 2000. Justice Ginsburg dismissed this theory, finding that the city had expressly allowed the business to operate during the appeal.

Lorillard Tobacco Corp. v. Reilly

Since the 1960s, the federal government has required TOBACCO companies to place warning labels on their consumer packaging and on their print advertising. Moreover, the law bans tobacco advertising on television. In the 1990s, most states filed lawsuits against the tobacco companies, alleging that they conspired to withhold information from the public about the health dangers associated with tobacco. These lawsuits have been settled, yet the tobacco companies continue to face legal obstacles in the marketing of their products. For example, the state of Massachusetts imposed regulations that prohibited tobacco ads within one-thousand feet of public playgrounds, parks, and schools. The regulations also required indoor store advertising of tobacco products to be placed no lower than five feet from the floor and to place tobacco products behind counters. The tobacco companies challenged these state regulations in federal court and the Supreme Court, in *Lorillard Tobacco Corp. v. Reilly*, __U.S.__, 121 S.Ct. 2404, __ L.Ed.2d __ (2001), struck down all but the in-store restrictions on displaying tobacco products. The Court based its decision on federal PREEMPTION and First Amendment grounds.

Massachusetts sought to implement its regulations in early 1999, but 1,200 members of the tobacco industry went to court to block the new rules. The federal DISTRICT COURT concluded that the state regulations did not intrude on the regulatory scheme found in the Federal Cigarette Labeling and Advertising Act (FCLAA), and they did not violate the tobacco industry's First Amendment rights. The Court of Appeals for the First Circuit agreed with the lower court, setting the stage for the Supreme Court appeal.

The Supreme Court ruled unanimously that the lower courts were wrong in their legal

Massachusetts Attorney General Thomas Reilly announces that the state of Massachusetts will regulate handguns like any other consumer product, including tobacco.

analysis. Justice SANDRA DAY O'CONNOR wrote the main opinion for the Court, though a number of justices also filed separate concurring opinions as to particular substantive and procedural issues surrounding the case. Justice O'Connor first addressed the federal preemption issue. Under the Constitution's SUPREMACY CLAUSE, federal laws may expressly bar states from enacting laws and regulations that conflict with federal statutes. For example, the National Labor Relations Act, which governs COLLECTIVE BARGAINING between employers and labor unions, prohibits the states from intruding into this area. In general, when Congress propounds a comprehensive regulatory scheme, the courts find that federal law preempts state action in that area.

Justice O'Connor found just such a comprehensive scheme in FCLAA. The act's numerous regulations as to advertising clearly justified the invocation of the Supremacy Clause. She pointed out that Congress had amended the original law to restrict state action beyond cigarette packaging. The amendment barred the states from imposing any "requirement or prohibition based on smoking and health . . . with respect to the advertising or promotion of any cigarettes the packages of which are labeled in conformity" with FCLAA. Thus, it was clear that Congress did not want the states to intrude and upset the federal regulatory framework. Though Justice O'Connor recognized that the states wish "to attempt to prevent minors from using tobacco products be-

fore they reach an age where they are capable of weighing for themselves the risks and potential benefits of tobacco use," FCLAA placed "limits on policy choices available to the states." States were free to use zoning restrictions to limit the size and location of advertisements of all products, not just tobacco products.

Justice O'Connor also declared the state regulations unconstitutional under the First Amendment. The amendment protects commercial as well as individual speech rights; the Court has set out a four-part test that analyzes whether a regulation meets constitutional muster. In this case there was no dispute as to the first two parts of the test, as the tobacco advertising was protected by the First Amendment, and the state of Massachusetts had a substantial interest in seeking to regulate the speech. The third and fourth parts of the test, however, were in dispute. The third prong requires the regulation to advance the state's substantial interest, but the fourth prong requires the regulation to be no "more extensive than is necessary to serve that interest."

The one-thousand foot restriction on advertising met the third prong's requirement, as it would keep tobacco advertising away from areas where children congregate. This regulation failed the fourth part of the test, however, because the regulation was too broad. Justice O'Connor noted that adults may purchase and consume tobacco products legally. The regulation went too far in restricting the ability of adults to receive information about tobacco products. As to the indoor, point-of-sale regulation, this failed both the third and fourth prongs of the test. O'Connor pointed out that not all children are shorter than five feet. In addition, children can look up and see advertising. Thus, the regulation did not advance the state's interest, and it exceeded what was necessary to serve that interest.

The Court upheld, however, the in-store restrictions on displaying and selling tobacco products. Requiring the purchaser of tobacco products to obtain them from a cashier rather than selecting them personally did not seriously compromise the First Amendment. Moreover, this regulation served a substantial interest in preventing MINORS from obtaining tobacco products.

United States v. United Foods, Inc.

The federal regulation of business has grown considerably since the 1930s. Despite the perception that businesses dislike government regulation, certain parts of the economy have actually sought government assistance as a way to stabilize their particular market. This type of government-business partnership has been most pronounced in agriculture, where growers of particular crops have used federal legislation to help inform consumers about the benefits of their produce. Despite the general appeal of these regulatory schemes, some individual processors object to the imposition of an assessment to help pay for generic product advertising.

The Supreme Court addressed this issue again in *United States v. United Foods, Inc.*, ___U.S.___, 121 S.Ct. 1711, 149 L.Ed.2d 722 (2001). The Court ruled that an assessment levied against producers of fresh mushrooms for generic advertising violated the First Amendment rights of producers who objected to assessment. In so ruling, the Court distinguished a recent ruling that appeared to find no First Amendment issues at stake in a case involving tree fruit advertising.

The Mushroom Production, Research and Consumer Information Act authorized the creation of a Mushroom Council made up of mushroom producers and importers, to further the goal of promoting the consumption of fresh mushrooms. The council, which is supervised by the United States Department of AGRICULTURE (USDA), was empowered to levy an assessment on fresh mushrooms up to one cent per pound of domestic or imported fresh mushrooms. Though the act authorized the council to spend the money collected through the assessment on a number of activities, most of the money was expended on generic advertising touting the qualities of fresh mushrooms.

United Foods, Inc., a large producer of fresh mushrooms located in Tennessee, refused to pay the assessment in 1996, arguing that the forced generic advertising violated the First Amendment. It preferred to spend its money on advertising the qualities of its brand of mushrooms. The federal government then filed suit in federal court demanding payment of the assessment. Though the district court ruled that United Foods must pay the assessment, the Court of Appeals for the Sixth Circuit reversed that decision.

The Supreme Court, in a 6–3 decision, affirmed the circuit court's determination that the assessment violated United Foods's First Amendment rights. Justice ANTHONY M. KENNEDY, writing for the majority, stated that the question to be resolved was whether "the government may underwrite and sponsor speech with a certain viewpoint using special subsidies," even when members of the subject class "object to the idea being advanced." He noted that the First Amendment does not just address the banning of speech; it also prevents the government from forcing persons to express views with which they disagree.

Justice Kennedy agreed that the views over mushrooms that were in dispute may appear to be minor. The majority of producers were happy with expressing the view that fresh mushrooms are good, while United Foods sought to impress consumers with the special qualities of their own mushrooms. Nevertheless, United Foods was within its rights to object to having to pay for a message it did endorse. Kennedy worried that the First Amendment was placed in jeopardy if the government can compel a citizen to pay for speech that supports the government's—that is, the Mushroom Council's—point of view. Thus, there was a compelling interest at stake.

Justice Kennedy acknowledged that a 1997 Court ruling seemed to contradict this concern. In that case, California producers of tree fruits paid a similar assessment to promote fruit. Kennedy concluded, however, that this precedent did not apply because the California advertising was just one part of a much larger effort to develop the fruit industry through restrictions on "marketing autonomy." In contrast, the mushroom assessment was spent almost entirely on generic advertising, suggesting that this was the only aim of the regulatory structure. The key to analyzing these types of assessments was the "entire regulatory program." In comparing the fruit and mushroom programs, Kennedy found that while the fruit growers had traded competition for cooperation, the mushroom industry still remained a competitive field for the producers. Therefore, the majority concluded that the assessment violated the First Amendment. United Foods should be free to spend its money on advertising that reflects its views rather than those of a government program and its competitors.

Justice STEPHEN G. BREYER, in a dissenting opinion, contended that the majority had split hairs in comparing the tree fruit and mushroom program assessment schemes. In his view, both programs involved issues of economic policy rather than free speech. In both cases the assessments did not fund political or ideological views, nor did they restrain the freedom of growers like United Foods to communicate their own advertising messages.

WHAT IS APPROPRIATE USE OF THE CONFEDERATE FLAG?

After months of open and contentious debate, the General Assembly of the State of South Carolina agreed in May 2000 that the Confederate flag would be placed at the Confederate Soldiers' Monument, instead of in its former position on the State House dome. State Governor Jim Hodges signed the bill, which was supported by the South Carolina Chamber as part of the Business Agenda and the Courage to Compromise coalition, on May 30. "Today, we bring this debate to an honorable end. Today, the descendants of slaves and the descendants of Confederate soldiers join together in the spirit of mutual respect," Hodges stated in a speech just prior to the signing. The actual relocation of the flag on July 1, 2000, complete with formal pomp and circumstance, was attended by 3,000 persons. The official ceremony lasted eight minutes. The fallout lasted for eight months.

In 1994 Governor of Alabama, Jim Folsom, Jr., decided to move a Confederate flag from the state capitol's roof to a nearby war memorial. His decision was partially in response to pressure from the NATIONAL ASSOCIATION FOR THE ADVANCEMENT OF COLORED PEOPLE (NAACP). Afterward, South Carolina was the only former member of the Confederate States of America to fly the Confederate flag on its capitol building, though some Southern states still used it as part of their flag design. The issue waxed and waned in South Carolina's legislature for the next several years without resolution. In late 1999, the NAACP again mobilized, calling for a boycott of all state tourism, athletic contests, cultural events, and film-making in South Carolina until the flag was removed.

Benedict College, an historically black institution, canceled its September 2, 2000, football game with South Carolina State University after the latter refused to move the game from its campus in Orangeburg, South Carolina, to Charlotte, North Carolina. This was followed by Bryn Mawr College, Haverford College, and Swarthmore College all canceling spring-break trips to South Carolina's coast. Furthermore, the National Collegiate Athletic Association's Division I Board of Directors threatened to move games in the men's basketball tournament out of South Carolina if the flag was not removed from the state dome.

The issue returned to the state legislature's general assembly, where, following several weeks of emotional and grueling battle, a compromise agreement was reached in May 2000 by a House vote of 66–43 and a Senate vote of 35–8. The flag came down and took up its new home at the Soldiers' Memorial. Senator Arthur Ravenel claimed, "The only people that seem to be unhappy are the extremists."

The NAACP, however, took umbrage with the new location, complaining that the flag had become more visible than ever. It sent out mailings, urging the continuation of its state boycott and arguing that the flag also should be removed from all state grounds, including the Soldiers' Memorial. State Senator Robert Ford, a black supporter of the compromise, defended the new location, stating that, contrary to the NAACP's contentions, the flag was not "in anybody's face" in its new location. House majority leader Rick Quinn remarked that the NAACP

CROSS REFERENCES
Prior Restraint; Supremacy Clause; Tobacco; Wiretapping

FOURTEENTH AMENDMENT

Brentwood Academy v. Tennessee Secondary School Athletic Association

Some federal CIVIL RIGHTS laws are based on the provisions of the Fourteenth Amendment. The Supreme Court of the United States has consistently held that such laws can only be applied against government officials and not against private citizens because the Fourteenth Amendment requires "state action." However, the Court has also found that in some circumstances a private individual or organization has become so entwined with government that it becomes a state actor and may be sued under federal civil rights cases. This was the case in *Brentwood Academy v. Tennessee Secondary School Athletic Ass'n*, 531 U.S. 288, 121 S.Ct. 924, 148 L.Ed.2d 807 (U.S. Feb 20, 2001), where the Court held that a state athletic association was so closely connected with the public schools as to become a state actor.

The case arose over the efforts of the Tennessee Secondary School Athletic Association to curtail the alleged football recruiting abuses of Brentwood Academy, a private school with a enormously successful football program. Brentwood Academy, a member of the association, was accused of violating an "undue influence" rule when it contacted new students and their parents about spring football practice. In 1997, the association brought an enforcement proceeding against the school. This proceeding led the association to place Brentwood's athletic

had "essentially become professional agitators and I think someone needs to stand up to them." Several hundred flag supporters gathered at the ceremony and vowed that the flag would again rise above the state capitol.

After the flag's removal in South Carolina, Georgia followed. In January 2001, Georgia governor Roy Barnes persuaded lawmakers to shrink the Confederate battle emblem prominently displayed on the state flag to a small box in the corner of the flag. One month later, during a remodeling project, Florida quietly removed its Confederate flag, one of four flags flying over the state capitol.

Mississippi, the last bastion of the old South, held its ground. In April 2001, by a two-thirds split along mostly racial lines, voters overwhelmingly rejected a bill to replace the state's "Southern Cross" on its flag, which dates back to 1894. Mississippi, the poorest state in the Union, showed little concern for any threatened boycotts.

The flag controversy revolves around the intended meaning of the flag. Clearly, if a state's flag represents "symbolic speech," there must be an intent to convey a particular message that is understood by those who view it, in order to invoke FIRST AMENDMENT consideration. Under these conditions, the time, place, and manner of display may be controlled if it can be proven that its display would cause violence or mayhem. According to the NAACP, the Confederate battle flag and emblem "have been embraced as the primary symbols for the numerous modern-day groups advocating white supremacy." The NAACP has referred to the flag as a "banner of secession and slavery." Some Southern whites see it as a banner of honor, however, for the Confederate soldiers who lost their lives during the U.S. CIVIL WAR. Furthermore, they interpret the war to have been more about state and federal power and states' rights to secede from a union that they had joined voluntarily and less as a war to end the institution of slavery. Still further, others see the flag as a banner of "treason against the United States government."

The flag's significance on the state building seems to send two messages. Some have charged that it was more than coincidence that the South Carolina Confederate flag first flew over the state capitol in the early 1960s: it was raised in a centennial celebration of the Civil War. Others believe it was also meant to send a message to the grass-roots CIVIL RIGHTS MOVEMENT, which was just beginning to mobilize. In a country where historians still debate the reasons for the Civil War, the flag's message has been interpreted according to passing ideological or economic battles.

Issues regarding Southern heritage and the Confederate flag also were fought over in schools. In October 2000 the Supreme Court of the United States declined review of the Eleventh Circuit's decision in *Denno v. School Board of Volusia County*, No. 98–2718, which upheld a school's right to discipline a student for displaying a small Confederate flag at school. The school had argued that the flag was such a controversial symbol that its display invited disruption. The Atlanta-based Eleventh Circuit panel first issued an opinion allowing the student to proceed with his case against the school board, then later withdrew its opinion and issued a dismissal.

Students in Kentucky, North Carolina, and Virginia also have been disciplined in recent years for wearing Confederate symbols or flags on their clothing. Notwithstanding, in March 2001, the U.S. Court of Appeals for the Sixth Circuit REMANDED to the trial court a suit by two Kentucky students who were suspended for wearing Hank Williams, Jr., shirts with the Confederate flag (*Castorina v. Madison County School Board*, No. 98–00068; March 8, 2001). The APPELLATE COURT stated that the school needed to better explain its reason for the ban, such as whether there had been any racial violence.

program on four years' probation, banned its football and boy's basketball programs from the playoffs for two years, and fined the school $3,000. The association officials who imposed these penalties were all public school administrators.

In response, Brentwood filed a federal suit against the association and its chief executive under 42 U.S.C.A. § 1983, arguing that implementation of the rule was a state action and against the First and Fourteenth Amendments. The district court agreed with the school and entered judgment in its favor, ordering the association not to enforce its penalties. *Brentwood Academy v. Tennessee Secondary School Athletic Ass'n*, 13 F.Supp.2d 670 (M.D.Tenn. Jul 29, 1998). In holding the Association to be a state actor under § 1983 and the Fourteenth Amendment, the court found that the state had given authority over high school athletics to the association, characterized the ties between the association and its public school members as mutualistic, and stressed the overtly public character of the association's members and leaders. However, the U.S. Court of Appeals for the Sixth Circuit reversed this holding. *Brentwood Academy v. Tennessee Secondary School Athletic Ass'n*, 180 F.3d 758 (6th Cir.(Tenn.) Jun 21, 1999). It found that there was not a mutualistic liaison between the state and the association and stressed that the association did not engage in a customary and designated public function nor did it respond to state mandate. Further, the court said that the athletic association, a private voluntary organization, was not arm of government, nor were its actions fairly attributable to state of Tennessee, and, thus, a member school could not bring a § 1983 claim against the association. Therefore, the case had to be dismissed.

The Supreme Court, on a 5–4 vote, rejected the Sixth Circuit's reasoning and found that the association was a state actor. Justice DAVID H. SOUTER, writing for the majority, noted that prior rulings of the Court had identified numerous factors that could lead to the conclusion that a person was a state actor. The general principle governing this determination was whether there is such a "close nexus between the State and the challenged action" that seemingly private behavior "may be fairly treated as that of the State itself." Based on this principle, Souter looked for facts that would suggest "public entwinement."

Justice Souter found a host of facts that indicated public entwinement. Most of the state's public high schools were members of association, representing 84 percent of the association's membership. School officials made up the voting membership of the association's governing council and control board, which typically held meetings during regular school hours. Souter also pointed out that association staff, although not state employees, were permitted to join the state retirement system. The association had substantial regulatory powers, setting membership standards and student eligibility rules and has the power to penalize any member school that violates those rules. The state board of education has long acknowledged the association's role in regulating interscholastic competition in public schools, and its members sit as nonvoting members of the association's governing bodies.

Reviewing these facts, Souter concluded that the association was a state actor. He stated that the association's "nominally private character is overborne by the pervasive entwinement of public institutions and public officials in its composition and workings, and there is no substantial reason to claim unfairness in applying constitutional standards to it." Because of its overwhelming public school membership, the association's body of public school officials were acting in their official capacity to make available a vital part of secondary public schooling, interscholastic athletics. Souter held that there would be "no recognizable Association without the public school officials, who overwhelmingly determine and perform all but the Association's purely ministerial acts." Therefore, Brentwood Academy was entitled to sue the association under the federal civil rights law.

Justice CLARENCE THOMAS, in a dissenting opinion, argued that that "entwinement " was not enough to find state action. Thomas adopted the Sixth Circuit's reasoning, contending that a private organization's acts constituted state action only when it can be shown that the organization performed a public function, was "created, coerced, or encouraged by the government," or acted in a symbiotic relationship with the government. In this case, the association was a private organization that had not been created or funded by the state of Tennessee. Moreover, the state had no involvement in the particular action challenged by Brentwood Academy.

New York City Settles Class Action for Illegal Strip Searches

In January 2001, New York City agreed to settle a CLASS ACTION lawsuit stemming from illegal strip-searches conducted by the city's Department of Corrections in Manhattan and Queens from July 1996 to June 1997. At least 50,000 people stand to receive between $250 and $22,500 each after a federal judge approved the settlement in a June 2001 fairness hearing.

The lawsuit stemmed from a strip-search policy that the Department of Corrections implemented in 1996 when it took over responsibility from the Police Department for pre-arraignment detention cells. To protect the safety of all detainees, the Corrections Department strip-searched every person brought in for detention. That policy violated the FOURTH AMENDMENT of the U.S. Constitution, which protects the public from unreasonable SEARCHES AND SEIZURES. In 1986, the U.S. Second Circuit Court of Appeals said it is unlawful under the Fourth Amendment to conduct a strip-search or body-cavity search of a person accused of a MISDEMEANOR or minor offense absent reasonable suspicion that the person is concealing a weapon or contraband.

Danni Tyson, a retail consultant and personal shopper in Manhattan, became a victim of the illegal policy. One afternoon in April 1997, Tyson was on the subway to get her daughter at swim practice when she got into an argument with a police officer. Tyson soon found herself under arrest for DISORDERLY CONDUCT and resisting arrest. During pre-arraignment detention, two female correction officers took Tyson into a room, ordered her to take off all of her clothes, and looked under her breasts. Although police dropped the charges, Tyson and her daughter—who had no idea where her mother was during the arrest—were traumatized by the event.

One month later in May 1997, Tyson filed a class action lawsuit against New York City. Although it denied any wrongdoing, the Corrections Department soon changed its strip-search policy to bring it into compliance with the Fourth Amendment. During the DISCOVERY phase of the lawsuit, lawyers learned that more than 50,000 people were subjected to illegal strip-searches between July 1996 and June 1997. Men usually had to strip down in groups, while women typically were alone with corrections officers. In court papers, the Corrections Department admitted that it conducted what it called "strip-frisks" of each arrestee's armpits, mouth, ears, nose, and navel while the arrestee was undressed. Tyson's lawyers claimed that arrestees often had to lift their breasts or genitals and then squat down and cough to expel any weapons or contraband being hidden in their anal or vaginal cavities.

One of the arrestees, Debra Ciraolo, filed her own lawsuit against New York City and, in 1999, received a verdict of $19,600 for medical expenses, pain, and suffering, and $5 million for PUNITIVE DAMAGES. A federal court of appeals later reversed the award of punitive damages, and in November 2000, the U.S. Supreme Court declined to review the case. Ciraolo's $19,600 award for COMPENSATORY DAMAGES, however, remained intact, making New York City's exposure in Tyson's class action lawsuit on behalf of 60,000 people very high.

In January 2001, Tyson's lawyer, Richard D. Emery, and New York City announced that they had reached a settlement of the class action case. The settlement would provide a minimum award of $250 to anyone who experienced an illegal strip-search when the Corrections Department policy was in place. Arrestees who experienced more severe physical or psychological damage could apply for higher awards, up to $22,500. Arrestees also could choose to opt-out of the class action, meaning they would not receive any money but would have the right to file their own lawsuit against New York City. Under federal rules for class action cases, Judge John S. Martin, Jr., of the Federal District Court in Manhattan had to approve the settlement as fair before it went into effect, which he did in June 2001.

CROSS REFERENCES
Civil Rights; Education Law; Fourth Amendment; Stop and Frisk

FOURTH AMENDMENT

Ferguson v. City of Charleston

The Fourth Amendment prohibits warrantless and nonconsensual searches in most circumstances, however, the Supreme Court of the United States has made exceptions, recognizing for example that "special needs" may justify searches that serve ends other than law enforcement. In this context the Court has upheld the right of employers to administer drug tests to employees and for schools to give drug tests to student athletes. The scope of the "special needs" exception was addressed in *Ferguson v. City of Charleston*, ___U.S.___, 121 S.Ct. 1281, 149 L.Ed.2d 205 (2001). The Supreme Court ruled that the exception could not be applied to drug tests conducted by hospitals on pregnant women suspected of cocaine use because the results were given to law enforcement officials for prosecution. Under these circumstances the Court ruled that such tests required either a SEARCH WARRANT or the INFORMED CONSENT of the patient.

The case grew out of efforts to deter cocaine use by pregnant women by the Charleston, South Carolina, public hospital operated by the Medical University of South Carolina (MUSC). In 1989 MUSC began testing maternity patients suspected of drug abuse. If the test was positive, the hospital referred the patient to the county substance abuse agency for counseling and drug treatment. MUSC staff soon concluded that this scheme had not reduced cocaine use among its patients and sought to develop a more effective policy. MUSC contacted the local prosecutor and offered its cooperation in prosecuting mothers whose children tested positive for drugs at birth. The prosecutor jumped at the offer and organized a series of meetings with various law enforcement agencies. Out of these meetings came a policy that MUSC adopted. This policy established how patients suspected of drug use would be identified, described the chain of CUSTODY needed for the drug tests, and detailed how the threat of prosecution would be used to get women into drug treatment. If a woman tested positive for cocaine she was to be arrested for distributing the drug to a minor.

Ten women who received obstetrical services at MUSC and "who were arrested after testing positive for cocaine challenged the constitutionality of the tests." The women argued that the nonconsensual tests were unconstitutional warrantless searches. Local government officials and hospital representatives defended the policy, contending that the women had consented to the tests. Moreover, even if they had not consented, they were justified by the "special needs" of local authorities to reduce the use of crack cocaine by pregnant women. The federal DISTRICT COURT upheld the policy, and the women appealed to the Court of Appeals for the Fourth Circuit. The APPELLATE COURT agreed that the policy was constitutional because of these special needs. The court used a balancing test, finding that the interest in minimizing pregnancy complications and costs outweighed what it considered minimal intrusion on the PRIVACY of the patients.

The Supreme Court, on a 6–3 vote, reversed the appeals court. Justice JOHN PAUL STEVENS, writing for the majority, noted that because MUSC is a public hospital, its staff members were government actors subject to the provisions of the Fourth Amendment. Stevens concluded that the policy did not demonstrate that the hospital "had probable cause to believe" a patient was using cocaine or that it had "reasonable suspicions of such use." Therefore, the hospital drug test was a search that could only be constitutional if it came within the "closely guarded category of constitutionally permissible suspicionless searches."

Justice Stevens examined the cases cited by the Fourth Circuit as permitting a warrantless search because of special needs. He pointed out that the invasion of privacy in the present case was much greater than in the preceding cases, in which drug tests were used to disqualify an employee promotion or to prevent a student from participating in an extracurricular activity. The persons taking these tests also knew the purpose of the tests. Moreover, the test results were not turned over to law enforcement. In contrast, the maternity patients at MUSC had a reasonable expectation that the results of diagnostic tests would "not be shared with nonmedical personnel."

While acknowledging that the purpose of MUSC's testing program was to get women into treatment, Justice Stevens stated that "the immediate objective of the searches was to generate evidence *for law enforcement purposes* in order to reach that goal." In this situation hospitals "have a special obligation to make sure that the patients are fully informed about their constitutional rights, as standards of knowing waiver require." Without such consent the drug tests were unreasonable searches and the evidence collected could not be used against the women.

Justice ANTONIN SCALIA, in a dissenting opinion joined by Chief Justice WILLIAM H. REHNQUIST and Justice CLARENCE THOMAS, argued that doctors "often obtain incriminating evidence." Moreover, the Charleston law enforcement officials used the tests in a "benign" way, as only 30 of the 252 women testing positive for cocaine were arrested and only two were prosecuted.

Illinois v. McArthur

The Fourth Amendment's prohibition against unreasonable SEARCH AND SEIZURE has been subjected to numerous court tests since the 1960s. Though the Fourth Amendment requires police to obtain a SEARCH WARRANT before entering a residence, the Supreme Court of the United States has permitted exceptions under certain circumstances. These exceptions have been conditioned on reasonableness. The Court again applied the reasonableness standard in *Illinois v. McArthur*, 531 U.S. 326, 121 S.Ct. 946, 148 L.Ed.2d 838 (2001), ruling that police acted constitutionally when they prevented a man from entering his home while they obtained a search warrant to look for marijuana inside his residence.

In 1997 Tera McArthur asked two police officers to accompany her to the trailer where she lived with her husband, Charles, so that they could keep the peace while she removed her belongings. She went inside and retrieved her belongings while Charles remained inside. The officer remained outside during this period. When she left the trailer she told the officers that Charles had marijuana and that he had put it under the couch. One of the officers then knocked at the door and told Charles what Tera had said and asked permission to enter the trailer. When he refused, the second officer left the site to get a search warrant. Charles soon joined the officer on the front porch but was told he could not reenter the residence unless the officer accompanied him. During the next two hours, Charles reentered the trailer two or three times to get cigarettes and to make phone calls. Each time the officer stood just inside the door to observe what Charles did. After the second officer returned with a warrant they searched the trailer and found a small amount of marijuana and drug paraphernalia. Charles McArthur was charged with misdemeanor possession.

McArthur moved to suppress the paraphernalia and marijuana as evidence on the GROUNDS that they were the "fruit" of an unlawful police SEIZURE. He claimed that unlawful seizure was the refusal to let him reenter the trailer unaccompanied, which would have permitted him, he said, to "have destroyed the mar-

John Love stands outside Charles McArthur's trailer in Sullivan, Illinois, where he had monitored McArthur for 2 hours while awaiting a search warrant's arrival in 1997.

ijuana." The trial court agreed with McArthur and suppressed the evidence. The Supreme Court of Illinois affirmed this decision, but the U.S. Supreme Court agreed to hear the state's appeal.

The Court, in an 8–1 decision, reversed the Illinois courts. Justice STEPHEN G. BREYER, writing for the majority, held that the brief seizure of the premises was permissible under the Fourth Amendment. Breyer restated the Court's position that the Fourth Amendment's central requirement is one of reasonableness. He also noted that the Court has made exceptions to the search warrant requirement involving "special law enforcement needs, diminished expectations of privacy, minimal intrusions" and other circumstances. In this case the circumstances involved a "plausible claim of specially pressing or urgent law enforcement need."

Justice Breyer refused to invoke a PER SE rule of unreasonableness in these circumstances, which would have made all cases like McArthur's automatically illegal. Instead, Breyer used a balancing test, setting McArthur's PRIVACY concerns against law enforcement-related concerns to determine if the intrusion was reasonable. He concluded that the restriction was reasonable, based on a combination of circumstances. First, police had PROBABLE CAUSE to believe that McArthur's residence contained evidence of illegal drugs. This probable cause was based on his wife's statement, which

appeared to be very reliable. Second, the police had good reason to fear that McArthur would destroy the drugs before they returned with a search warrant if they did not restrain him. Third, the police made reasonable efforts to balance their law enforcement needs with the "demands of personal privacy." Justice Breyer pointed out that the police "neither searched the trailer nor arrested McArthur before obtaining a warrant." Instead "they imposed a significantly less restrictive restraint" on him. Fourth, the police imposed the restraint for a limited period of time, namely two hours. This time period was no longer than reasonably necessary for police to obtain the search warrant.

Justice Breyer buttressed his argument by citing other cases where circumstances dictated the need for police to impose temporary restraints to preserve evidence until a search warrant could be obtained. In fact, Breyer could find no case where the Court had not upheld a temporary seizure that was "supported by probable cause and was designed to prevent the loss of evidence while the police diligently obtained a warrant in a reasonable period of time." Therefore, the search was legal and the evidence seized could be used against McArthur.

Justice JOHN PAUL STEVENS, in a dissenting opinion, contended that the Illinois courts had correctly placed more emphasis on the privacy interests at stake in this case. The invasion of these interests for the sake of prosecuting a very minor offense was unreasonable in Stevens's view.

Indianapolis v. Edmond

In *City of Indianapolis v. Edmond*, 531 U.S. 32, 121 S.Ct. 447, 148 L.Ed.2d 333 (2000), the Supreme Court of the United States struck down a drug interdiction checkpoint program operated by police officers on public roadways during a four-month period in 1998. The court held that the program violated the Fourth Amendment's protection against unreasonable SEARCH AND SEIZURE because it allowed police to stop motorists without a warrant, PROBABLE CAUSE, or a reasonable suspicion of criminal activity.

The case began in 1998 when the Indianapolis Police Department created a vehicle checkpoint program to help stop illegal drug trade in the city. The program ran from August to November and normally operated during daytime hours. Checkpoints were established in six high-crime areas, with 30 officers stationed at each one. The officers were instructed to select five to seven cars in a row for inspection and allow the rest to pass through. Once pulled over, the cars had to be inspected in the order they were stopped, and every motorist was subject to the same procedure.

Drivers were asked to produce a license and registration and were observed for signs of impairment. Officers performed an open-view inspection of all vehicles from the outside. Drug-sniffing dogs checked the exterior of each vehicle for the smell of drugs and narcotics. Officers were prohibited from conducting a complete search of vehicles or motorists unless they either obtained CONSENT or formed a particularized suspicion of criminal activity based on their preliminary investigation.

A police officer later testified that 1,161 vehicles were stopped at the roadblocks. One hundred and four arrests were made, fifty-five for drug-related crimes. Vehicles that were not subject to further processing were stopped for an average of two to three minutes. The program was terminated when aggrieved motorists filed a CLASS ACTION lawsuit against the city, the mayor, and certain members of the police department. But a police sergeant said Indianapolis would resume the program if the defendants eventually prevailed.

The case was tried in the U.S. District Court for the Southern District of Indiana. The plaintiffs asked the court to issue a preliminary injunction against the city's drug interdiction checkpoint program on the grounds that the program allowed motorists to be randomly pulled over by police officers who lacked reasonable suspicion or probable cause to justify a search or seizure. The plaintiffs argued that, unlike alcohol sobriety checkpoints, which the Supreme Court had previously upheld, drug checkpoints do not advance the safety of public roadways. Instead, the plaintiffs contended that the only purpose of drug checkpoints is to catch illegal drug traffickers.

The district court disagreed in *Edmond v. Goldsmith*, 38 F.Supp.2d 1016 (1998), finding that the city's drug interdiction program complied with the Fourth Amendment. Pointing to the 55 drug-related arrests that resulted from the program, the court observed that, like sobriety checkpoints, drug checkpoints are effective in combating a significant societal problem. The court said that the short length of an average stop minimized the intrusion upon the motorist's PRIVACY. Advance notice of the checkpoints was made publicly available. Therefore, motorists who wished to stay off the roadways on the scheduled dates and times could avoid those paths. Finally, the court said that the program restricted officers' discretion so that individual motorists could not be arbitrarily targeted for a search.

The plaintiffs appealed. In a 2–1 decision, the U.S. Court of Appeals for the Seventh Circuit reversed in *Edmond v. Goldsmith*, 183 F.3d 659 (1999). Chief Judge Richard Posner wrote the majority opinion. Ordinarily, the court wrote, a search or seizure will be deemed reasonable under the Fourth Amendment only if it is conducted by a police officer who is acting pursuant to a warrant, probable cause, or a reasonable suspicion that a particular individual is engaged in criminal wrongdoing. An exception to that rule is made when law enforcement is pursuing a purpose higher than ordinary crime detection. Sobriety checkpoints, the court said, further a higher purpose in highway safety. Suspicionless searches and seizures are allowed at sobriety checkpoints because law enforcement has demonstrated their necessity in making public roadways safe from drunk drivers. With drug checkpoints, the court found, no such higher purpose exists. Instead, the court ruled that drug checkpoints are just a pretext for ordinary crime prevention. As a result, they are the very kind of search the Fourth Amendment prohibits absent a warrant or probable cause.

The defendants appealed to the U.S. Supreme Court. Fifteen states, the U.S. Conference of Mayors, and the JUSTICE DEPARTMENT submitted AMICUS CURIAE briefs on their behalf. Justice SANDRA DAY O'CONNOR wrote the majority opinion and was joined by Justices STEPHEN G. BREYER, RUTH BADER GINSBURG, ANTHONY M. KENNEDY, DAVID H. SOUTER, and JOHN PAUL STEVENS. Justices ANTONIN SCALIA and CLARENCE THOMAS joined the dissenting opinion of Chief Justice WILLIAM H. REHNQUIST. Thomas also wrote a dissenting opinion of his own.

The Supreme Court agreed with the seventh circuit's analysis. Suspicionless searches pass constitutional muster, the court wrote, only when they are "designed to serve special needs beyond the normal need for law enforcement." The court provided several examples. Border patrol checkpoints are allowed because it would be highly impractical to require law enforcement agents to possess particularized suspicion of individual wrongdoing with the volume of immigration traffic along the nation's borders. The same rationale applies at government-run airports, where the need to guard against terrorism would be impeded if security personnel were required to establish probable cause before stopping and searching passengers. Finally, the court said that the "immediate, vehicle-bound threat to life and limb" presented by drunk drivers justifies sobriety checkpoints.

In this case the court said that the constitutionality of drug checkpoints must be determined by balancing the competing interests of law enforcement with motorists' privacy rights. The court acknowledged that "traffic in illegal narcotics creates social harms of the first magnitude." The court also conceded that the streets of America would no doubt be safer if random, suspicionless drug checkpoints were permitted to continue. The court even agreed that without drug checkpoints police would encounter more difficulty in distinguishing innocent motorists from those trafficking in narcotics.

Nonetheless, the court concluded that those interests were insufficient to overcome motorists' countervailing right to be free from unreasonable, warrantless searches. "We have never approved a checkpoint program whose primary purpose was to detect evidence of ordinary criminal wrongdoing," the court wrote, and the primary purpose of the Indianapolis narcotics checkpoint program "was in the end to advance the general interest in crime control." Thus, the court concluded that it must invalidate drug checkpoints now "to prevent such in-trusions from becoming a routine part of American life."

In their dissenting opinions Justices Rehnquist and Thomas said that they were not persuaded by the majority's attempt to distinguish illegal drug checkpoints from constitutionally permissible sobriety checkpoints. Rehnquist thought that both types of programs served valid law enforcement interests of fighting crime and promoting public safety. Thomas said the majority's decision was contrary to existing precedent governing border-patrol checkpoints.

Kyllo v. United States

The dramatic growth in surveillance technology has worried many advocates of personal privacy. The ability of law enforcement officers to penetrate the exteriors of homes with electronic signals and obtain evidence of criminal activity has led to calls for an extension of the Fourth Amendment's warrant requirement to cover such intrusions. The debate over this issue was resolved by the Supreme Court of the United States in a landmark ruling that establishes a new standard for such searches. In *Kyllo v. United States*, ___U.S.___, 121 S.Ct. 2038, ___ L.Ed.2d ___ (2001), an alliance of conservative and liberal justices ruled that police must apply for a warrant from court before using a device that can obtain details of a private home that would previously have been unknowable without physical intrusion. If police fail to secure a warrant, the search will be regarded as "presumptively unreasonable" and the evidence the search produced will be inadmissible at trial.

The case involved the use of thermal imaging technology to detect the amount of heat inside a home where police suspected marijuana was being grown. Police in Florence, Oregon, received a tip that Danny Kyllo was growing marijuana inside his home. Because marijuana cultivation requires the use of high-intensity lamps, police used a thermal imager to scan Kyllo's residence. The imager detects infrared radiation, which is invisible to the naked eye. The machine converts the radiation into images based on relative warmth. The police conducted the scan across the street from Kyllo's home, accomplishing the task in just a few minutes. The scan disclosed that a part of his house was substantially hotter than any other unit in his triplex. Based on the scan, utility bills and tips from informants, police secured a search warrant and found that Kyllo had indeed been growing marijuana. He was indicted on a federal drug charge, and after the court refused to

Danny Lee Kyllo stands outside his house where narcotics agents used a thermal imaging device to detect marijuana plants growing in his attic.

suppress the evidence taken in the search, Kyllo entered a conditional guilty plea.

Kyllo appealed the admissibility of the evidence because of the thermal imaging scan. The Court of Appeals for the Ninth Circuit upheld the constitutionality of the scan, concluding that Kyllo had not shown a subjective expectation of privacy because he had made no effort to conceal the heat escaping from his home. Moreover, the scan itself did not disclose any "intimate details" of his life but rather showed "hot spots" on the roof and exterior wall.

The Supreme Court, in a 5–4 decision, overturned the appeals court. The composition of the court majority was striking, as liberal Justices DAVID H. SOUTER, RUTH BADER GINSBURG, and STEPHEN G. BREYER joined conservative Justices ANTONIN SCALIA and CLARENCE THOMAS. Justice Scalia, writing for the majority, acknowledged that in previous cases the Court had ruled that aerial surveillance of private homes and surrounding areas was not a search. However, the present case involved "more than naked-eye surveillance of a home," and the Court had "reserved judgment as to how much technological enhancement of ordinary perception from such a vantage point, if any, is too much." Therefore, the Court could work from a clean slate.

Justice Scalia noted that the degree of privacy guaranteed by the Fourth Amendment had been affected by technological developments.

The question became "what limits there are upon this power of technology to shrink the realm of guaranteed privacy." In his view, individuals had, as a baseline criterion, a "minimum expectation of privacy" that the interiors of their homes were not subject to warrantless police searches. Thus, the use of "sense-enhancing technology" that could obtain information that would otherwise only be obtainable by a physical search was a "search." This meant that any information obtained by the thermal imager was the product of a search. Scalia's analysis led to the legal conclusion that such a search was unreasonable and could only be justified if it was made pursuant to a warrant.

Scalia rejected the government's position that the thermal scan merely captured heat that was radiating from external surfaces. This "off-the-wall" approach made no sense in his view, as a powerful microphone might pick up sounds emanating from a house or a satellite might pick up light emanating from a home. To allow the capturing of information emanating from the home "would leave the homeowner at the mercy of advancing technology-including technology that could discern all human activity in the home." Though the thermal imaging used in Kyllo's case was "relatively crude," Scalia emphasized that the Court's new rule "must take account of more sophisticated systems that are already in use or in development." Therefore, when law enforcement "uses a device that is not in general public use, to explore details of the home that would previously have been unknowable without physical intrusion, the surveillance is a 'search' and is presumptively unreasonable without a warrant." The Court remanded the case to the district court to determine whether the search warrant was supported by probable cause even without the inclusion of the thermal imaging information. But beyond the particulars of the Kyllo case, the Court sharply limited the use of technological surveillance without court oversight.

Justice JOHN PAUL STEVENS, in a dissenting opinion joined by Chief Justice WILLIAM H. REHNQUIST and Justice SANDRA DAY O'CONNOR and ANTHONY M. KENNEDY, argued that the majority's bright line rule was "unnecessary, unwise, and inconsistent with the Fourth Amendment." Stevens endorsed the "off-the-wall" emanation theory proposed by the government. As long as the government did not go "through the wall" with its surveillance technology, it did not perform a Fourth Amendment "search."

Milligan v. City of Slidell

Though all U.S. citizens have constitutional rights, the federal courts have generally been more tolerant about restrictions placed on high school students by school administrators. Numerous court cases have involved the extent and application of First, Fourth, and FIFTH AMENDMENT rights to students. The courts have tried to balance the legitimate rights of students against the rights of school administrators to run safe schools. In general, the courts have given schools latitude with respect to constitutional rights when special circumstances occur. Such was the case in *Milligan v. City of Slidell*, 226 F.3d 652 (5th Cir. 2000), where a federal appeals court ruled that the detention and questioning of students about a potential fight did not violate the Fourth Amendment's prohibition against unreasonable SEARCH AND SEIZURE.

The case grew out of a 1997 fight that involved students attending Salmen and Slidell High Schools in Slidell, Louisiana. Louis Thompson, the father of two sons attending Slidell High, received information from a student that a retaliatory fight would take place against his sons. Thompson contacted a local police officer, Sgt. John Emery, who discussed the possible fight with the Salmen High football coach and Thompson. Thompson compiled a list of Salmen students who might be involved, and Sgt. Emery requested that the vice principal call certain students in for questioning. The vice principal called in the football coach and some

players, who confirmed a fight involving baseball bats was going to happen that afternoon outside Slidell High. Sgt. Emery and a fellow officer warned the students that their parents would be contacted if they were involved in the fight. The meeting ended after fifteen minutes, and the fight did not occur.

Several students filed a CIVIL RIGHTS lawsuit in federal court against the police officers and the city, alleging that their Fourth Amendment rights had been violated when they were called to the meeting with school and police officials. At a BENCH TRIAL, where the judge determined both fact and law, the judge dismissed the city from the lawsuit but found "the two officers had violated the plaintiffs' Fourth Amendment rights." The plaintiffs had not proved that they suffered any harm that required the payment of COMPENSATORY DAMAGES, so the judge awarded them NOMINAL DAMAGES in the amount of one dollar. By awarding nominal damages, the attorneys for the students could not have their attorneys' fees paid by the officers. Both sides appealed.

A three-judge panel of the Court of Appeals for the Fifth Circuit overturned the district court's ruling that the police officers violated the Fourth Amendment. Judge Edith H. Jones, writing for the court, concluded that the district court had misapplied legal precedents to the facts. The district court had characterized the meeting with the students as an "investigative detention" that required "reasonable suspicion of past or incipient criminal activity." Judge Jones stated, "Even if this analysis [is] generally correct for investigative activities . . . it fails in this case because it neglects the all-important school context."

Judge Jones pointed out that the U.S. Supreme Court had examined the role of the Fourth Amendment in the context of schools. Though the Court stated that the protection of the Fourth Amendment applied in schools, "the nature of those rights is what is appropriate for children in school." Whether a search is reasonable "must take into account the schools' custodial and tutelary responsibility for children." In addition, the Court held that students have a "lesser expectation of privacy than members of the population generally."

Judge Jones applied these principles to the Salmen High School meeting. She found that it was unclear whether the students had any PRIVACY interests not to be summoned or detained in a school office for questioning on school discipline issues. Jones rejected the students' claim that they had "a right to remain in class unhindered during the school day." As to the government interest at stake, Jones concluded, "The school sought to protect its students" and deter possible violence. The immediacy of the concerns was apparent, as the fight was to take place in a few hours. Finally, Jones pointed out that questioning by police officers did not change the situation, as school officials could have done the questioning themselves.

The AMERICAN CIVIL LIBERTIES UNION took strong issue with the opinion, feeling it made schools tantamount to prisons, where students forfeited their rights to administrators once they entered the building. In the wake of the Columbine High School shooting and other issues of school safety that have risen in recent years, however, the appeals court ruled that the students' privacy rights did not outweigh the interests of school officials. School officials have the right to control the movement of students in school. The court held that "the officers' actions were reasonable and therefore constitutional."

CROSS REFERENCES
Drugs and Narcotics; Fruit of the Poisonous Tree; Schools; Search and Seizure

FREEDOM OF INFORMATION ACT

A federal law (5 U.S.C.A. § 552 et seq.) providing for the disclosure of information held by ADMINISTRATIVE AGENCIES to the public, unless the documents requested fall into one of the specific exemptions set forth in the statute.

Department of the Interior v. Klamath Water Users Protective Association

The federal Freedom of Information Act (FOIA) seeks to give individuals access to government information. The act makes exceptions, however, to the release of certain information. These exceptions have generated much litigation over their scope and application. The U.S. Supreme Court addressed such issues in *Department of the Interior v. Klamath Water Users Protective Association*, ___ U.S. ___, 121 S.Ct. 1060, 149 L.Ed.2d 87 (2001). In this case the Court ruled that a federal agency could not withhold communications it received from an American Indian tribe based on the claim that the information was attorney work product related to a pending lawsuit.

The case arose when the INTERIOR DEPARTMENT's Bureau of Reclamation sought to develop new water allocations for the Klam-

ath Irrigation Project, which uses water from the Klamath River to irrigate parts of Oregon and California. After the bureau began to formulate allocations of water for tribal and non-tribal users, it asked the Klamath Indian tribe and other tribes to consult with it on the matter. The bureau and the tribes signed a memorandum of understanding that called for consultation between the parties on the impact of the new plan on tribal trust resources. At the same time another Department of Interior agency, the Bureau of Indian Affairs, filed water allocation claims on behalf of the Klamath tribe in Oregon state court. Since this bureau is charged with administering land and water held in trust for Indian tribes, it consulted with the Klamath tribe, and the two exchanged written documents on the appropriate scope of the claims ultimately submitted by the government for the benefit of the tribe.

WATER RIGHTS have always been a source of tension in the West. The Klamath Water Users Protective Association was formed by members who receive water from the irrigation project and "whose interests were adverse" to the Indian tribes. Faced with the prospect of less water in the future, the association sought as much information as it could from the Department of Interior. The association specifically asked, under the FOIA, for communications between the two bureaus and the Indian tribes. The Bureau of Indian Affairs did not turn over everything shared between itself and the affected Indian tribes, however, citing the attorney WORK PRODUCT RULE as its justification.

The association sued in federal district court to compel the release of the seven withheld documents. Three of the documents addressed the irrigation plan, three were concerned with the lawsuit in state court, and one pertained to both topics. The Department of the Interior argued that an exemption to the FOIA protected "from disclosure inter-agency or intra-agency memorandums or letters which would not be available by law to a party other than an agency in litigation with the agency." The district court agreed with the government and dismissed the request. The Court of Appeals for the Ninth Circuit reversed the lower court, however, ruling that the documents generated by the Indian tribes were not "intra-agency" communications. Therefore, the association was entitled to receive the documents.

The Supreme Court, in a unanimous decision, upheld the Ninth Circuit's decision. Justice DAVID H. SOUTER, writing for the Court, noted that to qualify under the FOIA exemption, "a document must satisfy two conditions: its source must be a government agency and it must fall within the ambit of a privilege against discovery under judicial standards that would govern litigation against the agency that holds it." As to the second condition, Justice Souter agreed that it is necessary to allow officials to candidly communicate among themselves without fear that their words will be used in court or become front-page news. He determined that this policy was not at issue in this case, however. The central issue was whether the documents were prepared by a government agency.

Some courts of appeals have held that in certain circumstances a document prepared by a non-government, outside consultant may qualify under the FOIA exemption. Justice Souter had no trouble in acknowledging the propriety of this stance, as the government had hired the consultant from whom it received the communication. He did not agree, though, with the Department of the Interior's contention that the Indian tribes were identical with hired consultants. Souter found that consultants did not communicate with the government in their own interest or on behalf of any person or group whose interest might be affected by the government action addressed by the consultants. He said that the Indian tribes consulted in this case, however, had "their own, albeit entirely legitimate, interests in mind." This fact alone distinguished tribal communications from the consultants' examples recognized by several courts of appeals. Looking at the seven documents in question, Souter found them to be argumentative texts that supported tribal claims. Therefore, the documents were not intra-agency documents that could be exempted from disclosure by the FOIA.

CROSS REFERENCES
Native American Rights; Water Rights

FREEDOM OF SPEECH

The right, guaranteed by the First Amendment to the U.S. Constitution, to express beliefs and ideas without unwarranted government restriction.

Good News Club v. Milford Central School

The debate over separation of church and state is a recurrent one. The Supreme Court of the United States has confronted the issue numerous times in a variety of contexts. One troublesome area has involved the use of public school space by religious organizations for after school activities. Proponents of allowing such organizations access contend that they have as much right as any other organization to use public space and that to refuse such requests violates freedom of speech. Opponents invoke a different part of the First Amendment, arguing that the Establishment Clause prohibits the use of public schools for religious purposes. The Supreme Court resolved the issue in *Good News Club v. Milford Central School,* ___U.S.___, 121 S.Ct. 2093, 154 Ed.LawRep. 45 (2001), when it ruled that a private Christian organization could not be denied use of the public school space for after school activities. The Court emphasized that the Establishment Clause could not serve as a barrier to the organization's exercise of its free speech rights.

The case began when the administration at the Milford Central School in Milford, New York, denied the request of Stephen and Darleen Fournier to use the school's facilities after school to conduct a weekly meeting of the Good News Club. This club, which is a private Christian organization open to children ages 6 to 12, has children memorize Bible verses, sing songs, and listen to a Bible lesson. The administration refused the request because these activities are not discussion-based but are the equivalent of religious instruction. Though the school allowed many other groups, including the Boy Scouts, to use school facilities, the school board concluded that the Good News Club was not acceptable under its community use policy. The Fourniers and the Good News Club filed a federal CIVIL RIGHTS lawsuit in federal court alleging that the denial violated their freedom of speech and violated their EQUAL PROTECTION rights as guaranteed under the FOURTEENTH AMENDMENT. The district court dismissed the lawsuit, and the Court of Appeals for the Second Circuit affirmed the ruling. The appeals court held that because the Club's activities were religious, the school board was entitled to discriminate based on the subject matter. Because other circuit courts of appeal had ruled differently, the Supreme Court agreed to hear the appeal to resolve the issue.

The Court, in a 6–3 decision, reversed the Second Circuit. Justice CLARENCE THOMAS, in his majority opinion, first addressed the freedom of speech argument. He noted that the school was a limited public forum; therefore, the state was not required to permit persons "to engage in every type of speech." However, the state's ability to restrict speech was not unlimited. In addition, the state could not discriminate against speech on the basis of viewpoint. Justice Thomas found the school district decision had unlawfully imposed this requirement. He pointed to recent Supreme Court decisions that had forbade states from preventing religious groups from using public facilities or receiving funding for a college student organization.

Justice Thomas noted that the school board's policy required after school activities to pertain to the "welfare of the community." The Good News Club may have presented its viewpoint from a religious perspective, but it fostered and promoted "morals and character development" that were clearly in the community's interest. Nevertheless, the school excluded the club from its space. Justice Thomas dismissed the appeals court's conclusion that the club's "Christian viewpoint" disqualified it from the use of public space. In the Court's view, for purposes of the Free Speech Clause of the First Amendment, "we can see no logical difference in kind between the invocation of Christianity by the Club and the invocation of teamwork, loyalty, or patriotism by other associations to provide a foundation for their lessons." Thus, the school's refusal constituted viewpoint discrimination and was impermissible.

Milford had contended that even if they had committed viewpoint discrimination, it was justified by the school board's concern not to violate the Establishment Clause. Though Justice Thomas noted that a state interest in avoiding an Establishment Clause violation is "compelling," he concluded that the school district had not established a valid Establishment Clause interest. Thomas based this conclusion on several factors. The club's meetings were held after school, the school did not sponsor them, and they were open to any student who had obtained parental consent, not just to club members. These factors, coupled with the district's policy of making space available to other organizations, minimized any perception that the district favored a particular religion. Thomas also found unpersuasive Milford's argument that students would feel pressured to join the club. The club did not seek special favors but wished to be treated neutrally like other groups. Moreover, children would not feel pressure to join the club because parents had to give permission to have their children attend. The prospect that parents would feel pressure or be confused about whether the school was endorsing religion made little sense. Therefore, the Establishment Clause did not bar the school from allowing the club to use the school facilities.

Justice JOHN PAUL STEVENS, in a dissenting opinion joined by Justices RUTH BADER GINSBURG and DAVID H. SOUTER, equated the club's speech with political advocacy. It was one thing for a group to discuss a topic from a religious or political point of view; it was quite another thing to allow the "Democratic Party, the Libertarian Party or the Ku Klux Klan to hold meetings" in a public facility for the purpose of recruiting members. In his view, "School officials may reasonably believe that evangelical meetings designed to convert children to a particular faith pose the same risk."

CROSS REFERENCES
First Amendment; Religion

GAMING

The act or practice of gambling; an agreement between two or more individuals to play collectively at a game of chance for a stake or wager, which will become the property of the winner and to which all involved make a contribution.

State v. 192 Coin-Operated Video Game Machines

The U.S. gaming industry has grown dramatically since the 1980s. Even though most states permit some form of legalized gambling, the gaming industry must comply with strict laws and regulations. Forms of gambling that are illegal are subject to criminal prosecution. The ability of states to confiscate and destroy illegal gambling devices was challenged but upheld by the supreme court of Carolina in *State v. 192 Coin-Operated Video Game Machines*, 338 S.C. 176, 525 S.E.2d 872 (S.C. Feb 7, 2000), rehearing denied (Mar 9, 2000).

In 1997 a confidential informant told the South Carolina Law Enforcement Division (SLED) that the Collins Entertainment Corporation (CEC) was storing illegal video gambling machines at two sites in Greenville. SLED agents posed as potential buyers of a pool table and visited the sites. They were admitted to both locations and "personally observed the allegedly illegal machines." Armed with this knowledge, SLED obtained a SEARCH WARRANT and seized 192 "Cherry Master" and "8-Liner" video machines. As required by South Carolina law, a judicial MAGISTRATE examined the machines, determined they violated the law, and ordered them destroyed. CEC appealed the destruction

on a number of GROUNDS and the case eventually reached the South Carolina Supreme Court.

The court unanimously upheld the destruction order. Justice E.C. Burnett, writing for the court, noted that the case before them was a civil FORFEITURE action. The prime issue before the court was whether the possession of the machines was unlawful. Justice Burnett, after reviewing the statute's definition of illegal gambling devices concluded that the "machines in question are prohibited by the STATUTE." In addition, CEC had admitted in an AFFIDAVIT that it knew the machines were illegal. Nevertheless, CEC argued that the statute should not be applied.

CEC first argued that a federal law, the Gambling Devices Transportation Act (15 USCA § 1171 et seq.), preempted South Carolina law. It contended that Congress designated these machines as legal and "preempted the power of South Carolina to act when the gambling machines have been placed in the stream of interstate commerce with a destination into any state." Justice Burnett dismissed the PREEMPTION claim. In reviewing the federal law, he found that Congress had not intended to occupy the field of gambling regulation. Instead, he concluded that the federal law was designed to work "in concert with state laws prohibiting gambling." He also found that "the machines in question were not in the stream of interstate commerce" but were articles that had been housed in South Carolina warehouses for two years. It was not enough for CEC to assert that it intended to send the machines to Georgia.

Gamblers play at video poker game machines—similar to those banned in South Carolina—at the Riverfront Station in St. Charles, Missouri, 1996.

CEC also argued that the machines could only be illegal and subject to destruction if they were fully operational. It contended that modern video game machines are really "just a box containing a computer" that "could be configured to play a variety of games," both legal and illegal. Justice Burnett agreed that the technology of slot machines had changed but concluded that the law did not take this difference into account. If the legislature had wanted, it could have modified the statute "to outlaw only the operation, not the mere possession, of gambling machines when it last amended the statute in 1977." Burnett found that the plain language of the law made clear the legislature's intent to outlaw mere possession of gambling machines. Therefore, regardless of their intended use, possession was illegal.

Burnett also rejected the idea that the legislature intended to protect mere storage of the machines. In 1996 the South Carolina Supreme Court invalidated a county-by-county REFERENDUM on video poker. The legislature responded by passing a law that protected owners of video machines who stored them as the counties went through the referendum process again. CEC in this case argued that the law gave them similar protection, as they only stored the machines. Burnett disagreed, noting that the machines in issue "did not become illegal as a result of that referendum, therefore possession of these illegal machines is not protected."

CEC also argued that a local prosecutor had offered advice on how to store the machines in such a way as to make possession of them lawful. Justice Burnett found this defense inapplicable, however, as the question of INTENT is central to criminal charges. This case was a civil forfeiture action, and the official's advice did not make possession of the illegal machines lawful. Burnett also dismissed a host of claims that challenged the legality of the search warrant and the validity of the magistrate's order.

CROSS REFERENCES
Preemption; Search and Seizure

GERRYMANDER

The process of dividing a particular state or territory into election districts in such a manner as to accomplish an unlawful purpose, such as to give one party a greater advantage.

Hunt v. Cromartie

The national debate over race and politics has moved beyond guaranteeing all Americans the right to vote to examining legislative districting based on race. Traditionally, districts in the South were drawn in ways that made it difficult, if not impossible, for African Americans to be elected to Congress. The federal courts have intervened in a number of states, issuing orders that require state legislatures to draw voting districts in nondiscriminatory ways. However, attempts to create districts with a majority of African American voters have led to lawsuits by whites who contend such attempts are nothing more than racial gerrymandering.

Nowhere has the issue of racial gerrymandering been as visible and long-standing as in the state of North Carolina. After the 1990 census a new congressional district was created that followed a major interstate highway through North Carolina. The district stretched 160 miles from Gastonia to Durham, hugging the thin line of Interstate 85. The district was so narrow at one point that drivers in the northbound lane were in the district, while drivers in the southbound lane were in another district. Of the ten counties through which the district passed, five cut into three different districts, with some towns divided. The serpentine district held a majority of African American voters who elected Mel Watts in 1992 to Congress. Watts, along with another candidate, were the first African Americans from North Carolina to hold a congressional seat since 1901. However, opposition to the district sparked a lawsuit by white voters and the North Carolina Republican Party. The case refused to end, leading to three Supreme Court decisions in the 1990s. In *Hunt v. Cromartie*, ___U.S.___, 121 S.Ct. 1452, 149 L.Ed.2d 430 (2001), the Supreme Court of the United States finally put the issue to rest, ruling that a largely black district is constitutional if it is drawn to satisfy political rather than racial motives.

The first lawsuit was dismissed by a three-judge panel, but the Supreme Court reinstated the suit in 1993. It held that the plaintiffs had a cause of action under the FOURTEENTH AMENDMENT's Equal Protection Clause. The Court stated that race-based districts will be considered suspect if they disregard traditional districting principles "such as compactness, contiguity, and respect for political subdivisions." The three-judge panel reviewed the plan again but reiterated that the Twelfth District plan was constitutional. On the second appeal to the Supreme Court, the Court again reversed the lower court. In its 1996 decision it ruled that the redrawing of the district into a "bizarre-looking" shape so as to include a majority of African-Americans violated the Equal Protection Clause. The North Carolina then redrew the district, reducing it to 71 miles in length. The number of African American voters dropped from 57 percent to 47 percent. However, the white plaintiffs still contested the plan as being racially biased and in violation of the Equal Protection Clause.

A third appeal to the Supreme Court came after the three-judge panel ruled the new district unconstitutional. In its 1999 decision the Court held that the lower court had erred by ruling in the plaintiffs' favor on a summary judgment motion. The Court stated that summary judgment is only appropriate where the facts are not in dispute. In this case, North Carolina argued that it had legitimate, nondiscriminatory reasons to justify the new district. The principle justification was that African Americans voters overwhelmingly vote for Democratic Party candidates, an acceptable political reason for creating the district, as such considerations have traditionally been the focus of redistricting. Therefore, the Court sent it back to the three-judge panel for a full hearing. After the hearing the panel again ruled that the plan used race as a predominant factor, which is constitutionally impermissible. This set the stage for the Supreme Court's fourth and final review of the redistricting plan.

The Court, in a 5–4 decision, concluded that the three-judge panel's findings were clearly erroneous and must be reversed. Justice STEPHEN G. BREYER, writing for the majority, stated that the only issue before the Court was whether the three-judge panel had found sufficient evidence to justify its finding that race rather than politics motivated the legislature's redistricting plan. Moreover, the burden was on the plaintiffs to prove that only race could explain the plan. As to the panel's conclusions, Breyer dismissed them as inadequate. The panel had concentrated on voter registration rather than voter behavior. The former emphasized the raw number of African Americans. However, by focusing on the behavior of black voters, a neutral explanation emerged. The legislature had sought to create a "safe" Democratic seat because African Americans tended to vote heavily Democratic.

The majority also rejected statistical evidence provided by the plaintiffs and concentrated on comments by state legislators that indicated that race was only one of several factors that were take into account. Justice Breyer stated that the "Constitution does not place an *affirmative* obligation upon the legislature to avoid creating districts that turn out to be heavily, even majority, minority." As long as "political or traditional" districting motivations proved dominant, the district did not violate the Equal Protection Clause. This ruling seemed to give guidance to legislatures as they prepared again to redraw congressional districts following the 2000 census.

CROSS REFERENCES
Fourteenth Amendment; Voting

GUN CONTROL

Chicago's and Philadelphia's Lawsuits Against Gun Industry Dismissed

The gun industry enjoyed two victories in 2000 year as judges in separate lawsuits in Chicago and Philadelphia dismissed the cities' cases against the industry. Charging the industry with a public nuisance, both cities sought to recover the public costs of gun violence, including medical care, police protection, emergency services, and prison costs. Using a legal theory from recent TOBACCO litigation against cigarette manufacturers, the cities argued that gun manufacturers and distributors were responsible for these costs because they knowingly or negligently sold guns to dealers who then supplied them to criminals. At the time of this book's publication, both cities had appealed the rulings against them.

Chicago filed its lawsuit in November 1998 after an undercover police investigation concluded that gun dealers in Chicago's suburbs were flooding the city with illegal guns. Chicago has a strict ordinance that essentially bans private ownership of handguns, yet handguns proliferate in the city. Undercover officers posing as gang members went into suburban shops and successfully bought guns without a permit—a FELONY offense—often boasting that they would use the guns for criminal activity in the city.

In its lawsuit, Chicago looked to recover $433 million from "22 manufacturers, 12 stores, and 4 distributors" for creating a public nuisance by creating costs for hospitals, police, and fire departments. Announcing the lawsuit in 1998, Mayor RICHARD M. DALEY (see *American Law Yearbook 1999*) said the defendants "knowingly market and distribute their deadly weapons to criminals in Chicago and refuse to impose even the most basic controls." Daley added, "If money is the only language they understand, then money is the language we will use to make them understand that they have no business in Chicago." Spokespeople for the gun industry criticized the lawsuit. The American Shooting Sports Council said, "We, as an industry, really feel there is no basis for a suit against the legitimate sale of a product." The industry argued that the appropriate remedy for illegal gun sales is to enforce existing gun control laws, including prosecuting gun dealers who violate such laws.

Chicago's public nuisance theory was a tactic designed to defeat specific legal defenses anticipated by the plaintiffs. Manufacturers sometimes escape LIABILITY because they have no direct connection with the person who is injured by, or who causes injury with, the manufacturer's product, a legal requirement called PRIVITY. Under the public nuisance theory, Chicago argued that all manufacturers and dealers are responsible for public costs caused by gun violence in proportion to their share of the gun market even without privity. Chicago also intended to use the public nuisance theory to defeat a defense based on the SECOND AMENDMENT to the U.S. Constitution, which protects the right to bear arms: the Second Amendment does not provide manufacturers and distributors the inalienable right to *sell* guns.

Chicago's lawsuit received a boost in June 1999 when the U.S. Bureau of ALCOHOL, TOBACCO, AND FIREARMS (ATF) released a report showing that just 1 percent of federally licensed gun dealers are the source for 45 percent of guns used in crimes in which the guns could be traced back to their dealers. ATF, however, would not release national gun trace and multiple gun purchase data requested by Chicago for the lawsuit. The city had to file a separate lawsuit against ATF to get the data.

In March 2000, under pressure from many lawsuits nationwide, Smith & Wesson, the nation's oldest and largest manufacturer of handguns, entered into a settlement to end many of the cases. Under the agreement, Smith & Wesson agreed to place tamper-proof serial numbers on handguns to prevent criminals from scratching them off. It also promised to manufacture its handguns with trigger locks and to develop "smart-gun technology" to prevent them from being fired by unauthorized users. Smith & Wesson also established a "code of conduct" intended to prohibit its dealers from selling guns at trade shows to buyers without background checks. Chicago, however, chose not to dismiss Smith & Wesson from its lawsuit because the agreement did not provide financial compensation for the public costs of gun violence.

On September 15, 2000, Judge Stephen Schiller of Cook County Circuit Court in Chicago dismissed the city's lawsuit against the gun industry. Judge Schiller opined that Chicago's statistical data did not prove that gun manufacturers are responsible for public costs resulting from criminal gun violence. He suggested that

Chicago use law enforcement to crack down on violators of gun control laws.

Chicago appealed the ruling to the Illinois Court of Appeals, which is reviewing the case as of press time. Meanwhile, the judge in Chicago's case against ATF ruled that the Bureau must release gun trace and purchase data to the city. U.S. District Judge George Lindberg decided that the public need for the data outweighed PRIVACY interests in it. Chicago hoped to use the data to bolster its case against the industry.

Philadelphia filed its lawsuit on April 11, 2000, charging 14 handgun makers with negligently distributing guns to make it easy for criminals and juveniles to buy them. Like Chicago, Philadelphia included Smith & Wesson as a defendant because the manufacturer's March 2000 agreement did not provide financial compensation for public costs of gun violence. In addition to compensation for such costs, Philadelphia aimed to force manufacturers to add safety features to their handguns.

Philadelphia's lawsuit faced a quick defeat, however. Under the Pennsylvania Uniform Firearms Act (PUFA)—for which the gun industry lobbied—Pennsylvania has sole authority to regulate the industry at the state level. On December 20, 2000, U.S. District Judge Berle M. Schiller dismissed Philadelphia's lawsuit, saying that Philadelphia was trying to use the lawsuit to do what cities cannot do by ordinance because of PUFA. Judge Schiller said that a 1999 amendment to PUFA was designed "to prohibit this very case." Judge Schiller also ruled that even without PUFA, Philadelphia could not prove that gun manufacturers could foresee that their guns would be used in crimes. It would be unfair, he concluded, to hold manufacturers responsible for the public costs of criminal gun violence absent such proof.

Philadelphia appealed Judge Schiller's ruling. The city claimed that PUFA only bars lawsuits concerning the legal marketing of guns, not lawsuits concerning manufacturers that knowingly market to criminals. It also alleged that PUFA was unconstitutional as applied to its case. The city's appeal was pending before the U.S. Court of Appeals for the Third Circuit at press time.

HABEAS CORPUS

[*Latin, You have the body.*] A WRIT (court order) that commands an individual or a government official who has restrained another to produce the prisoner at a designated time and place so that the court can determine the legality of CUSTODY and decide whether to order the prisoner's release.

Duncan v. Walker

With the passage of the Anti-terrorism and Effective Death Penalty Act of 1996 (AEDPA), Congress sought to streamline post-conviction appeals proceedings and to curtail the time prisoners could use to seek habeas corpus relief. The AEDPA contains numerous provisions concerning time limits for appeals. In legal parlance these are referred to as STATUTES OF LIMITATIONS. In addition, the statute contains provisions that suspend or toll these statutes of limitations if certain legal actions take place. Though these provisions can be viewed as technical requirements, they play a critical part in limiting post-conviction proceedings. A petition for habeas corpus that misses a statutory deadline must be dismissed.

The Supreme Court of the United States has been called upon several times to interpret the provisions of the AEDPA. In *Duncan v. Walker*, __U.S.__, 121 S.Ct. 2120, __ L.Ed.2d __ (2001), the Court examined a tolling provision. The issue was whether the one-year limitation on filing a federal habeas corpus petition was only tolled by the filing of a state post-conviction proceeding or whether a prior federal habeas petition tolled the deadline as well. The Court held that the tolling provision only applied to state post-conviction proceedings and justified its decision on the plain language of the statute and the purposes behind the law.

Sherman Walker had been convicted of several armed robbery charges in New York state courts. After his last conviction became final with the end of all direct state appeals, Walker filed a habeas corpus petition in federal court in April 1996. In July 1996 the federal district court dismissed the petition because it appeared that Walker had not exhausted all his state post-conviction remedies. However, Walker failed to go back to state court on these issues and chose to file in May 1997 another federal habeas petition in the same federal district court, alleging the same claims as in his first petition. The court dismissed the petition a year later, ruling that under the AEDPA he had until April 1997 to file the petition.

Walker appealed this ruling, and the Court of Appeals for the Second Circuit overruled the district court. The appeals panel reviewed a tolling provision of the AEDPA that states: "The time during which a properly filed application for State post-conviction or other collateral review with respect to the pertinent judgment or claim is pending shall not be counted toward any period of limitation under this subsection." The court agreed with Walker that the time during which his first federal habeas petition was pending should have been excluded when calculating the one-year limitation for his second habeas petition. By tolling this period Walker's second petition would be timely. Because other circuit courts of appeal had ruled to the contrary, the

Supreme Court agreed to hear the case and resolve the issue.

The Supreme Court, in a 7–2 decision, overruled the Second Circuit's interpretation of the AEDPA tolling provision. Justice SANDRA DAY O'CONNOR, writing for the majority, applied rules of statutory interpretation to reach this conclusion. O'Connor noted that Walker and the appeals court had read the word "State" to apply only to the term "post-conviction" and not to the phrase "other collateral review." By dividing the phrase, the first part applied to state proceedings, and the second part could apply to either state or federal proceedings. In her view, however, this was a complete misreading of the provision. Congress had used the word "State" but had not mentioned "Federal" in the sentence. In other parts of the AEDPA, Congress has expressly mentioned "Federal" review. Quoting the law, O'Connor wrote that under a fundamental rule of statutory construction, "'[w]here Congress includes particular language in one section of a statute but omits it in another section of the same Act, it is generally presumed that Congress acts intentionally and purposefully in the disparate inclusion or exclusion." Therefore, the deletion of the term "Federal" was significant. Justice O'Connor concluded that Congress would not have failed to use the term if so intended because the subject matter of the AEDPA was "federal collateral review of state court" decisions.

In addition, Justice O'Connor found that Walker's construction of the statute would make the use of the word "State" superfluous. Again using a rule of statutory interpretation, O'Connor sought to give effect to each word used in the statute and to avoid treating "State" as "surplusage." In addition, she invoked other rules of construction to cement her conclusion that the tolling of the federal deadline was limited to state post-conviction proceedings.

Justice O'Connor also justified the majority's reading of the provision by examining congressional intent. Congress had sought to encourage the full use of state possibilities before allowing a state prisoner to file a federal habeas petition. If the provision were to be applied to federal habeas petitions, as in Walker's case, this purpose would be frustrated and the "piecemeal litigation that the exhaustion requirement" was intended to address would return. The "clear purpose" of the AEDPA was to "encourage litigants to pursue claims in state court prior to seeking federal collateral review." Therefore, the tolling of the one-year filing period for a federal habeas petition applied only to state proceedings.

Justice STEPHEN G. BREYER, in a dissenting opinion joined by RUTH BADER GINSBURG, argued that the Second Circuit decision was correct. He contended that the issue before the court was not a mere technicality but a significant one. It is common for federal courts to dismiss habeas petitions such as Walker's first one because the inmate failed to exhaust all state remedies first. The prisoner loses months of the one-year federal limitations period for making this mistake, and this lost time can result, as in Walker's case, in a dismissal of the second petition for being untimely. Breyer pointed out that it takes federal district courts an average of 268 days to dismiss petitions on procedural grounds. Thus, many federal petitions will miss the deadline. In addition, Breyer argued that the majority's use of rules of statutory construction did not solve the problem because the provision was ambiguous.

Tyler v. Cain

The Supreme Court has sought to strictly enforce the terms of the federal Antiterrorism and Effective Death Penalty Act of 1996 (AEDPA) in a series of rulings on specific provisions of the acts. These rulings have usually been required to resolve conflicting interpretations by the CIRCUIT COURTS of appeals. Though these AEDPA decisions have turned on close readings of STATUTORY language, the rulings have reinforced the congressional desire to limit petitions for habeas corpus by criminals convicted of very serious crimes. The AEDPA places strict limits on the filing of federal habeas petitions and only allows more than one to be filed under two exceptions. One provision requires a prisoner to file a motion asking permission of a circuit court of appeals to file a second habeas petition. In short, the AEDPA seeks to limit a prisoner's postconviction appeal rights and to restrict the discretion of the lower federal courts in making exceptions to the one-habeas-petition requirement.

The Supreme Court, in *Tyler v. Cain*, ___U.S.___, 121 S.Ct. 2478, ___ L.Ed.2d ___ (2001), reaffirmed these policy goals. The Court reviewed the retroactivity provision of the AEDPA, which permits a prisoner to file a second habeas corpus petition in federal court if the prisoner can show that his or her "claim relies on a new rule of constitutional law, made retroactive to cases on COLLATERAL review by the Supreme Court, that was previously unavailable." The Court analyzed this provision and concluded that only a specific ruling by the Court making it constitutionally RETROACTIVE would satisfy this requirement. Such a ruling could not be inferred from the sense of the opinion, nor could it be drawn from a later case that appeared to make the legal principle retroactive.

The case of Melvin Tyler demonstrates what Congress sought to end when it passed the AEDPA. Tyler was convicted in Louisiana state court of second-degree murder for the 1975 shooting and killing of his newborn daughter. The state courts upheld his conviction on direct appeal. Tyler then filed a series of five postconviction RELIEF petitions in state court, alleging constitutional deficiencies at his trial. All of these petitions were denied; by the late 1980s, he had shifted his focus to the federal courts. He filed a habeas corpus petition in federal district court, but it was denied in 1990. Shortly after his petition was denied, the Supreme Court ruled that a jury instruction is unconstitutional if there is a reasonable likelihood a jury understood that it could convict a defendant without finding him guilty beyond a reasonable doubt. Tyler took heart because the decision came out of a Louisiana case, and he believed the same unlawful instruction had been used at his trial.

In 1997 Tyler followed the procedure set out in the AEDPA and asked permission of the Court of Appeals for the Fifth Circuit to file a second federal habeas petition, arguing that the 1990 Supreme Court decision granted him this right. The appeals court granted permission because Tyler had made a PRIMA FACIE case about the applicability of the 1990 ruling. However, Tyler lost his argument in the district court. On appeal, the Fifth Circuit concluded that the 1990 case could not be applied retroactively and that his petition should have been dismissed by the district court. Because other federal circuit courts had come to the opposite conclusion about the retroactivity provision in the AEDPA, the Supreme Court agreed to hear Tyler's appeal.

The Court, in a 5–4 decision, upheld the Fifth Circuit decision. Justice CLARENCE THOMAS, writing for the majority, looked closely at the provision of the AEDPA in question. In analyzing the clause, Thomas concluded that the law's use of the word "made" is synonymous with the word "held." Thus, a new rule of constitutional law is retroactive and hence can be used by a prisoner, only if the Supreme Court's holding states that the rule is retroactive. Thomas emphasized that neither a federal district court or a federal appeals court could "make" the rule retroactive. Moreover, Thomas stated that the Court's reading of the clause was "necessary for the proper implementation of the collateral review structure created by AEDPA." Because an appeals court only has thirty days to consider an application to file a petition for habeas corpus, this "stringent time limit" suggested to Thomas that a court could not conduct exhaustive examination of the legal issues but had to rely on the Supreme Court holdings on retroactivity.

Justice Thomas then examined the 1990 decision that Tyler claimed was retroactive. Thomas concluded that the Court had not made a holding that the rule it announced was retroactive; the Court had only held that the jury instruction in question violated the FOURTEENTH AMENDMENT's DUE PROCESS Clause. In addition, he rejected the claim that a later case had built upon the 1990 decision and that the two decisions, taken together, mandated retroactive application of the rule. Finally, Thomas declined Tyler's request that the 1990 decision should not be made retroactive. Tyler was caught in a "catch 22." Thomas ruled that Tyler had no standing to make the request because his case must be dismissed due to his failure to show that the 1990 decision could be applied retroactively.

Justice STEPHEN G. BREYER, in a dissenting opinion, argued that the two cases dealing with the jury instruction could be said to constitute a "holding." Moreover, Breyer believed the decision in this case would breed more complexity in litigation and would generate "serious additional unfairness" to prisoners seeking habeas relief.

CROSS REFERENCES
Appeal; Statute of Limitations

HATE CRIME

A crime motivated by racial, religious, gender, sexual orientation, or other PREJUDICE.

Aryan Nations Bankrupted by $6.3 Million Verdict

On September 7, 2000, a jury in Kootenai County, Idaho, returned a $6.3 million verdict against Aryan Nations leader Richard Butler and other members of his white supremacist organization. The case grew out of an incident on July 1, 1998, when Aryan Nations guards chased down Victoria Keenan and her son Jason outside the group's compound then held them at

Morris Dees led the hate crime case against the Aryan Nations.

gunpoint and threatened to kill them. The verdict forced Richard Butler to declare BANKRUPTCY in October 2000.

Aryan Nations is a supremacist organization that believes white people are God's true children, Jews are Satan's children, and all minorities are inferior to white people. Richard Butler, an aerospace engineer from California and the group's self-appointed leader, waged the Aryan Nations' campaign from its armed, guarded headquarters in northern Idaho beginning in 1974. There he acted as pastor of the Church of Jesus Christ Christian, which held services in a chapel that used the Israeli flag as a doormat.

On July 1, 1998, Victoria Keenan and her son Jason were traveling home from a wedding in their 1977 Datsun when they stopped outside the Aryan Nations' compound to retrieve Jason's wallet, which had fallen out of the vehicle. When the Keenans started their car to continue on their way, it backfired. Hearing the sound, Aryan Nations guards Jesse Warfield, John Yeager, and Shane Wright jumped into a truck and chased the Keenans for two miles. They later claimed that they thought it was gunfire from militant Jews beginning an attack. Using deadly weapons, including an SKS assault rifle, the guards fired at the Datsun, flattening a tire and sending it off the road into a ditch.

The three men then accosted the Keenans and held them at gunpoint. Warfield grabbed Victoria's hair, yelled at her, hit her with the butt of his weapon, and threatened to kill her

and Jason. One of the men also hit Jason with a hard object. When Victoria begged for her son's life, the men asked if the Keenans were American Indian. Victoria, who is part Cherokee, said she was just a poor white farm girl. Believing the Keenans to be "untainted" whites, the guards let them go.

The Keenans turned to attorney Morris S. Dees, Jr., of the Southern Poverty Law Center (SPLC) for help with their case. Operating from Montgomery, Alabama, often called the birthplace of the CIVIL RIGHTS MOVEMENT, SPLC specializes in helping minorities redress hate crimes and other acts of intolerance. Attorney Dees has developed a legal strategy called "damage litigation" by which he puts hate groups out of business by holding them financially responsible for their members' wrongdoing. Using this strategy, Dees has collected $40 million for plaintiffs in lawsuits against the Ku Klux Klan, bankrupting some groups in the process.

Representing the Keenans in a civil lawsuit in Idaho, Dees set out to bankrupt the Aryan Nations as well. On January 25, 1999, Dees filed a complaint against Butler, the Aryan Nations, and the three guards who attacked the Keenans. Later, Dees added Butler's chief of staff, Michael Teague, to the case as a defendant. Dees charged the defendants with familiar forms of misconduct, such as ASSAULT, BATTERY, and FALSE IMPRISONMENT. He also accused Butler and his organization with RECKLESSNESS and NEGLIGENCE for using Warfield and Yeager as security guards.

The case went to trial in summer 2000. Dees used the theater of the courtroom to put the Aryan Nations' racist beliefs on trial. He urged the jury to be the conscience of the community and to send a message to Butler that the community does not share Butler's vision of America. Warfield and Yeager, both serving time in prison for the attack, testified that they were not members of the Aryan Nations and that they did not act for Butler or his organization when they attacked the Keenans. Yeager testified that he was so drunk during the attack that he could not remember anyone shooting at the Keenans' car. Edgar Steele, the lawyer for Butler and the Aryan Nations, said his clients could not be responsible for the unauthorized acts of drunken security guards.

On September 7, 2000, the jury sent a strong message to hate groups in America by returning a $6.3 million verdict in favor of the Keenans. The verdict was divided into $330,000 for COMPENSATORY DAMAGES and $6 million for PUNITIVE DAMAGES. The jury assessed $4.8 million of the punitive award against Butler and the Aryan Nations, $600,000 against chief of staff Teague, $500,000 against Warfield, and $100,000 against Yeager. In interviews after delivering the verdict, jurors said the question never was whether to punish Butler, but how much to punish him.

Steve Judy, mayor of the small town haunted by the case, said the verdict sent a strong message that Coeur D'Alene cares about human rights and that white supremacists are a small minority in northern Idaho. Attorney Dees also welcomed the verdict, saying he would use it to take the compound away from the hate group and force it to stop using its name. Butler scoffed at the whole case, calling it an attack on white people and a "rape of the American justice system." Speaking to reporters over the shouts of protestors telling him to leave the state, Butler said the Aryan Nations has "planted seeds" in northern Idaho with people who have "escaped multiculturalism or diversity or whatever you want to call it." Teague added, "we will continue the message of Aryan Nations and the white race as long as we live."

Attorney Steele asked Judge Charles Hosack either to reduce the size of the verdict or give his clients a new trial, both of which the judge declined to do. Although Butler considered filing an appeal, he eventually agreed to use the compound to satisfy the verdict and to retire use of the Aryan Nations' name. In the end, Butler had to file for bankruptcy, so the Keenans bought the 20-acre compound at a bankruptcy court sale for $250,000 in February 2001. Attorney Dees suggested that the compound could be used as a center to promote tolerance. Jason Keenan said he and his mother might sell it to a human rights organization "to get the evilness out of there and turn it around to something positive."

Soon thereafter, online Prodigy creator Greg Carr donated $250,000 to buy the compound from the Keenans. Carr plans to turn the site into a human rights center with a museum, peace park, and education center. Carr wants the center to teach local children, "Each person has their own worth, and everyone should have the opportunity to pursue their dreams." In a parallel move, millionaire R. Vincent Bertollini, founder of the racist 11th Hour Remnant Messenger group, bought a home five miles from Coeur d'Alene and minutes from the old compound for Butler to continue his Aryan Nations campaign.

Growing Number of Hate Sites on the Internet

Although the concept of hate is not a new one, the technological advancement of the Internet has provided a new forum for the topic, allowing dangerous and provocative messages to be sent into homes across the nation. The increasing number of hate sites on the Internet has prompted wide-ranging debates concerning weighty issues such as the scope of FREEDOM OF SPEECH, racism, anti-Semitism, and speech-induced violence. The effect of the increasing number of hate sites on the Internet, which has more than doubled over the past few years, has been most notable within the context of various civil and criminal lawsuits on the state and federal level.

An example of one such lawsuit that captured the nation's attention originated in the town of Reading, Pennsylvania. There, a hate group leader named Ryan Wilson faced a civil lawsuit brought in federal court for his alleged threats on the life of a local fair-housing advocate named Bonnie Jouhari. A white woman with a bi-racial daughter, Jouhari orchestrated a seminar on how hate groups use the Internet for recruitment and intimidation. In connection with her work in his arena, Jouhari appeared on a cable news television program where she detailed her employment as a CIVIL RIGHTS activist. Wilson took photographs from this interview and posted Jouhari's image on the website named Alpha HQ, hosted by his own Philadelphia-based neo-Nazi group by the same name. The caption accompanying her photo labelled Jouhari as a "race traitor" and stated that eventually she would be "hung from the neck from the nearest tree or lamppost."

When state officials became aware of these threats, the Pennsylvania ATTORNEY GENERAL filed suit in federal court for equitable RELIEF. In particular, the attorney general sought a permanent INJUNCTION that would serve to prevent Wilson and Alpha HQ from using the website to make such threats. In October 1998 the cause of action was found to be meritorious and, consequently, the website was removed from the Internet at that time. The termination of the Alpha HQ website did not, however, put an end to the controversy surrounding Jouhari's work. To the contrary, death threats continued to be made toward Jouhari and her daughter, Dani. These threats were so pervasive that Jouhari and Dani chose to flee their Reading home, only to have the threats travel with them to their new destination. At this point, the Department of

HOUSING AND URBAN DEVELOPMENT (HUD) decided to take action.

In a case believed to be the first of its kind, HUD brought a lawsuit in federal court, alleging that defendants Wilson and other members of Alpha HQ violated the Fair Housing Act by utilizing the Internet to make death threats against the fair housing advocate. In December 1998 HUD won the case by default when the defendants failed to appear in court. In May 2000 Roy Frankhouser, a former Pennsylvania Ku Klux Klan leader convicted in the lawsuit, agreed to pay Jouhari and her daughter 10 percent of his annual income for ten years and to formally apologize to them on his cable television program.

The growing number of hate sites on the Internet is said to be caused by several factors. The Internet is a broad communication tool, which is a relatively inexpensive means of reaching a large number of prospective recruits for any organization. As opposed to other media, no mailing lists are required, and the attention of many young people may be easily gained. This recruitment of teenagers and even young children is one of the principal reasons why the topic of hate sites on the Internet evokes such intensely heated debate.

For instance, a youth-targeted website sponsored by the Ku Klux Klan features characters from television's *Sesame Street* program. On that particular site, the character Bert is shown waving the Klan flag and standing beside a hooded Klansman. The caption accompanying this image reads, "Bert Supports the Klan." Whether this usage of the character was approved by the holders of its COPYRIGHT remains to be seen. The result, however, is that the advertisement reaches children. Another hate site targeted toward children was started by the eleven-year-old son of Don Black, the man referred to as the founder of the Internet's first hate site, Stormfront.com.

While organizations such as the AMERICAN CIVIL LIBERTIES UNION argue that hate speech is a protected form of expression per the U.S. Constitution, other advocates seek to ban such speech from the Internet entirely. A discussion concerning this issue necessarily involves a balancing of competing interests. Among other concerns, the importance of freedom of speech as provided in the FIRST AMENDMENT must be weighed against the effects of the hate speech.

CROSS REFERENCES
Damages; First Amendment; Freedom of Speech

HEALTH CARE LAW

Maine Faces Court Battle to Save Prescription Drug Cost Cutting Legislation

Given skyrocketing prescription drug prices in America and the failure of Congress to control them, Maine enacted the first state legislation to cut costs on May 11, 2000. Three months later, the prescription drug industry, led by Pharmaceutical Research and Manufacturers of America (PhRMA), filed a federal lawsuit challenging the Maine Rx Program as unconstitutional. On October 26, 2000, a federal judge issued a PRELIMINARY INJUNCTION to prevent the law from taking effect as planned on January 1, 2001. In his decision, Judge D. Brock Hornby said the law probably is unconstitutional, so Maine may not enforce the law pending a full and final decision in the case. Maine appealed the preliminary injunction to the First Circuit Court of Appeals, where the case was pending at press time.

Maine's law was the result of a curious situation faced by Americans with respect to prescription drugs. The National Institutes of Health uses federal taxpayer money to fund pharmaceutical research and then transfers the PROPERTY RIGHTS in new drugs to private corporations, which turn around and make huge profits selling the drugs to the public that funded the research in the first place. Americans often pay two to four times as much for these drugs as people pay in Canada, Great Britain, Australia, Mexico, and other countries where the national government negotiates with American manufacturers for lower prices on behalf of its citizens. In the United States, prescription drug prices continue to rise 15 percent annually, outpacing inflation and making the pharmaceutical industry one of the most profitable industries in the world.

Americans with private health insurance that pays for prescription drugs often do not notice the high prices involved. Those without insurance, however, and many poor and elderly people covered by MEDICAID must pay retail prices out of their own pockets. A 1998 report from the U.S. House of Representatives showed that the average retail price is 86 percent higher for the elderly than the price charged to the federal government and health maintenance organizations (HMOs), each of which having substantial bargaining power.

Uninsured people respond to this predicament in many ways. Some travel to Canada to buy prescription drugs, where prices on average are 37 percent lower than in Maine. Some are forced to choose between buying food and filling their prescriptions. Others skip doses, split pills, or decline to fill their prescriptions at all.

On May 11, 2000, Maine enacted an "Act to Establish Fairer Pricing for Prescription Drugs." The Act directs the Commissioner of Maine's Department of Human Services to negotiate with drug manufacturers for rebates for the half million Maine citizens who lack insurance for prescription drugs. The Commissioner must place the rebate money into a fund to compensate pharmacies for the lower prices they receive from Maine Rx Program participants. The Act directs the commissioner to identify publicly those manufacturers refusing to participate in the rebate program and also to place their drugs on the state's Medicaid "prior authorization" program. Under that program, the state Medicaid administrator must approve a drug before it may be dispensed to a Medicaid recipient.

The Act also sets up a 12-person commission to review drug prices and availability in the state. If the commission determines as of January 5, 2003, that prices are not reasonable, the state may begin imposing price limits instead of just negotiating for rebates. Any manufacturer who is guilty of "profiteering" under the Act— for example, by charging excessive prices or restricting drug supplies— would face penalties of up to $100,000 per incident.

Governor Angus King signed the Act after it passed overwhelmingly in the state legislature, announcing, "If the industry can consolidate and increase its market power, so can we." Maine Senator Chellie Pingree said, "This makes Maine the first state to say, 'Americans shouldn't be subsidizing low prices for prescription drugs around the world.'" Speaking for the industry, however, President Alan F. Holmer of PhRMA said the new law would hurt Maine's biotechnology industry, discourage investment in the state, and restrict drug supplies. PhRMA spokeswoman Gabrielle Williams added that price controls would remove the financial incentive for drug research and development. After Maine enacted the law, Holmer called it "the most antibusiness state in the United States." Governor King called the accusation "utter nonsense."

In early August 2000, drug manufacturer SmithKline Beecham announced that it would stop shipping drugs to wholesalers in Maine, restricting its supplies to wholesalers outside the state. SmithKline spokesman Thomas Johnson said the decision would not hurt drug supplies in the state because wholesalers would still ship drugs to Maine. Maine Commissioner of Human Services, Kevin W. Concannon, however, said the move would increase drug prices because of the costs of transportation from out-of-state.

Weeks later, PhRMA filed a lawsuit in the U.S. District Court for the District of Maine. PhRMA seeks to strike down the Maine Rx Program as unconstitutional. The industry says the law violates the Commerce Clause of the U.S. Constitution, which gives the U.S. Congress, not the states, the power to regulate commerce between the states. PhRMA says the Act regulates the price that out-of-state manufacturers receive for out-of-state sales of drugs that patients eventually purchase at retail in Maine. PhRMA also says the Act violates the SUPREMACY CLAUSE of the U.S. Constitution, which says federal laws are supreme and must be obeyed by the states. The Act violates the Supremacy Clause, according to PhRMA, by placing drugs on the Medicaid prior authorization program—a *federal* program—for reasons not authorized by federal Medicaid legislation or regulations.

Maine says the Commerce Clause does not apply to the Act because Maine is not regulating commerce but rather is acting as a market participant by negotiating with drug manufacturers for lower drug prices. The U.S. Supreme Court has said that the Commerce Clause does not apply when a state acts as a market participant and not a regulator. Even if the Commerce Clause applies, Maine says the Act is not unconstitutional because it does not burden commerce between the states. Manufacturers are asked for rebates whether they are in or out of state and whether or not they ship drugs across state lines. Finally, Maine claims the Act is valid under the Supremacy Clause because the federal Medicaid program allows states to place drugs on the prior authorization program, which states do all the time. Finally, Maine asserts that the Act does not permit the imposition of prior authorization if to do so would deprive Medicaid recipients of the drugs they need, thus satisfying federal Medicaid laws.

PhRMA filed a motion for a preliminary injunction, asking the court to stop Maine from enforcing the Act's "profiteering" provision and from penalizing manufacturers who fail to participate in the rebate program pending a final decision in the case. On October 26, 2000, Judge

Hornby granted the motion, going so far as to assess PhRMA's chances of winning the lawsuit as "overwhelming." Maine appealed that decision to the First Circuit Court of Appeals, which heard arguments in early March 2001.

During oral arguments before the U.S. Circuit Court of Appeals in Boston, Massachusetts, PhRMA attorney Kathleen Sullivan said the statute amounts to "an extra-territorial regulation of a transaction that is not taking place in Maine." Ms. Sullivan, who is dean of the Stanford University Law School, said the law would allow Maine to tax out-of-state sales. "The state is saying, 'You shall enter into a rebate agreement and there's a hammer if you don't.'" Maine reiterated its previously stated arguments against the allegations. A decision from the First Circuit was pending at press time.

Reynolds Metal Co. v. Ellis

Employers have seen employee health insurance costs skyrocket during the 1990s. As these costs have risen, employers have sought reimbursement for out-of-pocket health care costs from employees who have received large damage AWARDS for their injuries. Moreover, these companies have included reimbursement clauses in their health insurance agreements that employees must sign. Despite this company action, FEDERAL COURTS are split as to whether federal law permits such reimbursement. The U.S. Court of Appeals for the Ninth Circuit in *Reynolds Metal Co. v. Ellis*, 202 F.3d 1246 (9th Cir.2000) rejected such an approach by an employer. It ruled that absent some type of fraud or wrongdoing on the part of the employee, federal law did not permit such reimbursement. The law remains unclear in this area, however, because of a contrary ruling by the Court of Appeals for the Eleventh Circuit. The Supreme Court agreed to hear Reynolds Metal's appeal in this case, but ultimately Reynolds Metal asked that its appeal be dismissed, leaving the issue unsettled. The issue remains an important one as health care costs continue to burden U.S. employers.

The case began when Robert Ellis, a Reynolds Metal employee, was seriously injured in an automobile accident. The medical costs, which amounted to over $561,000, were paid for by Reynolds Metal's group medical plan. Three years after his accident, Ellis secured a settlement from those who caused the auto accident. The settlement was in excess of the medical costs absorbed by the health plan. Until the 1990s, that would have been the end of it, but the Reynolds Metal health plan included a con-

tractual reimbursement clause. This clause stated that if Ellis received any payment from a third party, he was obligated to reimburse the plan for his medical costs up to, but no more than, the amount of the third party settlement. When Reynolds Metal became aware of the financial settlement, it asked Ellis to reimburse it the $561,000. He refused, and Reynolds Metal filed a lawsuit in federal court demanding reimbursement.

Reynolds Metal based its civil action on the federal EMPLOYEE RETIREMENT INCOME SECURITY ACT (ERISA), a complicated STATUTE that governs retirement and benefit obligations for employers. Reynolds Metal sought enforcement of its contract clause by relying on a claims procedure set out in ERISA. Reynolds Metal pointed to one of the nine enforcement provisions which states that a FIDUCIARY can seek "appropriate equitable relief" to redress a violation of a health care plan. In this case there was no question that Reynolds Metal was an ERISA fiduciary, meaning it was in a TRUST relationship with another person. Therefore, the sole issue was whether Reynolds Metal was seeking equitable or legal RELIEF.

Civil remedies are divided into legal and equitable relief. Legal relief is the most easily understood, as the plaintiff asks the court for money DAMAGES. Equitable relief is much different; the plaintiff asks the judge, rather than a jury, for an order that directs the defendant to do or not to do something. In some cases this action may involve the return of something of value. In other cases it comes in the form of restitution; in this form the plaintiff alleges that the defendant was unjustly enriched by unlawfully taking the plaintiff's property. In the case at hand, the distinction between legal and equitable relief meant either that Reynolds Metal was entitled to total reimbursement or to none at all. The federal district court ruled that Reynolds Metal could claim nothing. Reynolds Metal then appealed to the Ninth Circuit.

Circuit Judge Betty B. Fletcher, writing for the three-judge appeals panel, ruled that Reynolds Metal may have sought a court order, also known as an INJUNCTION, that would require Ellis to reimburse the health plan but what Reynolds Metal really wanted was money. In Fletcher's view, Reynolds Metal was trying to mischaracterize its claim in order to qualify for ERISA jurisdiction. Fletcher noted that the law on this issue had been settled in the Ninth Circuit in a prior case, *MC Medical Plan v. Owens*, 122 F.3d 1258 (9th Cir. 1997). Reynolds Metal conceded as much, yet demanded that the full Ninth Circuit hear its appeal, because it believed the CIRCUIT COURT had strayed from a recent U.S. Supreme Court ruling.

Judge Fletcher and the panel were not persuaded that the Ninth Circuit was in error. Fletcher pointed out that the facts in *Owens* were almost identical to the present case. In the prior decision the court had rejected the claim that the employer was seeking equitable SUBROGATION. Subrogation allows a person to step into the shoes of another person to pursue a third party TORTFEASOR. This did not make sense because Reynolds Metal did not seek to go after the parties that injured Ellis; instead, Reynolds Metal wanted to be reimbursed from the proceeds Ellis obtained himself. Fletcher examined several other technical theories of equitable relief offered by Reynolds Metal but found those wanting, too. Finally, she disputed the idea that the circuit had misapplied Supreme Court precedent. She noted that none of the factual or legal underpinnings of the Supreme Court decision was pertinent to the Reynolds Metal claim. Therefore, the *Owens* precedent dictated that the claim for reimbursement be dismissed.

CROSS REFERENCES
Commerce Clause; Medicaid; Supremacy Clause

HOMELESS PERSON

An individual who lacks housing, including an individual whose primary residence during the night is a supervised public or private facility that provides temporary living accommodations, an individual who is a resident in transitional housing, or an individual who has as a primary residence a public or private place not designed for, or ordinarily used as, a regular sleeping accommodation for human beings.

New York City's Employed Homeless Win Back Pay Award

In October 2000 approximately 200 homeless persons in New York City received the first distribution of an $816,000 settlement award stemming from work they performed in the 1990s for $1 an hour. The settlement was in the form of back wages owed by two business districts, licensed by the city, that hired the plaintiffs to perform menial jobs. The plaintiffs had actually won their seven-year case against the districts in 1998 but never received the award because of an appeal.

Defendants Grand Central Partnership and 34th Street Partnership were two of 40 "business improvement districts" (BIDs) under contract with New York City administrators to provide private sanitation, security, and tourism services to local business areas in return for additional city-authorized property tax assessments. First created by the state legislature in 1982, New York City's BIDs had been largely successful in rehabilitating and reviving several failing intra-city business districts. While they were subject to AUDIT and loss of contract, the BIDs generally operated independently—with a president and a managing board—and managed their own budgets. Defendant Grand Central Partnership (GCP) managed a $10 million contract to provide services in the area bound by 35th and 54th Streets and 2nd to 5th Avenues in Manhattan.

Despite the general success, several BIDs had come under increasing scrutiny for such violations as questionable bookkeeping practices, making illegal loans, using illegal immigrants for cheap labor, and entangling with local businesses to the point of patent conflicts of interest. More serious complaints surfaced in 1995 when the *New York Times* reported that GCP "outreach workers," organized to offer homeless persons referral services for food, shelter, and counseling, were in fact rousting up persons, beating them, and physically forcing them off sidewalks and out of the BID areas. Following formal investigation, the Department of HOUSING AND URBAN DEVELOPMENT (HUD) canceled its $500,000 grant to GCP for homeless programs. The self-described "goon squad" incident also served as the basis for the present lawsuit.

In the CLASS ACTION case of *Archie v. Grand Central Partnership, Inc.*, 997 F. Supp. 504 (S.D.N.Y., 1998), the plaintiffs had worked and performed various services for the defendant BIDs during the 1990s, including security services, street cleaning, maintenance, food service, and clerical/administrative duties, all for $1 an hour. Complaints eventually reached the nonprofit advocacy group of the Urban Justice Center, which did the initial legal work. They were joined by advocates from the Coalition for the Homeless. Plaintiffs' counsel also enlisted the help of several local corporate lawyers, headed by attorney Jennifer L. Kroman, who jointly waived more than $1 million in legal fees to assist. Suit was filed in the U.S. District Court for the Second District in Manhattan, alleging, among other things, violations of federal

Among the homeless workers who received retroactive compensation were those who cleaned the street around the Grand Central Terminal, seen here in 1991.

MINIMUM WAGE laws. The Manhattan DIS-TRICT ATTORNEY also brought several criminal INDICTMENTS for the alleged physical AS-SAULTS upon the homeless persons.

In March 1998 U.S. District Court Judge Sonia Sotomayor held that the defendant BIDs unlawfully had paid the plaintiffs sub-minimum wages, used the cheap labor to undercut competitors and padded executive salaries with the excess. Daniel Biederman, president of Defendant GCP, was also in violation of city rules that prohibited individuals from heading more than one BID. Biederman's yearly compensation was approximately $335,000 plus benefits. In July 1998 New York Mayor RUDY GIULIANI terminated the GCP's contract; the city itself offered the additional services until businesses in the area voted to form a new BID.

Following the decision, the defendants appealed. Their key defense was that plaintiffs were participating in job-training programs and were accordingly not entitled to minimum wages. During the protracted appellate proceedings, a settlement was reached in which defendants agreed to pay $816,000 to approximately 198 plaintiffs. On October 26, 2000, the first $400,000 of the settlement was disbursed to about 70 plaintiffs. The volunteer corporate counsel for the plaintiffs also succeeded in negotiating with local banks to offer free accounts for low-income plaintiffs.

Notwithstanding settlement of the matter, other challenges to the BIDs have continued. In *Kessler v. Grand Central District Management Association*, 158 F.3d 92 (2nd Circuit, 1998), non-property-owning citizens challenged the voting structure for the BID's management board, alleging that it violated the constitutional guarantee of "one person, one vote." While the case turned on the fact that the BID was meant to supplement, rather than substitute for, the services provided by the city, constitutional issues remain. Votes are weighted by the value of land owned, and the same is true for membership on the managing board. According to the Court of Appeals for the Second Circuit, the thin veil of distinction is that properly-structured BIDs are private entities assisting local governments; they are accountable to the business owners and not to the governments themselves. One of the proofs supporting this distinction is that governments may sever or terminate their relationship or funding to the BIDs, whereas a government could not terminate funding to or sever its own arm or subdivision.

CROSS REFERENCES
Back Pay Award; Employment Law

IMMUNITY

Exemption from performing duties that the law generally requires other citizens to perform, or from a penalty or burden that the law generally places on other citizens.

Saucier v. Katz

The Supreme Court of the United States has made it increasingly more difficult for individuals to sue law enforcement officers for damages for allegedly violating their CIVIL RIGHTS. The Court has used official immunity as the vehicle for this policy. Unlike legislators and judges, who enjoy absolute immunity from civil damages lawsuits, enforcement officers only possess a qualified immunity. A court must review their applications for immunity and determine if they qualify. The qualifications for immunity have undergone a number of modifications since the 1960s, but the Supreme Court settled on a formula in late 1980s that remains good law. Nevertheless, the Court was called upon in *Saucier v. Katz*, ___U.S.___, 121 S.Ct. 2151, ___ L.Ed.2d ___ (2001), to decide how this formula applied to cases where the plaintiff alleges that the officer used excessive force. The Court reasserted its general belief that law officers must be given the benefit of the doubt that they acted lawfully in carrying out their day-to-day activities.

The case arose out of an attempted 1996 political demonstration by Elliot M. Katz, president of the organization In the Defense of Animals. A ceremony was held at the Presidio, in San Francisco, California, in which Vice President AL GORE, gave a speech that marked the conversion of the military base to a national park. Katz, concerned that the Presidio's medical facilities would be used to experiment with animals, concealed a cloth banner under his coat when he entered the base. The banner stated: "Please Keep Animal Torture Out of Our National Parks." Located at the front of the public seating area, Katz jumped to his feet and unfurled the banner as Gore began to speak. Military officer Donald Saucier and another officer immediately grabbed and picked up Katz. They took Katz, half-walking, half-dragging, to a nearby military van. Katz alleged that they shoved or threw him into the van. Katz caught himself to avoid any injury. He was driven to a military police station and was released a short time later.

Katz sued Saucier for violating his FIRST AMENDMENT right to free speech and for violating his FOURTH AMENDMENT rights by using excessive force to arrest him. It was at this point that Saucier claimed immunity from the lawsuit and asked the court to dismiss the action. Though the court dismissed a number of Katz's claims, it refused to dismiss the excess force claim because there was a dispute over the facts. The Court of Appeals for the Ninth Circuit upheld the ruling. In interpreting Supreme Court immunity tests, it first established that the law governing the issue was "clearly established." However, it declined to apply the second part of the test, which is to determine if a "reasonable officer could have believed, in light of the clearly established law, that his conduct was unlawful." The appeals court declined to apply the second step because it believed the qualified immunity inquiry and the merits of the

Fourth Amendment excessive force claim were identical. Therefore, it denied Saucier immunity so both sides could present to a jury evidence of the reasonableness of the force.

The Supreme Court, in an 8–1 decision, overturned the Ninth Circuit decision. Justice ANTHONY M. KENNEDY, writing for the majority, concluded that the appeals court had failed to follow the proper sequence of analysis and had ignored the policy behind the qualified immunity test. One goal of qualified immunity is removing the defendant from the lawsuit as quickly as possible, thereby reducing legal costs. Kennedy restated the principle that immunity is not a "mere defense" to liability but an "immunity from suit." Therefore, immunity issues must be resolved as early as possible.

Justice Kennedy then undertook the qualified immunity analysis that the Ninth Circuit cut short. He agreed that as to the first step the case revealed a "general proposition" that excessive force is contrary to the Fourth Amendment. However, a more specific inquiry must take place to see whether a reasonable officer "would understand that what he is doing violates that right." As to this second step, Justice Kennedy rejected the idea that because the plaintiff and the officer disputed certain facts there could be no short-circuiting of this step. He stated: "The concern of the immunity inquiry is to acknowledge that reasonable mistakes can be made as to the legal constraints on particular police conduct." Officers have difficulty in assessing the amount of force that is required in a particular circumstance. If their "mistake as to what the law requires is reasonable, however, the officer is entitled to the immunity defense."

Kennedy concluded that Saucier was entitled to immunity as his conduct was reasonable. He found that Saucier "did not know the full extent of the threat . . . how many other persons there might be" who could have posed a threat to Vice President Gore. Therefore, the court directed that Saucier be granted immunity and his case dismissed.

Justice DAVID H. SOUTER dissented only as to the Court's determination of immunity. He believed the case should have been sent back to the district court for a full application of the immunity test to see if Saucier qualified.

CROSS REFERENCES
Civil Rights; First Amendment; Fourth Amendment

IMPEACHMENT

A process used to charge, try, and remove public officials for misconduct while in office.

New Hampshire's Chief Justice Not Impeached

Though the U.S. Constitution, as well as state constitutions, give the legislature the power to impeach an executive branch or JUDICIARY officer, the impeachment process is seldom used. Because legislatures are political bodies, impeachment is often viewed as a political rather than a legal process. This perception can cause deep divisions within the populace and diminish respect for the three branches of government. Nevertheless, when official conduct appears to violate legal and ethical standards, impeachment may be used in an attempt to remove an official from office.

Such was the case in the state of New Hampshire when Supreme Court Chief Justice David Brock faced charges of lying under oath to impede an investigation into his court. Though the New Hampshire House of Representatives voted to impeach Brock, the Senate acquitted him of all charges in October 2000. Brock retained his office, but the damage to the reputation of the state supreme court was severe after the public learned of serious charges of misconduct by Brock and other members of the court.

The controversy began when Justice Stephen Thayer "tried to influence the appointment of judges to hear an appeal in his own divorce case." Such conduct violates the canons of judicial conduct. When a judge has a conflict of interest in a case to be heard by the court, the judge is supposed to RECUSE him or herself. This means that the judge will not participate in the case in *any* way. By doing so, the judge maintains the neutrality of the court and prevents the appearance of impropriety. At a February 2000 court meeting, however, Chief Justice Brock mentioned to the assembled judges, including Thayer, the name of a judge who would sit on Thayer's appeal. Instead of remaining silent, Thayer discussed the wisdom of the appointment. He later claimed that Brock solicited his opinion about the divorce panel outside the conference room, which would have been both unethical and illegal.

The clerk of the New Hampshire Supreme Court, Howard Zibel, learned of the incident and wrote a memorandum to the state's attorney general, Peter McLaughlin, reporting the details of the incident and his unease at the conduct.

McLaughlin launched an investigation. By March 2000, McLaughlin threatened to seek a GRAND JURY indictment against Thayer for allegedly violating the state's improper influence and OBSTRUCTION OF JUSTICE laws. Thayer ended this part of the controversy by resigning on March 31 in return for immunity.

Thayer's resignation did not end the inquiry. The House of Representatives voted in April to have its judiciary committee determine whether Brock and two associate justices were guilty of impeachable offenses. In July the committee recommended only the impeachment of Brock, and a week later the house voted for articles of impeachment. Brock was charged with soliciting Thayer's opinion on the replacement judges, calling a trial judge in 1989 who had ruled in a lawsuit involving a powerful legislator, lying to the judiciary committee about a number of matters, and failing to administer a proper judicial recusal policy. As to the last issue, the investigation discovered that judges who had recused themselves from hearing specific cases nevertheless read the draft opinions in such cases and made suggestions.

Chief Justice Brock, a member of the state supreme court since 1978 and chief justice since 1986, vigorously defended himself at the Senate trial held in October 2000. As to the charge of making an improper phone call on behalf of a state senator, Brock testified that he had called a court clerk to check on the status of the case because the senator had complained that nothing was happening. He also claimed that the trial court judge then called him. The former senator also testified that he never asked Brock for special treatment. However, the trial court judge testified that he had never initiated a call to the chief justice. In addition, Brock was charged with failing to inform his colleagues of the phone call when the case came before them on appeal. Brock admitted skirting the truth when he answered questions asked by investigators, but he claimed some of the questions were confusing. He also said that in maintaining the confidentiality of court proceedings he was less than candid.

On October 11, 2000, the Senate acquitted Brock of all four counts. None of the votes were close. A number of senators characterized Brock's conduct as unintended mistakes and lapses in judgment. Brock returned to the bench and sought to reestablish the credibility and integrity of the institution. In response to the failure of judges to remove themselves totally from cases in which they had an interest, the

David Brock stands in the courtroom after his impeachment trial ends with an acquittal.

court adopted a new disqualification policy. Under this policy judges will have to recuse themselves completely from all matters relating to any case in which they have an interest. Brock admitted at the impeachment trial that he had made a mistake when he continued the old, ineffective recusal policy after he became chief justice in 1986.

CROSS REFERENCES
Ethics; Judge; Separation of Powers

INCARCERATION

Confinement in a jail or prison; imprisonment.

Atwater v. City of Lago Vista

The FOURTH AMENDMENT protects citizens against unreasonable SEARCHES AND SEIZURES by law enforcement officers. An arrest must be based on PROBABLE CAUSE that the suspect has committed a criminal act. Though many minor acts, including traffic offenses, are crimes, the penalty for many of these offenses is a fine. In *Atwater v. City of Lago Vista*, ___U.S.___, 121 S.Ct. 1825, 149 L.Ed.2d 889 (2001), the Supreme Court of the United States, for the first time in history, had to consider whether police violated the Fourth Amendment if they arrested persons for misdemeanors that are only penalized by fines. The Court ruled that such arrests are permissible as long as they are based on probable cause. Therefore, police officers enjoy a qualified immunity and may not be sued for damages for such arrests. The decision, one of the most publicized of the Court's term, drew a vigorous dissent from Justice Sandra Day O'Connor, who concluded that the

Gail Atwater of Lago Vista, Texas, sits with her two children after her arrest for the family not wearing seatbelts.

decision gave police too much discretion to arrest and incarcerate individuals for minor offenses.

The facts of the case were stark and disturbing for the entire Court. Gail Atwater, a 16-year resident of Lago Vista, Texas, was driving her pickup truck through a residential area of town. With her in the front seat were her 3-year-old son and 5-year-old daughter. Neither of the children nor Atwater was wearing a seatbelt. Lago Vista police officer Bart Turek stopped Atwater for not wearing a seatbelt. Turek, who had pulled over Atwater several months before on a mistaken belief her child was not seatbelted, approached the truck in an loud and abusive manner, stating that Atwater was going to jail for her offense. When she asked to take her scared children to a nearby friend's home, Turek denied the request. However, the friend arrived and took the children to her house. Turek handcuffed Atwater, placed her in the squad car, and took her to the police station. At the station, she was required to take off her shoes, jewelry, and glasses and empty her pockets. Officers obtained a "mug shot" and then put her in a cell. After an hour, she was brought before a judge and posted $310 bail. She later pleaded no contest to the seatbelt offenses and was fined $50.

Atwater and her husband, Michael Haas, proceeded to sue Turek, the city of Lago Vista, and the police chief under 42 U.S.C.A. § 1983, a federal CIVIL RIGHTS statute. The Atwaters sought money damages for the injuries suffered to their family by the arrest. For example, the two children had been required to undergo counseling to deal with the trauma surrounding the arrest. The federal DISTRICT COURT and the Fifth Circuit Court of Appeals dismissed the lawsuit, finding that the arrest was not unreasonable and that, therefore, Turek enjoyed a qualified immunity from civil lawsuits for his actions.

The Supreme Court, on a 5–4 vote, upheld the lower courts. Justice DAVID H. SOUTER, writing for the majority, concluded that neither COMMON LAW nor prior Court precedents provided any grounds for placing limits on police authority to arrest individuals for minor criminal offenses. Because the Atwaters based much of their argument on legal history, Souter conducted a review of English and American common law. He noted that the use of such history is important for reading the Fourth Amendment, as the principles governing at the time of its drafting would have been understood to be incorporated into the provision. In reviewing the common law of the 1700s, Souter acknowledged that some commentators believed arrest was not permitted for minor crimes except for breach of the peace. However, other commentators held a contrary view. In addition, the British Parliament had passed many criminal laws that had given police without a warrant express authority to arrest persons for minor offenses. Finally, an historical review of American legal history failed to demonstrate that there had been a tradition of prohibiting arrests for petty crimes. All fifty states had laws on the book that permitted the arrest of individuals for minor crimes. Therefore, Justice Souter concluded that the historical argument failed.

The majority also found no legal precedents to support an arrest prohibition. Justice Souter admitted that it would be easy to "derive a rule exclusively to address the uncontested facts of this case." Though the "gratuitous humiliation" imposed by officer Turek showed that he exercised "extremely poor judgment," Souter found that it would be difficult to craft a rule that would cover each fact situation. Police may not know when they apprehend someone that the ultimate charge may be minor. It would be difficult and unfair to ask police to determine if an offense is jailable or punished only by a fine. Police might not risk an arrest if they believed they might be sued. Therefore, Justice Souter stated a new rule: as long as police have probable cause, they may proceed to make an arrest regardless of the seriousness of the offense or the possible penalty.

Justice SANDRA DAY O'CONNOR, in a dissenting opinion, lamented the majority's ruling, believing that it was unreasonable for police to arrest a person for such a minor offense. In such situations where the offense is clearly fine only, O'Connor believed that an arrest should not take place unless the officer can articulate good reasons for it. Finally, she argued that the Court had given too much authority to the police to use their discretion, as fine-only offenses constitute a large part of the misdemeanors prosecuted each year.

CROSS REFERENCES
Fourth Amendment; Probable Cause; Search and Seizure

INTELLECTUAL PROPERTY

A&M Records, Inc. v. Napster, Inc.
The Internet has changed the entertainment habits of millions of people. The popularity of sharing audio recordings over the Internet has been facilitated by an audio compression format that produces MP3 files, which dramatically reduce the amount of data sent over computer networks. What originally was an individual, unorganized activity became an international phenomenon when programmer Shawn Fanning developed a peer-to-peer software system that allowed individuals to search and download MP3 files from computers around

the world. (Peer-to-peer means that the Napster servers communicate the host user's Internet address to the requesting user; the requesting user's computer uses this information to establish a connection with the host user's computer and to download a copy of the contents of the MP3 file from it.) Fanning's software business, Napster, had more than 50 million registered users by 2001. Not surprisingly, recording companies objected to the Napster concept, arguing that it permitted the wholesale pirating of COPYRIGHTED music. In addition, many recording artists complained that it deprived them of ROYALTIES. The federal courts agreed with the recording industry in a series of rulings issued in 2000 and 2001. By April 2001 the effect of these legal rulings had drastically reduced the use of Napster.

In July 2001, U.S. chief district court judge Marilyn Hall Patel issued a preliminary INJUNCTION at the request of the Recording Industry Association of America (RIAA). The RIAA alleged that Napster had cost the recording industry billions of dollars in lost profits. Judge Patel, agreeing that the RIAA's allegation of copyright infringement was strong, ordered Napster to block users from exchanging copyrighted material. She stayed this order, however, to give Napster the opportunity to file an appeal.

The Court of Appeals for the Ninth Circuit, in *A&M Records, Inc. v. Napster, Inc.*, 239 F.3d 1004 (9th Cir. 2001), upheld much of Judge Patel's ruling but ordered her to revise the injunction because it was overbroad. Judge Robert R. Beezer, writing for the three-judge panel, found that the plaintiffs had satisfied the two requirements necessary to prove a prima facie case of direct copyright infringement. The plaintiffs demonstrated that they owned "the allegedly infringed material" and "that the alleged infringers violate[d] at least one exclusive right granted to copyright holders" under the federal Copyright Act. As to the first requirement, the plaintiffs had shown that they owned as much as 70 percent of the files available on Napster. The second requirement proved even easier to satisfy, as the evidence established that the majority of Napster users used the service to download and upload copyrighted music.

Napster had argued that its users had not directly infringed on the copyrighted works because the users were engaged in the fair use of the material. Under the Copyright Act fair use does not constitute infringement. Napster proposed three fair uses: making temporary copies for sampling before purchasing the music, using

Left to right: Hank Berry, Andreas Schmidt, Thomas Middelhoff, and Shawn Fanning display Napster t-shirts.

Napster to access music its users already owned in audio CD format, and permissive distribution of recordings by new and established artists. Judge Beezer endorsed the views of Judge Patel on these affirmative defenses to infringement. The sampling of works remained a commercial use even if some users eventually bought the music. Moreover, the recording industry had shown the market for audio CDs and online distribution of music had been affected by Napster. Judge Beezer also found that, upon remand to the trial court, the plaintiffs were likely to prove that the Napster service involved the wholesale transferring of copyrighted work rather than the mere copying of a CD into a cassette tape or portable MP3 player. The permissive distribution argument did not affect the plaintiffs' case because they did not seek to enjoin Napster from distributing these works.

The appeals court upheld Judge Patel's legal conclusions but found that the injunction needed modification. As originally crafted, the injunction held Napster strictly liable (*see* STRICT LIABILITY) for the existence of the system. Judge Beezer stated that Napster could be held liable if it receives actual notice from the plaintiffs of the specific MP3 files with copyrighted work or if it knows or *should know* such files are available and then fails to prevent distribution of the works. Judge Beezer found that Napster had the ability to "patrol its system and preclude access to potentially infringing files in its search index." Therefore, upon remand, the

plaintiffs had the burden of providing Napster with lists of recordings, and Napster had the burden of promptly removing them from its system.

On March 5, 2001, Judge Patel issued a modified injunction incorporating the process described by the appellate court. *A&M Records, Inc. v. Napster, Inc.*, 2001 WL 227083 (N.D.Cal. Mar 05, 2001). Napster agreed to begin using screening technology that would block the distribution of files named by the recording industry. Intrepid MP3 users sought to thwart the system by deliberately misnaming files, but by mid-March Napster usage had suffered a steep decline. Judge Patel appointed a special master to oversee the blocking process, but the recording industry and Napster continued to spar over the effectiveness of Napster's efforts.

CROSS REFERENCES
Copyright; Injunction; Music Publishing

INTERNAL REVENUE SERVICE

The federal agency responsible for administering and enforcing all internal revenue laws in the United States, except those relating to ALCOHOL, TOBACCO, firearms, and explosives, which are the responsibility of the Bureau of ALCOHOL, TOBACCO AND FIREARMS.

Western Center for Journalism
v. Cederquist

The Internal Revenue Service (IRS) possesses enormous authority to investigate potential tax fraud or the misapplication of tax-exempt status. Critics have periodically charged that the IRS has been used for political purposes by presidential administrations to punish their opponents. President RICHARD M. NIXON, for example, allegedly used the IRS for such purposes during his scandal-plagued administration. In 1996 the Western Center for Journalism, doing business as the Western Journalism Center (WJC), made a similar charge against President BILL CLINTON's administration, accusing the IRS of conducting an AUDIT of its tax-exempt status in retaliation for the center's investigative journalism. The Court of Appeals for the Ninth Circuit, in *Western Center for Journalism v. Cederquist* 235 F.3d 1153 (9th Cir. 2000), threw out the WJC's lawsuit against the IRS agent who conducted the audit, Thomas Cederquist, and the IRS commissioner, Margaret Milner Richardson. The APPELLATE COURT ruled that the WJC had waited too long to file its civil damage suit.

The WJC is a media organization with conservative political ties that funded an investigative journalist's probe into the death of Clinton White House aid Vincent Foster. Foster committed suicide in a local park, but conservative opponents of Clinton contended that he had been murdered to prevent him from disclosing incriminating information about White House activities. In July 1996 WJC discovered that the IRS was auditing its 1995 tax returns to ascertain whether its tax-exempt status was merited. Several months later WJC claimed it had obtained a White House memorandum that stated the audit had been done in retaliation for its anti-Clinton journalism. On October 25, 1996, a date that would prove crucial to the case, WJC's founder, Joseph Farah, published an opinion article in the *Wall Street Journal.* Farah alleged that "the unconstitutional harassment of [WJC] is a smoking gun that proves that the White House is manipulating the IRS for political purposes."

Agent Cederquist conducted the audit for the IRS. WJC alleged that on two occasions he made statements that suggested the audit was in retaliation for the center's journalism. In addition, WJC claimed that the IRS broadened its audit to include the 1994 tax year after Farah published his opinion piece. The center also alleged that the IRS audited its two largest individual charitable donors. In April 1997 the IRS reassigned the audit to another agent, and

within two months the agent filed a report recommending that the IRS continue WJC's tax-exempt status.

The WJC filed a lawsuit in May 1998 asking for more than $10 million in DAMAGES from Cederquist and Commissioner Richardson. It alleged that the audit violated the center's FIRST AMENDMENT and FOURTH AMENDMENT rights. The IRS moved the U.S. District Court for the Eastern District of California to dismiss the lawsuit. The DISTRICT COURT did so, ruling that WJC could not sue the IRS employees because the IRS had its own remedial scheme for raising such claims.

On appeal, the Ninth Circuit upheld the dismissal but on different GROUNDS. The court, in a PER CURIAM opinion, concluded that the STATUTE OF LIMITATIONS prevented the suit from going forward. Statutes of limitations require a person to file a lawsuit within a certain amount of time. These time periods vary based on the type of lawsuit and the state where the alleged injury took place. A federal court is generally governed by the statutes of limitations in the state in which it sits. WCJ is headquartered in California, thus the appeals court noted that the state's personal injury statute of limitations was one year. The federal courts, however, have the authority to determine when the statute of limitations period begins to run. The Ninth Circuit panel pointed to CASE LAW in the circuit concerning civil lawsuits against federal officials for constitutional violations. In this particular cause of action, the clock typically starts to run when the plaintiff knows or has reason to know of the injury.

The IRS argued that the time period had already expired when WCJ filed its lawsuit in May 1998. WCJ countered that the statute of limitations did not start to run until May 1997 and that it beat the limitations period by two weeks. The appeals court concluded that the time period had expired before the lawsuit was filed because the clock had started to run no later than October 22, 1996, when Farah's op-ed piece appeared in print. The gist of WCJ's claim was that the IRS had retaliated against it for exercising its First Amendment rights. Farah's article had made the same allegation. Therefore, WJC knew of its injury on that date or earlier. The statute of limitations period expired on October 22, 1997, making the May 1998 action untimely, and thus the Ninth Circuit held that WCJ's suit had been properly dismissed by the district court.

CROSS REFERENCES
Statute of Limitations

INTERNET

A worldwide telecommunications network of business, government, and personal computers.

Howard v. America Online, Inc.

The growth of the Internet in the 1990s led to the creation of various service providers. America Online (AOL) emerged as a dominant Internet Service Provider (ISP) through aggressive marketing campaigns and affordable prices. Nevertheless, AOL also received its share of criticism from subscribers who complained of deceptive advertising and billing. AOL reached a settlement with a class of subscribers, which was approved by a California state superior court in 1997. The subscribers alleged various deceptive billing practices. In the settlement agreement, which defined the class as all subscribers of AOL in the United States from July 1991 to March 1996, the parties agreed that the settlement barred any subscriber from suing on these matters again. Nevertheless, another group of subscribers sued AOL, alleging violations of the RACKETEER INFLUENCED AND CORRUPT ORGANIZATIONS ACT (RICO), FALSE ADVERTISING, fraud, and unfair business practices. AOL sought to dismiss this lawsuit under the terms of the 1997 settlement agreement, and the Court of Appeals for the Ninth Circuit agreed in *Howard v. America Online Inc.*, 208 F.3d 741 (9th Cir. 2000).

The plaintiffs specifically alleged that AOL had engaged in fraudulent billing practices, SECURITIES fraud, fraudulent promotion of its "flat-fee" program, improper charges to subscribers, and violations of its duty to protect subscribers' PRIVACY rights and COPYRIGHTS.

The America Online Headquarters is located in Chantilly, Virginia.

The federal district court dismissed the lawsuit, finding that the plaintiffs were within the 1997 settlement class and that they had not opted out of the settlement class. The court saw their lawsuit as an "attempt to repackage the claims asserted and settled" in the 1997 case.

A three-judge panel of the Ninth Circuit upheld the district court's ruling. Judge Robert R. Beezer, writing for the court, noted that the plaintiffs sought to establish RICO violations by offering evidence against AOL relating to acts covered by the 1997 settlement. Without these "predicate acts," the plaintiffs could not present a pattern of corrupt acts as required by RICO. The plaintiffs contended that the RICO pattern concerning billing allegations was not completed at the time of the 1997 settlement and that, therefore, they could use these as predicate acts. Judge Beezer concluded that this argument was "meritless."

Judge Beezer pointed out that "claim preclusion in federal court can be based on a state court settlement." Under California state law the 1997 settlement precluded further litigation on the same cause of action, as the court entered a final judgment on the matter. The appeals court rejected the plaintiffs' contention that the requisite RICO pattern had not been developed at the time of the settlement. The plaintiffs were part of the 1997 class and "asserted identical billing claims that occurred during the same time period." The 1997 settlement class could have alleged a RICO violation based on the billing fraud but did not do so. Nevertheless, Judge Beezer found that by failing to make that allegation, the class of subscribers had forfeited the opportunity to raise the RICO charge later.

The court also rejected the claim that AOL committed securities fraud as part of a pattern of racketeering activity. It found that the plaintiffs could not use these claims to establish a RICO violation because a federal securities law barred the use of RICO for this purpose. Judge Beezer then examined the allegation concerning AOL's "flat-fee program, which charged subscribers a monthly fee for unlimited Internet access." This led to an overload of the network that prevented subscribers from accessing the Internet. The plaintiffs claimed that AOL was aware that it could not handle the traffic and that it distributed false and misleading advertising to promote the flat-fee program. However, Judge Beezer ruled that the plaintiffs had failed to show a series of related acts extending over a substantial period of time. Without this showing, the plaintiffs could not use RICO. Nor could plaintiffs demonstrate that "AOL engaged in an open-ended pattern of racketeering activity."

The plaintiffs also alleged that AOL had violated the federal Communications Act "by making unreasonable charges, practices, classifications or regulations." The appeals court agreed with the district court "that AOL is not a common carrier" as defined by the act "and therefore did not violate" the law. The Federal Communications Commission (FCC), which enforces the Communications Act, has declared that ISPs are not common carriers like radio and television stations. *In re Non-Accounting Safeguards*, 11 F.C.C.R. 21905, 22034, 1996 WL 734160 (1996) (proposed rule) (citing 47 U.S.C. § 153(10)). The FCC has distinguished ISPs from radio and television stations by stating that common carriers offer "basic" information transport rather than "enhanced" services, which implicate the transfer and storage of information that subscribers can access." *In re Second Computer Inquiry*, 77 F.C.C.2d 384, 417–23 (1980) (final decision); 47 C.F.R. 64.702(a). The appeals court ruled that the FCC's construction of the term "common carrier" was a reasonable interpretation of an "ambiguous statute."

CROSS REFERENCES

Class Action; Federal Communications Commission

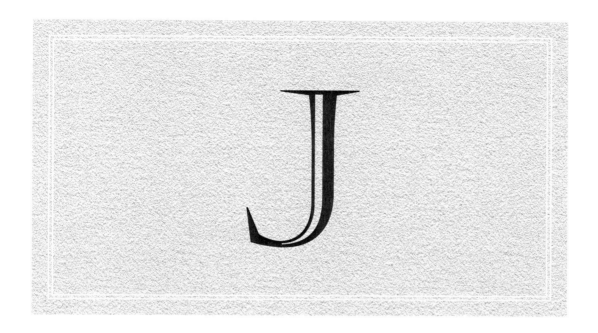

JUDICIARY

The branch of government that is endowed with the authority to interpret and apply the law, adjudicate legal disputes, and otherwise administer justice.

United States v. Hatter

The independence of the federal judiciary is insured by lifetime tenure, subject only to IMPEACHMENT by the Congress. In addition, Article III of the Constitution contains the Compensation Clause, which states that compensation for federal judges "shall not be diminished during their Continuance in Office." This clause prevents Congress from reducing the salary of federal judges and thus removes this threat from the minds of the judges. This clause is rarely litigated, but a change in Social Security and MEDICARE taxation policies for federal employees in the early 1980s triggered a challenge by a number of federal judges. This litigation, which lasted over a decade, was finally resolved by the Supreme Court in *United States v. Hatter*, ___U.S.___, 121 S.Ct. 1782, 149 L.Ed.2d 820 (2001). The Court overturned a 1920 precedent in ruling that a nondiscriminatory tax of general application does not violate the Compensation Clause. The Court did rule, however, that judges appointed to the bench before 1984 did not have to pay Social Security taxes because Congress had unfairly singled them out.

The case arose after Congress changed taxation policies for federal employees in the early 1980s. In 1982 Congress passed a law that required all federal employees to pay the Medicare tax that all other American workers paid. This law, which went into effect on January 1, 1983, was followed a year later by a change in the Social Security laws. Congress mandated that all new employees hired after January 1, 1984, would pay Social Security taxes. As for all current employees, Congress permitted, but did not require, about 96 percent of these workers to participate in Social Security. The remaining four percent of employees encompassed high-ranking Executive Branch employees as well as the federal judiciary. From this group, Congress allowed employees to opt out of Social Security taxes if they contributed to a qualified pension plan. This exception effectively made federal judges the only employees who were required to pay Social Security, as the judicial pension plan did not require contributions by the judges.

In 1989 eight federal judges filed suit, arguing that the Compensation Clause prohibited the imposition of these taxes on judges appointed before 1983 because their effect was to reduce the judges' net salary. The case remained unsettled in the federal courts for more than ten years, with a first appeal to the Supreme Court failing because most of the justices disqualified themselves since they had been appointed before 1983. Finally, in 2000 a federal appeals court decided in favor of the judges. The U.S. government then appealed to the Supreme Court, contending that the Compensation Clause did not apply. Moreover, the government argued that a 1984 judicial pay raise increased judicial salaries by an amount greater than the new taxes.

The Court made separate decisions on the two taxes. With two justices not participating,

THE POLITICIZING OF AMERICAN JURISPRUDENCE

An old saying goes, "A judge is a lawyer who knew a governor (or senator or president)." The inference in unavoidable, and some think all too true, as evidenced by the 2000 elections and campaign spending in races for judicial posts.

Only federal judges and a handful of state judges are appointed for life, barring IMPEACHMENT. In all other states and in local governments, most judges are elected and re-elected by popular vote and for a specific term. Voters tend to elect persons who share their views. The same is true for most gubernatorial appointments, although in many states this tendency is tempered by senatorial confirmation. The development of platforms that represent the most popular, prevailing, or promising views is a political process.

In the words of JOHN ADAMS's Massachusetts constitution, it has always been the desire to make judges "as free, impartial and independent as the lot of humanity will admit." In a political system where party politics are defined by social issues and where jurisprudence affects social issues, however, party alignment of judges seems inevitable, either by default or by declaration. Does this truly constitute partisan politics or is it merely that politics have come to be defined by associative process: Democratic liberalism versus Republican conservatism? Whether elected by the people, or appointed by a governor, judges assume the bench based on how others perceive they will run the court: conservatively or liberally, favorable to special interests or disfavorable to them, notwithstanding ethical standards requiring disinterested and unbiased opinions, which most judges honor.

IN FOCUS

Ostensible checks and balances exist, however. Most states have a CODE OF JUDICIAL CONDUCT and/or ethics, mostly fashioned from that of the AMERICAN BAR ASSOCIATION (ABA). These codes proscribe many instances of campaign conduct for prospective and current judges. Judges cannot personally solicit or accept campaign funds and often are prohibited from identifying themselves with any political party. They often must run on a non-partisan ticket.

These restrictions do not prevent partisan groups from contributing to a prospective or current judge's campaign. Furthermore, many believe that controlling or limiting campaign funds will not help prevent partisan politicking. Said Dick Wilcox, president of the Business and Industry Political Education Committee in Mississippi, "You can't restrict dollar amounts (donated) from individuals or an entity. . . . [P]eople will figure out ways to spend whatever funds they want to allocate to the process. If PACs (political action committees) are limited, people go out and create more PACs. If wealthy individuals are restricted, they give money to their secretaries, wives, or children to contribute. I don't think limiting contributions accomplishes anything." Of the four states in which judicial elections were held in 2000—Alabama, Michigan, Mississippi, and Ohio—Mississippi spent the least amount of money in campaigns. Michigan spent an estimated $16 million, leading that state's Senator Ken Sikkema to introduce a bill in 2001 for a CONSTITUTIONAL AMENDMENT allowing the governor to appoint justices to a single 14-year term. His idea is similar to that of one of the state's own supreme court justices, Elizabeth Weaver.

An alternative for Michigan and several other states, including Texas, is a variant of what political scientists refer to as the Missouri system, after the state where it was pioneered. Under this system, a governor appoints all state trial and appellate judges, with the advice and

the Court ruled 7–0—only seven votes because Justices SANDRA DAY O'CONNOR and JOHN PAUL STEVENS recused themselves—that the Medicare tax did not violate the Compensation Clause. On a 5–2 vote, however, the Court ruled that the Social Security tax could not be imposed on judges appointed before 1984. Justice STEPHEN G. BREYER, writing for the Court, acknowledged that a 1920 decision barred the government from imposing federal taxes on federal judges appointed before Congress enacted the tax in 1918. The Court overruled this decision, however, with Breyer stating that the Compensation Clause does not apply to "a generally applicable, nondiscriminatory tax" on ju-

dicial salaries, whether or not the judges were appointed before the passage of the new tax law.

As to the Medicare tax, the lower courts and the plaintiffs did not contend that it was a discriminatory tax. Therefore, the Court reversed the appeals court and concluded that federal judges could be taxed for Medicare without violating the Compensation Clause. As to the Social Security tax, however, Justice Breyer saw constitutional problems with its imposition on pre-1983 judges. In examining the law, Breyer pointed out that the practical effect of the statute "imposed a new financial obligation upon sitting judges, but it did not impose a new financial burden upon any other group of (then) current federal employees." He noted that "nearly every

consent of the legislature. Still another variation would require a governor to select among nominees submitted by a selection panel or special nominating committee.

For those who favor such changes, there is the knowledge that these alternative systems may cure ills and weaknesses more than just out-of-control campaign spending. For one, they would eliminate so-called "negative campaigning." Michigan Supreme Court Chief Justice Maura Corrigan believes negative campaigns create perceptions among voters that justices are "bought" by special interests. For instance, judges may be curbed from writing some opinions because they fear writing an opinion that will end up in a negative campaign ad.

Another blemish that could potentially be cured is that of real or perceived lawyer lobbying. It has been known for years that attorneys, in particular plaintiffs' lawyers, have contributed more to state judicial campaigns than the largest oil or automotive companies in those states. The ABA has spoken out sharply against attorneys contributing to campaigns of judges before whom they do frequent business or from whom they wish to gain court-appointed business. Attorneys have rights, too, however, and cannot be prevented from contributing to a candidate or party of their choice since it is protected speech under the FIRST AMENDMENT.

Just how much politics may play into judicial decision-making became all too apparent during the 2000 presidential election campaign. When Florida Circuit Judge Nikki Ann Clark, an African American and a Democrat, was assigned one of the election cases seeking to invalidate as many as 15,000 absentee ballots from Florida's Seminole County, candidate GEORGE W. BUSH's attorneys requested that she RECUSE herself from the case. Just weeks before, Bush's brother, Florida Governor Jeb Bush, had declined to pick her from a short list of nominees for a state APPELLATE COURT vacancy. She refused to recuse herself. Her decision in the matter was disfavorable to Bush and favorable to Florida's African-American voters. The appellate court upheld her decision as did the Florida Supreme Court, all of whom had been appointed by Democratic governors. The media wasted no time in characterizing the players by race and party, adding to the perception of political bias in the judicial process.

The Supreme Court of the United States later found that the manual recount of votes ordered by the Florida Supreme Court violated the EQUAL PROTECTION clause of the Constitution by treating voters' ballots differently and by being conducted erratically and arbitrarily without proper standards. Despite all the media analysis and characterization of each Supreme Court justice's ide-ological tendencies, the Court's decision still surprised many. Some were openly skeptical about an undercurrent of a "results-oriented" majority seeking a high-minded legal rationale to front its own political leanings.

While the Supreme Court's historic PER CURIAM majority opinion was debated and re-debated across the country, an article appeared in the January 1, 2001, issue of *Newsweek*, giving cause for thought. It told of an election-night party, attended by Supreme Court Justice SANDRA DAY O'CONNOR and her husband John O'Connor, a Washington lawyer. Apparently, as the first critical returns were broadcast and CBS television's anchor Dan Rather called Florida for Democratic presidential hopeful and former vice-president AL GORE, O'Connor uncharacteristically dropped her guard and expressed her unhappiness. "This is terrible," she reportedly exclaimed and left the room to get some refreshments. Her husband explained that his wife was upset "because they wanted to retire to Arizona," but if Gore won the election, they might wait: she did not want Gore to name her successor. Responding through a high court spokesperson to questions about her remark, O'Connor had "no comment" for the media. She is considered a moderate on the Court and often makes the "swing vote" in controversial issues.

current federal employee, but not federal judges," avoided the new tax. In addition, Breyer ruled that the tax adversely affected most judges, requiring them to pay $2,000 per year into a system that all but a handful of judges had qualified for prior to taking the bench. In his view, the law imposed this obligation "with little or no expectation of substantial benefit for most of them." The judicial retirement system, which is noncontributory, is based on lifetime tenure. A judge continues to collect a salary for life by remaining on the bench, even if in a limited capacity. This system, which was placed in the Constitution to foster judicial independence, led to adverse treatment by Congress. Therefore, the tax had the effect of reducing a judge's income and ran afoul of the Compensation Clause. Justice Breyer also rejected the idea that the tax no longer mattered because of a 1984 judicial pay raise. He noted that the Congress provided the increase not to remedy the tax payment but rather to restore the real value of the salary that had been hurt by inflation over a number of years.

CROSS REFERENCES
Social Security

JURY

In trials, a group of people selected and sworn to inquire into matters of fact and to reach a verdict on the basis of the evidence presented to it.

Sea Hawk Seafoods, Inc. v. Alyeska Pipeline Service Co.

When the U.S. oil tanker Exxon *Valdez* ran aground on a reef in Prince William Sound, Alaska, in March 1989, it dumped more than 260,000 barrels of oil into the water, creating the largest oil spill in U.S. history. Clean up by the Exxon Corporation and Alyeska Pipeline Service Company came slowly, leaving 1,100 miles of Alaska shoreline coated with oil. The environmental damage was enormous, but the oil spill also devastated the fishing and tourist industries. Lawsuits were soon filed asking for DAMAGES from the companies. A 1994 trial resulted in a $5 billion PUNITIVE DAMAGES claim against Exxon and Alyeska. Since then the defendants have filed numerous appeals in an effort to overturn the jury verdict. The Court of Appeals for the Ninth Circuit resolved one issue in *Sea Hawk Seafoods, Inc. v. Alyeska Pipeline Service Co.*, 206 F.3d 900 (9th Cir.2000), when it ruled that a new trial was not warranted because a bailiff told a member of the jury a tasteless joke about another juror. Moreover, the testimony of a juror who claimed to have been threatened by the bailiff and fellow jurors was determined not to be credible.

The rather bizarre set of facts that characterized the appeal demonstrated the pressures of a high-profile trial where jurors are kept in seclusion for many months. A retired Florida police officer served as a bailiff during the trial and deliberations of the jury that eventually awarded the injured parties $5 billion in punitive damages. The bailiff was responsible for maintaining court security, escorting the jury to and from the courtroom, and attending to the requests of jurors for food and other needs. The punitive damages phase of the trial extended over a period of four months. As a result, the bailiff became well acquainted with the jurors. In 1996 an Anchorage newspaper published an article that recounted this stressful period for the jury. It noted that Juror A was emotionally distressed and did not get along with the other jurors. Her behavior became so odd that jurors sent the judge notes expressing concern about her welfare.

After the newspaper publication, the federal district court held a hearing and had the jurors answer questions about possible irregularities. Juror B testified that the bailiff took her aside during deliberations and commiserated about Juror A's problems. He then "pulled out his gun, took out a bullet and said 'maybe if you put her out of her misery or something.'" Juror B took it as a tasteless joke rather than a threat, but it disturbed her enough to tell the jury foreman. Juror A was never told about this remark. The bailiff initially denied making the remark, and the judge believed him. Nevertheless, the U.S. Marshal's service conducted an internal investigation and administered polygraphs to both Juror B and the bailiff. After the bailiff did poorly

The Exxon *Valdez* oil spill, a 1989 environmental disaster off the Alaskan coast, is cleaned up using hot and cold water jets.

on his exam, he admitted to making the statement. He resigned five minutes after he was told that termination proceedings would begin immediately. A few months later he died of a heart attack.

Through a twist of fate following the $5 billion jury award, the defendants learned of the bailiff's admission and asked the court for a new hearing. At this hearing they also presented Juror A to testify about what happened during deliberations. She testified that the bailiff and most of the jurors had threatened her. Moreover, she had voted to award the punitive damages because of these threats. Based on this evidence the defendants asked for a new trial. The district court, however, denied their motions.

The Ninth Circuit upheld the district court rulings. Judge Andrew J. Kleinfeld, writing for a unanimous three-judge panel, ruled that the bailiff's remarks, while tasteless, did not amount to conduct that warranted a new trial. Kleinfeld noted that prior court rulings had distinguished between the introduction of "extraneous evidence" to the jury and EX PARTE contacts with a juror that do not include the imparting of any information about the case to the juror. If extraneous evidence is introduced, the party opposing a new trial must demonstrate the absence of PREJUDICE. With EX PARTE contacts, the party seeking the new trial has the burden of showing prejudice.

Judge Kleinfeld concluded that the bailiff had not introduced any extraneous evidence to the juror by making the tasteless joke. Therefore, the defendants had the burden of proving prejudice. The appeals court deferred to the trial court's decision that the bailiff had neither meant to make a threat nor had Juror B interpreted his remarks in that way. The fact that Juror A did not know about the remark clarified that it did not have an effect on the outcome of the damages award.

The defendants also argued that Juror A had been threatened by the bailiff and other jurors. The trial court had found her testimony unbelievable, as it contradicted previous statements made by her and her husband. She admitted that the 1996 newspaper article had jogged her memory, but the trial judge pointed out that she had kept a journal during the trial and had never commented on being threatened by anyone. The appeals court agreed that her statements were bizarre, especially her claim that nine of the jurors had threatened her and that one had forced her to vote for the damage award out of fear that her daughter would be harmed.

These facts, coupled with Juror A's suicide attempt, led the court to discredit her testimony. Therefore, the appeals court upheld the trial court on these issues. The underlying issue of whether the $5 billion punitive damages award is the right amount remains disputed in the appeals process.

CROSS REFERENCES
Civil Procedure; Damages

JUVENILE LAW

An area of the law that deals with the actions and well-being of persons who are not yet adults.

Extending Sex Offender Registration to Juveniles

On Saturday, August 19, 2000, seven-year-old Kristi Blevins and her twelve-year-old friend were playing outside of Kristi's home in Oilton, Oklahoma, when they suddenly disappeared. When searchers located the two girls approximately three hours after their disappearance, they were in a nearby abandoned home in the presence of nineteen-year-old Robert Rotramel. Kristi had been strangled to death, and her twelve-year-old friend had been raped. Rotramel, who had previously served time in a juvenile detention facility for the crime of forcible sodomy, was arrested on first-degree murder, first-degree rape, forced sodomy, lewd molestation, and two counts of kidnapping in connection with the incident.

Rotramel became acquainted with Kristi Blevins when her brother began work in a bait shop owned by Rotramel's father. On occasion, Kristi visited the bait shop when Rotramel was there. At the time, Kristi's parents were unaware of the fact that Rotramel was a convicted juvenile sex offender. As a juvenile at the time of the forcible sodomy offense, Rotramel was not required to comply with Oklahoma's Sex Offenders Registration Act.

The Act is one version of a law passed in all fifty states often referred to as Megan's Law. The name of the law refers to Megan Kanka, a young girl raped and murdered by a convicted sex offender who, unbeknownst to her family, lived just across the street from them. The law requires convicted sex offenders to register with local police and allows the community to be notified that the offender resides in the area.

Twenty-one previous states had passed laws to include juvenile offenders, and in June 2001, Oklahoma passed Senate Bill 157, titled the "Juvenile Sex Offender Registration Act." The act requires the establishment of a separate registry of juvenile sex offenders, who must re-register each year; failure to do so constitutes a misdemeanor charge. In addition, prosecutors may petition courts to have the offender included in the adult registry once they become 21 years old. But the case in Oklahoma raises the issues that similar laws in other states have brought up.

While statistics reflect that sex offenses committed by juvenile offenders have been on the rise, whether those offenders, once convicted, should be required to register with local law enforcement officials upon their release from juvenile detention facilities remains a highly controversial issue. Those individuals that oppose required registration for juvenile sex offenders argue that such registration undermines the very principals behind juvenile justice in America. In 1999, the U.S. celebrated the 100th anniversary of the founding of the first juvenile court in the world. It was established in Chicago, Illinois, by individuals who believed that children should be treated differently than adults. To that end, those individuals created a system in which the concepts of prevention and rehabilitation constitute the benchmark of juvenile justice. The individuals that support this system assert that requiring juvenile sex offenders to register necessarily circumvents any attempts they make to live a normal life. As such, they contend that the registration requirement thereby negates the possibility that the juvenile sex offender could ever become rehabilitated.

In contrast, other individuals argue that the trend of increasingly violent crimes being committed by juveniles warrants children accused of a crime being treated the same as adults. That is, proponents of extending the registration requirement to juvenile sex offenders argue that the importance of public safety, proper punishment, and individual accountability mandate that these individuals continue to be held responsible for their actions. In addition, some argue that sex offenders, juvenile or otherwise, are untreatable because various well known studies demonstrate an extremely high RECIDI-VISM rate, indicating that individuals who have a propensity to commit such crimes are often unamenable to any type of rehabilitation. Consistent with this approach, states such as Idaho require juvenile sex offenders to comply with their state's equivalent of Megan's Law. There, the statute requires juvenile sex offenders above the age of thirteen to register each year with local law enforcement officials. These convicted sex offenders must have committed a sexual crime that would have been a felony if they were tried in court as an adult. The Idaho statute further requires the names of these juvenile offenders to be automatically removed from the registry when they reach the age of twenty-one, unless a prosecutor is able to persuade a judicial officer that the continued registration, in the context of that particular case, is in the best interest of the public.

CROSS REFERENCES
Recidivism; Sex Offenses

LABOR UNIONS

An association, combination, or organization of employees who band together to secure favorable wages, improved working conditions, and better work hours, and to resolve grievances against employers.

National Labor Relations Board v. Kentucky River Community Care, Inc.

The National Labor Relations Act (NLRA) governs union-management relations. The National Labor Relations Board (NLRB) enforces this federal law and also promulgates regulations that further clarify how the law will be applied in specific circumstances. Congress and the courts have given the NLRB broad discretion to interpret these provisions, believing it best to have one body with great expertise to manage labor relations. At times, however, the courts will be called on to decide whether the NLRB's interpretations are legally justified. Such was the case in *National Labor Relations Board v. Kentucky River Community Care, Inc.* ___U.S.___, 121 S.Ct. 1861, ___ L.Ed.2d ___ (2001), when a slim majority of the Supreme Court of the United States agreed with a lower FEDERAL COURT that the board had been mistaken in labeling registered nurses as nonsupervisory employees who could join a union. In so ruling, the Court concluded that the board had read more into the STATUTE than was there.

The case involved the successful efforts of a carpenters' union to organize the employees of the Caney Creek Developmental Complex in Pippa Passes, Kentucky. Caney Creek is a care facility for individuals who are developmentally disabled or who are mentally ill. It is owned by Kentucky River Community Care, Inc., which employs 110 professional and nonprofessional employees. Kentucky River objected to the union's plan to include all 110 employees in the election to determine if the union could represent the employees as a single bargaining unit. It argued that six registered nurses were supervisors as defined by the NLRA and, therefore, must be excluded from the class of employees subject to the NLRA's provisions. The board's regional director required Kentucky River to carry the burden of proving the nurses were supervisors, a burden that the director concluded they did not meet. The election resulted in the union being certified as the representative of every Caney Creek employee.

Because the NLRA prevents direct JUDICIAL REVIEW of such issues as the status of the nurses as supervisors, Kentucky River sought indirect review by refusing to bargain with the union. The NLRB's hearing on this refusal to bargain did not help Kentucky River on the supervisor issue because the board's regulations prevented relitigating the issue absent new evidence. Nevertheless, Kentucky River appealed to the U.S. Court of Appeals for the Sixth Circuit (193 F.3d. 444). The APPELLATE COURT made two rulings: (1) the burden of proving the nurses were not supervisors should have fallen on the board; and (2) the nurses were not employees covered by the NLRA because they exercised independent judgment in their duties.

The Supreme Court ruled unanimously that the Sixth Circuit erred in its first ruling, but ruled 5–4 that the appeals court had correctly found that the nurses were supervisory personnel. Justice ANTONIN SCALIA, writing for the Court, noted as to the first issue that the NLRA does not contain any provisions as to "allocating the burden of proof" over a challenge of an employee's supervisory status. Therefore, the NLRB has applied a rule that requires that the party claiming the employee is a supervisor to bear the burden. Justice Scalia found this rule consistent with the general rule of statutory construction that the burden of proof generally falls on the person who claims the benefit. In the case of this provision, it was far easier to prove an employee is a supervisor than to disprove an employee's authority to exercise certain supervisory functions. Thus, the board's allocation of the burden of proof was correct.

Edward Hirsch
Levi

The majority of the justices found, however, that the Sixth Circuit's ruling on the MERITS of the controversy was correct. Justice Scalia pointed out that the applicable provision of the NLRA lists twelve functions that may confer supervisory status on an employee. These functions include the authority to "hire, transfer, suspend, lay off, recall, promote, discharge, assign, reward or discipline other employees, or responsibly direct them, or to adjust their grievances, or effectively to recommend such action." The provision articulates a three-step test to determine supervisory status. Employees are supervisors if they hold the authority to engage in any of the twelve named supervisory functions; their "exercise of such authority is not of a merely routine or clerical nature, but requires the use of independent judgment, and . . . their authority is held 'in the interest of the employer.'" The NLRB had interpreted "independent judgment" as not applying to the nurses when they exercised ordinary professional or technical judgment in directing lesser-skilled employees. Justice Scalia found no basis in the statute for this qualification of independent judgment and questioned whether the board's approach would "virtually eliminate 'supervisors' from the Act." Finding no justification for this interpretation, the majority upheld the appeals court and found that the nurses should be excluded from the bargaining unit.

John V. Lindsay

Justice JOHN PAUL STEVENS, in a dissenting opinion, contended that the Kentucky River had failed to prove the nurses were supervisors. Stevens argued that the only evidence to support this claim was the use of two nurses as "building supervisors" on weekends. These nurses received no extra compensation for this responsibility, however, and could not compel employ-

ees to follow their directions. Apart from the factual issue, Stevens expressed concern that the Court had intruded on the NLRB's domain and had redefined supervisor in such a way as to exclude many employees that Congress wanted within a collective bargaining unit.

LEVI, EDWARD HIRSCH

Obituary notice

Born on June 26, 1911, in Chicago, Illinois; died March 7, 2000, in Chicago, Illinois. Edward Hirsch Levi is best known as the U.S. attorney general who helped restore confidence and respect to an embattled U.S. JUSTICE DEPARTMENT after the WATERGATE scandal and resignation of President RICHARD M. NIXON. Levi was chosen by President GERALD FORD to head the Justice Department in February 1975. Levi served many functions within the government prior to becoming attorney general, including helping to draft the 1946 Atomic Energy Act. Levi also held many positions with the University of Chicago, including being named president in 1968 and appointed professor emeritus after his retirement from full-time teaching in 1985.

LINDSAY, JOHN V.

Seventy-nine-year-old John V. Lindsay, the dashing Ivy League mayor of New York City during the late 1960s and early 1970s, died of natural causes on December 19, 2000, in a hospital near his Hilton Head, South Carolina, residence. Having previously come in and out of favor with the public, Lindsay, an outspoken and high-profile activist during his political career, left the world virtually impoverished and forgotten at the time of his death.

A native New Yorker, John Vliet Lindsay and a twin brother were born in Manhattan on November 24, 1921. One of five children, Lindsay was the son of investment banker George Nelson and Eleanor (Vliet) Lindsay. He graduated from the private St. Paul's High School in Concord, New Hampshire, then continued his education at Yale University, earning his bachelor's degree in 1944 and a law degree in 1948. Concurrently, he served as a gunnery officer in the U.S. Naval reserves from 1943 to 1946, earning five battle stars and rising to the rank of senior lieutenant in the process. After graduation from law school, Lindsay joined the New York City law firm of Webster & Sheffield in 1949 as associate counsel. By 1953 he had become a partner and continued his association with this firm for the remainder of his career, albeit interrupted by subsequent political appointments.

In 1949 Lindsay married Mary Harrison, a graduate of nearby prestigious Vassar College. They eventually had four children together. Lindsay took his first leave from the law partnership in 1955 to serve as executive assistant to U.S. ATTORNEY GENERAL Herbert Brownell. A liberal Republican, Lindsay next decided to take a chance on running for a seat in New York City's 17th Congressional District in 1958 and won. For the next three successful re-elections, Lindsay's margin of victory in the polls grew larger each time. He had earned a reputation as a shirt-sleeve warrior of liberal idealism, enjoying a particular popularity with ethnic and minority groups. For example, he refused to support Senator BARRY M. GOLDWATER's 1964 presidential campaign.

By 1965 Lindsay was riding high on a wave of popularity and decided to run for mayor of New York. In his mid-forties, he carried a striking image as a tall, handsome, and patrician-looking man who exuded calmness and self-confidence, often being dubbed the "Republican Kennedy." The three-way mayoral race was memorable, in which Lindsay ran against Democrat Abraham Beame (who succeeded Lindsay to the office in later years) and William F. Buckley, Jr., editor of the *National Review*. Backed by Governor Nelson A. Rockefeller and endorsed by the *New York Times* and the *New York Post*, Lindsay was elected with 45 percent of the vote. A few months later, he guest hosted *The Tonight Show*, entering to Ed McMahon's refrain of "Heeeere's Johnny!"

Lindsay's tenure as mayor of New York brought national focus to the city. In the turbulent political years of the latter 1960s, Newark, Los Angeles, Detroit, and other major cities suffered race riots and fires, but New York remained essentially stable. Lindsay was given the credit. He would appear on inner-city streets or in ethnic neighborhoods, interacting with the "hippies," blacks, and Hispanics. People were seen trying to touch him or his clothes, and his very presence sent a message that he heard their concerns.

Lindsay's initially ubiquitous appeal began to disintegrate, however, when his idealistic advocacy started to polarize the communities he served. When Lindsay ordered the American flag atop City Hall lowered to half-mast in protest of the VIETNAM WAR, the blue-collar

JOHN V. LINDSAY

1921	Born in New York City, New York
1948	Graduated from Yale Law School; joined law firm of Webster & Sheffield
1955	Served as executive assistant to U.S. Attorney
1958	Won Congressional seat in New York's 17th district
1965	Became New York City's 103rd mayor, serving two terms
1971	Switched to Democratic Party, but was not nominated for 1972 presidential primary
1973	Left office and politics and returned to law practice
1991	Retired as presiding partner at Webster & Sheffield
2000	Died

worker who climbed the building to re-raise the flag became a hero. When Lindsay tried to make peace with New York's powerful public-employee unions by giving in to all of their demands, the taxpaying residents took umbrage. He alienated the Jewish community by advocating school decentralization, and his aggressive activism on behalf of minorities cost him votes with non-minorities who represented the bulk of his constituency and felt ignored. By the end of his first term in office, he was denied renomination for re-election by his own Republican party. Notwithstanding, Lindsay tried running as a Liberal candidate and was re-elected in 1969, successfully beating both the Republican and Democratic candidates.

In an attempt to regain his former appeal, Lindsay then denounced the Republican Party and formally became a Democrat, hoping to position himself for the 1972 Democratic presidential nomination. Both gestures proved disastrous at the polls, and, in 1973 Lindsay left the office of mayor and politics forever.

In 1974 Lindsay returned to his law practice in Manhattan and also furthered his avocation of creative writing. He had previously written

Journey Into Politics (1966) and *The City* (1970). He added his first novel, *The Edge* in 1976. He took a bit part in Otto Preminger's film, *The Rosebud*, and served as a political commentator in the press and on television's *Good Morning America*. Lindsay was a board member emeritus of the Lincoln Center for the Performing Arts and chairman emeritus of the Lincoln Center Theatre Company.

Lindsay formally retired as presiding law partner of Webster & Sheffield in 1991. Following a series of medical problems in the ensuing years, he left the area in 1999 to settle in an adult retirement community near Hilton Head. Following news of his death, a memorial service, which included a performance by the internationally renowned Harlem Boys Choir, was held in his memory in Manhattan on January 26, 2001.

MAIL FRAUD

A crime in which the perpetrator develops a scheme using the mails to defraud another of money or property. This crime specifically requires the intent to defraud, and is a federal offense governed by § 1341 of title 18 of the U.S. Code. The mail fraud statute was first enacted in 1872 to prohibit illicit mailings with the Postal Service (formerly the Post Office) for the purpose of executing a fraudulent scheme.

Cleveland v. United States

The federal mail fraud statute, 18 U.S.C.A. § 1341, seeks to protect individual property rights by prohibiting the use of the mail system to further criminal fraud. The statute, which has a long history, is used to combat consumer fraud as well as RACKETEERING activities such as MONEY LAUNDERING and other corrupt practices. Because the states have primary authority for policing criminal activity, the U.S. Supreme Court has limited the scope of the mail fraud statute since its enactment in 1872. This desire was illustrated in *Cleveland v. United States*, 531 U.S. 12, 121 S.Ct. 365, 148 L.Ed.2d 221 (2000), where the Court held that government licenses are not "property" within the meaning of the mail fraud statute.

In 1992 Carl Cleveland, a New Orleans, Louisiana, attorney, assisted Fred Goodson and his family in forming a limited partnership, Truck Stop Gaming, Ltd. (TSG), in order to participate in the video poker business at their truck stop in Slidell, Louisiana. Cleveland helped prepare TSG's application for a video poker license. The application required TSG to identify its partners and to submit personal financial statements for all partners. It also required TSG to affirm that the listed partners were the sole beneficial owners of the business and that no partner held an interest in the partnership merely as an agent or nominee, or intended to transfer the interest in the future. The application listed Goodson's adult children as the sole beneficial owners of the partnership, though Goodson and Cleveland were the actual owners. The application further stated that Goodson and Cleveland's law firm loaned the Goodson children the money for the partnership. The state approved the application in 1992 and issued a license to TSG. TSG successfully renewed the license in 1993, 1994, and 1995.

In 1996 the FEDERAL BUREAU OF INVESTIGATION (FBI) discovered that Cleveland and Goodson had participated in a scheme to bribe state legislators to vote in a manner favorable to the video poker industry. Federal prosecutors charged Cleveland and Goodson with money laundering, racketeering, CONSPIRACY, and mail fraud. The government alleged that the pair had fraudulently concealed that they were the true owners of TSG in the initial license application and three renewal applications mailed to the state. They concealed their ownership interests, according to the government, because they had tax and financial problems that could have undermined their suitability to receive a video poker license.

Before trial, Cleveland moved the court to dismiss the mail fraud charges because the alleged fraud did not deprive the state of "property" as defined by the federal mail fraud statute. The district court denied the motion, concluding that licenses are property even before they are issued by the state. Cleveland was convicted on two of the mail fraud counts and on other counts that were predicated on the mail fraud. He appealed, arguing that Louisiana had no property interest in video poker licenses, relying on several court of appeals decisions holding that the government does not relinquish "property" for purposes of the mail fraud statute when it issues a permit or license. The Court of Appeals for the Fifth Circuit rejected his argument and upheld the conviction. The U.S. Supreme Court agreed to hear Cleveland's appeal but only on the issue of whether the licenses constitute property under the mail fraud statute.

In a unanimous decision, the Supreme Court reversed the Fifth Circuit decision, concluding that unissued government licenses are not "property." Justice RUTH BADER GINSBURG, writing for the Court, noted that the federal mail fraud statute is "limited in scope to the protection of property rights." A previous decision, *McNally v. United States*, 483 U.S. 350, 360 (1987), had examined the history of the mail fraud statute and found that "the original impetus for the law was to protect the people from schemes to deprive them of their money or property."

As to the issue at hand, Justice Ginsburg rejected the idea that a government license is property for the purposes of the mail fraud statute. She found that the core interest in issuing a video poker license is to regulate an activity that a private citizen cannot take without official authorization. The government argued that the state had a property interest because "it received substantial sums of money in exchange for each license and continued to receive payments as long as the license remained in effect." Justice Ginsburg concluded that most of the expected revenue came *after* the license was issued. To accept the government's argument, Ginsburg said, would give "the state property rights in drivers' licenses, medical licenses, and other licenses requiring upfront" license fees. Justice Ginsburg stated that the government's reading of the mail fraud statute would lead to a "sweeping extension of federal criminal jurisdiction in the absence of a clear statement by Congress." Equating issuance of a license or permit with deprivation of property would give federal prosecutors authority to regulate conduct that has traditionally been handled by state and local authorities. Absent congressional direction, the Court refused to take this step. Therefore, the Court reversed the conviction and remanded the case back to the lower courts.

CROSS REFERENCES
Federalism; Property Law

MANSLAUGHTER

The unjustifiable, inexcusable, and intentional killing of a human being without deliberation, premeditation, and MALICE. The unlawful killing of a human being without any deliberation, which may be involuntary, in the commission of a lawful act without due caution and circumspection.

Man Takes Life Preserver from Child to Save Self

In October 2000 Troy Lee Carlisle, convicted of manslaughter earlier that year, received the maximum sentence of twenty years in prison for the May 2000 drowning death of 7-year-old Dallas Reinhardt. At the sentencing hearing, Mississippi's DeSoto Circuit Court Judge George Ready said to Carlisle about his conduct that it was "one of the most cowardly of acts I have ever heard of. I don't know how any reasonable man could have done what you did." He was alluding to the fact that the little girl had drowned after a frightened Carlisle pulled off her life preserver jacket to save his own life. At the time of the drowning, Carlisle was already facing charges of cocaine possession in an unrelated matter but was free on posted bond.

On May 7, 2000, Carlisle, who was a live-in friend of the child's mother and stepfather, had joined the family for a fishing trip. Kerri Peeples, the little girl's mother, had stayed behind, although in the past the entire family often spent time with Carlisle on the boat. Carlisle had worked for the Peeples family in their automotive shop before it closed down just one week prior to the incident. Kerri Peeples and her husband offered him shelter in their two-bedroom apartment and even paid for his attorney on the drugs and narcotics charges. Little Dallas and her 4-year-old brother Garrett often played with him and referred to him as "Troy Boy."

According to authorities, on the day of Dallas Reinhardt's death, Carlisle had joined Dallas, Garrett, and stepfather Kenneth on the family boat. Both children were wearing life preservers and left the boat to swim nearby when the current caused them to drift away. Neither man was wearing a life jacket. Kenneth jumped overboard to rescue Garrett, and Carlisle swam toward Dallas. After swallowing water in the strong current, however, he panicked. Carlisle later told police, "I was thinking I was going to die or she was going to die . . . I didn't really want both of us to die, so I figured I'd take it off her and put it around my arm . . . but she slipped out of my hand."

More than three-hundred law officers assisted in the search at Arkabutla Lake near Southaven, Mississippi, to find the girl, whose body was recovered three days later by her step-father Kenneth. At that time, Carlisle was accused of "depraved heart murder" under Mississippi law; several days later he was formally indicted by GRAND JURY. The indictment charged that Carlisle "did willfully, unlawfully and feloniously, knowingly and intentionally, drown and kill Dallas Reinhardt, while the said TROY CARLISLE was engaged in the commission of an act eminently dangerous to others and evincing a depraved heart."

Prosecutors originally sought conviction for murder under Mississippi's "depraved heart murder" law, which does not require specific INTENT. Akin to third-degree murder in some states, it is premised upon conduct that shows extreme RECKLESSNESS while in the commission of an eminently dangerous activity and with such disregard for the safety and well-being of others that the activity is continued even though the actor knows it may cause grave harm or death to another. As a result of such wanton behavior in the face of a reasonable expectation of it causing injury to another, the intent to cause great harm or death is *presumed* as a matter of law. Such a crime differs from first- and second-degree murders in that it does not require an element of premeditation or an intent to take the life of a specific individual.

Instead of depraved heart murder, however, the jury found Carlisle guilty of manslaughter and culpable NEGLIGENCE. Carlisle was sentenced to twenty years in prison. While the burden of proof does not leave the prosecutor, a verdict of manslaughter is premised upon the introduction of evidence that tends to show EXTENUATING CIRCUMSTANCES that preceded or precipitated the HOMICIDE, such as provocation, fear for one's life—especially in self-defense—or, in few states, impaired CAPACITY. According to Jack Jones, Carlisle's court-appointed attorney, the conviction was being appealed on both substantive and procedural GROUNDS.

CROSS REFERENCES
Appendix: Mississippi's Murder Statutes; Murder

Troy Carlisle is seen here at the Rankin County Courthouse after being convicted of manslaughter in the death of Dallas Reinhardt.

MARRIAGE

The legal status, condition, or relationship that results from a contract by which one man and one woman, who have the CAPACITY to enter into such an AGREEMENT, mutually promise to live together in the relationship of HUSBAND AND WIFE in law for life, or until the legal termination of the relationship.

Covenant Marriages

As of early 2001, Arizona and Arkansas were the only states to join Louisiana in legislatively approving "covenant marriages." The concept is a new one aimed at saving marriages in which couples agree to impose upon themselves limitations on their ability to divorce one another. Twenty other states have considered but refrained from adopting similar bills.

A COVENANT is technically a promise. When combined with the tendering of CONSIDERATION or the receipt thereof, it becomes contractually binding. Covenants differ from laws in that they are private contracts between parties, in this case, parties to a marriage. In covenant marriages, the parties mutually reject "no-fault divorce," agree to enroll in premarital or post-wedding counseling and also agree to divorce only under certain, more limiting conditions—DOMESTIC VIOLENCE, ABANDONMENT, ADULTERY, imprisonment of a spouse, or lengthy SEPARATION, for example. States which pass bills recognizing covenant marriages do not actually *require* such marriages but rather formally acknowledge them as legally viable, thus creating legal recourse under the law for breaches of such covenants.

Louisiana passed its covenant marriage law in 1997. At the time, it was touted as the first substantive effort in two centuries to make divorce more difficult, and lawmakers had hoped that other states would follow suit. Since then, however, fewer than five percent of Louisiana couples have opted to enter such marriages. Arizona's version of the law is less restrictive in that it permits an additional reason for divorce based on the mutual CONSENT of the parties.

The most common objection to covenant marriages comes from those who view such measures as undue government intrusion into family matters. The counterargument is that states increasingly have viewed divorce as a legitimate matter of public concern because of its extensive costs and the havoc it causes to primary and extended social and economic relationships. In this regard, covenant marriages are no more intrusive than state laws that permit or deny divorce based on certain articulated GROUNDS.

Another objection, the most vociferous proponent of which is the AMERICAN CIVIL LIBERTIES UNION (ACLU), is that covenant marriages seemingly infringe upon the separation of church and state because the mandatory premarital counseling contained in the two existing laws is often provided by clergy. Other opponents to the attempted legislative measures in other states have either expressed reservation for laws that seem to limit adult autonomy and choice or have themselves been active in the "divorce industry." This resistance was apparently the case in Texas and Oklahoma, where covenant marriage bills failed because of opposition by key committee chairmen who were divorce attorneys.

In addition to failed legislative attempts to pass covenant marriage bills in other states, different tactics to curb divorce have been tried. For example, Florida passed its Marriage Preparation and Preservation Act in 1998, but no state has followed Florida in requiring a marriage-education curriculum for public high schools. The Minnesota legislature attempted to pass a law that would have lowered marriage license fees for couples who sought pre-marital counseling, but it was vetoed by Minnesota Governor Jesse Ventura. In Wisconsin, a federal judge struck down a new state law that earmarked WELFARE money for clergy who encouraged long-married couples to mentor younger cou-

ples. According to the judge, the measure unfairly and unconstitutionally favored ministers over lay persons such as judges or JUSTICES OF THE PEACE. Texas recently passed a law allocating $3 from every marriage license fee to be used for marriage education research and reform. Nationwide, a group of activists called Americans for Divorce Reform sought to educate lawmakers, the media, and the general public on the true negative aspects of divorce, but the group did not advocate any specific reform such as covenant marriages.

Federal measures explicitly addressing marriage include the 1996 Defense of Marriage Act—limiting marriage to heterosexuals—and a 1996 welfare law that promoted two-parent marriages. Statistics indicated that in 2000 nearly one-third of all births were to unmarried women; nearly 40 percent of children do not live with both of their biological parents; and nearly half of all marriages in the United States end in divorce. There has been increasing interest in developing U.S. family policy through philanthropic commitments, state and federal policy initiatives, and the use of research as a basis for sound policy making.

CROSS REFERENCES
Appendix: Louisiana's Covenant Marriage Statute; Divorce

MILITARY LAW

The body of laws, rules, and regulations developed to meet the needs of the military. It encompasses service in the military, the constitutional rights of service members, the military criminal justice system, and the international law of armed conflict.

Army Sergeant Convicted of Child Rape and Murder in Kosovo

In July 2000, Staff Sergeant Frank Ronghi, who was serving as a peacekeeper in the NATO-led force in Kosovo, forewent full trial and entered a plea of guilty to charges of murder, forcible SODOMY, and indecent acts in the death of Merita Shabiu. Ronghi, a 36-year-old Army soldier from Niles, Ohio, was sentenced in August 2000 to life imprisonment without parole for the January 2000 rape and murder of an 11-year-old Albanian girl. He was given the maximum allowable sentence at the general COURT-MARTIAL hearing, but sat impassively as the verdict was read. The Ronghi case was the first time a soldier from any country had been accused of a serious crime since the arrival of the international peace-keeping force into Kosovo, the Serbian province where NORTH ATLANTIC TREATY ORGANIZATION (NATO) bombing in 1999 had ended Yugoslav President Milosevic's persecution of Albanian separatists. In unrelated incidents, however, five more soldiers from Ronghi's battalion had been caught and punished for abuse of Kosovar civilians.

On January 20, 2000, the U.S. Army announced that it would begin investigation into charges filed against Ronghi during the previous week. The formal Article 32 UNIFORM CODE OF MILITARY JUSTICE (UCMJ) investigation, complete with witness testimony, is comparable to a civilian pre-trial GRAND JURY investigation in that it is used to determine whether sufficient evidence exists to court-martial an accused. The key testimony at the Article 32 investigation was from fellow soldiers, who stated that Ronghi had repeatedly bragged to them about raping several young girls in other countries. He boasted of a nine-year-old victim in Haiti and two young sisters elsewhere.

A month prior to Merita Shabiu's murder, Ronghi allegedly had taken his squad to a remote hillside location near some woods, telling them "it was a good place to dump a body" because no one would hear any screaming. The soldiers allegedly failed to report any of these conversations to officers for fear of Ronghi's retaliation. Ronghi's defense attorneys told the investigative court in opening remarks, however, that their client was "an ordinary person" who encountered a culture of excessive violence and abuse of power during his military duty in Kosovo.

In June 2000 the Army announced that sufficient evidence existed for a full court-martial, held at the First Infantry Division courtroom at Leighton Barracks in Wuerzberg, Germany. Ronghi had been held in confinement at an Army facility in Mannheim, German, during the interim. According to prosecutors, evidence revealed that Ronghi knocked on the girl's apartment door on January 13, 2000, looking for a 23-year-old woman with whom he had recently been flirting. Merita Shabiu and her sister grew uncomfortable at Ronghi's presence and left him with their brother. Ronghi encountered the victim as he was leaving the building and persuaded her to go with him to the basement of the building. After the sexual assault, Ronghi killed her to stop her screaming. He placed the body in two U.N. food sacks and hid it under the stairs, covering up bloodstains with flour. He later returned to the scene with another soldier, even

Staff Sergeant
Frank J. Ronghi

though he had been summoned by radio to respond to a situation elsewhere in town. After burying the body in the snow, he allegedly advised his companion, "what happens in the squad stays in the squad." Nevertheless, the soldier related the information to fellow soldiers, who returned to the location that night and found a trail of pinkish blood in the snow. After removing some surface snow, they discovered the body of the dead girl. The private who originally had accompanied Ronghi to the scene then reported the incident to superiors.

Ronghi initially denied any knowledge of the body. When the evidence against his claims grew stronger, he "confessed" that he had found the girl's body in an apartment building, became frightened, and buried her on a hill nearby. After the Article 32 investigation required a full court-martial, Ronghi still did not enter a plea in his defense. One week before the scheduled court-martial trial, however, he voluntarily entered a plea of guilty to charges of murder, forcible sodomy, and three counts of indecent acts with a child. Although conviction of murder could have resulted in the death penalty for Ronghi, the matter had been referred to court-martial as a "non-capital" matter. Ronghi also was to be stripped of his rank and pay and dishonorably discharged. He will most likely serve his sentence in the high-security military prison facility in Fort Leavenworth, Kansas.

In December 2000 Merita Shabiu's father approached an Army checkpoint for food, telling soldiers his family was starving. His murdered daughter was buried in a grave about an hour's distance away, marked only with sticks and a water bottle used by the family to wash her prior to burial. In early 2001 American soldiers in Kosovo collected money to purchase a headstone for the little girl's gravesite.

MISREPRESENTATION

An assertion or manifestation by words or conduct that is not in accord with the facts.

Sweepstakes Settlements and Legislation

Until the late 1990s, it was fairly commonplace for Americans to open their residential mailboxes to find an envelope boldly claiming "You Are a Winner" of millions of dollars, only to be disappointed by the reality that they have not won anything. Such was the practice of the multimillion-dollar sweepstakes industry until recent years. In response to this practice of inducing individuals to believe that they had won something, a multitude of lawsuits erupted on behalf of citizens across the United States.

In February 2000 a federal judge approved a $30 million settlement against Publishers Clearing House, ending a CLASS ACTION lawsuit brought on behalf of people who bought magazines and other items from the sweepstakes company because they had been led to believe such purchases would increase their chances of winning a grand prize. This class-action litigation accused Publishers Clearing House of misleading the recipients of its mailings. The settlement also included terms under which the company agreed to make fundamental changes in the manner in which it conducts its business.

A similar nationwide class action lawsuit was filed against sweepstakes sponsor American Family Publishers. Like the lawsuit filed against Publishers Clearing House, this class action alleged that the defendant engaged in deceptive mailing practices that were designed to lure recipients into falsely believing that if they purchased merchandise, their odds of winning would be greatly increased. In September 2000 a U.S. DISTRICT COURT judge approved a settlement of the action in the amount of $33 million. In addition, the company agreed to make broad changes to their practices which include circulating new literature that conspicuously indicates that no purchase is necessary to win.

Many individuals, particularly the elderly, testified to spending as much as $11,000 per year in merchandise with the hope of winning a grand prize. One particular individual broke down in tears when testifying before the U.S. Senate about the $15,000 he had spent on unnecessary purchases bought in response to the sweepstakes mailings. In many instances, the funds needlessly spent on sweepstakes items were needed to support the buyers and often their families. For example, a Florida man named Eustace Hall testified before a Senate committee that he became so addicted to sweepstakes gimmicks that he squandered the money he had saved for his child's law school education hoping that his many purchases would increase his chances of winning a large sum of money. Other individuals reportedly spent their Social Security checks and even their life savings in order to purchase unwanted merchandise. When the various class action lawsuits filed across the country made this information apparent to lawmakers, new legislation was adopted on the federal level to prevent the deceptive mailing practices used by the sweepstakes industry.

On December 12, 1999, then-President BILL CLINTON signed into law Senate Bill 335, which contained the Federal Deceptive Mail Prevention and Enforcement Act. The purpose of the legislation is to protect unsuspecting Americans against exploitation by sweepstakes companies that occurs in response to misleading mailings. This law, which went into effect in April 2000, requires that sweepstakes literature contain a clear notice that purchases will not increase the chances of winning. The sweepstakes companies also are responsible for notifying recipients that if they wish to be removed from the company's mailing list, they may do so by calling a toll-free telephone number. Moreover, the STATUTE provides that any individual who receives sweepstakes promotional materials despite an election to be excluded from the mailing list is entitled to bring a private action in state court to ENJOIN the company from sending any more mailings. The individual may also file a private action to recover monetary loss caused from the violation, if any, or to receive $500 in DAMAGES for each such violation, whichever is greater. Sweepstakes companies that are discovered to be in violation of the Act face hefty fines for any deceptive practices used to induce recipients to purchase their products. Thus, these companies no longer have the right to tell an individual that they are "a guaranteed winner," when they have not won anything. The Act further prevents these companies from hiding the actual odds of winning in fine print in an attempt to induce the individual into buying magazines, compact discs, home videos, and other items. In accordance with this Act, the estimated odds and contest rules must now be in large type. The law is predicted to have a profound effect, not only on the way the sweepstakes industry conducts its business, but also on the magazine industry, which derives nearly one-third of all new subscriptions through sweepstakes entries.

MONOPOLY

An economic advantage held by one or more persons or companies deriving from the exclusive power to carry on a particular business or trade or to manufacture and sell a particular item, thereby suppressing competition and allowing such persons or companies to raise the price of a product or service substantially above the price that would be established by a free market.

Handicomp, Inc. v. United States Golf Association

Small companies often have a difficult time competing with large, entrenched companies that have close ties to their customers. The federal ANTITRUST LAW is designed to deter unfair competition but it is very difficult and expensive to prove that a business is monopolizing a market. This difficulty is demonstrated in *Handicomp, Inc. v. United States Golf Association*, 2000 WL 426245 (3rd.Cir. 2000), in which a computer software company unsuccessfully alleged that the United States Golf Association (USGA) illegally tried to dominate the business of computerized golf handicap calculations.

The case involved the seemingly innocuous calculation of a golfer's handicap. In the game of golf, a course is designed with eighteen holes. Beyond this golf course, designers establish the regulation number of strokes that a skilled golfer will need to tour the course. The number of strokes is referred to as par. Although most touring professional golfers usually can meet or break par, most amateur golfers take many more strokes to complete the course. In an effort to make the game fairer and more fun to play, the concept of the golf handicap was developed. A player's scores are recorded and averaged on a regular basis. The difference between the average score and par is known as the handicap. Thus, a player who averages 82 strokes on a par 72 course will have a handicap of 10. Because golf courses vary in difficulty, each golf course is given a course rating or slope. This slope calculation is included in determination of a golfer's handicap. Amateur players can then deduct their uniformly-calculated handicaps at the end of the round or tournament to help determine who won.

In 1968 Handicomp established a computerized handicap business to sell its software product to golf associations, golf courses, and country clubs. The software enabled a person at the course or club to maintain a record of the individual scores of golfers and to calculate the handicap. In 1981 the USGA formed the Golf Handicap & Information Network (GHIN) and began selling its own handicap calculation software. Over time more and more state and regional golf associations signed exclusive contracts with USGA for the GHIN system. By the mid-1990s USGA had such agreements with 70 percent of the associations.

Handicomp filed an antitrust lawsuit against USGA in 1996. It alleged a CONSPIRACY between the USGA and its regional associations to violate the SHERMAN ANTI-TRUST ACT and the Clayton Act. Handicomp brought this action under § 2 of the Sherman Act (15 U.S.C. § 2) and § 4 of the Clayton Act (15 U.S.C. § 15). Among its allegations was that the USGA changed handicap rules to frustrate other handicap software makers. The federal district court in New Jersey chose to ignore the Clayton Act claims, stating, "Because the parties are familiar with the facts and proceedings, our discussion will not be extensive and will be limited to a discussion of the Sherman Act allegations." The court ruled against Handicomp on April 13, 1999, finding it had failed to prove that the USGA had controlled prices or harmed competition. The judge attributed Handicomp's financial losses to legitimate business competition.

A three-judge panel of the Court of Appeals for the Third Circuit upheld the district court ruling. Judge Ruggero J. Aldisert, writing for the court, stated that to establish a claim under the Sherman Act, Handicomp needed to demonstrate that the USGA had "monopoly power" in the golf handicapping market and that the USGA had willfully acquired or maintained that power. Handicomp had to prove that the USGA's domination of the market could not be explained as a consequence of a superior product, business acumen, or historic accident. Judge Aldisert recognized that golf associations are the entire market for golf handicapping services because they are the only bodies entitled to grant a player a USGA Handicap Index. Though the USGA's 72 percent market share was an important factor, by itself it did not mean that the company had illegal monopoly power. The key issue was whether the USGA excluded competition.

Judge Aldisert found that Handicomp was "unable to prove substantial barriers to entry" into the market. The development of software and computing power made it possible that "a skilled teen age hacker today would have no difficulty in programming a data processing system to register the rating slope of a golf course and the gross score of the golfer and produce a handicap." Moreover, Handicomp's president had admitted that software was now easier to write and that it would take just three weeks to develop a competitive product and place it on the market. Based on this finding, Aldisert concluded that there were "no barriers to entry in the handicap data processing market similar to services provided by the parties before us." Without barriers to entry there can be no violation of the Sherman Act.

In re Independent Service Organizations Antitrust Litigation CSU, L.L.C.

When a manufacturer of a machine holds patents on the machine's components, it has the right to refuse to sell replacement parts to a service organization in competition with its own repair service. In some circumstances the manufacturer may be compelled to sell these parts to a competitor but such circumstances are limited and rare. This situation is illustrated in *In re Independent Service Organizations Antitrust Litigation CSU, L.L.C.*, 203 F.3d 1322 (Fed.Cir.2000), where a federal appeals court ruled that the Xerox Corporation did not have to sell patented parts, copyrighted manuals, and diagnostic software to photocopier repair companies. In so ruling the court rejected the claim that Xerox violated federal ANTITRUST LAWS because it held a monopoly over these parts, manuals, and software.

Xerox manufactures, sells, and services copiers that are used in all sectors of the economy. In 1984 it implemented a policy of "not selling parts unique to one series of copiers to independent service organizations (ISOs), including CSU, unless they were end-users of the copiers." The company expanded this policy in 1987 to include another copier line and cut off CSU's direct purchase of restricted parts. Xerox also began to track aggressively the sale of repair parts to insure that ISOs were not using the parts to repair copiers they did not own. The policy first applied to the six largest ISOs, which included CSU.

This policy severely undermined CSU's ability to service Xerox equipment for its customers. It was forced to recycle parts from other Xerox machines and to purchase parts from other ISOs and some of its customers. For a year it was able to import parts from a European affiliate of Xerox, but Xerox soon forced an end to this practice. In 1994 Xerox reached an out of court settlement with a group of ISOs on an antitrust suit, agreeing to freeze its restrictive parts policy for six and one-half years and to supply diagnostic software for four and one-half years. CSU did not participate in the settlement and instead filed a lawsuit alleging that "Xerox had violated the Sherman Act by setting prices on its patented parts much higher for ISOs than for end-users." This would "force ISOs to raise their prices" and make them uncompetitive in relation to the services offered by Xerox to end-users.

A federal district court dismissed CSU's lawsuit, ruling that Xerox had a lawful right as a patent and COPYRIGHT holder to refuse to sell or license its patented inventions or copyrighted expression. Such actions did not violate the antitrust laws. CSU appealed this decision. The Court of Appeals for the Federal Circuit upheld the district court decision. Chief Judge H. Robert Mayer, writing for the court, noted that "[i]ntellectual property rights do not confer a privilege to violate the antitrust laws." However, he also pointed out that antitrust laws do not negate the right of a patentee to exclude others from its property.

Judge Mayer stated that a patent alone does not establish market power under the antitrust laws. The patentee's right to exclude is supported by the U.S. Department of JUSTICE, the Federal Trade Commission, and the federal Patent Act. Despite this ability not to sell parts to competitors, Judge Mayer recognized two exceptions to this blanket rule. CSU could prevail if it proved Xerox either "obtained its patent through knowing and willful fraud" or that Xerox's counter-suit for patent infringement was a "sham to cover what is actually no more than an attempt to interfere directly with the business relationships of a competitor." The first exception did not apply because CSU never alleged that Xerox obtained its patents through fraud.

As to the second exception, CSU was required to "prove that the suit was both *objectively* baseless and *subjectively* motivated" to injure the competitive position of CSU. CSU argued that Xerox had sought to leverage its dominance in parts and equipment into dominance of the service market by tying the two together. Judge Mayer found no evidence that Xerox tied the sale of patented parts to the sale of other non-patented goods and services, however.

Having found that Xerox had not violated antitrust laws by refusing to sell patented parts, the court examined its refusal to sell copyrighted manuals and software to service competitors. Judge Mayer noted that the Copyright Act gives the copyright owner the exclusive right to distribute the protected work. CSU had sought to inquire into the subjective motivations Xerox had for not selling this material but the appeals court refused to take this approach. Absent evidence that the copyrights were obtained illegally or were used to gain monopoly power, according to Mayer's opinion, Xerox "was squarely within the rights granted by Congress to the copyright holder." Its refusal to sell or license its copyrighted work did not violate the antitrust laws.

PepsiCo v. Coca-Cola

Finding that "PepsiCo has not proffered sufficient evidence . . . [to warrant a full trial,]" on September 19, 2000, Judge Loretta A. Preska of the U.S. District Court for the Southern District of New York granted SUMMARY JUDGMENT against PepsiCo in its ANTITRUST lawsuit against competitor, the Coca-Cola Company. PepsiCo's principal claim, in *PepsiCo Inc. v. The Coca-Cola Company*, 98 Civ. 3282, was that Coca-Cola held an unlawful monopoly on the distribution of soda fountain syrup by controlling independent distributors of food source products through "loyalty agreements" and conflict of interest policies.

PepsiCo alleged that the problem began in 1997 when it DIVESTED its restaurant division by spinning off Kentucky Fried Chicken (KFC), Pizza Hut, and Taco Bell, and turning its fountain supply chain over to INDEPENDENT CONTRACTORS. According to the suit filed by PepsiCo, Coca-Cola controls 90 percent of the nation's independent food service distribution. Independent industry analysts estimate that Coca-Cola holds two-thirds of the fountain business, compared to PepsiCo's one-fourth. They also estimate that Coca-Cola controls 44 percent of the $54 billion U.S. carbonated soft drink market, compared to Pepsi's 31 percent. Globally, Coca-Cola controls just under half of the world market while PepsiCo holds 20.3 percent.

PepsiCo filed the original suit in May 1998, seeking unspecified DAMAGES and injunctive RELIEF to prohibit Coca-Cola from executing its exclusionary "loyalty agreements," which required independent service distributors to carry only Coca-Cola products on their trucks. Such distributors supply fountain drinks to restaurants, movie theaters, retail outlets, college campuses, among other locations. PepsiCo alleged that Coca-Cola had strong-armed distributors to drop PepsiCo products. According to the suit, Coca-Cola's business practices halted the flow of PepsiCo at fountains and inflated prices for consumers. By preventing distributors from delivering PepsiCo, chains were forced "to remain with Coke without being able to put [their] requirements out for fair and competitive bids."

Under the SHERMAN ANTI-TRUST ACT, exclusivity contracts are not illegal. Both PepsiCo and Coca-Cola have executed numerous multi-million-dollar "exclusive" contracts with various entities in the past. For example, PepsiCo signed several contracts with colleges and universities, such as the $14 million, 12-year contract with Pennsylvania State University—complete with cash incentives and high commissions—to make Pepsi-Cola the exclusive soft drink sold on that campus. Coca-Cola has entered into similar contracts elsewhere.

Furthermore, having a monopoly is not necessarily illegal. In fact, proponents of monopolistic economies, such as economist Joseph Schumpeter, have argued in the past that monopolist entities may have greater access to low-cost internal finance and may be better able to take advantage of scale economies in research and development, thereby facilitating full appropriation of the value of new ideas. What is often relevant in alleged antitrust activity, however, is whether there has been a misuse of monopolistic power such that competition in the relevant market is substantially lessened or made impossible. This argument was made by PepsiCo.

Technically, the judge's dismissal of the three-year old suit hinged on PepsiCo's failure to prove an important element in all monopoly cases: the "relevant market" affected by the alleged monopoly. In what the judge referred to as a "gerrymandered customer definition," PepsiCo tried to define the customer base at issue as large chain accounts with limited franchising, centralized management, and predictable needs since they served their meals with fountain drinks but not with bottled or canned drinks. Judge Loretta A. Preska referred to this as creating a "strange red-haired, bearded, one-eyed-man-with-a-limp classification." Accordingly, the judge ruled, "PepsiCo has chosen to define the elements of the relevant market to suit its desire for high Coca-Cola market share, rather than letting the market define itself. . . . Regardless of the substance of the proffered customer definition or the method by which it was arrived at, PepsiCo has not proffered sufficient evidence from which a finder of fact could conclude that the customer base should be viewed so narrowly."

The judge did not find that the "bundle" of other services provided along with the fountain syrup delivery comprised a separate market, as argued by PepsiCo. Preska found that there was insufficient evidence to show that bottled and canned soft drink distributors, through price reductions or marketing strategies, were not able to "lure significant numbers of customers into buying fountain syrup [from them]." The judge also agreed with Coca-Cola's argument that the relevant market could not be limited to fountain drinks from commissaries because customers could just as easily obtain syrup concentrate directly from bottlers. In fact, one of PepsiCo's own officers had testified in the case that the relevant market was fountain syrup, irrespective of the delivery method.

The decision concluded that PepsiCo had attempted to define the product at issue as the distribution method itself, not the product being distributed. Since the distribution method is not a product of either PepsiCo or Coca-Cola, but rather derives from the distributors and bottlers, "this factor weighs against the finding of a separate market for distribution through systems distributors because PepsiCo and Coca-Cola do not engage in the distribution line of commerce."

CROSS REFERENCES
Antitrust Law

MURDER

The unlawful killing of another human being without justification or excuse.

Doctor Convicted of Multiple Poisonings

Charged with killing three patients while he was on the staff of the Veteran's Affairs Medical Center in Northport, New York, in 1993, Dr. Michael J. Swango is suspected of as many as 50 other deaths. Proof of such charges could mark him as one of history's most prolific serial killers. The three patients died from injections of a drug that stopped their hearts. No attempt was made to revive them because Swango had forged orders that said, "Do Not Resuscitate." He was also charged with lying about his past, which may involve more poisoning and ASSAULT charges being filed. At first declaring his innocence, Swango later pleaded guilty to the murders in September 2000, which spared him the death penalty. He was sentenced to life without parole. Two weeks later, he was charged with, and pleaded guilty to, the 1984 injection death of 19-year-old Cynthia Ann McGee at Ohio State University Hospital.

Swango was born in Fort Lewis, Washington, in 1954. According to relatives, his mother and father were emotionally-detached as parents. After the family moved to Quincy, Illinois, in 1967, Swango went to a Catholic high school, graduating as valedictorian in 1972. He left Millikin University in Decatur after two years to join the U.S. Marines. Discharged honorably in 1976, he graduated from Quincy College with majors in biology and chemistry. He wrote his senior chemistry thesis on the poisoning murder of Georgi Markov, the Bulgarian writer.

At Southern Illinois University Medical School, fellow students began to notice Swango's seeming disregard for the patients he treated. He gained the nickname "Double-O-Swango," after James Bond's "007" who had a "license to kill," because so many of his patients died after he attended them. The connection between Swango and the unusual number of deaths, however, was considered coincidental.

Swango graduated in April 1983 and began a neurosurgery residency at Ohio State University in Columbus in July. He was investigated the following February when a student nurse said Swango had injected an elderly patient shortly before the patient died. Although there was concern about the rise in deaths since Swango's arrival, he was cleared and allowed to finish the year. Despite the fact that the school did not renew his residency, he was granted a permanent license to practice medicine from the Ohio State Medical Board.

Back in Quincy, Swango began work as a paramedic with the Adams County Ambulance Corps. At one point when asked why he kept so many clippings about poisons in a scrapbook, he reportedly replied, "It's a good way to kill people." After a number of colleagues became ill at various times, suspicion fell on Swango. At one point, doctors on Swango's shift ate some chicken he had brought for them. They vomited so violently that they broke blood vessels in their eyes. Finally, after more strange happenings,

Swango's apartment was searched and a home-made poison lab uncovered. He served two years in prison and was released in 1987. Although his conviction resulted in the loss of his medical license, Swango sought out and won a residency at the University of South Dakota in 1992. He worked at the Veterans Affairs Medical Center in Sioux Falls, South Dakota, until hospital administrators learned the truth about his suspicious past, which Swango had concealed by falsifying facts on his application.

Swango's dismissal from the hospital did not deter him from seeking out another medical position. In 1993 he again received a residency, this time at the State University of Stony Brook Medical School, which placed him in its Northport Veterans Affairs Medical Center facility in New York. To gain the residency, Swango misrepresented his conviction in Illinois as stemming from a bar fight. Apparently, no one checked his credentials. "He was a pathological charmer," said Stephen Villano, associate medical school dean. During his time at the hospital, Swango administered toxic substances to patients George Siano, Aldo Serini, and Thomas Sammarco. He told colleagues that the patients' families had ordered them not to be resuscitated, which later proved to be a lie.

Less than a year into his residency, Swango was again dismissed. Facing impending charges of making a false statement to federal officials and improperly using controlled substances in the hospital, Swango left the country before they could be filed. He took a job with the Zimbabwe Association of Church Hospitals, working at the Mnene Hospital. Between May and July of 1995, he poisoned two of his patients, both of whom survived. Hospital administrators became suspicious of Swango, and suspended him in July.

Within two years, Swango obtained another medical position, this time in Dharan, Saudi Arabia. However, his flight to the Middle East first took him to Chicago, where he was arrested in June of 1997 on the charges filed against him shortly after he moved to Zimbabwe. During the course of his 42-month prison sentence, investigators focused on the suspicious deaths at the various hospitals in which Swango worked. Only a few days before Swango's scheduled release, prosecutors charged him with the three murders in New York, and later the one in Ohio. Added to the indictment were assault charges in connection with another Northport patient, Barron Harris, who survived his poisoning, and the two patients in Zimbabwe.

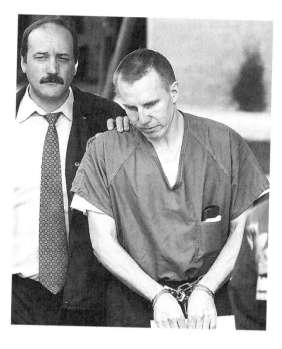

Former physician Michael Swango is escorted by a U.S. Marshal out of Federal Court in Uniondale, New York.

Swango initially proclaimed his innocence, but then changed to a guilty plea in September of 2000 in order to avoid the death penalty and to prevent his extradition to Zimbabwe, where he was wanted in connection with suspected poisonings. His conviction and the media coverage of his trial inspired a campaign for more thorough background checks into those applying for medical positions. Pulitzer-prize winning author James B. Stewart was one of the outspoken critics of the medical profession, which he accused of unwittingly aiding Swango's murder spree by ignoring warning signs. Stewart outlined his argument in the 1999 book, *Blind Eye: How the Medical Establishment Let a Doctor Get Away with Murder*, which he had written before murder charges were filed against Swango. According to Stewart, Swango operated undetected in so many different institutions because the authority of doctors is rarely questioned in a hospital setting, making it difficult for nurses and patients to introduce suspicions about their conduct.

Handyman Convicted of Yosemite Decapitations

On July 22, 1999, the headless body of 26-year-old naturalist Joie Armstrong was discovered in Yosemite National Park, California. Cary Stayner, a shy motel handyman and long-time resident of the park, later confessed to the crime and was sentenced to life imprisonment without parole in November 2000. In addition, he is charged with first-degree murder for strangling two women and slashing the throat of

Cary Stayner is escorted into a Mariposa County courtroom to face charges that he killed three female Yosemite Park tourists.

another, also in Yosemite. A guilty verdict for these crimes could bring the death penalty. Experts stated their belief that Stayner, 37-years old at the time of the murders, is a sociopath whose deep fury is directed toward women.

Stayner grew up in Merced, California, where he went to high school. He was a loner and about the only thing that interested him was drawing. As he grew older, he liked being alone in the mountains and wilderness of Yosemite. He claimed to have once seen the legendary Bigfoot. Perhaps he preferred the solitude to the publicity his family had received over their personal tragedies. In 1972, Stayner's younger brother Steven was kidnapped by a pedophile and held for seven years. He finally came home and was something of a celebrity for a while with an NBC movie on his experience called *I Know My First Name Is Steven*. Tormented by his ordeal and under the influence of drugs, Steven died in a motorcycle crash in September 1989 at the age of 24. The following December, an uncle of Stayner's, with whom he lived for a time, came home from work one day to find an intruder in the house. The intruder, who has never been identified, killed him with a shotgun.

In 1995, while Stayner was working for Merced Glass Company, he confessed to a friend that he was "freaking out" and felt like killing their boss. The friend told the boss that Stayner needed help, and, obligingly, the boss took Stayner to the Merced County Mental Health Center. Stayner stayed only a few hours,

though, returning to Merced Glass only to quit. He said he was going to Santa Cruz. He never got there, however. Instead, he just stayed in the mountains, spending much of his time alone and using drugs. In the spring of 1997, Stayner began work as handyman for the Cedar Lodge, a remote motel on Highway 140, leading into Merced. People liked him because he was quiet, neat, and could fix almost anything.

On the night of February 15, 1999, Stayner knocked on the door of Carole Sund's Cedar Lodge motel room where she was staying with her daughter Juli, 15, and Juli's friend, Silvina Pelosso, 16, on a vacation in Yosemite. Although he actually had been laid off for the winter, Stayner claimed to be a handyman called to fix a bathroom leak. Carole let him in. Once inside the motel room, Stayner reportedly produced a gun and locked the girls in the bathroom. He first strangled Carole and then Silvina, stuffing their bodies into their rental car. He then spent hours forcing Juli to perform sex acts. Finally, in the early morning hours he drove her, still alive, in the rental car to a deeply wooded trail where he cut her throat. He drove the car to an old logging road where he left it and walked miles to a pay phone to call a cab. The bodies were not found for a month. When authorities later went to the motel where the women had last been seen alive, Stayner appeared very helpful in answering all their questions. Authorities dismissed him as a suspect since he had no prior history of violence.

In July, Stayner spotted naturalist Joie Armstrong outside her cabin. After a struggle, he got her into his jeep. Although partially bound by duct tape, Armstrong managed to escape through an open window of the moving vehicle and fled into the woods. Stayner caught up with her and, now in a rage, cut off her head. He threw it in a stream.

This time there was a witness, although not to the actual murder. A firefighter in Yosemite spotted Stayner's truck on the road and later remembered that it had stayed there a long time. The crime scene produced blood, fingerprints, and hair. Until Armstrong's remains were found, Stayner was not a suspect in the earlier murders. In fact, the authorities believed they were looking for at least two killers. One reason was an anonymous letter that had been mailed from Stockton, California, about a month after the three women were murdered, and another was Sund's wallet, which was found in Modesto, a city some 90 miles away. Police later concluded that Stayner was responsible for mailing the letter—in which he taunted them about the murder spree—and planting the wallet. Although he initially denied involvement with Armstrong's death, Stayner unexpectedly confessed to both that murder and the murders of the other three women during a television interview. He later repeated his confession to authorities.

Stayner later regretted his confession and pleaded not guilty to killing Armstrong. He was tried in federal court because the murder occured inside the national park, which is federal territory. The federal death penalty law of 1994 was invoked by the prosecution, to which Stayner's attorney objected. His challenge was denied in July 2000, thus officially allowing the prosecution to seek CAPITAL PUNISHMENT. At the trial, however, he changed his pleas to guilty for all counts—kidnapping, premeditated murder, and sexual assault. In a tearful statement at his sentencing he apologized to Armstrong's family for killing their daughter, blaming his actions on the "terrible dark dreams" that drove him to murder. On November 30, 2000, he was sentenced to life imprisonment without parole. Although he avoided the death penalty in Armstrong's murder, that may not be the case in his trial for the murders of the three Yosemite tourists, which got underway in June 2001. Since Stayner's confessions included details that the police say only the killer could know, authorities are rechecking at least five other murders in the area, including the still-unsolved shooting of Stayner's uncle in 1990.

The victims' families filed WRONGFUL DEATH lawsuits in Fresno County Superior Court against the lodge where Stayner worked. The Sund family alleged that Stayner's "unusual, bizarre or violent manner" should have been recognized by his employers, much as it had been by his boss at Merced Glass in 1995. At the very least, the lawsuits claimed, a sufficient background check was not done on Stayner before employing him.

Rae Carruth, NFL Player, Convicted for Murdering His Girlfriend

On November 16, 1999, Cherica Adams, 24-years old and pregnant, was fatally shot in Charlotte, North Carolina. Hours after the attack, her baby, Chancellor Lee Adams, was delivered by caesarean birth. He is developmentally disabled and suffers from cerebral palsy, probably because he was six weeks early. Cherica Adams died a month later. Her boyfriend, father of the child, and star wide receiver for the Carolina Panthers, Rae Lamar Carruth, was charged

Rae Carruth listens as witnesses testify during his murder trial.

with first-degree murder, the first active National Football League (NFL) player ever to be so charged. In January 2001 he was acquitted of first degree murder but convicted of CONSPIRACY to commit murder for shooting into an occupied vehicle and trying to kill an unborn child. Carruth was sentenced to 24 years and 4 months in prison without the possibility of parole.

Carruth was at the top of his world in 1997 when he became a first-round pick—number 27—in the NFL draft. A wide receiver, he was chosen by the Carolina Panthers and signed a four-year, $3.7-million contract. This income immediately distanced him from his youth in Sacramento, California, where he was born on January 20, 1974. His real name is Rae Lamar Wiggins, but he took the name of his stepfather when his mother remarried. After they divorced, his mother raised him alone. He grew up talented enough in football to earn a scholarship to the University of Colorado. While there, a son was born to Carruth and a girlfriend. Later, he was ordered by the court to pay $3,500 a month in CHILD SUPPORT.

Friends in college and in the pros describe Carruth as distant and somewhat mysterious, genial but not close to anyone. He performed brilliantly during his first professional season, however, racking up a total of 545 yards and leading all NFL rookies with 44 catches. Then injuries hampered his career. He broke his right foot and sat out nearly the entire 1998 campaign. After catching 14 passes in the first five games of 1999, he sprained his right ankle and was force to the sidelines again.

When Carruth learned that Adams, whom he began dating in 1998, was pregnant, he asked her to think about an abortion. She declined, but according to the testimony of her mother, Saundra, Carruth then began to take an interest in the coming baby, even going to prenatal care visits for a while. After his injury, he began to worry openly about his pro career and how much the child was going to cost, despite the fact that Adams was a successful real estate agent. He still had $3,500 monthly payments for the child born in Colorado. Additionally Carruth was being sued for reneging on the purchase of a house in Charlotte.

Prosecutors at the trial theorized that Carruth planned the murder because he did not want to pay child support. According to the prosecution and trial testimony, shortly after midnight on November 19, 1999, Adams was driving behind Carruth as they returned from a movie. Carruth called another car from his cell phone. In it were Van Brett (some sources say William) Watkins, who worked at odd jobs for Carruth; Michael E. Kennedy, who had recently pleaded guilty to a gun possession charge in South Carolina; and a 19-year-old laborer, Stanley Abraham, Jr. While Carruth blocked Adams's car from escaping, the car containing the three men pulled alongside, and she was shot in the neck, chest, and stomach.

All four men were charged with conspiracy to commit murder, but when Adams died, the charge became first-degree murder. The Panthers, who had put Carruth on unpaid leave, cut him. When an arrest warrant went out, Carruth disappeared. He was picked up by the FEDERAL BUREAU OF INVESTIGATION (FBI) less than a day later hiding in the trunk of a car in a motel parking lot in Tennessee. With him was $3,900 in cash. The tip to the FBI had come from his mother, Theodry, who feared that his flight might result in a violent confrontation with unsympathetic police.

Carruth declared his innocence. According to his explanation, the shooting was the result of a drug deal gone wrong. An exchange was supposed to take place on the night of the shooting, but Carruth claimed that he refused to finance it. Enraged by the change of plans and in retaliation, Watkins and Kennedy allegedly shot Carruth's girlfriend. Kennedy testified, however, that Carruth paid him to buy the gun, recruited him to drive the car, and said that the murder was planned because of the coming

baby. Watkins, who pleaded guilty to second-degree murder, had agreed to testify against Carruth but was not called. An ex-girlfriend of Carruth's, Candace Smith, also testified that Carruth told her he was involved in the murder.

Carruth denied involvement. He explained his flight from arrest charges by asking, "[W]ho was going to speak up for me?" He repeatedly declared his innocence at the trial. "I was not there," he said. "I didn't see the shooting." However, his claim was refuted by the words of Cherica Adams herself. After the attack and badly wounded, she called 911 from her car. On tape, which was played at the trial, and later at the hospital, she said that Carruth's car had blocked her own. When asked where Carruth had gone after the shooting, she said, "He just left."

Because he spent 14 months in jail awaiting trial, Carruth may have his sentence cut by about five years if his behavior is good. Thus, he would serve a minimum of 18 years and 11 months without parole. As his sentence was read, the former star player showed no emotion. He said of the shooting, "I feel guilty about none of it. I didn't have anything to do with it." His attorney notified the court that he intended to appeal on several grounds, including the fact that no black males were on the jury.

Ray Lewis, NFL Star, Evades Murder Charges

Two men were stabbed to death in Atlanta, Georgia, following a post-Super Bowl party on January 31, 2000. Baltimore Ravens linebacker Ray Lewis and two co-defendants were charged with the murders. Lewis was released on a $1 million bond. In June, he pleaded guilty to a misdemeanor, and the murder charges were dropped. The crimes are still unsolved. Lewis returned to Baltimore and the football team for the next season. He was named the game's Most Valuable Player after the Ravens victory over the New York Giants in Super Bowl XXXV, in January 2001.

Ray Anthony Lewis, born May 15, 1975, was drafted by the Baltimore Ravens out of the University of Miami, Florida, in 1996 and was named to *USA Today*'s All-Rookie team that year. A native of Lakeland, Florida, he developed into a linebacker with amazing speed and toughness. He won honors as the National Football League's (NFL) most valuable defensive player for the 2000 season. The Baltimore Ravens took the American Conference championship that year and played National Conference winners, the New York Giants, in the Super Bowl held in Tampa, Florida, on January 28, 2001.

A year earlier, on January 31, police in Atlanta, Georgia, were called to the Cobalt Lounge at about 4:00 A.M. to investigate a shooting at a post-Super Bowl party. Instead, they discovered two men, Jacinth Baker, 21, and Richard Lollar, 24, suffering from fatal stab wounds. Both deaths were judged HOMICIDES. It was believed that the killings had resulted from a brawl that erupted at the lounge, with Baker and Lollar teaming against Lewis and several others in his group.

An eyewitness led police to a stretch limousine, leased by Lewis, about one block from the crime scene. A search revealed blood in the passenger compartment. The limousine driver said he saw Lewis fighting with one of the victims. At first Lewis gave incorrect names to police concerning who had entered the limousine with him after the stabbing. Lewis, Reginald Oakley, 31, and Joseph Sweeting, 34, were charged with murder. Protesting his innocence, Lewis claimed he had tried to break up the fight and was at least 60 feet away when the stabbings occurred. "I am very sorry about the tragedy," he said when he was out on bail and back at the Ravens' training camp. "You've heard it many times before. Now you get to hear it from me: I am innocent."

The $1 million bond was issued on a first-degree murder charge because the superior court judge ruled that Lewis, with no prior felony convictions, was not likely to flee the country. After the pro star was released, he returned home to Maryland, where he lives in Owings Mills. In June 2000 he pleaded guilty to a misdemeanor charge, one count of OBSTRUCTION OF JUSTICE. In exchange for admitting he had misled police after the stabbing and had initially told witnesses "to keep their mouths shut," he was sentenced to one year of probation. During the probation period, Lewis must remain employed, must not use alcohol or other drugs, and must be at home no later than 9 P.M. every night. The prosecution agreed to the deal apparently because there were too many inconsistencies in the testimonies of various witnesses to firmly establish the guilt of any of the defendants.

Also as part of his plea, Lewis agreed to testify for the prosecution. At the trial he said that co-defendant Sweeting showed a knife after the fight and that Sweeting had admitted to "hitting" one of the victims. Even though past criminal records of the victims were not admissi-

ble, the defense attacked the character of the dead men at trial. Baker was wanted on gun possession and drug charges, and Lollar had been arrested three times in 1996 and 1997. Both Sweeting and Oakley were later acquitted of the murders. Lewis's change of plea allowed him to return to his job as linebacker for the Baltimore Ravens.

The families of the murdered men are bitter about the resolution of the trial. They vowed that they would not let the matter rest. "If [Lewis] wasn't in the NFL," said Baker's aunt, "he'd be just another person sitting in the penitentiary." In the event that Lewis's athletic ability eventually leads him to the Pro Football Hall of Fame, family members said they would be present for the induction ceremony: "We'll be out there with our signs."

Immediately after the misdemeanor plea, the Baltimore Ravens welcomed Lewis back to the team. Although he was cleared of murder and AGGRAVATED ASSAULT charges, the NFL indicated Lewis would be suspended for two to six weeks. The league did not specify when that suspension would occur.

Skakel to Stand Trial on 26-Year-Old Murder Charge

A court decision has ordered 40-year-old Michael Skakel, nephew of Ethel Kennedy, to stand trial as an adult for the 1975 murder of Martha Moxley. Skakel was 15-years old at the time of the killing, the same age as the victim. When he was charged in 2001, he hoped to be tried as a juvenile or have the case dismissed on this 26-year-old crime. The long-unsolved murder gained new life when differences were noted

Baltimore Ravens linebacker Ray Lewis testifies in Fulton Superior Court during the murder trial of Joseph Sweeting and Reginald Oakley.

Michael Skakel (*center*) leaves with his attorney after a court hearing for the 1975 murder of Skakel's childhood neighbor Martha Moxley.

in Skakel's statements made after the killing and again in 1992 when he spoke to private investigators whom his father had hired to clear the family name.

Michael Skakel is one of seven children born to wealthy industrialist Rushton Skakel, brother of Ethel Kennedy, and his wife Ann, who died in 1973. In 1975 young Skakel lived at the family home in Belle Haven, an upper-class area of Greenwich, Connecticut, that was guarded by a private security detail. Just 16 months earlier, Dorthy and David Moxley and their two teenage children had moved from Piedmont, California, to a home across the street from the Skakel family. David, an accountant, had been recommended by Skakel for membership at Manhattan's University Club, and Dorthy felt assured about the safety of her children in this neighborhood of privilege.

So it was a relaxed Dorthy Moxley who waved goodbye to 15-year-old Martha as she set off to join the neighborhood kids in some pre-Halloween pranks. The group often included Michael Skakel and his brother Tommy. It was cold that October 30, 1975, and Martha wore her blue down jacket. That was the last Dorthy Moxley saw of her daughter. Anxious hours spent watching at the front window turned to panic before dawn. Several hours later, the body of the teenager was found beneath a tree on the Moxley property. Martha had been killed with a six-iron golf club, so viciously attacked that her skull was crushed and the club shattered. The killer had stabbed her in the neck with the broken shaft. The handle of the club was missing. The girl's jeans and underclothing were around her ankles, but she had not been raped. The

killing was described as one of appalling savagery.

After investigation by the Greenwich Police Department, which had little experience in HOMICIDE, the search for Martha Moxley's murderer went into virtual limbo for the next 15 years. The Moxleys remained friendly with the Skakel household for a time until they became convinced that some member of that family had to be the perpetrator. They moved to New York City and then to Annapolis, Maryland, where David Moxley died in 1988. His wife, herself troubled by depression, felt that their daughter's murder contributed to his heart attack.

The main reason for the lack of progress in the hunt for the killer was lack of evidence. Stephen Carroll, a Greenwich detective at the time who later retired, admitted that perhaps the police had not been aggressive enough, which he blamed on the fact that they were novices in this area. There had been no quick AUTOPSY, so the time of death was imprecise. Although the golf club found at the murder site belonged to Ann Skakel, there was no police search of the Skakel home. The handle of the club, which might have held the killer's fingerprints, was never found. Investigators apparently assumed a teenager could not have committed such a vicious crime. Tommy and Michael Skakel, although interviewed by police after the murder, were not considered as possible suspects until several months had passed. Another suspect, 23-year-old Kenneth Littleton, a tutor who had moved into the Skakel household on the day of the murder, was also suspected. He failed three polygraph tests but, in part because he barely knew the victim, he was never charged.

For a time, the Skakels cooperated with the investigation. However, when police began to zero in on Tommy as a suspect, his father became angry and refused further cooperation. Michael, who was dyslexic, remained a troubled youth who drank heavily. In 1978 he was arrested for drunk driving in upstate New York. His father sent him to Elan School in Maine, a tough love institution for rich children. Michael ran away on several occasions. Another Elan student at the time later testified that Michael Skakel admitted to killing Moxley, though Skakel denied it. After two years, he left Elan and spent the next several years on ski slopes and golf courses and in and out of substance abuse rehabilitation clinics, backed financially by his father. He nearly qualified for the 1992 Olympics in speed skating. Friends who knew him then said he was a friendly, gentle person, but a

Greenwich resident, who published an account of the murder in 1998, said he was ill tempered and cruel to animals.

Skakel seemed to straighten out his life in the early 1990s when he married Margot Sheridan, a golf pro. They had one son, George. Skakel graduated from Curry College in Milton, Massachusetts, in 1993 and worked for the 1994 re-election campaign of Senator Edward Kennedy, his uncle.

Perhaps the Moxley killing would have faded into the background of Skakel's life, but in 1991, William Kennedy Smith, a cousin, was charged with rape in West Palm Beach, Florida. Although he was acquitted, the trial resurrected the rumors, which proved false, that he had been at the Skakel home on the night of the murder in 1975. Angered by the old suspicions that swirled around the case, Rushton Skakel ordered a private investigation to clear the family name.

It had just the opposite effect. Investigators discovered that both Michael and Tommy had changed their stories dramatically. Tommy initially said he last saw Martha at 9:30 P.M.; now he said the two indulged in "heavy petting" on her home grounds around 10 P.M. Michael originally said he was nowhere near the Moxley home on that night; now he said he had been in a tree outside the girl's bedroom.

Michael Skakel was charged with the 26-year-old murder. He turned himself in to police in Greenwich in February 2001. He was released on bond and returned to his home in Hobe Sound, Florida. His hopes for being tried as a juvenile, which meant that he could face as little as four years in jail if convicted, were dashed in March when the court ordered that he be tried as an adult. In that case, he could get life if convicted. Skakel's troubles did not end with the court decision. His wife sued him for divorce and CUSTODY of their son.

The Kennedy family stood behind Skakel. "This has ruined his life," a relative said. As for Dorthy Moxley, much of her own money as well as media attention through the years have kept interest in the case alive. She realizes that without physical evidence linking Skakel to the 26-year-old crime, a conviction may be difficult, but she feels that any progress is some satisfaction.

CROSS REFERENCES
Juvenile Law

NATIONAL RIFLE ASSOCIATION

As of 2001 the National Rifle Association (NRA) had replaced the American Association of Retired Persons as Washington's most powerful lobbying group according to *Fortune* magazine's top 25 list. The 130-year-old organization reported a membership of 4.3 million, which included 1 million new members in the previous year alone. With a 2001 budget of $200 million, the NRA comfortably maintained its own $35 million state-of-the-art lobbying machine, complete with an in-house telemarketing department, its own newscast, and one million political organizers at the precinct level. The NRA considers itself America's foremost defender of the SECOND AMENDMENT of the U.S. Constitution, which preserves the right of the people to keep and bear arms. The NRA is a tax-exempt organization focused on raising and ensuring financial support for several firearms-related activities benefiting youth, women, hunters, competitive shooters, gun collectors, and law enforcement agents. Its platform prefers gun safety programs and the intensified enforcement of *existing* federal gun laws to an increase in the number of restrictions on gun owners.

Formed by New York charter in 1871, the NRA's original goal was to "promote and encourage rifle shooting on a scientific basis," according to co-founder and U.S. CIVIL WAR veteran Colonel William C. Church. He and fellow co-founder, fellow Union veteran General George Wingate, were dismayed by the lack of marksmanship shown by Union troops and wanted to set up a rifle range for practice. With contributions from New York State, the new organization purchased the Creed Farm on Long Island in 1872 and opened it to members in 1873 under the name of "Creedmoor," the NRA's first official shooting range. When political opposition to the promotion of marksmanship arose in New York, Creedmoor was deeded back to the state. A new site was established in Sea Girt, New Jersey.

The NRA targeted America's youth from the onset, and by 1903 was promoting shooting sports and competition matches through the establishment of rifle clubs at all major colleges, universities, and military academies. In addition to training and education in marksmanship, the association published *The American Rifleman*, which helped keep its members abreast of new BILLS and laws affecting firearms. In 1934 the NRA formed its Legislative Affairs Division, which engaged in direct mail efforts to apprise members of legislative facts and analyses on pending bills. Although it was not involved in direct lobbying efforts at that time, the NRA later formed the Institute for Legislative Action (ILA) in 1975, a lobbying entity organized "for political defense of the Second Amendment."

During WORLD WAR II, the association offered its shooting ranges to the U.S. government and helped develop training materials for personal and industrial security. NRA members also volunteered to reload ammunition for those guarding war plants. Through a series of GUN CONTROL laws enacted between the first and second world wars, Britain found itself virtually disarmed and vulnerable when Germany began its European invasions. The NRA's efforts to encourage assistance for Britain in 1940 resulted in the collection of more than 7,000 firearms for Britain's defense against German invasion.

Wayne LaPierre, executive vice-president of the NRA, speaks at a Washington news conference, accompanied by Eddie Eagle, the mascot for the GunSafe Program.

Following the war, the NRA concentrated on the hunting community and in 1949, in conjunction with the state of New York, set up the first hunter education program. In 1973 it launched its second magazine, *The American Hunter*. Although hunter education courses eventually became the assumed responsibility of state fish and game departments, the NRA continued to manage its Youth Hunter Education Challenge (YHEC), a program currently active in 43 states and three Canadian provinces, with youth enrollment of approximately 40,000.

Since 1956 the association has been instrumental in law enforcement training as well. With the introduction of its Police Firearms Instructor Certification Program in 1960, the NRA became the only national trainer of law enforcement officers, and by 2000 there were 10,000 NRA-certified program graduates. The association's certified instructors train about 750,000 civilian gun owners each year, conducting gun safety campaigns for children in addition to personal security and protection seminars, as well as marksmanship training, for adults.

Also in the 1990s, the association announced the publication of its third periodical, *The American Guardian*, which proved to be less esoteric in content and catering more to topics such as recreational use of firearms and self-defense. Concomitant with the new publication was an internal effort to purge the organization of radical, right-wing gun enthusiasts and develop more general appeal. Since 1997 actor Charlton Heston has served as the organization's president.

Politically and historically, supporters for both the NRA and the gun-control movement have split along party lines. The NRA essentially backed so-called conservative candidates and views, such as those typically held by the Republican Party or the LIBERTARIAN PARTY; those who sought stricter limitations on gun ownership tended to support Democrats, or so-called liberal candidates and ideas. At the end of the twentieth century, the delineation became more nebulous, not only among politicians but also between lobbying groups. While the organization generally opposes all forms of gun control as abridgments upon individuals' constitutional rights, many NRA members had aligned with what they referred to as "common-sense" gun control efforts. The militant gun control movement, however, splintered into extremist and middle-ground factions within their own ranks. The NRA generally holds that criminals create gun violence, not the 48 percent of the electorate who constitute law-abiding gun owners.

CROSS REFERENCES

Gun Control

NATIVE AMERICAN RIGHTS

Atkinson Trading Company v. Shirley

The legal debate over the limits of Native American tribal sovereignty continues to generate lawsuits. The Supreme Court of the United States has been called upon to resolve many technical issues concerning civil and criminal LIABILITY as well as taxation policy for non-Indians on tribal lands. Moreover, because there are many parcels of non-Indian land located within Indian reservations, additional litigation has contested whether tribes may impose taxes on services originating from this non-tribal property. The Supreme Court, in *Atkinson Trading Company v. Shirley,* ___U.S.___, 121 S.Ct. 1825, 149 L.Ed.2d 889 (2001), addressed this issue, ruling that the Navajo Nation could not impose a hotel occupancy tax on a hotel located within the reservation's BOUNDARIES but owned by a nonmember.

The genesis of the dispute can be traced to 1916, when Hubert Richardson purchased land from the United States near Cameron, Arizona. Richardson built the Cameron Trading Post, located adjacent to the Navajo Nation Reservation. In 1934, however, the United States enlarged the boundaries of the reservation and Richardson's property came within the new boundaries. Nevertheless, he was permitted to own non-Indian land within the reservation, a not uncommon occurrence. By the early 1990s the trading post had evolved from a one-room cabin to a business complex containing a hotel, restaurant, cafeteria, gallery, and other shops and tourist facilities. The current owner, Atkinson Trading Company, Inc., benefitted from the post's location near the Grand Canyon National Park.

In 1992 the Navajo Nation imposed an 8 percent hotel occupancy tax on any hotel room located within the exterior boundaries of the reservation. The hotel guests pay the tax, but the hotel must collect and remit the proceeds to the Navajo Tax Commission. Annual tax collections averaged $84,000. Atkinson first challenged the tax within the Navajo judicial system. After these efforts proved unsuccessful, the company filed suit in federal DISTRICT COURT. Both the district court and the Court of Appeals for the Tenth Circuit, however, upheld the tax in *Atkinson Trading Company v. Shirley,* 210 F.3d 1247 (2000). The Tenth Circuit acknowledged that the hotel sat on non-Indian land but concluded this was but one factor to consider in evaluating the legitimacy of the tax. In this case the court found that the tax was legitimate because the

guests consent to paying the tax when they take a room. If guests object to the tax, they can refrain from staying at the hotel.

The Supreme Court, in a unanimous vote but with three written opinions, overturned the APPELLATE COURT's decision. Chief Justice WILLIAM H. REHNQUIST, writing for the Court, stated as a threshold position that tribal sovereignty is limited. The Navajo could justify the tax only if it was "expressly conferred . . . by a federal statute or treaty," or if it could be justified "upon their retained or inherent sovereignty." Moreover, the Court's previous decisions had made clear "that Indian tribe power over nonmembers on non-Indian-owned land is sharply circumscribed." The general rule is that the "inherent sovereign powers of an Indian tribe do not extend to the activities of nonmembers." In *Montana v. United States,* 450 U.S. 544 (March 24, 1981), however, the Court had created two bases for tribal jurisdiction over non-Indian land. The first BASIS is a consensual relationship between the tribe and nonmembers, such as through commercial dealings and contracts. A second basis is the need for the tribe to regulate conduct of non-members that has a "direct effect on the political integrity, the economic security, or the health or welfare of the tribe."

Because Congress had not authorized the hotel tax, the Navajo were required to use one of these two bases to justify the tax. Chief Justice Rehnquist rejected the claim that the Navajo and the hotel guests had entered into a consensual relationship. It was not enough to claim that the provision of police and fire services to the area rose to the level of tribal services that demonstrated "civil authority over nonmembers on non-Indian fee land." Moreover, the consensual relationship had to arise from commercial dealings and not from the "actual or potential receipt of tribal police, fire, and medical services." If such an interpretation was applied, "the exception would swallow the rule" and tribes would be permitted to tax all non-member property. The Court also rejected the claim that Atkinson consented to the tax by becoming an "Indian trader." There was no consensual relationship between the trading post and the tribe on this issue. Rather, the relationship was between the trading post hotel and its guests. As for the second basis, the tribe contended that the hotel had an effect on the Navajo Nation because of its location and its employment of 100 Navajo Indians. Rehnquist did not dispute the business's effect on the tribe, but he concluded that the hotel's effect did no harm to the political, economic, or physical well-being of the Indian community around it.

C&L Enterprises, Inc. v. Citizen Band Potawatomi Indian Tribe of Oklahoma

The Supreme Court of the United States has long recognized that Native American tribes are sovereign nations that enjoy immunity in state and federal courts. In *Kiowa Tribe of Oklahoma v. Manufacturing Technologies, Inc.*, 523 U.S. 751, 118 S.Ct. 1700, 140 L.Ed.2d 981 (1998), the Court held that an Indian tribe is not subject to a lawsuit in state court for off-reservation conduct unless "Congress authorizes such suits or the tribe has waived its immunity." Three years later the Court was called on to determine whether another tribe had waived its immunity in a construction contract. The Court, in *C&L Enterprises, Inc. v. Citizen Band Potawatomi Indian Tribe of Oklahoma* ___U.S.___, 121 S.Ct. 1589, 149 L.Ed.2d 623 (2001), ruled that the tribe had clearly waived its immunity and was subject to the lawsuit and judgment lodged against it in state court.

The facts of the case illustrate the difficulties inherent in SOVEREIGN IMMUNITY disputes. The tribe contracted with C&L for the installation of a roof on a tribe-owned bank building located off reservation property. The tribe prepared a standard form contract that contained two important provisions. The first provision required the parties to submit to ARBITRATION if any disputes arose over the performance of the contract. Second, the contract stated that contract would "be governed by the law of the place where the Project is located." The bank building was located in Shawnee, Oklahoma, thus making Oklahoma state law the relevant legal code. After the parties signed the contract but before C&L started work on the roof, the tribe changed the design of the roof which meant that the roofing material changed from foam to rubber guard. The tribe took new bids on this design and awarded a new contract. C&L argued that it had a valid contract and demanded the tribe enter into arbitration as specified by the contract. The tribe refused to arbitrate, and C&L proceeded to arbitration alone. The arbitrator awarded the company $25,400 in DAMAGES plus attorney's fees and costs.

C&L then filed a lawsuit in state court to enforce its AWARD. The tribe appeared in court for the purpose of disputing the jurisdiction of the court to hear the case. It asserted sovereign immunity and asked that the case be dismissed. The trial court denied the motion, however, and entered judgment in C&L's favor. The Oklahoma Court of Civil Appeals ultimately ruled that under the 1998 *Kiowa* decision the tribe was immune from the lawsuit. It concluded that the tribe had not clearly and unequivocally waived its immunity by signing the contract with the arbitration and choice of law clauses. The Supreme Court agreed to hear C&L's appeal because other state and federal courts have ruled that arbitration clauses such as the one in this case do expressly waive tribal immunity.

The Court, in a unanimous decision, ruled that the Potawatomi had indeed waived their immunity by signing the contract. Justice RUTH BADER GINSBURG, writing for the Court, reaffirmed its prior ruling in *Kiowa* that Indian tribes are immune from lawsuits unless Congress abrogates this immunity or the tribe does so itself. Therefore, the only issue was whether the tribe itself waived immunity when it signed the contract. The arbitration clause clearly stated that the parties would resolve disputes through binding arbitration and that "any arbitration award could be entered in any federal or state court having jurisdiction." The choice of law clause was even clearer, making Oklahoma state courts the place for a party to enforce an arbitration award. After a thorough review of these provisions, Justice Ginsburg concluded that the tribe had agreed "by express contract, to adhere to certain dispute resolution procedures." Even more telling was the fact that the tribe had prepared and submitted the contract to C&L. Though the contract did not explicitly state that the tribe waived its tribal immunity, Ginsburg read the language as clearly constituting a knowing waiver.

Nevertheless, the tribe argued that the arbitration clause was not a waiver and that the choice of law clause did not settle the issue. Indeed, the tribe's counsel at oral argument stated that "no court on earth or even on the moon" had jurisdiction over C&L's lawsuit. Justice Ginsburg rejected these claims and found it unreasonable to read the arbitration clause as merely acknowledging that the parties would not seek a court trial to resolve any disputes. The overall structure of the agreement demonstrated that it had a "real world" objective. Finally, Ginsburg rejected outright the tribe's claim that a form contract that is used mostly by parties with no immunity to waive could not be used to establish a waiver of tribal immunity. Under COMMON LAW rules of interpretation, the provisions of a contract that are ambiguous must be construed "against the interests of the party that drafted it." In this case the tribe had submitted the contract, which was not ambiguous. Therefore, the tribe had waived its tribal immunity.

Federal Government Mishandled Native American Trust Accounts

In *Cobell v. Norton*, 240 F3d 1081 (D.C. Cir. 2001) (formerly *Cobell v. Babbitt*), a unanimous panel of the U.S. Court of Appeals for the District of Columbia Circuit upheld an earlier decision by a federal district judge, which found the U.S. government responsible for the mismanagement of a multi-billion-dollar TRUST fund for Native Americans. A separate trial to determine the amount of monies lost as a result of the malfeasance was scheduled for later in 2001. The government did not appeal the matter to the Supreme Court. More than 300,000 Indians were included in the CLASS ACTION suit.

The trust accounts are the result of the General Allotment Act of 1887, also known as the Dawes Act, which divided certain reservation lands into smaller plots for individual Indians. Under the law, some 90 million acres and approximately two-thirds of all Indian lands have been held in trust for the Indians by the federal government and cannot be sold or taxed. The land is leased for mining, logging, oil drilling, or grazing, and the proceeds are ostensibly deposited into Individual Indian Money (IIM) trust accounts for the benefit of the Indians. The Bureau of Indian Affairs (BIA) within the INTERIOR DEPARTMENT is vested with the responsibility of pooling and investing the funds. Proceeds amount to approximately $500 million each year.

Elouise Cobell, one of five original plaintiffs to the action and a member of the Blackfeet tribe, had worked for the BIA as a student. She experienced initial misgivings about the government's handling of the accounts when she discovered that her tribe was losing, not earning money. Attempts to query into the matter led to a BIA AUDIT and the 1994 passage of the Indian Trust Fund Management Reform Act by Congress. The Act provided for the appointment of a special TRUSTEE for American Indians (Paul Homan), who concluded, among other things, that the BIA had never set up an accounts receivable system, which made it impossible to track the amount of money in the system. He also discovered that more than $50 million had never been paid to individual account holders because the BIA had lost track of them and that 21,000 accounts were in the names of deceased persons.

The $540 million *Cobell* suit that followed was filed in 1996 by the Boulder, Colorado-based Native American Rights Fund, naming the BIA as key defendant. In December 1999, federal DISTRICT COURT judge Royce Lamberth ruled that the accounts had been so badly mismanaged that the system represented "fiscal and governmental irresponsibility in its purest form." *Cobell v. Norton*, 91 F.Supp.2d 1 (D.D.C. 1999). Judge Lamberth ruled that the plaintiff Indians had a judicially enforceable right to an accounting of their money, and that the secretaries of the Interior and TREASURY were in breach of their duties as trustees to the Indian beneficiaries. He also cited Secretary of the Interior Bruce Babbitt, Assistant Interior Secretary Kevin Gover, and Secretary of the Treasury Robert Rubin for CONTEMPT and fined them $600,000 for withholding and destroying government documents in response to DISCOVERY requests. Finally, the judge retained jurisdiction over the matter for five years, to monitor trust reform efforts and ordered Interior officials to file quarterly reports of progress with the court.

On behalf of the federal government in January 2000, the JUSTICE DEPARTMENT appealed Lamberth's ruling. The essence of the appeal was that the decision went beyond the scope of law and the intent of Congress in relation to the 1994 Indian Trust Reform Act and that the judge had overreached his authority by retaining jurisdiction to oversee reform efforts. The government argued that prior to 1994, its responsibilities were unclear, and that *after* 1994, the new Act limited its responsibility and did not require a timetable to accomplish reform.

Judge David Sentelle, writing for the three-member appeals panel on the Court of Appeals for the D.C. Circuit, agreed with the earlier decision finding that the Interior and Treasury Departments clearly had violated their duties to the Indians. The APPELLATE COURT rejected all of the government's arguments, finding that district judge Lamberth was correct in exercising the district court's equitable powers to oversee reforms because previous efforts had been "a day late and a dollar short." The court went on to say that governmental record keeping and data collection had been so bad that the government could not even execute "the most fundamental of trust duties, an accurate accounting."

The government had in fact admitted mismanagement of the accounts dating back to 1887, with monies being lost, stolen, never collected, or transferred to other federal programs. As of 2001, the federal government held approximately $450 million in more than 500,000 individual Indian trust accounts, of which records were missing for approximately $100 million. Another $2.4 billion still remained unreconciled for an estimated 2,000 tribal trust accounts.

In May 2001 the plaintiffs again filed charges with Judge Lamberth to hold Secretary of the Interior Gale Norton in contempt of court and to grant injunctive RELIEF to stop the government from shredding documents relating to the above case. These allegations followed an earlier court-appointed investigator's findings—following an unannounced visit to the BIA—of case-related documents having been found in a paper shredder. The government responded that the documents were computer printouts used to test the computer system's storage of records and were destroyed because they contained social security numbers. Also pending was a special counsel's finding that there was reason to believe that BIA officials had retaliated against an employee who had provided testimony in the *Cobell* litigation. This information was reported just prior to the appellate decision, however.

Nevada v. Hicks

The struggle to define the jurisdictional boundaries between Native American tribal courts and state courts has occupied the federal courts for many years. Though Indian reservations are deemed sovereign states, both Congress and the U.S. Supreme Court have placed limitations on their sovereignty. Therefore, as specific issues arise about tribal court jurisdiction, the federal courts must intervene to decide these cases. Such was the case in *Nevada v. Hicks* ___U.S.___, 121 S.Ct. 2304, ___ L.Ed.2d ___ (2001), in which the Supreme Court ruled that tribal courts do not have jurisdiction to hear federal CIVIL RIGHTS lawsuits concerning allegedly unconstitutional actions by a state government officer on tribal land. The case severely limited the scope of tribal jurisdiction and sought to establish principles to resolve future jurisdictional disputes.

Floyd Hicks, a member of the Fallon Paiute-Shoshone Tribes of western Nevada, came under suspicion for having killed a California big horn sheep outside the tribe's reservation. Such killings are illegal under Nevada state law. A Nevada game warden secured search warrants from both the state court and the tribal court to search Hick's premises. He found no evidence of a big horn sheep, but a year later the game warden was told that Hicks had two big horn sheep heads mounted in his home. Again

the warden secured search warrants from both courts and inspected Hicks's home. He found no evidence of the big horn sheep. Hicks responded by filing a federal civil rights lawsuit against the game warden and numerous government entities, alleging that the search had violated his rights. Hicks filed his lawsuit in tribal court.

The tribal court dismissed all the defendants except the game warden in his individual capacity and declared that it had jurisdiction to hear the case. The warden and the state of Nevada then filed an action in federal DISTRICT COURT, seeking a dismissal of the lawsuit for want of jurisdiction. The district court and the Circuit Court of Appeals for the Ninth Circuit rejected the motion to dismiss, finding that the warden would have to exhaust all tribal court remedies before seeking federal court relief. Moreover, the appeals court found that because the alleged violation took place on tribal land, the tribal court had jurisdiction to hear the case.

The U.S. Supreme Court overturned these rulings in a decision that saw all nine justices agreeing to the basic result but disagreeing about the reasons for the decision. Justice ANTONIN SCALIA, writing for the six-judge majority, based his opinion on two principles. Prior cases had established that tribal courts had jurisdiction when it was needed to "protect tribal self-government or to control internal relations," or when Congress specifically granted it by law. Scalia rejected a reading of prior decisions that suggested jurisdiction was vested automatically if the alleged injury took place on tribal land. Instead, the "ownership status of the land" was but one factor for a court to consider. Justice Scalia also reiterated that state sovereignty could be imposed on reservation land if the state's interests were implicated. In this case, the need for a state game warden to enter the reservation to execute a search warrant was a valid state interest. Though the tribal government had a competing interest, it was "not essential to tribal self-government or internal relations." The effect on state enforcement of game regulations would be substantial if state officers were not allowed to execute process on tribal lands.

Justice Scalia then turned to the issue of explicit grants of jurisdiction by Congress. The tribe argued that it had general jurisdictional powers from Congress that justified its authority to hear the federal civil rights suit. Scalia disagreed with this argument, concluding that, "Nothing in the federal statutory scheme prescribes, or even remotely suggests, that state officers cannot enter a reservation . . . to investigate or prosecute violations of state law occurring off the reservation." Moreover, he found that tribal courts are not courts of "general jurisdiction" that are authorized to hear federal civil rights lawsuits. Although state courts can hear these types of actions, tribal courts do not fit into this category. Tribal courts only have limited jurisdiction, based on legislative acts, to hear certain cases.

Therefore, the next issue was whether Congress had authorized tribal courts to hear federal civil rights lawsuits. Justice Scalia noted that though Congress had given tribal courts authority to hear cases under the Indian Child Welfare Act and other federal statutes, Congress had not provided for tribal court jurisdiction over federal civil rights laws claims. Without express congressional authorization the courts could not recognize such jurisdiction.

Finally, Justice Scalia found that the game warden did not have to exhaust all tribal court remedies before moving an action to federal court. In light of the lack of jurisdiction by tribal courts to hear federal civil rights suits, the exhaustion requirement was not necessary.

CROSS REFERENCES
Arbitration; Sovereign Immunity; Trust

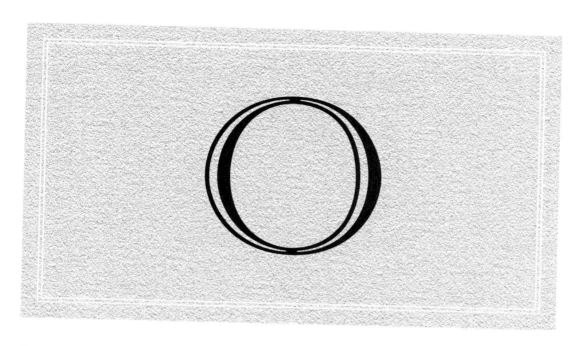

OLSON, THEODORE B.

Theodore B. Olson became widely known in November 2000 when GEORGE W. BUSH selected him to represent Bush in the Florida election recount dispute. Olson took Bush's case before the Supreme Court in an emergency appeal and won, thereby clearing the way for George W. Bush to become president of the United States. In turn, Bush named Olson for the position of SOLICITOR GENERAL, and a Republican-majority Senate confirmed his nomination prior to a shift in power which gave Democrats a majority.

Olson was born on September 11, 1940, in Chicago, Illinois. He received his bachelor's degree from the University of Pacific and in 1965 graduated from the University of California at Berkeley, Boalt Hall School of Law, where he was a member of the California Law Review and Order of the Coif. Olson then entered private practice with the prominent law firm of Gibson, Dunn, and Crutcher, where he specialized in APPELLATE oral arguments in the firm's Los Angeles office for 16 years.

In 1981, Olson was appointed as assistant ATTORNEY GENERAL by then-U.S. President RONALD REAGAN to head the JUSTICE DEPARTMENT's Office of Legal Counsel. He served until 1984 and then returned to Gibson, Dunn, and Crutcher. In spite of his return to private practice, however, there was still unfinished business remaining from his position as assistant attorney general. In 1985, the House Judiciary Committee accused Olson of giving false and misleading statements during an investigation of the ENVIRONMENTAL PROTECTION AGENCY. An

INDEPENDENT COUNSEL was appointed to investigate the matter. This action became the basis for Olson's constitutional challenge of the Ethics in Government Act, which was passed in 1978 following the WATERGATE scandal and which established the government's authority to appoint an independent counsel. Pursuant to this Act, the independent counsel was to be given full power to investigate and prosecute cases assigned by the Department of Justice. Olson challenged the constitutionality of the independent counsel on the basis that it violated the SEPARATION OF POWERS doctrine.

In *Morrison v. Olson*, 487 U.S. 654, 108 S.Ct. 2597 (1988), the Supreme Court of the United States upheld the constitutional validity of the act, maintaining it did not violate the separation of powers doctrine as it did not invade upon the powers of the executive branch and it did not give the JUDICIARY or the legislature any additional powers. Shortly after the Court's decision, the independent counsel dropped the case against Olson, clearing Olson of any wrongdoing.

Throughout the independent counsel ordeal, Olson continued to work with Gibson, Dunn, and Crutcher. He started a CONSTITUTIONAL LAW practice for the firm's Washington, D.C., office and handled many Supreme Court cases himself. He also represented former president Ronald Reagan on several personal matters and continued to support Republican Party politics.

As an appellate advocate, Olson usually pursued conservative rulings, asking for limits on regulations pertaining to environmental pro-

Theodore B. Olson

THEODORE B. OLSON

1940 Born in Chicago, Illinois

1965 Graduated from the University of California at Berkley, Boat Hall and joined the law firm of Gibson, Dunn & Crutcher, LLP

1981 Appointed U.S. Assistant Attorney General by then-President Ronald Reagan

2000 Represented George W. Bush in the Supreme Court case, *Bush v. Gore,* a case which would clear the way for George W. Bush to become President

2001 Appointed U.S. Solicitor General by President George W. Bush

tection, sexual discrimination, and AFFIRMATIVE ACTION. In 1996 Olson represented the Virginia Military Institute in an unsuccessful fight to continue its all-male enrollment policy. He argued to the Supreme Court that the school's character would be fundamentally altered if women were to enroll. The Supreme Court was not persuaded, and forced the Institute to lift the restriction against female enrollment. In 2000, however, Olson was successful in another case before the Court challenging an election law in Hawaii, which favored only aboriginal Hawaiians. To date, Olson has made 15 appearances before the U.S. Supreme Court.

Olson's most historic victory involved the disputed presidential election in the year 2000. On November 8, 2000, the day after the votes were cast in the race between George W. Bush and AL GORE, the result came down to one state: Florida. The results in Florida showed that Bush had won, but only by a margin of less than one half of one percent, which was not enough to declare him a winner. An automatic machine recount was ordered pursuant to the Florida election laws, which showed Bush to still be the winner, but by even fewer votes.

Gore then requested a manual recount of four counties pursuant to Florida's election protest laws. As the manual recount began, the controversy mounted as disputes evolved re-

garding, among other things, confusing ballots and voter intent. Both sides began taking their case to the courts. During the election battle, Olson appeared twice before the Supreme Court, and it was his second appearance that decided the election outcome.

In *Bush v. Gore* 531 U.S. 98, 121 S.Ct. 525 (2000), the Supreme Court found the recounting systems utilized in each of the counties failed to develop uniform standards for deciding voter intent and that the arbitrary treatment of votes violated each citizen's guaranteed right to vote under the EQUAL PROTECTION clause of the Constitution. Since there was not enough time to develop uniform rules, the Court ordered that the hand recount be terminated immediately. Shortly thereafter, Al Gore conceded defeat, and George W. Bush was declared the president-elect.

In recognition of Olson's service, President Bush selected him to serve as solicitor general. However, Olson's appointment elicited controversy because of his involvement with the *American Spectator,* a conservative magazine. During the 1990s, he served on the board of directors for the magazine, which during that time spent millions of dollars to investigate former president and first lady, BILL and HILLARY RODHAM CLINTON. Olson claims that he was not involved in the controversial "Arkansas Project" and that, in fact, he helped to terminate it. Nonetheless, the Senate Judiciary Committee was split with a 9–9 vote on his appointment, thereby necessitating a vote before the entire Senate. The Republican majority in the Senate managed to push through his nomination on May 24, 2001, shortly before a power shift resulted in a Democratic majority. As solicitor general, Olson decides which cases should go before the U.S. Supreme Court and argues many of them on behalf of the federal government.

CROSS REFERENCES
Solicitor General

ORGAN DONATION LAW

Federal Organ Distribution Rules Survive Legal Challenge

As the successful medical transplantation of organs has become an almost "routine" activity, the demand for human organs has continued to greatly exceed the supply. State and federal laws have publicized and promoted organ donation registration programs in hopes of increasing the supply. Despite these efforts thousands of people die each year while waiting for a donated heart, liver, kidney, or lung. In the mid-1990s the U.S. Department of Health and Human Services (HHS) initiated a review of how organs are distributed. From this review came new regulations that gave HHS more oversight and control of the process. In addition, the new regulations mandated a significant change in how organs are distributed.

The regulations, which were first issued in April 1998, changed the distribution and allocation of organs by broadening transplant areas. The old system of distribution and allocation allowed organs to be distributed locally first. Therefore, a person who needed a liver in New York would get a donated liver from a New York donee even though a person living in New Jersey who needed a liver was much sicker and closer to death. This policy was based on the belief that local distribution gave states and local medical institutions an incentive to promote organ donation. If the organ were to be distributed regionally or nationally, states and hospitals might conclude that successful promotion of organ donations turned the state into a supplier for other states that did not do as good a job encouraging donations.

These concerns were raised during the administrative process that preceded the implementation of the final HHS regulations. Nevertheless, HHS concluded that major changes needed to be made in a system that had grown more complex as medical science evolved. The new regulations "stripped the United Network for Organ Sharing (UNOS) . . . of the power to decide how organs should be allocated." The department replaced UNOS, a private agency, with HHS's own Health Resources and Services Administration, which oversees the U.S. organ transplantation system.

The new regulations angered a number of states and hospitals. The State of Wisconsin, the University of Wisconsin Hospitals and Froedert Memorial Lutheran Hospital filed a lawsuit in federal district court. The two hospitals are major transplant centers and concluded that the new regulations would reduce the number of organs available to their patients. The plaintiffs alleged that HHS lacked legislative authority to broaden the regional organ sharing networks and to take away the power of UNOS to decide how organs are allocated. In addition, the plaintiffs claimed the regulations would injure the hospitals financially because they would have to

NATIONAL TRANSPLANT WAITING LIST BY ORGAN TYPE (JUNE 1997)

Organ Needed	Number Waiting
Kidney	36,148
Liver	8,447
Heart	3,777
Lung	2,452
Kidney-Pancreas	1,565
Pancreas	334
Heart-Lung	222
Intestine	85

Source: Colorado Health Net. http://www.coloradohealthnet.org/transplant/trans_main.html

pay a larger amount of the transplantation network's operating costs.

In November 2000, U.S. District Court Judge Barbara Crabb issued an unpublished ruling in *Wisconsin v. Department of Health and Human Services.* By this time the state of New Jersey and the Oregon Health Sciences University in Portland, Oregon, had joined the case as plaintiffs, testifying to the national interest in this issue. Judge Crabb dismissed the case and never reached the merits of the substantive issues because she found that the plaintiffs lacked standing to file the lawsuit. Standing is a judicial doctrine that requires a plaintiff to have been actually injured by the defendant's conduct in order to file a civil lawsuit. Because the U.S. Constitution requires that courts only handle actions that involve a "case or controversy," courts of law routinely examine whether the plaintiff has been injured and thus has a real stake in the outcome.

Judge Crabb concluded that the states and the hospitals lacked standing. She ruled that the plaintiffs were not entitled to sue because no one "had suffered an actual injury." In addition, they lacked standing because they had sued on their own behalf rather than on behalf of the national transplantation network. This was significant because the hospitals were not alleging that their policies would be subjected to an allegedly unconstitutional review. Instead it was the policies of the "organ procurement and transplantation network that are subject to such review."

Judge Crabb also ruled that the plaintiffs had not proved that the new rules would cause financial injury. She found it more likely that the

As these numbers suggest, the high demand for transplant organs can cause tense debates regarding how available organs should be distributed to patients.

hospitals would pass the costs onto their patients.

Despite the court decision opponents of the regulations may have other options. Though Congress failed to overturn the regulations in October 2000, it might be persuaded to in the future. More importantly, President GEORGE W. BUSH appointed Wisconsin governor Tommy Thompson secretary of HHS in January 2001. Thompson had led the fight to overturn the rules while governor.

CROSS REFERENCES
Administrative Law; Health and Human Services Department

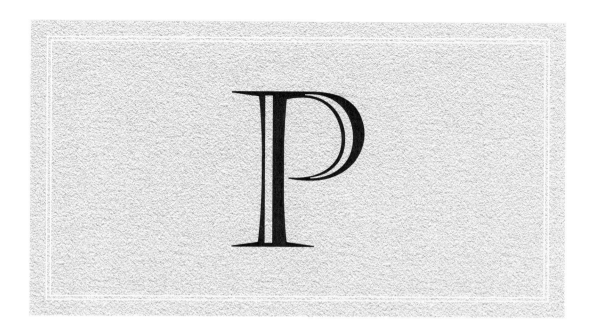

PARENT AND CHILD

The legal relationship between a father or mother and his or her offspring.

Forced Separation of Conjoined Twins

One of the most sensitive and emotionally-charged cases of 2001 was the decision by a British APPELLATE COURT to allow surgical separation of conjoined twins against the parents' religious and personal convictions. Surgical separation meant certain death for one of the twins, who were fused at the spine and shared several vital organs including heart and lungs. The parents, devout Catholics, refused to consent to the operation on religious grounds, stating that the intentional taking of one's life for the benefit of the other was morally wrong. They steadfastly repeated their wishes that nature should be allowed to take its course, without human intervention, even if that meant eventual death for both twins.

From their home in the small country of Malta, the parents had flown to England at the behest of a local physician after learning that the yet-unborn fetuses were conjoined. The twins were born on August 8, 2000, at St. Mary's Hospital in Manchester. Doctors advised the parents that one twin was physically dependent upon the other for survival and recommended separation with likely survival of the stronger twin, at the expense of the weaker one. The devastated parents refused CONSENT. The hospital filed suit, petitioning the court to intervene and compel surgical separation. In late August 2000, British judge Robert Johnson heard private arguments from both sides then ruled that the twins should be separated, even though one would die in the process and even though such ruling was against the parents' religious beliefs and personal convictions.

The Vatican announced that it would provide "safe haven" for the family, including health and medical benefits for the natural lives of the twins, whose life expectancies were limited if they remained conjoined. An attorney for the parents advised instead that they take the matter to the London Court of Appeals. At stake was the issue of whose or what interest should prevail, pitting parents against doctors, medicine against religion, and personal autonomy and privacy against governmental intrusion. British law puts a child's interest above that of the parents, yet even when considering the interests of one child, one infant twin's interest would inevitably be pitted against the other's. Must the stronger twin's life be threatened by the physiological strain of supporting the weaker twin? Conversely, must the weaker twin give up her life in order that the stronger one survive?

Adding to the complexity of the matter was English criminal law, which does not permit one person to be killed for the benefit of another. The seminal case in this area is that of *Dudley*, (1884) wherein two seamen were convicted of murder for taking the life of a cabin boy and devouring him in order to stay alive after being adrift without food or water for twenty days. The key defense in that case was a reliance upon British COMMON LAW's "doctrine of necessity," a concept familiar to American jurisprudence as well. The doctrine of NECESSITY excuses harm caused to another under justifiable circumstances, as when saving a life.

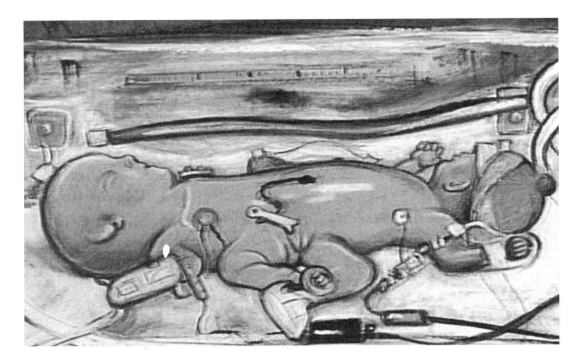

An artist's impression of female twins depicts how the twins were conjoined. The stronger twin (*left*) survived the court-ordered separation but the weaker twin did not.

In the case of the twins, lawyers for the hospital argued that the matter of the twins was distinguishable from *Dudley*. They argued that since the weaker twin had no functioning heart or lungs, she could not be regarded as an individual under the law. In other words, because she relied on another for life itself, she had not been "born alive." Moreover, attorneys for the doctors and hospital argued that in reality, the weaker twin, by draining oxygenated blood from the other twin, was in effect inflicting an assault upon her sibling. They argued that the operation would ensure the survival of the stronger twin with a reasonable quality of life, which she could not have if she remained conjoined.

Simon Taylor, attorney for the parents, argued that, "maybe [the weaker twin] is relying on her sister, but nevertheless she was born alive." He argued that both the parents and the hospital had "regarded the babies as two individuals, not one." Therefore, it would be an unlawful killing to intervene affirmatively on behalf of one and hasten the death of the other. As Lord Justice Ward noted: "The moment the knife goes into that united body, it touches the body of the unhappy little [weaker twin]. You cannot pretend that is not actively engaged in assaulting [the weaker twin's] integrity." Thus, the appellate court also needed to consider how extreme circumstances had to be to justify an otherwise unlawful killing.

The British appellate court, declaring itself "a court of law, not a court of morals," ruled unanimously on September 22, 2000, that doctors could operate to separate the twins, even against the parents' wishes, and even though surgery would result in death for one twin. The parents' religious convictions were not as weighty as the conflicting interests of the two twins themselves. In upholding the lower court's decision, the high court reasoned that the healthy twin's right to life outweighed that of the weaker, dependent twin, whose life could not be sustained without reliance on her sister's heart and lungs. The judges relied on medical evidence tending to show that the stronger twin would herself succumb if the strain of sustaining two bodies were to continue.

Characterizing its duty as one of deciding whether it could put the interest of one twin ahead of the other, the Court concluded that the "weaker twin was incapable of independent existence and was threatening the life of the other with her dependency." Under the circumstance, the court concluded that it could permit doctors "to choose the lesser of two evils . . . the death of one twin instead of the death of both."

The parents had a vested right to appeal to Britain's highest court, the House of Lords, and feasibly to the European Court of Human Rights in Strasburg. Approximately ten days after the decision, however, the parents announced that they would not further appeal the matter. In late November 2000, the three-month-old conjoined twins were separated following a twenty-hour operation at St. Mary's Hospital. The weaker twin died. The cemetery site in Malta where the baby girl is buried was dedicated by the parents as a shrine to unborn babies.

CROSS REFERENCES
Necessity

PRISONER'S RIGHTS

The nature and extent of the privileges afforded to individuals kept in CUSTODY or confinement against their will because they were convicted of performing an unlawful act.

Alabama v. Bozeman

It is not uncommon for a person to be charged with crimes in different states or jurisdictions. Once a person is convicted of a crime in one jurisdiction and is incarcerated, another jurisdiction may wish to prosecute the inmate on criminal charges. Sometimes these prosecutions take place while the inmate is serving time in the first jurisdiction, and sometimes they are postponed until the inmate is about to be released from prison. Until the 1950s the procedures used by states and the federal government to arrange for these prosecutions were confusing and disparate. Oftentimes an inmate would be released from prison, and the second jurisdiction would not be able to find the person. Under growing pressure to correct these problems, the Council on State Governments drafted in 1956 the Interstate Agreement on Detainers. The agreement was overwhelmingly endorsed by the states, and Congress enacted the agreement as well as an interstate compact.

Within the agreement were standard procedures for filing and carrying out DETAINERS, which are legal orders that allow a state to hold a prisoner who has finished his sentence due to another state wanting to try that prisoner on separate charges. Because the federal government and the District of Columbia have joined the compact, they are considered states under the compact. The agreement contains ten articles and has been examined in court cases from time to time, but overall it has not been a controversial law.

However, the Supreme Court of the United States was required to address the statutory interpretation of one article in *Alabama v. Bozeman*, ___U.S.___, 121 S.Ct. 2079, ___

L.Ed.2d ___ (2001). This case involved Article IV's provision concerning the movement of a prisoner while incarcerated from one state (the sending state) to another state (the receiving state) for prosecution. The article states that "the receiving State shall begin the prisoner's trial 'within one hundred and twenty days of arrival of the prisoner in the receiving State.'" In addition, the article prohibits return of the prisoner to the sending state before that trial is complete. If the receiving state fails to complete the trial during the time period the criminal charge must be dismissed by the court "with prejudice": Thus, the inmate can never be tried on that charge.

Michael H. Bozeman was serving a sentence in January 1997 in a federal prison in Marianna, Florida. Convicted of federal drug charges, Bozeman was also wanted by the state of Alabama for discharging firearms. Therefore, Alabama lodged a detainer with federal authorities and sought temporary custody of Bozeman under Article IV in order to arraign him on the firearms charge and to appoint defense counsel. Alabama authorities picked him up at the prison and drove him 80 miles to Covington County, Alabama. He spent the night in jail. The next morning he was arraigned, and the court appointed a defense attorney. He was back at the federal prison that evening. About a month later Bozeman was brought back to Alabama for trial. His attorney objected to the prosecution and asked that the charges be dismissed on the grounds that Article IV prohibited returning Bozeman to the federal prison prior to trial. The trial court rejected this argument, believing that it made sense to return Bozeman to prison to continue rehabilitation rather than let him sit in a county jail for a month. The Alabama COURT OF APPEALS affirmed this decision, but the Alabama Supreme Court reversed. It held that the literal language of the detainer compact mandated dismissal of the charges. Because there were conflicting interpretations of this provision in the lower courts, the U.S. Supreme Court agreed to hear Alabama's appeal.

The Court, in a unanimous decision, upheld the Alabama Supreme Court. Justice STEPHEN G. BREYER, writing for the Court, noted that Alabama admitted it violated the literal language of Article IV. Instead, the state contended that the basic purpose of the provision was to avoid shuttling the prisoner back and forth between jurisdictions, which would interrupt the prisoner's rehabilitation. The state characterized the violation as "harmless" and "technical." Justice Breyer relied on the article's plain language. He pointed out that the language was absolute. The provision states that "when a prisoner is 'returned' before trial, the indictment, information, or criminal complaint 'shall not be of any further force or effect, and the court shall enter an order dismissing the same with prejudice." Moreover, the article did not contain any exceptions to this command. It did not matter if the prisoner was returned in one day or 100 days. If the trial is not completed by the end of 120 days, the charges must be dismissed.

Justice Breyer also rejected the idea that the quick return of Bozeman prevented the interruption of his rehabilitation. Though this might be a laudable purpose, a larger purpose was decreasing "the number of days the prisoner will spend in the sending State." The sending state saved money when the prisoner was sent to the receiving state. This purpose was frustrated by the one day turnaround of Bozeman and implied that Alabama did not want to spend money housing Bozeman before trial. Therefore, both the literal language and the underlying goal of the interstate compact required the dismissal of the charges against Bozeman.

Artuz v. Bennett

After a person convicted of a crime has exhausted all direct appeals, the person may seek postconviction relief by petitioning for a writ of HABEAS CORPUS. In applying for a writ of habeas corpus, the inmate alleges that he or she should be released from custody because of constitutional violations by the prosecutor or the trial court. Beginning in the 1960s, prisoners began filing habeas petitions at a steadily increasing rate, due in large part to the expanding set of procedural rights established by the Supreme Court of the United States under its then-chief justice, EARL WARREN.

By the 1990s, however, critics called for greater restrictions on the filing of habeas petitions. Congress responded by passing the Antiterrorism and Effective Death Penalty Act of 1996 (AEDPA), 110 Stat. 1224, which includes time restrictions on the filing of habeas petitions. Since the enactment of the AEDPA, the U.S. Supreme Court has been called on to determine how these restrictions should be applied. Such was the case in *Artuz v. Bennett*, ___U.S.___, 121 S.Ct. 361, 148 L.Ed.2d 213 (2000), where the Court held that the failure of the trial judge to issue a written ruling on the prisoner's motion to VACATE his conviction suspended or "tolled" the law's time period. Thus, the prisoner's habeas petition was timely.

In 1984, a New York state jury convicted Tony Bennett of attempted murder, criminal possession of a weapon, reckless endangerment, criminal possession of stolen property, and unauthorized use of a motor vehicle. Though he appealed his conviction, the New York state appellate courts upheld the verdict. In 1991, he unsuccessfully pursued state postconviction relief, and he tried again in 1995 when he filed a motion to vacate his conviction. The state trial judge held a hearing in November 1995 and denied the motion in an oral decision recorded by the court reporter. The judge gave no reasons for denying Bennett's motion, and Bennett claimed that he never received a copy of a written order reflecting the denial, despite several written requests.

In 1998, Bennett filed a petition for a writ of habeas corpus in New York federal district court, alleging that: (1) the state trial court's refusal to allow a defense witness to testify deprived him of his right to a fair trial and his right to present witnesses in his own defense; (2) that his absence from a pretrial hearing violated due process; and (3) that his trial counsel was constitutionally ineffective in failing to object to allegedly improper remarks made by the prosecutor in summation. However, the district court summarily dismissed the petition as untimely, noting that it had been filed more than one year and nine months after the effective date of the AEDPA. Under the AEDPA, a state prisoner has a one-year statute of limitations to file a federal habeas petition. The one-year term period begins to run from the date of the state court decision denying postconviction relief. Depending on circumstances of a case, this one year period can be suspended, or "tolled."

Bennett appealed to the U.S. Court of Appeals for the Second Circuit, which reversed the district court ruling. The appeals court concluded that the one-year period of limitations should also toll the one-year grace period that began in April 1996 after the enactment of the AEDPA. It assumed that Bennett had not yet received a written order denying his 1995 motion to vacate the conviction. Bennett could not appeal this decision without a written order and therefore the case was still pending for the purposes of the AEDPA. The court rejected the state's claim that Bennett's 1995 motion was not properly filed for the purposes of the AEDPA because it improperly raised issues that could only have been raised on direct appeal.

The Supreme Court, in a unanimous ruling, affirmed the Second Circuit decision. Justice ANTONIN SCALIA, writing for the Court, rejected the state's claim that postconviction review is not "properly filed" for purposes of the AEDPA unless it complies with all mandatory state-law procedural requirements that would bar review of the merits of the application. Justice Scalia noted that an application is "filed" when it is delivered to and accepted by the appropriate court officer for placement in the court record. Moreover, the question whether an application has been "properly filed" was "quite separate" from the question whether the claims contained in the application were meritorious or barred by court procedure.

Justice Scalia concluded that Bennett's application for state postconviction relief may have contained procedurally-barred claims yet this did not render it improperly filed under the AEDPA. The state procedural bars at issue in the case placed conditions on obtaining relief but did not place conditions on the actual filing of Bennett's motion. Therefore, Bennett was entitled to consideration of his federal habeas petition.

Booth v. Churner

Prisoner lawsuits have been the bane of the federal courts. From the late 1960s through the early 1990s, thousands of inmates filed federal civil rights suits concerning matters both compelling and frivolous. These lawsuits consumed enormous amounts of time for both prison officials and federal courts. This circumstance led Congress to pass the Prison Litigation Reform Act of 1995, a piece of legislation that sought to drastically curtail prisoner lawsuits in the federal courts. One major provision requires prisoners to exhaust all administrative procedures provided by state correctional facilities before they pursue a federal court case. The drafters of this provision believed that this process would lead some prisoners to accept the state procedure, while others might become discouraged at the prospect of pursuing administrative remedies and abandon their claims. The Supreme Court of the United States reaffirmed this provision in *Booth v. Churner*, ___U.S.___, 121 S.Ct. 1819, 149 L.Ed.2d 958, (2001), holding that a prisoner must exhaust all administrative procedures, even if these steps cannot provide the relief, namely money, that the inmate is seeking.

Timothy Booth was an inmate at a Pennsylvania correctional facility who sought to bypass the exhaustion requirement in his federal CIVIL RIGHTS lawsuit. Booth alleged that prison guards had assaulted him and denied him medical attention in violation of the EIGHTH AMENDMENT's Cruel and Unusual Punishment Clause. Booth sought injunctive relief, including a transfer to another prison, and several hundred thousand dollars in money damages. The Pennsylvania Department of Corrections provided an administrative grievance system that addressed issues such as excessive force and abuse. However, an inmate could not recover money damages through this administrative process. Though Booth filed a grievance based on some of the alleged abuse, he did not pursue his remedies through the intermediate or final steps of review after prison authorities denied relief. Instead, Booth filed his federal civil rights lawsuit.

The federal district court, applying the provision of the Prison Litigation Reform Act, dismissed Booth's case because he had failed to exhaust the administrative procedures available to him. The U.S. Court of Appeals for the Third Circuit upheld this ruling, though it admitted that several other circuit courts had found an exception to the exhaustion requirement when the inmate grievance procedure could not provide monetary damages as could a federal civil rights suit. Because of this conflict the Supreme Court agreed to hear Booth's appeal.

The Court, in a unanimous ruling, upheld the Third Circuit's decision on the issue. Justice DAVID H. SOUTER, writing for the Court, made clear that exhaustion of administrative procedures is not required where the administrative procedure cannot provide any relief to the inmate. However, the question in this case was whether exhaustion was required if the state could provide some, if not all, forms of relief requested by the inmate. To answer this question, the Court examined the language of the provision and the congressional intent behind the law. It acknowledged that Booth's argument had "some intuitive appeal." If the intent of the law was to keep cases out of the courts, it was clear in cases such as Booth's that the "odds of keeping the matter out of court are slim." But the Court also acknowledged the state's position. Requiring the exhaustion of administrative procedures "would produce administrative results that would satisfy at least some inmates who start out asking for nothing but money, since the very act of being heard and prompting administrative change can mollify passions even when nothing ends up in the pocket." Moreover, this procedure may eliminate "frivolous claims and foster better-prepared litigation once a dispute did move to the courtroom."

The Court examined the words of the provision and concluded that the word "exhaust" must be read in conjunction with processes rather than forms of relief. Hence, a prisoner must exhaust the process regardless of whether the particular remedy is all that he or she desires. Failure to go through these steps will bar a federal civil rights lawsuit. In addition, the Court referred to the history of Prison Litigation Reform Act. Before its enactment, federal law gave courts the discretion to require an inmate to exhaust administrative remedies but "only if those remedies were plain, speedy, and effective." That scheme was now "a thing of the past," as Congress had eliminated both these provisions. This change was significant in the Court's view because of a 1992 Supreme Court case in which it had ruled that exhaustion was not required because the failure of the administrative remedy to provide money damages meant that the remedy was not "effective" under the statute. Thus, the Court concluded that Congress sought to overturn this ruling and reasoning by deleting the term "effective" from the statute. Because Congress had "mandated exhaustion clearly enough, regardless of the relief offered through administrative procedures," inmates cannot sue in federal court until they have exhausted these procedures.

Shaw v. Murphy

The law governing prisons and prisoners' rights is based on the special requirements that come with overseeing the long-term incarceration of large numbers of individuals. The courts have always been exceedingly deferential to the needs of prison administrators to maintain order and security. These needs often override constitutional rights of prisoners; with few exceptions the courts permit authorities to restrict individual liberties. Such was the case in *Shaw v. Murphy*, ___U.S.___, 121 S.Ct. 1475, ___ L.Ed.2d ___ (2001), in which the Supreme Court of the United States ruled that prisoners do not possess a FIRST AMENDMENT right to provide legal advice to other prisoners. In so ruling the Court permitted prison officials to discipline inmates who do not have authority to assist other inmates with their legal problems.

The case arose out of the conduct of Montana state prison inmate Kevin Murphy. Murphy was one of a number of inmates who were designated "inmate law clerks" by prison authorities. Administrators designated certain inmates who could consult with Murphy on their legal problems and have him assist them with filling out paper work. The use of inmate clerks, who in more informal roles have been labeled "jailhouse lawyers," provides inmates with inexpensive and accessible counseling. However, Montana authorities maintained control over the clerks by preventing them from consulting with inmates without prior approval.

Murphy ignored this rule when he wrote a letter to another inmate who had been accused of assaulting a correctional officer. In the letter Murphy accused the officer of prior brutalities and urged the inmate not to plea bargain. Moreover, he volunteered his assistance on the case. Prison officials intercepted the letter, which is standard operating procedure in prisons. These officials initiated disciplinary proceedings against Murphy, charging him with insolence, interference with a due process hearing, and conduct that disrupts prison security. He was convicted of the first two charges and was given a suspended sentence of 10 days' detention and a number of demerits that could affect his custody level at the prison.

Murphy filed a federal CIVIL RIGHTS lawsuit against the prison administrators, alleging that his First Amendment rights had been violated. The federal district court dismissed the lawsuit, but the Ninth Circuit Court of Appeals reversed. The appellate court ruled that it had to balance the prisoner' rights against the government's interest to determine whether there had been a violation of free speech. The court concluded that inmates have a First Amendment right to assist other inmates with their legal claims. This ruling was in conflict with other circuit court decisions, thus requiring the Supreme Court to resolve the issue.

The Supreme Court, in a unanimous opinion, overruled the Ninth Circuit. Justice CLARENCE THOMAS, writing for the Court, noted that a prior ruling on prisoner-to-prisoner communications required that restrictions must be "reasonably related to legitimate and neutral government objectives." Therefore, the sole question was whether legal correspondence merited a blanket exception to this rule. The Court rejected the idea that there was a special right for legal communications, basing its analysis on a tradition of noninterference by the courts in the administration of prisons. Though the Supreme Court has ruled that prisoners have some constitutional protections, it has made clear that these rights are limited in scope and much less than those enjoyed by free individuals. The First Amendment provided a number of examples to illustrate these limitations. Thus, prisoners may not be permitted to give media interviews, organize a prison labor union, or be allowed uncensored correspondence among inmates. These limitations have been based on the belief that prison officials are in the best position to assess what is best for the security of the institution.

Having disposed of the idea that legal correspondence enjoyed heightened First Amendment protection, the Court examined whether the regulation governing Murphy was reasonably related to the legitimate needs of prison administrators. The Court found that it was a neutral regulation that was grounded on rational conclusions. Moreover, the Court made clear it did not want to examine the content of prison communications, as this would invite numerous lawsuits that would have to be determined on the individual facts of each communication. Prison officials should be given the discretion to determine which communications are harmful to the prison environment.

The Court also stated that even if it were to give special protection to certain types of speech based on a content, "we would not do so for speech that includes legal advice." To do so would undermine prison administrators as they addressed the complex problems of everyday life in a correctional facility. In addition, the Court pointed out that some inmate law clerks play a disruptive role in prisons and threaten to undermine prison discipline. Finally, some legal correspondence has been used to communicate illicit and illegal information.

CROSS REFERENCES
Criminal Procedure; Detainer; Due Process of Law; Exhaustion of Remedies; First Amendment; Habeas Corpus; Statutory Interpretation

PRIVACY

In constitutional law, the right of people to make personal decisions regarding intimate matters; under the COMMON LAW, the right of people to lead their lives in a manner that is reasonably secluded from public scrutiny, whether such scrutiny comes from a neighbor's prying eyes, an investigator's eavesdropping ears, or a news photographer's intrusive camera; and in statutory law, the right of people to be free from unwarranted drug testing and electronic surveillance.

Norman-Bloodsaw v. Lawrence Berkeley Laboratory

Genetic testing in the workplace is a controversial topic involving the right to privacy. Concerns about the use of DNA testing for certain medical conditions without the employee's consent led to an important federal lawsuit. In *Norman-Bloodsaw v. Lawrence Berkeley Laboratory*, 135 F.3d 1260 (9th Cir. 1998), a federal appeals court held that seven employees of the government laboratory could assert constitutional and STATUTORY rights against their employer. For many years the laboratory had tested prospective employees for syphilis, pregnancy, and sickle-cell traits without their consent.

Marya Norman-Bloodsaw and six other employees filed the lawsuit against Lawrence Berkeley Laboratory, a research facility operated by the University of California under contract with the U.S. ENERGY DEPARTMENT. Since 1981 the department has required contractors, such as the laboratory, to conduct "preplacement examinations" of individuals who have been offered employment but who have not yet started working. During the physical examination the employees gave blood and urine samples and were questioned about numerous medical conditions. All employee samples were tested for syphilis, women were tested for pregnancy, and African Americans were tested for sickle-cell anemia. The testing of these three categories ended in 1995. Laboratory officials claimed that signs were posted in health examination rooms and reception areas stating that these tests would be administered.

After the plaintiffs filed their lawsuit in 1995, the laboratory asked the court to dismiss the case. The DISTRICT COURT agreed to this request, basing the decision primarily on statute of limitation GROUNDS. The court ruled that the time period for filing a lawsuit began to run when the tests were taken, not when the plaintiffs found out that the specific genetic screenings had taken place.

The Court of Appeals for the Ninth Circuit overturned most of the district court's ruling. Judge Stephen Reinhardt, writing for the three-judge panel, concluded that the district court judge had erred on the STATUTE OF LIMITATIONS issue. He found that there were MATERIAL issues of fact in dispute that could only be resolved at trial. It was premature to dismiss the case when it was unclear if the plaintiffs "knew or had reason to know of the nature of the tests" when they agreed to the preplacement examination.

A scientist examines a DNA sequencing autoradiogram.

Judge Reinhardt also disagreed with the lower court's decision that the laboratory had not violated the plaintiffs' right to privacy because the intrusion was minimal. Reinhardt noted, "The constitutionally protected privacy interest in avoiding disclosure of personal matters clearly encompasses medical information and its confidentiality." He characterized the medical tests as SEARCHES AND SEIZURES under the FOURTH AMENDMENT. The court had to balance the government's interest in conducting medical tests against public employees' expectations of privacy. In viewing this issue, Reinhardt could "think of few subject areas more personal and more likely to implicate privacy interests than that of one's health or genetic make-up." The pregnancy and syphilis tests were even more disturbing because employers are not allowed to inquire into an employee's "personal sexual matters that have no bearing on job performance." Because factual matters still existed, the APPELLATE COURT concluded that they should be resolved at trial. For much the same reasons, the appeals court sent back issues involving the right to privacy based on the California state constitution.

Judge Reinhardt also considered whether the testing had violated Title VII of the Civil Rights Act of 1964. The act bars discrimination in employment based on a number of categories, including race, gender and pregnancy. The appeals court found that "plaintiffs' claims fall neatly into a Title VII framework" because "The plaintiffs allege that black and female em-

ployees were singled out for additional nonconsensual testing," thereby having their privacy "invaded on the basis of race, gender, and pregnancy." Because the preplacement examinations were conditions of employment, they fell within the employment relationship covered by Title VII.

The Department of Energy, which was a defendant, contended that it should be dropped from the lawsuit because it had stopped requiring testing for syphilis in 1992. Judge Reinhardt rejected the department's contention that the case was MOOT. He ruled that the department and the laboratory "have not carried their heavy burden of establishing either that their alleged behavior cannot be reasonably expected to recur, or that interim events have eradicated the effects of the alleged violation." Therefore, the appeals court ordered the case be REMANDED to the district court for trial.

In July 2000 the parties agreed to a settlement of $2.2 million, which amounted to $4,050 per person. The laboratory agreed to restrictive consent rules for the use of genetic information and a monitor was appointed to oversee the examination process.

CROSS REFERENCES
Employment Law; Fourth Amendment

PRODUCT LIABILITY

The responsibility of a manufacturer or vendor of goods to compensate for injury caused by a defective good that it has provided for sale.

Fen-Phen Diet Drug Class Actions Continue

Litigation continued in 2001 concerning fen-phen, the diet drug combination of fenfluramine and phentermine. American Home Products Corporation (AHPC) manufactured fenfluramine, a drug that alters seratonin levels in the brain to suppress feelings of hunger, under the brand name Pondimin. In 1997 AHPC removed Pondimin and Redux, a chemical cousin, from the market after a Mayo Clinic study linked the fenfluramine/phentermine combination to heart valve damage. At that time, more than 6 million people had taken the drug. Since then, AHPC has faced more than 9,000 lawsuits from people claiming heart injuries from fen-phen. Phentermine is still on the market although plaintiffs attorneys say there is a question whether it alone causes heart damage.

In August 2000 Judge Louis C. Bechtle of the U.S. District Court for the Eastern District of Pennsylvania approved a $3.75 billion settlement of a CLASS ACTION case against AHPC. Fen-Phen users who participate in the settlement could receive between $30 and $1.5 million each, depending on the length of time they took the drugs and the severity of their injuries. Patients who took the drugs for in excess of sixty days but who have not yet developed injuries could receive money for medical monitoring to determine if they develop injuries in the future. The settlement does not cover the several hundred people who claim the drugs gave them primary pulmonary hypertension, a fatal lung disorder. The class action attorneys who ran the case for the plaintiffs stood to recover up to $430 million in legal fees under the settlement.

AHPC and class action attorney Stanley Chesley called the settlement a fair resolution of the claims of most people who have suffered heart damage from fen-phen. Some objectors said the settlement did not give injured patients enough money and gave the class action attorneys too much money. Representing a group of objectors, attorney Edward F. Blizzard called the settlement unfair for fen-phen users who might develop heart problems in the future. Those users will not recover money from AHPC for their injuries and will not be allowed to file their own lawsuits unless they opted-out of the class action case by March 30, 2000.

Approximately 45,000 people opted-out, meaning AHPC still faces considerable litigation over the drug. Some evidence suggests that AHPC knew or should have known that fenfluramine could cause heart valve damage, meaning the company faces PUNITIVE DAMAGES in litigation brought by individual plaintiffs.

In one such case in Oregon, a jury awarded Juanita Batson and her son, Richard Wirt, $29.1 million for heart damage caused by fenfluramine. The award included $25.3 million in punitive damages. AHPC attorney Mark Spooner called the case a "lottery litigation wherein the plaintiffs were absolutely healthy" until their attorneys "took them aside and told them they weren't." AHPC nevertheless settled the case weeks later for an undisclosed sum of money in exchange for abandoning an appeal of the verdict.

In October 2000, on the second day of a trial in Mississippi concerning more than 2,000 fen-phen users, AHPC settled the case for $200 million. The lead plaintiff in that case, Penny Lucky, required open heart surgery to replace a leaky valve that she said was caused by fenfluramine.

John Denver Plane Crash

In September 2000 the heirs of singer John Denver settled their WRONGFUL DEATH lawsuit against several defendants who manufactured and sold a fuel valve installed in Denver's two-seater private airplane. Denver was piloting the plane on a routine sightseeing flight on October 12, 1997, when it suddenly plunged and crashed just off the coast of Monterey, California. Denver was killed though the accident occurred from an altitude of only 300–500 feet. The original suit, filed in October 1998, charged that the fuel selector valve malfunctioned, ultimately causing the crash and Denver's death. The parties settled the case in late-September 2000.

Denver, who died without a will, was born Henry John Deutschendorf, Jr., in 1943. Plaintiffs in this action included Denver's children, Jesse Belle Denver, a minor, and adults Zachary and Anna Kate Deutschendorf. His mother, Erma Deutschendorf, was also named a plaintiff. Shortly after the suit was filed, attorneys representing the plaintiffs requested, and were granted, a court extension to compile a definitive list of defendants.

As in all product liability cases, the plaintiffs would have had the burden of proving a design or manufacturing defect that proximately caused the accident. The lengthy list of defendants filed with the court in March 1999 included Mark IV

Erma Deutschendorf, mother of the late John Denver, arrives with son Ron Deutschendorf for a public memorial at the Faith Presbyterian Church in Aurora, Colorado.

Industries; Imperial Eastman Company, the ostensible manufacturer of the fuel valve; Dayco Eastman; Gould Electronics Inc.; and Aircraft Spruce & Specialty Company. Several of the defendants were successor entities as Imperial Eastman had been bought and sold several times between the date when the subject valve had been manufactured, purchased, and installed in Denver's plane. Mark IV Industries was also bought out, by the European investment company BC Partners. Complicating the list of defendants, as well as the ability to establish PROXIMATE CAUSE, was the fact that Denver's Long EZ canard plane was a "kit-built" one in which the parts and functions had been significantly "customized." Substantial deviation from a designer's or manufacturer's plans often severs LIABILITY.

Prior to the filing of listed defendants in March 1999, the NATIONAL TRANSPORTATION SAFETY BOARD (NTSB) published its investigative report and findings on the crash. Contrary to earlier rumors that bird feathers had been found in the wreckage, that Denver had been intoxicated or suicidal, and that the plane had been repainted prior to the crash, the NTSB report focused on the *location* of the fuel selector valve within the plane. Its findings little resembled the initial legal theories upon which liability had been premised.

The subject fuel selector valve is used to access on-board fuel distributed between left and right holding tanks in the wing bases. As it is meant to function, a dashboard gauge indicates low fuel in one of the tanks, at which point a pilot can switch the fuel selector valve to access fuel in another tank.

The plaintiffs' theory of liability was that "the fuel tank was frozen between the left-tank and right-tank positions [and] . . . could not be moved." Denver was the third owner of the aircraft. There was evidence that the plane's prior owner had complained the valve required lubrication and was increasingly hard to use. To neutralize this evidence and its significance as tending to show contributory NEGLIGENCE on the part of Denver for attempting flight with a faulty valve, the plaintiffs countered with evidence that the valve was working prior to takeoff. This could be established by facts that Denver, first having attempted to start the plane with the valve off and failed, then turned it on and successfully started the plane.

Another likely defense theory would have been that Denver failed to refuel prior to takeoff. Because Denver had purchased the plane just two week before the crash, the defense might have claimed that he was inadequately trained or knowledgeable in the working of the fuel selector valve. With the added benefit of the NTSB report, defendants were prepared to show that the valve was fully functional at the time of the accident but that the *location* of the valve had caused Denver to inadvertently or awkwardly apply pressure to the right rudder while trying to switch the valve.

Undisputed facts were that the airplane had been heading west when it suddenly pitched slightly upward then diverted to a nosedive and that the plane had turned or banked steeply to the right. Witnesses noted a reduction in engine noise before the dive. Consistent with these eyewitness reports, the NTSB had found that when its inspectors twisted around to reach behind their shoulders to access the fuel valve, they inadvertently pressed down on the right rudder pedal. The witnesses' description of a slight upward pitch followed by a right roll and dive was consistent with such a sudden unintentional application of the right rudder.

The NTSB report also indicated that the plane's builder, Adrian Davis, had not placed the valve in front of the pilot for fear of running fuel lines in the cockpit, and in case of their bursting in a landing on the bottom of the plane. According to NTSB's findings, the probable cause of the accident was "the pilot's diversion of attention from the operation of the airplane and his inadvertent application of right rudder that resulted in the loss of airplane control while attempting to manipulate the fuel selector handle. . . . The pilot's inadequate preflight planning and preparation, specifically his failure to refuel the airplane" was also found to be "causal." Finally, the report listed "the builder's decision to locate the unmarked fuel selector handle in a hard-to-access position" and Denver's "inadequate" transition training as noncausal "factors in the accident."

As is true in many product liability cases, proofs against each defendant may tend to undermine the liability. Furthermore, jurors may become confused by conflicting technical expert testimony. With a high risk for jury confusion and the likelihood of protracted and costly trials, a high percentage of cases settle, as did this one. The settlement amount was not publicly disclosed, and there was no admission of guilt by the defendants.

CROSS REFERENCES
Wrongful Death

RACKETEER INFLUENCED AND CORRUPT ORGANIZATIONS ACT

Cedric Kushner Promotions v. Don King

The Racketeer Influenced and Corrupt Organizations Act (RICO) was passed as a means of punishing businesses run by organized crime. RICO also has civil provisions that are designed to punish illegal activity through the recovery of DAMAGES. This is standard in civil lawsuits, but RICO enhances the award by allowing treble damages, which means that after the jury awards the plaintiff damages, the court automatically triples that amount. In addition, the defendant must pay the plaintiff's legal fees and costs. Like RICO's criminal provisions, these provisions seek to weaken and destroy organized crime. Civil attorneys have convinced federal courts that RICO also applies to business activities *not* contemplated by the drafters of the law. The courts have interpreted the civil provisions to encompass any business activities by a corporation that were fraudulent.

The courts also have been required to interpret the finer points of these provisions. Such was the case in *Cedric Kushner Promotions, Ltd. v. King*, ___U.S.___, 121 S.Ct. 2087, ___ L.Ed.2d ___ (2001), where the Supreme Court resolved whether the only shareholder in a tightly controlled corporation could be sued under civil RICO provisions. The Court used basic law on corporate personhood in concluding that the corporation and the sole owner are legally separate and distinct persons. Thus, the STATUTORY requirement of the RICO law were satisfied and such a RICO action could proceed against the corporate owner.

Cedric Kushner Promotions, Ltd., is a corporation that promotes boxing matches. It filed a RICO lawsuit against the flamboyant and powerful boxing promoter, Don King, who is the president and sole shareholder of Don King Productions. Kushner alleged that King had conducted the boxing-related affairs of his corporation in part through a RICO "pattern." Under RICO, a pattern is the commission of two or more statutorily defined crimes. In this case, Kushner alleged that King had committed at least two acts of fraud and other RICO crimes.

King moved to dismiss the complaint, alleging that RICO did not apply to him because the law required two separate legal entities: a "person" and a "distinct enterprise." The specific provision, Justice STEPHEN G. BREYER explained, "makes it 'unlawful for any person employed by or associated with any enterprise . . . to conduct or participate . . . in the conduct of such enterprise's affairs' through the commission of two or more statutorily defined crimes." King argued that because he owned the corporation there was only one legal entity: himself. Therefore, RICO could not apply. The DISTRICT COURT, applying precedent from the Court of Appeals for the Second Circuit, agreed and dismissed the lawsuit. The Second Circuit affirmed this decision, and the Supreme Court agreed to hear Kushner's appeal because four other CIRCUIT COURTS of appeal took a contrary position.

The Court, in a unanimous decision, overturned the Second Circuit's decision and interpretation of the RICO provision. Justice Breyer, writing for the Court, noted that the only issue was whether there were two distinct legal en-

Don King, who faces charges of insurance fraud, is seen here following opening statements at New York's Federal Court on April 20, 1998.

tities: a "person" and a separate "enterprise." The Second Circuit had concluded that King was part of, and not separate from, the corporation he owned. Thus, there was no person distinct from the enterprise who improperly conducted the enterprise's affairs. Breyer rejected this analysis, though he did acknowledge that two distinct entities are required, because RICO does not permit labeling the same "person" with two different names.

Breyer based his analysis on corporate law principles. It is undisputed that a corporation is a distinct legal "person." The creation of this personhood is one of the reasons this type of business organization has flourished. As a distinct entity it shields individual owners of the corporation from personal LIABILITY for the corporation's debts. In this case Don King is a natural person and an employee of the corporation he owns. Don King Productions is a separate legal person, as it is a legally chartered corporation and has different rights and responsibilities. In examining the RICO provision, Justice Breyer could find nothing in the law that "requires more 'separateness' than that." Don King is both an employee of the corporation and the sole owner of the corporation. Though he may totally control the corporation, the corporation is a distinct legal entity.

The Court's interpretation was justified in Breyer's view by RICO's basic purpose to protect both "a legitimate 'enterprise' from those who would use unlawful acts to victimize it" and "the public from those who would unlawfully use an 'enterprise' (whether legitimate or illegitimate) as a 'vehicle' through which 'unlawful . . . activity is committed'." In addition, there was

nothing in RICO's history that "significantly favored an alternative interpretation."

CROSS REFERENCES
Corporations

REFUGEES

Individuals who leave their native country for social, political, or religious reasons, or who are forced to leave, as a result of any type of disaster, including war, political upheaval, and famine.

Advocacy for Refugee Children

According to a 2000 statement by the Women's Commission for Refugee Women and Children, a nonprofit, nonpartisan ADVOCACY organization, more than 80 percent of the world's 40 million displaced persons and refugees are women and children. The United Nations High Commission on Refugees agrees that children comprise half of the refugee population alone. The U.S. Immigration and Naturalization Office (INS) reported that 4,600 unattended, unaccompanied children entered the United States illegally in 1999, a number that represented only those children officially apprehended by the INS.

If the INS cannot locate the refugee child's family or a sponsor, the government temporarily houses him or her. According to the INS, unclaimed or unidentified children spend an average of thirty days in governmental shelter, but many cases have continued for months or years. While many of these children are housed in private shelters under contract with the INS, at least one third are housed in juvenile detention centers or jails, with commensurately inferior living conditions and direct commingling with youthful offenders. Eventually, the children must appear at immigration court hearings, where decisions are made as to whether they should be deported. Fewer than half of the children have attorneys, and they do not have a right to one since they are ALIENS and not U.S. citizens or legal residents of the country.

The plight of these children has instigated the mobilization of several ADVOCACY efforts to represent them and their plea for political ASYLUM, the most frequently-cited reason for child immigration. The 1980 Refugee Act requires that those who seek political asylum must prove they have a "well-founded fear" of persecution because of their race, national origin, or membership in a political or social group if they are returned home. Children bear the same evidentiary burden as adults although some children are eligible for other types of VISAS. One in four children voluntarily agrees to DEPORTATION, however, largely because he or she does not understand the legal options or the evidence needed to warrant the granting of a visa.

First among efforts to come forward and help these children was a one-year program begun in the fall of 2000 to provide volunteer advocates for unaccompanied child refugees in the Phoenix, Arizona, area. The Women's Commission for Refugee Women and Children, the University of Chicago, the Lutheran Immigration and Refugee Service, and the Florence, Arizona Immigrant and Refugee Rights Project collaborated on the program with the Executive Office for Immigration Review—a U.S. JUSTICE DEPARTMENT agency that oversees immigration courts—and the INS. Under the Phoenix Pilot Project for Children and Immigration Proceedings, trained "friends of the children" volunteers were assigned to work with unaccompanied children at the local detention facilities and continue assisting them until the time they appeared before an immigration judge. The program cost an estimated $250,000. It also called for a separate immigration docket for juveniles, who would each receive a rights package with written, video, and live presentations, along with individual appointed counsel. The Arizona Bar Association had coordinated free legal representation for many of the children. Finally, the detention centers were to be staffed with social workers and volunteers who would assist children in adjusting to daily life in the United States.

Another key initiative was the introduction of Bill S121, brought forward by Senator Diane Feinstein (D-CA), proposing the "Unaccompanied Alien Child Protection Act." The bill "would establish an Office of Children Services within the Department of Justice to help ensure refugee children's access to appointed counsel and guardians" AD LITEM, in other words for the pending legal matter. Existing standards that governed the treatment of children in INS custody had been laid out in the 1997 settlement of *Flores v. Reno*, 507 U.S. 292 (1993). Many advocates wished to eliminate a perceived conflict of interest in the existing procedures, namely, placing children "in the custody of the INS, the very agency prosecuting them" for deportation. The Women's Commission backed Feinstein's legislation and also induced the national law firm of Latham & Watkins to do PRO BONO lobbying on the bill's behalf. Latham then com-

U.S. Navy crewmen aboard USS *Blue Ridge* carry two Vietnamese refugee children brought in by a Vietnamese Air Force helicopter.

mitted its lawyers across the country to represent individual refugee children in detention. The AMERICAN BAR ASSOCIATION (ABA) also provided $40,000 in matching grants to state and local bar associations whose lawyers assisted refugee children.

In late 2000 the UNITED NATIONS worked to bring approximately 600 Sudanese children to the United States. Known as the "lost boys" of the Sudan, they were almost all male and under the age of eighteen. The United States was the only country accepting refugees from the wartorn country, where homeless children were forced to survive war, disease, starvation, and attacks from wild animals. The boys were to be placed in foster homes in a few selected cities, including Seattle, Washington.

Efforts on behalf of refugee children are also being made in other areas of the world. In March 2001 at a two-day conference on children held by the European Union, Grace Machel, wife of former South African President Nelson Mandela, made a special appeal for more aid and attention to be directed toward refugee children, especially those affected by wars. The European Union hoped to "find common minimum guarantees" for children seeking asylum. Britain already provides such children with legal counsel.

RELIGION

Adler v. Duval County School Board

The division in the federal appellate courts over the constitutionality of student-initiated prayers led the Supreme Court of the United States in June 2000 to announce its decision in

Santa Fe Independent School District v. Doe, 530 U.S. 290, 120 S.Ct. 2266, 147 L.Ed.2d 295 (2000). The Court affirmed the Court of Appeals for the Fifth Circuit (*Doe v. Santa Fe Independent School Dist.*, 168 F.3d 806 (5th Cir.(Tex.) Feb 26, 1999), which ruled that a Texas public school district could not let its students lead prayers over the public address system before its high school football games. In so ruling, the Supreme Court reaffirmed its prior decisions on the separation of church and state and its interpretation of the FIRST AMENDMENT's Establishment Clause. The school district's sponsorship of the public prayers by elected student representatives was impermissible because the schools could not coerce anyone to support or participate in religious activities.

However, three months prior to the Supreme Court's decision, the Court of Appeals for the Eleventh Circuit ruled the other way in *Adler v. Duval County School Board*, 206 F.3d 1070 (11th Cir. 1999). The Eleventh Circuit upheld the school board's policy in Duval County, Florida, which allowed the graduating students to vote on whether a student would be allowed to make a speech in which subject matter was decided upon by the speaker. The court found that since the state was not involved in choice of speaker, subject matter, or whether anyone would speak at all provided for a suitable non-state sponsored format.

The facts surrounding the Florida case were similar to the facts in the *Santa Fe* case. Until 1992, clergy and others traditionally offered invocations, benedictions, and other religious prayers or messages at public high school commencement ceremonies in the Duval County School District. In that year, however, the Supreme Court in *Lee v. Weisman*, 505 U.S. 577, 112 S.Ct. 2649, 120 L.Ed.2d 467 (1992), held that a Providence, Rhode Island high school principal who brought in a local clergyman to deliver a nondenominational prayer had in fact acted with the school board in violating the Establishment Clause. In response the Duval school superintendent stopped the traditional practice. In 1993, the school district adopted the policy that generated the lawsuit, allowing students at each high school to vote on the whether to have a student deliver a personal message at the graduation ceremony. The district made clear that the administration and faculty would not be involved in the decision-making process. The policy was immediately challenged in court on Establishment Clause grounds, but the courts were at first hostile to First Amendment

arguments that would prohibit the policy and practice. In the first year under the new policy, student speakers at 10 of the 17 high school graduation ceremonies delivered a religious message of some kind. At the remaining seven ceremonies there were either no student messages or the messages were completely secular in theme.

Though the first lawsuit was dismissed, a second one was filed in 1998 challenging the policy. The federal district again ruled in favor of the school board but a three-judge panel of the Eleventh Circuit reversed. The school board then appealed this ruling to the full bench of the circuit, which vacated the panel decision and granted a rehearing before the full court.

The Eleventh Circuit, with two dissenting votes, agreed with the district court that the policy did not violate the Establishment Clause. Judge Stanley Marcus, writing for the majority, concluded that the policy was constitutional on its face. Marcus stated that the policy did not violate the First Amendment "merely because an autonomous student *may* choose to deliver a religious message." In reviewing Establishment Clause cases, Marcus emphasized that a line must be drawn between a student's private message, which may be religious in character, and a state-sponsored religious message. The private message is protected while the state-sponsored message is not.

Judge Marcus found that the absence of state involvement in each of the central decisions surrounding the selection of a graduation speaker "insulates the School Board's policy from constitutional infirmity on its face." In examining *Lee v. Weisman*, Marcus concluded that the Supreme Court based its ruling on the school system's policy of ordering and directing the performance of a religious exercise by deciding to include a prayer in the graduation ceremony and by inviting a clergyman to give prayer. Moreover, the school district provided the clergyman with guidelines for the prayer. In addition, students felt compelled to attend graduation and join their peers by either standing as a group or remaining quiet during the prayers. Judge Marcus distinguished the facts in Duval County. In the Florida district, school officials did not direct a formal religious exercise and students were not required to deliver a religious message at graduation. Therefore, the policy did not offend the Establishment Clause. Judge Marcus stated that to rule otherwise "would come perilously close to announcing an absolute rule that would excise *all* private expression from a public graduation ceremony, no matter how neutral" the process. On October 2, 2000, the Supreme Court granted certiorari but immediately vacated the decision in light of its ruling in *Santa Fe* and remanded it to the Eleventh Circuit.

Chandler v. Siegelman

The courts remain filled with cases challenging the constitutionality of state laws that permit students to lead prayers at school-related events. The Supreme Court of the United States, in *Santa Fe Independent School District v. Doe*, 530 U.S. 290, 120 S.Ct. 2266, 147 L.Ed.2d 295 (2000) [see also, "Religion: Santa Fe Independent School District v. Doe" essay in *American Law Yearbook 2000*], ruled 6–3 that a Texas public school district could not let its students lead prayers over the public address system before its high school football games. In so ruling, the Court reaffirmed its prior decisions on the separation of church and state. The school district's sponsorship of the public prayers by elected student representatives was deemed impermissible because the schools could not coerce anyone to support or participate in religion.

Following this decision, the Court vacated and remanded a decision of the Circuit Court of Appeals for the Eleventh Circuit, *Chandler v. James*, 180 F.3d 1254 (11th Cir. 1999), that upheld an Alabama statute permitting nonsectarian, non-proselytizing student-initiated prayer at school-related events. The Court asked the Eleventh Circuit to reconsider its decision in light of the *Santa Fe* ruling. In a somewhat surprising move, the appeals court reinstated its ruling, holding that the decision was not in conflict with the *Santa Fe* decision. *Chandler v. Siegelman*, 230 F.3d 1313 (11th Cir. 2000).

In its original decision, the appeals court had overturned a federal district court's order that the statute on its face was unconstitutional because it violated the Establishment Clause of the FIRST AMENDMENT. The district court injunction prohibited all prayers or devotional speech by students or other private individuals in school situations that were not purely private, such as prayers said aloud in the classroom, over the public address system, or as part of a school-relate event such as a graduation ceremony. The appeals court struck down this part of the order, holding that so long as school personnel did not participate in or actively supervise student-initiated speech, the school district could not "constitutionally prohibit students from speaking religiously."

On remand, the Eleventh Circuit panel reinstated its ruling. Judge James C. Hill, writing for the court, stated that its original decision was not in conflict with the *Santa Fe* decision. Hill believed the Supreme Court in *Santa Fe* had condemned school sponsorship of student prayer. In the Alabama case, however, the appeals court had condemned school censorship of student prayer. Viewed in this way, Judge Hill concluded the two cases were "complimentary rather than inconsistent."

Judge Hill pointed out that the Supreme Court had reaffirmed that the Establishment Clause prohibits a school district from taking affirmative steps to create a vehicle for prayer to be delivered at a school function. The Santa Fe school district violated this prohibition by passing a policy that allowed student-led prayer and established a selection process for choosing the student who would deliver it. Thus, the district was not "merely providing a neutral accommodation of private religious speech." In Hill's view, the "fatal flaw" in Santa Fe's efforts was its attempt "to disentangle itself from the religious messages by instituting the student election process." By allowing majority rule to guide the selection of speakers, the district ensured that only "appropriate" messages would be delivered.

In its decision, the Supreme Court emphasized that not every message delivered at school-related events can be attributed to the government, Judge Hill observed. In Hill's view, the Court had condemned the prayer in *Santa Fe* because it was not private. Based on this analysis, the appeals court returned to the Alabama law and the district court's injunction that it had struck down. Judge Hill noted that it had held the injunction was overbroad "to the extent that it equated all student religious speech in any public context at school with State speech." This was wrong because the Establishment Clause "does not require the elimination of private speech endorsing religion in public places." To rule otherwise would mean that "the exercise of one's religion would not be free at all."

The critical distinction for the appeals court was not the public context that makes some speech the state's speech; it was the "entanglement with the State." What the Supreme Court banned in *Santa Fe* was not private speech endorsing religion "but the delivery of a school-sponsored prayer." In Hill's view, removing school sponsorship removed the Establishment Clause issues. Once that was done, "the prayer is private" and, under the Eleventh Circuit's first decision, the prayer must be permitted.

The Eleventh Circuit reiterated its views that private speech endorsing religion is constitutionally protected in school. Such speech is not "the school's speech even though it occurs in school." Moreover, such speech is not "unconstitutionally coercive even though it may occur before non-believer students."

Freedom from Religion Foundation, Inc., v. City of Marshfield

In *Freedom from Religion Foundation, Inc., v. City of Marshfield*, 203 F.3d 487 (7th Cir. 2000), The U.S. Court of Appeals for the Seventh Circuit ruled that a statue of Jesus located in a city park and visible from a major public thoroughfare violated the Establishment Clause of the FIRST AMENDMENT to the U.S. Constitution, even though the statue itself was located on private property. The seventh circuit remanded the case to federal DISTRICT COURT, which ordered the city to erect a fence around the statue and maintain a disclaimer that the statue is located on private property.

The statue was originally given to the city of Marshfield, Wisconsin, in 1959 by the John Eisen Assembly, Fourth Degree Knights of Columbus. The city placed it in what was then known as Wildwood Park, an undeveloped area owned by the city. The statue is made of white marble and stands fifteen feet tall. It depicts Jesus, arms open in prayer, standing on top of a large sphere, which in turn rests on a base bearing an inscription in twelve-inch block letters: *Christ Guide Us On Our Way.* The statue faces Highway 13, the main thoroughfare into Marshfield from the south and is clearly visible to travelers using the roadway.

In 1964 Henry Praschak, a Knights of Columbus member, offered to construct a comfort station near the statue, adding signs, picnic tables, and outdoor grills. The city agreed to reserve the area for city-park purposes and to build the infrastructure necessary to support it. The city also agreed to provide electrical service and maintain the statue. In recognition of Praschak's contribution, Wildwood Park was renamed Praschak Wayside Park.

In 1993 Marshfield businessman Clarence Reinders objected to the presence of the statue on public property. Reinders, a member of the Freedom from Religion Foundation, Inc. (FFRF), told the city that he avoided using the park because of the white marble Jesus and was forced to take alternate routes to work to avoid viewing the statue from Highway 13. The city refused to take action. Five years later FFRF filed suit against the city in the U.S. District Court for the Western District of Wisconsin. The plaintiff sought an order declaring the statue's presence in a public park a violation of the First Amendment's Establishment Clause. FFRF also requested an INJUNCTION ordering the city to remove it.

Soon after the lawsuit was filed, the city placed a DISCLAIMER in front of the statue. It provided that the "location of this statue . . . does not reflect an endorsement of a religious sect or belief by the city of Marshfield." A group of Marshfield citizens then formed the Henry Praschak Memorial Fund (HPMF), and purchased the 0.15 acres of land upon which the statue sits. The fund paid $21,560 for the land, the highest price per square foot that the city had ever received for a parcel of property. The city also separated the electrical service required to light the statue from the system that serves the rest of the public park.

SUMMARY JUDGMENT motions were brought by both sides following the sale of the land. The federal district court said the case no longer required a decision on the MERITS of the plaintiff's First Amendment claims. Instead, the court found that the sale of land had rendered those claims MOOT because the statue was no longer located on public property. The court rejected FFRF's claim that the sale itself constituted an endorsement of religion. The sale had complied with all applicable laws, the court observed, and the city had since taken steps to disassociate itself from the marble Jesus. The plaintiffs appealed.

The seventh circuit VACATED the district court's decision and remanded the case for further proceedings. Under the Establishment Clause of the First Amendment, the court wrote, governmental entities are prohibited from promoting or endorsing any religious doctrine or organization. According to the so-called Lemon test enunciated in *Lemon v. Kurtzman*, 403 U.S. 602, 91 S.Ct. 2105, 29 L.Ed.2d 745 (1971), the seventh circuit said that government action will not constitute the endorsement of religion if (1) the action has a secular purpose; (2) the action does not have the principle or primary effect of advancing or inhibiting religion; and (3) the action does not foster excessive government entanglement with religion.

The court found that the statue violated the first two prongs of the Lemon test. The statue's inscription, the court said, left "no doubt as to the obvious religious message imparted" by the inscription. The court also found that the statue had the primary effect of advancing religion because of the statue's physical location and its historical association with the city-owned land. No visual boundaries currently exist to physically differentiate the private property on which the statue rests from the surrounding public property, the court noted. Thus, the court concluded that a reasonable but unknowledgeable observer could perceive the statue as a governmental monument erected by the city to convey a message in favor of a particular religion, namely Christianity. The disclaimer placed below the statue was insufficient to offset this perception.

At the same time, the court was reluctant to order the statue removed from the park. The court said that the park was a traditional public forum that for "time out of mind" had been used "for purposes of assembly, communicating thoughts between citizens, and discussing public questions." Traditional public forums must remain "open to all on equal terms," the court emphasized, and HPMF could not be compelled to limit its expression in a manner more restrictive than would be applied to other religious groups wishing to express themselves in the park. Conversely, HPMF could not be given preferential access to the park, as it was when the city sold it the land where the statue could permanently reside in a prominent location.

To balance these competing interests the court ordered the city to construct "some defining structure, such as a permanent gated fence or wall, to separate city property from [the HPMF] property." The permanent structure, the court ruled, must be accompanied by a clearly visible disclaimer that would prevent a reasonable person from confusing the marble statue as an expressive message endorsed by the city. The seventh circuit then remanded the case for the federal district court to conduct a hearing on the matter.

On REMAND FFRF asked the district court to order the city to build a ten-foot cement wall around the statue, while the city wanted a three-foot fence. On June, 16, 2000, the court issued an unpublished decision ordering the city to build a four-foot wrought-iron fence around the statue stating that it is a private park along with the disclaimer:

THIS PROPERTY IS NOT OWNED OR MAINTAINED BY THE CITY OF MARSHFIELD, NOR DOES THE CITY ENDORSE THE RELIGIOUS EXPRESSION THEREON.

The words "private park" were to be in ten-inch block letters, while the accompanying text was to be in four-inch block letters. The order did not indicate whether the message should be displayed on marble, stone, paper, or other material. Although FFRF said it was disappointed with the ruling, it has not filed an appeal.

CROSS REFERENCES
First Amendment; Judicial Review

RIGHT TO COUNSEL

Texas v. Cobb

Since the 1960s, the Supreme Court of the United States has wrestled with various issues surrounding the SIXTH AMENDMENT's right to counsel provision. Though the Court has mandated that criminal suspects placed in custody must be allowed to consult with an attorney, it has also declined to throw out confessions and convictions in some cases where the suspect has not consulted with an attorney. In *Texas v. Cobb*, ___U.S.___, 121 S.Ct. 1335, 149 L.Ed.2d 321 (2001), the Court refused to reverse a murder conviction where the suspect's attorney was not informed that the police were interrogating the suspect about related crimes. The Court concluded that the right to counsel is "offense specific."

Raymond L. Cobb was accused of burglarizing the Walker County, Texas home of a neighbor in December 1993. In addition, the wife and 16-month-old daughter of the home's owner were reported missing after the burglary. After an anonymous informer named Cobb as a suspect, police arrested him on an unrelated charge. While in custody the police questioned him about the burglary and disappearance of the two residents. Cobb at first denied any role in the crime but eventually signed a statement confessing to the burglary. However, he claimed he knew nothing about the disappearances. Soon after he was charged, an attorney was appointed to represent him. Several times over the next year the police asked and received permission from Cobb's attorney to question him about the disappearances.

In November 1995 Cobb was awaiting trial on the burglary trial and staying with his father in another town. His father contacted the local sheriff to report that his son had confessed to killing the mother. The sheriff contacted the Walker County sheriff's office, which obtained an arrest warrant and faxed it to the sheriff.

Once in custody, Cobb was advised of his right to counsel but waived it. Within a short time he confessed to murdering both the mother and child, admitting that the mother had confronted him during the burglary. He stabbed the mother and buried her and the child in a hole a few hundred yards from the house. Based on this confession, a jury convicted Cobb of capital murder and sentenced him to death. However, the Texas Court of Criminal Appeals reversed Cobb's conviction. The court held that once Cobb's right to counsel attached for the burglary, it attached "to any other offense that is very closely related factually to the offense charged." This declaration meant that police should have contacted Cobb's attorney to secure permission to question Cobb about the murders. Therefore, his confession was inadmissible, and its introduction was not harmless error.

The Supreme Court, in a 5–4 decision, reversed the Texas appeals court. Chief Justice WILLIAM H. REHNQUIST, writing for the majority, noted that the Court had addressed when the right to counsel arises in *McNeil v. Wisconsin*, 501 U.S. 171, 111 S.Ct. 2204, 115 L.Ed.2d 158 (1991). In this case the Court stated that the right to counsel is "offense specific" and "cannot be invoked once for all future prosecutions." Therefore, the Court ruled that a defendant's statements concerning offenses for which he had not been charged were admissible despite the attachment of the right to counsel for previously charged offenses. Despite this ruling many state and federal courts had interpreted *McNeil* to include an exception to the offense-specific definition for crimes that are factually related to a charged offense. Chief Justice Rehnquist rejected this exception as being outside the Court's decision.

William Pierce
Rogers

The Court dismissed the concern that police would use the offense-specific rule to commit what Cobb's lawyer called "unwanted and uncounseled interrogations." Rehnquist pointed out that this rule still required police to advise a suspect of the right against self-incrimination and the right to counsel; the suspect was free not to talk to police until counsel was present. Moreover, "it is critical to recognize that the Constitution does not negate society's interest in the ability of police to talk to witnesses and suspects, even those who have been charged with other offenses."

Having established the policy behind its decision, Rehnquist sought to make sure the lower courts understood what the word "offense" meant in this Sixth Amendment context. Citing

Charles Frederick
Carson Ruff

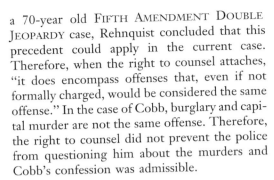

a 70-year old FIFTH AMENDMENT DOUBLE JEOPARDY case, Rehnquist concluded that this precedent could apply in the current case. Therefore, when the right to counsel attaches, "it does encompass offenses that, even if not formally charged, would be considered the same offense." In the case of Cobb, burglary and capital murder are not the same offense. Therefore, the right to counsel did not prevent the police from questioning him about the murders and Cobb's confession was admissible.

Justice STEPHEN G. BREYER, in a dissent joined by Justices JOHN PAUL STEVENS, DAVID H. SOUTER, and RUTH BADER GINSBURG, argued that the right to counsel had been undercut by the majority's ruling. He contended that the Court's technical definition of "offense" thwarted the right to counsel's "central role in ensuring the fairness of criminal proceedings in our system."

CROSS REFERENCES
Sixth Amendment

ROGERS, WILLIAM PIERCE

Obituary notice

Born on June 23, 1913, in Norfolk, New York; died January 2, 2001, in Bethesda, Maryland. Rogers served as U.S. ATTORNEY GENERAL during President DWIGHT D. EISENHOWER's administration and SECRETARY OF STATE during President RICHARD M. NIXON's administration. He played a major role in the writing and enacting of the CIVIL RIGHTS ACT of 1957. While U.S. attorney general, he made the Civil Rights Division a permanent division within the JUSTICE DEPARTMENT. As secretary of state, Rogers was able to negotiate a truce in 1970 between Egypt and Israel along the Suez Canal. In 1986, Rogers was chosen as chair of the commission set up to determine the cause of the space shuttle *Challenger* explosion.

RUFF, CHARLES FREDERICK CARSON

Charles Frederick Carson Ruff, the attorney who defended former President BILL CLINTON during IMPEACHMENT proceedings in 1999, died of natural causes on November 19, 2000. A high-profile litigator who formerly served as a special prosecuting attorney on the WATERGATE legal team in the 1970s, Ruff also was well known for representing ANITA HILL in her sexual harassment claim against U.S. Supreme Court nominee CLARENCE THOMAS in 1991. He was a familiar name and face in Washington legal circles, having represented some of the most elite and powerful figures in politics.

Born in Cleveland, Ohio, on August 1, 1939, Charles Ruff graduated from Swarthmore College in 1960, then earned a law degree from Columbia University School of Law in 1963. Shortly after graduation, Ruff accepted a Ford Foundation grant to teach law at the University of Liberia on the west coast of Africa. While in that country, he contracted a suspected tropical disease that left him a paraplegic. He remained wheelchair-bound for the remainder of his life.

Ruff returned from Liberia during the years of JIMMY CARTER's presidency and began an impressive career with the federal government. Starting as a federal prosecutor for the U.S. JUSTICE DEPARTMENT's organized crime section, he also served briefly as a deputy inspector general for the U.S. Department of Health, Education and Welfare. Later, as a member of the Watergate Special Prosecution Force, Ruff was assigned to work on the case against President RICHARD M. NIXON's chief fund-raisers who had been charged with accepting illegal campaign contributions. On a subsequent assignment, he conducted inquiry into allegations of President GERALD FORD's misuse of campaign funds, but found no impropriety. He also served as both an associate and acting deputy attorney general during the Justice Department's prosecution of members of Congress in the notorious Abscam bribery scandal. From 1979 to 1982, Ruff served as U.S. Attorney for the District of Columbia.

In 1982 Ruff left governmental practice to join the Washington, D.C., law firm of Covington & Burling. He developed a reputation as a formidable legal foe, displaying both intelligence and integrity in his style and substantive arguments. He became one of the most powerful and expensive lawyers in Washington. During this period, Ruff defended Senators John Glenn and Charles Robb in the "Keating Five" scandal involving bank savings and loan chief Charles Keating. Five senators, including Glenn and Robb, were investigated for partiality in voting on legislation favorable to Keating, who had contributed large donations to their respective political campaigns. Ruff also represented former White House aide Ira Magaziner.

Although he had become a partner at his law firm, Ruff left the lucrative practice in 1995 to accept a position as counsel for the District of

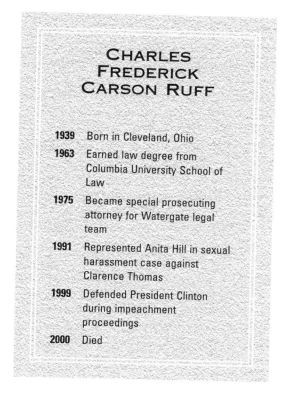

CHARLES FREDERICK CARSON RUFF

1939 Born in Cleveland, Ohio

1963 Earned law degree from Columbia University School of Law

1975 Became special prosecuting attorney for Watergate legal team

1991 Represented Anita Hill in sexual harassment case against Clarence Thomas

1999 Defended President Clinton during impeachment proceedings

2000 Died

Columbia Corporation. He would later address the Senate during presidential impeachment proceedings by stating: "My name is Charles Ruff. I'm from the District of Columbia. And we don't have a vote in the Congress of the United States."

In 1997 President Clinton asked him to serve as White House legal counsel, succeeding Abner Mikva, a former federal judge. At this time, the Clintons were caught up in the legal and political wranglings surrounding WHITEWATER, the Arkansas land deal being investigated by independent counsel KENNETH STARR. During Starr's expanded investigation in 1998, which brought in the Monica Lewinsky matter, Ruff became Clinton's chief defender. Concurrently enmeshed with these scandals was the Paula Jones sexual misconduct litigation, in which Ruff also defended the president.

Ruff's clever and skilled representation of Clinton resulted in a Senate decision against impeachment of the president for PERJURY and OBSTRUCTION OF JUSTICE. The House had already voted for impeachment, notwithstanding Ruff's first appearance before the House Judiciary Committee. The defense of President Clinton at the Senate trial was premised upon arguments that, "Impeachment should be reserved for those cases in which the President's very capacity to govern may be in question." Substantively, he engaged in several rounds of legal "hairsplitting" over the definition of sexual relations to undermine the perjury charges and argued that the obstruction article was unconstitutionally VAGUE because Clinton was charged with engaging in "one or more" acts to cover up his relationship with Lewinsky.

Charles Ruff was discovered dead in his home, apparently the victim of an accident. He is survived by his wife and two daughters. President Clinton saluted Ruff, commenting, "Every single day, I was so profoundly grateful that my counsel was so strong and wise and good, and that he believed so profoundly in our Constitution and rule of law."

SCHOOLS AND SCHOOL DISTRICTS

Kansas Votes on Evolution in State-Funded Education

Following a November 2000 local election that put more moderate Republicans and Democrats on the Kansas Board of Education, the new board reversed its 1999 position and voted 7–3 in February 2001 to approve new science standards that emphasize the theory of evolution. The new standards also included a revised tolerance statement intended to be less antagonistic toward religion. The old standards contained a statement declaring that there was nothing in the U.S. or Kansas Constitution that required teachers to consider religious views in teaching the beginnings of man or the cosmos. The standards are guidelines that outline academic content and identify topics that Kansas students should learn and be tested on, mostly in biology classes. The new Spring 2001 exams contained questions about evolution.

The concept of evolution, usually credited to the work of nineteenth-century English naturalist Charles Darwin, considers the earth to be billions of years old; life-forms, including humans, evolved from simple forms over the millenia through a process called natural selection. Conversely, "creationism" proposes that the earth and most life forms came into existence suddenly—approximately 6,000 years ago, according to Judeo-Christian reckoning—although intra-species changes are the result of natural selection over the years. While critics have viewed this theory as a guise for promoting the Biblical book of Genesis, in fact, the theory is premised more on respected hypotheses of many nonpartisan and nonreligious scientists and educators who collectively believe in "the idea that the design and complexity of the design of the cosmos requires an intelligent designer."

A 1999 Gallup poll of the American public found that nearly 70 percent favored the teaching of both creationism and evolution in public school science curricula. While Kansas's dilemma turned out to be one of the most closely-watched cases in recent U.S. education history, Kansas had been but one of several states, including Alabama, Arizona, Illinois, Nebraska, New Mexico, and Texas, where school boards had down-played evolutionary concepts or removed evolution from state science standards.

Kansas's problems began in May 1999 when, during the school board's monthly meeting, two versions of science standards were presented. One, written by the state board committee, defined evolution as a concept that unified all scientific disciplines. The other proposed standard, authored by the Creation Science Association for Mid-America and others, eliminated all but one reference to evolution and added a definition of creation that incorporated an intelligent designer of the cosmos. Neither version met board approval. Three board members then re-wrote the standards, removing the requirement that students be taught about evolution and wholly eliminating correlative information such as the Big Bang theory. The rewritten standards also took out references to major evolutionary changes that create new species—called macroevolution—but retained the terms "microevolution," or changes within species, and "natural selection." The standards deferred to the discretion of local school districts whether to teach evolution, therefore eliminating the concept from required learning and testing material. A new definition of science as "the human activity of seeking logical explanation" was also included. The board adopted the revised standards by a 6–4 vote in August 1999.

All appeared well until a month later when three national science groups, on whose work the Kansas science writing committee based its standards, revoked permission for Kansas to use their COPYRIGHTED texts, citing that the standards did not "embrace the vision and content" of their materials. Later in 1999, the Thomas B. Fordham Foundation retained California State University professor emeritus Lawrence Lerner to review the science standards of forty-six states; Kansas's received an "F."

The battle raged through the state for the next year, with local and televised debates, public meetings, and international attention for what many perceived as the school board's abandonment of prevailing scientific thought. State Governor Bill Graves publicly declared the board's action as "terrible, tragic and embarrassing." As the months went on, the controversy focused upon upcoming elections to the Board of Education. It also divided the state's Republican Party, which had heretofore been divided on the issue of abortion. When two of the six original board members who voted for the 1999 standards were not re-elected, moderates regained control of the board. The new board members publicly declared their intention to reinstate critical scientific ideas, including evolution, to the science standards.

The new standards, authored by a 27-member committee of science educators, are supported by the American Association for the Advancement of Science, the National Academy of Sciences and National Research Council, and the National Science Teachers Association. Although the media polarized opposition to the new standards as premised upon religious conservatism, the opposing board members merely reiterated their belief that the new standards kept students from thinking critically about science and evolution. The Intelligent Design Network, a local organization that proffered another alternative revision allowing "discussion of evidence against Darwinism," referred to the new standards as "a victory for censorship and viewpoint discrimination." The main objection to the new standards was *not* the inclusion of evolution, but rather that the standards explicitly prohibited the classroom discussion of any dissent-

ing scientific opinions on Darwinism or the inference of design from evidence in nature.

Following the vote, the Intelligent Design Network planned to take its case to school boards across the country. Meanwhile, an organized group of scientific and education professionals supporting intelligent-design theories held a briefing for Congress in June. Both sides to the controversy admitted that the issue had yet to reach final resolution.

Zero Tolerance Policies

In September 2000 an eleven-year-old Georgia girl received the maximum punishment of ten days suspension because a ten-inch chain connecting her wallet to two key rings violated the school district's zero-tolerance weapons policy. Earlier in the school year, the students were lectured by school officials about the school's policy and were shown several items that the school considered potential weapons, including a two-foot section of chain. The students were warned that anyone caught with any of the items would be suspended automatically. Furthermore, anyone breaking the rules would receive the same maximum punishment, with few exceptions.

Although sixth-grader Ashley Smith had viewed the school's two-foot chain during the warning seminar, she did not believe hers resembled it enough to be considered a weapon under school policy. Initially, she and her parents were told that the suspension could not be appealed because it was "short-term." School officials stated that Smith and her parents knew that chains were banned and that similar chains had been used in the past as weapons, with any number of devices attached to them.

After eventual pressure from the AMERICAN CIVIL LIBERTIES UNION (ACLU), the school district dropped the suspension. Smith's case, however, was one of several that made headlines around the country in reference to an increasing number of schools with zero-tolerance policies. Some of the more publicized incidents included a Pittsburgh kindergartner who was disciplined because his Halloween firefighter costume included a plastic axe, an eight-year-old boy disciplined for aiming a piece of chicken at a teacher like a gun, and a high schooler who unintentionally shot a lunchroom employee with a paper clip propelled by a rubber band.

While these incidents appeared to many as examples of benign adolescent behavior, the focus of zero tolerance is on the message, not the means. When thirteen-year-old T. J. West of

Derby, Kansas, drew a Confederate flag on a scrap of paper, he was suspended for racial harassment and intimidation, because the school had warned students that the flag was considered a hate symbol. The boy and his parents sued, lost in FEDERAL COURT, and lost again in the Tenth Circuit Court of Appeals. The Supreme Court of the United States refused to hear the case, letting stand the appellate decision.

Fashioned loosely after federal and state laws passed in the 1990s, which incorporated mandatory sentencing and "three strikes and you're out" policies, zero tolerance was first used against students who brought guns to school, in response to the growing incidence of school violence. The federal Drug Free School Act and Gun Free School Act require the expulsion and arrest of students who bring illegal drugs and firearms to schools. At the heart of all such laws and policies is safety and prevention. Eventually, zero-tolerance policies were broadened to include an array of infractions, including the wearing of clothing associated with gangs and threats directed at other persons. The policy expansion followed published psychological and police profiling of potentially-dangerous students and also served to help assuage doubts as to whether tragedies were predictable and could have been prevented.

In a highly-publicized case involving seven African-American youths from Decatur, Illinois, two-year expulsions under the school's zero-tolerance policy followed a no-weapons fight at a football game. Two of the students were seniors about to graduate, and none of the students was allowed to have his parents or legal counsel intervene in his behalf. After JESSE JACKSON brought national attention to the case, the expulsions were reduced to one year but were still enforced (see *American Law Yearbook 2000* 206–208).

While critics of zero-tolerance policies would like to see punishments more commensurate with their offenses, school officials believe such considerations are secondary to a school's need to respond swiftly and decisively in order to maintain control and discipline. They must weigh established disciplinary rules that treat all students and offenses the same against other policies that permit discretion and could be construed as discriminatory. By meting out consistent mandatory punishments, schools are able to eliminate protracted fact-finding in search of MITIGATING or EXTENUATING CIRCUMSTANCES. For example, in the case of Ashley Smith's keychain, the school might have needed

to interview her about why she had a chain of that length and maybe question friends and classmates as to whether they had ever seen her use it in a threatening manner. Schools also avoid battles over the policies' application because all applications are identical. Instead, school proponents argue, they can carry an unequivocal message: zero tolerance means zero tolerance.

In early 2001 the AMERICAN BAR ASSOCIATION issued a statement that zero-tolerance rules failed to consider the circumstances of each case or the individual student's history and called for their demise. Spokespersons for the ABA were quick to defend that the issue was a matter of fairness, not one of lost attorney fees for those who might have represented students in such individual cases.

CROSS REFERENCES
Scopes, John T.; Weapons

SELF-INCRIMINATION

Giving testimony in a trial or other legal proceeding that could subject one to criminal prosecution.

Tankleff v. Senkowski

The U.S. Supreme Court denied CERTIORARI from an appeal of a teenage defendant who claimed that his conviction for murdering his parents should be overturned because the allegedly deceptive and coercive circumstances of his initial confession tainted the subsequent confession he gave after being read the MIRANDA warnings. *Tankleff v. Senkowski*, ___U.S.___, 121 S.Ct. 654, 148 L.Ed.2d 558 (2000).

The case officially began at 6:17 A.M. on September 17, 1988, when the Long Island police received a 911 call from a wealthy section of Belle Terre, New York. The call was placed by 17-year-old Martin Tankleff, who said that someone had murdered his parents. At the crime scene Tankleff told investigating officers that he had first discovered the bodies when he awoke for school. The officers reported that Tankleff's mother had died from multiple stab wounds. The officers observed that Tankleff's father was still alive, however, lying unconscious from what appeared to be a blunt-head injury. The teenager named his father's former business partner as a suspect, informing police that the partner had been at their home the night before and owed his father a great deal of money.

At 7:40 A.M. the police placed Tankleff in a squad car for questioning by a series of detectives. The detectives noted several inconsistencies in Tankleff's accounts of the morning's events and took him to police headquarters for further questioning. The drive to the police station lasted 40 minutes, during which Tankleff was asked more questions by a detective. At 9:40 Tankleff was escorted to a ten-foot by ten-foot windowless room were he was interviewed continuously for the next two hours. At trial the defense portrayed the two hours of questioning as increasingly hostile. Although the detectives disputed this characterization, they did admit that they openly expressed doubt about Tankleff's account, telling him it was "ridiculous" and "unbelievably absurd."

The detectives also admitted to deceiving the teenager. At 11:45 A.M. one of the detectives left the interview room and faked receiving a telephone call from an officer who was supposedly at the hospital with Tankleff's father. The detective spoke loudly enough so he could be heard by Tankleff in the interview room. The detective then returned to the interview room and falsely told Tankleff that his father woke from his coma to identify his son as the murderer. Less than ten minutes later Tankleff began to incriminate himself, at which time he was read his Miranda rights for the first time. The suspect waived his rights and gave a full confession, stating that he had killed his parents because they made him drive an old car to school. Tankleff's father never awoke from his coma and died a few weeks later.

In 1990 Tankleff was convicted on two counts of murder in Suffolk County Court and was sentenced to two consecutive terms of twenty-five years to life in prison. The trial court allowed into evidence the defendant's first pre-Mirandized confession as well as his second confession after he was properly Mirandized. On direct appeal the defendant argued that both confessions should have been deemed inadmissible. However, his conviction was affirmed by the New York Supreme Court, Appellate Division in *People v. Tankleff*, 199 A.D.2d 550, 606 N.Y.S.2d 707 (App.Div.1993), and by the New York Court of Appeals, the state's highest court. *People v. Tankleff*, 84 N.Y.2D 992, 622 N.Y.S.2d 503, 646 N.E.2d 805 (1994).

On February 7, 1996, Tankleff sought to collaterally attack his state-court conviction by filing a HABEAS CORPUS petition with the U.S. District Court for the Eastern District of New York. In his petition Tankleff argued that the first confession was inadmissible because it was given before he was Mirandized. Since the first confession was illegally obtained, Tankleff maintained, the second confession was a "fruit of the poisonous tree" and should also have been ruled inadmissible. Tankleff also argued that the police had used extreme pressure and deceptive tactics to extract both confessions, and thus he maintained that neither confession was voluntarily given. The district court denied the petition, *Tankleff v. Senkowski*, 993 F.Supp. 151 (1997), and Tankleff appealed.

On review, the U.S. Court of Appeals for the Third Circuit held that the first confession was illegally obtained and was erroneously admitted into evidence by the trial judge. Stressing that all defendants are entitled to Miranda warnings prior to custodial interrogation, the federal court of appeals found that Tankleff was effectively taken into custody when he was placed in the squad car, driven to the police station, and escorted to a windowless room. No reasonable person in the defendant's shoes would have felt free to leave, the court said. The questions put to the defendant during this period constituted "interrogation," the court continued, clearly designed to illicit incriminating responses.

The third circuit, however, found that Tankleff was not harmed by the trial court's error in admitting the first confession into evidence because the two confessions were substantially similar. Only if the second confession was "irredeemably" tainted by the first confession was the defendant entitled to have both confessions suppressed. The issue was a "close one," the court said. It acknowledged that the "use of improper tactics in obtaining an initial confession may warrant a presumption of compulsion as to the second one," thus entitling the defendant to have each confession excluded. The record simply provided "no indication" for the court to conclude that Tankleff misunderstood the Miranda warnings prior to his second confession. Nor was the court satisfied that his waiver of those rights was "anything but knowing and voluntary."

Nevertheless, the court remanded the case to the district court for further proceedings on an unrelated issue. During the preliminary examination of prospective jurors, or VOIR DIRE, Tankleff objected to the prosecution's PEREMPTORY CHALLENGE of several African-American jurors. The trial court overruled the defendant's objection on GROUNDS that Tankleff was himself a Caucasian. Only an African-American defendant, the trial court ruled, may object to the race-based exclusion of a prospective African-American juror. The third circuit disagreed, holding that defendants and excluded jurors need not be the same race before defendants can raise a so-called Batson challenge—because of the Supreme Court ruling in *Batson v. Kentucky*, 476 U.S. 79, 106 S.Ct. 1712, 90 L.Ed.2d 69 (1986)—to a race-based removal from the jury pool.

CROSS REFERENCES

Confession; Miranda v. Arizona

SENTENCING

The postconviction stage of the criminal justice process, in which the defendant is brought before the court for the imposition of a penalty.

Buford v. United States

The United States Sentencing Guidelines (USSG) direct federal DISTRICT COURT judges to sentence convicted offenders in specific ways. Sometimes the guidelines severely limit a judge's discretion, while others are more ambiguous. When there is ambiguity in a sentencing provision, different judges will rule differently, thereby inviting appeals. What standard an APPELLATE COURT uses to review a lower court decision regarding sentencing often dictates the outcome of their appellate review. Such was the case in *Buford v. United States*, ___U.S.___, 121 S.Ct. 1276, 149 L.Ed.2d 197 (2001), where the Supreme Court of the United States ruled that appellate courts should review certain sentencing guidelines' provisions deferentially and should not conduct a DE NOVO review. A de novo review permits an appellate court to ignore the trial court decision and to review the facts as if it were a trial court.

Paula Buford contested her classification as a career offender under the federal sentencing guidelines, a classification that brings with it severe punishment. The guidelines define a career offender as "an offender with 'at least two prior FELONY convictions' for violent or drug-related crimes." The guidelines also provide that "a sentencing judge must count as a single prior felony conviction all those that are 'related' to one another." In the applications notes the guidelines advise "that prior convictions are 'related' to one another when . . . they 'were consolidated for . . . sentencing.'" The Court of Appeals for the Seventh Circuit further refined this "prior conviction" doctrine: "It has held that two prior convictions might have been 'consolidated for sentencing,' and therefore

'related,' even if the sentencing court did not enter any formal order of consolidation." In such an instance, a court should decide whether the convictions were nonetheless "functionally consolidated," which means that the convictions were "factually or logically related, and sentencing was joint."

Buford pleaded guilty to armed bank ROBBERY in federal court. The federal sentencing judge had to decide whether her five 1992 Wisconsin state-court convictions were "related" to one another, and consequently counted as one single prior conviction, or whether they should count as more than one. The federal prosecutor conceded that four of the five prior convictions, involving a string of gas station robberies, were related to one another. All four had been the subject of a single criminal INDICTMENT, and Buford had pleaded guilty to all four at the same time in the same court.

The prosecution, however, did not concede that the fifth conviction, possession of cocaine with intent to deliver, was related to the other four. The drug crime had taken place about the same time as the fourth robbery, and Buford claimed that the robberies had been motivated by her drug addiction. The only evidentiary link among the crimes was that the police had discovered the cocaine when searching Buford's house after her arrest for the robberies. Moreover, the state had charged the drug offense in a separate indictment and had assigned a different prosecutor to handle the drug case.

Buford produced different facts to show the drug crime was related to the robberies. She showed that the drug crime conviction had been consolidated with the robbery convictions for sentencing, rendering her drug conviction and robbery convictions "related." She pointed out that the state had sent the four robbery cases for sentencing to the same judge who had heard and accepted her plea of guilty to the drug charge. The judge had heard arguments about sentencing in all five cases at the same time in a single proceeding and had issued sentences for all five crimes at the same time. Finally, the judge ordered the sentences for the drug crime and the robberies to be served concurrently.

The federal district court favored the government's argument and ruled that the drug conviction and the robbery convictions were not related, thus giving Buford two prior felony offenses. This meant she had to be sentenced as a career offender. Buford appealed to the Seventh Circuit, which upheld the district court decision. The appeals court ruled that the standard of review for such cases was based on deference to the trial court. This meant that it would overturn the decision only if the judge abused his or her discretion. This standard is very difficult for a defendant to overcome. Buford appealed to the U.S. Supreme Court, noting that two other circuit courts of appeal used de novo review, under which the appeals court could make a legal determination without regard to the lower court's analysis.

A unanimous Supreme Court rejected Buford's call for de novo review. Justice STEPHEN G. BREYER, writing for the Court, noted that the case raised "a narrow question of sentencing law." Breyer pointed out that the sentencing guidelines required a reviewing court not only to accept a district court's findings of fact, unless clearly erroneous, but also to "give due deference to the court's application of the guidelines to the facts."

Justice Breyer reasoned that "the district court is in a better position than the appellate court to decide whether a particular set of individual circumstances demonstrates 'functional consolidation'." Breyer believed that district judges were more familiar with sentencing practices and could "draw the proper inferences from the procedural descriptions provided." Therefore, an appellate court must treat district court decisions deferentially.

Daniels v. United States

Since the 1980s state and federal governments have imposed longer sentences on career criminals who have a violent past. The federal Armed Career Criminal Act of 1984 (ACCA) is particularly severe, requiring a minimum 15-year sentence on anyone who has been convicted of three prior violent FELONIES or serious drug offenses. Because of its severity, the ACCA has spawned numerous lawsuits by prisoners seeking to have their prior convictions thrown out because of constitutional defects. The Supreme Court of the United States has had to decide what types of federal postconviction proceedings prisoners may use to raise these issues. Overall, the Court has been reluctant to allow such actions because they prevent finality and seek to overturn cases that may be 15 or 20 years old. In *Daniels v. United States* , ___U.S.___, 121 S.Ct. 1578, 149 L.Ed.2d 590 (2001), the Court prohibited the use of federal postconviction proceedings to contest the constitutionally of prior convictions except in the most unusual circumstances.

Earthy D. Daniels, Jr. was convicted in 1994 of being a felon in possession of a firearm, a federal crime. He had two previously convictions each in California for robbery (1978 and 1981) and for first degree burglary (1977 and 1979). With these four prior convictions for violent crimes, the ACCA had to be applied. Thus, his sentence was set at 176 months rather than the 120-month sentence he would have received if he had not been an armed career criminal. Daniels appealed his conviction and sentence, arguing that his two BURGLARY convictions did not apply for ACCA purposes. After he lost this direct appeal, Daniels filed a postconviction motion to vacate his sentence. In this proceeding Daniels focused on his two robbery convictions, contending that they were unconstitutional because his guilty pleas were not of his own volition and because he had received inadequate legal advice. The federal DISTRICT COURT dismissed his motion to vacate, and this ruling was affirmed by the Ninth Circuit Court of Appeals. The APPELLATE COURT held that a 1994 Supreme Court ruling barring such claims in federal sentencing proceedings must be extended to include postconviction sentencing proceedings. Because the circuit courts of appeal were divided over this issue, the Supreme Court agreed to hear Daniels' appeal.

The Supreme Court, in a 5–4 decision, affirmed the Ninth Circuit's interpretation of its 1994 decision. Justice SANDRA DAY O'CONNOR, writing for the majority, noted that the 1994 decision matched the facts as set out in the present case. The earlier decision had been grounded on two points: the ease of administration of justice and the need for a final judgment. The question of administration was important because courts would have to "rummage through" old trial court records and transcripts if such attacks on prior convictions were allowed. As to the finality of judgments, Justice O'Connor pointed out that allowing prisoners to attack prior convictions would produce delay "and deprive the state court judgments of conviction of their normal force and effect."

Daniels had argued that these considerations did not apply to his postconviction sentencing proceeding. O'Connor rejected this assertion, concluding that district courts would have just as difficult a time locating "decades-old state court records and transcripts." In Daniels' case, a court would have to reach back over 20 years to examine the record. Justice O'Connor found it telling that Daniels had not placed these transcripts in the record and had indicated the

1978 transcript was missing from the state court record. Thus, attempting to decide constitutional issues surrounding his convictions would be at best "an almost futile exercise for a district court." As to the issue of finality, Daniels argued that because he had served his sentences for the prior convictions there would be little consequence if the convictions were now overturned. Justice O'Connor dismissed this argument as well, finding that the state had a powerful interest in maintaining these convictions even after release. For example, felons are prohibited from holding public office or possessing firearms.

The majority viewed Daniels' efforts as just the latest effort to use the federal courts to correct errors that were the proper province of the state courts. Moreover, Daniels had the right to seek a writ of HABEAS CORPUS in federal court on the issue. Justice O'Connor stated that "[t]hese vehicles for review, however, are not available indefinitely and without limitation." STATUTES OF LIMITATIONS and various court rules place limits on the ability of a prisoner to adjudicate constitutional claims. Therefore, O'Connor concluded that if a prior conviction has not been set aside at the time of sentencing under the ACCA, "that conviction is presumptively valid and may be used to enhance the federal sentence." The only exception would be convictions where defendants argue that they were denied legal counsel as guaranteed by the SIXTH AMENDMENT. Apart from that exception the Court was resolute: "No other constitutional challenge to a prior conviction may be raised in the sentencing forum." Moreover, after sentencing under ACCA, the prisoner "is without recourse" to challenge prior convictions.

Lopez v. Davis

The criminal sentences imposed on federal defendants are governed by congressional statutes, sentencing guidelines, judicial orders, and federal Bureau of Prison (BOP) regulations. Since the 1980s defendants have received sentences based on federal sentencing guidelines that impose mandatory sanctions depending on the crime committed and the defendant's prior criminal history. This approach has reduced judicial discretion and prevented judges from shaping a sentence based on the defendant's particular circumstances. Congress recognized in the 1990s that prisoners who complete a drug treatment program stand a better chance of staying out of trouble after being released from prison. Therefore, it authorized the BOP to release these prisoners up to a year earlier from prison but limited eligibility to prisoners con-

victed of nonviolent crimes. This apparently benign provision generated numerous court cases over BOP regulations that implemented this approach. The U.S. Supreme Court finally resolved these issues in *Lopez v. Davis*, 531 U.S. 230, 121 S.Ct. 714, 148 L.Ed.2d 635 (2001), finding that the BOP has discretion to deny early release for inmates convicted of drug crimes if they carried, possessed, or used a firearm in the commission of their crimes.

In 1997, Christopher A. Lopez was convicted of possession with intent to distribute methamphetamine. His sentences was "enhanced" or increased under federal sentencing guidelines because he possessed a firearm in connection with his offense. After he was incarcerated, Lopez requested substance abuse treatment. Though the BOP found him qualified for its residential drug abuse program, he was categorically ineligible under BOP regulations. These regulations stated that prisoners are not eligible for early release for successful completion of drug treatment if they possessed a firearm in connection with their offense.

Lopez then filed a petition for a WRIT of HABEAS CORPUS in federal district court in South Dakota challenging this regulation. The district court granted Lopez's petition, finding that the BOP regulation had overstepped the law passed by Congress, which authorizes early release. The court acknowledged that the statute stated that the BOP "may" allow early release, thus making such a decision on which nonviolent offenders were eligible a discretionary act. The court concluded, however, that the BOP could not categorically disqualify inmates whose underlying conviction was for a nonviolent crime. Therefore, it ordered the BOP to reconsider Lopez's eligibility for early release. The BOP appealed to the Court of Appeals for the Eighth Circuit, which reversed the trial court. The appeals court found that the BOP had the discretion to make such decisions on eligibility. The Supreme Court agreed to hear Lopez's appeal because other circuit courts of appeals had ruled that the BOP had exceeded its authority in this area.

The Supreme Court, on a 5–3 vote, affirmed the Eighth Circuit's interpretation of the law. Justice RUTH BADER GINSBURG, writing for the majority, agreed with the BOP's position that the underlying statute had established two prerequisites for sentence reduction: conviction of a nonviolent offense and successful completion of drug treatment. If those prerequisites are met, the bureau "may," but also may not, grant early release. Ginsburg found that Congress had not addressed how the bureau should exercise its discretion within the class of inmates who satisfy the statutory requirements for early release. Therefore, the BOP may choose to exclude inmates either categorically as in this case or on a case-by-case basis as long as it interpreted the statute reasonably. Ginsburg concluded that the bureau had acted reasonably, as its denial of early release for inmates who possessed a firearm rationally reflected the view that such inmates displayed a readiness to endanger another's life. Thus, in the interests of public safety, such prisoners should not be released months in advance of completing their sentences.

Justice Ginsburg rejected the idea that the statute prevented the BOP from making categorical exclusions and she denied that it required individual assessments. In the absence of clear statutory language, the bureau had discretion under its rulemaking authority to resolve issues as it sees fit. To require individual assessments of eligibility for early release would generate thousands of cases each year and could "invite favoritism, disunity, and inconsistency." Justice Ginsburg found that it was appropriate for the bureau to resolve issues "fairly and efficiently" in a single rulemaking proceeding.

Justice JOHN PAUL STEVENS, in a dissenting opinion joined by Chief Justice WILLIAM H. REHNQUIST and Justice ANTHONY M. KENNEDY, contended that the bureau had exceeded its authority because Congress had "directly spoken" on the eligibility criteria. The statute and the legislative history surrounding it indicated that Congress had unambiguously disqualified prisoners convicted for "violent offenses" from eligibility for a sentence reduction. Nonviolent offenses, such as drug possession, clearly did not disqualify an inmate from a sentence reduction. Though Stevens acknowledged that sentences "may" be reduced, he concluded that the statute "guarantees nonviolent offenders who successfully complete a drug treatment program consideration for such a reduction."

Mild Sentence for Convicted Perjurer

In October 2000, U.S. District Judge James A. Parker sentenced Ruben Renteria Sr., a convicted perjurer, to fifteen months in prison rather than the five years recommended by federal sentencing guidelines. Judge Parker, an appointee of RONALD REAGAN, said it was unfair for the U.S. Department of JUSTICE to seek a harsh sentence when its own boss, former President BILL CLINTON, pleaded for leniency after

lying under oath in the Paula Jones sexual harassment case.

The PERJURY case against Renteria grew out of a drug CONSPIRACY case. In October 1992, federal law enforcement agents arrested Renteria and charged him and other defendants with conspiracy to distribute more than one-thousand kilograms of marijuana. During his arrest, Renteria signed a CONSENT form giving the federal agents permission to search his home.

During his conspiracy trial, Renteria filed a motion to suppress evidence found during the search. At a suppression hearing, Renteria testified that he did not sign the consent form and argued that the search violated his rights under the FOURTH AMENDMENT to be free from unreasonable SEARCHES AND SEIZURES. Renteria's son, Ruben Renteria Jr., testified at the suppression hearing that he, not his father, signed the consent form, which, if true, could have invalidated the search.

Renteria, however, withdrew his motion to suppress before the judge ruled on it, and after a jury trial, he was acquitted of conspiracy. Unsatisfied with that result, the U.S. District Attorney's office charged Renteria and his son with perjury for lying under oath at the suppression hearing. On November 15, 1995, a jury convicted both men of perjury in violation of federal law.

At an original sentencing hearing in March 1996, Judge Parker had to decide whether sentencing guidelines required him to use five years or fifteen months as the baseline for determining Renteria's prison sentence. Federal sentencing guidelines require a sentence of 10–16 months for first time offenders, but certain qualifiers can make the crime more severe. In an opinion dated April 11, 1996, Judge Parker said fifteen months was the appropriate baseline. In March 1998, however, the U.S. Tenth Circuit Court of Appeals said five years was the appropriate baseline. The Tenth Circuit remanded the case to Judge Parker for a new sentence determination.

After further briefing and hearings, Judge Parker announced his new decision in October 2000. Starting with five years as the baseline, Judge Parker again knocked the sentence down to 15 months using various MITIGATING CIRCUMSTANCES criteria, including the fact that the government had been unable to prove at the conspiracy trial how much marijuana Renteria allegedly had smuggled and the fact that Renteria already had served his 1996 perjury sentence and was doing well at a full-time job.

In a startling announcement, however, Judge Parker also said he was being lenient on Renteria because then-President Clinton had pleaded for leniency after lying under oath in the Paula Jones sexual harassment case. At the time of Judge Parker's ruling, Clinton had been found in CONTEMPT of court and fined $90,000 for lying under oath in the Jones case about his affair with White House intern Monica Lewinsky. When a state court panel recommended that Arkansas DISBAR Clinton for his misconduct, Clinton said disbarment would be a harsh punishment for perjury.

In handing down a fifteen month sentence to Renteria, Judge Parker said, "I think it demonstrates how terribly unfair it is for the president's Department of Justice to be attempting to pillorize Mr. Renteria when the president, for similar conduct, or what is probably more egregious conduct in terms of its consequences, is claiming that the prospect of not being allowed to practice as an attorney in Arkansas is too harsh." Judge Parker had expressed similar frustration with the Department of Justice and the FEDERAL BUREAU OF INVESTIGATION (FBI) in September 2000 when the government dismissed charges against former Los Alamos scientist Dr. Wen Ho Lee (see updated essay on this case under ESPIONAGE). Speaking in court at that time, Judge Parker apologized to Dr. Lee for his unfair treatment at the hands of the federal government and said the executive branch misled him into imposing a harsh pretrial confinement. The misleading conduct, according to press reports, included false statements by FBI agent Robert Messemer.

If Judge Parker's 15 month sentence survives appeal, Renteria will incur no more jail time because he already served the original sentence from 1996. After Judge Parker's October 2000 announcement, the U.S. District Attorney's office said it was considering an appeal but could not make a final decision until Judge Parker filed a written decision and final judgment against Renteria.

CROSS REFERENCES
Habeas Corpus; Judicial Review; Perjury; Prisoners' Rights; Regulations

SEPARATION OF POWERS

The division of state and federal government into three independent branches.

Campbell v. Clinton

The U.S. Constitution divides governmental authority between a legislature, an executive branch, and a JUDICIARY. Each independent branch possesses unique powers and responsibilities, yet the Constitution also employs various checks and balances to prevent one branch from exercising too much power. In the areas of foreign policy and the national defense, the president is given broad powers as commander-in-chief. Nevertheless, Congress must appropriate funds to fight wars, which serves as a significant check on a president's war powers.

In the aftermath of the VIETNAM WAR, Congress sought to place limits on presidential war power. The War Powers Resolution of 1973 restricts the ability of the president to conduct an undeclared war, meaning one that has not been sanctioned by a congressional declaration of war. When the president commits American forces to a foreign country, the president must submit a report to Congress. In addition, the resolution limits the length of time military forces may be committed without congressional authorization and gives Congress the ability to force a recall of troops at any time.

The War Powers Resolution has not curtailed U.S. military intervention, nor has it significantly limited presidential war power authority. At times congressional frustration has boiled over at the ineffectiveness of the resolution. The latest example occurred in March 1999 when President BILL CLINTON authorized the start of an air and missile campaign by NORTH ATLANTIC TREATY ORGANIZATION (NATO) forces against Yugoslavia. Clinton submitted a report to Congress within days of the start of the campaign, as required by the resolution. Many members of the U.S. House of Representatives disagreed with American involvement that was designed to stop Serbian oppression and genocide in Kosovo. In late April, Congress voted on four resolutions concerning this conflict. It overwhelmingly voted down a declaration of war but deadlocked 213–213 over "authorizing" air strikes. It also defeated a resolution calling for the immediate end to U.S. participation in the conflict. Finally, Congress voted to fund the military campaign.

Dissatisfied with these results, seventeen members of the House of Representatives—fifteen Republicans and two Democrats led by Tom Campbell of California—opposed to the military intervention filed a lawsuit in federal court asking the court to issue a declaratory judgment that President Clinton's use of

Collection of London newspapers with headlines reporting the NATO bombing of Serbia.

American forces was unlawful under the War Powers Resolution and the War Powers Clause of the Constitution. *Campbell v. Clinton*, 203 F.3d 19 (D.C. Cir. 2000). Another fourteen congressmen—twelve Republicans and two Democrats—joined the suit later. The members of Congress alleged that under the resolution Clinton was required to end U.S. involvement after 60 days unless Congress enacted a specific authorization. Because Congress did not specifically authorize continuation in its April votes, continued involvement was unlawful.

The Clinton administration refused to respond in court to the merits of the plaintiffs' case. Instead it asserted that the court had no jurisdiction to hear the case, alleging that the members of Congress did not have STANDING to bring the lawsuit. Judge Laurence H. Silberman, writing for the Court of Appeals for the District of Columbia Circuit agreed with the administration that the plaintiffs lacked standing. Judge Silberman pointed to the recent U.S. Supreme Court case of *Raines v. Byrd*, 521 U.S. 811, 117 S.Ct. 2312, 138 L.Ed.2d 849 (1997), as a precedent for answering the standing question. In this case a group of congressmen "sought to challenge the constitutionality" of the Line Item Veto Act, arguing that the law diminished the "institutional power of Congress." The Supreme Court held that members of Congress do not have "legislative standing" to assert "an institutional injury." The Court concluded that the members of Congress had an "adequate po-

litical remedy" because they could vote to repeal the act or exempt individual spending bills from the act's reach. The High Court also emphasized the need to preserve the separation of powers as embodied in the Constitution.

Judge Silberman acknowledged, however, a 1939 Supreme Court case, *Coleman v. Miller*, 307 U.S. 433, 59 S.Ct. 972, 83 L.Ed. 1385, in which the Court determined that a challenge by twenty Kansas state senators of a state constitutional amendment vote could go forward. The Court ruled that the senators had standing because they had a legal interest "in maintaining the effectiveness of their votes." Judge Silberman noted that the Court in *Raines* had distinguished the Kansas case on the grounds that the federal separation of powers issue was not present in the earlier case. The Court also held that the congressmen could not assert that "their votes had been completely nullified." Applying these principles to the present case, Judge Silberman concluded that the plaintiffs' votes had not been completely nullified because "they continued, after the votes, to enjoy ample legislative power to have stopped prosecution of the 'war'." They sought and failed to end the funding of the Yugoslavia action and to formally authorize the president to withdraw troops. Though they lost, the congressmen were free to introduce similar resolutions later. To allow the courts to intervene in this matter would violate the separation of powers and subvert the legislative process.

SEX OFFENSES

A class of sexual conduct prohibited by the law.

Seling v. Young

One of the most controversial developments in U.S. law in the 1990s was the enactment by many states of "sexual predator" laws, in which states created the ability to continue to confine inmates convicted of sexual crimes after completion of their prison sentences. Such laws are characterized as civil, rather than criminal, in nature. The U.S. Supreme Court upheld the constitutionality of a Washington state act after reviewing a plaintiff's facial challenge of it. The Court also agreed that they are civil proceedings. Despite these rulings, inmates have continued to challenge their confinement, which will not end until medical personnel have certified that they no longer threaten to commit sex crimes upon release. Therefore, despite less stringent criminal sentencing guidelines, inmates may serve a "life sentence" if their mental condition does not improve.

The Supreme Court, in *Seling v. Young*, ___ U.S. ___, 121 S.Ct. 727, ___ L.Ed.2d ___ (2001), rejected a new theory challenging these laws. In this ruling, the Court held that federal courts may *not* deem sexual predator statutes punitive as applied to an individual inmate, making it a criminal, and not a civil, proceeding. The distinction between civil and criminal procedures is of utmost importance. Persons labeled as sexual predators under the new statutes most likely would be able to succeed with an appeal on the GROUNDS that continuing to limit their rights after serving their jail time amounts to DOUBLE JEOPARDY. Such persons also would be able to challenge the statutes on the grounds that they were applied EX POST FACTO—or "after the fact" of the original conviction.

Over a period of three decades, Andre Brigham Young committed rape, was incarcerated for the crime, spent time in jail, gained his release, and repeated the cycle. One day prior to his release from the state of Washington's correctional system in October 1990, the state filed a petition to commit Young as a sexually violent predator, as permitted under the state's Community Protection Act. Based on the testimony of the state's expert medical witness, a jury concluded that Young remained a sexually violent predator. Young appealed this finding to the Washington Supreme Court, which upheld the finding and rejected his contention that the statute was criminal in nature. The court upheld the act's constitutionality and found that the commitment proceedings were civil in nature and thus not reversible on the grounds of double jeopardy and *ex post facto* arguments.

After exhausting his direct state appeals, Young filed for a WRIT of HABEAS CORPUS in federal district court. The district court ultimately denied his petition, but this ruling was reversed by the Court of Appeals for the Ninth Circuit. The appellate court found that the "linchpin" of Young's argument "was whether the act was punitive 'as applied' to Young." It reasoned that actual conditions of a person's confinement could strip a statute that was valid on its face of its civil label if it can be shown by the clearest proof that the statutory scheme was punitive in effect. In reviewing Young's claims, the Ninth Circuit concluded that the "conditions of his confinement . . . were punitive and did not comport with due process."

The U.S. Supreme Court, in an 8–1 decision, reversed the Ninth Circuit's decision. Justice SANDRA DAY O'CONNOR, writing for the majority, ruled that the Washington statute, which had been found to be civil, could not be deemed punitive "as applied" to a single individual in violation of the prohibitions against double jeopardy and *ex post facto* laws. O'Connor noted that in the Court's previous examination of sexual predator laws, it applied the principle that determining whether an act is civil or punitive in nature must begin with a reference to its text and legislative history. In addition, she pointed out that the Court had clearly disapproved of evaluating the civil nature of an act by referring to its effect on a single individual. Instead, the Supreme Court had held that courts must take into consideration many factors that relate to the statute on its face. Furthermore, only the most conclusive proof can justify overriding legislative intent and concluding that an act labeled civil is in fact punitive in purpose or effect.

Based on these principles, Justice O'Connor concluded that the Ninth Circuit's reasoning was "fundamentally flawed." A proper analysis of Young's claims should be grounded on the assumption that the Washington state law was civil, as both the Washington Supreme Court and the Ninth Circuit acknowledged. The "as-applied" analysis was both wrong and "unworkable." In O'Connor's view, "Such an analysis would never conclusively resolve whether a particular scheme is punitive and would thereby prevent a final determination of the scheme's validity under the Double Jeopardy and Ex Post Facto Clauses." Allowing the as-applied challenge would "invite an end run around the Washington Supreme Court's decision that the Act is civil when that decision is not before this Court."

Justice O'Connor stated that Young and others in his situation had other legal remedies in state court. Young could ask the Washington courts to determine whether the facility in which he is housed operates in accordance with the law. In addition, O'Connor noted that a federal CIVIL RIGHTS action was currently pending against the facility and that the facility was operating under an INJUNCTION requiring it to take steps to improve confinement conditions.

Justice JOHN PAUL STEVENS, in a dissenting opinion, argued that the majority had "incorrectly assume[d] the law was 'necessarily civil.'" He contended that the Court should have allowed Young to prove that the conditions of his confinement were evidence of the punitive purpose and effect of the Washington statute.

CROSS REFERENCES

Civil Law; Criminal Law; Double Jeopardy; Ex Post Facto

SEXUAL ABUSE

Illegal sex acts performed against a MINOR by a parent, guardian, relative, or acquaintance.

Catholic Church Apologizes and Settles Abuse Claims

In one of the largest cases involving the Roman Catholic Church to date, the Archdiocese of Portland, Oregon, publicly apologized in October 2000 for the sexual abuse of children by some of its priests and agreed to pay an undisclosed amount of money to twenty-two plaintiffs who had alleged such abuse. The apology was read during mass in each parish of the archdiocese.

All of the plaintiffs were male and all alleged that Father Maurice Grammond, 80-years old at the time of the settlement, had enticed them into sexual acts from 1950—when Grammond was ordained—to 1974. The plaintiffs, ranging in age from 39 to 61, had sued for $44 million. In addition to naming Grammond as key defendant, the civil lawsuits also charging that the Portland archbishop and the archdiocese of Portland did not inform members of the parish about Grammond's previous acts, did not keep watch on his current activities, and did not include other adults in addition to Grammond on trips involving children.

Oregon law permits civil lawsuits to be filed up to three years from the time a victim "discovers . . . significant injury in his life" resulting from molestation. All of the plaintiffs stated that they kept quiet about the abuse for decades, but decided to come forward after the filing in 1999 of the first suit against Grammond by Joe Elliot, a local hairdresser living in Portland. Several weeks prior to the filing of the suit, Elliot telephoned the 80-year-old Grammond while his attorney recorded the conversation. In it, Grammond told Elliot that he and others "threw themselves" at Grammond for "some kind of excitement." Grammond then told Elliot that he was sorry for what happened in the past, then asked Elliot, "Aren't you?"

According to plaintiffs' attorney, David Slader, the STATUTE OF LIMITATIONS had already expired for criminal prosecution. Moreover, at the time of suit, Grammond resided in the Alzheimer's unit of a retirement home in Portland. He admitted nothing, but the archdiocese issued a statement in May 2000 saying that it had previously confronted Grammond in 1991 following an accusation at that time from a resident of Seaside, Oregon, who said that Grammond abused him as a boy. Grammond had denied the claims. Although he had been retired for health reasons since 1986, the diocese discreetly removed Grammond from any priestly responsibilities after the incidents in 1991.

From the mid-1950s to the mid-1980s, Grammond had been assigned to work in parishes in the coastal town of Seaside and a logging town in the western foothills of the Cascades, as well as several years at a home for troubled boys in Portland. Most of the plaintiffs had been altar boys in Seaside, where Grammond served for almost twenty years prior to his retirement in 1986.

The archdiocese's apology was part of the settlement. In addition to the apology and the monetary consideration, the settlement also contained a provision wherein the church agreed to formalize in writing the 1991 suspension of Grammond from priestly duties. The archdiocese agreed to head a taskforce to examine the way the archdiocese handles abuse complaints and recommend policies to avoid future incidents. It also agreed to review files of active priests who had previously been subjects in abuse complaints, and to offer counseling to other victims. A COVENANT of confidentiality shielded the dollar amount of the settlement from publication.

The reaching of a settlement was announced publicly by plaintiffs' attorney at a press conference outside the Multnomah County Courthouse. Dennis O'Donovan, vicar general of the archdiocese, also spoke at the conference, noting that the alleged abuse occurred 25 to 50 years ago and stating that "for a number of years, policies and practices have been in place in the archdiocese to guard against similar incidents." In fact, prior to this case, the archdiocese had been subjected to very few allegations of abuse by priests.

Every one of the 188 Catholic dioceses throughout the country has faced sexual abuse lawsuits. In many states, archdioceses may be held liable for the wrongdoing of a priest under such circumstances where GROSS NEGLIGENCE can be found: usually plaintiffs must show that the archdiocese knew of prior abuse and failed to take action or took grossly inadequate action to avoid future occurrence. One of the largest cases ever was that of Father James Porter of Massachusetts, who pleaded guilty in 1993 to molesting at least 28 of the 99 claimants when they were children; he received a sentence of 18 to 20 years in prison. In 1997 a Dallas jury awarded a record $118 million to 11 plaintiffs, one who ultimately committed suicide, who were allegedly abused by Father Rudolph Kos. In the last decade, the Catholic church paid an estimated $650 million in medical and legal costs to settle abuse cases, though, as mentioned above, the frequency of allegations has been on the decline.

SEXUAL HARASSMENT

Unwelcome sexual advances, requests for sexual favors, and other verbal or physical conduct of a sexual nature that tends to create a hostile or offensive work environment.

Pollard v. E.I. du Pont de Nemours & Company

Title VII of the CIVIL RIGHTS ACT of 1964 prohibits sexual harassment in the workplace. Until the early 1990s victims of sexual harassment could not sue for damages for their injuries. Instead, they were limited to job reinstatement, back pay, and front pay. Front pay is money awarded for lost compensation during the period between the entry of judgment in the civil rights lawsuit and reinstatement; moreover, if the plaintiff does not opt for reinstatement due to workplace hostility or psychological injuries,

Sharon Pollard is seen here at her home near Memphis, Tennessee.

the front pay will be awarded as a substitute. In 1991 Congress amended Title VII to allow plaintiffs to sue for COMPENSATORY DAMAGES and PUNITIVE DAMAGES in cases of intentional discrimination. However, the law placed a cap of $300,000 on these damages.

Since the change in the law the circuit courts have, with one exception, found that front pay is not classified as compensatory damages and thus is not subject to the $300,000 cap. The Court of Appeals for the Sixth Circuit held to the contrary, which triggered an appeal to the Supreme Court of the United States. In *Pollard v. E.I. du Pont de Nemours & Company*, ___U.S.___, 121 S.Ct. 1946, ___ L.Ed.2d ___ (2001), the Court unanimously rejected the Sixth Circuit interpretation and found that front pay cannot be included in the $300,000 cap amount.

Sharon Pollard sued DuPont, alleging that it had subjected her to a hostile work environment. Harassment by her male co-workers led Pollard to take a medical leave of absence for psychological counseling. DuPont fired her after she refused to return to the same hostile work environment. At trial the court awarded Pollard $107,000 in back pay and benefits, $252,000 in attorney's fees and $300,000 in compensatory damages. In so awarding the statutory maximum of $300,000, the trial court noted that the amount was insufficient to compensate Pollard, but it was bound by the Sixth Circuit's interpretation that front pay was subject to the cap. On appeal, the Sixth

Circuit rejected Pollard's contention that front pay is not compensation but a replacement for the reinstatement remedy. Moreover, Pollard pointed to language in the 1991 amendment to Title VII that explicitly excludes remedies traditionally available under the law from the $300,000 cap.

The Supreme Court, on an 8–0 decision with Justice SANDRA DAY O'CONNOR not participating, overturned the Sixth Circuit decision. Justice CLARENCE THOMAS, writing for the Court, concluded that front pay is not "an element of compensatory damages." The Court first looked at the National Labor Relations Act (NLRA) and its provisions on back pay. It noted that Title VII had been modeled on provisions of the NLRA and that the National Labor Relations Board (NLRB) had consistently awarded "backpay up to the date the employee was reinstated or returned to the position he should have been in had the violation of the NLRA not occurred, even if such event occurred after judgment." The courts in Title VII actions later awarded this pay, which is now called "front pay." Thus, it existed before Congress amended the law in 1991 to include damage remedies. The Court pointed out that the courts found front pay to be a good remedy when reinstatement is not a viable option.

Though the 1991 law used "future pecuniary losses" as one measure of a damages remedy, front pay did not fit into this category. While the two terms might look similar in the "abstract," the Court rejected the idea of reading these terms in isolation. Looking to the 1991 amendment, it noted that Congress had stated that victims of employment discrimination needed "additional remedies" under federal law. Moreover, Congress did not indicate a desire to curtail any previously available remedies. The Court concluded that the plain language of the new law showed that the new remedies were in addition to the old ones. With this statutory construction in place, the Court reasserted the history of front pay by the NLRB and the federal courts in Title VII cases, making it clear that front pay was a prior remedy.

The Court pointed out that front pay can be awarded for the period preceding reinstatement as well as when reinstatement does not occur. It could see "no logical difference" between front pay awards in either situation. In addition, distinguishing between the two situations would produce a "strange result": "employees could receive front pay when reinstatement eventually is available but not when reinstatement is not an option." As a result, "the most egregious offenders could be subject to the least sanctions." Based on the statutory language, the Court held that front pay is a remedy not limited by the statutory cap on damages.

CROSS REFERENCES
Civil Rights Acts; Labor Law

SHIELD LAWS

STATUTES affording a privilege to journalists not to disclose in legal proceedings confidential information or sources of information obtained in their professional capacities.

Journalists Fined for Refusing to Divulge Interview Notes

In December 2000 COMMON PLEAS Court Judge Jane Cutler Greenspan ordered *Philadelphia Inquirer* reporter Mark Bowden and *Philadelphia Tribune* columnist Linn Washington, Jr., to turn over notes of interviews with Brian Tyson, who was on trial in Philadelphia for murder. The journalists refused to do so. Testifying at Tyson's trial, Mark Bowden also refused to answer any questions except those related to what he published in a three-part story about the case in 1998. Judge Greenspan held the journalists in CONTEMPT of court and fined them each $100 per minute for the duration of the trial, which allowed the fines to grow to $64,000.

The Tyson case began the night of September 27, 1997, when Brian Tyson shot and killed Damon Lovelle Millner, a cocaine dealer who terrorized the people in Tyson's Philadelphia neighborhood. Tyson, who had been on a personal crusade to stop Millner and his gang's illegal activities, was due in court the next day to testify against Kareem Jones, a friend of Millner's who tried to rob Tyson's hotdog stand. When Tyson went out that night to remove the battery from his car to prevent it from being stolen, he smelled gasoline around the car and then was hit from behind. Panicked, he ran down an alley and saw members of Millner's gang at the other end. When he saw a flash and heard a gunshot, Tyson pulled his own gun and fired five times, killing Millner. Witnesses, mostly friends and acquaintances of Millner, claimed that Tyson fired without provocation, so Tyson faced charges of first-degree murder.

In the summer of 1998, the *Philadelphia Inquirer* ran a three-part story by Mark Bowden about Tyson. Bowden, who interviewed Tyson, told the story of Tyson's crusade against the cocaine dealers in his neighborhood of Feltonville. In the story, Bowden described Tyson's fruitless efforts to get city, state, and federal officials to clean up the neighborhood. Tyson explained how Millner's gang shot out the windows of his car after Tyson's employee, Ron Nicholson, testified against Kareem Jones before a GRAND JURY. Tyson shared the frightening details of feeling ambushed the night he pulled his gun allegedly in SELF-DEFENSE and killed Millner.

At Tyson's murder trial in autumn 2000, Assistant District Attorney Emily Zimmerman subpoenaed notes that both Bowden and *Tribune* columnist Linn Washington, Jr., had taken in interviews with Tyson. Zimmerman said the notes might contain statements that contradicted Tyson's self-defense argument. Greenspan ordered the journalists to produce their notes, saying, "In a criminal case, what the defendant says about the incident is crucial."

Relying on the FIRST AMENDMENT and Pennsylvania law, Bowden and Washington refused to share their confidential notes. They claim that FREEDOM OF THE PRESS, a privilege under the First Amendment, allows reporters to maintain the confidentiality of information they gather. Pennsylvania also has a shield law that prevents reporters from being forced to reveal confidential sources of information.

District Attorney Zimmerman asked Judge Greenspan to imprison the journalists to persuade them to comply. Instead, Judge Greenspan held the journalists in contempt of court and fined them $100 per minute, saying the shield law did not apply to this case because Tyson was not a confidential source. At the end of testimony, the fines had amounted to $64,000 each. Even without information from the notes, the jury rejected Tyson's self-defense argument and found him guilty of second-degree murder, which carries a 10 to 30 year prison sentence.

Meanwhile, the *Inquirer* and *Tribune* posted a bond for the fines for their journalists and appealed the contempt citations. *Inquirer* editor Robert Rosenthal said the newspaper respects the JUDICIARY and the executive branch of government but added, "The job of a newspaper is not to serve as an investigative arm of the prosecution." The prosecution has no right to interview a criminal defendant without his consent. Rosenthal said Pennsylvania's reporter shield law is important because "it protects a newspaper's ability to tell the public about important issues, such as crime and safety in our neighbor-

hoods." The plain language of the law, however, says it only protects the identity of confidential sources of information, not the information itself. The reporters argue that CASE LAW has extended its protection to unpublished information. At press time for *American Law Yearbook 2001*, the appeal was pending before the Pennsylvania Superior Court.

CROSS REFERENCES
Freedom of the Press

SIXTH AMENDMENT

Glover v. United States

The Sixth Amendment gives every person accused of a serious crime the right to legal counsel. The Supreme Court of the United States has extended this constitutional provision to include the right to *effective* legal counsel. Since the 1960s many persons convicted of crimes have asserted that ineffective assistance by their lawyers led to their conviction. The Supreme Court has examined these claims and attempted to provide the lower courts with clear standards on how to judge these claims. In *Glover v. United States,* ___ U.S. ___, 121 S.Ct. 696, ___ L.Ed.2d ___ (2001), the U.S. Supreme Court addressed the issue of ineffective assistance during the sentencing phase of the criminal trial. In doing so the Court rejected a subjective standard that would have prevented such a claim if a court did not believe the increased sentence was sufficiently prejudicial to the defendant.

Paul Glover served as the vice president and general counsel of a Chicago union during the 1980s and early 1990s. He was prosecuted and convicted in federal court for using "his control over the union's investments to enrich himself and his co-conspirators through kickbacks." The probation office put together a report prior to sentencing stating that, under the United States Sentencing Commission Guidelines Manual, Glover's labor racketeering, MONEY LAUNDERING, and tax evasion convictions should be grouped together for the purposes of sentencing since they "involv[ed] essentially the same harm." The federal sentencing guidelines use a matrix of factors to calculate a prison sentence that the trial judge has little discretion to change. The prosecution objected to grouping the money laundering counts with the other two counts and a hearing was held on the matter. The federal district court ruled that the money laundering counts should not be grouped with Glover's other offenses. During this sentencing phase, Glover's attorney did not submit papers or offer extensive oral arguments to rebut the government's claims. By separating the money laundering counts from the other convictions, Glover's offense level under the guidelines was increased by two levels, yielding an increase in the sentencing range. He was sentenced to 84 months in prison, which was in the middle of the guidelines range of 78 to 97 months.

Glover's attorney did not question whether the money laundering conviction should have been grouped with the others during the appeal, concentrating instead on the alleged wrongful admission of certain testimony at trial. After the Circuit Court of Appeals for the Seventh Circuit upheld Glover's conviction and sentencing, Glover personally filed a motion to correct his sentence. He noted that another panel of Seventh Circuit judges had recently ruled that a grouping of counts similar to his was acceptable under the sentencing guidelines. He contended that the failure of his lawyer "to press the grouping issue" amounted to "ineffective assistance," as his lawyer's conduct "fell below a reasonable standard both at sentencing . . . and on appeal." Glover argued that had his attorney brought up the grouping of the convictions during his appeal, his prison sentence would have been anywhere from 6 to 21 months, far fewer than the 84 months to which he was sentenced.

The district court denied his motion, concluding that the increase in Glover's sentence was "not significant enough to amount to prejudice" that would merit a hearing before the court on his ineffective assistance claim. Therefore, the court did not decide "whether the performance of Glover's lawyer fell below a reasonable standard of competence." The Seventh Circuit affirmed this ruling, agreeing with the government that the increased sentence was not sufficiently prejudicial to merit consideration.

The Supreme Court disagreed, ruling unanimously that Glover was entitled to a hearing to attempt to prove that his counsel's competency was below a reasonable standard. Justice ANTHONY M. KENNEDY, writing for the Court, stated that the appellate court was in error when it denied relief to Glover because the sentence error did not meet some "baseline standard of prejudice." He found that there was no legal authority to conclude that even "a minimal amount of additional time in prison cannot constitute prejudice." Moreover, prior rulings of the Court had made clear "that any amount of actual jail time has Sixth Amendment significance."

Kennedy also emphasized the weakness of the Seventh Circuit rule. In the Court's view "there is no obvious dividing line by which to measure how much longer a sentence must be for the increase to constitute substantial prejudice." Although the amount of the increase of the defendant's sentence may be a factor in deciding whether counsel's failure to argue the point constitutes ineffective assistance, "it cannot serve as a bar to a showing of prejudice." Kennedy found it important that this case did not involve trial strategies which might have led to a harsher sentence. This case simply involved "a [sentencing] calculation resulting from a ruling which, if it had been in error, would have been correctable on appeal."

CROSS REFERENCES
Sentencing

SODOMY

Anal or oral intercourse between human beings, or any sexual relations between a human being and an animal, the act of which may be punishable as a criminal offense.

Louisiana v. Smith

The sexual practice of sodomy has been regarded as deviant for hundreds of years, however, since the 1970s many states have repealed their criminal sodomy statutes, which often were defined in terms of "crimes against nature." Most states that have removed these laws from the books have used the legislative process, though a few state supreme courts have ruled these laws unconstitutional. The U.S. Supreme Court, in *Bowers v. Hardwick*, 478 U.S. 186, 106 S.Ct. 2841, 92 L.Ed.2d 140 (1986), explicitly rejected a PRIVACY rights claim challenge to sodomy laws, specifically holding that the U.S. Constitution does not prohibit states from enacting laws that prohibit private acts of consensual sodomy between adults. Because of this ruling subsequent legal challenges have been based on state constitutional provisions dealing with the right to privacy.

Such was the case in *State v. Smith*, 99–2094 (La.7/6/00), 766 So.2d 501 (2000), where a man convicted of a crime against nature challenged the Louisiana criminal sodomy law. Mitchell Smith contended that the law was unconstitutional on its face because it violated the right to privacy expressly guaranteed by the Louisiana Constitution. Though Smith convinced an appeals court of the soundness of his arguments, the Supreme Court of Louisiana rejected this reasoning, holding that the legislature had not overstepped its bounds when it ruled that sodomy was illegal. In the ruling, the majority emphatically rejected the idea that it had the authority to strike down the law.

Smith met a woman at a bar and they eventually ended up in a motel. The woman contacted the police the next day and alleged that Smith had raped her and had forced her to have anal intercourse. Smith was charged "with one count of aggravated crime against nature" and one count of "simple rape." Smith testified that the sex had been consensual and had been limited to oral sex. After a bench trial—where there is no jury and the judge determines the facts—the judge acquitted Smith of the rape charge but found him guilty of the lesser offense of simple crime against nature as defined in Louisiana's criminal statutes. Smith appealed his conviction, arguing that the law violated the state constitution's right to privacy provision to the extent that it criminalized the performance of private, consensual, non-commercial acts of sexual intimacy between individuals legally capable of CONSENT. The appeals court agreed with Smith's argument and reversed his conviction.

The Louisiana Supreme Court reversed the appeals court decision, however. Justice Chet D. Traylor, writing for the majority, noted that the state constitution's privacy clause expressly guarantees that every individual shall be secure against unreasonable invasions of privacy. Traylor also acknowledged that the state provision "affords more stringent protection of individual liberty than the Fourteenth Amendment to the Federal Constitution." Nevertheless, Traylor rejected the idea that the privacy clause gave individuals the right to engage in oral or anal sex.

Justice Traylor cited with approval the *Bowers v. Hardwick* decision, restating the fact that Smith had no constitutional right to engage in the acts forbidden by the statute. Echoing that case, Traylor examined the history of the Louisiana sodomy statute, concluding that for almost 200 years the state had prohibited sodomy. He also pointed out that, despite the repeal of many state sodomy laws, 17 states still had some form of law outlawing sodomy between consenting adults.

Justice Traylor carefully reviewed the Louisiana law, describing it as a comprehensive statute that covered "heterosexual and homosexual acts, both private and public acts, and both commercial and non-commercial acts." First enacted in 1805 when Louisiana was still a territory, the "crime against nature" originally carried with it a mandatory life sentence. The law was revised in 1856 to make rape a separate offense and to reduce the penalty to a sentence of between two and ten years in prison. In 1896 the law was amended to include oral sex as well as anal sex and sex with animals. The law was revised in 1942 to more fully describe the prohibited acts and was left unchanged until 1975, when the legislature inserted language to make clear "that crime against nature did not include those acts which would constitute rape."

As to the right of privacy argument, Traylor found it absurd to argue that individuals had a constitutional right to engage in consensual anal and oral sex when it had been "legislatively determined to be morally reprehensible." A constitutional right to privacy could not include the right to engage in private acts "which were condemned as criminal, either by statute or case law interpretation thereof, at the very time the Louisiana Constitution was ratified." In Traylor's view the question was not one of what is "good or wise for Louisiana society," but rather whether the voters who approved the constitution intended to deprive the legislature of the power to deal with sodomy. He concluded that there was no such evidence. Therefore, it was up to the Louisiana legislature, not the courts, to repeal or amend the sodomy law.

CROSS REFERENCES
Criminal Law; Privacy

SPORTS LAW

The laws, regulations, and judicial decisions that govern sports and athletes.

NHL Player McSorley Convicted for On-Ice Incident

On February 21, 2000, National Hockey League (NHL) veteran Marty McSorley used his hockey stick to strike an opponent, Donald Brashear, in the head during a game between the Boston Bruins and the Vancouver Canucks. He was found guilty by a judge in the Provincial Court in British Columbia, Canada, for criminal ASSAULT with a weapon.

Martin James McSorley, known by his fans as Marty, entered the NHL in 1983 with the Pittsburgh Penguins and continued to play in the league for 17 years. McSorley built his reputation in the game as an "enforcer," a player whose physical play and willingness to fight helps intimidate opponents. He had accumulated the third

Marty McSorley (*left*) fights Tie Domi in 1997. In 2000 he faced assault charges for an on-ice incident.

highest number of penalty minutes in league history and was suspended seven times for intentional violence. He was retired hockey legend Wayne Gretzky's protector when they both played for the Edmonton Oilers in the 1980s and later with the Los Angeles Kings. In addition to being a tough guy, McSorley was also one of the better defensemen in the league, helping the Edmonton Oilers win the NHL championship in 1987 and 1988.

At 36-years of age, McSorley is 6-feet 2-inches tall, weighs 230 pounds, and possesses great strength. He has, however, suffered from many injuries over the last few years and only had a one-year contract with the Boston Bruins. Some have speculated that, as one of the older players in the league, he felt pressured to salvage his waining career, which may have contributed to his actions on February 21, 2001.

The infamous slash in the last remaining seconds was the culmination of events throughout the game. McSorley and Brashear fought early in the game, and McSorley came out the worse of the two. Throughout the game, McSorley attempted to start another fight with Brashear, but Brashear would not be provoked. Later in the game, Brashear fell on the Bruins' goalie and afterward skated past their bench flexing his muscles. The Bruins coach, Pat Burns, shouted to his players, "Are we going to take that or are we going to stand up for our rights?"

With only 20 seconds left in regulation, McSorley was put into the game just after Brashear also skated onto the ice. McSorley assumed that his coaches sent him in to fight with Brashear. With only three seconds left, McSorley aggressively skated up behind Brashear, who did not have the puck, and swung his stick, hitting Brashear on the right temple. Brashear fell onto the ice, hit his head and began having a seizure. While Brashear ultimately recuperated and rejoined his team more than a month later, he still suffered from occasional headaches and drowsiness.

Fighting has always been a part of professional hockey, from the NHL to the junior leagues, and fans have grown to expect violent brawls. McSorley's actions, however, did not qualify as a typical altercation, and his violent record in the league did not help either. NHL Commissioner Gary Bettman suspended McSorley for the remaining 23 games of the season as well as any Bruins playoff games, the longest suspension in league history. McSorley was also prosecuted in the Provincial Court in British Columbia for assault with a weapon. It was the first time an incident during an NHL game was prosecuted since 1988. McSorley pleaded not guilty, and the case went to trial.

The week-long trial took place in the courtroom of Judge William Kitchen. The prosecutor, Mike Hick, opened his case with the game officiator, Brad Watson, who described the events of the game leading up to the blow. He called Canucks' trainer, Mike Burnstein, to testify about Brashear's condition immediately after the incident. Dr. Rui Avelar also testified about his medical condition, diagnosing the concussion as a very serious "Grade 3". The doctor further stated that the injuries came from McSorley's strike and not from the fall.

The Criminal Code of Canada, Part VIII § 265, states that a person commits assault when, without the CONSENT of another person, he applies force intentionally to that other person directly or indirectly. McSorley's lawyers, Bill Smart and Jim Williams, did not dispute the fact that McSorley applied force with his hockey stick. Instead they argued, first, that McSorley had no INTENT to injure Brashear and, second, that NHL players consent to the risk of injuries from hits during the game as that is the nature of hockey.

On the third day of the trial, McSorley testified, explaining that he was only trying to provoke Brashear by hitting him on the shoulder. McSorley claimed that his own prior shoulder and wrist injuries affected his ability to control his stick. Further complicating his attempt to strike Brashear's shoulder was Brashear's movement at the time of the incident. These factors caused McSorley to miss Brashear's shoulder and hit him in the temple instead. A slower version of the video did, indeed, show that the stick first hit the victim's shoulder and then moved up to his head. He further explained to the court that his role as a "policeman" on the ice was to protect his teammates by intimidating other club's players. The defense also called another NHL player, Steve Heinze, to testify that hits in the head are common in hockey. Bruins team trainer, Don Del Negro, affirmed that McSorley did suffer from shoulder and wrist injuries and that they could have affected his control over the stick.

On Friday, October, 6, 2000, Judge Kitchen announced his verdict of guilty, finding that Marty McSorley did intentionally commit assault with a weapon when he deliberately struck Donald Brashear. Judge Kitchen stated that McSorley would have to live with the consequences, yet he believed that McSorley was truly sorry for his actions. He therefore did not impose jail time, but instead issued an 18-month conditional discharge, during which time McSorley must not play in a game in which Donald Brashear is playing. If McSorley follows the conditions, he will not have a criminal record. A month later, NHL commissioner, Gary Bettman, lengthened McSorley's suspension to one year, through February 20, 2001.

CROSS REFERENCES
Assault

SUPREMACY CLAUSE

The clause of Article VI of the U.S. Constitution that declares that all laws and treaties made by the federal government shall be the "supreme law of the land."

Buckman Company v. Plaintiffs' Legal Committee

The American constitutional framework is based on the concept of FEDERALISM, under which certain powers are delegated to the states, certain powers reside exclusively with the federal government, and other powers are shared by the state and federal governments. The Framers of the federal Constitution drafted the Supremacy Clause to clarify this often murky concept. U.S.C.A. Const. Art. VI cl. 2. The Supremacy Clause prohibits states from legislating or regulating certain activities exclusively within the province of the federal government. The Supreme Court of the United States has been called on frequently to determine whether the Supremacy Clause preempts state actions. Finally, the Court has also reviewed cases to see if a federal regulatory scheme prevents plaintiffs from filing private lawsuits. This was the case in *Buckman Co. v. Plantiffs' Legal Committee*, 121 S.Ct. 1012, 2001 WL 167647, 148 L.Ed.2d 854 (2001). The Court ruled that plaintiffs claiming injury caused by a medical device could not bring an action in state court alleging that the defendant made fraudulent representations to the FOOD AND DRUG ADMINISTRATION (FDA) in its request for approval of the device. In so ruling, the Court reaffirmed the need to maintain a uniform regulatory framework for pharmaceuticals and medical devices.

The Plaintiffs' Legal Committee (PLC) represented more than 5,000 plaintiffs who claimed injuries resulting from the use of orthopedic bone screws implanted in pedicles of the spine. The PLC sued the Buckman Company, which assisted AcroMed Corporation, the screw's manufacturer, in obtaining FDA approval of the device. The PLC alleged that Buckman had made fraudulent representations to the FDA about how the screws would be marketed and used. It argued that but for these misrepresentations the FDA would not have approved the screws and the plaintiffs would not have been injured by the implantations of the screws. The FDA had denied AcroMed approval of the screws for spinal surgery in 1984 and 1985, citing potential health risks. The company, with the aid of Buckman, filed a third application in 1985. In this application, the screws were renamed as "nested bone plates" and "cancellous bone screws" and their intended use was for the long bones of the leg and arm, not the spine. The FDA approved this application in 1986. However, the screws were used in spinal surgeries, resulting in the lawsuits by the PLC. The PLC contended that the 1986 application was awarded under a false pretext because the company intended to market them for use in spinal surgery.

A federal district court supervising the lawsuits dismissed these "fraud-on-the-FDA" claims. It ruled that the actions were preempted by the federal Medical Devices Amendments of 1976 (MDA) and that there was no private right of action under the MDA (*In re Orthopedic Bone Screw Products Liability Litigation*, 1997 WL 305257 (E.D.Pa. Mar 28, 1997)). On appeal, the Court of Appeals for the Third Circuit reversed this decision, concluding that the fraud claims were neither expressly nor implicitly preempted by the MDA (*In re Orthopedic Bone Screw Products Liability Litigation*, 159 F.3d 817, (3rd Cir.(Pa.) Nov 17, 1998)). Because other circuit courts of appeal had ruled differently on this issue, the Supreme Court accepted Buckman's appeal to resolve the conflict.

The Supreme Court unanimously reversed the Third Circuit decision. Chief Justice WIL-LIAM H. REHNQUIST, writing for the Court, noted that policing fraud against federal agencies is not a field that the states have traditionally occupied. Instead, the relationship between a "federal agency and the entity it regulates is inherently federal in character because the relationship originates from, is governed by, and terminates according to federal law." In reviewing the MDA and the regulatory process mandated by this legislation, Rehnquist concluded that the fraud-on-the-FDA claims were in conflict with federal law and were implicitly preempted by that law. The "federal statutory scheme amply empowers the FDA to punish and deter fraud against the Agency." Moreover, the "delicate balance" that agency strives to maintain among many statutory objectives would be skewed by allowing private lawsuits to proceed under this fraud theory.

Chief Justice Rehnquist pointed out that the FDA is empowered to investigate suspected fraud and citizens may report wrongdoing to the agency. In addition to the general criminal law against making false statements to the federal government, the FDA may respond to fraud by seeking injunctive relief and civil penalties, seizing the devices, and pursuing criminal prosecutions. In analyzing the regulatory approval process, Rehnquist emphasized the need for the FDA to retain flexibility as it regulated medical devices "without intruding upon decisions statutorily committed to the discretion of health care professionals."

The Court was concerned that allowing the fraud claims to go forward would complicate the FDA's work. In addition, potential applicants would have to contend with the tort laws of the 50 states as well as the FDA's regulations. Such a heavy burden might, in Rehnquist's view, discourage device manufacturers from seeking approval for devices with "potentially off-label uses for fear that such use might expose the manufacturer or its associates to unpredictable civil liability." Moreover, this fear might result in a device maker submitting an overwhelming amount of data not needed by the FDA in order to protect against state tort claims. Therefore, the Court concluded that the need to maintain the FDA regulatory framework mandated the rejection of a private right of action for fraud against the agency.

California's Milk Standards Take Precedence Over Federal Standards

In December 2000 the California Supreme Court ruled that out-of-state milk producers must meet California's stricter standards for milk content than what federal standards require. The Supreme Court of the United States declined INTERLOCUTORY review of the matter earlier in 1999. In *People v. Shamrock Foods Company*, 24 Cal.4th 415, 101 Cal.Rptr.2d 200, 11 P.3d 956 (2000), California's high court reversed the decision of the state's Court of Appeal for the Fourth Appellate District and reinstated the 1996 decision of the Superior Court of San Diego County.

The relevant laws at issue included the Federal Food, Drug, and Cosmetic Act, the Nutrition Labeling and Education Act of 1990 (NLEA), the Federal Agriculture Improvement and Reform Act of 1996 (FAIRA), and California's Milk and Milk Products Act of 1947. The federal laws include "standards of identity," which define foods and list their components. Milk and milk products are essentially composed of water, milkfat, and nonfat solids. Additional nutrients such as fat, cholesterol, sodium, protein, carbohydrates, vitamins, and calcium are contained within the milkfat and nonfat milk solids. Federal standards of identity set the maximum and/or minimum percentage of water, milkfat, and nonfat milk solids to be contained in whole milk, lowfat milk, and skim milk products.

California's Milk and Milk Products Act does the same, except that the state standards of identity "require higher percentages of nonfat milk solids than the federal standards." For example, California requires that nonfat milk contain 8.2 grams of protein per eight liquid ounces of milk, while federal rules only require 7.5. California also requires higher calcium content. Generally, the higher percentage does not occur naturally and is achieved by the addition of these nutrients. According to the defendants, this resulted in a 13–20 cent increase in the cost of production per gallon. California is the only state to require such enrichment of milk.

Also playing into the equation was the NLEA, which prohibits a state from establishing a new standard of identity or labeling requirement or maintaining a previous standard of identity or labeling requirement for any food in interstate commerce unless it is the same as a federal counterpart, if one exists. This is considered a preemption provision. The NLEA provides for an exception to its rule whereby the Secretary of HEALTH AND HUMAN SERVICES may exempt a state by petition. In 1990 California filed such a petition for administrative exemption from the NLEA's rule of preemption, and it was granted. Moreover, before California's petition had been acted upon, Section 144 of the FAIRA granted California a STATUTORY exemption from the federal standards of identity and declared that "nothing ... shall be construed to preempt, prohibit, or otherwise limit the authority of the State of California, directly or indirectly, to establish or continue to effect any law, regulation, or requirement ... regarding, among other things, standards of identity for whole milk, lowfat milk, and skim milk."

Shamrock Foods of Phoenix was Arizona's largest milk producer and also maintained offices in San Diego County, California. On July 24, 1996, the People of the State of California by way of the ATTORNEY GENERAL filed suit in the Superior Court of San Diego County against Shamrock for violations of the Milk and Milk Products Act of 1947. To wit, the complaint alleged, among other things, that Shamrock "sold and delivered whole milk, lowfat milk, and nonfat milk that did not meet the state standards

of identity" and failed to disclose the same. The suit alleged that such practice victimized elderly and disabled persons and constituted unfair competition in that it deceptively sold a product inferior to the state's requirements, to the detriment of state-complying competitors and the consumer market at large.

Shamrock answered the complaint with an affirmative defense that Section 32912 of the Agricultural Code of the Milk and Milk Products Act expressly adopted the less stringent federal standards as alternatives to the more stringent state standards for milk. The superior court ruled against Shamrock, finding that Section 32912 did not adopt the less stringent standards; that Shamrock had violated the Milk and Milk Products Act by selling products that did not meet the state standards and failing to disclose same; and that Shamrock had conducted its business in bad faith solely to serve its own interest. By order of the court, the company was ENJOINED from selling or delivering any more non-complying milk and was fined $700,000. Shamrock appealed.

The Court of Appeal reversed the judgment of the superior court, finding that the "plain meaning" of section 32912 was indeed to adopt the less stringent federal standards of identity for milk and milk products as alternatives to more stringent standards. The State of California then filed petition for review with the California Supreme Court.

The question before the state's high court was the proper construction of Section 32912 of the state Milk Act. Included with the petition was a letter to the superior court by the author of the bill that added Section 32912 to the Act, who patently responded that Section 32912 did *not* adopt less stringent standards. The clear intent of the section was to address *labeling nomenclature* and labeling requirements for milk and milk products. The bill mandated that milk products that did not meet the state standards were to be properly labeled as not meeting those requirements, in accordance with the applicable provisions of Title 21 of the Code of Federal Regulations (CFR). In other words, the intent of the bill was "to bring ... state [labeling] nomenclature into line with" federal.

In finding that the Court of Appeal erroneously construed Section 32912, the California Supreme Court reversed the appellate decision and remanded the case back to the superior court for further review on other issues not part of the appeal.

CROSS REFERENCES
Food and Drug Administration; Fraud

SUPREME COURT HISTORICAL SOCIETY

The Supreme Court Historical Society (the Society) is a nonprofit organization incorporated in the District of Columbia and recognized as a (501)(c)(3) organization by the INTERNAL REVENUE SERVICE (IRS). It is dedicated to expanding public awareness of the history and heritage of the Supreme Court of the United States and to preserving historical documents and artifacts relating to the Court's history. The Society conducts public and educational programs, publishes books and periodicals, supports historical research, and collects antiques and period pieces to enhance an appreciation of the history behind the U.S. Constitution and its first interpreters. It supports its programs through member contributions, grants, gifts, and a small endowment. The Society is located in the Opperman House on East Capitol Street in Washington, D.C. It also maintains its own website located at <http://www.supremecourthistory.org/>.

Founded in 1974 by the late Chief Justice WARREN E. BURGER, the Society has approximately 6,000 individual members who volunteer services on its standing and AD HOC committees; the committees report to an elected Board of Trustees. The Chief Justice of the United States serves as Honorary Chairman of the Society. Former Chief Justice Burger served as the Society's first chairman. Retired Associate Justice BYRON R. WHITE is an honorary member of the Board of Trustees.

The Society's most ambitious historic project to date has been the research and publication of the first six volumes of the *Documentary History of the Supreme Court, 1789 to 1800*. This series is projected to require at least two more volumes and represents the reconstruction of an accurate record of the development of the federal JUDICIARY in the formative decade between 1789 and 1800. The series has been published by the Columbia University Press. Another scholarly publication is the Society's *Supreme Court of the United States 1789–1990: An Index to Opinions Arranged by Justice*, which is updated periodically. The three-volume publication is the only printed resource of all the opinions of each justice and thus provides easy reference to each individual's contribution to the United States Reports, the official record of the Court's opinions. Additionally, a pilot program of oral recorded histories, documenting the careers and service of retired Supreme Court Justices, has been in progress. Thus far, the Society has completed oral histories of the late Associate Justices HARRY BLACKMUN, WILLIAM J. BRENNAN, JR., THURGOOD MARSHALL, and LOUIS F. POWELL.

Semi-annually, the Society publishes the *Journal of Supreme Court History*, which features articles by the justices, noted academicians, solicitors general, and other noted contributors. Special topic publications by the Society include *The Supreme Court in the Civil War, The Jewish Justices of the Supreme Court Revisited: Brandeis to Fortas*, and *The Supreme Court in World War II*. The Society's quarterly newsletter for its members contains short historical articles and news of programs and activities.

For the general public, the Society co-publishes an ongoing illustrated history of the Court, *Equal Justice Under Law*, in conjunction with the National Geographic Society. In cooperation with Congressional Quarterly, Inc., the Society published *The Supreme Court Justices: Illustrated Biographies, 1789–1995, a collection of biographies of 108 current and former justices*.

Another important part of the Society's activities is its co-sponsorship of the National Heritage Lecture, rotating the hosting of the annual event with the White House Historical Association and the U.S. Capitol Historical Society. Along with Street Law, Inc., it also conducts the Supreme Court Summer Institute, a program for secondary school teachers to help them develop in their students an awareness of

United States Supreme Court, Washington, D.C.

their rights and duties as citizens. It has developed a special "landmark cases" volume as an education tool for teachers, that provides extensive information on some of the Court's most important cases, many of which have been included in states' standards for teaching history and government. In 2000 the Society launched a special initiative for high school teachers in the Washington, D.C., public schools.

Finally, the Society conducts an acquisition program, working closely with the Court Cura-

tor's office, to locate, acquire, and display the Court's permanent collection of busts and portraits of justices, as well as period furnishings, original documents, and private papers, and other artifacts relating to the Court and its history. Many of these items are on display or otherwise made available for the benefit of the Court's one million annual visitors.

CROSS REFERENCES
Supreme Court of the United States

TAXATION

The process whereby charges are imposed on individuals or property by the legislative branch of the federal government and by many state governments to raise funds for public purposes.

United Dominion Industries, Inc. v. United States

The U.S. Tax Code is a lengthy and complicated legal document that is the special province of accountants and lawyers specializing in taxation. Over the years Congress has passed many tax laws and the INTERNAL REVENUE SERVICE (IRS) has written regulations that seek to impose administrative coherence on arcane STATUTORY provisions. While the tax code is complex for individual taxation, it is even more so for businesses, which spend enormous sums of money analyzing code provisions in hopes of using every legal advantage to reduce their tax burdens. Not surprisingly, there are many gray areas where the IRS and business taxpayers dispute the proper interpretation of a tax law. This dispute sometime leads to litigation. The courts generally defer to the IRS because the IRS has the most expertise and because judges are not enamored of analyzing tax laws and then writing opinions that explain their decisions. Such was the case in *United Dominion Industries, Inc. v. United States*, ___U.S.___, 121 S.Ct. 1934, ___ L.Ed. ___ (2001). In this case, the Supreme Court of the United States ruled against an IRS interpretation on a business deduction method.

Regarding United Dominion Industries, Inc., a large corporation that serves as the parent of an affiliated group of corporations, the issue that confronted the courts was the proper method for calculating a corporation's net operating loss (NOL). Under the tax code a NOL results from deductions in excess of gross income for a given year. More simply, if a business's expenses exceed its profits, it has suffered a net operating loss. NOLs are important to businesses because the code allows a taxpaying business to carry them into other tax years, either past or future. Thus, a business that has a very good year can use a net operating loss from a prior year to reduce its tax liability from the profitable year.

Specifically at issue in this case was the use of product liability losses (PLLs) when calculating a net operating loss. PLLs include fees paid out to consumers due to the failure of a given product created by the company. A product liability loss is the total of a taxpayer's product liability expenses (PLEs). A company's PLL cannot exceed the amount of its NOL, however. For example, a taxpayer corporation with a positive income, who thereby has no net operating loss, may have product liability expenses but can claim no product liability losses. Thus, a business with any income cannot deduct any PLEs.

The issue grows even more complicated when an affiliated group of corporations, such as those controlled by United Dominion, file a corporate tax return as a single, consolidated entity. IRS regulations provide that such a group's consolidated taxable income (CTI) or its consolidated net operating loss (CNOL) is calculated by taking into account several items. The first is the separate taxable income (STI) of each group member. The calculation of the separate taxable income requires each member

213

to disregard certain items, such as capital gains and losses, even though these items are factored into the consolidated taxable income or consolidated net operating loss for the entire group of corporations acting as one. For four tax years United Dominion reported a consolidated net operating loss exceeding the combined total of its twenty-six individual members' product liability expenses. Five group members with PLEs reported positive separate taxable incomes, but United Dominion included these product liability expenses in determining its consolidated product liability loss for a carryback under a "single entity" approach. This approach compares the group's CNOL and total PLEs to determine the group's total PLL.

The IRS challenged the single-entity approach. Instead, it contended that United Dominion should have used the "separate-member" approach. Under this method, the corporation compares each affiliate's separate taxable income and product liability expenses to determine whether each affiliate individually suffers a product liability loss. Only then can the corporation combine any affiliates' PLLs to calculate a *consolidated* PLL. PLEs incurred by an affiliate with a positive STI cannot contribute to a consolidated PLL.

United Dominion applied for refunds for two tax years based on its single-entity approach. The court ruled in its favor, but a congressional committee that oversees refunds reversed this decision. United Dominion then filed a refund lawsuit in U.S. District Court for the Western District of North Carolina. The DISTRICT COURT adopted the single entity theory and ruled in favor of United Dominion. This ruling was overturned by the U.S. Court of Appeals for the Fourth Circuit, which concurred with the IRS's separate-entity approach.

The Supreme Court, in an 8–1 decision, reversed the Fourth Circuit's separate-entity approach interpretation. Justice DAVID H. SOUTER, writing for the majority, restated the complicated scenario before examining both approaches. He found that the single-entity approach to calculating an affiliated group's product liability loss is "straightforward." He noted that the tax laws definition of a net operating loss was a "consolidated" NOL. There was no definition of an NOL for separate group members. Because the tax statutes and regulations did not make such a distinction, a corporation with affiliated members must be treated as a conventional corporate taxpayer. Justice Souter rejected the IRS's contention that single-entity calculations

should be invalid since they could be abused to avoid paying taxes. He noted, however, that the IRS has the authority to disallow deductions that are designed to avoid taxes. For instance, the IRS could amend its regulations to remove the single-entity approach. Since it had not done so, the IRS could not object to corporations using a method that proved to be in their favor.

United States v. Cleveland Indians Baseball Company

The INTERNAL REVENUE SERVICE (IRS) is charged with enforcing federal tax laws and its own regulations. Though there are many lawsuits filed each year that dispute how the IRS interprets the law, the Supreme Court of the United States rarely hears appeals on such cases. In general, the Court pays great deference to the IRS and supports its interpretation of its laws and regulations as long as they are reasonable. This judicial attitude was displayed again in *United States v. Cleveland Indians Baseball Company,* ___U.S.___, 121 S.Ct. 1433, ___ L.Ed.2d ___ (2001), in which the Court heard an appeal concerning the year in which back wages should be taxed. The decision affirmed the IRS's position that Social Security, MEDICARE, and unemployment taxes must be based on the year the back wages were actually paid, not the year they should have been paid.

The case arose out of a settlement between players and owners of Major League Baseball (MLB) over the players' free agency rights. The clubs agreed to pay $280 million to players who could prove they had been injured because of limitations placed on their ability to negotiate with any team in MLB. The Cleveland Indians baseball team owed twenty-two players a total in excess of $2 million in back wages for the years 1986 and 1987. When the team prepared to make the payments it became uncertain as to how to deduct Federal Insurance Contributions Act (FICA) taxes that fund Social Security and Medicare. In addition, it had to pay its portion of FICA taxes as well. Moreover, the ball club was solely responsible for paying Federal Unemployment Tax Act (FUTA) taxes to the IRS. The issue centered on which tax years to base the tax calculations. The team decided to pay the taxes based on the current 1994 tax year but immediately filed for a refund with the IRS for overpayment.

The differences in the tax burden for the club and the players was significant. The tax rates for both FICA and FUTA had risen between 1986 and 1994. Moreover, the STATUTORY ceiling on taxable wages, which limits the amount of annual wages subject to tax, also had changed to the detriment of the taxpayers. In 1986 the Social Security tax on employees and employers was 5.7 percent of wages up to $42,000. By 1994 the rate had risen to 6.2 percent of wages up to $60,600. The Medicare tax remained constant at 1.45 percent of wages, but Congress had removed the wage ceiling on this tax by 1994. The FUTA tax rose slightly, from 6.0 percent to 6.2 percent between 1986 and 1994. In this case the ballplayers who received their back wages in 1994 had already collected wages exceeding the statutory maximum in 1986 and 1987. Thus, there would be no additional tax liability for the players or the club if they could use the two years rather than 1994 for calculating the tax. If they had to pay based on 1994, they were exposed to a significant tax liability.

After the IRS denied the club's refund request, the club filed suit in federal district court, asking the court to rule that the wages should be taxed on the years they should have been paid rather than when they actually were paid. The DISTRICT COURT, which was governed by CIRCUIT COURT precedent, ruled in the ball club's favor. On appeal to the Sixth Circuit Court of Appeals, the court reaffirmed its precedent and upheld the lower court. The Supreme Court agreed to hear the government's appeal because there were conflicting rulings in the circuit courts.

The Court, in a unanimous decision, reversed the Sixth Circuit. Justice RUTH BADER GINSBURG, writing for the Court, stated that the decision was based on the Court giving the IRS "due respect" to the agency's "reasonable, longstanding construction of the governing statutes and its own regulations." Nevertheless, Ginsburg rejected the government's assertion that this was a simple case and could be decided on a reading of the plain language in the controlling FICA and FUTA provisions. These provisions regularly refer to "wages . . . paid . . . during a calendar year." Thus, the government contended that "[w]ages are taxed according to the calendar year" in which they are actually paid.

Ginsburg rejected this simple explanation and agreed with the Cleveland ball club that a 1946 Supreme Court case on the crediting of Social Security benefits went in the other direction, *Social Security Board v. Nierotko*, 327 U.S. 358 (1946). In that case, the back pay in a labor dispute was credited to the years when the worker should have received the money for purposes of Social Security eligibility. This rejection of the "year in which it was actually paid" approach complicated the analysis, but Ginsburg ultimately found that the case was directed at benefits rather than the payment of taxes. Therefore, the decision had no dispositive precedential weight.

Finding that neither side had a compelling legal argument, the Court fell back into its deferential role to the IRS. Justice Ginsburg noted that the Court has consistently declined to sit as a "committee of revision" to refine the federal tax code. Instead, the Court agreed that the IRS had maintained its position on taxing income in the year that it was actually paid since the 1940s. This consistent interpretation led the Court to side with the IRS. Justice ANTONIN SCALIA, in a concurring opinion, felt the payments to players could not be considered wages "within the normal meaning of that term." The FICA and FUTA provisions made no mention for how to assess taxes on such AWARDS, and, therefore, he agreed that the Court had to defer to the IRS's consistent interpretation of its own regulations.

CROSS REFERENCES
Baseball; Corporations

TELECOMMUNICATIONS

The transmission of words, sounds, images, or data in the form of electronic or electromagnetic signals or impulses.

Omnipoint Communications Enterprises v. Newtown Township

The U.S. Court of Appeals for the Third Circuit unanimously ruled that the federal Telecommunications Act of 1996 does not prohibit a township from denying a wireless communication service provider the right to install antennas that would fill a "gap" in the provider's coverage when the township's zoning ordinance lawfully excludes the installation of such antennas and when competing wireless telecommunication services are reasonably available to the residents. *Omnipoint Communications Enterprises, L.P. v. Newtown Township*, 219 F.3d 240 (3rd Cir. 2000). On November 6, 2000, the Supreme Court of the United States let the lower court's decision stand, denying CERTIORARI without comment. *Omnipoint Communications Enterprises, L.P. v. Newtown Township*, ___U.S.___, 121 S.Ct. 441, ___ L.Ed.2d ___ (2000).

The lawsuit began in 1997 when the plaintiff, Omnipoint Communications Enterprises, L.P., a personal communication service provider

THE POPULARITY OF TELEVISION'S JUDGE SHOWS

It began in 1981, with the premiere of Judge Joseph Wapner's *The People's Court*. The show remained consistently popular for many years but faced no real competition. As the millennium approached, "reality television," including shows such as *Survivor*, *Cops*, and *World's Funniest Home Videos*, garnered high ratings for television program viewing. The trend of reality TV, in combination with live television broadcasts such as the unfolding drama of the O.J. SIMPSON murder trial and the IMPEACHMENT proceedings of then-President BILL CLINTON, left a palpable void that needed to be filled, and America's fascination with the televised courtroom began in earnest.

By the start of the 2000–2001 television season, there were no fewer than ten court shows being scheduled on the networks, five of them newly premiering. This figure did not include regular television drama series focusing on the law or lawyers, such as *The Firm*, *The Practice*, and more than one variation on *Law and Order*. Rather, all ten involved real-life courtroom drama, real judges,

real cases, and real parties. "Judge shows," sometimes referred to as "court TV," unequivocally dominated the syndicated programs television lineup for the Fall 2000 television season. By January 2001, the syndicated *Judge Judy*, reigning queen of the court TV genre, pulled a 6.9 Nielsen rating, placing the show squarely in the top three syndicated programs, just behind long-standing gameshows *Wheel of Fortune* and *Jeopardy*.

IN FOCUS

But just as TV viewers were growing accustomed to the "All rise" command, the gavel came down. In Spring 2001 one judge show was canceled and two others were approaching a similar sentence. Critics referred to an "oversaturated market." Others believed it was simply a shakedown to eliminate the losers and focus on the winners. Still others believed "the jury [was] still out" on the future of court TV and its sustaining power for the Fall 2001 season. "Any time you take the novelty out of an individual program or emerging genre by too much replication, you'll hurt the

original shows," said Johnny Rash, senior vice president and director of broadcast negotiations for Campbell-Mithun.

Those court shows that appeared to have some staying power included: *Judge Judy* (leading by an appreciable margin), *Judge Joe Brown*, *Divorce Court*, (the only one whose audience actually grew from the previous season), *Power of Attorney*, and *Judge Mathis*. Following behind these were *Judge Hatchett*, *The People's Court*, *Judge Mills Lane* (canceled for Fall 2001), *Curtis Court*, and *Moral Court*. Related new shows for the season included *Single Court*, *Attorney*, and *Arrest and Trial*.

Who are the judges who preside over these programs, and who are their litigants? Most of the judges, although they were not household names prior to television, were in fact practicing on the bench when they were pursued by television networks. Judy Sheindlin, better known as Judge Judy, graduated first in her class from New York Law School. She was a cut-to-the-chase jurist in Manhattan Family Court when she was approached by TV producers. Her show

that has since been acquired by VoiceStream Wireless Corp., entered into a lease with the owner of an apartment building known as Newtown Towers in Newtown Township, Pennsylvania. The lease specifically authorized Omnipoint to install wireless communication antennas on the apartment building rooftop. The plaintiff then applied for a building permit to install antennas. Newtown Township's Zoning Officer denied the application. The officer stated in a letter that the proposed antennas were not a *use* or an *accessory use* permitted in the area because the antennas were slated for commercial purposes and Newtown had been zoned as an Apartment Office District only. Omnipoint appealed, but the township's Zoning Hearing Board upheld the zoning officer's decision.

Omnipoint then filed a civil action in the U.S. District Court for the Eastern District of

Pennsylvania. The action sought to overturn the zoning board's decision on the GROUNDS that it violated the federal Telecommunications Act of 1996, 47 U.S.C.A. 332, which bars any state or local government from taking action that "prohibits or has the effect of prohibiting the provision of wireless services." Responding to a motion for SUMMARY JUDGMENT, the DISTRICT COURT agreed with the plaintiff. In an opinion written by Magistrate Judge Charles B. Smith, the court concluded that the zoning board's decision had the effect of prohibiting Omnipoint from providing personal wireless services in Newtown Township and the surrounding communities. *Omnipoint Communications Enterprises, L.P. v. Newtown Township*, 1999 WL 269936 (E.D. Pa. 1999).

The court observed that the township's zoning ordinance prohibited placement of wireless service antennas anywhere in the vicinity,

first aired in 1996. She is married to Gerald Sheindlin, otherwise known as "Judge Jerry" on *The People's Court*. In 2001, Sheindlin, who took over the show from former New York Mayor Ed Koch in 1999, passed the gavel to Marilyn Milian, a Miami Circuit Court judge. Judge Mills Lane, billed as "Justice You Can Trust," hails from Reno, Nevada. He returned to his Reno practice after the show was canceled in Spring 2001. A prior district attorney and district judge, Lane was also professional boxing's most recognized and respected referee before agreeing to arbitrate legal battles on TV in 1998.

Most of the shows gather prospective litigants from advertising, such as through a toll-free number posted during the broadcast. Judge Hatchett, from the Fulton County Juvenile Court in Georgia, was recruited expressly to "young down" the court-show circuit on television. She agreed to take the job as long as the producers would give her wide latitude in dealing with the mostly youthful litigants. In return, she hoped that, through her innovative sentencing remedies, combined with a genuine sense of compassion, she could reach out to people in the viewing audience and make a difference in their lives as well. Her program, thus far rated in the middle of the pack, is characterized by more narrowly-tailored sentences such as treatment and counseling programs and "scared-straight" interventions. Unlike many of her court-TV colleagues, Hatchett maintains a professional legal staff that not only follows up and monitors the progress of her subjects after sentencing but also screens and manages the pool of applicants being referred from the toll-free line, SMALL CLAIMS COURT, and even local social service agencies. Similar to other shows, the "ordinary people" whose cases are accepted for television must sign releases before they appear on the show. Even with the glut of court shows, there appears to be no scarcity of available litigants willing to tell their problems to the televised world.

Though the shows are numerous, they are not redundant. Each tries to distinguish itself by taking on a different twist. According to Mary Duffy, senior executive producer at King World Productions, judge shows like this provide "more order, more resolution" than on-and-on talk shows. *Judge Judy* remains the top no-nonsense, bottom-line judge. *Curtis Court* offers a more "touchy-feely" judge than some of other leading contenders. *Power of Attorney* relies on famous counsel, such as O.J. Simpson prosecutor Christopher Darden, for its appeal. *Moral Court* focuses on ethical problems not resolvable by legal precedent. Still, "The industry thrives on imitation," said Dick Kurlander, a Petry TV executive. "It is an irresistible human trait to seize on the success of *Judge Judy* and some of the others."

What remained to be seen for the Fall 2001 season was the final list of court shows that would be asked to return. Another consideration too early to predict was whether viewers' image of the bar was heightened or hurt by the on-air presentations. A study released in June 2001, "Changing Images of Government in TV Entertainment," updated a previous 1999 report examining entertainment television's depiction of the public sector and people in government from the 1950s to 1998. According to the findings, seven out of ten shows in the 1990s depicted the legal system as unjust, discriminatory, and/or ineffective. Conversely, in current series, eight out of ten shows portray a functioning, fair, and just legal system. Judges and prosecuting attorneys were the most favorably portrayed occupational group.

except possibly for one area zoned as Light Industrial Business. The Light Industrial area, however, was owned almost exclusively by a single proprietor who had refused to do business with the plaintiff. The court found that Omnipoint should not have been forced to negotiate with a single owner who had the power to arbitrarily exclude the company's business operation from the area. The court also found that Newtown had "looked the other way" when competing businesses installed wireless communication antennas within the township's limits. Thus, the court held that the zoning board's denial of the building permit unreasonably left a gap in Omnipoint's wireless service coverage. The board's denial also permitted competing services to maintain continuous coverage in the same area, the court said. As a result, Omnipoint was granted summary judgment, and Newtown was ordered to take all steps necessary for the plaintiff to install the wireless communication antennas as proposed by the plaintiff.

Newtown appealed, and the third circuit reversed. The CIRCUIT COURT acknowledged that the Telecommunications Act was intended to promote competition by limiting the ability of local authorities to regulate and control the expansion of wireless technologies. At the same time, the court noted that the act authorizes state and local governments to exercise some authority over personal wireless services. The court said that zoning boards are still permitted to enact ordinances restricting designated areas to residential and non-residential uses. In this case, the court observed that the Apartment Office zoning designation was consistent with a residential-only use. The only question that remained, the court wrote, was whether the gap created in Omnipoint's wireless coverage for

Erection of a cellular telephone tower, like this one in Clackamas, Oregon, led to a Supreme Court ruling.

Newtown residents was by itself a violation of the act.

In holding that the Telecommunications Act of 1996 was not violated, the court said that not all gaps in a wireless provider's service will run afoul of federal law. The court reasoned that it is not sufficient for a cellular phone company to show that it has been denied the chance to fill a gap in its own coverage. Rather, the Court emphasized, cellular phone companies such as the plaintiff must show that all wireless service providers have been denied the opportunity to service the residents of a particular community. The court found that neither the district court nor the local zoning authorities had heard much evidence on this point. So the court REMANDED the case to the district court for further fact-finding consistent with its opinion.

Omnipoint filed a petition for certiorari before the U.S. Supreme Court. AT&T Wireless Services, Nextel Communications, SAC Wireless, Sprint Spectrum, and Dobson Communications all filed AMICUS CURIAE briefs supporting the appellant. They argued that competition would be stifled and costs would soar if local governments were allowed to grant a monopoly to one wireless service provider at the expense of all others. The appeal was refused a hearing in the nation's highest court, however, so the case will proceed back to federal district court as ordered by the third circuit.

TERRORISM

The unlawful use of force or violence against persons or property in order to coerce or intimidate a government or the civilian population in furtherance of political or social objectives.

Execution of Timothy McVeigh

Timothy McVeigh was executed by lethal injection on June 11, 2001, at a federal prison in Terra Haute, Indiana, becoming the first federal prisoner to suffer the death penalty in thirty-eight years. McVeigh had been found guilty in 1997 of the April 19, 1995, bombing of the Alfred P. Murrah building in Oklahoma City, which killed 168 people and wounded hundreds more. Though McVeigh had abandoned an appeal of his conviction in late 2000, the surprising disclosure in May 2001 that the Federal Bureau of Investigation (FBI) had failed to turn over three-thousand documents to McVeigh's lawyers led newly-appointed attorney general JOHN ASHCROFT to delay McVeigh's execution for one month. During this period, McVeigh's lawyers sought a longer STAY of execution in hopes of persuading the trial judge to throw out the case and force a retrial. These efforts proved fruitless but placed the events of 1995 and McVeigh's motivations back in the headlines.

McVeigh, a young Persian Gulf war veteran, was arrested ninety minutes after the truck bomb exploded in front of the Murrah building. Within days Terry Nichols, a friend of McVeigh's, was arrested and charged with participating in the bombing. McVeigh's trial was moved to Denver, Colorado to ensure a fair hearing. On June 2, 1997, a jury found him guilty on all counts. Though McVeigh did not testify, the trial revealed that he held radical right-wing, anti-government beliefs and had sought to punish the federal government for the way it had conducted the 1993 siege of the Branch Davidian compound in Waco, Texas.

U.S. District Court Judge Richard Matsch formally sentenced McVeigh to death in August 1997. The following month, Terry Nichols went on trial in Denver for his role in the bombing. A jury convicted him of CONSPIRACY and involuntary MANSLAUGHTER but acquitted him of taking part in the bombing. After the jury deadlocked over whether to sentence him to death, Judge Matsch sentenced Nichols to life imprisonment without chance of parole.

Following sentencing, McVeigh changed his legal representation. His new lawyers compiled a long list of issues that they believed prej-

Mementos and a newspaper announcing Timothy McVeigh's death sentence on the fence of the Murrah Federal Building in Oklahoma City.

udiced McVeigh's ability to receive a fair trial. Legal commentators fully expected McVeigh to exhaust all legal avenues, including his direct appeal and post-conviction proceedings. On December 12, 2000, McVeigh informed Judge Matsch that he wished to drop his appeal, however, and asked the judge to set an execution date. Judge Matsch granted McVeigh's requests two weeks later. On January 16, 2001, the U.S. JUSTICE DEPARTMENT set May 16 as McVeigh's execution date.

During early 2001, McVeigh granted a number of press interviews, including a televised appearance. Though he had never admitted in court that he had committed the bombing, McVeigh was more forthcoming in these interviews. He told reporters from a Buffalo, New York, newspaper that he had bombed the Murrah building, but he refused to provide any details about the planning of the crime or other participants. Moreover, he declined to apologize or express regret for killing 168 people, including 19 young children. He described the deaths of the children as "collateral damage."

As the May 16 execution deadline drew closer, surviving bombing victims and family members of deceased victims participated in a lottery to see who would witness McVeigh's execution in person. In a macabre moment, an Internet company requested permission to show the execution online. The Justice Department promptly refused the request, but it agreed to transmit a closed-circuit television feed of the execution to an Oklahoma City facility where the remaining victims and victims' families could watch.

Then on May 11, just five days before the scheduled execution, attorney general Ashcroft announced that the FBI had failed to turn over to McVeigh's attorneys all files that it had accumulated during the investigation. This failure occurred despite directives from the FBI leadership that all bureaus send their material on the bombing to the Justice Department so as to comply with a 1996 DISCOVERY agreement. Ashcroft announced that he was postponing the execution until June 16 so that McVeigh's lawyers could review the 3,100 pages of documents. He also ordered the FBI to search its files again and transmit any other pertinent documents. This request came in spite of eleven previous searches.

McVeigh's defense team began to review the documents and shortly thereafter asked their client to allow them to file a motion with Judge Matsch asking for additional time beyond that given by Ashcroft. In late May McVeigh agreed, and his attorneys filed a motion on May 31 asking the judge to delay the execution. The attorneys argued in their motion that the federal government had perpetrated a "fraud on the court" that might merit a full review of the fairness of the trial. Attorney general Ashcroft opposed the motion, concluding that nothing in the 3,100 pages changed the conclusion that McVeigh had committed the bombings. The fact that Mc-Veigh had admitted as much to reporters also hurt his case. Nevertheless, his trial and appellate attorneys believed that the new files suggested that a third person had been involved in the bombing and that this might reduce Mc-Veigh's CULPABILITY. In addition, Terry Nichols's attorneys filed an appeal with the Supreme Court asking for a review of his case based on this new information.

On June 6, Judge Matsch denied McVeigh's motion, ruling that the missing 3,100 pages did not materially change the outcome of the case. McVeigh's attorney immediately appealed to the Court of Appeals for the Tenth Circuit, but on June 7 the circuit court refused to intervene. Though McVeigh could have made an emergency appeal to the Supreme Court, he instructed his attorneys not to file such an action. On June 10 McVeigh was moved to the "death house," a small, windowless building. He met with his lawyers, and on the morning of his execution took last rites from a Catholic priest.

On Monday, June 11, McVeigh entered the execution chamber. He did not speak but provided a handwritten statement that quoted the poem "Invictus," which states in part that "I am the master of my fate: I am the captain of my soul." At 8:00 A.M., McVeigh was injected with three chemicals. Fourteen minutes later he was declared dead.

INS Holds Arab Immigrant Secretly for Three Years

In November 1999 the federal government released an Arab immigrant, Nasser Ahmed, after imprisoning him for three and a half years on secret charges. The Immigration and Naturalization Service (INS) arrested Ahmed in 1996. Under the sweeping powers of a then-new federal anti-terrorism law, officials sought to deport Ahmed while declining to reveal charges or evidence against the Egyptian-born engineer. He responded by seeking political asylum. As his incarceration drew protests from Arab-American groups, both an immigration judge and an appeals board ruled in his favor, and Attorney General JANET RENO declined to block his release. Ahmed's freedom was championed by critics of secret evidence rules, who say they have been used unfairly in twenty cases since 1996, mainly against Arabs.

Ahmed immigrated to the United States in 1986. Along with his wife, Salwa, a physician, he raised three children in Brooklyn. The family joined New York's Abu Bakr mosque, where Ahmed became a board member and treasurer. There he met the outspoken Egyptian cleric Sheikh Omar Abdel Rahman, who was subsequently convicted in New York in 1995 of conspiring to blow up the United Nations building and other landmarks. At the sheikh's trial, Ahmed served as a court-appointed translator and paralegal. He made no secret of his admiration for the sheikh's harsh opposition to the Egyptian government, although he never avowed terrorism.

Ahmed's legal troubles began during the sheikh's trial. The FEDERAL BUREAU OF INVESTIGATION (FBI) approached him seeking his assistance in the case. When he refused, FBI agents allegedly threatened him and his family with DEPORTATION. Shortly afterwards, the INS arrested him for having overstayed his visa and then released him. In April 1996 the INS detained him again and began deportation proceedings. This time, Ahmed's attorneys could not learn why he was under arrest. Held for two years in the Metropolitan Correctional Center in Manhattan, with frequent periods of solitary confinement, he was eventually moved to the federal prison at Otisville, New York. In protest, he went on a hunger strike and was ultimately force-fed in a hospital.

The INS asserted its authority to hold Ahmed under the 1996 Anti-Terrorism and Effective Death Penalty Act. Passed by Congress in response to the Oklahoma City bombing, the law expanded the normally broad powers of the INS. Previously, only limited forms of DUE PROCESS were available to defendants in immigration cases, but the anti-terrorism law allowed the agency new powers in cases of national security. The INS can arrest and detain aliens while keeping secret the charges, evidence, and even their accusers' identities, while also restricting attorneys' access to their clients. The law is intended to prevent any support, financial or otherwise, for anti-American terrorist groups and their supporters, as it is believed that such groups use legal means to enlist support for illegal activities.

Ahmed applied for bond and political asylum, asserting that his status as a critic of the Egyptian government meant he would face torture if repatriated. Both applications were denied due to the government's secret evidence. One year later, a small break in the case came. Having found that Ahmed's fears of torture were valid, federal immigration judge Donn Livingston ordered INS officials to provide defense attorneys with an unclassified summary of the charges. The agency responded with a single written sentence declaring that Ahmed was associated with a terrorist organization, although they refused to say which one.

The case had attracted the attention of several prominent attorneys who agreed to represent Ahmed for free. Among them was Georgetown University law professor David D. Cole, who has represented more than a dozen clients similarly charged under the anti-terrorism law. These attorneys pressed the INS in federal court to reveal its secret evidence, and the INS divulged some of its case. It charged that Ahmed belonged to the terrorist organization el-Gama'a el-Islamiyya; that he had sought to mail a bomb manual abroad; that he had relayed a threat by the imprisoned Sheikh Abdel Rahmen that led to a bombing in Egypt; and that he had threatened the leader of the Abu Bakr mosque. Ahmed denied the charges.

In mid-1999, Judge Livingston rejected the government's case and granted Ahmed's asylum request. The INS appealed, but the Board of Immigration Appeals agreed with Judge Livingston that Ahmed posed no national security threat: it ordered him released while it reviewed the asylum decision. In a final attempt to prevent his release, INS Commissioner Doris Meissner directly requested that Attorney General Reno exercise her authority to intervene. After Reno refused to respond to the request, Meissner summarily announced that the agency had reversed its position on the case, without explaining why. On November 29, Ahmed was released on bond and reunited with his family.

The case elicited strong reactions. Ahmed denounced the federal government for holding him without explanation for so long. Aly R. Abuzzaakouk, executive director of the American Muslim Council, told the *New York Times*, "Should we celebrate tonight, or should we decry the fact that in America, a man was behind bars for so many years on the basis of secret evidence?" Attorney Cole said he expected a positive outcome for Ahmed's asylum request, which was still pending more than a year later.

Following Ahmed's release, the use of secret evidence drew more fire. Two other cases grabbed headlines: in 1999 federal authorities released Hany Kiareldeen, a Palestinian man held on suspicion of terrorism for 19 months; in December 2000 they freed Mazen Al-Najjar, a Palestinian and former University of South Florida professor held for three years. Amid accusations of bias by Arab-American groups, repeal of secret evidence rules appeared to be

Nasser Ahmed, former associate of convicted terrorist Omar Abdel-Rahman, speaks during an undated prison interview.

gaining political momentum. President GEORGE W. BUSH had been critical of the rules while campaigning in 2000, and in January 2001, Representative David E. Bonior (D-Mich.) promised to reintroduce repeal legislation that had gained support but stalled in the previous session of Congress.

The Lockerbie Trial

On the evening of December 21, 1988, shortly after Pan Am Flight 103 departed from Heathrow Airport in London, England, the aircraft suddenly exploded in mid-air as it passed over the small town of Lockerbie, Scotland. A total of 270 people were killed in the disaster, including eleven residents of Lockerbie. One-hundred eighty-nine passengers on board the flight destined for New York City were Americans returning home for the holiday season. Two male members of the Libyan Intelligence Service named Abdel-baset Ali Mohmed Al-Megrahi and Al Amin Khalifa Fhimah were charged with the bombing. The trial of this matter began on May 3, 2000, in an old school building at Camp Zeist, a former NORTH ATLANTIC TREATY ORGANIZATION air base in the Netherlands, which was temporarily declared a Scottish territory for purposes of the trial.

The establishment of the Camp Zeist site raised interesting legal questions that authorities were forced to deal with before a trial could commence. The initial issue was one of jurisdiction, because the suspects were Libyan, the crime occurred in Scottish air space, but many of the victims were American and English. Consequently, both the American and English governments wanted to try the suspects in their own justice systems. Libya had refused to hand the suspects over due to UNITED NATIONS trade sanctions against the country, instituted for its suspected part in the bombing. After years of negotiations and stalemates, progress began to be made in 1998, as the suggestion for Scottish jurisdiction and a neutral site were accepted by all interested nations. In early 1999 a deal was brokered in which Libya would hand over the suspects in exchange for the sanctions being dropped.

Further legal details remained, such as the establishment of the base at Camp Zeist. For the duration of the trial the grounds would be considered Scottish soil and subject to its laws. To enable this unique turn of events, a treaty was signed to change the nationality of the camp for the trial. Scottish policemen were flown in to patrol the camp, and all judicial matters were conducted according to Scottish law. The suspects were tried in front of a three judge panel, with one alternate judge in case of illness.

Upon commencement, the prosecution first called an air traffic controller employed at Heathrow, who recounted the aircraft disappearing from his radar screen on the night of the bombing. The prosecution then followed with witnesses Stephen Charles Tegel, Roland Stevenson, Jasmine Bell, and Ian Wood, who submitted detailed eyewitness accounts of the explosion seen from the ground in Lockerbie. In addition to this emotional layperson testimony,

the prosecutors presented expert testimony concerning the contents of the wreckage and the arguable link from bomb-building paraphernalia found therein to the defendants. On July 11, 2000, the prosecution presented the highly-controversial but certainly damaging testimony of a Maltese shopkeeper named Tony Gauci. He claimed to remember a man who resembled Al-Megrahi buying clothing from him a few weeks prior to the bombing. The same clothes were determined by forensic science to have been packed in a suitcase around the bomb that brought down Pan Am Flight 103. He testified as to remembering Al-Megrahi's purchase in his small family-owned business because Al-Megrahi took no interest in the items that he chose. In total, the prosecutors called 232 witnesses before they rested their case-in-chief in early December 2000.

The defense strategy concentrated on trying to show that the bombing could have been perpetrated by Palestinians, including a prosecution witness named Mohammed Abu Talb. The attorneys for the defendants opened their case by challenging the CREDIBILITY of the Maltese shopkeeper who said that he remembered selling the clothes to Al-Megrahi on a rainy day. The defense countered with a meteorologist's testimony that it was unlikely to have been rainy on that particular day. Among several of the witnesses notably subject to questioning by the defense was former Pan Am security director Martin Huebner. His testimony apparently supported the defense theory that it could have been Palestinians, and not the defendants, who placed the bomb on the plane in Frankfurt, Germany. After calling three witnesses, counsel for the defendants rested their case.

The responsibility of resolving the case was finally given to the three-judge panel after a total of nine months of evidence. Upon considering the matter, the finders of fact came to a unanimous decision. In an 82-page verdict, the three judges all reached the conclusion that there was no doubt as to Al-Megrahi's guilt with respect to the crime of murder in connection with Pan Am Flight 103. Upon review of the CIRCUMSTANTIAL EVIDENCE that led to the conviction, the judges ordered that Al-Megrahi be sentenced to life in prison. Al-Megrahi's co-defendant Fhimah, however, was found not guilty. While Fhimah was set free, Al-Megrahi remains in custody pending the outcome of his appeal of the verdict through the Scottish legal system.

Some wreckage of Pan Am Flight 103 lying in a field outside the village of Lockerbie, Scotland, after it was downed by a terrorist bomb in 1988.

Although the family and friends of the victims who perished in Pan Am Flight 103 find solace in the fact that at least one person is being held responsible for the bombing, many express dissatisfaction that relevant officials have yet to charge the person they believe ordered the attack, Libyan leader Colonel Moammar Khadafi. Many experts in this area suggest that once Al-Megrahi's appeals are exhausted, the next logical step is to move up the chain-of-command and, thus, prosecute Khadafi himself.

CROSS REFERENCES
Capital Punishment

TOBACCO

Allegheny General Hospital v. Philip Morris, Inc.

During the late 1990s, many private and public entities sued U.S. tobacco companies for the reimbursement of costs they absorbed in treating individuals with tobacco-related illnesses. The tobacco companies have aggressively defended themselves and have had success in preventing non-government entities from fully asserting their claims. This was demonstrated in *Allegheny General Hospital v. Philip Morris, Inc.*, 228 F3d 429 (3rd Cir.2000), where a federal APPELLATE COURT ruled that a group of Pennsylvania hospitals did not have legal STANDING to bring claims against the tobacco companies under federal ANTITRUST and racketeering laws as well as under state COMMON LAW claims such as fraudulent MISREPRESENTATION and civil CONSPIRACY. The court found that the hospitals were not quasi-governmental entities and further ruled that the alleged DAMAGES were too speculative and the alleged injuries too remote from the tobacco companies' alleged wrongdoing.

The sixteen hospitals that sued the tobacco companies were required, as charitable non-profit corporations, to provide medical services to indigent people. This requirement caused financial problems because the state of Pennsylvania only reimbursed the hospitals for a portion of these costs. Thus, the hospitals sought payment from the tobacco companies for the financial shortfall sustained over forty years. The hospitals claimed that the tobacco companies had participated in a conspiracy to conceal the health risks associated with tobacco use, out of fear that such information would decrease sales. The hospitals specifically claimed that the companies had suppressed scientific research and had falsely claimed that the use of tobacco was safe

and even beneficial to the user's health. This behavior led millions of people to consume tobacco and to become seriously ill from its consumption. For indigent patients suffering from tobacco-related diseases—including various cancers and heart or lung problems—this meant that the hospitals had been forced to diagnose and treat them with hospital monies. Though the lawsuit did not seek RELIEF for these individual tobacco users, it did seek millions of dollars for reimbursement of the hospital expenses.

The hospitals employed two theories of injury. The indirect theory alleged that the tobacco companies used deception to cause nonpaying patients to smoke, inducing significant tobacco-related diseases. The direct theory alleged that the companies conspired to conceal information about the risks of tobacco and to prevent the development of safer cigarettes. These actions hampered the hospitals' efforts to reduce tobacco consumption among nonpaying patients. The hospitals sought to use federal antitrust laws, the RACKETEER INFLUENCED AND CORRUPT ORGANIZATIONS ACT (RICO), and various state common law claims such as fraudulent misrepresentation, breach of special duty, public nuisance, and civil conspiracy.

The tobacco companies asked the federal DISTRICT COURT to dismiss all the claims, arguing that the hospitals did not have legal standing to use the federal laws and had no BASIS to assert the state law claims. The district court agreed and dismissed the case. The Court of Appeals for the Third Circuit upheld the decision in all respects. Judge Julio M. Fuentes, writing for the appeals court, noted that this was a case of FIRST IMPRESSION in terms of whether hospitals with a legal duty to treat indigent persons suffering from tobacco-related diseases had standing to assert antitrust and RICO claims against tobacco companies. The hospitals needed to show they had such standing or their claims had to be dismissed.

The hospitals argued that they had standing to assert a violation of state laws, arguing that though they were private entities, the state's requirement that they serve poor patients, as well as other state laws and regulations, had delegated to the hospitals the traditionally *public* function of providing health care to those without means. Therefore, the hospitals claimed they were "quasi-governmental" units, which gave them the right to sue the tobacco companies as if they were a part of state government. Judge Fuentes rejected this argument, finding that no state law authorized them to sue and that they could not claim quasi-governmental standing.

The hospitals attempted to gain standing under the federal antitrust and RICO laws by demonstrating that the tobacco companies' alleged conduct was the PROXIMATE CAUSE of their injuries. Judge Fuentes concluded, however, that the hospitals' injuries were remote from the alleged conspiracy and that the alleged damages were "highly speculative." Therefore, the hospitals could not sue under the federal antitrust and RICO laws. Judge Fuentes dismissed the remaining state law claims on a variety of reasons, but all were grounded on the conclusions that the alleged injuries were too remote and indirect.

Engle et al. v. R.J. Reynolds et al.

On July 14, 2000, a six-person jury awarded Florida's smokers a record $145 billion PUNITIVE DAMAGES award in the first CLASS ACTION lawsuit against tobacco companies to go to trial. Under many state statutes, punitive damages may be awarded in addition to COMPENSATORY DAMAGES, if there is a finding of intentional misconduct or intentional/fraudulent misrepresentation. This verdict came on the heels of the same jury's earlier $12.7 million verdict for compensatory damages the preceding April and one year after the tobacco companies were found guilty of making a defective product. The lawsuit is far from over, however.

The lawsuit was filed in 1994 in Miami-Dade County Circuit Court. It was certified a class-action with three sick smokers representing 300,000 to 700,000 Florida smokers or their heirs. The plaintiffs' legal team was headed by Stanley and Susan Rosenblatt, whose children went to lead plaintiff, pediatrician Howard Engle. The lawsuit named as defendants: Philip Morris, R.J. Reynolds Tobacco Co., Brown & Williamson Tobacco Corp., Lorillard Tobacco Co., Liggett Group, Inc., the Council for Tobacco Research, and the Tobacco Institute. Presiding over the suit was Circuit Judge Robert Kaye, who, interestingly, is a member of the class in this suit.

During the trial, the plaintiffs claimed that the tobacco companies had intentionally misled the public regarding the danger of smoking, hid the results of research they had conducted, produced advertisements aimed at those under the legal smoking age, and had ceased research on producing cigarettes that were safer. The tobacco companies countered that no positive scientific link between smoking and illnesses existed, that risks associated with smoking were common knowledge, and that they had changed their business practices, including curtailing much of their advertising and creating youth anti-smoking programs.

The jury agreed with the plaintiffs. Jurors indicated that they did not believe the defense as presented by the defendants' lawyers and believed the companies to be "arrogant." In July 1999, the defendants were found guilty of "engag[ing] in extreme and outrageous conduct . . . with the intent to inflict severe emotional distress." The following April, the jury handed down a compensatory judgment of $12.7 million. In July 2000, the jury issued a record-setting punitive award of $145 billion against the tobacco companies, lower than the almost $200 billion sought by the plaintiffs. These awards came on top of a $246 billion settlement reached between tobacco companies and almost forty states during the previous year to cover treatment of smoking-related illnesses. The settlement prevented the states from suing the tobacco companies, but individuals were not prevented from doing so. Judge Kaye upheld the award in November 2000. The next phase of the trial is hearing the claims of individual members of the class to ascertain equitable distribution of the judgment amount.

The next phase of the lawsuit depends, however, on the outcome of any appeal filed by the tobacco companies. Many experts believe that the award may be decreased on appeal. Of the five awards handed down by juries against the tobacco industry, three have been overturned and two are currently being appealed. The question has been raised as to whether the

Jurors of a class-action lawsuit against the tobacco industry listen to the judge as they learn about the second phase of the trial at the Miami-Dade County (Fla.) Courthouse.

lawsuit should have been certified a class-action. The tobacco companies will argue that a "one size fits all" class-action cannot accurately take into account differences associated with each person's situation. Also, Florida law prevents punitive awards that would bankrupt a company, which the tobacco companies claim would happen to them if the verdict remained.

Critics to the findings in the current Florida suit believe that individuals should have some responsibility for their actions. In particular, the victims should have known that using tobacco products can damage their health. Yet they used the tobacco products anyway. These critics believe that enough information about the dangers of tobacco use has been provided to the public over the years so that smokers are at least partially to blame for their tobacco-related illnesses. This theory is expected to be closely scrutinized by the APPELLATE COURT. The defendant companies can provide evidence that they have in fact made the public more aware of the dangers of tobacco and have taken steps to minimize advertising the product. In addition, the tobacco companies contend that they have made special efforts to reduce the desire of children to smoke, as required by the Tobacco Pilot Project. The defendant companies are expected to present a case indicating that they have done their fair share in the effort to prevent tobacco induced illnesses, by complying with those requirements that are meant to raise public awareness of the problem. In essence the tobacco industry will be claiming that they are being misjudged.

U.S. Government Sues Tobacco Companies

After a mixed ruling in September 2000, the U.S. JUSTICE DEPARTMENT proceeded with controversial litigation against the tobacco industry, *United States v. Philip Morris, et al.*, Civil Action No. 99–2496 (GK). The federal civil lawsuit seeks billions in DAMAGES from eleven defendants. Filed in 1999 at the behest of the Clinton administration, the suit accuses major tobacco companies and trade groups of CONSPIRACY and fraud in an attempt to shift the burden of health care costs from tobacco-related illnesses onto U.S. taxpayers. Decrying the lawsuit as political mischief, the defendants asked a federal court for a dismissal. On September 28, a federal judge dismissed two counts but permitted a third and broader count to proceed when the case comes to trial in 2003. Its future, however, remained uncertain as well as politically-charged.

The federal lawsuit arose in the wake of staggering legal defeats for the tobacco industry. After almost effortlessly fending off legal troubles for decades, the industry began suffering setbacks in the 1980s that culminated, a decade later, in its agreement to settle $246 billion in lawsuits with state ATTORNEYS GENERAL. Because the 1998 settlement did not preclude future federal litigation, anti-tobacco forces saw possibilities to press the industry further. That same year, the administration of President BILL CLINTON announced strong support for litigation to recover federal health care expenditures due to smoking.

Ambitiously, the Justice Department responded with a massive lawsuit. In general, the suit asserted that smoking caused cancer and other serious illnesses. These illnesses cost the federal government $25 billion annually in health care claims. It sought to recover more than four decades' worth of expenses, plus damages.

The lawsuit advanced three distinct theories of LIABILITY. First, the suit asserted that the federal government was entitled to use the Medical Care Recovery Act (MCRA) of 1962 to recover health care costs for treating individuals injured by tobacco industry misconduct. Specifically, it sought reimbursement for MEDICARE and Federal Employees Health Benefit Act (FEHBA) expenditures. Second, the suit contended that the federal government was entitled to recover Medicare costs for tobacco-related illnesses paid for by private insurers. Third, the lawsuit invoked the RACKETEER INFLUENCED AND CORRUPT ORGANIZATIONS ACT (RICO), a law originally intended to fight organized crime. This claim accused the tobacco industry of conspiracy to fraudulently hide knowledge about the damaging effects of cigarettes—a four-decade long pattern of activities ranging from making false and deceptive statements to concealing and destroying documents. In this way, said the suit, the industry shielded itself from liability and shifted health-care costs to third parties, including the U.S. government. The suit sought to use RICO's provision for treble damages while also asking for a court order forbidding the industry from making false product claims in the future.

Publicly, the tobacco industry denounced the lawsuit as a political maneuver. Noting that Congress had rejected strong anti-smoking legislation in 1998, the industry accused President Clinton of resorting to the courts to achieve the goals his administration failed to achieve through the legislature. In court filings seeking to have the suit dismissed, the defendants challenged the health care reimbursement claims as having no BASIS in law. In response to the RICO claims, they argued that the government failed to demonstrate that the unlawful activity would continue into the future. Moreover, they asserted, the 1998 settlement with the states assured that the opposite was true.

On September 28, 2000, Judge Gladys Kessler of the U.S. District Court for the District of Columbia issued a mixed ruling on the tobacco industry's motion to dismiss. Favorably for the tobacco industry, Judge Kessler threw out the lawsuit's health care reimbursement claims. She ruled that Congress never intended for the MCRA to be used to recover Medicare or FEHBA costs. Indeed, she opined, the law had been designed to allow the government to recover medical expenses from third parties only for its own employees. Judge Kessler also dismissed the lawsuit's claim for reimbursement of Medicare expenses by private insurers, again citing Congressional intent. The judge allowed the RICO claims to go forward, however. At this stage in the litigation, the Justice Department had met the law's minimum requirements: it adequately demonstrated that the defendants formed an enterprise that engaged in a pattern of racketeering activity. "[W]hether the government can prove it remains to be seen," the judge wrote in her memorandum opinion.

Following the ruling, both sides predictably claimed victory. One of the plaintiffs, Philip Morris, called the ruling "a big step in the right direction." The Justice Department vowed to fight on, and in March 2001, amended its lawsuit seeking to resurrect the health benefits claims dismissed by Judge Kessler. A trial date was scheduled for July 15, 2003, but whether the suit would even come to trial was uncertain. Twice in 2000, Republican congressional foes had blocked funding for the litigation, which the Clinton administration only barely restored by diverting funding from various federal departments. The election of President GEORGE W. BUSH, a critic of the litigation, raised conservative hopes that the suit would be dropped or settled in a manner favorable to the tobacco industry. By spring 2001, new Attorney General JOHN ASHCROFT—another critic of the suit and one with authority to decide if it would continue—was said to be reviewing it.

CROSS REFERENCES
Racketeer Influenced and Corrupt Organizations Act; Standing

TRADEMARKS

Distinctive symbols of authenticity through which the products of particular manufacturers or the salable commodities of particular merchants can be distinguished from those of others.

Kellogg Company v. Exxon Corporation

Corporations zealously protect the marks of their corporate identity through the enforcement of federal trademark laws. Because advertising and marketing rely on corporate logos and images, it is not unusual for a large corporation to allege trademark infringement against smaller, lesser known companies. However, such was not the case when two major U.S. corporations sparred over the use of cartoon tigers in *Kellogg Company v. Exxon Corporation*, 209 F.3d 562 (6th Cir. 2000). Kellogg alleged that Exxon had infringed on Kellogg's "Tony the Tiger" trademark when it used a cartoon tiger first to sell petroleum products and later to promote its convenience food stores. The appeals court rejected a lower court decision that held that Kellogg had waited too long, over 30 years, to allege infringement.

Kellogg first introduced Tony the Tiger in 1952 to promote a sugared cereal called "Kellogg's Frosted Flakes." Kellogg registered the cartoon tiger with the U.S. PATENT AND TRADEMARK OFFICE and has maintained the tiger as an integral part of its cereal product marketing and advertising. In 1959 Exxon first introduced a cartoon tiger to promote its gasoline. It registered its "Whimsical Tiger" in 1965 with the trademark office and embarked on a popular advertising campaign based on the slogan, "Put a Tiger in Your Tank." Kellogg did not object to Exxon's tiger during this period. After officially changing the corporate name from Standard Oil Company to Exxon along with a $100 million ad campaign featuring the slogan "Energy for a Strong America" along with the tiger, Exxon reduced its use of the tiger through the 1970s and into the 1980s. By the mid-1980s Exxon officials had ordered the tiger logo removed from all its gas stations. However, in the early 1990s Exxon began to use the tiger inside its redesigned convenience stores to promote food products. These stores eventually became labeled "Tiger Marts."

Kellogg became aware of Exxon's new commitment to the cartoon tiger and asked for examples of its use. Exxon provided 14 pieces of promotional material used in the United States, but none of the items disclosed Exxon's use of its tiger to promote food and beverage items or its

Tiger Mart stores. In 1996 Kellogg filed a trade-mark infringement against Exxon in federal DIS-TRICT COURT, *Kellogg Co. v. Exxon Corp.*, 50 U.S.P.Q.2d 1499 (W.D.Tenn. Aug 31, 1998), asking the court to prohibit Exxon from using its cartoon tiger in connection with the sale of food items. Exxon asked the court for a SUMMARY JUDGMENT to dismiss the claims, and this re-quest was granted because the district found that Kellogg had waited too long to allege infringe-ment.

The U.S. Court of Appeals for the Sixth Circuit reversed this decision. Judge Alice M. Batchelder, writing for the three-judge panel, concluded that the lower court had misapplied basic principles of trademark law. The court looked at three central issues: ACQUIESCENCE, progressive encroachment, and ABANDON-MENT. Exxon had raised the defense of acquies-cence, which, in the judge's opinion, needed "finding of conduct on the plaintiff's part that amounted to an assurance to the defendant, ex-press or implied, that plaintiff would not assert his trademark rights against the defendant." In essence, Exxon argued that Kellogg had known about the tiger for 30 years and had done noth-ing to stop its use. Therefore, it would be unfair to require Exxon to stop using it now.

Judge Batchelder examined Kellogg's pro-gressive encroachment theory as part of her ac-quiescence analysis. Progressive encroachment applies in cases where the defendant has infringed the plaintiff's trademark, but the plaintiff does not bring a claim right away be-cause it has not reached a level to justify litiga-tion. Central to progressive encroachment is whether there is the "likelihood of confusion" between the two marks as the defendant moves to compete with the plaintiff in certain markets.

In the present case Judge Batchelder con-cluded that the case should not have been dis-missed based on acquiescence. Though Kellogg waited for more than 30 years to raise an in-fringement claim, the length of time was not a DISPOSITIVE FACT, that is, a fact that completely settles the matter on its own. The key factor was Exxon's move from selling gasoline to selling food items at its revamped gas and convenience stores. Kellogg had not been obligated to bring an action when Exxon was only selling gasoline with the tiger, as there would have been no likelihood of confusion between the products. Once Exxon began marketing food items, how-ever, Judge Batchelder agreed that Kellogg had "a duty to defend its trademark." It was from

this "point that any delay must be measured" for determining acquiescence.

Judge Batchelder also found that a factual dispute existed over when Kellogg was put on notice about the use of the tiger in promoting food items. When such a factual dispute exists, it is inappropriate for a district court to dismiss an action. In addition, Kellogg had raised a valid claim that Exxon had abandoned the cartoon tiger trademark in the 1970s and 1980s. There-fore, the court reversed the trial court and remanded the case for trial. In 2000 the U.S. Supreme Court denied CERTIORARI in *Exxon Mobil Corp. v. Kellogg Co.*, 121 S.Ct. 340, 148 L.Ed.2d 273 (U.S. Oct 16, 2000).

Tony the Tiger with (*left-right*) Richard Grasso, New York Stock Exchange Chairman, Carlos M. Gutierrez of Kellogg, and Sam K. Reed of Keebler Foods.

Smirnov Vodka v. Smirnoff Vodka

The famous Smirnoff brand of vodka was founded in Russia during the 1860s by Pyotr Smirnov. All private property was confiscated following the Russian Revolution, and the fam-ily distillery was nationalized by the Soviet gov-ernment in 1917, eventually being turned into a state garage. Meanwhile, family members fled the country for Italy and France.

Vladimir Smirnov, one of Pyotr's three sons, emigrated from the Soviet Union in the early 1920s, changed the spelling of his surname to Smirnoff, and started production of the fam-ily vodka in Poland. He later set up production facilities in Paris and New York. Vladimir, desti-tute, later sold the Smirnoff name and trade-mark to Heublein Inc. in the mid-1930s. The Smirnoff brand of vodka failed to gain apprecia-bly in the American market until the 1950s, when martinis became popular and Smirnoff eventually became the world's best-selling vodka. Heublein, now known as UDV North America, is a Connecticut-based company held by the British giant Diageo, PLC, which was formed in 1997. UDV also owns such famous brands as Bacardi, Bailey's Irish Cream, Gordon's, and Johnny Walker. Its parent company, Diageo, is the world's largest drinks company.

Following the collapse of the Soviet Union, relatives and heirs of Pyotr, in particular his two great-great-grandsons, Boris and Andrei, reestablished the family distillery under the name of "Trade House of Descendants of Peter Smirnov, Official Purveyor to the Imperial Court."

The legal battle over rights to the Smirnoff name began in 1995 when the Russian company challenged UDV/Diageo's rights to it. In essence, Smirnov became a best-selling vodka in Russia and a competitor of Smirnoff vodka, imported from the United States. UDV had been selling its vodka in Russia for at least the previous ten years. Smirnov sued in U.S. District Court for the District of Delaware to regain use of the Smirnov name and sell their vodka in America, but in 1999, the district judge dismissed its case. Delaware was the court of jurisdiction because Diageo is incorporated in that state.

In 2000, Smirnov, through counsel, asked the Third Circuit Court of Appeals to reverse the dismissal. Boris Smirnov, on the plaintiffs' side, charged that Vladimir Smirnov, their uncle, was the rogue "black sheep" of the family and did not have the right to sell the family name. Smirnov asked for the right to market its Smirnov vodka in the United States.

Oral arguments in *Joint Stock Society v. UDV North America, Inc.*, No. 99–5433, were heard in the summer of 2000, but one member of the three-judge appellate panel was RECUSED for undisclosed reasons. Oral arguments were heard before a reconvened panel in late September 2000. At the hearing, Chief Justice Edward R. Becker challenged Smirnov's counsel in U.S. trademark law, noting that trademark rights are lost if the party fails to assert rights or remain associated with a product. In this case, there was no association for at least seventy years. Smirnov argued that in the former Soviet Union, civil law requires documents, and not testimony, to establish such property rights. The family had tried repeatedly over the years to obtain documents from the Russian government to prove their ownership, but it was not until the collapse of the Soviet government that third-generation family members were able to do so. Notwithstanding, the chief justice also challenged UDV

attorneys, noting that it appeared that UDV (Heublein, Inc.) had purchased the Smirnoff name from "nothing but a rogue."

Meanwhile, Boris Smirnov, founder and owner of half the company stock in The Trade House of the Descendants of Peter Smirnov, had a falling out with his cousin Andrei, who allegedly sold *his* 50 percent interest to an offshore concern, the Alfa Group. In September 2000 Alfa began marketing a fourth Smirnov vodka outside Moscow. In November, police raided Boris's Trading House offices to enforce a local court order recognizing Alfa-Eko as the authorized distillery, after Alfa filed suit. Boris charged that Alfa's intention was to "sell [out] to the Americans," referring to talks between Alfa and UDV.

In March 2001 UDV signed a five-year contract not with Alfa, but with the LIVIZ distillery in Moscow, by which LIVIZ will be licensed by UDV to produce Smirnoff vodka, with the stated intent of enhancing UDV's strategic position in the region. UDV had been working with LIVIZ in Russia since 1997. Boris, in turn, threatened to turn over his interest to the Russian state to ensure that the brand and the family's secret formula and traditions, remained in Russia.

The U.S. case before the Third Circuit had not been decided as of Spring 2001. In October 2000, however, the U.S. Supreme Court denied review of a similar trademark case involving domestic and foreign adversaries, in *Havana Club Holdings v. Bacardi*, No. 99–1957. Despite the similarities in the two cases, the latter relied on Section 211 of the Omnibus Appropriations Bill of 1998, which blocks U.S. courts from recognizing certain trademarks of Cuban origin, which clearly is not an issue in the *Smirnoff* case.

Wendt v. Host International, Inc.

In today's mass entertainment industry, participants in successful television programs, movies, and recording projects zealously guard their name and celebrity against unapproved commercial exploitation. Federal trademark law offers some protection, and the state of California has enacted legislation that gives all individuals the "right of publicity," which confers upon an individual the right to recover DAMAGES when another individual or company uses his or her name, voice, signature, photograph, or likeness for purposes of advertising or selling without the person's CONSENT. For example, recording artists such as Bette Midler and Tom Waits have recovered damages from companies

Norm (left; George Wendt) and Cliff (John Ratzenberger) sit at their usual bar stools facing Sam (Ted Danson) and Diane (Shelly Long) from the television sitcom *Cheers*.

that used singers to impersonate their unique vocal styles in television commercials.

Claims for violations of the right of publicity and trademark law were asserted by actors George Wendt and John Ratzenberger, who played the characters Norm and Cliff in the popular television show *Cheers*. In the early 1990s, Host International secured permission from Paramount Pictures Corporation, the COPYRIGHT holder of the *Cheers* program, to build a number of airport bars called Cheers. In these drinking establishments, which resembled the television program's main set, Host placed two animatronic robotic figures (robots) that Wendt and Ratzenberger claimed were based upon their likenesses. Because they had not consented to the production and placement of these robots, the actors sought damages. Host and Paramount moved the court for SUMMARY JUDGMENT. In a summary judgment proceeding, which occurs very early in the CIVIL PROCEDURE, the defendant alleges that there are no genuine issues of MATERIAL fact for a jury to decide and that the court should apply the law and dismiss the case. In this case, the federal DISTRICT COURT agreed with the defendants and granted the motion for summary judgment. Wendt and Ratzenberger successfully appealed the decision to the Court of Appeals for the Ninth Circuit in 1995, which found that there were disputed material facts about whether the robots appropriated Wendt's and Ratzenberger's likenesses. The APPELLATE COURT spe-

cifically ruled that the mere "comparison of photographs" of the actors and the robots was not sufficient.

When the trial court again took up the matter it granted Host and Paramount's new summary judgment motion. This time the judge had the robots brought to court for inspection. The court concluded that it could not find any resemblance beyond that one of the robots, like one of the plaintiffs, weighed more than the other. In addition, the court found no similarities in facial features. Wendt and Ratzenberger again appealed.

In *Wendt v. Host International, Inc.*, 125 F.3d 806 (9th Cir.1997), the appeals court again overturned the district court's summary judgment decision. Judge Betty B. Fletcher, writing for the court, first examined the application of California's STATUTORY right of publicity. Judge Fletcher concluded, "The degree to which these robots resembled, caricatured, or bore an impressionistic resemblance to Wendt and Ratzenberger" clearly supported their claim under the state law. Turning to the evidence before the court, Fletcher found that after the appeals courts' inspection of the robots "[m]aterial facts existed that might have caused a reasonable jury to find them sufficiently 'like'" the plaintiffs to violate the right of publicity law.

Judge Fletcher noted that California also has a "common law right of publicity" (§ 3344) that is similar to the statutory right. Under the

COMMON LAW right it is unlawful to appropriate a name or likeness for the defendant's commercial advantage without the person's consent. Host and Paramount argued that the robots appropriated only the identities of the characters Norm and Cliff, to which Paramount owns the copyrights, and not the identities of Wendt and Ratzenberger. In the defendants' view, the actors merely portrayed those characters on television and retained no licensing rights to them. Wendt and Ratzenberger conceded that they did not retain any rights to the characters of Norm and Cliff. Instead, they "argue[d] that the robotic figures, named 'Bob' and 'Hank', [were] not related to Paramount's copyright of the creative elements of the characters Norm and Cliff. They argue[d] that it was the physical likeness to Wendt and Ratzenberger, not Paramount's characters, that ha[d] commercial value to Host."

Judge Fletcher agreed with the plaintiffs, reasoning that "an actor or actress does not lose the right to control the commercial exploitation of his or her likeness by portraying a fictional character." Because the actors had raised material facts as to whether the robots were based on their likeness, summary judgment was inappropriate. Wendt and Ratzenberger had the right to present their case to a jury to determine the facts.

As to federal trademark law issues, Judge Fletcher agreed with the plaintiffs that the federal Lanham Act of 1946 "prohibits ... any symbol or device which is likely to deceive consumers" as "to the association, sponsorship, or approval of goods or services by another person" (§ 43(a), 15 U.S.C.A. § 1125(a). In this case, the appeals court found that a reasonable jury might conclude that Host's alleged conduct violated the Lanham Act by creating the likelihood of consumer confusion over whether Wendt and Ratzenberger approved of the Cheers bars or were otherwise associated with it. Therefore, the appeals court REMANDED the case to the district court for trial.

CROSS REFERENCES
Copyright; Summary Judgment

TRESPASS

An unlawful intrusion that interferes with one's person or property.

Missouri Sues Benetton for Death Row Ads

The Benetton Group, creator and marketer of the "United Colors of Benetton" line of trendy clothing, has long been known for its controversial advertising. By the 1990s, its attention-hoarding advertising campaign had gone from multicultural, multi-ethnic models to more shocking ads, such as a nun kissing a priest or the bloody uniform of a Bosnian soldier. While Benetton's advertising creative director, Oliviero Toscani, once bragged, "There's no such thing as going too far," in truth, the connection between the ads and the product advertised was becoming increasingly nebulous. In 1995 German retailers sued Benetton—headquartered in Treviso, Italy—charging that Benetton's ads sabotaged the retailer's efforts to sell Benetton merchandise. In France, another court ruled that the company had exploited human suffering in its photograph advertising campaign in which AIDS patients had "HIV Positive" stamped on buttocks and other body parts. Benetton was ordered to pay DAMAGES to French HIV victims.

The company, controlled by the Benetton family, had managed a small presence in the United States, operating between 150 and 200 struggling stores nationwide. Another 400 Benetton outlets had already gone out of business. After a $100 million pending deal with Sears, Roebuck & Company to boost its U.S. market with a private-label line, Benetton launched a new advertising campaign that may have pushed it over the edge in the States: using death row inmates as models.

Some of the convicts featured in its ads were: Jeremy Sheets, who had raped and murdered a 17-year-old honors student in Nebraska; Jerome Mallett, who had beaten a Missouri state trooper and shot him in the head; and Cesar Francesco Barone, who had sexually assaulted and murdered three women in Oregon. At least one of them, Jerome Mallett, was paid $1,000 for working as a model for Benetton. On each photo-ad appearing in publications and on billboards was the company's trademark symbol, a small green triangle that read, "The United Colors of Benetton." The ad campaign, "We, On Death Row," ran from January to April 2000 and appeared in such publications as *Vanity Fair*, *Rolling Stone*, and *Talk* magazines.

At the commencement of the campaign, *AP Worldstream* ran a news piece describing the campaign, the crimes committed by the models appearing in the ads, and comments from crime

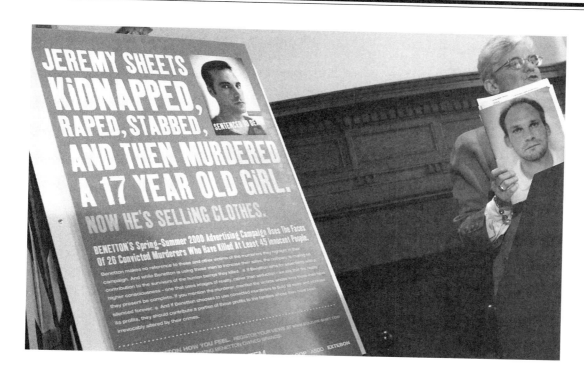

Philly's D.A.,
Lynne Abraham
displays
Benetton's ads
showcasing a
convicted
murderer during a
press conference
to announce a
boycott of the
campaign.

victims and survivors. The article noted that Italians in general were longtime opponents of the death penalty and had engaged in other crusades at home and abroad. The article stated they could not reach anyone at Benetton headquarters to comment on the ads for their article.

By February 9, 2000, the State of Missouri, through its ATTORNEY GENERAL, Jay Nixon, had filed suit against Benetton, alleging that its agents had lied to officials at the state's Department of Corrections to gain access to inmates at Missouri's Potosi prison center. Within days of filing, protesters marched in front of a Sears store in Texas, decrying the glamorization of death row inmates. In mid-February, Sears canceled its contract with Benetton. In early April, Benetton issued a statement announcing the severance of its 18-year professional relationship with advertising creator and director Toscani. No reason for the break-up was given in the statement.

Missouri's multi-million dollar civil suit named the Benetton company; Toscani, who photographed the campaign; Ken Shulman, a free-lance copywriter who worked on the text that accompanied each photographic ad; and Thomas "Speedy" Rice, director of international relations for the National Association of Criminal Defense Lawyers (NACDL). The suit alleged that Rice, who also teaches law at Gonzaga University in Spokane, Washington, sent letters to several prisons to request access for Shulman and

Toscani. He presented the purpose as a journalistic "photo essay," and did not disclose any commercial purpose. Moreover, the suit alleged that Shulman represented himself to Missouri officials as working for *Newsweek*, and the suit further charged that the three men represented to Department of Corrections officials that they were journalists working on a project for NACDL. Documents in court showed that Shulman signed in as a representative of Benetton when he arrived at Potosi, however.

Under Missouri and COMMON LAW, even though CONSENT to enter upon, or gain access to, the property of another may have been granted, a cause of action for trespass will lie if such consent was procured through false pretenses or other illegal means. In order to prove fraudulent MISREPRESENTATION, Missouri officials must show that the defendants knowingly made false or misleading statements to gain a particular benefit and that Missouri officials relied on these false statements in granting permission. According to Missouri's assistant attorney general, Chuck Hatfield, "A key issue in this case will be whether the defendants can convince the court that this campaign was not part of an advertising strategy, that it was indeed journalism." The trial date for the case was set for October 2001. The state of North Carolina was also looking into the legality of Benetton's advertising campaign in its state, but as of Spring 2001, no other state had yet pursued vigorous legal action.

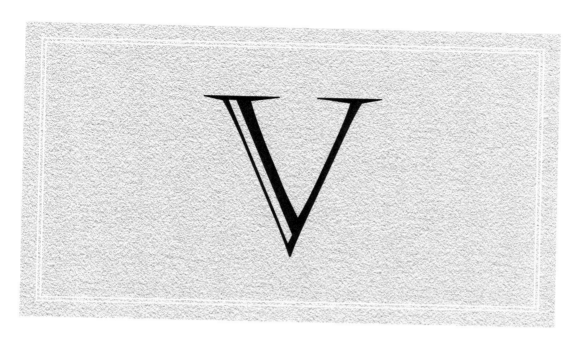

VENTO, BRUCE F.

Congressman Bruce F. Vento, a liberal Democrat and a leading advocate for environmental preservation, homeless persons, and Hmong and Laotian veterans who fought with U.S. forces during the VIETNAM WAR, died at the age of 60 on October 10, 2000. Vento was diagnosed with a rare form of cancer, malignant Mesothelioma, which he contracted by breathing in asbestos fibers when he worked for ten years as a state-paid laborer in St. Paul, Minnesota.

Vento was born October 7, 1940, in St. Paul, Minnesota, and grew up under the influence of his politically active parents and German and Italian immigrant grandparents. He received a B.S. degree with honors from Wisconsin State University and an M.S. degree from the University of Minnesota. He went on to teach science and social studies in junior high school for ten years. At the age of 30, Vento was elected to the Minnesota House of Representatives and served for three consecutive terms, eventually becoming the assistant majority leader. In 1976 the Fourth Congressional District elected him to serve in the U.S. House of Representatives and continued to re-elect him for twelve more terms, until his death in 2000.

When Vento entered Congress, Democratic President JIMMY CARTER was in office and the Democrats controlled the House. Vento was able to make a difference from the very beginning. During his early years, he focused on such issues as Social Security, MEDICARE, and financial and banking reform. He chaired the Resolution Trust Corporation, which investigated the

SAVINGS AND LOAN crisis during the 1980s. He also served on the Banking and Financial Services Committee where he supported the ability of banks to merge and branch on a national basis. During the modernization of the banking industry, he called for consumer PRIVACY. Finally, he was a strong advocate of the 1999 Graham-Leach-Bliley Act, which brought the banking, insurance, and SECURITIES industries together.

Bruce F. Vento

Vento proved to be a strong advocate for less fortunate persons when he worked to help preserve the Federal Housing Authority. He was also the main sponsor of the Stuart B. McKinney Homeless Assistance Act, which provided for $1.3 billion to create outreach programs for homeless persons, including emergency shelter and transitional housing. He later became a ranking member of the Housing and Community Opportunity subcommittee.

Vento is best known, however, for his efforts to protect the environment, his true passion. For ten years, Vento served as chairman of the House subcommittee on Parks and Public Lands whose efforts preserved and expanded millions of acres of trails, scenic rivers, wilderness, and national park land, including the creation of Great Basin National Park in Nevada and the Mississippi National River and Recreation Area. He is also greatly responsible for the establishment and preservation of the Boundary Waters Canoe Area Wilderness, a 1.1 million acre parkland along the Minnesota-Canada border where logging, mining, and snowmobiling are prohibited. During his leadership, over 300 environmental bills were steered into law. Vento also went to battle for the protection of the

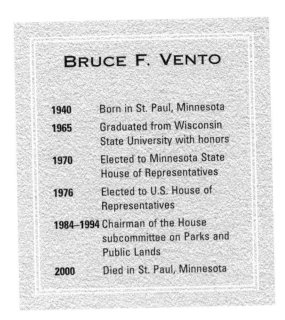

BRUCE F. VENTO

1940	Born in St. Paul, Minnesota
1965	Graduated from Wisconsin State University with honors
1970	Elected to Minnesota State House of Representatives
1976	Elected to U.S. House of Representatives
1984–1994	Chairman of the House subcommittee on Parks and Public Lands
2000	Died in St. Paul, Minnesota

redwood forests and tropical rainforests and the safeguard of California's desert from recreational off-road vehicles, mining interests, and military operations.

In 1994 Vento received the Ansel Adams Conservation Award from the Wilderness Society for his efforts to protect the Arctic National Wildlife Refuge from oil drilling. Vento also worked to prohibit commercial and recreational trapping on national wildlife refuges and to protect the endangered species of the wilderness. The lifelong resident of Minnesota is being recognized for his environmental achievements with the Bruce Vento Trail, a paved bicycle and pedestrian path, which will connect downtown St. Paul and the Mississippi river with the eastern historic neighborhoods and the northern suburban communities of that city. Additionally, thirty trees will be planted in honor of his thirty years of service, first with the Minnesota state legislature and then as a Congressman. As former Vice President AL GORE stated, "His conservation legacy will endure for many generations to come."

During the last several years of his service, Vento worked hard to reverse U.S. refugee policy. He hoped that thousands of Laotian and Hmong veterans who fought with U.S. forces during the Vietnam War and their families could leave refugee camps in Thailand and immigrate to the United States. He authored the Hmong Veterans Naturalization Act of 2000, which assists the Hmong and Laotian veterans in becoming U.S. citizens by allowing them to take the citizenship test with the help of a trans-

lator. Congress approved the measure, and then-President BILL CLINTON signed the act into effect in May 2000.

As a former teacher, Vento worked to establish a scholarship fund for training future high school science teachers. He also helped create the Urban Recreation and At-Risk Youth Act, which expanded park and recreational activities for youth in high crime urban areas. The elementary school he attended was renamed, Bruce F. Vento Elementary in recognition of his deeds while in office.

Vento discovered that he had cancer just six months before his death. At that time he announced that he would not seek re-election. He described his service best when he said, "I have been a member of Congress for the past 24 years, dedicated to making federal government work for the people, to do for our community and state and, yes, even internationally—that which we cannot do for ourselves. The federal government can and should make a difference."

VOTING

Puerto Ricans Lose Bid to Vote in Presidential Elections

In April 2000, a group of Puerto Ricans filed a federal lawsuit to force the United States to allow Puerto Ricans to vote in presidential elections, a privilege they have been denied since attaining U.S. citizenship in 1917. In August 2000, Federal District Judge Jaime Pieras, Jr., ordered Puerto Rico to develop a system to allow Puerto Ricans to vote and to appoint ELECTORS for selecting the president under Article II of the Constitution, *Igartua de la Rosa v. United States*, 113 F.Supp.2d 228 (D.Puerto Rico Aug 29, 2000). Less than one month before the November 2000 election, the First Circuit Court of Appeals, *Igartua de la Rosa v. United States*, 229 F.3d 80 (1st Cir.(Puerto Rico) Oct 13, 2000), reversed, saying that under prior case law interpreting the Constitution, only states can appoint electors to select the president. Puerto Rico, which is a territory and not a state, does not have that right according to the First Circuit.

The United States took Puerto Rico from Spain during the Spanish-American War of 1898. When General Nelson Miles arrived at Puerto Rico, he said "American forces came 'bearing the banner of freedom' and would bring to the Puerto Ricans 'the fostering arm of a nation of free people, whose greatest power is in justice and humanity to all those living within its fold'." At that time America promised to "bestow upon [the Puerto Ricans] the immunities and blessings of the liberal institutions of our Government . . . [and] the advantages and blessings of enlightened civilization."

The United States has struggled to make these lofty promises come to fruition. Although Puerto Ricans attained U.S. citizenship in 1917 and the power to run their own commonwealth government in 1940, Puerto Rico is still a territory of the United States. Puerto Ricans do not pay federal income taxes, but they are subject to other federal laws and have fought for the United States in every war beginning with World War I.

Although they fight for the United States, Puerto Ricans have not been allowed to vote for its president, the commander-in-chief of the very armed forces in which they have served. Article II of the Constitution says electors appointed by each State select the president. Congress receives and counts votes from this so-called ELECTORAL COLLEGE to determine who wins an election. Because the U.S. territories of Puerto Rico and Guam are not states, federal courts have held that residents of those territories may not vote for the president in general elections, *Igartua de la Rosa v. United States*, 32 F.3d 8 (1st Cir. 1994); *Guam v. United States*, 738 F.3d 1017 (9th Cir. 1984). The Supreme Court of the United States has declined to review this ruling.

In April 2000, eleven individuals filed another lawsuit challenging the system. They did not rely solely on the argument that Puerto Ricans should be allowed to vote for the president. Instead, they argued that as United States citizens, Puerto Ricans have the constitutional right to appoint electors to select the president under the Article II mechanism for doing so. They said that the ability to elect the president is a fundamental component of democracy, liberty, citizenship, and representative government.

In July 2000, the plaintiffs enjoyed an early victory when Judge Pieras denied a motion by the United States to dismiss the case. Judge Pieras said that the prior cases concerning voting did not apply because the plaintiffs sought not only the right to vote but also the right to appoint electors. Judge Pieras used strong words in his order:

The present political status of Puerto Rico has enslaved the United States cit-izens residing in Puerto Rico by preventing them from voting in Presidential and Congressional elections and therefore it is abhorrent to the most sacred of the basic safeguards contained in the Bill of Rights of the Constitution of the United States—freedom.

Judge Pieras also called the United States to task for using Puerto Ricans in wars while denying them the right to vote, saying, "It is . . . preposterous that the United States can fight for the freedom of others abroad and ignore the lack of liberty of citizens at home." Judge Pieras concluded, "The right to vote freely for the candidate of one's choice is the essence of a democratic society, and any restrictions on that right strike at the heart of representative government."

The following month, Judge Pieras ordered Puerto Rico to set up a mechanism for U.S. citizens residing in Puerto Rico to vote in presidential elections and to appoint electors, adding that the electoral votes must be counted in Congress. He said no constitutional amendment was necessary to do this. Relying on *Brown v. Board of Education*, 347 U.S. 483, 47 S. Ct. 686, 98 L. Ed. 873, the case in which the Supreme Court ended segregation in schools, Judge Pieras suggested that courts are allowed to disregard prior case law when necessary to end unconstitutional treatment of citizens.

On September 10, 2000, the legislature of Puerto Rico enacted and Governor Pedro Rossello signed Law No. 403 to put Judge Pieras' order into effect. Puerto Ricans were only two months away from casting their first votes for the president in a general election. Meanwhile, the United States appealed Judge Pieras' order to the First Circuit Court of Appeals.

On October 13, 2000, the First Circuit reversed Judge Pieras' order. Relying on its prior case of *Igartua de la Rosa* and the 9th Circuit's decision in *Guam*, the First Circuit said the plaintiffs had no grounds to argue that they have a constitutional right to vote in presidential elections. The First Circuit said it made no difference that the plaintiffs also sought the right to appoint electors to select the president under Article II. The First Circuit said that under the Constitution, only states have the privilege of appointing electors, and Puerto Rico is not a state. In a concurring opinion, Judge Juan Torruella said he only voted in favor of reversal because he felt bound by prior case law. Judge Torruella urged either the Congress or the U.S.

Supreme Court to change prior law to give Puerto Ricans the right to vote in presidential elections.

Despite the ruling, Puerto Rico planned to use Law No. 403 to allow Puerto Ricans to vote in the November 2000 presidential election. Although the votes would not be counted without Puerto Rico's representation in the Electoral College, many thought it would be a way to attract attention to the issue of its political enslavement. Unfortunately for Puerto Ricans interested in voting, the Supreme Court of Puerto Rico struck down Law No. 403, saying it would not be appropriate to use public funds to gather and tally votes that would not count in the presidential election.

For Puerto Rico and Guam, then, the struggle to attain voting rights continues. One way to accomplish this is to amend the Constitution. The Twenty-Third Amendment, for example, allows the District of Columbia to appoint electors even though it is not a state. Another option is to make Puerto Rico a state. Most Puerto Ricans oppose this, in large part because they would have to pay federal income taxes. Voter turnout, however, is generally 80% percent in Puerto Rico, and a large number of Puerto Ricans want to have a say in who becomes president of the United States of America. Gregorio Igartua de la Rosa, the lead plaintiff and attorney in the case before the First Circuit, said he is waiting for developments in other cases before continuing his legal bid to get the vote for Puerto Ricans.

CROSS REFERENCES
Constitution; Electoral College

WALD, PATRICIA MCGOWAN

In July 1999 UNITED NATIONS Secretary-General Kofi Annan appointed Judge Patricia M. Wald to serve on the International War Crimes Tribunal for Yugoslavia. Wald, who had served as a judge on the U.S. Court of Appeals for the District of Columbia for twenty years and as vice president of the American Law Institute for ten years, had the necessary background and experience to tackle the difficult task of determining the guilt or innocence of those accused of crimes committed during the war between Serbians and Croatians in the early 1990s.

Born Patricia McGowan on September 16, 1928, and raised in the manufacturing town of Torrington, Connecticut, Wald spent her summers working in the brass mills. Through this experience, she became involved in her first cause—the protection of working class people. Later, after graduating first in her class from Connecticut College for Women, she decided she could better help people if she obtained a law degree. She enrolled in Yale University's Law School. At a time when female law students were rare, she was among fewer than a dozen other women in her class.

After graduating from Yale in 1951, Wald accepted a clerkship with Judge Jerome N. Frank of the U.S. Court of Appeals for the Second Circuit. She was the first female clerk in the CIRCUIT COURT. In 1952 she married Robert Wald, a Navy reservist stationed in Norfolk, Virginia, and moved to Washington, D.C., to be closer to her new husband. Wald went to work as an associate attorney with the firm of Arnold, Fortas and Porter. She took leave of the firm in

1953, however, when she was eight-months pregnant. While they told her that she could return when she was ready, she chose to stay home to care for her child.

Ten years and four more children later, Wald returned to the practice of law. She quickly became involved in several research projects, including the Kerner Commission Report on the cause and prevention of violence, as well as the President's Commission on Crime in the District of Columbia. In 1963 Wald gave a presentation at the National Conference of Bail and Criminal Justice challenging the bail system of the time. She argued for additional factors to be considered in determining bail, apart from the mere ability of the accused to pay the amount set by the court. One factor Wald suggested was ties the accused had to the community. One year later, her ideas became a book, *Bail in the United States* (1964), and the bail system was reformed.

That same year, Wald became an attorney with the JUSTICE DEPARTMENT's Office of Criminal Justice, but soon thereafter she left to join the innovative Neighborhood Legal Services Program in Washington, D.C. This position exposed her for the first time to litigation, which she would later say was helpful in making her a more understanding judge. In 1972 she became an attorney for the Mental Health Law Project where, between 1975 and 1977, she served as director.

In 1977 JIMMY CARTER took office as U.S. president and appointed Wald to the U.S. Justice Department position of assistant attorney general for legal affairs. Only two years later, Wald made it to the top of President Carter's list

PATRICIA M. WALD

1928	Born in Torrington, Connecticut
1951	Graduated from Yale Law School
1977	Appointed Assistant Attorney General for Legal Affairs
1979	Appointed to U.S. Court of Appeals for the D.C. Circuit
1986–1991	Chief Justice of the U.S. Court of Appeals for the D.C. Circuit
1999	Judge on International War Crimes Tribunal for Yugoslovia

again and was appointed to a judgeship on the U.S. Court of Appeals for the District of Columbia Circuit. There she made history once more, as she was the first woman to serve as a judge on a U.S. Court of Appeals. The D.C. Circuit is often referred to as the country's second-most important court—the Supreme Court of the United States being the first—because it hears many issues of national importance due to its location in the nation's capital. Wald served as chief justice of the court between 1986 and 1991.

In 1997 Wald sat on a three-judge panel to hear part of the Justice Department's ANTITRUST case against Microsoft. The panel was to review a lower court order that prohibited Microsoft from forcing computer makers to purchase the Microsoft Internet Explorer browser as a condition of buying Microsoft Windows, which was a necessary standard for most computers. Microsoft argued that the two products were integrated, therefore, they were not in violation of the order. The panel decided 2–1 in favor of Microsoft. Wald gave the dissenting opinion, arguing that the products were not integrated. Her opinion was later echoed by Judge Thomas Penfield Jackson, who ruled that Microsoft did indeed violate the antitrust laws. By the end of her career on the court of appeals, Wald had authored more than 800 opinions.

In 1999 Judge Wald left the D.C. Circuit Court of Appeals to join the International War Crimes Tribunal for Yugoslovia. The tribunal was created by the United Nations in 1993 to judge those accused of crimes against humanity during the massacres in Croatia, Serbia, and Bosnia. This new position would entail her leaving behind her family and moving to The Hague, The Netherlands, in order to serve a two-year term on the bench. The position meant a great deal to Wald, however, because she had served for the past five years on the Executive Board of the AMERICAN BAR ASSOCIATION's Central and Eastern European Law Initiative and had aided in the monitoring of elections and the creation of new constitutions in Eastern Europe.

The International War Crimes Tribunal is made up of fourteen judges from various nations. The process is based on two legal systems: British COMMON LAW and European civil law. There are two official languages: French and English. Wald faced an incredibly large case load, much of which involved such disturbing acts as murder, rape, and torture.

WAR CRIMES

Those acts that violate the international laws, treaties, customs, and practices governing military conflict between belligerent states or parties.

Rome Treaty Would Create International Criminal Court

At the very end of his tenure, former president BILL CLINTON authorized the signature of the United States to the controversial Rome Treaty, which intends to create a permanent international criminal court (ICC). The court's purpose is to adjudicate war crimes, GENOCIDE, and crimes against humanity. U.S. Negotiator David J. Scheffer signed the ACCORD on December 31, 2000, without protesting the absence of the changes and amendments for which he had been fighting. In a statement released with his decision, Clinton noted that the treaty had "some flaws" and that he would not submit it for Senate RATIFICATION in its present form. GEORGE W. BUSH's administration also made it clear that there was no intention of forwarding the treaty for ratification in its then-current form.

The United States cannot participate in the court unless the Senate ratifies the treaty, making the Clinton administration's signature largely symbolic. If it had not been signed, however, the United States would have forfeited the right to help select the judges and prosecutors who will serve on the tribunal. The original treaty was created and adopted in Rome in July 1998, with 120 affirmative votes, 21 abstentions, and 7 negative votes, including those of the United States and China. By September 2000, 138 nations had signed the treaty, but only 27 had completed the formal process of ratification. A minimum of 60 nations must ratify the treaty in order for the court to be formed. A coalition of grass-roots groups has set an arbitrary deadline of July 2002 for ratification.

Ever since the UNITED NATIONS Declaration of Human Rights in 1948, the creation of an international forum for justice has not been a new concept. Following WORLD WAR I, there were discussions of trying Germany's leader Kaiser Wilhelm for war crimes. The NUREMBERG TRIALS and the TOKYO TRIAL after WORLD WAR II were established by the legal authority of Germany and Japan, with limited power to adjudicate only those crimes committed on their soil. More recently, tribunals have been set up at The Hague for crimes in Bosnia and in Tanzania for alleged genocide in Rwanda, but these are AD HOC tribunals whose authority and purpose will cease with the specific adjudications for which they were chartered. Even the enforcement powers of the UN's INTERNATIONAL COURT OF JUSTICE are usually limited to multinational boycotts, which can be defeated by majority votes.

By contrast, the proposed ICC is intended to be permanent and multi-jurisdictional but to have jurisdiction limited to prosecuting war crimes and genocide. It is to be further restricted to handling only those cases not addressed by the judicial system of any country. Technically, this arrangement would mean that a member of the armed forces who is found guilty of wrongdoing by a COURT-MARTIAL system could not face a second trial before the ICC.

This point was a key issue of concern to most U.S. Congressmen who had reservations about the propriety of signing the treaty. They believe that the United States would be opening itself up to frivolous charges and claims such as an accusation that the bombings of Serbia and Kosovo in 1999 were illegal because civilians were harmed. Senator Jesse Helms, a vociferous opponent to the signing of the treaty, was co-sponsor of a BILL introduced in June 2000, called the American Servicemembers' Protection Act, which would make U.S. troops immune from prosecution. Further, the U.S. rejected a clause in the treaty that would give the ICC "universal jurisdiction," allowing it to prosecute crimes

perpetrated anywhere, even if countries do not agree to its jurisdiction or ratify the treaty.

In March 2001 countries that had signed the treaty met for a two-week UN session to negotiate final operating rules and continue attempts to work out differences, such as the universal definition of "crimes of aggression." The United States sent a two-person technical delegation, but maintained a low profile. It is clearly understood that U.S. involvement is critical to the success of the ICC. First, there is the issue of monetary support, as the United States contributes about one-fourth of UN operating costs. Second, only the United States has the international leadership and influence to ensure that the ICC will have the necessary clout to pursue other powerful countries that commit such jurisdictional crimes. Another important factor is that American intelligence is crucial to the success of international justice, as evidenced in Yugoslavia and Rwanda. Even by early 2001, America's influence was felt when other nations began to articulate the same concerns of unwarranted prosecutions as earlier expressed by the United States.

Most countries, including the United States, agree in principle that there is a pressing need for a new level of global governance. Generally, a country can only punish those over whom the country has authority to govern. But when it is a country's government that is the wrongdoer—or a ratifying principal behind the wrongdoing—other countries are often powerless to eliminate the wrong with any weapon other than economic reprisal. When human lives are at issue, this limited sanction is often impotent and creates a black market for boycotted goods or services. Thus, it is hoped by those nations ratifying the treaty that an international court of sufficient authority and power to deter and punish may someday be instrumental in eliminating unconscionable war crimes, genocides, and other crimes of inhumanity.

UN War Crimes Tribunal Metes Out Stiff Sentences

After the end of WORLD WAR II, the NUREMBERG TRIALS adjudicated and punished Nazi leaders for committing GENOCIDE and other war crimes. Europeans vowed "never again" to permit genocide on their continent. Despite that vow, Europeans subsequently watched as Bosnian Serbs and Croats—mostly military, but some civilian, leaders from the Bosnian wars that followed the disintegration of the former Yugoslavia—were prosecuted by the UNITED NATIONS War Crimes Tribunal in

Bosnian Croat Army General Tihomir Blaskic, faced charges before the UN's War Crimes Tribunal.

The Hague, Netherlands. By January 2001 the tribunal had thirty-nine persons in custody or in provisional release and had completed seventeen trials. There were fifteen convictions and two acquittals, one of which was under appeal by prosecutors. Four defendants were serving sentences between five and twenty years. The forty-five year sentence handed down to Tihomir Blaskic, former Bosnian Croat army commander, was under appeal, as were eleven others. Charges had been dropped in eighteen other cases, and eight suspects had died. Approximately ninety-eight persons had been publicly indicted.

The AD HOC tribunal was established in 1993 by the UN Security Council to prosecute those responsible for atrocities in the Balkans, mostly occurring between 1992 and 1995. This action followed the Bosnian Serb Nationalists' rebellion against Bosnia's declaration of independence from Yugoslavia in 1992. The most comprehensive case before the tribunal involved the massacre of Bosnian Muslims in an alleged attempt at "ethnic cleansing." The issue at trial was whether such killings constituted genocide, the most serious international crime.

During the ensuing conflict, Srebenica, in Eastern Bosnia, was set up as a UN "safe haven." Approximately 1,500 Dutch troops were employed to guard the UN area, infiltrated with thousands of Serbian soldiers. About 20,000 Muslims sought shelter at the Srebenican compound. There were repeated assurances of protection from the UN.

It was alleged at trial, however, that Serb army forces separated men and boys from the women, then slaughtered all of them. When word of the executions got out, the Serbs allegedly dug up many bodies and buried them elsewhere to conceal the massacre. Following five years of forensic investigation at hundreds of mass graves, 2,500 bodies had been recovered; another 4,500 remained missing. These killings have been referred to as the worst massacre on European soil since the Holocaust.

Blaskic's forty-five year prison sentence followed a twenty-five month trial with 158 witnesses and 30,000 pages of documents. It took the three-judge panel seven months for a decision. Because the Croatian government was implicated, Blaskic also was charged with grave breaches of the 1949 GENEVA CONVENTIONS, which sought to protect civilians caught in warfare. In addition to Blaskic, who had received the sentence for his soldiers' 1993 massacres in Muslim villages, Goran Jelisic, a Bosnian Serb, was sentenced to forty years for slaughters committed while he was a shift commander at the notorious Luka prison camp in Northern Bosnia. France's Claude Jorda, the presiding judge, told Jelisic that he had committed crimes that "shocked the conscience of mankind." Jelisic's lawyer had asked for leniency because Jelisic, a prior farm mechanic, had only been twenty-three years old when the crimes were committed.

In another tribunal trial, an appellate ruling upheld a finding that the Serbian-led government of Slobodan Milosevic was also involved in the Bosnian conflict. Milosevic had remained at large ever since his ouster from power in October 2000. He was arrested by local soldiers in March 2001, however, at his villa in Belgrade, following a twenty-six-hour siege, to be prosecuted for fraud and abuse of power. He was also facing charges from the tribunal for his role in the deaths of thousands of ethnic Albanians in Kosovo, and the persecution and/or displacement of 700,000 more. If and when he were to be prosecuted, Milosevic was anticipated to receive life imprisonment, the most severe punishment allowable under the tribunal's sentencing guidelines.

As of May 2001, Yugoslavian President Vojislav Kostunica had refused to turn Milosevic over to tribunal authorities, stating that Yugoslavia will try "its own" war crimes suspects at home. Earlier, in October 2000, Kostunica had agreed to allow the UN to reestablish a tribunal office in Belgrade, hoping that his country could regain economic aid after a decade of international sanctions. The United States and other

Western powers continued to withhold about $50 million in aid to Yugoslavia until Milosevic was made available to the tribunal. Kostunica had previously stated that the tribunal was a puppet of American foreign policy, and he vowed not to extradite any suspects.

Another key trial completed in early 2001 was that of Dario Kordic, former vice president of the self-proclaimed Bosnian Croat State. He was sentenced to twenty-five years in prison for his role in death campaigns that targeted ethnic Albanians, most of whom are Muslims. A key development in that trial was the finding that Bosnian Croats had engaged in a widespread campaign against Bosnian Muslims, designed to annihilate them, capture their territory, and create a Greater Croatia.

CROSS REFERENCES

Appendix: Rome Treaty Approval Justification Letter; Treaty

WEAPONS

A comprehensive term for all instruments of offensive or defensive combat, including items used in injuring a person.

Musician "Puffy" Combs Beats Rap on Gun Possession

On March 16, 2001, hip-hop megastar Sean "Puffy" Combs was found not guilty of illegal gun possession and bribery charges. After a seven-week trial for a 1999 shooting in a Manhattan nightclub that injured three people and for the attempted bribery of his chauffeur, the 31-year-old rap mogul might have faced 15 years in prison if found guilty. However, he still faces other civil suits resulting from the incident with DAMAGES that may run into the millions. The nightclub shooting was the second incident involving Combs and the law that year. Earlier in 1999 he was charged with ASSAULT for beating Steven Stoute, a record executive, breaking his arm and jaw. Combs, who pleaded to the lesser charge of harassment, was ordered to submit to counseling.

The trouble began on December 27, 1999, when Combs, then known as Puff Daddy, entered Club New York shortly after midnight. Accompanied by his former girlfriend and fellow-celebrity Jennifer Lopez, among others, he joined a party for members of the rap music industry. Reportedly, Combs and his entourage were not searched for weapons, unlike regular patrons of the club. After some hours of partying, witnesses testified that a fight broke

out between Matthew Allen, a patron, and Combs's group. Insults were traded, and Allen threw a wad of money at Combs. Minutes later, three patrons were shot, one in the face.

Combs, along with Lopez, his bodyguard Anthony Jones, and driver Wardel Fenderson, fled the nightclub in the star's vehicle. After it ran several red lights, the car was stopped by New York City police, who searched it and found what later proved to be a stolen handgun.

Charges were brought against Combs for illegal gun possession and for bribery. Fenderson testified that Combs offered him $50,000 while in the police precinct to say that the gun belonged to the chauffeur. Bodyguard Jones was also charged with gun possession and bribery. A third defendant and a Combs protege, Jamaal Barrow, who was also with the rap star that night, was charged with attempted murder.

Combs stoutly maintained his innocence: "I do not own a gun. I do not carry a gun." He retained well-known criminal lawyer JOHNNIE COCHRAN to help with his defense. Prosecution witnesses testified to seeing both Combs and Barrow with guns that night in the club. The defense, in cross-examination, was able to bring out many inconsistencies in their testimony, however. As a result, the verdict on March 16 was not guilty for Combs and bodyguard Jones and guilty on five of eight charges for Barrow, who could face 25 years in prison.

Combs continues to have other legal problems to overcome. He is being sued on CIVIL RIGHTS charges from the nightclub incident. Damages in that case could run into the millions. He is also being sued by fashion model

Sean "Puffy" Combs speaks in New York City, 1998.

Kim Porter, the mother of his three-year-old son, Christian. She is seeking $2 million and $20,000 monthly for CHILD SUPPORT, on which she claims Combs has reneged.

However the legal problems are resolved, Combs toned down his image during and after the trial. He often appeared in court looking uncharacteristically subdued in a pin-striped suit. In a *New York Times* interview shortly after his acquittal, Combs admitted to some doubts about his Puff Daddy reputation, saying that he had a lot of time during the trial to think about such things. He concluded that he has spent too much time advertising his wealth, power, and bad-boy style. He seemed surprised that the public does not understand that much of his public persona is just a role he plays. He also announced that he would vanish from the public eye for a time and reappear with a new name, later announced as P Diddy. As he said, "I am definitely the fault of my own image."

WELFARE

Government benefits distributed to impoverished persons to enable them to maintain a minimum standard of well-being.

Legal Services Corporation v. Velazquez

Individuals who seek to obtain welfare benefits sometimes have to go to court to achieve this result. Such persons may be eligible to receive free legal assistance through local legal aid organizations. These organizations have been funded in part by the LEGAL SERVICES CORPORATION (LSC), a District of Columbia nonprofit corporation established by Congress in 1974. The LSC's mission is to distribute funds appropriated by Congress to eligible local legal aid organizations. In 1996, after a vote split almost exactly down party lines, the Republican-controlled Congress passed the Omnibus Consolidated Rescissions and Appropriations Act. This new legislation imposed restrictions on the use of LSC funds, prohibiting legal aid organizations from representing clients in a lawsuit where the action seeks to amend or challenge existing welfare law. Proponents of the restriction intended it to prevent federal funds from being used inappropriately to challenge state or federal laws. Opponents argued that the restriction violated the FIRST AMENDMENT. The U.S. Supreme Court, in *Legal Services Corporation v. Velazquez*, 531 U.S. 533, 121 S.Ct. 1043, 149 L.Ed.2d 63 (2001), resolved this dispute by ruling the restriction unconstitutional.

After Congress imposed this funding restriction, the LSC interpreted the law as preventing an attorney from arguing to a court that a state law conflicts with a federal statute, or that either a state or federal statute by its terms or in its application violated the U.S. Constitution. Lawyers who worked for the New York City LSC—along with private contributors to the LSC, indigent clients of the LSC, and state and local public officials of governments which contributed to organizations funded by the LSC—filed suit against the LSC, challenging this restriction in federal district court.

Carmen Velazquez was a grandmother who had lost her welfare benefits because she failed to participate in a job search program. She claimed her termination was wrong because state regulations did not provide her with a pre-termination hearing at which she could present evidence of a physical impairment that kept her from working. The lawsuit sought to invalidate the funding restriction law, but the court denied a preliminary injunction. The U.S. Court of Appeals for the Third Circuit approved the injunction against the enforcement of the provision, however, as an "impermissible viewpoint-based discrimination" under the First Amendment.

The Supreme Court, in a 5–4 vote, upheld the circuit court decision. Justice ANTHONY M. KENNEDY, writing for the majority, acknowledged that Congress had placed restrictions on the use of LSC funds since it created the LSC in 1974. Congress has prohibited recipients from using funds on behalf of political parties, political campaigns, or for use in advocating or opposing any ballot measures. The law also bars funding of most criminal proceedings and in litigation involving nontherapeutic abortions, secondary school desegregation, military desertion, or violations of the Military Selective Service Act. In addition, fund recipients are barred from bringing CLASS ACTION lawsuits unless the LSC grants express approval.

Despite these funding restrictions, Justice Kennedy concluded that the prohibition on challenging welfare laws went too far. Congress did not have to create the LSC or to continue funding it, but once Congress appropriated funds for providing legal assistance to private citizens, First Amendment rights are implicated. The LSC program was designed to facilitate private speech rather than to promote a government message. An LSC attorney "speaks on behalf of a private, indigent client in a welfare benefits claim, while the Government's message is delivered by the attorney defending the benefits decision." Therefore, the LSC attorney's advice to the client and advocacy to the court was private speech that could not be restricted by the government.

Justice Kennedy was also troubled that the government sought to control speech in the legal system, which distorted its normal functioning. The restriction prevented LSC attorneys from advising the courts of "serious statutory validity questions." Moreover, the funding restriction threatened "severe impairment of the judicial function by sifting out cases presenting constitutional challenges in order to insulate the Government's laws from judicial inquiry." Such restrictions would impair the credibility of legal advice given by an LSC attorney, as the client and the public would not be sure if there was a constitutional or statutory question at stake. Kennedy concluded that the First Amendment did not permit "the government to confine litigants and their attorneys in this manner."

Justice ANTONIN SCALIA, in a dissenting opinion joined by Chief Justice WILLIAM H. REHNQUIST and Justices SANDRA DAY O'CONNOR and CLARENCE THOMAS, argued that the majority had adopted "a novel and unsupportable interpretation" of prior Court rulings on the First Amendment. Scalia contended that the LSC funding did not prevent anyone from speaking, nor did it coerce anyone to change his or her expression.

CROSS REFERENCES
First Amendment; Legal Aid

WHISTLEBLOWING

FMC Settles Bradley Vehicle Lawsuit

In October 2000 a former defense contractor settled a long-running fraud lawsuit with an ex-employee for $80 million. Chicago-based manufacturer FMC Corporation agreed to pay the settlement to Henry Boisvert, a whistleblower who charged that the company defrauded the U.S. Army by falsifying reports for the trouble-plagued Bradley Fighting Vehicle. Between 1986 and 1998, Boisvert fought a legal battle that culminated with a federal jury imposing a $125 million judgment against FMC under the federal False Claims Act. After a court reduced the judgment, both sides appealed and then reached a mediated settlement.

The case dated to the nation's extensive military buildup of the mid-1980s. A former military draftee who joined FMC in the 1970s, Boisvert had risen to the position of testing

supervisor in charge of reviewing the company's production of Bradley vehicles. The Bradley was a lucrative contract for FMC, which produced some 9,000 of the armored fighting troop transports for the U.S. Army at costs of up to $1.5 million each. Its popularity was due partly to the manufacturer's claim that the vehicle could "swim"—remain airtight through submersion in water and lakes. Boisvert became alarmed, however, when he found that the vehicle leaked, a problem that could potentially drown its passengers. In 1986 his discovery cost him his job. First, his attempt to inform the outside world about the problem was allegedly thwarted by a company official, and later, when he refused to sign his name to allegedly falsified reports, he was fired.

Boisvert brought two legal actions. He successfully sued for WRONGFUL DISCHARGE, collecting $200,000 in DAMAGES in a California state court jury trial in 1992. His second lawsuit was a claim under the False Claims Act. Dating to the CIVIL WAR era, the federal law (31 USCA §§ 3729–3731) was originally designed to encourage private citizens with information about corrupt defense contractors to come forward in lawsuits in behalf of the Union. In 1986, amid sharp complaints about a new era of defense contractor fraud, Congress revived the moribund law to fit modern needs. The 1986 amendments (Pub.L. 99–562, Oct. 27, 1986, 100 Stat. 3153) sought to encourage citizen whistleblowing: they provided for up to 30 percent of the damages collected in these so-called QUI TAM ACTIONS to be shared with citizens; the other 70 percent goes to the federal treasury. Additionally, the amendments added new sting to the law by providing in some instances for doubling and trebling of damages.

As provided under the law, the federal government privately reviewed Boisvert's qui tam claim against FMC to determine whether to assist it. Upon review, the JUSTICE DEPARTMENT declined to participate—a decision that, strategically, meant that Boisvert had an uphill battle. Nevertheless, he pursued the civil case on his own for twelve years, during which time he was unable to find permanent employment. During this period the Bradleys came under considerable attack from critics in and out of Congress. The vehicle frequently malfunctioned and fell far short of expectations. FMC, meanwhile, exited the defense contractor business but still had Bradley-related problems. In 1996 it agreed to pay the federal government a $13 million settlement in a different whistleblower case alleging that it had deliberately inflated the vehicle's price tag.

In 1998, Boisvert's case finally came before a jury in U.S. District Court in San Jose, California. During the four-month-long trial, the plaintiff presented shocking testimony from assembly line welders who said their work schedule allowed them no time to seal gaps properly in the allegedly water-proof Bradleys; instead, they had used mere putty. Boisvert's own testimony alleged that rigged quality-control procedures were used to ensure that vehicles would pass tests. FMC disputed the testimony and pointed to the Bradley's success in the Gulf War, but its arguments failed to persuade the ten-member jury. On April 14, 1998, after more than a week of deliberations, the jury returned a $125 million judgment against FMC. Subject to doubling and trebling under the law's harsh penalties, the damages could have risen as high as $310 million.

In post-trial arguments in December 1998, FMC persuaded the DISTRICT COURT to reject $100 million of the claim as well as one-half of the penalties. Both FMC and Boisvert then appealed, the company seeking to reverse the verdict and the plaintiff seeking to have penalties increased. Just as the first appeal was set to be heard in October 2000, the company and Boisvert concluded settlement talks with a mediator. Boisvert dropped the suit in return for $80 million, including interest and legal fees. For its part, FMC stated in the agreement that it admitted neither error nor LIABILITY in connection with its production of the Bradley.

WHITEWATER

Kenneth Starr's Spokesman Acquitted of Contempt Charges

In October 2000 another legal chapter closed in the Office of the INDEPENDENT COUNSEL's (OIC) probe of former President BILL CLINTON. Charles Bakaly III, an attorney and former spokesman for Independent Counsel KENNETH STARR, was acquitted on criminal CONTEMPT charges after a four-day federal BENCH TRIAL—a trial before a federal judge sitting without a jury. Since 1999, Bakaly had stood accused of lying and engaging in a cover-up of his role in allegedly leaking secret information to the *New York Times*. His acquittal concluded a process that had begun with the White House accusing Bakaly and Starr of violating federal GRAND JURY secrecy laws.

Charles Bakaly III speaks in Washington, D.C., 1998.

On January 31, 1999, the *Times* article, "Starr is Weighing Whether to Indict Sitting President" hit newsstands in the midst of the U.S. Senate's IMPEACHMENT trial of President Clinton. In addition to his impeachment, Clinton also faced a potential INDICTMENT on charges of PERJURY and OBSTRUCTION OF JUSTICE. The article reported that Starr had decided he had the authority to indict and that prosecutors in the OIC favored doing so. The article attributed the information to unidentified "associates" of Starr, but it also quoted his spokesman Bakaly as saying, "We will not discuss the plans of this office or the plans of the grand jury in any way, shape or form."

One day later, the White House filed a criminal complaint. For months, attorneys for the president had publicly accused the OIC of leaking information to the press in violation of grand jury secrecy rules. They asked the District Court for the District of Columbia to hold the OIC and Bakaly in contempt for violating Federal Rule of Criminal Procedure 6(e). The rule forbids government attorneys from publicly disclosing a broad range of information about grand jury cases.

The complaint set in motion several events. First, Bakaly appeared on television the same day denying that the OIC had provided information to the *Times* reporter, Don Van Natta, Jr. Next, Starr conducted an internal investigation with the assistance of the FEDERAL BUREAU OF INVESTIGATION (FBI). In March 1999 this probe ended dramatically: Starr forced Bakaly to resign, and he referred the case to the JUSTICE DEPARTMENT for criminal investigation and possible prosecution.

In response, the DISTRICT COURT issued a preliminary ruling in July ordering Bakaly and the OIC to show why they should not be held in civil contempt, and it ruled that the *Times* article contained information that was, on its face, a violation of Rule 6(e). On appeal, however, the OIC argued successfully that the district court had misinterpreted the secrecy rule. In September 1999 a three judge APPELLATE COURT panel of the U.S. Court of Appeals for the D.C. Circuit overturned the lower court, ruling that the information in the article was not protected, *In re Sealed Case No. 99–3091 (Office of Independent Counsel Contempt Proceeding)*. "(W)e have never read Rule 6(e) to require that a 'veil of secrecy be drawn over all matters occurring in the world that happen to be investigated by a grand jury'," the panel wrote.

While the panel's decision was a victory for Starr's office, Bakaly still personally faced contempt charges. Before his case came to trial, however, he earned a reprieve. The Justice Department decided against indicting him, announcing that the matter would be better addressed through the contempt case. In July 2000 Bakaly's case came before U.S. District Judge Norma Holloway Johnson, the district court's chief judge with authority to oversee all grand jury secrecy issues in Washington. At her request, the Justice Department agreed to serve as prosecutor during his six-day non-jury trial.

At trial, both sides offered evidence concerning the veracity of statements made by Bakaly in a submission to Judge Johnson's court in 1999. Prosecutors made use of FBI interviews conducted with Bakaly in which he appeared to have changed his story and conceded to having given the *Times* information. Prosecutor Alan Gershel accused him of "many falsehoods and lies," but defense attorneys contended that their client had always told the truth. Defense attorney Michele Roberts argued that all Bakaly had told the newspaper was "garden variety" information, while never giving it information about the OIC's intentions. In that sense, Roberts told the court, Bakaly had been truthful in his submission to the court. Moreover, Starr's office had omitted information from a court submission that her client had wanted included—with damaging results to Bakaly.

In a 50-page ruling issued on October 6, 2000, Judge Johnson acquitted Bakaly on all charges. The judge wrote that some of his statements were "misleading" because they implied that Bakaly was not a source of information to the newspaper. But "such a finding does not provide a sufficient basis for a criminal contempt conviction for making false statements," the judge concluded.

CROSS REFERENCES

Contempt

WHITMAN, CHRISTINE TODD

Christine Todd Whitman took office as Administrator of the U.S. ENVIRONMENTAL PROTECTION AGENCY on January 31, 2001. Whitman came to Washington, D.C., from New Jersey, where, since 1994, she had served as the state's fiftieth governor. Whitman's environmental record in New Jersey drew alternating praise and criticism from business, industry, and environmental groups, giving her a moderate appearance that led to the Senate's unanimous confirmation of her nomination to head the EPA.

Whitman was born Christine Temple Todd on September 26, 1946, in New York City. She grew up in Hunterdon County, New Jersey, where her parents, Eleanor and Webster Todd, were prominent Republicans in a family of GOP adherents. Whitman attended Wheaton College, where she graduated with a degree in government in 1968. In 1974 she married John R. Whitman, a New York investment banker, with whom she had two children.

Whitman's government career began in 1983, as she won election to the Somerset County Board of Freeholders, where she served until 1988. She also served on the New Jersey Board of Public Utilities from 1988 until, in 1990, she launched a close but unsuccessful campaign against Bill Bradley for a seat in the U.S. Senate. Her strong showing against the popular Democratic senator convinced Whitman that she was in a position to challenge incumbent Democratic Governor James Florio in 1993.

Florio faced an uncertain future in New Jersey, as his economic policies were blamed for New Jersey's severe recession. Whitman faced problems of her own, though. Her first media advisor, Larry McCarthy, quit under pressure for his role in developing the racist "Willie Horton" advertisements that George H. W. Bush used in his presidential campaign against Michael Dukakis in 1988. Her combined annual family income of almost $4 million hurt her image among the "common man." Finally, Jewish citizens criticized Whitman for using the Holocaust to characterize Florio's welfare program. Whitman, nevertheless, managed to win the election by 26,000 votes.

When she was inaugurated on January 18, 1994, Whitman announced that New Jersey was "Open for Business." Facing a $1 billion deficit did not stop her from implementing her number one campaign promise—tax cuts. Within two years, New Jersey had slashed taxes 30 percent in an effort to revive New Jersey's economy. As New Jersey's first female governor, Whitman appointed New Jersey's first African American State Supreme Court justice, its first female State Supreme Court Chief Justice, and its first female ATTORNEY GENERAL. In 1995, Whitman became the first governor and first woman to give the Republican Party's formal response to the President's State of the Union Address.

A proponent of "Smart Growth," Whitman supported plans to save 1 million acres of open

Christine Todd Whitman

CHRISTINE TODD WHITMAN

1946   Born in New York City

1968   Graduated from Wheaton College

1983–1988   Served on Somerset County Board of Freeholders

1988–1990   Served on New Jersey Board of Utilities

1990   Lost in election bid for U.S. Senate seat to Bill Bradley

1993–2000   Served as Governor of New Jersey

2001   Confirmed as Administrator of U.S. Environmental Protection Agency

space and farmland from development while encouraging responsible development of other land. She also used the State Development and Redevelopment Plan to encourage renovation of abandoned buildings and new growth in cities where roads, sewerage, and schools already existed. The Natural Resources Defense Council praised New Jersey for the best beach monitoring system in the nation. Business leaders said Whitman was responsible for cleaning up thousands of industrial sites in New Jersey, setting ambitious water quality standards, and leading the way for removing greenhouse gases, which cause global warming.

Whitman said in a 1998 public address, "We want [our grandchildren] to breathe the freedom from excessive government regulation, but we also want them to inhale clean air." Many environmentalists, however, expressed disappointment with Whitman's record as governor. Whitman slashed the budget for the New Jersey Department of Environmental Protection (DEP) by 30 percent, leading to an 80 percent reduction in fines assessed on polluters. Whitman ordered the DEP to prevent state environmental regulations from being stricter than federal rules. She eliminated the position of environmental prosecutor, allowing companies to regulate themselves and giving them grace periods during which they could stop polluting instead of immediately levying fines for viola-

tions. The EPA opposed her administration's removal support for two development projects that could ruin some of New Jersey's remaining wetlands. The EPA also rejected the New Jersey DEP's proposed water quality regulations that the EPA claimed would have let hundreds of millions of gallons of carcinogens and other pollutants into waterways.

Whitman considered criticism an indicator of good job performance. "The fact that we're being attacked by both sides leads me to believe that we're probably right where we need to be . . . to find some kind of common ground," Whitman said in December 2000. She urged critics to assess air and water quality when evaluating her record. Such scrutiny yielded mixed results, though, as a report from New Jersey's DEP in December 2000 showed that streams classified as "severely impaired" decreased between 1993 and 1998 but there were fewer pollution-free waterways in the same period.

With a controversial environmental record, President GEORGE W. BUSH nominated Whitman to head the EPA in January 2001. During Bush's election bid in 2000, Whitman campaigned in twenty states and served as a Bush spokeswoman. In her first two months atop the EPA, Whitman remained firm about "freedom from excessive government regulation." She announced that the Bush administration would support the previous administration's rules to cut sulfur pollution from diesel gasoline but followed that with policies that seemed to favor coal, mining, and other industries. She supported President Bush's decision to *not* to regulate carbon dioxide emissions from power plants, which had been a campaign promise. Under her leadership, the EPA also chose to pursue further scientific studies before accepting new arsenic limits for water supplies. Finally, Whitman announced that the United States would not enact the Kyoto Treaty, a strongly-debated international agreement aimed at reducing greenhouse gases.

Business leaders praised Whitman's early record at the EPA as appropriately sensitive to the needs of America's halting economy and growing energy crisis. Environmentalists rejected Whitman's pro-environment rhetoric, fearing that catering to the economy would hurt the health of Americans and the environment.

CROSS REFERENCES
Environmental Protection Agency

WILL

A document in which a person specifies the method to be applied in the management and distribution of his or her ESTATE after his or her death.

Anna Nicole Smith Inheritance Feud Continues

In May 2001 Anna Nicole Smith, the 33-year-old actress, model, and widow of Texas oil billionaire J. Howard Marshall II, had another setback in her years-long legal battle with Marshall's two sons over the considerable inheritance. District Court Judge David Carter threw out a California BANKRUPTCY court decision that granted Smith almost $475 million of her husband's estate over eight months earlier, stating that he would make a decision on whether to award Smith a portion of the estate after reviewing the facts of the case. Anna Nicole Smith claims that Marshall promised her half of his $1.6 billion estate, although none of his six wills reflect that promise. The wills support Marshall's son, E. Pierce Marshall, in his claim to half of the estate. Complicating the case further are the claims to the estate of Marshall's other son, J. Howard Marshall III, reportedly disinherited after a soured business deal with his father.

Smith, whose birth name is Vicki Lynn Hogan, first met J. Howard Marshall II while she was working as a stripper in Houston. Their difference in age—she was 26-years old and he was 89—did not prevent the couple from marrying in 1994. Marshall's deteriorating physical and mental health during their fourteen-month marriage led his son, Pierce, to petition a court to grant him POWER OF ATTORNEY and appoint him as legal guardian. As such, he froze all of his father's accounts, cutting off Smith's $5,000 weekly allowance and restricting her visits to the elder Marshall. When Marshall died in August 1995, Smith and Pierce fought over his ashes in court. Each received half of the ashes, which they then used to hold separate funerals.

Under the terms of the will, neither Smith nor Marshall's other son, J. Howard III, had legal claim to any of Marshall's estate. When the disinherited son, J. Howard III, sued his brother Pierce in COURT OF PROBATE, Smith joined as a claimant, charging that Pierce had defrauded her of $500–800 million, which was her share of her late husband's $1.6 billion estate. In addition to the litigation surrounding the inheritance, Smith faced a SEXUAL HARASSMENT lawsuit brought against her by a former nanny. Smith

Anna Nicole Smith cries as she testifies against E. Pierce Marshall in probate court.

lost the case, and the court ruled that she owed $850,000.

The lawsuit proved to be a blessing in disguise. Smith filed for bankruptcy in a California court in 1996 and listed as one of her assets, her claim to part of J. Howard Marshall's fortune. Smith based her claim on oral promises made to her by Marshall and introduced witnesses, including J. Howard III in support of her claims that Marshall had promised to adopt her son and give her half of his estate. Marshall's previous estate attorney offered other evidence on her behalf, testifying that at one time Marshall had debated between adopting Smith or marrying her before proceeding with the latter course of action.

In September 2000 the California federal bankruptcy judge awarded Smith $450 million. Because Texas is a COMMUNITY PROPERTY state, assets earned while married are jointly held by husband and wife. Smith's award in this case was equivalent to the amount that stock in Marshall's company rose during their marriage. In the court's written opinion, the judge ruled that Smith also was entitled to PUNITIVE DAMAGES because Pierce had deliberately altered documents in an attempt to defraud her. One such example was a document entitled the "J. Howard Marshall II Post Nuptial Fine Tuning of Estate Plan," which the federal judge concluded had been altered. The court opinion, citing Pierce's quick actions "to preserve his own entitlement to the entire estate and to cut

[Smith] out of any inheritance," later determined punitive damages in the additional amount of $25 million. The award prompted Smith to drop her claim in the litigation still ongoing in Harris County, Texas, between Marshall's sons in January 2001. Pierce Marshall, however, countersued Smith, prompting her continued participation in the inheritance case.

The Harris County probate court jury was not informed of the California bankruptcy judgment or of Smith's withdrawal of probate claims. Smith returned to court in February to testify in the countersuit against her, which charged that she induced her late husband to make promises to her in a tape recording while she disrobed in front of him. This suit was supported by the purported testimony of a healthcare worker who witnessed Smith removing her clothing and urging her debilitated husband to say into the tape recorder that he would leave her half of the estate and adopt her son.

In addition to determining that Smith should receive nothing from the estate, the jury ordered J. Howard III to pay $30 million in punitive damages for having interfered with the inheritance right of his brother as outlined in his father's will. Furthermore, District Court Judge David Carter determined that Smith's $475 million award from the bankruptcy court was invalid because the bankruptcy court did not have jurisdiction to decide such a matter. Instead, Judge Carter determined that he would make a decision after a review of the facts of the case. Both sides hailed the decision as a victory: Pierce Marshall because the $475 million award had been invalidated, and Anna Nicole Smith because the judge had rejected Marshall's assertion that the case did not belong in a federal court.

WRONGFUL DEATH

The taking of the life of an individual resulting from the willful or negligent act of another person or persons.

El Salvadoran Generals Cleared of Nuns' Death

In 1980 four U.S. religious workers in El Salvador were raped and murdered by soldiers. After discovering that two of the soldiers' generals were living comfortably in Florida, the victims' families filed a wrongful death suit against them in federal DISTRICT COURT. The generals' Florida residency gave the U.S. District Court for the Southern District of Florida jurisdiction over them in *Ford et al v. Garcia and Vides Casa-nova.* Defendants Jose Guillermo Garcia and Carlos Eugenio Vides Casanova, both former defense ministers in El Salvador, retained local Florida counsel for their defense. The suit was premised on the 1992 federal Torture Victim Protection Act, and it alleged that under the "theory of command" principle, superior officers may be liable for their subordinates' extrajudicial violence if they ordered, tolerated, or failed to prevent the actions or failed to punish the perpetrators. The Lawyers Committee for Human Rights was instrumental in bringing the suit and contributed greatly through its research and persistence. The suit asked for $25 million for the family of each woman, in COMPENSATORY DAMAGES and unspecified PUNITIVE DAMAGES.

The victims were four of an estimated 75,000 persons who lost their lives in El Salvador's Civil War, mostly to right-wing death squads or marauding military men. The war ended in 1992. Forty-year old Sister Ita Ford and forty-nine-year old Sister Maura Clarke were Maryknoll nuns from Ossining, New York. Forty-year old Sister Dorothy Kazel was an Ursuline nun from Cleveland, Ohio, and twenty-seven-year old Jean Donovan was a lay missionary from Florida. Kazel and Donovan had dined with another missionary and the U.S. ambassador in the capital city of San Salvador on December 1, 1980, then headed for the airport the next day to pick up the two Maryknoll nuns. Their bullet-ridden bodies and burned-out vehicle were found by local peasants. They had been taken to a wooded area, raped, then shot in the head. In 1984 five low-ranking members of El Salvador's National Guard were convicted by a Salvadoran jury for the murders. Many years later, four of the five convicted men stated that they had acted on orders from superiors. Although the Salvadoran military and government maintained that the five men acted alone and that their motive was robbery, a suspicion persisted that the guardsmen would not have committed the crimes without direction or encouragement from higher-ranking officials.

The defense team was able to show that the country's twelve-year civil war was a time of chaotic uprisings and turbulent political mayhem in El Salvador, with various factions gaining and losing control. The nuns in this case were among other religious persons murdered in a short period. Defense attorney Kurt Klaus, Jr., showed the jurors a film of one of the defendant generals asking troops to respect the human rights of fellow Salvadorans. The defense

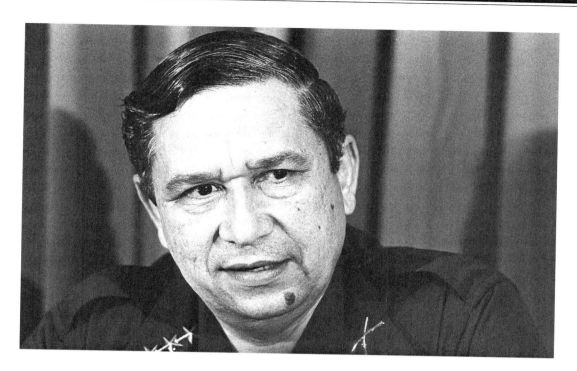

Colonel Jose Guillermo Garcia is the former defense minister of El Salvador.

also noted that these generals were praised publicly by the Reagan administration for helping to wage Washington's war against Marxist insurgents in El Salvador. In fact, Garcia received the Legion of Merit, the highest honor the U.S. government can bestow on a foreign dignitary. The defense implied that if the jurors found the generals guilty, they would be implying that the Reagan administration AIDED AND ABETTED the criminal acts of the Salvadoran government.

The plaintiffs charged that the Salvadoran military command created a culture that sanctioned sadism and repression. Plaintiffs' counsel elicited admissions from the defendants that they knew that thousands of innocent people were being killed by death squads. Apparently the nuns were suspected of sympathizing with leftist guerrillas and insurgents. The plaintiffs' attorneys argued that the defendants knew of these abuses by troops under their command and did nothing to stop them.

The civil trial began on October 10, 2000, and jury deliberation lasted only two hours into the second day of deliberations. The unanimous verdict was "not guilty." The jury had struggled with various evidentiary elements in conjunction with the jury instructions. U.S. District Court Judge Daniel Hurley instructed that, to find the two ex-generals guilty, jurors would have to believe that the two generals possessed or should have possessed clear knowledge of abuses by those under their command and then failed to halt those abuses. They concluded that the defendants did not bear "command responsibility" for the slayings because they did not have *effective* control over the troops.

Lawyers for the victims' families sought a new trial, based on what they considered to be an erroneous jury instruction. They also argued that the verdict was contrary to the evidence admitted at trial. In December 2000, Judge Hurley denied the request for a new trial. The one-sentence written order of the court was handed down without explanation for the denial. Both generals, however, faced another unrelated trial in May 2001 for the alleged torture and kidnapping of four Salvadorans now living in the United States.

Riverside, California, Settles with Victim of Police-shooting

On December 28, 1998, nineteen-year-old Tyisha Shenee Miller was shot and killed by four policemen in Riverside, California, a racially-mixed community of about 250,000 located sixty miles east of Los Angeles. The civil lawsuit filed by her family against the City of Riverside, the four officers, and their supervisor was settled for $3 million in November 2000. Federal inquiry into the case as well as into city police practices was still ongoing as of Spring 2001, but the officers were initially cleared of criminal wrongdoing by the local DISTRICT ATTORNEY.

Miller, an athlete and high school dropout, was attending evening make-up classes and was

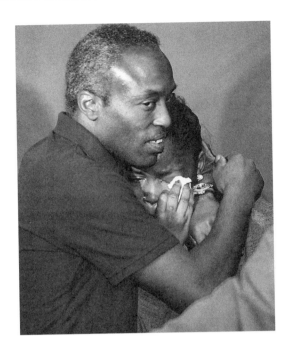

David Miller embraces his daughter as they enter a news conference where attorney Johnnie Cochran announced the filing of a federal civil rights lawsuit.

on probation at the time of her death for attacking another eighteen-year-old girl. There had been questions about her wearing the plaid Pendleton jacket favored by a local gang. Earlier on the evening of her death, she told protesting friends that she would leave two illegal guns, which she had agreed to hide for a boyfriend, at her parents' house. Instead, she took them with her.

Earlier in the day, Miller borrowed her aunt's car and drove four friends to a Riverside amusement park. One of the friends became upset over the two handguns she saw under the vehicle's seat. In response, Miller drove to her mother's house and pretended to leave them there. Later, the girls bought orange juice and gin, and Miller began drinking.

Around midnight, Miller and one of the four female friends had planned to go to a party, but the car suffered a flat tire. They pulled off the road, and a white male, Michael Horan, attempted to help them. Although he changed their tire for them, the spare tire was as flat as the other, and not inflatable. They removed the car to a nearby gas station. Horan and the friend then left Miller with the car while they went for help. When they returned at about 1:30 A.M., they found Tyisha in what appeared to be a drunken stupor, sitting behind the wheel, with the engine running and the radio blaring at full volume. She had an unlicensed semi-automatic handgun in her lap. All doors and windows were locked. Her friend and Horan were unable to

arouse her despite loud poundings on the windows and repeated shouting. Her friend, afraid that Miller might become disoriented and shoot at them, called 911.

Within minutes, four police officers arrived and began shouting, "Police! Police! Unlock the car!" When she remained unresponsive, with foamy exudate oozing from her mouth, the officers started to smash in the windows. Investigators determined that the officers believed Miller reached for her gun to try and shoot one officer who had broken the driver's side window and who tried to reach inside. A volley of shots followed, all fired by the police, and when the engine revved up, as though the gas pedal were being depressed, another round followed. In all, twenty-three shots were fired, twelve of them striking Miller. Miller died instantly.

The fact that Miller was an African American and all four officers were Caucasian or Hispanic gave the incident instant racial overtones. The shooting and lack of criminal charges against the officers touched off a series of demonstrations and national protests by CIVIL RIGHTS leaders, who immediately charged that the killing was racially motivated.

The officers, all in their twenties with good work histories, were exonerated of criminal wrongdoing by the Riverside district attorney, who found their tactics faulty but not criminally CULPABLE. They were nonetheless fired from their jobs, along with their sergeant. Riverside Police Chief Jerry Carroll stated that he believed their actions were not racist but that their actions "were not reasonable." For instance, he cited that "They never got on the radio to call for medical help." The officers, who believe they were "scapegoated" in the case, appealed their terminations. Said one of their attorneys, Bill Hadden, "What if they didn't do anything, and Tyisha Miller died?"

Meanwhile, Miller's family filed a wrongful death lawsuit, asking for $10 million. During the course of DISCOVERY in the ensuing litigation, toxicology evidence was introduced that showed that Miller's body contained alcohol, marijuana, and the hallucinogen GHB, which is also called "ecstasy." City attorneys had intended to use this to explain "her confused and paranoid response, her totally unanticipated behavior, in bolting for the gun." The case never got that far.

In July 2000 U.S. District Judge Robert J. Timlin removed the defense attorneys from the case, citing a conflict of interest because they already had represented the individual officers in the same matter. Rather than further protract the matter while new counsel acquainted itself with the voluminous materials, the parties agreed to settle.

The settlement involved more than just money. The city appointed nine community leaders to a Police Review Commission that would investigate complaints against the department, including those for excessive force and discrimination. In early 2001 Riverside also signed a legal police reform agreement with California's attorney general requiring changes in the police department over the next five years.

Waco Victims' Family Members Sue Federal Government

On February 28, 1993, Bureau of ALCOHOL, TOBACCO AND FIREARMS (ATF) agents attempted to arrest David Koresh, the leader of the Branch Davidians, at their compound in Waco, Texas. The government reportedly gained information that Koresh was preparing the Davidians for war by stockpiling illegal weapons and training his followers how to use these weapons. In the context of the attempted arrest, a gun battle started between the arresting officials and sect members, which left four ATF agents and six Davidians dead. As a result, a nationally-televised, fifty-one-day standoff ensued between the officials and sect members.

The standoff finally came to an end on April 19, 1993. On that date, agents of the Federal Bureau of Investigation (FBI) used tanks to fire tear gas into the Davidian compound, seeking to put an end to the dispute. At the same time, a fire erupted in the compound. Eighty Davidians died in connection with the incident, including leader David Koresh. The numerous deaths were later attributed to gunshot wounds and the fire.

Thereafter, approximately one hundred plaintiffs comprised of the surviving sect members and family members of the deceased, filed a lawsuit for wrongful death against the government in federal court. In setting forth a claim of excessive force, the plaintiffs sought a total of $675 million in DAMAGES. U.S. District Judge Walter Smith was assigned to preside over the case. Judge Smith assembled a five-member advisory panel to assist him with findings of fact concerning the April 19 incident. Under the federal rules governing lawsuits against the U.S. government, however, Judge Smith was not bound to follow the advisory panel's decision in reaching his verdict. Judge Smith requested that this advisory jury decide the following issues: (1)

The Branch Davidian compound burns following the 1995 disaster in Waco, Texas.

whether ATF agents were excessive in their actions; (2) whether the FBI displayed NEGLIGENCE in the way it handled the Waco situation; (3) whether the Davidians were negligent in their actions; and (4) if both the FBI and the Davidians were negligent, what was the percent of each party's responsibility.

The trial lasted more than three weeks. After hearing all of the evidence, including audio tapes made inside the compound prior to the raid and numerous autopsy reports, the advisory jury deliberated for only two and one half hours before reaching a conclusion. In its suggested verdict, the advisory jury found that ATF agents used an appropriate amount of force in responding to actions by sect members. The advisory jury found that the FBI was not negligent, and, furthermore, that Koresh bore all of the responsibility for the events that transpired on April 19. Consequently, the jury recommended a dismissal of the wrongful death action against the government in its entirety.

In September 2000, Judge Smith issued a decision similar to the advisory panel's findings. In particular, Judge Smith held that cult leader David Koresh was responsible for the tragedy and that both the ATF and the FBI had acted reasonably under the circumstances. Based upon these findings, Judge Smith dismissed the case against the government. This resolution of the wrongful death trial was consistent with the findings of John Danforth, who served as a special counsel appointed by the government to complete an independent investigation into the matter.

Upon the announcement of the verdict in favor of the defendants, attorneys for the plaintiffs announced their intention to file an appeal. The primary basis for appeal is the alleged BIAS demonstrated by the trial judge. Counsel for the plaintiffs contend that Judge Smith ignored all of the evidence presented on their behalf, and that he had demonstrated hostility toward the Davidians since the inception of the lawsuit.

Although the Waco disaster took place in 1993, certain individuals argue that its effects continue to the present day, as seen in various violent acts committed by anti-government groups across the nation. For example, the tragic end the Waco standoff allegedly inspired Timothy McVeigh to bomb the Alfred P. Murrah Federal Building in Oklahoma City. This horrific bombing by McVeigh occurred precisely two years to the day after the Waco siege. For this reason, some officials argue that the bombing, at least in part, was intended to avenge the government's actions at the Branch Davidian compound.

GLOSSARY OF LEGAL TERMS

This section includes definitions from West's Encyclopedia of American Law *for difficult or uncommon legal terms that are highlighted in the preceding entries by being set in small caps. Though also set in small caps, proper names of acts, cases, organizations, persons, etc., do not appear in this glossary, nor do simple or common terms such as* JUDGE *or* PLAINTIFF.

Abandonment: The surrender, relinquishment, disclaimer, or cession of property or of rights. Voluntary relinquishment of all right, title, claim and possession, with the intent of not reclaiming it.

The giving up of a thing absolutely, without reference to any particular person or purpose, as vacating property with the intention of not returning, so that it may be appropriated by the next comer or finder. The voluntary relinquishment of possession of thing by owner with intention of terminating ownership, but without vesting it in any other person. The relinquishing of all title, possession, or claim, or a virtual, intentional throwing away of property.

Term includes both the intention to abandon and the external act by which the intention is carried into effect. In determining whether one has abandoned property or rights, the intention is the first and paramount object of inquiry, for there can be no abandonment without the intention to abandon.

Abandonment differs from surrender in that surrender requires an agreement, and also from forfeiture, in that forfeiture may be against the intention of the party alleged to have forfeited.

Abrogation: The destruction or annulling of a former law by an act of the legislative power, by constitutional authority, or by usage. It stands opposed to *rogation;* and is distinguished from derogation, which implies the taking away of only some part of a law; from subrogation, which denotes the substitution of a clause; from *dispensation,* which only sets it aside in a particular instance; and from *antiquation,* which is the refusing to pass a law.

Abuse of discretion: A failure to take into proper consideration the facts and law relating to a particular matter; an arbitrary or unreasonable departure from precedents and settled judicial custom.

Accord: An agreement that settles a dispute, generally requiring a compromise or satisfaction with something less than what was originally demanded.

Acquiescence: Conduct recognizing the existence of a transaction and intended to permit the transaction to be carried into effect; a tacit agreement; consent inferred from silence.

Ad hoc: [*Latin, For this; for this special purpose.*] An attorney ad hoc, or a guardian or curator ad hoc, is one appointed for a special purpose, generally to represent the client or infant in the particular action in which the appointment is made.

Adjudication: The legal process of resolving a dispute. The formal giving or pronouncing of a judgment or decree in a court proceeding; also the judgment or decision given. The entry of a decree by a court in respect to the parties in a case. It implies a hearing by a court, after notice, of legal evidence on the factual issues(s) involved. The equivalent of a determination. It indicates that the claims of all the parties thereto have been considered and set at rest.

Ad litem: [*Latin, For the suit; for the purposes of the suit; pending the suit.*] A guardian ad litem is a guardian appointed to prosecute or defend a suit on behalf of a party who is legally incapable of doing so, such as an infant or an insane person.

Administrative agency: An official governmental body empowered with the authority to direct and supervise the implementation of particular legislative acts. In addition to *agency*, such governmental bodies may be called commissions, corporations (e.g., F.D.I.C.), boards, departments, or divisions.

Administrative law and procedure: *Administrative law* is the body of law that allows for the creation of public regulatory agencies and contains all the statutes, judicial decisions, and regulations that govern them. It is the body of law created by administrative agencies to implement their powers and duties in the form of rules, regulations, orders, and decisions. *Administrative procedure* constitutes the methods and processes before administrative agencies, as distinguished from judicial procedure, which applies to courts.

Adultery: Voluntary sexual relations between an individual who is married and someone who is not the individual's spouse.

Advocacy: The act of pleading or arguing a case or a position; forceful persuasion.

Affidavit: A written statement of facts voluntarily made by an affiant under an oath or affirmation administered by a person authorized to do so by law.

Affirmative action: Employment programs required by federal statutes and regulations designed to remedy discriminatory practices in hiring minority group members; i.e. positive steps designed to eliminate existing and continuing discrimination, to remedy lingering effects of past discrimination, and to create systems and procedures to prevent future discrimination; commonly based on population percentages of minority groups in a particular area. Factors considered are race, color, sex, creed, and age.

Aggravated assault: A person is guilty of aggravated assault if he or she attempts to cause serious bodily injury to another or causes such injury purposely, knowingly, or recklessly under circumstances manifesting extreme indifference to the value of human life; or attempts to cause or purposely or knowingly causes bodily injury to another with a deadly weapon. In all jurisdictions statutes punish such aggravated assaults as assault with intent to murder (or rob or kill or rape) and assault with a dangerous (or deadly) weapon more severely than "simple" assaults.

Aid and abet: To assist another in the commission of a crime by words or conduct.

Aliens: Foreign-born persons who have not been naturalized to become U.S. citizens under federal law and the Constitution.

Ambiguity: Uncertainty or doubtfulness of the meaning of language.

Amendment: The modification of materials by the addition of supplemental information; the deletion of unnecessary, undesirable, or outdated information; or the correction of errors existing in the text.

Amicus curiae: Literally, friend of the court. A person with strong interest in or views on the subject matter of an action, but not a party to the action, may petition the court for permission to file a brief, ostensibly on behalf of a party but actually to suggest a rationale consistent with its own views. Such amicus curiae briefs are commonly files in appeals concerning matters of a broad public interest; e.g., civil rights cases. They may be filed by private persons or the government. In appeals to the U.S. courts of appeals, an amicus brief may be filed only if accompanied by written consent of all parties, or by leave of court granted on motion or at the request of the court, except that consent or leave shall not be required when the brief is presented by the United States or an officer or agency thereof. See also FRIEND OF THE COURT.

Antitrust law: Legislation enacted by the federal and various state governments to regulate trade and commerce by preventing unlawful restraints, price-fixing, and monopolies, to promote competition, and to encourage the production of quality goods and services at the lowest prices, with the primary goal of safeguarding public welfare by ensuring that consumer demands will be met by the manufacture and sale of goods at reasonable prices.

Appellant: A person who, dissatisfied with the judgment rendered in a lawsuit decided in a lower court or the findings from a proceeding before an administrative agency, asks a superior court to review the decision.

Appellate: Relating to appeals; reviews by superior courts of decisions of inferior courts or administrative agencies and other proceedings.

Appellate court: A court having jurisdiction to review decisions of a trial-level or other lower court.

Arbitration: The submission of a dispute to an unbiased third person designated by the parties to the controversy, who agree in advance to comply with the award—a decision to be issued after a hearing at which both parties have an opportunity to be heard.

Assault: At common law, an intentional act by one person that creates an apprehension in another of an imminent harmful or offensive contact.

Assent: An intentional approval of known facts that are offered by another for acceptance; agreement; consent.

Asylum: See ALIENS.

Autopsy: The dissection of a dead body by a medical examiner or physician authorized by law to do so in order to determine the cause and time of the death that appears to have resulted from other than natural causes.

Award: To concede; to give by judicial determination; to rule in favor of after an evaluation of the facts, evidence, or merits. The decision made by a panel of arbitrators or commissioners, a jury, or other authorized individuals in a controversy that has been presented for resolution. A document that memorializes the determination reached in a dispute.

Back pay award: A legally enforceable decree ordering an employer to pay to an employee retroactively a designated increase in his or her salary that occurred during a particular period of employment. A decision rendered by a judicial or quasi-judicial body that an employee has a legal right to collect accrued salary that has not been paid out to him or her.

Bankruptcy: A federally authorized procedure by which a debtor—an individual, corporation, or municipality—is relieved of total liability for its debts by making court-approved arrangements for their partial repayment.

Basis: The minimum, fundamental constituents, foundation, or support of a thing or a system without which the thing or system would cease to exist. In accounting, the value assigned to an asset that is sold or transferred so that it can be determined whether a gain or loss has resulted from the transaction. The amount that property is estimated to be worth at the time it is received for tax purposes.

Battery: At common law, an intentional unpermitted act causing harmful or offensive contact with the "person" of another.

Bench trial: A trial conducted before a judge presiding without a jury.

Bill: A declaration in writing. A document listing separate items. An itemized account of charges or costs. In equity practice, the first pleading in the action, the paper in which the plaintiff sets out his or her case and demands relief from the defendant.

Boundaries: Natural or artificial separations or divisions between adjoining properties to show their limits.

Burglary: The criminal offense of breaking and entering a building illegally for the purpose of committing a crime therein.

Capacity: The ability, capability, or fitness to do something; a legal right, power, or competency to perform some act. An ability to comprehend both the nature and consequences of one's acts.

Cartel: A combination of producers of any product joined together to control its production, sale, and price, so as to obtain a monopoly and restrict competition in any particular industry or commodity. Cartels exist primarily in Europe, being illegal in the United States by antitrust laws. Also, an association by agreement of companies or sections of companies having common interests, designed to prevent extreme or unfair competition and allocate markets, and to promote the interchange of knowledge resulting from scientific and technical research, exchange of patent rights, and standardization of products.

In war, an agreement between two hostile powers for the delivery of prisoners or deserters, or authorizing certain nonhostile intercourse between each other that would otherwise be prevented by the state of war, for example, agreements between enemies for intercommunication by post, telegraph, telephone, or railway.

Case law: Legal principles enunciated and embodied in judicial decisions that are derived from the application of particular areas of law to the facts of individual cases.

Certiorari: [*Latin, To be informed of.*] At common law, an original writ or order issued by the Chancery (old English court headed by the king's secretary) or King's/Queen's Bench (formerly the highest court in England), commanding officers of inferior courts to submit the record of a cause pending before them to give the party more certain and speedy justice.

A writ that a superior appellate court issues in its discretion to an inferior court, ordering it to produce a certified record of a particular case it has tried, in order to determine whether any irregularities or errors occurred that justify review of the case.

A device by which the Supreme Court of the United States exercises its discretion in selecting the cases it will review.

Charter: A grant from the government of ownership rights in land to a person, a group of people, or an organization such as a corporation.

A basic document of law of a municipal corporation granted by the state, defining its rights, liabilities, and responsibilities of self-government.

A document embodying a grant of authority from the legislature or the authority itself, such as a corporate charter.

The leasing of a mode of transportation, such as a bus, ship, or plane. A *charter-party* is a contract formed to lease a ship to a merchant in order to facilitate the conveyance of goods.

Circuit court: A specific tribunal that possesses the legal authority to hear cases within its own geographical territory.

Circumstantial evidence: Information and testimony presented by a party in a civil or criminal action that permit conclusions that indirectly establish the existence or nonexistence of a fact or event that the party seeks to prove.

Citation: A paper commonly used in various courts—such as a probate, matrimonial, or traffic court—that is served upon an individual to notify him or her that he or she is required to appear at a specific time and place.

Reference to a legal authority—such as a case, constitution, or treatise—where particular information may be found.

Civil action: A lawsuit brought to enforce, redress, or protect rights of private litigants—the plaintiffs and the defendants—not a criminal proceeding.

Civil law: Legal system derived from the Roman *Corpus Juris Civilus* of Emperor Justinian I; differs from a common-law system, which relies on prior decisions to determine the outcome of a lawsuit. Most European and South American countries have a civil law system. England and most of the countries it dominated or colonized, including Canada and the Unites States, have a common-law system. However, within these countries, Louisiana, Quebec, and Puerto Rico exhibit the influence of French and Spanish settlers in their use of civil law systems.

A body of rules that delineate private rights and remedies and govern disputes between individuals in such areas as contracts, property, and family law; distinct from criminal or public law.

Civil procedure: The methods, procedures, and practices used in civil cases.

Civil rights: Personal liberties that belong to an individual owing to his or her status as a citizen or resident of a particular country or community.

Civil rights acts: Federal legislation enacted by Congress over the course of a century beginning with the post-Civil War era that implemented and extended the fundamental guarantees of the Constitution to all citizens of the United States, regardless of their race, color, age, or religion.

Class action: A lawsuit that allows a large number of people with a common interest in a matter to sue or be sued as a group.

Code of judicial conduct: A collection of rules governing the conduct of judges while they serve in their professional capacity.

Collateral: Related; indirect; not bearing immediately upon an issue. The property pledged or given as a security interest, or a guarantee for payment of a debt, that will be taken or kept by the creditor in case of a default on the original debt.

Collective bargaining: The process through which a labor union and an employer negotiate the scope of the employment relationship.

Collective bargaining agreement: The contractual agreement between an employer and a labor union that governs wages, hours, and working conditions for employees and which can be enforced against both the employer and the union for failure to comply with its terms.

Collusion: An agreement between two or more people to defraud a person of his or her rights or to obtain something that is prohibited by law.

A secret arrangement wherein two or more people whose legal interests seemingly conflict conspire to commit fraud upon another person; a pact between two people to deceive a court with the purpose of obtaining something that they would not be able to get through legitimate judicial channels.

Color of law: The appearance of a legal right.

Commerce clause: The provision of the U.S. Constitution that gives Congress exclusive power over trade activities between the states and with foreign countries and Indian tribes.

Common law: The ancient law of England based upon societal customs and recognized and enforced by the judgments and decrees of the courts. The general body of statutes and case law that governed England and the American colonies prior to the American Revolution.

The principles and rules of action, embodied in case law rather than legislative enactments, applicable to the government and protection of persons and property that derive their authority from the community customs and traditions that evolved over the centuries as interpreted by judicial tribunals.

A designation used to denote the opposite of statutory, equitable, or civil, for example, a common-law action.

Common pleas: Trial-level courts of general jurisdiction (i.e., jurisdiction over a particular geographic region). One of the royal common-law courts in England existing since the beginning of the thirteenth century and developing from the *Curia Regis*, or the King's Court.

Community property: The holdings and resources owned in common by a husband and wife.

Compensatory damages: A sum of money awarded in a civil action by a court to indemnify (compensate) a person for the particular loss, detriment, or injury suffered as a result of the unlawful conduct of another.

Compliance: Observance; conformity; obedience.

Consent: Voluntary acquiescence to the proposal of another; the act or result of reaching an accord; a concurrence of minds; actual willingness that an act or an infringement of an interest shall occur.

Consideration: Something of value given by both parties to a contract that induces them to enter into the agreement to exchange mutual performances.

Conspiracy: An agreement between two or more persons to engage jointly in an unlawful or criminal act, or an act that is innocent in itself but becomes unlawful when done by the combination of its actors.

Constitutional amendment: The means by which an alteration to the U.S. Constitution, whether a modification, deletion, or addition, is accomplished.

Constitutional law: The written text of the state and federal constitutions. The body of judicial precedent that has gradually developed through a process in which courts interpret, apply, and explain the meaning of particular constitutional provisions and principles during a legal proceeding. Executive, legislative, and judicial actions that conform with the norms prescribed by a constitutional provision.

Contempt: An act of deliberate disobedience or disregard for the laws, regulations, or decorum of a public authority, such as a court or legislative body.

Controller: The key financial officer of a state, private, or municipal corporation, who is charged with certain specific responsibilities related to its financial affairs. See also COMPTROLLER in *WEAL*.

Controversy: An actual dispute between individuals who seek judicial resolution of their grievances that have arisen from a conflict of their alleged legal rights.

Copyright: An intangible right granted by statute to the author or originator of certain literary or artistic productions, whereby, for a limited period, the exclusive privilege is given to the person to make copies of the same for publication or sale.

Corporations: Artificial entities that are created by state statute, and that are treated much like individuals under the law, having legally enforceable rights, the ability to acquire debt and pay out profits, the ability to hold and transfer property, the ability to enter into contracts, the requirement to pay taxes, and the ability to sue and be sued.

Court-martial: A tribunal that tries violations of military criminal law. Often, the entire military justice process, from actual court proceedings to punishment.

Court of appeal: An intermediate federal judicial tribunal of review that is found in thirteen judicial districts, called circuits, in the United States.

A state judicial tribunal that reviews a decision rendered by an inferior tribunal to determine whether it made errors that warrant the reversal of its judgment.

Court of probate: A judicial body that exercises jurisdiction over the acceptance of wills as valid documents and over the management and settlement of the estates of minors or of spendthrifts, of mentally incompetent persons, and of habitual drunkards.

Covenant: An agreement, contract, or written promise between two individuals that frequently constitutes a pledge to do or refrain from doing something.

Credibility: Believability. The major legal application of the term *credibility* relates to the testimony of a witness or party during a trial. Testimony must be both competent and credible if it is to be accepted by the trier of fact as proof of an issue being litigated.

Criminal law: A body of rules and statutes that defines conduct prohibited by the government because it threatens and harms public safety and welfare and that establishes punishment to be imposed for the commission of such acts.

Criminal procedure: The framework of laws and rules that govern the administration of justice in cases involving an individual who has been accused of a crime, beginning with the initial investigation of the crime and concluding either with the unconditional release of the accused by virtue of acquittal (a judgment of not guilty) or by the imposition of a term of punishment pursuant to a conviction for the crime.

Culpable: Blameworthy; involving the commission of a fault or the breach of a duty imposed by law.

Custody: The care, possession, and control of a thing or person. The retention, inspection, guarding, maintenance, or security of a thing within the immediate care and control of the person to whom it is committed. The detention of a person by lawful authority or process.

Damages: Monetary compensation that is awarded by a court in a civil action to an individual who has been injured through the wrongful conduct of another party.

Decree: A judgment of a court that announces the legal consequences of the facts found in a case and orders that the court's decision be carried out. A decree in equity is a sentence or order of the court, pronounced on hearing and understanding all the points in is-sue, and determining the rights of all the parties to the suit, according to equity and good conscience. It is a declaration of the court announcing the legal consequences of the facts found. With the procedural merger of law and equity in the federal and most state courts under the Rules of Civil Procedure, the term *judgment* has generally replaced *decree*.

Defamation: Any intentional false communication, either written or spoken, that harms a person's reputation; decreases the respect, regard, or confidence in which a person is held; or induces disparaging, hostile, or disagreeable opinions or feelings against a person.

De novo: [*Latin, Anew*] A second time; afresh. A trial or a hearing that is ordered by an appellate court that has reviewed the record of a hearing in a lower court and sent the matter back to the original court for a new trial, as if it had not been previously heard nor decided.

Deportation: Banishment to a foreign country, attended with confiscation of property and deprivation of civil rights.

The transfer of an alien, by exclusion or expulsion, from the United States to a foreign country. The removal or sending back of an alien to the country from which he or she came because his or her presence is deemed inconsistent with the public welfare, and without any punishment being imposed or contemplated. The grounds for deportation are set forth at 8 U.S.C.A. § 1251, and the procedures are provided for in §§ 1252-1254.

Detainer: The act (or the juridical fact) of withholding from a lawfully entitled person the possession of land or goods, or the restraint of a person's personal liberty against his or her will; detention. The wrongful keeping of a person's goods is called an unlawful detainer although the original taking may have been lawful.

A request filed by a criminal justice agency with the institution in which a prisoner is incarcerated asking the institution either to hold the prisoner for the agency or to notify the agency when release of the prisoner is imminent.

Disbar: To revoke an attorney's license to practice law.

Disclaimer: The denial, refusal, or rejection of a right, power, or responsibility.

Discovery: A category of procedural devices employed by a party to a civil or criminal action, prior to trial, to require the adverse party to disclose information that is essential for the preparation of the requesting party's case and that the other party alone knows or possesses.

Discrimination: In constitutional law, the grant by statute of particular privileges to a class arbitrarily designated from a sizable number of persons, where no reasonable distinction exists between the favored and disfavored classes. Federal laws, supplemented by court decisions, prohibit discrimination in such areas as employment, housing, voting rights, education, and access to public facilities. They also proscribe discrimination on the basis of race, age, sex, nationality, disability, or religion. In addition, state and local laws can prohibit discrimination in these areas and in others not covered by federal laws.

Disorderly conduct: A broad term describing conduct that disturbs the peace or endangers the morals, health, or safety of a community.

Dispositive fact: Information of evidence that unqualifiedly brings a conclusion to a legal controversy.

District and prosecuting attorneys: The elected or appointed public officers of each state, county, or other political subdivision who institute criminal proceedings on behalf of the government.

District court: A designation of an inferior state court that exercises general jurisdiction (i.e., jurisdiction over a particular geographic region) that it has been granted by the constitution or statute which created it. A U.S. judicial tribunal with original jurisdiction to try cases or controversies that fall within its limited jurisdiction.

Divest: To deprive or take away.

Domestic violence: Any abusive, violent, coercive, forceful, or threatening act or word inflicted by one member of a family or household on another can constitute domestic violence.

Double jeopardy: A second prosecution for the same offense after acquittal (a judgment of not guilty) or conviction or multiple punishments for same offense. The evil sought to be avoided by prohibiting double jeopardy is double trial and double conviction, not necessarily double punishment.

Drugs and narcotics: *Drugs* are articles intended for use in the diagnosis, cure, mitigation, treatment, or prevention of disease in humans or animals, and any articles other than food intended to affect the mental or body function of humans or animals. *Narcotics* are any drugs that dull the senses and commonly become addictive after prolonged use.

Due process of law: A fundamental constitutional guarantee that all legal proceedings will be fair and that one will be given notice of the proceedings and an opportunity to be heard before government acts to take away one's life, liberty, or property. Also, a constitutional guarantee that a law shall not be unreasonable, arbitrary, or capricious.

Elector: A voter who has fulfilled the qualifications imposed by law; a constituent; a selector of a public officer; a person who has the right to cast a ballot for the approval or rejection of a political proposal or question, such as the issuance of bonds by a state or municipality to finance public works projects.

A member of the electoral college—an association of voters elected by the populace of each state and the District of Columbia—which convenes every four years to select the president and vice president of the United States.

Electoral college: Nominated persons, known as electors, from the states and the District of Columbia, who meet every four years in their home state or district and cast ballots to choose the president and vice president of the United States.

Eminent domain: The power to take private property for public use by a state, municipality, or private person or corporation authorized to exercise functions of public character, following the payment of just compensation to the owner of that property.

Employment law: The body of law that governs the employer-employee relationship, including individual employment contracts, the application of tort and contract doctrines, and a large group of statutory regulation on issues such as the right to organize and negotiate collective bargaining agreements, protection from discrimination, wages and hours, and health and safety.

En banc: [*Latin, French. In the bench.*] Full bench. Refers to a session where the entire membership of the court will participate in the decision rather than the regular quorum. In other countries, it is common for a court to have more members than are usually necessary to hear an appeal. In the United States, the Circuit Courts of Appeal usually sit in panels of judges but for important cases may expand the bench to a larger number, when the judges are said to be sitting *en banc.* Similarly, only one of the judges of the U.S. Tax Court will typically hear and decide on a tax controversy. However, when the issues involved are unusually novel or of wide impact, the case will be heard and decided by the full court sitting *en banc.*

Enjoin: To direct, require, command, or admonish.

Equal protection: The constitutional guarantee that no person or class of persons shall be denied the same protection of the laws that is enjoyed by other persons or other classes in like circumstances in their lives, liberty, property, and pursuit of happiness.

Espionage: The act of securing information of a military or political nature that a competing nation holds secret. It can involve the analysis of diplomatic reports, publications, statistics, and broadcasts, as well as spying, a clandestine activity carried out by an individual or individuals working under a secret identity for the benefit of a nation's information gathering techniques. In the United States, the organization that heads most activities dedicated to espionage is the Central Intelligence Agency.

Estate: The degree, quantity, nature, and extent of interest that a person has in real and personal property. An estate in lands, tenements, and hereditaments (anything that can be passed by an individual to heirs) signifies such interest as the tenant has therein. *Estate* is commonly used in conveyances in connection with the words *right, title,* and *interest,* and is, to a great degree, synonymous with all of them.

When used in connection with probate proceedings, the term encompasses the total property of whatever kind that is owned by a decedent prior to the distribution of that property in accordance with the terms of a will, or when there is no will, by the laws of inheritance in the state of domicile of the decedent. It means, ordinarily, the whole of the property owned by anyone, the realty as well as the personalty.

In its broadest sense, the social, civic, or political condition or standing of a person; or a class of persons considered as grouped for social, civic, political purposes.

Estoppel: A legal principle that precludes a party from denying or alleging a certain fact owing to that party's previous conduct, allegation, or denial.

Exhaustion of remedies: Doctrine requiring that procedures established by statute, common law, contract, or custom must be initiated and followed in certain cases before an aggrieved party may seek relief from the courts. After all other available remedies have been exhausted, a lawsuit may be filed.

Ex parte: [*Latin, On one side only.*] Done by, for, or on the application of one party alone.

Ex post facto laws: [*Latin, "After-the-fact" laws*] Laws that provide for the infliction of punishment upon a person for some prior act that, at the time it was committed, was not illegal.

Extenuating circumstances: Facts surrounding the commission of a crime that work to mitigate or lessen it.

Extortion: The obtaining of property from another induced by wrongful use of actual or threatened force, violence, or fear, or under color of official right.

False imprisonment: The illegal confinement of one individual against his or her will by another individual in such a manner as to violate the confined individual's right to be free from restraint of movement.

Federal courts: The U.S. judicial tribunals created by Article III of the Constitution, or by Congress, to hear and determine justiciable controversies.

Federal register: A daily publication that makes available to the public the rules, regulations, and other legal notices issued by federal administrative agencies

Felony: A serious crime, characterized under federal law and many state statutes as any offense punishable by death or imprisonment in excess of one year.

Fiduciary: An individual in whom another has placed the utmost trust and confidence to manage and protect property or money. The relationship wherein one person has an obligation to act for another's benefit.

Final decision: The resolution of a controversy by a court or series of courts from which no appeal may be taken and that precludes further action. The last act by a lower court that is required for the completion of a lawsuit, such as the handing down of a final judgment upon which an appeal to a higher court may be brought.

First impression: The initial presentation to, or examination by, a court of a particular question of law.

Forfeiture: The involuntary relinquishment of money or property without compensation as a consequence of a breach or non-performance of some legal obligation or the commission of a crime. The loss of a corporate charter or franchise as a result of illegality, malfeasance (any wrongful act), or nonfeasance (intentional failure to perform a required duty or obligation). The surrender by an owner of her or his entire interest in real property mandated by law as a punishment for illegal conduct or negligence. In old English law, the release of land by a tenant to the tenant's lord due to some breach of conduct, or the loss of goods or chattels (articles of personal property) assessed as a penalty against the perpetrator of some crime or offense and as a recompense to the injured party.

Fraud: A false representation of a matter of fact—whether by words or by conduct, by false or misleading allegations, or by concealment of what should have been disclosed—that deceives and is intended to deceive another so that the individual will act upon it to her or his legal injury.

Freedom of association: The right to associate with others for the purpose of engaging in constitutionally protected activities.

Freedom of speech: The right, guaranteed by the First Amendment to the U.S. Constitution, to express beliefs and ideas without unwarranted government restriction.

Freedom of the press: The right, guaranteed by the First Amendment to the U.S. Constitution, to gather, publish, and distribute information and ideas without government restriction; this right encompasses freedom from prior restraints on publication and freedom from censorship.

Friend of the court: A person who has a strong interest in a matter that is the subject of a lawsuit in which he or she is not a party. See also AMICUS CURIAE.

Fruit of the poisonous tree: The principle that proscribes the use of evidence directly derived from an illegal search and seizure.

Gag order: A court order to gag or bind an unruly defendant or remove her or him from the courtroom in a trial. In a trial with a great deal of notoriety, a court order directed to attorneys and witnesses not to discuss the case with the media—such order being felt necessary to assure the defendant of a fair trial. A court order, directed to the media, not to report certain aspects of a criminal investigation prior to trial.

Genocide: The crime of destroying or conspiring to destroy a national, ethnic, racial, or religious group.

Grand jury: A panel of citizens that is convened by a court to decide whether it is appropriate for the government to indict (proceed with the prosecution against) someone suspected of a crime.

Grant: To confer, give, or bestow. A gift of legal rights or privileges, or a recognition of asserted rights, as in treaty.

Gross negligence: An indifference to, and a blatant violation of, a legal duty with respect to the rights of others.

Grounds: The basis or foundation; reasons sufficient in law to justify relief.

Guardian ad litem: A guardian appointed by the court to represent the interests of infants, the unborn, or incompetent persons in legal actions.

Gun control: Government regulation of the manufacture, sale, and possession of firearms.

Habeas corpus: [*Latin, You have the body.*] A writ (court order) that commands an individual or a government official who has restrained another to produce the prisoner at a designated time and place so that the court can determine the legality of custody and decide whether to order the prisoner's release.

Homicide: The killing of one human being by another human being (cf. MURDER).

Immigration: The entrance into a country of foreigners for purposes of permanent residence. The correlative term *emigration* denotes the act of such persons in leaving their former country. See also ALIENS.

Impeachment: A process used to charge, try, and remove public officials for misconduct while in office.

Independent contractor: A person who contracts to do a piece of work according to her or his own methods and is subject to another's control only as to the end product or the final result of the work.

Independent counsel: An attorney appointed by the federal government to investigate and prosecute federal government officials.

Indictment: A written accusation charging that an individual named therein has committed an act or omitted to do something that is punishable by law.

Informed consent: Assent to permit an occurrence, such as surgery, that is based on a complete disclosure of facts needed to make the decision intelligently, such as knowledge of the risks entailed or alternatives.

The name for a fundamental principle of law that a physician has a duty to reveal what a reasonably prudent physician in the medical community employing reasonable care would reveal to a patient as to whatever reasonably foreseeable risks of harm might result from a proposed course of treatment. This disclosure must be afforded so that a patient—exercising ordinary care for his or her own welfare and confronted with a choice of undergoing to the proposed treatment, alternative treatment, or none at all—can intelligently exercise judgment by reasonably balancing the probable risks against the probable benefits.

Infringement: The encroachment, breach, or violation of a right, law, regulation or contract.

Injunction: A court order by which an individual is required to perform or is restrained from performing a particular act. A writ framed according to the circumstances of the individual case.

Intent: A determination to perform a particular act or to act in a particular manner for a specific reason; an aim or design; a resolution to use a certain means to reach an end.

Interlocutory: Provisional; interim; temporary; not final; that which intervenes between the beginning and the end of a lawsuit or proceeding to either decide a particular point or matter that is not the final issue of the entire controversy or prevent irreparable harm during the pendency of the lawsuit.

Judicial review: A court's authority to examine an executive or legislative act and to invalidate that act if it is contrary to constitutional principles.

Judiciary: The branch of government that is endowed with the authority to interpret and apply the law, adjudicate legal disputes, and otherwise administer justice.

Jurisdiction: The geographic area over which authority extends; legal authority; the authority to hear and determine causes of action.

Just cause: A reasonable and lawful ground for action.

Justice of the peace: A judicial officer with limited power whose duties may include hearing cases that involve civil controversies, conserving the peace, performing judicial acts, hearing minor criminal complaints, and committing offenders.

Juvenile law: An area of the law that deals with the actions and well-being of persons who are not yet adults.

Labor law: An area of the law that deals with the rights of employers employees, and labor organizations.

Legal aid: A system of nonprofit organizations that provide legal services to people who cannot afford an attorney.

Liability: A comprehensive legal term that describes the condition of being actually or potentially subject to a legal obligation.

Libel and slander: Two torts that involve the communication of false information about a person, a group, or an entity such as a corporation. Libel is any defamation that can be seen, such as a writing, printing, effigy, movie, or statue. Slander is any defamation that is spoken or heard.

Magistrate: Any individual who has the power of a public civil officer or inferior judicial officer, such as a justice of the peace.

Mail fraud: A crime in which the perpetrator develops a scheme using the mails to defraud another of money or property. This crime specifically requires the intent to defraud, and is a federal offense governed by §1341 of title 18 of the U.S. Code. The mail fraud statute was first enacted in 1872 to prohibit illicit mailings with the Postal Service (formerly the Post Office) for the purpose of executing a fraudulent scheme.

Malice: An intentional commission of a wrongful act, absent justification, with the intent to cause harm to others; conscious violation of the law that injures another individual; a mental state indicating a disposition in disregard of social duty and a tendency toward malfeasance (the commission of any wrongful act).

Manslaughter: The unjustifiable, inexcusable, and intentional killing of a human being without deliberation, premeditation, and malice. The unlawful killing of a human being without any deliberation, which may be involuntary, in the commission of a lawful act without due caution and circumspection.

Material: Important; affecting the merits of a case; causing a particular course of action; significant; substantial. A description of the quality of evidence that possesses such substantial probative value as to establish the truth or falsity of a point in issue in a lawsuit.

Medicaid: A joint federal-state program that provides health care insurance to low-income persons.

Medicare: A federally funded system of health and hospital insurance for persons age sixty-five and older and for disabled persons.

Merits: The strict legal rights of the parties to a lawsuit.

Minimum wage: The minimum hourly rate of compensation for labor, as established by federal statute and required of employers engaged in businesses that affect interstate commerce. Most states also have similar statutes governing minimum wages.

Minor: An infant or person who is under the age of legal competence. A term derived from the civil law, which described a person under a certain age as *less than* so many years. In most states, a person is no longer a minor after reaching the age of 18 (though state laws might still prohibit certain acts until reaching a greater age; e.g., purchase of liquor). Also, less; of less consideration; lower; a person of inferior condition.

Minority: The state or condition of a minor; infancy. Opposite of majority. The smaller number of votes of a deliberative assembly; opposed to majority. In context of the Constitution's guarantee of equal protection, *minority* does not have merely numerical denotation by refers to identifiable and specially disadvantaged groups such as those based on race, religion, ethnicity, or national origin.

Misdemeanor: Offenses lower than felonies and generally those punishable by fine, penalty, forfeiture, or imprisonment other than in a penitentiary. Under federal law, and most state laws, any offense other than a felony is classified as a misdemeanor. Certain states also have various classes of misdemeanors (e.g., Class A, B, etc.).

Misrepresentation: An assertion or manifestation by words or conduct that is not in accord with the facts.

Mistrial: A courtroom trial that has been terminated prior to its normal conclusion. A mistrial has no legal effect and is considered an invalid or nugatory trial. It differs from a "new trial," which recognizes that a trial was completed but was set aside so that the issues could be tried again.

Mitigating circumstances: Circumstances that may be considered by a court in determining culpability of a defendant or the extent of damages to be awarded to a plaintiff. Mitigating circumstances do not justify or excuse an offense but may reduce the severity of a charge. Similarly, a recognition of mitigating circumstances to reduce a damage award does not imply that the damages were not suffered but that they have been partially ameliorated.

Money laundering: The process of taking the proceeds of criminal activity and making them appear legal.

Moot: An issue presenting no real controversy.

Murder: The unlawful killing of another human being without justification or excuse.

Music publishing: The contractual relationship between an songwriter or music composer and a music publisher, whereby the writer assigns part or all of his or her music copyrights to the publisher in exchange for the publisher's commercial exploitation of the music.

Necessity: A defense asserted by a criminal or civil defendant that he or she had no choice but to break the law.

Negligence: Conduct that falls below the standards of behavior established by law for the protection of others against unreasonable risk of harm. A person has acted negligently if he or she has departed from the conduct expected of a reasonably prudent person acting under similar circumstances.

Negligence is also the name of a cause of action (facts that give a person the right to seek judicial solution to a problem) in the law of torts. To establish negligence, a plaintiff must prove that the defendant had a duty to the plaintiff, the defendant breached that duty by failing to conform to the required standard of conduct, the defendant's negligent conduct was the cause of the harm to the plaintiff, and the plaintiff was, in fact, harmed or damaged.

Nominal damages: Minimal money damages awarded to an individual in an action where the person has not suffered any substantial injury or loss for which he or she must be compensated.

Obstruction of justice: A criminal offense that involves interference, through words or actions, with the proper operations of a court or officers of the court.

Original jurisdiction: The authority of a tribunal to entertain a lawsuit, try it, and set forth a judgment on the law and facts.

Parent and child: The legal relationship between a father or mother and his or her offspring.

Paternity: The state or condition of a father; the relationship of a father.

Pecuniary: Monetary; relating to money; financial; consisting of money or that which can be valued in money.

Per curiam: [*Latin, By the court.*] A phrase used to distinguish an opinion of the whole court from an opinion written by any one judge.

Peremptory challenge: The right to challenge a juror without assigning, or being required to assign, a reason for the challenge.

Perjury: A crime that occurs when an individual willfully makes a false statement during a judicial proceeding, after he or she has taken an oath to speak the truth.

Per se: [*Latin, In itself.*] Simply as such; in its own nature without reference to its relation.

Power of attorney: A written document in which one person (the principal) appoints another person to act as an agent on his or her behalf, thus conferring authority on the agent to perform certain acts or functions on behalf of the principal.

Preemption: A doctrine based on the Supremacy Clause of the U.S. Constitution that holds that certain matters are of such a national, as opposed to local, character that federal laws preempt or take precedence over states laws. As such, a state may not pass a law inconsistent with the federal law.

A doctrine of state law that holds that a state law displaces a local law or regulation that is in the same field and is in conflict or inconsistent with the state law.

Prejudice: A forejudgment; bias; partiality; preconceived opinion. A leaning toward one side of a cause for some reason other than a conviction of its justice.

Preliminary injunction: A temporary order made by a court at the request of one party that prevents the other party from pursuing a particular course of conduct until the conclusion of a trial on the merits.

Presidential powers: The executive authority given to the president of the United States by Article II of the Constitution to carry out the duties of the office.

Price-fixing: The organized setting of what the public will be charged for certain products or services agreed to by competitors in the marketplace in violation of the Sherman Anti-Trust Act (15 U.S.C.A. § 1 et seq.).

Prima facie: [*Latin, On the first appearance.*] A fact presumed to be true unless it is disproved.

Prior restraint: Government prohibition of speech in advance of publication.

Prisoners' rights: The nature and extent of the privileges afforded to individuals kept in custody or confinement against their will because they were convicted of performing an unlawful act.

Privacy: In constitutional law, the right of people to make personal decisions regarding intimate matters; under the common law, the right of people to lead their lives in a manner that is reasonably secluded from public scrutiny, whether such scrutiny comes from a neighbor's prying eyes, an investigator's eavesdropping ears, or a news photographer's intrusive camera; and in statutory law, the right of people to be free from unwarranted drug testing and electronic surveillance.

Privilege: A particular benefit, advantage, or immunity enjoyed by a person or class of people that is not shared with others. A power of exemption against or beyond the law. It is not a right but, rather, exempts one from the performance of a duty, obligation, or liability.

Privileges and immunities: Concepts contained in the U.S. Constitution that place the citizens of each state on an equal basis with citizens of other states in respect to advantages resulting from citizenship in those states and citizenship in the United States.

Privity: A close, direct, or successive relationship; having a mutual interest or right.

Probable cause: Apparent facts discovered through logical inquiry that would lead a reasonably intelligent and prudent person to believe that an accused person has committed a crime, thereby warranting his or her prosecution, or that a cause of action (facts that give a person the right to seek judicial solution to a problem) has accrued, justifying a civil lawsuit.

Pro bono: Short for *pro bono publico* [*Latin, For the public good*]. The designation given to the free legal work done by an attorney for indigent clients and religious, charitable, and other non-profit entities.

Promissory estoppel: In the law of contracts, the doctrine that provides that if a party changes his or her position substantially either by acting or forbearing from acting in reliance upon a gratuitous promise, then that party can enforce the promise although the essential elements of a contract are not present.

Property right: A generic term that refers to any type of right to specific property whether it is personal or real property, tangible or intangible; e.g., a professional athlete has a valuable property right in his or her name, photograph, and image, and such right may be saleable by the athlete.

Prosecuting attorney: See DISTRICT AND PROSECUTING ATTORNEYS.

Proximate cause: An act from which an injury results as a natural, direct, uninterrupted consequence and without which the injury would not have occurred.

Publishing law: The body of law relating to the publication of books, magazines, newspapers, electronic materials, and other artistic works.

Punitive damages: Monetary compensation awarded to an injured party that goes beyond that which is necessary to compensate the individual for losses and that is intended to punish the wrongdoer.

Qui tam actions: Civil actions maintained by private persons on behalf of both themselves and the government to recover damages or to enforce penalties available under a statute prohibiting specified conduct. The term *qui tam* is short for the Latin *qui tam pro domino rege quam pro se ipso in hac parte sequitur*, which means "who brings the action for the king as well as for himself."

Ratification: The confirmation or adoption of an act that has already been performed.

Rational basis test: A judicial standard of review that examines whether a legislature had a reasonable and not an arbitrary basis for enacting a particular statute.

Recidivism: The behavior of a repeat or habitual criminal. A measurement of the rate at which offenders commit other crimes, either by arrest or conviction baselines, after being released from incarceration.

Recklessness: Rashness; heedlessness; wanton conduct. The state of mind accompanying an act that either pays no regard to its probably or possibly injurious consequences, or which, though foreseeing such consequences, persists in spite of such knowledge.

Recuse: To disqualify or remove oneself as a judge over a particular proceeding because of one's conflict of interest. Recusal, or the judge's act of disqualifying himself or herself from presiding over a proceeding, is based on the maxim that judges are charged with a duty of impartiality in administering justice.

Referendum: The right reserved to the people to approve or reject an act of the legislature, or the right of the people to approve or reject legislation that has been referred to them by the legislature.

Regulation: A rule of order having the force of law, prescribed by a superior or competent authority, relating to the actions of those under the authority's control.

Relief: Financial assistance provided to the indigent by the government. The redress, or benefit, given by a court to an individual who brings a legal action.

Remand: To send back.

Remittitur: The procedural process by which an excessive verdict of the jury is reduced. If money damages awarded by a jury are grossly excessive as a matter of law, the judge may order the plaintiff to remit a portion of the award.

Republic: That form of government in which the administration of affairs is open to all the citizens. A political unit or "state," independent of its form of government.

Rescind: To declare a contract void—of no legal force or binding effect—from its inception and thereby restore the parties to the positions they would have occupied had no contract ever been made.

Restraining order: A command of the court issued upon the filing of an application for an injunction, prohibiting the defendant from performing a threatened act until a hearing on the application can be held. See also TEMPORARY RESTRAINING ORDER.

Retroactive: Having reference to things that happened in the past, prior to the occurrence of the act in question.

Ripeness: The mandate contained in Article III of the Constitution that requires an appellate court to consider whether a case has matured into a controversy worthy of adjudication before it can hear the case.

Robbery: The taking of money or goods in the possession of another, from his or her person or immediate presence, by force or intimidation.

Royalty: Compensation for the use of property, usually copyrighted works, patented inventions, or natural resources, expressed as a percentage of receipts from using the property or as a payment for each unit produced.

Savings and loan association: A financial institution owned by and operated for the benefit of those using its services. The savings and loan association's primary purpose is making loans to its members, usually for the purchase of real estate or homes.

School desegregation: The attempt to end the practice of separating children of different races into distinct public schools.

Search and seizure: In international law the right of ships of war, as regulated by treaties, to examine a merchant vessel during war in order to determine whether the ship or its cargo is liable to seizure

A hunt by law enforcement officials for property or communications believed to be evidence of crime, and the act of taking possession of this property.

Search warrant: A court order authorizing the examination of a place for the purpose of discovering contraband, stolen property, or evidence of guilt to be used in the prosecution of a criminal action.

Securities: Evidence of a corporation's debts or property.

Seizure: Forcible possession; a grasping, snatching, or putting in possession. See also SEARCH AND SEIZURE.

Self-defense: The protection of one's person or property against some injury attempted by another.

Sentencing: The postconviction stage of the criminal justice process, in which the defendant is brought before the court for the imposition of a penalty.

Separation: A termination of cohabitation of husband and wife either by mutual agreement or, in the case of *judicial separation*, under the decree of a court. See also DIVORCE.

Separation of powers: The division of state and federal government into three independent branches.

Sex offenses: A class of sexual conduct prohibited by the law.

Sexual harassment: Unwelcome sexual advances, requests for sexual favors, and other verbal or physical conduct of a sexual nature that tends to create a hostile or offensive work environment.

Slander: See LIBEL AND SLANDER.

Small claims court: A special court, sometimes called conciliation court, that provides expeditious, informal, and inexpensive adjudication of small claims.

Sodomy: Anal or oral intercourse between human beings, or any sexual relations between a human being and an animal, the act of which may be punishable as a criminal offense.

Solicitor general: An officer of the U.S. Department of Justice who represents the U.S. government in cases before the U.S. Supreme Court.

Sovereign immunity: The legal protection that prevents a sovereign state or person from being sued without consent.

Standing: The legally protectible stake or interest that an individual has in a dispute that entitles him to bring the controversy before the court to obtain judicial relief.

State's evidence: A colloquial term for testimony given by an accomplice or joint participant in the commission of a crime, subject to an agreement that the person will be granted immunity from prosecution if he or she voluntarily, completely, and fairly discloses his or her own guilt as well as that of the other participants.

Statute: An act of legislature that declares, proscribes, or commands something; a specific law, expressed in writing.

Statute of limitations: A type of federal or state law that restricts the time within which legal proceedings may be brought.

Statutory: Created, defined, or relating to a statute; required by statute; conforming to a statute.

Stay: The act of temporarily stopping a judicial proceeding through the order of a court.

Stop and frisk: The situation where a police officer who is suspicious of an individual detains the person and runs his or her hands lightly over the suspect's outer garments to determine if the person is carrying a concealed weapon.

Strict liability: Absolute legal responsibility for an injury that can be imposed on the wrongdoer without proof of carelessness or fault.

Subrogation: The substitution of one person in the place of another with reference to a lawful claim, demand, or right, so that he or she who is substituted succeeds to the rights of the other in relation to the debit or claim, and its rights, remedies, or securities.

Summary judgment: A procedural device used during civil litigation to promptly and expeditiously dispose of a case without a trial. It is used when there is no dispute as to the material facts of the case and a party is entitled to judgment as a matter of law.

Supremacy clause: The clause of Article VI of the U.S. Constitution that declares that all laws and treaties made by the federal government shall be the "supreme law of the land."

Temporary restraining order: A court order that lasts only until the court can hear further evidence. See also RESTRAINING ORDER.

Terrorism: The unlawful use of force or violence against persons or property in order to coerce or intimidate a government or the civilian population in furtherance of political or social objectives.

Tortfeasor: A wrongdoer; an individual who commits a wrongful act that injures another and for which the law provides a legal right to seek relief; a defendant in a civil tort action. See also TORT LAW.

Tort law: A body of rights, obligations, and remedies that is applied by courts in civil proceedings to provide relief for persons who have suffered harm from the wrongful acts of others. The person who sustains injury or suffers pecuniary damage as the result of tortious conduct is knows as the plaintiff, and the person who is responsible for inflicting the injury and incurs liability for the damage is known as the defendant or tortfeasor.

Trademarks: Distinctive symbols of authenticity through which the products of particular manufacturers or the salable commodities of particular merchants can be distinguished from those of others.

Treaty: A compact made between two or more independent nations with a view to the public welfare.

Trust: A relationship created at the direction of an individual, in which one or more persons hold the individual's property subject to certain duties to use and protect it for the benefit of others.

Trustee: An individual or corporation named by an individual, who sets aside property to be used for the benefit of another person, to manage the property as provided by the terms of the document that created the arrangement.

Vacate: To annul, set aside, or render void; to surrender possession or occupancy.

Vague: Imprecise; uncertain; indefinite.

Visa: An official endorsement on a passport or other document required to secure an alien's admission to a country.

Voir dire: [*Old French, To speak the truth.*] The preliminary examination of prospective jurors to determine their qualifications and suitability to serve on a jury, in order to ensure the selection of a fair and impartial jury.

Water rights: A group of rights designed to protect the use and enjoyment of water that travels in streams, rivers, lakes, and ponds, gathers on the surface of the earth, or collects underground.

Weapons: A comprehensive term for all instruments of offensive or defensive combat, including items used in injuring a person.

Welfare: Government benefits distributed to impoverished persons to enable them to maintain a minimum standard of well-being.

Wiretapping: A form of electronic eavesdropping accomplished by seizing or overhearing communications by means of a concealed recording or listening device connected to the transmission line.

Work product rule: A legal doctrine that provides that certain materials prepared by an attorney who is acting on behalf of his or her client during preparation for litigation are privileged from discovery by the attorney for the opposition party.

Writ: An order issued by a court requiring that something be done or giving authority to do a specified act.

Wrongful death: The taking of the life of an individual resulting from the willful or negligent act of another person or persons.

Wrongful discharge: The cause of action (facts that give a person the right to seek judicial solution to a problem) for at-will employees against their former employer, alleging that their discharge was in violation of state or federal antidiscrimination statutes, public policy, an implied contract, or an implied covenant of good faith and fair dealing.

ABORTION: LOUISIANA'S ABORTION MALPRACTICE LAW

Also known as Act 825, the Louisiana state law regarding the liabilities of abortion doctors was challenged by several physicians and five health care clinics. They claimed the law made the procedure so legally risky that even licensed doctors would cease considering them, thereby eliminating the right for women to have abortions. Dr. Okpalobi et al lost their case, however, due to issues regarding the court's jurisdiction over the named defendants.

RS 9:2800.12

§2800.12. Liability for termination of a pregnancy

A. Any person who performs an abortion is liable to the mother of the unborn child for any damage occasioned or precipitated by the abortion, which action survives for a period of three years from the date of discovery of the damage with a peremptive period of ten years from the date of the abortion.

B. For purposes of this Section:

(1) "Abortion" means the deliberate termination of an intrauterine human pregnancy after fertilization of a female ovum, by any person, including the pregnant woman herself, with an intention other than to produce a live birth or to remove a dead unborn child.

(2) "Damage" includes all special and general damages which are recoverable in an intentional tort, negligence, survival, or wrongful death action for injuries suffered or damages occasioned by the unborn child or mother.

(3) "Unborn child" means the unborn offspring of human beings from the moment of conception through pregnancy and until termination of the pregnancy.

C.(1) The signing of a consent form by the mother prior to the abortion does not negate this cause of action, but rather reduces the recovery of damages to the extent that the content of the consent form informed the mother of the risk of the type of injuries or loss for which she is seeking to recover.

(2) The laws governing medical malpractice or limitations of liability thereof provided in Title 40 of the Louisiana Revised Statutes of 1950 are not applicable to this Section.

Acts 1997, No. 825,§ 1.

ELECTIONS: MISSOURI'S TERM LIMITS AMENDMENT

Sections 15–22 of this amendment to the Missouri Constitution led to changes in ballot language for Missouri elections involving U.S. Representatives and U.S. Senators. The ballot language was deemed unconstitutional by the Supreme Court in Cook v. Gralike.

Missouri Constitution, Article VIII Sections 16–18

Section 16. CONGRESSIONAL TERM LIMITS AMENDMENT

(a) No person shall serve in the office of United States Representative for more than three terms, but upon ratification of this amendment no person who has held the office of the United States Representative or who then holds the office shall serve for more than two additional terms.

(b) No person shall serve in the office of United States Senator for more than two terms, but upon ratification of this amendment no person who has held the office of United States Senator or who then holds the office shall serve in the office for more than one additional term.

(c) Any state may enact by state constitutional amendment longer or shorter limits than those specified in section "a" or "b" herein.

(d) This article shall have no time limit within which it must be ratified to become operative upon the ratification of the legislatures of three-fourths of the several States.

Therefore, We, the people of the State of Missouri, have chosen to amend the state constitution to inform voters regarding incumbent and non-incumbent federal candidates' support for the above proposed CONGRESSIONAL TERM LIMITS AMENDMENT.

Section 17. VOTER INSTRUCTION ON TERM LIMITS FOR MEMBERS OF CONGRESS

(1) We, the Voters of Missouri, hereby instruct each member of our congressional delegation to use all of his or her delegated powers to pass the Congressional Term Limits Amendment set forth above.

(2) All primary and general election ballots shall have printed the information "DISREGARDED VOTERS' INSTRUCTION ON TERM LIMITS" adjacent to the name of any United States Senator or Representative who:

(a) fails to vote in favor of the proposed congressional Term Limits Amendment set forth above when brought to a vote or;

(b) fails to second the proposed Congressional Term Limits Amendment set forth above if it lacks for a second before any proceeding of the legislative body or;

(c) fails to propose or otherwise bring to a vote of the full legislative body the proposed Congressional Term Limits Amendment set forth above if it otherwise lacks a legislator who so proposes or brings to a vote of the full legislative body the proposed Congressional Term Limits Amendment set forth above or;

(d) fails to vote in favor of all votes bringing the proposed Congressional Term Limits Amendment set forth above before any committee or subcommittee of the respective house upon which he or she serves or;

(e) fails to reject any attempt to delay, table or otherwise prevent a vote by the full legislative body of the proposed Congressional Term Limits Amendment set forth above or;

(f) fails to vote against any proposed constitutional amendment that would establish longer term limits than those in the proposed Congressional Term Limits Amendment set forth above regardless of any other actions in support of the proposed Congressional Term Limits Amendment set forth above or;

(g) sponsors or cosponsors any proposed constitutional amendment or law that would increase term limits beyond those in the proposed Congressional Term Limits Amendment set forth above, or;

(h) fails to ensure that all votes on Congressional Term Limits are recorded and made available to the public.

(3) The information "DISREGARDED VOTERS' INSTRUCTION ON TERM LIMITS" shall not appear adjacent to the names of incumbent candidates for Congress if the Congressional Term Limits Amendment set forth above is before the states for ratification or has become part of the United States Constitution.

Section 18. VOTER INSTRUCTION ON TERM LIMIT PLEDGE FOR NON- INCUMBENTS

(1) Non-incumbent candidates for United States Senator and Representative shall be given an opportunity to take a "Term Limit" pledge regarding "Term Limits" each time they file to run for such office. Those who decline to take the "Term Limits" pledge shall have the information "DECLINED TO PLEDGE TO SUPPORT TERM LIMITS" printed adjacent to their name on every primary and general election ballot.

(2) The "Term Limits" pledge shall be offered to non-incumbent candidates for United States Senator and Representative until a Constitutional Amendment which limits the number of terms of United States Senators to no more than two and United States Representatives to no more than three shall have become part of our United States Constitution.

(3) The "Term Limits" pledge that each non-incumbent candidate, set forth above, shall be offered is as follows:

I support term limits and pledge to use all my legislative powers to enact the proposed Constitutional Amendment set forth in the Term Limits Act of 1996. If elected, I pledge to vote in such a way that the designation "DISREGARDED VOTERS' INSTRUCTION ON TERM LIMITS" will not appear adjacent to my name.

(Adopted November 5, 1996)

(1998) Article VIII, sections 15–22 are a facially unconstitutional violation of plaintiff's first amendment rights and also violate articles I and V of the U.S. Constitution. *Gralike v. Cook*, 996 F.Supp. 917 (W.D. Mo.).

EMPLOYMENT LAW: OSHA LETTER ON WORK-AT-HOME EMPLOYEES

The Occupational Safety and Health Administration's opinion letter below regarding work-at-home employees caused great confusion and concern in the business world until its complete withdrawal January 5, 2000, one day after it was widely reported in the news media. It seemed to imply that all employers were responsible for the day-to-day safety of their employees no matter where they worked. (Note: minor contact information and names have been omitted.)

November 15, 1999

Mr. T. Trahan

CSC Credit Services

[address]

Dear Mr. Trahan:

Thank you for your August 21, 1997 letter to the Occupational Safety and Health Administration's (OSHA's) Directorate of Compliance Programs (DCP), requesting information on OSHA's policies concerning employees working at home. We apologize for the delay in responding.

Specifically, you state that your company will be placing some of its sales executives in home office environments. You state that the home office is generally a single room within the home of the sales executive that would have a desk, chair, file cabinet, business telephone, desktop or laptop computer, printer and a fax machine. You ask several specific questions that would apply specifically to your sales executives, as well as general questions that could apply to many other types of home work situations.

Question #1:

What is the employer's obligation within the home work environment?

Response #1: WITHDRAWN 1/5/2000

The OSH Act applies to work performed by an employee in any workplace within the United States, including a workplace located in the employee's home. All employers, including those which have entered into "work at home" agreements with employees, are responsible for complying with the OSH Act and with safety and health standards.

Even when the workplace is in a designated area in an employee's home, the employer retains some degree of control over the conditions of the "work at home" agreement. An important factor in the development of these arrangements is to ensure that employees are not exposed to reasonably foreseeable hazards created by their at-home employment. Ensuring safe and healthful working conditions for the employee should be a precondition for any home-based work assignments. Employers should exercise reasonable diligence to identify in advance the possible hazards associated with particular home work assignments, and should provide the necessary protection through training, personal protective equipment, or other controls appropriate to reduce or eliminate the hazard. In some circumstances the exercise of reasonable diligence may necessitate an on-site examination of the working environment by the employer. Employers must take steps to reduce or eliminate any work-related safety or health problems they become aware of through on-site visits or other means.

Certainly, where the employer provides work materials for use in the employee's home, the employer should ensure that employer-provided tools or supplies pose no hazard under reasonably foreseeable conditions of storage or use by employees. An employer must also take appropriate steps when the employer knows or has reason to know that employee-provided tools or supplies could create a safety or health risk.

Question #2:

Is the employer responsible for compliance with the home itself?

Response #2: WITHDRAWN 1/5/2000

An employer is responsible for ensuring that its employees have a safe and healthful *workplace*, *not* a safe and healthful *home*. The employer is responsible only for preventing or correcting hazards to which employees may be exposed in the course of their work. For example: if work is performed in the basement space of a residence and the stairs leading to the space are unsafe, the employer could be liable if the employer knows or reasonably should have known of the dangerous condition.

Question #3:

Is the employer required to do periodic compliance inspections in the home, which may include safety, health, fire, and environmental issues?

Response #3: WITHDRAWN 1/5/2000

There is no general requirement in OSHA's standards or regulations that employers routinely conduct safety inspections of all work locations. However, certain specific standards require periodic inspection of specific kinds of equipment and work operations, such as:

* ladders (§1910.25(d)(1)(x) and §1910.26(c)(2)(vi));

* compressed gas cylinders (§1910.101(a));

* electrical protective equipment (§1910.137(b)(2)(ii));

* mechanical power-transmission equipment (§1910.219(p));

* resistance welding (§1910.255(e)); and

* portable electric equipment (§1910.334(a)(2)).

Although some of these operations may not be found in home-based workplaces, nevertheless, if an employer of home-based employees is aware of safety or health hazards, or has reason to be aware of such hazards, the OSH Act requires the employer to pursue all feasible steps to protect its employees; one obvious and effective means of ensuring employee safety would be periodic safety checks of employee working spaces.

This letter addresses only the employer's responsibilities under the OSH Act. Depending on what kind of business the "at home" employer is engaged in, he or she may have additional responsibilities under other federal labor or environmental laws, as well as under state laws of general applicability, such as public health, licensing, zoning, fire and building codes, and other matters.

Question #4:

What would be OSHA's inspection procedures in a private home?

Response #4: WITHDRAWN 1/5/2000

OSHA's health and safety inspection program is directed primarily toward industrial and commercial establishments and construction sites. We do not ordinarily conduct inspections of home-based workplaces, although from time to time we have visited private homes or apartments to investigate reports of sweatshop-type working conditions in the garment industry and other businesses. We would also investigate work-related fatalities occurring in home-based workplaces. Any OSHA enforcement visit must, of course, be conducted in compliance with the Fourth Amendment which would require that OSHA obtain either consent to inspect or a judicially-issued warrant.

Question #5:

Does the employer have to include these home locations in its file regarding record keeping on the OSHA 200 logs?

Response #5: WITHDRAWN 1/5/2000

Employers are not required to maintain an OSHA 200 Log for each home. As stated in 29 CFR 1904.14, which concerns employees not in fixed establishments, employers of employees engaged in physically dispersed operations may satisfy the provisions of 1904.2, 1904.4, and 1904.6 with respect to such employees by maintaining the required records for each operation or group of operations subject to common supervision (field superintendent, field supervisor, etc.) in an established central place.

Injuries and illnesses that occur to employees working at a home location are recordable on the employer's OSHA 200 Log, if they are work-related and meet the criteria for an OSHA recordable injury or illness under 29 CFR Part 1904.2 and the *Recordkeeping Guidelines for Occupational Injuries and Illnesses.* Injuries and illnesses that result from an event or exposure off the employer's premises are work-related if the worker was engaged in work-related activities or was present as a condition of his or her employment (see *Recordkeeping Guidelines,* page 35, Section 2). These criteria must be applied to employees who work at their homes. The *Recordkeeping Guidelines* are available from the Government Printing Office, OSHA's CD-ROM, and the OSHA website — www.osha.gov.

If an employee was injured or became ill while performing duties in the interest of the employer, the case would be considered work-related. If an employee was injured or became ill while performing normal living conditions (e.g., eating), the case would not be considered work-related. For example, when an employee who works at home doing typing develops carpal tunnel syndrome, it must be determined whether the employee's work duties in any way caused, contributed to, or aggravated the condition. If so, the condition is considered work-related for OSHA recordkeeping purposes.

Below are responses to other general questions.

WITHDRAWN 1/5/2000

Workplace Analysis and Hazard Prevention: The employer is responsible for correcting hazards of which it is aware, or should be aware. If, for example, the work requires the use of office equipment (computer, printer, scanner, fax machine, copying machine, etc.) in an employee's home, it must be done manner [sic]. For example, from a fire safety aspect the installation must not overload the home electrical circuits.

WITHDRAWN 1/5/2000

Training — Can the training be in written form? In addition to any training requirements imposed by specific standards, employee training is one way for an employer to meet its general responsibility under the OSH Act for preventing violations. In the absence of specific requirements, the type of training that should be provided will be measured by what a reasonably prudent employer would do under the circumstances, taking into consideration such factors as the nature of the potential hazards and the abilities of the employees. It will not always be necessary for training to be in written form. On the other hand, written training alone may not be sufficient.

WITHDRAWN 1/5/2000

Ergonomics: From the information you have provided, your employees could be exposed to ergonomic hazards. We have, therefore, enclosed a booklet entitled, *Working Safely with Video Display Terminals,* 1997 OSHA Publication 3092, which may be helpful in addressing these hazards. This publication is available on OSHA's CD-ROM and at the OSHA Internet site.

WITHDRAWN 1/5/2000

Fire Protection, Lighting, Cooling, Heating, and Ventilation: See response to Question #2, above.

WITHDRAWN 1/5/2000

Asbestos, Chemicals or Toxic Materials within the Home Itself — Would Material Safety Data Sheets (MSDS) be Required? The employer is responsible for making the workplace of its employees safe, not the entire home. If the employee will be performing work for the employer that involves exposure to any chemical substance for which an MSDS is required, then the MSDS must be present at the home worksite. However, an employer need not supply an MSDS if the hazardous chemical is a consumer product that is being used by an employee in the home office for the purpose intended by the manufacturer, and the use results in a duration and frequency of exposure which is not greater than that experienced by consumers.

WITHDRAWN 1/5/2000

Lockout/Tagout and Confined Spaces: If an employee is performing servicing and maintenance on machines or equipment which are used to perform his or her job, then the 1910.147 lockout/tagout standard applies. With regard to other equipment that may be in the home, the employer would have no responsibility. As long as the designated workplace is within the existing habitat space of the home, then the 1910.146 confined space standard would *not* apply. However, since you have not provided examples of such situations, we can give only general answers.

WITHDRAWN 1/5/2000

Bloodborne Pathogen Exposures: A home office for a sales executive is not covered by OSHA's bloodborne pathogen standard since the standard is intended to protect employees who are exposed or potentially exposed to blood or Other Potentially Infectious Materials (OPIM). This issue cannot be addressed further without knowing a specific factual situation in which employees in their own homes would be exposed to bloodborne pathogens while performing a work-related task.

WITHDRAWN 1/5/2000

Means of Ingress and Egress: Many building/fire codes require offices to have two entrances/exits. This, however, does not mean that OSHA would require installation of a second entrance/exit in an employee's workroom in the employee's home unless the nature of the work and the surroundings create a heightened risk of fire. However, see response to Question #3, above.

WITHDRAWN 1/5/2000

Personal Protective Equipment (PPE): The employer is required to assess the workplace to determine if hazards which necessitate the use of personal protective equipment (PPE) are present, or are likely to be present. If these hazards are or are likely to be present then the employer must provide both the PPE and the necessary training. Employees must be trained in the proper use and maintenance of personal protective equipment, and the employer must verify, through a written certification, that each affected employee has received and understands the required training.

OSHA requires employers to make sure employees have and use safe tools and equipment and that such equipment is properly maintained. Employers are also required to establish or update operating procedures and communicate them to employees so that they will follow safety and health requirements.

WITHDRAWN 1/5/2000

Emergency Plans, Medical Assistance Services, and First Aid Kits and Training: Until OSHA develops policies for these issues as they apply to employees working in their homes, enforcement will necessarily be on a case-by-case basis. The seriousness of the potential hazards will be an important consideration.

WITHDRAWN 1/5/2000

Lead Levels in Old Paint: See response to Question #2, above.

WITHDRAWN 1/5/2000

OSHA Consulting Services: Consultation is a voluntary activity; i.e., the service is not automatic, but must be requested by the employer — it cannot be requested by the employee. The service is provided chiefly at the worksite, but limited services may be provided away from the worksite via offsite training to employers and their employees. When an employer requests onsite Consultation services, the request is prioritized according to the nature of the workplace and any existing backlog of requests. In the case of home-based worksites, a Consultation visit would be classified as "high hazard" only if particularly dangerous work processes or work areas are within the "work zone" of the home.

Due to the limited resources available to the State Consultation Projects, requests from employers that cover only one employee at a home-based worksite would usually be given a very low scheduling priority, particularly when the requested service relates to low hazard activities. In all likelihood, therefore, a Consultation visit would occur only in unusual situations, and then only with the consent of the home-based employee. The inability of OSHA to provide such free onsite assistance in such cases does not, however, relieve the employer of the responsibility to continue to provide safe and healthful work and workplace conditions for all employees, including those based at home.

Other Consultation services are available to employers and their employees, such as dissemination of informational materials and providing telephone assistance on technical and compliance-related issues. Further, offsite technical assistance could be provided to employers and their employees at locations other than the employee's home-based worksite, such as in the State Consultation Project office. Offsite assistance is typically provided in situations where offsite training would be the best use of Consultation resources to address a training need common to a number of employers.

The involvement of employees is key:

* to ensuring the fullest protection of employees in the workplace;

* to properly identifying and assessing the nature and extent of hazards; and

* in determining the effectiveness of the employer's efforts to establish and maintain a workplace safety and management program.

However, in the case of home-based worksites, employees would be involved only where they had freely consented to the provision of assistance requested by the employer, and then only within the parameters defined above.

Americans with Disabilities Act (ADA) compliance and Workers' Compensation: An employer's responsibility under the ADA falls outside OSHA's statutory authority. Similarity, OSHA cannot address the responsibility for workers' compensation in this type of situation, since OSHA does not have statutory authority in this area. For information concerning an employer's responsibility for workers' compensation the employer should contact the workers' compensation agency in the State in which the workplace is located.

Thank you for your interest in occupational safety and health. We hope you find this information helpful. Please be aware that OSHA's enforcement guidance is subject to periodic review and clarification, amplification, or correction. Such guidance could also be affected by subsequent rulemaking. In the future, should you wish to verify that the guidance provided herein remains current, you may consult OSHA's website at www.osha.gov. If you have any questions, please feel free to contact [someone] in the Office of General Industry Compliance Assistance at [telephone number].

Sincerely,

Richard E. Fairfax, Director

Directorate of Compliance Programs

WITHDRAWN 1/5/2000

ENGLISH-ONLY LAWS: UTAH'S "INITIATIVE A"

Utah voters approved the following legislation to make English the official language of their state. It was challenged on several fronts, but unlike similar legislation in other states, it has not been ruled unconstitutional.

63-13-1.5. Official state language.

(1) English is declared to be the official language of Utah.

(2) As the official language of this State, the English language is the sole language of the government, except as otherwise provided in this section.

(3) Except as provided in Subsection (4), all official documents, transactions, proceedings, meetings, or publications issued, conducted, or regulated by, on behalf of, or representing the state and its political subdivisions shall be in English.

(4) Languages other than English may be used when required:

(a) by the United States Constitution, the Utah State Constitution, federal law, or federal regulation;

(b) by law enforcement or public health and safety needs;

(c) by public and higher education systems according to rules made by the State Board of Education and the State Board of Regents to comply with Subsection (5);

(d) in judicial proceedings, when necessary to insure that justice is served;

(e) to promote and encourage tourism and economic development, including the hosting of international events such as the Olympics; and

(f) by libraries to:

(i) collect and promote foreign language materials; and

(ii) provide foreign language services and activities.

(5) The State Board of Education and the State Board of Regents shall make rules governing the use of foreign languages in the public and higher education systems that promote the following principles:

(a) non-English speaking children and adults should become able to read, write, and understand English as quickly as possible;

(b) foreign language instruction should be encouraged;

(c) formal and informal programs in English as a Second Language should be initiated, continued, and expanded; and

(d) public schools should establish communication with non-English speaking parents of children within their systems, using a means designed to maximize understanding when necessary, while encouraging those parents who do not speak English to become more proficient in English.

(6) Unless exempted by Subsection (4), all state funds appropriated or designated for the printing or translation of materials or the provision of services or information in a language other than English shall be returned to the General Fund.

(a) Each state agency that has state funds appropriated or designated for the printing or translation of materials or the provision of ser-

vices or information in a language other than English shall:

(i) notify the Division of Finance that those monies exist and the amount of those monies; and

(ii) return those monies to the Division of Finance.

(b) The Division of Finance shall account for those monies and inform the Legislature of the existence and amount of those monies at the beginning of the Legislature's annual general session.

(c) The Legislature may appropriate any monies received under this section to the State School Board for use in English as a Second Language programs.

(7) Nothing in this section affects the ability of government employees, private businesses, non-profit organizations, or private individuals to exercise their rights under:

(a) the First Amendment of the United States Constitution; and

(b) Utah Constitution, Article 1, Sections 1 and 15.

(8) If any provision of this section, or the application of any such provision to any person or circumstance, is held invalid, the remainder of this act shall be given effect without the invalid provision or application.

Enacted by Statewide Initiative A, Nov. 7, 2000.

FIFTH AMENDMENT: NATIONALITY STATUTE ON CHILDREN BORN OUT OF WEDLOCK

The provisions of the following federal statute were challenged in Nguyen v. INS *on the grounds that the equal protection guaranteed to all U.S. citizens was not available in the case of determining citizenship for children born to unmarried couples. In this case the plaintiff claimed it was more difficult for a male U.S. citizen to establish citizenship for his children if the mother was not also a U.S. citizen, whereas the children of a female U.S. citizen and a non-U.S. citizen who is not her husband automatically receive U.S. citizenship.*

Title VIII, Sec. 1409. Children born out of wedlock

(a) The provisions of paragraphs (c), (d), (e), and (g) of section 1401 of this title, and of paragraph (2) of section 1408 of this title, shall apply as of the date of birth to a person born out of wedlock if –

(1) a blood relationship between the person and the father is established by clear and convincing evidence,

(2) the father had the nationality of the United States at the time of the person's birth,

(3) the father (unless deceased) has agreed in writing to provide financial support for the person until the person reaches the age of 18 years, and

(4) while the person is under the age of 18 years–

(A) the person is legitimated under the law of the person's residence or domicile,

(B) the father acknowledges paternity of the person in writing under oath, or

(C) the paternity of the person is established by adjudication of a competent court.

(b) Except as otherwise provided in section 405 of this Act, the provisions of section 1401(g) of this title shall apply to a child born out of wedlock on or after January 13, 1941, and before December 24, 1952, as of the date of birth, if the paternity of such child is established at any time while such child is under the age of twenty-one years by legitimation.

(c) Notwithstanding the provision of subsection (a) of this section, a person born, after December 23, 1952, outside the United States and out of wedlock shall be held to have acquired at birth the nationality status of his mother, if the mother had the nationality of the United States at the time of such person's birth, and if the mother had previously been physically present in the United States or one of its outlying possessions for a continuous period of one year.

MANSLAUGHTER: MISSISSIPPI'S MURDER STATUTES

All the definitions of murder under Mississippi law could not be fit conveniently into this Appendix: sections 97-3-15 through 97-3-47 all deal with homicides. Two portions of the state's code that apply to the death of Dallas Reinhardt, however, are displayed below. Troy Lee Carlisle was charged with Reinhardt's murder but was found guilty by the jury of manslaughter.

SEC. 97-3-19. Homicide; murder defined; capital murder.

(1) The killing of a human being without the authority of law by any means or in any manner shall be murder in the following cases:

(a) When done with deliberate design to effect the death of the person killed, or of any human being;

(b) When done in the commission of an act eminently dangerous to others and evincing a depraved heart, regardless of human life, although without any premeditated design to effect the death of any particular individual;

(c) When done without any design to effect death by any person engaged in the commission of any felony other than rape, kidnapping, burglary, arson, robbery, sexual battery, unnatural intercourse with any child under the age of twelve (12), or nonconsensual unnatural intercourse with mankind, or felonious abuse and/or battery of a child in violation of subsection (2) of Section 97-5-39, or in any attempt to commit such felonies.

(2) The killing of a human being without the authority of law by any means or in any manner shall be capital murder in the following cases:

(a) Murder which is perpetrated by killing a peace officer or fireman while such officer or fireman is acting in his official capacity or by reason of an act performed in his official capacity, and with knowledge that the victim was a peace officer or fireman. For purposes of this paragraph, the term "peace officer" means any state or federal law enforcement officer including but not limited to a federal park ranger, the sheriff of or police officer of a city or town, a conservation officer, a parole officer, a judge, prosecuting attorney or any other court official, an agent of the Alcoholic Beverage Control Division of the State Tax Commission, an agent of the Bureau of Narcotics, personnel of the Mississippi Highway Patrol, and the employees of the Department of Corrections who are designated as peace officers by the Commissioner of Corrections pursuant to Section 47-5-54, and the superintendent and his deputies, guards, officers and other employees of the Mississippi State Penitentiary;

(b) Murder which is perpetrated by a person who is under sentence of life imprisonment;

(c) Murder which is perpetrated by use or detonation of a bomb or explosive device;

(d) Murder which is perpetrated by any person who has been offered or has received anything of value for committing the murder, and all parties to such a murder, are guilty as principals;

(e) When done with or without any design to effect death, by any person engaged in the commission of the crime of rape, burglary, kidnapping, arson, robbery, sexual battery, unnatural intercourse with any child under the age of twelve (12), or nonconsensual unnatural intercourse with mankind, or in any attempt to commit such felonies;

(f) When done with or without any design to effect death, by any person engaged in the commission of the crime of felonious abuse and/or battery of a child in violation of subsection (2) of Section 97-5-39, or in any attempt to commit such felony;

(g) Murder which is perpetrated on educational property as defined in Section 97-37-17;

(h) Murder which is perpetrated by the killing of any elected official of a county, municipal, state or federal government with knowledge that the victim was such public official.

SOURCES: Codes, Hutchinson's 1848, ch. 64, art. 12, Title 2 (3, 4); 1857, ch. 64, art. 165; 1871, Sec. 2628; 1880, Sec. 2875; 1892, Sec. 1149; 1906, Sec. 1227; Hemingway's 1917, Sec. 957; 1930, Sec. 985; 1942, Sec. 2215; Laws, 1974, ch. 576, Sec. 6(1, 2); 1983, ch. 429, Sec. 1; 1992, ch. 508, Sec. 1, eff. from and after July 1, 1992. Laws, 1996, ch. 422, Sec. 3, eff. from and after passage (approved March 25, 1996); Laws, 1998, Ch. 588, § 1, SB 2868, eff. July 1, 1998. Amended by Laws 2000, Ch. 516, Sec. 134, HB666, eff. from and after passage (approved April 30, 2000).

* * *

SEC. 97-3-47. Homicide; all other killings.

Every other killing of a human being, by the act, procurement, or culpable negligence of another, and without authority of law, not provided for in this title, shall be manslaughter.

SOURCES: Codes, Hutchinson's 1848, ch. 64, art. 12, Title 3 (19); 1857, ch. 64, art. 182; 1871, Sec. 2645; 1880, Sec. 2893; 1892, Sec. 1166; 1906, Sec. 1244; Hemingway's 1917, Sec. 974; 1930, Sec. 1002; 1942, Sec. 2232.

MARRIAGE: LOUISIANA'S COVENANT MARRIAGE ACT

Louisiana Governor Mike Foster signed H.B. 756 into law on July 15, 1997, as Act 1380. H.B. 1631 was signed into law as Act 1298 of 1999 to amend and reenact 1380. This publication of the act should not be considered an authoritative or valid source for the forms required under Louisiana law to effect a covenant marriage.

Section 3. Part VII of Chapter 1 of Code Title IV of Code Book I of Title 9 of the Louisiana Revised Statutes of 1950, to be comprised of R.S. 9:272 through 275, is hereby enacted to read as follows:

Part VII. Covenant Marriage

272. Covenant marriage; intent; conditions to create

A. A covenant marriage is a marriage entered into by one male and one female who understand and agree that the marriage between them is a lifelong relationship. Parties to a covenant marriage have received counseling emphasizing the nature and purposes of marriage and the responsibilities thereto. Only when there has been a complete and total breach of the marital covenant commitment may the non-breaching party seek a declaration that the marriage is no longer legally recognized.

B. A man and woman may contract a covenant marriage by declaring their intent to do so on their application for a marriage license, as provided in R.S. 9:224(C), and executing a declaration of intent to contract a covenant marriage, as provided in R.S. 9:273. The application for a marriage license and the declaration of intent shall be filed with the official who issues the marriage license.

273. Covenant marriage; contents of declaration of intent

A. A declaration of intent to contract a covenant marriage shall contain all of the following:

(1) A recitation by the parties to the following effect:

"A COVENANT MARRIAGE

We do solemnly declare that marriage is a covenant between a man and a woman who agree to live together as husband and wife for so long as they both may live. We have chosen each other carefully and disclosed to one another everything which could adversely affect the decision to enter into this marriage. We have received premarital counseling on the nature, purposes, and responsibilities of marriage. We have read the Covenant Marriage Act, and we understand that a Covenant Marriage is for life. If we experience marital difficulties, we commit ourselves to take all reasonable efforts to preserve our marriage, including marital counseling.

With full knowledge of what this commitment means, we do hereby declare that our marriage will be bound by Louisiana law on Covenant Marriages and we promise to love, honor, and care for one another as husband and wife for the rest of our lives."

(2)(a) An affidavit by the parties that they have received premarital counseling from a priest, minister, rabbi, clerk of the Religious Society of Friends, any clergyman of any religious sect, or a marriage counselor, which counseling shall include a discussion of the seriousness of covenant marriage, communication of the fact that a covenant marriage is a commitment for life, a discussion of the obligation to seek marital counseling in times of marital difficulties, and a discussion of the exclusive grounds for legally terminating a covenant marriage by divorce or by divorce after a judgment of separation from bed and board.

(b) A notarized attestation, signed by the counselor and attached to or included in the parties' affidavit, confirming that the parties were counseled as to the nature and purpose of the marriage and the grounds for termination thereof and an acknowledging that the counselor provided to the parties the informational pamphlet developed and promulgated by the office of the attorney general, which pamphlet entitled the Covenant Marriage Act provides a full explanation of the terms and conditions of a covenant marriage.

(3)(a) The signature of both parties witnessed by a notary.

(b) If one or both of the parties are minors, the written consent or authorization of those persons required under the Children's Code to consent to or authorize the marriage of minors.

B. The declaration shall contain two separate documents, the recitation and the affidavit, the latter of which shall include the attestation either included therein or attached thereto. The recitation shall be prepared in duplicate originals, one of which shall be retained by the parties and the other, together with the affidavit and attestation, shall be filed as provided in R.S. 9:272(B).

274. Covenant marriage; other applicable rules

A covenant marriage shall be governed by all of the provisions of Chapters 1 through 4 of Title IV of Book I of the Louisiana Civil Code and the provisions of Code Title IV of Code Book I of Title 9 of the Louisiana Revised Statutes of 1950.

275. Covenant marriage; applicability to already married couples

A. On or after August 15, 1997, married couples may execute a declaration of intent to designate their marriage as a covenant marriage to be governed by the laws relative thereto.

B.(1) This declaration of intent in the form and containing the contents required by Subsection C of this Section must be presented to the officer who issued the couple's marriage license and with whom the couple's marriage certificate is filed. If the couple was married outside of this state, a copy of the foreign marriage certificate, with the declaration of intent attached thereto, shall be filed with the officer who issues marriage licenses in the parish in which the couple is domiciled. The officer shall make a notation on the marriage certificate of the declaration of intent of a covenant marriage and attach a copy of the declaration to the certificate.

(2) On or before the fifteenth day of each calendar month, the officer shall forward to the state registrar of vital records each declaration of intent of a covenant marriage filed with him during the preceding calendar month pursuant to this Section.

C.(1) A declaration of intent to designate a marriage as a covenant marriage shall contain all of the following:

(a) A recitation by the parties to the following effect:

"A COVENANT MARRIAGE

We do solemnly declare that marriage is a covenant between a man and a woman who agree to live together as husband and wife for so long as they both may live. We understand the nature, purpose, and responsibilities of marriage. We have read the Covenant Marriage Act, and we understand that a Covenant Marriage is for life. If we experience marital difficulties, we commit ourselves to take all reasonable efforts to preserve our marriage, including marital counseling.

With full knowledge of what this commitment means, we do hereby declare that our marriage will be bound by Louisiana law on Covenant Marriage, and we renew our promise to love, honor, and care for one another as husband and wife for the rest of our lives."

(b)(i) An affidavit by the parties that they have discussed their intent to designate their marriage as a covenant marriage with a priest, minister, rabbi, clerk of the Religious Society of Friends, any clergyman of any religious sect, or a marriage counselor, which included a discussion of the obligation to seek marital counseling in times of marital difficulties and the exclusive grounds for legally terminating a covenant marriage by divorce or by divorce after a judgment of separation from bed and board.

(ii) A notarized attestation, signed by the counselor and attached to the parties' affidavit, acknowledging that the counselor provided to the parties the information pamphlet developed and promulgated by the office of the attorney general, which pamphlet entitled the Covenant Marriage Act provides a full explanation of the terms and conditions of a covenant marriage.

(iii) The signature of both parties witnessed by a notary.

(2) The declaration shall contain two separate documents, the recitation and the affidavit, the latter of which shall include the attestation either included therein or attached thereto. The recitation shall be prepared in duplicate originals, one of which shall be retained by the parties and the other, together with the affidavit and attestation, shall be filed as provided in Subsection B of this Section.

Section 4. R.S. 9:307, 308, and 309 are hereby enacted to read as follows:

307. Divorce or separation from bed and board in a covenant marriage; exclusive grounds

A. Notwithstanding any other law to the contrary and subsequent to the parties obtaining counseling, a spouse to a covenant marriage may obtain a judgment of divorce only upon proof of any of the following:

(1) The other spouse has committed adultery.

(2) The other spouse has committed a felony and has been sentenced to death or imprisonment at hard labor.

(3) The other spouse has abandoned the matrimonial domicile for a period of one year and constantly refuses to return.

(4) The other spouse has physically or sexually abused the spouse seeking the divorce or a child of one of the spouses.

(5) The spouses have been living separate and apart continuously without reconciliation for a period of two years.

(6)(a) The spouses have been living separate and apart continuously without reconciliation for a period of one year from the date the judgment of separation from bed and board was signed.

(b) If there is a minor child or children of the marriage, the spouses have been living separate and apart continuously without reconciliation for a period of one year and six months from the date the judgment of separation from bed and board was signed; however, if abuse of a child of the marriage or a child of one of the spouses is the basis for which the judgment of separation from bed and board was obtained, then a judgment of divorce may be obtained if the spouses have been living separate and apart continuously without reconciliation for a period of one year from the date the judgment of separation from bed and board was signed.

B. Notwithstanding any other law to the contrary and subsequent to the parties obtaining counseling, a spouse to a covenant marriage may obtain a judgment of separation from bed and board only upon proof of any of the following:

(1) The other spouse has committed adultery.

(2) The other spouse has committed a felony and has been sentenced to death or imprisonment at hard labor.

(3) The other spouse has abandoned the matrimonial domicile for a period of one year and constantly refuses to return.

(4) The other spouse has physically or sexually abused the spouse seeking the divorce or a child of one of the spouses.

(5) The spouses have been living separate and apart continuously without reconciliation for a period of two years.

(6) On account of habitual intemperance of the other spouse, or excesses, cruel treatment, or outrages of the other spouse, if such habitual intemperance, or such ill-treatment is of such a nature as to render their living together insupportable.

308. Separation from bed and board in covenant marriage; suit against spouse; jurisdiction, procedure, and incidental relief

A. Unless judicially separated, spouses in a covenant marriage may not sue each other except for causes of action pertaining to contracts or arising out of the provisions of Book III, Title VI of the Civil Code; for restitution of separate property; for separation from bed and board in covenant marriages, for divorce, or for declaration of nullity of the marriage; and for causes of action pertaining to spousal support or the support or custody of a child while the spouses are living separate and apart, although not judicially separated.

B.(1) Any court which is competent to preside over divorce proceedings, including the family court for the parish of East Baton Rouge, has jurisdiction of an action for separation from bed and board in a covenant marriage, if:

(a) One or both of the spouses are domiciled in this state and the ground therefor was committed or occurred in this state or while the matrimonial domicile was in this state.

(b) The ground therefor occurred elsewhere while either or both of the spouses were domiciled elsewhere, provided the person obtaining the separation from bed and board was domiciled in this state prior to the time the cause of action accrued and is domiciled in this state at the time the action is filed.

(2) An action for a separation from bed and board in a covenant marriage shall be brought in a parish where either party is domiciled, or in the parish of the last matrimonial domicile.

(3) The venue provided herein may not be waived, and a judgment of separation rendered by a court of improper venue is an absolute nullity.

C. Judgments on the pleadings and summary judgments shall not be granted in any action for separation from bed and board in a covenant marriage.

D. In a proceeding for a separation from bed and board in a covenant marriage or thereafter, a court may award a spouse all incidental relief afforded in a proceeding for divorce, including but not limited to spousal support, claims for contributions to education, child custody, visitation rights, child support, injunctive relief and possession and use of a family residence or community movables or immovables.

309. Separation from bed and board in a covenant marriage; effects

A.(1) Separation from bed and board in a covenant marriage does not dissolve the bond of matrimony, since the separated husband and wife are not at liberty to marry again; but it puts an end to their conjugal cohabitation, and to the common concerns, which existed between them.

(2) Spouses who are judicially separated from bed and board in a covenant marriage shall retain that status until either reconciliation or divorce.

B.(1) The judgment of separation from bed and board carries with it the separation of goods and effects and is retroactive to the date on which the original petition was filed in the action in which the judgment is rendered, but such retroactive effect shall be without prejudice (a) to the liability of the community for the attorney fees and costs incurred by the spouses in the action in which the judgment is rendered, or (b) to rights validly acquired in the interim between commencement of the action and recordation of the judgment.

(2) Upon reconciliation of the spouses, the community shall be reestablished between the spouses, as of the date of filing of the original petition in the action in which the judgment was rendered, unless the spouses execute prior to the reconciliation a matrimonial agreement that the community shall not be reestablished upon reconciliation. This matrimonial agreement shall not require court approval.

(3) Reestablishment of the community under the provisions of this Section shall be effective toward third persons only upon filing notice of the reestablishment for registry in accordance with the provisions of Civil Code Article 2332. The reestablishment of the community shall not prejudice the rights of third persons validly acquired prior to filing notice of the reestablishment nor shall it affect a prior community property partition between the spouses.

Section 5. The office of attorney general, Department of Justice shall, prior to August 15, 1997, promulgate an informational pamphlet, entitled "Covenant Marriage Act', which shall outline in sufficient detail the consequences of entering into a covenant marriage. The informational pamphlet shall be made available to any counselor who provides marriage counseling as provided for by this Act.

Section 6. The provisions of Section 5 of this Act shall become effective upon signature by the governor or, if not signed by the governor, upon expiration of the time for bills to become law without signature by the governor, as provided in Article III, Section 18 of the Constitution of Louisiana. If vetoed by the governor and subsequently approved by the legislature, this

Act shall become effective on the day following such approval.

WAR CRIMES: ROME TREATY APPROVAL JUSTIFICATION LETTER

Lame-duck President Bill Clinton drafted this letter on the final day allowed by the "Rome Treaty" (also known as the International Criminal Court Treaty) for countries to become signatories. In it he explained the reasons for signing it despite having reservations regarding the proposed court's jurisdiction and despite knowing the reservations of the incoming George W. Bush administration.

President Clinton

Statement on Signature of the International Criminal Court Treaty, Washington, DC,

December 31, 2000

The United States is today signing the 1998 Rome Treaty on the International Criminal Court. In taking this action, we join more than 130 other countries that have signed by the December 31, 2000 deadline established in the Treaty. We do so to reaffirm our strong support for international accountability and for bringing to justice perpetrators of genocide, war crimes, and crimes against humanity. We do so as well because we wish to remain engaged in making the ICC an instrument of impartial and effective justice in the years to come.

The United States has a long history of commitment to the principle of accountability, from our involvement in the Nuremberg tribunals that brought Nazi war criminals to justice, to our leadership in the effort to establish the International Criminal Tribunals for the Former Yugoslavia and Rwanda. Our action today sustains that tradition of moral leadership.

Under the Rome Treaty, the International Criminal Court (ICC) will come into being with the ratification of 60 governments, and will have jurisdiction over the most heinous abuses that result from international conflict, such as war crimes, crimes against humanity and genocide. The Treaty requires that the ICC not supercede or interfere with functioning national judicial systems; that is, the ICC Prosecutor is authorized to take action against a suspect only if the country of nationality is unwilling or unable to investigate allegations of egregious crimes by their national, [sic] The U.S. delegation to the Rome Conference worked hard to achieve these limitation [sic], which we believe are essential to the international credibility and success of the ICC.

In signing, however, we are not abandoning our concerns about significant flaws in the Treaty. In particular, we are concerned that when the Court comes into existence, it will not only exercise authority over personnel of states that have ratified the Treaty, but also claim jurisdiction over personnel of states that have not. With signature, however, we will be in signature, we will not.[sic]

Signature will enhance our ability to further protect U.S. officials from unfounded charges and to achieve the human rights and accountability objectives of the ICC. In fact, in negotiations following the Rome Conference, we have worked effectively to develop procedures that limit the likelihood of politicized prosecutions. For example, U.S. civilian and military negotiators helped to ensure greater precision in the definitions of crimes within the Court's jurisdiction.

But more must be done. Court jurisdiction over U.S. personnel should come only with U.S. ratification of the Treaty. The United States should have the chance to observe and assess the functioning of the Court, over time, before choosing to become subject to its jurisdiction. Given these concerns, I will not, and do not recommend that my successor, successor, [sic] submit the Treaty to the Senate for advice and consent until our fundamental concerns are satisfied.

Nonetheless, signature is the right action to take at this point. I believe that a properly constituted and structured International Criminal Court would make a profound contribution in deterring egregious human rights abuses worldwide, and that signature increases the chances for productive discussions with other governments to advance these goals in the months and years ahead.

A.	Atlantic Reporter
A. 2d	Atlantic Reporter, Second Series
AA	Alcoholics Anonymous
AAA	American Arbitration Association; Agricultural Adjustment Act of 1933
AALS	Association of American Law Schools
AAPRP	All African People's Revolutionary Party
AARP	American Association of Retired Persons
AAS	American Anti-Slavery Society
ABA	American Bar Association; Architectural Barriers Act of 1968; American Bankers Association
ABC	
ABM	Antiballistic missile
ABM Treaty	Anti-Ballistic Missile Treaty of 1972
ABVP	Anti-Biased Violence Project
A/C	Account
A.C.	Appeal cases
ACAA	Air Carrier Access Act
ACCA	Armed Career Criminal Act of 1984
ACF	Administration for Children and Families
ACLU	American Civil Liberties Union
ACRS	Accelerated Cost Recovery System
ACS	Agricultural Cooperative Service
ACT	American College Test
Act'g Legal Adv.	Acting Legal Advisor
ACUS	Administrative Conference of the United States
ACYF	Administration on Children, Youth, and Families
A.D. 2d	Appellate Division, Second Series, N.Y.
ADA	Americans with Disabilities Act of 1990
ADAMHA	Alcohol, Drug Abuse, and Mental Health Administration
ADC	Aid to Dependent Children
ADD	Administration on Developmental Disabilities
ADEA	Age Discrimination in Employment Act of 1967
ADL	Anti-Defamation League
ADR	Alternative dispute resolution
AEC	Atomic Energy Commission
AECB	Arms Export Control Board

AEDPA	Antiterrorism and Effective Death Penalty Act
A.E.R.	All England Law Reports
AFA	American Family Association; Alabama Freethought Association
AFB	American Farm Bureau
AFBF	American Farm Bureau Federation
AFDC	Aid to Families with Dependent Children
aff'd per cur.	Affirmed by the court
AFIS	Automated fingerprint identification system
AFL	American Federation of Labor
AFL-CIO	American Federation of Labor and Congress of Industrial Organizations
AFRes	Air Force Reserve
AFSC	American Friends Service Committee
AFSCME	American Federation of State, County, and Municipal Employees
AGRICOLA	Agricultural Online Access
AIA	Association of Insurance Attorneys
AIB	American Institute for Banking
AID	Artificial insemination using a third-party donor's sperm; Agency for International Development
AIDS	Acquired immune deficiency syndrome
AIH	Artificial insemination using the husband's sperm
AIM	American Indian Movement
AIPAC	American Israel Public Affairs Committee
AIUSA	Amnesty International, U.S.A. Affiliate
AJS	American Judicature Society
Alcoa	Aluminum Company of America
ALEC	American Legislative Exchange Council
ALF	Animal Liberation Front
ALI	American Law Institute
ALJ	Administrative law judge
All E.R.	All England Law Reports
ALO	Agency Liaison
A.L.R.	American Law Reports
ALY	*American Law Yearbook*
AMA	American Medical Association
AMAA	Agricultural Marketing Agreement Act
Am. Dec.	American Decisions
amdt.	Amendment
Amer. St. Papers, For. Rels.	American State Papers, Legislative and Executive Documents of the Congress of the U.S., Class I, Foreign Relations, 1832–1859
AMS	Agricultural Marketing Service
AMVETS	American Veterans (of World War II)
ANA	Administration for Native Americans
Ann. Dig.	Annual Digest of Public International Law Cases
ANRA	American Newspaper Publishers Association
ANSCA	Alaska Native Claims Act
ANZUS	Australia-New Zealand-United States Security Treaty Organization
AOA	Administration on Aging
AOE	Arizonans for Official English
AOL	America Online
APA	Administrative Procedure Act of 1946
APHIS	Animal and Plant Health Inspection Service
App. Div.	Appellate Division Reports, N.Y. Supreme Court
Arb. Trib., U.S.-British	Arbitration Tribunal, Claim Convention of 1853, United States and Great Britain Convention of 1853
Ardcor	American Roller Die Corporation
ARPA	Advanced Research Projects Agency

ARPANET	Advanced Research Projects Agency Network
ARS	Advanced Record System
Art.	Article
ARU	American Railway Union
ASCME	American Federation of State, County, and Municipal Employees
ASCS	Agriculture Stabilization and Conservation Service
ASM	Available Seatmile
ASPCA	American Society for the Prevention of Cruelty to Animals
Asst. Att. Gen.	Assistant Attorney General
AT&T	American Telephone and Telegraph
ATFD	Alcohol, Tobacco and Firearms Division
ATLA	Association of Trial Lawyers of America
ATO	Alpha Tau Omega
ATTD	Alcohol and Tobacco Tax Division
ATU	Alcohol Tax Unit
AUAM	American Union against Militarism
AUM	Animal Unit Month
AZT	Azidothymidine
BAC	Blood alcohol concentration
BALSA	Black-American Law Student Association
BATF	Bureau of Alcohol, Tobacco and Firearms
BBS	Bulletin Board System
BCCI	Bank of Credit and Commerce International
BEA	Bureau of Economic Analysis
Bell's Cr. C.	Bell's English Crown Cases
Bevans	United States Treaties, etc. *Treaties and Other International Agreements of the United States of America, 1776–1949* (compiled under the direction of Charles I. Bevans, 1968–76)
BFOQ	Bona fide occupational qualification
BI	Bureau of Investigation
BIA	Bureau of Indian Affairs; Board of Immigration Appeals
BID	business improvement district
BJS	Bureau of Justice Statistics
Black.	Black's United States Supreme Court Reports
Blatchf.	Blatchford's United States Circuit Court Reports
BLM	Bureau of Land Management
BLS	Bureau of Labor Statistics
BMD	Ballistic missile defense
BNA	Bureau of National Affairs
BOCA	Building Officials and Code Administrators International
BOP	Bureau of Prisons
BPP	Black Panther Party for Self-defense
Brit. and For.	British and Foreign State Papers
BSA	Boy Scouts of America
BTP	Beta Theta Pi
Burr.	James Burrows, *Report of Cases Argued and Determined in the Court of King's Bench during the Time of Lord Mansfield* (1766–1780)
BVA	Board of Veterans Appeals
c.	Chapter
C³I	Command, Control, Communications, and Intelligence
C.A.	Court of Appeals
CAA	Clean Air Act
CAB	Civil Aeronautics Board; Corporation for American Banking
CAFE	Corporate average fuel economy
Cal. 2d	California Reports, Second Series
Cal. 3d	California Reports, Third Series
CALR	Computer-assisted legal research

Cal. Rptr.	California Reporter
CAP	Common Agricultural Policy
CARA	Classification and Ratings Administration
CATV	Community antenna television
CBO	Congressional Budget Office
CBS	Columbia Broadcasting System
CBOEC	Chicago Board of Election Commissioners
CCC	Commodity Credit Corporation
CCDBG	Child Care and Development Block Grant of 1990
C.C.D. Pa.	Circuit Court Decisions, Pennsylvania
C.C.D. Va.	Circuit Court Decisions, Virginia
CCEA	Cabinet Council on Economic Affairs
CCP	Chinese Communist Party
CCR	Center for Constitutional Rights
C.C.R.I.	Circuit Court, Rhode Island
CD	Certificate of deposit; compact disc
CDA	Communications Decency Act
CDBG	Community Development Block Grant Program
CDC	Centers for Disease Control and Prevention; Community Development Corporation
CDF	Children's Defense Fund
CDL	Citizens for Decency through Law
CD-ROM	Compact disc read-only memory
CDS	Community Dispute Services
CDW	Collision damage waiver
CENTO	Central Treaty Organization
CEO	Chief executive officer
CEQ	Council on Environmental Quality
CERCLA	Comprehensive Environmental Response, Compensation, and Liability Act of 1980
cert.	*Certiorari*
CETA	Comprehensive Employment and Training Act
C & F	Cost and freight
CFC	Chlorofluorocarbon
CFE Treaty	Conventional Forces in Europe Treaty of 1990
C.F. & I.	Cost, freight, and insurance
C.F.R	Code of Federal Regulations
CFNP	Community Food and Nutrition Program
CFTA	Canadian Free Trade Agreement
CFTC	Commodity Futures Trading Commission
Ch.	Chancery Division, English Law Reports
CHAMPVA	Civilian Health and Medical Program at the Veterans Administration
CHEP	Cuban/Haitian Entrant Program
CHINS	Children in need of supervision
CHIPS	Child in need of protective services
Ch.N.Y.	Chancery Reports, New York
Chr. Rob.	Christopher Robinson, *Reports of Cases Argued and Determined in the High Court of Admiralty* (1801–1808)
CIA	Central Intelligence Agency
CID	Commercial Item Descriptions
C.I.F.	Cost, insurance, and freight
CINCNORAD	Commander in Chief, North American Air Defense Command
C.I.O.	Congress of Industrial Organizations
CIPE	Center for International Private Enterprise
C.J.	Chief justice
CJIS	Criminal Justice Information Services
C.J.S.	Corpus Juris Secundum

Claims Arb. under Spec. Conv., Nielsen's Rept.	Frederick Kenelm Nielsen, *American and British Claims Arbitration under the Special Agreement Concluded between the United States and Great Britain, August 18, 1910* (1926)
CLASP	Center for Law and Social Policy
CLE	Center for Law and Education; Continuing Legal Education
CLEO	Council on Legal Education Opportunity; Chief Law Enforcement Officer
CLP	Communist Labor Party of America
CLS	Christian Legal Society; critical legal studies (movement), Critical Legal Studies (membership organization)
C.M.A.	Court of Military Appeals
CMEA	Council for Mutual Economic Assistance
CMHS	Center for Mental Health Services
C.M.R.	Court of Military Review
CNN	Cable News Network
CNO	Chief of Naval Operations
CNOL	Consolidated net operating loss
CNR	Chicago and Northwestern Railway
CO	Conscientious Objector
C.O.D.	Cash on delivery
COGP	Commission on Government Procurement
COINTELPRO	Counterintelligence Program
Coke Rep.	Coke's English King's Bench Reports
COLA	Cost-of-living adjustment
COMCEN	Federal Communications Center
Comp.	Compilation
Conn.	Connecticut Reports
CONTU	National Commission on New Technological Uses of Copyrighted Works
Conv.	Convention
COPA	Child Online Protection Act (1998)
COPS	Community Oriented Policing Services
Corbin	Arthur L. Corbin, *Corbin on Contracts: A Comprehensive Treatise on the Rules of Contract Law* (1950)
CORE	Congress on Racial Equality
Cox's Crim. Cases	Cox's Criminal Cases (England)
COYOTE	Call Off Your Old Tired Ethics
CPA	Certified public accountant
CPB	Corporation for Public Broadcasting, the
CPI	Consumer Price Index
CPPA	Child Pornography Prevention Act
CPSC	Consumer Product Safety Commission
Cranch	Cranch's United States Supreme Court Reports
CRF	Constitutional Rights Foundation
CRR	Center for Constitutional Rights
CRS	Congressional Research Service; Community Relations Service
CRT	critical race theory
CSA	Community Services Administration
CSAP	Center for Substance Abuse Prevention
CSAT	Center for Substance Abuse Treatment
CSC	Civil Service Commission
CSCE	Conference on Security and Cooperation in Europe
CSG	Council of State Governments
CSO	Community Service Organization
CSP	Center for the Study of the Presidency
C-SPAN	Cable-Satellite Public Affairs Network
CSRS	Cooperative State Research Service

CSWPL	Center on Social Welfare Policy and Law
CTA	*cum testamento annexo* (with the will attached)
Ct. Ap. D.C.	Court of Appeals, District of Columbia
Ct. App. No. Ireland	Court of Appeals, Northern Ireland
Ct. Cl.	Court of Claims, United States
Ct. Crim. Apps.	Court of Criminal Appeals (England)
Ct. of Sess., Scot.	Court of Sessions, Scotland
CTI	Consolidated taxable income
CU	Credit union
CUNY	City University of New York
Cush.	Cushing's Massachusetts Reports
CWA	Civil Works Administration; Clean Water Act
DACORB	Department of the Army Conscientious Objector Review Board
Dall.	Dallas's Pennsylvania and United States Reports
DAR	Daughters of the American Revolution
DARPA	Defense Advanced Research Projects Agency
DAVA	Defense Audiovisual Agency
D.C.	United States District Court; District of Columbia
D.C. Del.	United States District Court, Delaware
D.C. Mass.	United States District Court, Massachusetts
D.C. Md.	United States District Court, Maryland
D.C.N.D.Cal.	United States District Court, Northern District, California
D.C.N.Y.	United States District Court, New York
D.C.Pa.	United States District Court, Pennsylvania
DCS	Deputy Chiefs of Staff
DCZ	District of the Canal Zone
DDT	Dichlorodiphenyltricloroethane
DEA	Drug Enforcement Administration
Decl. Lond.	Declaration of London, February 26, 1909
Dev. & B.	Devereux & Battle's North Carolina Reports
DFL	Minnesota Democratic-Farmer-Labor
DFTA	Department for the Aging
Dig. U.S. Practice in Intl. Law	Digest of U.S. Practice in International Law
Dist. Ct.	D.C. United States District Court, District of Columbia
D.L.R.	Dominion Law Reports (Canada)
DMCA	Digital Millennium Copyright Act
DNA	Deoxyribonucleic acid
Dnase	Deoxyribonuclease
DNC	Democratic National Committee
DOC	Department of Commerce
DOD	Department of Defense
DODEA	Department of Defense Education Activity
Dodson	Dodson's Reports, English Admiralty Courts
DOE	Department of Energy
DOER	Department of Employee Relations
DOJ	Department of Justice
DOL	Department of Labor
DOMA	Defense of Marriage Act of 1996
DOS	Disk operating system
DOT	Department of Transportation
DPT	Diphtheria, pertussis, and tetanus
DRI	Defense Research Institute
DSAA	Defense Security Assistance Agency
DUI	Driving under the influence; driving under intoxication
DWI	Driving while intoxicated
EAHCA	Education for All Handicapped Children Act of 1975

EBT	Examination before trial
E.coli	Escherichia coli
ECPA	Electronic Communications Privacy Act of 1986
ECSC	Treaty of the European Coal and Steel Community
EDA	Economic Development Administration
EDF	Environmental Defense Fund
E.D.N.Y.	Eastern District, New York
EDP	Electronic data processing
E.D. Pa.	Eastern-District, Pennsylvania
EDSC	Eastern District, South Carolina
E.D. Va.	Eastern District, Virginia
EEC	European Economic Community; European Economic Community Treaty
EEOC	Equal Employment Opportunity Commission
EFF	Electronic Frontier Foundation
EFT	Electronic funds transfer
Eliz.	Queen Elizabeth (Great Britain)
Em. App.	Temporary Emergency Court of Appeals
ENE	Early neutral evaluation
Eng. Rep.	English Reports
EOP	Executive Office of the President
EPA	Environmental Protection Agency; Equal Pay Act of 1963
ERA	Equal Rights Amendment
ERDC	Energy Research and Development Commission
ERISA	Employee Retirement Income Security Act of 1974
ERS	Economic Research Service
ERTA	Economic Recovery Tax Act of 1981
ESA	Endangered Species Act of 1973
ESF	Emergency support function; Economic Support Fund
ESRD	End-Stage Renal Disease Program
ETA	Employment and Training Administration
ETS	Environmental tobacco smoke
et seq.	*Et sequentes* or *et sequentia* ("and the following")
EU	European Union
Euratom	European Atomic Energy Community
Eur. Ct. H.R.	European Court of Human Rights
Ex.	English Exchequer Reports, Welsby, Hurlstone & Gordon
Exch.	Exchequer Reports (Welsby, Hurlstone & Gordon)
Ex Com	Executive Committee of the National Security Council
Eximbank	Export-Import Bank of the United States
F.	Federal Reporter
F. 2d	Federal Reporter, Second Series
FAA	Federal Aviation Administration; Federal Arbitration Act
FAAA	Federal Alcohol Administration Act
FACE	Freedom of Access to Clinic Entrances Act of 1994
FACT	Feminist Anti-Censorship Task Force
FAIRA	Federal Agriculture Improvement and Reform Act of 1996
FAMLA	Family and Medical Leave Act of 1993
Fannie Mae	Federal National Mortgage Association
FAO	Food and Agriculture Organization of the United Nations
FAR	Federal Acquisition Regulations
FAS	Foreign Agricultural Service
FBA	Federal Bar Association
FBI	Federal Bureau of Investigation
FCA	Farm Credit Administration
F. Cas.	Federal Cases
FCC	Federal Communications Commission

FCIA	Foreign Credit Insurance Association
FCIC	Federal Crop Insurance Corporation
FCLAA	Federal Cigarette Labeling and Advertising Act
FCRA	Fair Credit Reporting Act
FCU	Federal credit unions
FCUA	Federal Credit Union Act
FCZ	Fishery Conservation Zone
FDA	Food and Drug Administration
FDIC	Federal Deposit Insurance Corporation
FDPC	Federal Data Processing Center
FEC	Federal Election Commission
FECA	Federal Election Campaign Act of 1971
Fed. Cas.	Federal Cases
FEHBA	Federal Employees Health Benefit Act
FEMA	Federal Emergency Management Agency
FFB	Federal Financing Bank
FFDC	Federal Food, Drug, and Cosmetics Act
FGIS	Federal Grain Inspection Service
FHA	Federal Housing Administration
FHAA	Fair Housing Amendments Act of 1998
FHWA	Federal Highway Administration
FIA	Federal Insurance Administration
FIC	Federal Information Centers; Federation of Insurance Counsel
FICA	Federal Insurance Contributions Act
FIFRA	Federal Insecticide, Fungicide, and Rodenticide Act
FIP	Forestry Incentives Program
FIRREA	Financial Institutions Reform, Recovery, and Enforcement Act of 1989
FISA	Foreign Intelligence Surveillance Act of 1978
FJC	Federal Judicial Center
FLSA	Fair Labor Standards Act
FMC	Federal Maritime Commission
FMCS	Federal Mediation and Conciliation Service
FmHA	Farmers Home Administration
FMLA	Family and Medical Leave Act of 1993
FNMA	Federal National Mortgage Association, "Fannie Mae"
F.O.B.	Free on board
FOIA	Freedom of Information Act
FOMC	Federal Open Market Committee
FPC	Federal Power Commission
FPMR	Federal Property Management Regulations
FPRS	Federal Property Resources Service
FR	Federal Register
FRA	Federal Railroad Administration
FRB	Federal Reserve Board
FRC	Federal Radio Commission
F.R.D.	Federal Rules Decisions
FSA	Family Support Act
FSB	Federal'naya Sluzhba Bezopasnosti (the Federal Security Service of Russia)
FSLIC	Federal Savings and Loan Insurance Corporation
FSQS	Food Safety and Quality Service
FSS	Federal Supply Service
F. Supp.	Federal Supplement
FTA	U.S.-Canada Free Trade Agreement of 1988
FTC	Federal Trade Commission
FTCA	Federal Tort Claims Act

FTS	Federal Telecommunications System
FTS2000	Federal Telecommunications System 2000
FUCA	Federal Unemployment Compensation Act of 1988
FUTA	Federal Unemployment Tax Act
FWPCA	Federal Water Pollution Control Act of 1948
FWS	Fish and Wildlife Service
GAL	Guardian ad litem
GAO	General Accounting Office; Governmental Affairs Office
GAOR	General Assembly Official Records, United Nations
GA Res.	General Assembly Resolution (United Nations)
GATT	General Agreement on Tariffs and Trade
GCA	Gun Control Act
Gen. Cls. Comm.	General Claims Commission, United States and Panama; General Claims United States and Mexico
Geo. II	King George II (Great Britain)
Geo. III	King George III (Great Britain)
GHB	Gamma-hydroxybutrate
GI	Government Issue
GID	General Intelligence Division
GM	General Motors
GNMA	Government National Mortgage Association, "Ginnie Mae"
GNP	Gross national product
GOP	Grand Old Party (Republican Party)
GOPAC	Grand Old Party Action Committee
GPA	Office of Governmental and Public Affairs
GPO	Government Printing Office
GRAS	Generally recognized as safe
Gr. Br., Crim. Ct. App.	Great Britain, Court of Criminal Appeals
GRNL	Gay Rights-National Lobby
GSA	General Services Administration
Hackworth	Green Haywood Hackworth, *Digest of International Law* (1940–1944)
Hay and Marriott	Great Britain. High Court of Admiralty, *Decisions in the High Court of Admiralty during the Time of Sir George Hay and of Sir James Marriott, Late Judges of That Court* (1801)
HBO	Home Box Office
HCFA	Health Care Financing Administration
H.Ct.	High Court
HDS	Office of Human Development Services
Hen. & M.	Hening & Munford's Virginia Reports
HEW	Department of Health, Education, and Welfare
HFCA	Health Care Financing Administration
HGI	Handgun Control, Incorporated
HHS	Department of Health and Human Services
Hill	Hill's New York Reports
HIRE	Help through Industry Retraining and Employment
HIV	Human immunodeficiency virus
H.L.	House of Lords Cases (England)
H. Lords	House of Lords (England)
HMO	Health Maintenance Organization
HNIS	Human Nutrition Information Service
Hong Kong L.R.	Hong Kong Law Reports
How.	Howard's United States Supreme Court Reports
How. St. Trials	Howell's English State Trials
HUAC	House Un-American Activities Committee
HUD	Department of Housing and Urban Development

Hudson, Internatl. Legis.	Manley Ottmer Hudson, ed., *International Legislation: A Collection of the Texts of Multipartite International Instruments of General Interest Beginning with the Covenant of the League of Nations* (1931)
Hudson, World Court Reps.	Manley Ottmer Hudson, ea., *World Court Reports* (1934–)
Hun	Hun's New York Supreme Court Reports
Hunt's Rept.	Bert L. Hunt, *Report of the American and Panamanian General Claims Arbitration* (1934)
IAEA	International Atomic Energy Agency
IALL	International Association of Law Libraries
IBA	International Bar Association
IBM	International Business Machines
ICBM	Intercontinental ballistic missile
ICC	Interstate Commerce Commission
ICJ	International Court of Justice
ICM	Institute for Court Management
IDEA	Individuals with Disabilities Education Act of 1975
IDOP	International Dolphin Conservation Program
IEP	Individualized educational program
IFC	International Finance Corporation
IGRA	Indian Gaming Regulatory Act of 1988
IJA	Institute of Judicial Administration
IJC	International Joint Commission
ILC	International Law Commission
ILD	International Labor Defense
Ill. Dec.	Illinois Decisions
ILO	International Labor Organization
IMF	International Monetary Fund
INA	Immigration and Nationality Act
IND	Investigational new drug
INF Treaty	Intermediate-Range Nuclear Forces Treaty of 1987
INS	Immigration and Naturalization Service
INTELSAT	International Telecommunications Satellite Organization
Interpol	International Criminal Police Organization
Int'l. Law Reps.	International Law Reports
Intl. Legal Mats.	International Legal Materials
IOC	International Olympic Committee
IPDC	International Program for the Development of Communication
IPO	Intellectual Property Owners
IPP	Independent power producer
IQ	Intelligence quotient
I.R.	Irish Reports
IRA	Individual retirement account; Irish Republican Army
IRCA	Immigration Reform and Control Act of 1986
IRS	Internal Revenue Service
ISO	Independent service organization
ISP	Internet service provider
ISSN	International Standard Serial Numbers
ITA	International Trade Administration
ITI	Information Technology Integration
ITO	International Trade Organization
ITS	Information Technology Service
ITT	International Telephone and Telegraph Corporation
ITU	International Telecommunication Union
IUD	Intrauterine device
IWC	International Whaling Commission
IWW	Industrial Workers of the World

JAGC	Judge Advocate General's Corps
JCS	Joint Chiefs of Staff
JDL	Jewish Defense League
JNOV	Judgment *non obstante veredicto* ("judgment nothing to recommend it" or "judgment notwithstanding the verdict")
JOBS	Jobs Opportunity and Basic Skills
John. Ch.	Johnson's New York Chancery Reports
Johns.	Johnson's Reports (New York)
JP	Justice of the peace
K.B.	King's Bench Reports (England)
KFC	Kentucky Fried Chicken
KGB	Komitet Gosudarstvennoi Bezopasnosti (the State Security Committee for countries in the former Soviet Union)
KKK	Ku Klux Klan
KMT	Kuomintang (Chinese, "national people's party")
LAD	Law Against Discrimination
LAPD	Los Angeles Police Department
LC	Library of Congress
LCHA	Longshoremen's and Harbor Workers Compensation Act of 1927
LD50	Lethal dose 50
LDEF	Legal Defense and Education Fund (NOW)
LDF	Legal Defense Fund, Legal Defense and Educational Fund of the NAACP
LEAA	Law Enforcement Assistance Administration
L.Ed.	Lawyers' Edition Supreme Court Reports
LI	Letter of interpretation
LLC	Limited Liability Company
LLP	Limited Liability Partnership
LMSA	Labor-Management Services Administration
LNTS	League of Nations Treaty Series
Lofft's Rep.	Lofft's English King's Bench Reports
L.R.	Law Reports (English)
LSAC	Law School Admission Council
LSAS	Law School Admission Service
LSAT	Law School Aptitude Test
LSC	Legal Services Corporation; Legal Services for Children
LSD	Lysergic acid diethylamide
LSDAS	Law School Data Assembly Service
LTBT	Limited Test Ban Treaty
LTC	Long Term Care
MAD	Mutual assured destruction
MADD	Mothers against Drunk Driving
MALDEF	Mexican American Legal Defense and Educational Fund
Malloy	William M. Malloy, ed., *Treaties, Conventions International Acts, Protocols, and Agreements between the United States of America and Other Powers* (1910–1938)
Martens	Georg Friedrich von Martens, ea., *Noveau recueil général de traités et autres act es relatifs azlx rapports de droit international* (Series I, 20 vols. [1843–1875]; Series II, 35 vols. [1876–1908]; Series III [1909–])
Mass.	Massachusetts Reports
MCC	Metropolitan Correctional Center
MCH	Maternal and Child Health Bureau
MCRA	Medical Care Recovery Act of 1962
MDA	Medical Devices Amendments of 1976
Md. App.	Maryland, Appeal Cases
M.D. Ga.	Middle District, Georgia

Mercy	Movement Ensuring the Right to Choose for Yourself
Metc.	Metcalf's Massachusetts Reports
MFDP	Mississippi Freedom Democratic party
MGT	Management
MHSS	Military Health Services System
Miller	David Hunter Miller, ea., *Treaties and Other International Acts of the United States of America* (1931–1948)
Minn.	Minnesota Reports
MINS	Minors in need of supervision
MIRV	Multiple independently targetable reentry vehicle
MIRVed ICBM	Multiple independently targetable reentry vehicled intercontinental ballistic missile
Misc.	Miscellaneous Reports, New York
Mixed Claims Comm., Report of Decs	Mixed Claims Commission, United States and Germany, Report of Decisions
M.J.	Military Justice Reporter
MLAP	Migrant Legal Action Program
MLB	Major League Baseball
MLDP	Mississippi Loyalist Democratic Party
MMI	Moslem Mosque, Incorporated
MMPA	Marine Mammal Protection Act of 1972
Mo.	Missouri Reports
MOD	Masters of Deception
Mod.	Modern Reports, English King's Bench, etc.
Moore, Dig. Intl. Law	John Bassett Moore, *A Digest of International Law*, 8 vols. (1906)
Moore, Intl. Arbs.	John Bassett Moore, *History and Digest of the International Arbitrations to Which United States Has Been a Party*, 6 vols. (1898)
Morison	William Maxwell Morison, *The Scots Revised Report: Morison's Dictionary of Decisions* (1908–09)
M.P.	Member of Parliament
MP3	MPEG Audio Layer 3
MPAA	Motion Picture Association of America
MPAS	Michigan Protection and Advocacy Service
MPEG	Motion Picture Experts Group
mpg	Miles per gallon
MPPDA	Motion Picture Producers and Distributors of America
MPRSA	Marine Protection, Research, and Sanctuaries Act of 1972
M.R.	Master of the Rolls
MS-DOS	Microsoft Disk Operating System
MSHA	Mine Safety and Health Administration
MSSA	Military Selective Service Act
N/A	Not Available
NAACP	National Association for the Advancement of Colored People
NAAQS	National Ambient Air Quality Standards
NAB	National Association of Broadcasters
NABSW	National Association of Black Social Workers
NACDL	National Association of Criminal Defense Lawyers
NAFTA	North American Free Trade Agreement of 1993
NAGHSR	National Association of Governors' Highway Safety Representatives
NALA	National Association of Legal Assistants
NAM	National Association of Manufacturers
NAR	National Association of Realtors
NARAL	National Abortion and Reproductive Rights Action League
NARF	Native American Rights Fund
NARS	National Archives and Record Service
NASA	National Aeronautics and Space Administration
NASD	National Association of Securities Dealers

NATO	North Atlantic Treaty Organization
NAVINFO	Navy Information Offices
NAWSA	National American Woman's Suffrage Association
NBA	National Bar Association; National Basketball Association
NBC	National Broadcasting Company
NBLSA	National Black Law Student Association
NBS	National Bureau of Standards
NCA	Noise Control Act; National Command Authorities
NCAA	National Collegiate Athletic Association
NCAC	National Coalition against Censorship
NCCB	National Consumer Cooperative Bank
NCE	Northwest Community Exchange
NCF	National Chamber Foundation
NCIP	National Crime Insurance Program
NCJA	National Criminal Justice Association
NCLB	National Civil Liberties Bureau
NCP	National contingency plan
NCSC	National Center for State Courts
NCUA	National Credit Union Administration
NDA	New drug application
N.D. Ill.	Northern District, Illinois
NDU	National Defense University
N.D. Wash.	Northern District, Washington
N.E.	North Eastern Reporter
N.E. 2d	North Eastern Reporter, Second Series
NEA	National Endowment for the Arts; National Education Association
NEH	National Endowment for the Humanities
NEPA	National Environmental Protection Act; National Endowment Policy Act
NET Act	No Electronic Theft Act
NFIB	National Federation of Independent Businesses
NFIP	National Flood Insurance Program
NFL	National Football League
NFPA	National Federation of Paralegal Associations
NGLTF	National Gay and Lesbian Task Force
NHL	National Hockey League
NHRA	Nursing Home Reform Act of 1987
NHTSA	National Highway Traffic Safety Administration
Nielsen's Rept.	Frederick Kenelm Nielsen, *American and British Claims Arbitration under the Special Agreement Concluded between the United States and Great Britain, August 18, 1910* (1926)
NIEO	New International Economic Order
NIGC	National Indian Gaming Commission
NIH	National Institutes of Health
NIJ	National Institute of Justice
NIRA	National Industrial Recovery Act of 1933; National Industrial Recovery Administration
NIST	National Institute of Standards and Technology
NITA	National Telecommunications and Information Administration
N.J.	New Jersey Reports
N.J. Super.	New Jersey Superior Court Reports
NLEA	Nutrition Labeling and Education Act of 1990
NLRA	National Labor Relations Act
NLRB	National Labor Relations Board
NMFS	National Marine Fisheries Service
No.	Number
NOAA	National Oceanic and Atmospheric Administration

NOC	National Olympic Committee
NOI	Nation of Islam
NOL	Net operating loss
NORML	National Organization for the Reform of Marijuana Laws
NOW	National Organization for Women
NOW LDEF	National Organization for Women Legal Defense and Education Fund
NOW/PAC	National Organization for Women Political Action Committee
NPDES	National Pollutant Discharge Elimination System
NPL	National priorities list
NPR	National Public Radio
NPT	Nuclear Non-Proliferation Treaty of 1970
NRA	National Rifle Association; National Recovery Act
NRC	Nuclear Regulatory Commission
NRLC	National Right to Life Committee
NRTA	National Retired Teachers Association
NSI	Network Solutions, Inc.
NSC	National Security Council
NSCLC	National Senior Citizens Law Center
NSF	National Science Foundation
NSFNET	National Science Foundation Network
NTIA	National Telecommunications and Information Administration
NTID	National Technical Institute for the Deaf
NTIS	National Technical Information Service
NTS	Naval Telecommunications System
NTSB	National Transportation Safety Board
NVRA	National Voter Registration Act
N.W.	North Western Reporter
N.W. 2d	North Western Reporter, Second Series
NWSA	National Woman Suffrage Association
N.Y.	New York Court of Appeals Reports
N.Y. 2d	New York Court of Appeals Reports, Second Series
N.Y.S.	New York Supplement Reporter
N.Y.S. 2d	New York Supplement Reporter, Second Series
NYSE	New York Stock Exchange
NYSLA	New York State Liquor Authority
N.Y. Sup.	New York Supreme Court Reports
NYU	New York University
OAAU	Organization of Afro American Unity
OAP	Office of Administrative Procedure
OAS	Organization of American States
OASDI	Old-age, Survivors, and Disability Insurance Benefits
OASHDS	Office of the Assistant Secretary for Human Development Services
OCC	Office of Comptroller of the Currency
OCED	Office of Comprehensive Employment Development
OCHAMPUS	Office of Civilian Health and Medical Program of the Uniformed Services
OCSE	Office of Child Support Enforcement
OEA	Organización de los Estados Americanos
OEM	Original Equipment Manufacturer
OFCCP	Office of Federal Contract Compliance Programs
OFPP	Office of Federal Procurement Policy
OIC	Office of the Independent Counsel
OICD	Office of International Cooperation and Development
OIG	Office of the Inspector General
OJARS	Office of Justice Assistance, Research, and Statistics
OMB	Office of Management and Budget

OMPC	Office of Management, Planning, and Communications
ONP	Office of National Programs
OPD	Office of Policy Development
OPEC	Organization of Petroleum Exporting Countries
OPIC	Overseas Private Investment Corporation
Ops. Atts. Gen.	Opinions of the Attorneys-General of the United States
Ops. Comms.	Opinions of the Commissioners
OPSP	Office of Product Standards Policy
O.R.	Ontario Reports
OR	Official Records
OSHA	Occupational Safety and Health Act
OSHRC	Occupational Safety and Health Review Commission
OSM	Office of Surface Mining
OSS	Office of Strategic Services
OST	Office of the Secretary
OT	Office of Transportation
OTA	Office of Technology Assessment
OTC	Over-the-counter
OTS	Office of Thrift Supervisors
OUI	Operating under the influence
OWBPA	Older Workers Benefit Protection Act
OWRT	Office of Water Research and Technology
P.	Pacific Reporter
P. 2d	Pacific Reporter, Second Series
PAC	Political action committee
Pa. Oyer and Terminer	Pennsylvania Oyer and Terminer Reports
PATCO	Professional Air Traffic Controllers Organization
PBGC	Pension Benefit Guaranty Corporation
PBS	Public Broadcasting Service; Public Buildings Service
P.C.	Privy Council (English Law Reports)
PC	Personal computer; politically correct
PCBs	Polychlorinated biphenyls
PCIJ	Permanent Court of International Justice
	Series A-Judgments and Orders (1922–30)
	Series B-Advisory Opinions (1922–30)
	Series A/B-Judgments, Orders, and Advisory Opinions (1931–40)
	Series C-Pleadings, Oral Statements, and Documents relating to Judgments and Advisory Opinions (1923–42)
	Series D-Acts and Documents concerning the Organization of the World Court (1922 –47)
	Series E-Annual Reports (1925–45)
PCP	Phencyclidine
P.D.	Probate Division, English Law Reports (1876–1890)
PDA	Pregnancy Discrimination Act of 1978
PD & R	Policy Development and Research
Pepco	Potomac Electric Power Company
Perm. Ct. of Arb.	Permanent Court of Arbitration
PES	Post-Enumeration Survey
Pet.	Peters' United States Supreme Court Reports
PETA	People for the Ethical Treatment of Animals
PGA	Professional Golfers Association
PGM	Program
PHA	Public Housing Agency
Phila. Ct. of Oyer and Terminer	Philadelphia Court of Oyer and Terminer
PhRMA	Pharmaceutical Research and Manufacturers of America
PHS	Public Health Service

PIC	Private Industry Council
PICJ	Permanent International Court of Justice
Pick.	Pickering's Massachusetts Reports
PIK	Payment in Kind
PINS	Persons in need of supervision
PIRG	Public Interest Research Group
P.L.	Public Laws
PLAN	Pro-Life Action Network
PLC	Plaintiffs' Legal Committee
PLE	Product liability expenses
PLI	Practicing Law Institute
PLL	Product liability loss
PLLP	Professional Limited Liability Partnership
PLO	Palestine Liberation Organization
PLRA	Prison Litigation Reform Act of 1995
PNET	Peaceful Nuclear Explosions Treaty
PONY	Prostitutes of New York
POW-MIA	Prisoner of war-missing in action
Pratt	Frederic Thomas Pratt, *Law of Contraband of War, with a Selection of Cases from Papers of the Right Honourable Sir George Lee* (1856)
PRIDE	Prostitution to Independence, Dignity, and Equality
Proc.	Proceedings
PRP	Potentially responsible party
PSRO	Professional Standards Review Organization
PTO	Patents and Trademark Office
PURPA	Public Utilities Regulatory Policies Act
PUSH	People United to Serve Humanity
PUSH-Excel	PUSH for Excellence
PWA	Public Works Administration
PWSA	Ports and Waterways Safety Act of 1972
Q.B.	Queen's Bench (England)
QTIP	Qualified Terminable Interest Property
Ralston's Rept.	Jackson Harvey Ralston, ed., *Venezuelan Arbitrations of 1903* (1904)
RC	Regional Commissioner
RCRA	Resource Conservation and Recovery Act
RCWP	Rural Clean Water Program
RDA	Rural Development Administration
REA	Rural Electrification Administration
Rec. des Decs. des Trib. Arb. Mixtes	G. Gidel, ed., *Recueil des décisions des tribunaux arbitraux mixtes, institués par les traités de paix* (1922–30)
Redmond	Vol. 3 of Charles I. Bevans, *Treaties and Other International Agreements of the United States of America, 1776–1949* (compiled by C. F. Redmond) (1969)
RESPA	Real Estate Settlement Procedure Act of 1974
RFC	Reconstruction Finance Corporation
RFRA	Religious Freedom Restoration Act of 1993
RIAA	Recording Industry Association of America
RICO	Racketeer Influenced and Corrupt Organizations
RNC	Republican National Committee
Roscoe	Edward Stanley Roscoe, ed., *Reports of Prize Cases Determined in the High Court Admiralty before the Lords Commissioners of Appeals in Prize Causes and before the judicial Committee of the Privy Council from 1745 to 1859* (1905)
ROTC	Reserve Officers' Training Corps
RPP	Representative Payee Program
R.S.	Revised Statutes
RTC	Resolution Trust Corp.

RUDs	reservations, understandings, and declarations
Ryan White CARE Act	Ryan White Comprehensive AIDS Research Emergency Act of 1990
SAC	Strategic Air Command
SACB	Subversive Activities Control Board
SADD	Students against Drunk Driving
SAF	Student Activities Fund
SAIF	Savings Association Insurance Fund
SALT	Strategic Arms Limitation Talks
SALT I	Strategic Arms Limitation Talks of 1969–72
SAMHSA	Substance Abuse and Mental Health Services Administration
Sandf.	Sandford's New York Superior Court Reports
S and L	Savings and loan
SARA	Superfund Amendment and Reauthorization Act
SAT	Scholastic Aptitude Test
Sawy.	Sawyer's United States Circuit Court Reports
SBA	Small Business Administration
SBI	Small Business Institute
SCCC	South Central Correctional Center
SCLC	Southern Christian Leadership Conference
Scott's Repts.	James Brown Scott, ed., *The Hague Court Reports*, 2 vols. (1916–32)
SCS	Soil Conservation Service; Social Conservative Service
SCSEP	Senior Community Service Employment Program
S.Ct.	Supreme Court Reporter
S.D. Cal.	Southern District, California
S.D. Fla.	Southern District, Florida
S.D. Ga.	Southern District, Georgia
SDI	Strategic Defense Initiative
S.D. Me.	Southern District, Maine
S.D.N.Y.	Southern District, New York
SDS	Students for a Democratic Society
S.E.	South Eastern Reporter
S.E. 2d	South Eastern Reporter, Second Series
SEA	Science and Education Administration
SEATO	Southeast Asia Treaty Organization
SEC	Securities and Exchange Commission
Sec.	Section
SEEK	Search for Elevation, Education and Knowledge
SEOO	State Economic Opportunity Office
SEP	Simplified employee pension plan
Ser.	Series
Sess.	Session
SGLI	Servicemen's Group Life Insurance
SIP	State implementation plan
SLA	Symbionese Liberation Army
SLAPPs	Strategic Lawsuits Against Public Participation
SLBM	Submarine-launched ballistic missile
SNCC	Student Nonviolent Coordinating Committee
So.	Southern Reporter
So. 2d	Southern Reporter, Second Series
SPA	Software Publisher's Association
Spec. Sess.	Special Session
SPLC	Southern Poverty Law Center
SRA	Sentencing Reform Act of 1984
SS	Schutzstaffel (German, "Protection Echelon")
SSA	Social Security Administration
SSI	Supplemental Security Income
START I	Strategic Arms Reduction Treaty of 1991

START II	Strategic Arms Reduction Treaty of 1993
Stat.	United States Statutes at Large
STS	Space Transportation Systems
St. Tr.	State Trials, English
STURAA	Surface Transportation and Uniform Relocation Assistance Act of 1987
Sup. Ct. of Justice, Mexico	Supreme Court of Justice, Mexico
Supp.	Supplement
S.W.	South Western Reporter
S.W. 2d	South Western Reporter, Second Series
SWAPO	South-West Africa People's Organization
SWAT	Special Weapons and Tactics
SWP	Socialist Workers Party
TDP	Trade and Development Program
Tex. Sup.	Texas Supreme Court Reports
THAAD	Theater High-Altitude Area Defense System
THC	Tetrahydrocannabinol
TI	Tobacco Institute
TIA	Trust Indenture Act of 1939
TIAS	Treaties and Other International Acts Series (United States)
TNT	Trinitrotoluene
TOP	Targeted Outreach Program
TPUS	Transportation and Public Utilities Service
TQM	Total Quality Management
Tripartite Claims Comm., Decs. and Ops.	Tripartite Claims Commission (United States, Austria, and Hungary), Decisions and Opinions
TRI-TAC	Joint Tactical Communications
TRO	Temporary restraining order
TS	Treaty Series, United States
TSCA	Toxic Substance Control Act
TSDs	Transporters, storers, and disposers
TSU	Texas Southern University
TTBT	Threshold Test Ban Treaty
TV	Television
TVA	Tennessee Valley Authority
TWA	Trans World Airlines
UAW	United Auto Workers; United Automobile, Aerospace, and Agricultural Implements Workers of America
U.C.C.	Uniform Commercial Code; Universal Copyright Convention
U.C.C.C.	Uniform Consumer Credit Code
UCCJA	Uniform Child Custody Jurisdiction Act
UCMJ	Uniform Code of Military Justice
UCPP	Urban Crime Prevention Program
UCS	United Counseling Service
UDC	United Daughters of the Confederacy
UFW	United Farm Workers
UHF	Ultrahigh frequency
UIFSA	Uniform Interstate Family Support Act
UIS	Unemployment Insurance Service
UMDA	Uniform Marriage and Divorce Act
UMTA	Urban Mass Transportation Administration
U.N.	United Nations
UNCITRAL	United Nations Commission on International Trade Law
UNCTAD	United Nations Conference on Trade and Development
UN Doc.	United Nations Documents

UNDP	United Nations Development Program
UNEF	United Nations Emergency Force
UNESCO	United Nations Educational, Scientific, and Cultural Organization
UNICEF	United Nations Children's Fund (formerly United Nations International Children's Emergency Fund)
UNIDO	United Nations Industrial and Development Organization
Unif. L. Ann.	Uniform Laws Annotated
UN Repts. Intl. Arb. Awards	United Nations Reports of International Arbitral Awards
UNTS	United Nations Treaty Series
UPI	United Press International
URESA	Uniform Reciprocal Enforcement of Support Act
U.S.	United States Reports
U.S.A.	United States of America
USAF	United States Air Force
USF	U.S. Forestry Service
U.S. App. D.C.	United States Court of Appeals for the District of Columbia
U.S.C.	United States Code; University of Southern California
U.S.C.A.	United States Code Annotated
U.S.C.C.A.N.	United States Code Congressional and Administrative News
USCMA	United States Court of Military Appeals
USDA	U.S. Department of Agriculture
USES	United States Employment Service
USFA	United States Fire Administration
USGA	United States Golf Association
USICA	International Communication Agency, United States
USMS	U.S. Marshals Service
USOC	U.S. Olympic Committee
USSC	U.S. Sentencing Commission
USSG	United States Sentencing Guidelines
U.S.S.R.	Union of Soviet Socialist Republics
UST	United States Treaties
USTS	United States Travel Service
v.	*Versus*
VA	Veterans Administration
VAR	Veterans Affairs and Rehabilitation Commission
VAWA	Violence against Women Act
VFW	Veterans of Foreign Wars
VGLI	Veterans Group Life Insurance
Vict.	Queen Victoria (Great Britain)
VIN	Vehicle identification number
VISTA	Volunteers in Service to America
VJRA	Veterans Judicial Review Act of 1988
V.L.A.	Volunteer Lawyers for the Arts
VMI	Virginia Military Institute
VMLI	Veterans Mortgage Life Insurance
VOCAL	Victims of Child Abuse Laws
VRA	Voting Rights Act
WAC	Women's Army Corps
Wall.	Wallace's United States Supreme Court Reports
Wash. 2d	Washington Reports, Second Series
WAVES	Women Accepted for Volunteer Service
WCTU	Women's Christian Temperance Union
W.D. Wash.	Western District, Washington
W.D. Wis.	Western District, Wisconsin
WEAL	*West's Encyclopedia of American Law*, Women's Equity Action League
Wend.	Wendell's New York Reports

WFSE	Washington Federation of State Employees
Wheat.	Wheaton's United States Supreme Court Reports
Wheel. Cr. Cases	Wheeler's New York Criminal Cases
WHISPER	Women Hurt in Systems of Prostitution Engaged in Revolt
Whiteman	Marjorie Millace Whiteman, *Digest of International Law*, 15 vols. (1963–73)
WHO	World Health Organization
WIC	Women, Infants, and Children program
Will. and Mar.	King William and Queen Mary (Great Britain)
WIN	WESTLAW Is Natural; Whip Inflation Now; Work Incentive Program
WIPO	World Intellectual Property Organization
WIU	Workers' Industrial Union
W.L.R.	Weekly Law Reports, England
WPA	Works Progress Administration
WPPDA	Welfare and Pension Plans Disclosure Act
WTO	World Trade Organization
WWI	World War I
WWII	World War II
Yates Sel. Cas.	Yates's New York Select Cases
YMCA	Young Men's Christian Association
YWCA	Young Women's Christian Association

INDEX
By Name and Subject

Page numbers appearing in boldface indicate major treatment
of entries. Italicized page numbers refer to photos.

reduction of, 195–196
Separation of church and state, 99–100
Separation of powers, **197–199**
Serbia, NATO air and missile campaign, 197–199
Sex offender registration, extension to juveniles, 133–134
Sex offenses, **199–200**
Sexual abuse, **200–201**
Sexual harassment, **201–202**
    Clinton, Bill, claim against, 47, 196–197
    DuPont, claim against, 201–202
    Thomas, Clarence, claim against, 186–187
Sexual materials or activities, banning or curtailing of traffic of, 84–85
Sexual predator laws, 199–200
Shabiu, Merita, 142–144
Shafer, Aaron, Jr., 25–26
Shamrock Foods, 209
Shandling, Gary, 16
Sheets, Jeremy, 230, *231*
Sheindlin, Gerald, 217
Sheindlin, Judy, 216–217
Sheridan, Margot, 155
Sherman Antitrust Act, 7, 145, 147
Shield laws, **202–203**
Shields, Gregg, 48
Shulman, Ken, 231
Siamese twins, forced separation of, 169–171
Sifford, Chris, 26
Sikkema, Ken, 130
Silberman, Laurence H., 198
Simpson, O. J., 216, 217
Sixth Amendment, **203–204**
Skakel, Ann, 154
Skakel, George, 155
Skakel, Michael, 153–155
Skakel, Rushton, 154, 155
Skakel, Tommy, 154
Slader, David, 200
Slidell, Louisiana, detention of students, 97–98
Smart, Bill, 207
Smirnov, Boris, 228
Smirnov, Pyotr, 227–228
Smirnov, Vladimir, 227–228
Smirnov/Smirnoff Vodka, 227–228
Smith, Anna Nicole, 247–248
Smith, Ashley, 190–191
Smith, James, 11–12
Smith, Mitchell, 204–205
Smith, Walter, 251–252
Smith, William Kennedy, 155
Smith & Wesson, 104
SmithKline Beecham, 113
Smokers, punitive damages award to, 224–225
Social Security taxes, 129–130, 214–215

Soda fountain syrup, distribution of, 147–148
Sodomy, **204–205**
Solid Waste Agency of Northern Cook County, 71–72
Sony Music, 37
Sotheby's, 6–7
Sotomayor, Sonia, 116
Souter, David H.
    arbitration, 13
    boundaries, 17–18
    cameras in court, 21–22
    civil rights, 29
    Election 2000, 64
    election campaign financing, 57–58
    English-only laws, 69
    Fifth Amendment, 80
    Fourteenth Amendment, 90
    Fourth Amendment, 95, 96
    Freedom of Information Act (FOIA), 99
    Freedom of Speech, 100
    immunity, 120
    incarceration, 122–123
    prisoners' rights, 173
    taxation, 214
South Carolina
    capital punishment, 25–26
    Confederate flag, flying of, 88–89
    drug tests, 91–92
Southeastern Legal Foundation, 47
Southern Poverty Law Center, 70, 110
Sparry, Chris, 22
Specter, Arlen
    cameras in court, 21
    electoral college, 60
Spielberg, Steven, 48
Spivey, Kenneth, 22
Spooner, Mark, 177
Sports law, **205–207**
Starr, Kenneth, 34, 47
    Whitewater, 187, 244–245
Statutes of limitations, 107–108, 125
Stayner, Cary, 149–151
Stayner, Steven, 150
Steele, Edgar, 110–111
Steele, Julie Hiatt, 34–35
Steinbrenner, George, 15–16
Stevens, John Paul
    arbitration, 13
    civil rights, 29
    copyright, 36
    damages, 42
    disabled persons, 44–45
    elections, 61, 64
    English-only laws, 69
    environmental law, 72, 73
    ex post facto laws, 77
    First Amendment, 83–84

ISBN 0-7876-4789-6

9 780787 647896

90000